"They were the proud providers of our vicarious sexual entertainment, capable of launching millions of wet dreams by allowing us to utilize their alluring assets for the fulfillment of our basest desires — essentially sinematic Circes beckoning us to crash upon their seductive shores. And as proudly presented by author Jill Nelson in *Golden Goddesses* — they are also fascinating, multi-talented human beings who strove to fit into the society that they satiated...once their carnal cinema careers ended. With a remarkably tender, almost adoptive tone, Nelson presents a cross-section of adult entertainment industry personalities, most of whom attained "legendary status" in the eyes of their fans as well as the minds of their peers, to give the reader a multi-dimensional look at a world that undulated under the letter X from the late Sixties into the mid-Eighties. And if one of your "fondling favorites" is missing here, perhaps Nelson can be convinced to do a follow-up called 'Vibrating Vixens.'"

WILLIAM MARGOLD, Adult Film Historian

"(*Golden Goddesses* is)...A personal and revealing look at 25 of the most important ladies in the history of the adult film industry. The ones who started it all! Presented in an oral history format, the book covers not only actresses, but also directors, screenwriters, and costumers, making it essential reading for anyone interested in Golden Age erotic cinema."

JASON S. MARTINKO, author, *The XXX Filmography, 1968-1988*

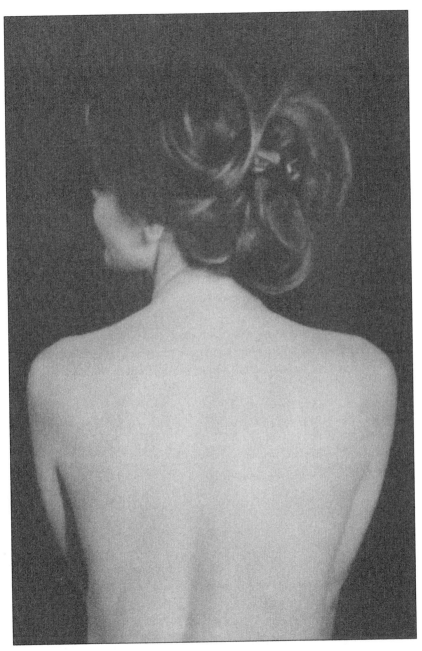

PHOTOGRAPHY BY TINA HUBBERT

Published in the USA by:
BearManor Media
PO Box 1129
Duncan, Oklahoma 73534-1129
www.bearmanormedia.com

ISBN 978-1-59393-298-5

Printed in the United States of America.

Front and Back Cover design by JSV Designs.
Front Cover image of Serena: Photography by Joel Sussman.
Front Cover images of Marilyn Chambers and Kay Parker and Back Cover
images of Ginger Lynn, Kelly Nichols, and Kay Parker: Photography by Kenji.
Back Cover creative by Kenji.

Book design by Brian Pearce | Red Jacket Press.

Golden Goddesses

25 Legendary Women of Classic Erotic Cinema 1968-1985

BY JILL C. NELSON

Table of Contents

Dedicated in loving memory
To my brother Chris

Acknowledgements

Golden Goddesses would not have been possible without the participation of the women profiled and/or highlighted in this book and the input of others who provided additional dialogue material.

For sharing with me in interviews, thank you: Penny Antine, Christy Canyon, Roberta Findlay, Valerie Gobos, Jane Hamilton/Veronica Hart, Nina Hartley, Laurie Holmes, Gloria Leonard, Mai Lin, Amber Lynn, Ginger Lynn, Porsche Lynn, Jody Maxwell, Carly Mills, Sharon Mitchell, Francesca "Kitten" Natividad, Kelly Nichols, Kay Parker, Rhonda Jo Petty, Candida Royalle, Seka, Serena, Georgina Spelvin, Annie Sprinkle, Julia St. Vincent, McKenna Taylor, and Greg Yedding. I would also like to acknowledge the contributions of Juliet Anderson, Marilyn Chambers, and Barbara Mills, all of whom passed away after their interviews.

Heartfelt thanks to Jennifer Sugar for this book's foreword, and for her initiative to pen "Inches," which inspired and gave rise to "Goddesses."

Special thanks to Bob Chinn for this book's title and for his acute memory, to Joel Sussman for his stunning "Serena" front cover photography, to JSV Designs for this book's exceptional and classy front/back cover design, to Kenji for this book's inspired back cover creative and beautiful front and back cover images, to "Papa Bear" Bill Margold for his wise counsel and enduring support, to Cass Paley for his sense of humor and feedback, to Sandra Deady for her keen eyes, to Richard Freeman for reading every single word, and to Dr. Vonda L. Pelto for providing professional insight and analysis on women working in the sex industry. I'd like to extend personal thanks to my publisher Ben Ohmart, BearManor Media Manager Sandy Grabman, Editor Dr. Wesley Britton, and book designer Brian Pearce.

I also appreciate the generosity of the people who have allowed me to use their photos and other resources in this book: Penny Antine, Rita Benton, Christy Canyon, Bob Chinn, *Carnal Comics*, Scott Church, Ian Culmell, Roberta Findlay, Peggy Giroux, Howie Gordon, Jane Hamilton,

Nina Hartley, Laurie Holmes, Tina Hubbert, Hustler Video, Paul Johnson, Kenji, Gloria Leonard, Amber Lynn, Ginger Lynn, Bill Margold, Jody Maxwell, Carly Mills, Mitchell Brothers Film Group, Steven Morowitz, Francesca Natividad, Kelly Nichols, Cass Paley, Kay Parker, Rhonda Jo Petty, Suze Randall, Candida Royalle, Seka, Serena, Georgina Spelvin, Annie Sprinkle, Julia St. Vincent, Joel Sussman, Arne Svensen, McKenna Taylor, and Greg Yedding.

Additionally, I'd like to give recognition to individuals, websites, distributors, and other source materials used for the compilation of this book: Alpha Blue Archives, Amber Guerra, *anniesprinkle.org*, Caballero Home Video, Cal-Vista, *candidaroyalle.com*, *Chic* Magazine, *Cronenberg on Cronenberg* (1992), David Sutton, Distribix blog, Donna Ann McAdams, *georginaspelvin.blogspot.com*, Hollywood Cinema Associates, original Ann Perry dialogue and script text from the motion picture *WADD: The Life & Times of John C. Holmes* provided by Hustler Video, I-Candy, *jodymaxwell.com*, *johnholmes.com*, *John Holmes: A Life Measured in Inches* (2008) by Jennifer Sugar and Jill C. Nelson, Julian Cash, *kaytaylorparker. com*, *kittenclub.com*, *Lights, Camera, Sex!* (2003) by Christy Canyon, *loveartlab.org*, New Line Home Video, Pacific Media Entertainment, *paulsfantasy.com*, *Playgirl* magazine, *seka.com*, Shriek Show/Media Blasters, Something Weird Video, Temple of *Schlock.blogspot.ca*, *The Devil Made Me Do It* (2008) by Georgina Spelvin, *www.suze.net*, TVX Home Video, *VCX.com*, Video-X-Pix, and Worth Mentioning Public Relations.

I would like to express my gratitude to friends, acquaintances, and loved ones who have encouraged me and championed the development of this book: Penny Antine, Judy Barker, Terri Beckwith, Cass Paley, Sam Caldwell, Bob Chinn, Heather Drain, Ted Fell, Tracy-Ann Francis, Kristine Fransden, Richard Freeman, Ann Gee, Peggy Giroux, Valerie Gobos, Howie Gordon, Jane Hamilton, Steve Hamilton, John Harrison, Laurie Holmes, Tina Hubbert, Tod Hunter, Kenji, Lyn & Terry Lawrence, Jason Martinko, Bill Margold, Jody Maxwell, Donna Morton, Steve & Wendy Morton, Christopher Neeme, Jan Nelson, Val Osher, Kay Parker, Ron Parry, Rhonda Jo Petty, Serena, Shaun Price, Candida Royalle, Joe Rubin, Casey Scott, Jeffrey Scull, the "Longos" Starbucks girls, Julia St. Vincent, Jennifer Sugar, Joel Sussman, Peggy Webber, and Adam Wilcox.

Last, but not least, thank you to Hud, Corey, and Andrea for much love and laughter. *xo*

A Foreword BY JENNIFER SUGAR

Three hundred miles and a twenty-five year age difference separated us, but Jill and I were united over our shared interest in John Holmes, in order to co-author the authorized, definitive biography, *John Holmes: a Life Measured in Inches*. I spent a bit over two years conducting interviews, experimenting with different writing styles, watching Holmes's films and researching before I asked Jill, whom I had recently met online, to co-author the book with me. Because I was finishing my bachelor's degree at Michigan State University, my John Holmes biography had lost steam compared to when I had started it at age 21. Fortunately, Jill agreed to join me in the project. As I had hoped, her passion for writing, and her care for our interview participants breathed new life into *Inches* and pushed us to publish within (Jill's goal of) two years.

Considering that both of us were first-time authors, living in two different countries, publishing *Inches* was a thrill! Following a well-attended launch at Book Soup in Los Angeles on the night of Friday, August 8, 2008 — which would have been John Holmes's 64th birthday — Jill and I went on to pursue our next adventures. For me, this meant beginning a full-time career, completing a master's degree, and starting a family. For Jill already with two, successful, adult children, and who had recently sold her small business — finishing *Inches* inspired her to write a second biography, that she would call *Golden Goddesses*.

It's the book in your hands right now. Its conception began sometime as we neared the finish line with *Inches*. During a walk along a California beach, Jill described her desire to explore the intimate details of the lives of women who had been involved as performers, directors, and writers in three decades of adult entertainment. Having just completed *Inches* helped Jill to obtain contact with these women, many of whom are self-protective and reluctant to participate in interviews, but Jill earned the trust of her interview subjects and frequently developed friendships. Each of these women has a unique, personal story to share regarding their childhood, entrance into the realm of adult entertainment, their lives afterward, retrospectives, and more.

Our credo for writing was to be honest and complete in reporting. Because of this, Jill's interview participants continue to be satisfied with the tasteful portrayal of their candid and emotional stories. Enjoy!

Golden Goddesses:
An Introduction

In 2008, while nearing completion of *John Holmes: A Life Measured in Inches*, it occurred to me it would be interesting to talk in depth to some of the females who have become synonymous with the classic era of films depicting sexual situations.

While participating in interviews for *Inches*, Jennifer Sugar and I had established connections with a handful of women known from the golden age, so it seemed a natural step to approach prospective females to gauge interest. In the beginning, I discussed with Jennifer the possibility of collaborating on the book as we had done before. Jennifer was very excited about the prospect and supportive, but she was about to start a brand new full time career so this would be a solo venture.

My idea for each woman to share her own story openly was surprisingly met with a positive reception when I pitched it to a few of the females I'd gotten to know. I remember speaking at first with Rhonda Jo Petty in the spring of 2009. Petty was enthusiastic about the concept and encouraged me to get started. In September 2009, I packed up my little black Yaris on a sunny Sunday morning, and traveled east to Montreal to interview Seka.

As luck would have it, Seka had accompanied her husband on a business trip to Montreal which was only a six-hour drive away from my home. We planned to meet outside of her deluxe hotel situated in quaint Old Montreal. Over the telephone, she had instructed me to look for her platinum head adjacent to another woman standing outside of the hotel, and was insistent that I address her by her real name, Dottie, and not by her stage name, Seka. Understandably, Seka was taking precautions to protect her husband's job security and didn't want to run the risk her friend might learn of her real identity. When I wondered whom I was supposed to be, Seka laughed and suggested I pretend I was "an old friend from Canada." About an hour later, I strode up to the hotel, and after exchanging a warm greeting (as "old friends" would) we walked a few blocks for crêpes and champagne breakfast before returning to Seka's room to begin the interview which I taped on a digital pocket recorder.

Afterwards, Seka promised to put me in touch with some of her legendary girlfriends: Kay Parker, Veronica Hart, Gloria Leonard and Annie Sprinkle. True to her word, by the end of September, I had established interview dates with all four ladies. One thing led to another, and soon I had enough material and additional contacts to begin piecing together a chronological history of the lives and times of these fascinating women.

On a sad note, a few months after their interviews were completed, Barbara Caron Mills and Juliet Anderson passed away unexpectedly. Barbara had been reluctant to talk about her past at first, but her daughter Carly reassured her mother she should not feel ashamed. I had fortunately interviewed Marilyn Chambers for *Inches* in June 2007, just two years before her death from a cerebral hemorrhage and brain aneurism, and was very surprised and moved when I learned about her untimely passing. We had hoped to meet up for dinner that summer in Santa Monica during my visit there, only Marilyn cancelled at the last minute. I was disappointed, but a few days later, she sent me a sweet e-mail apologizing for changing plans. Among a few other things, she wrote, "Jill, you are a breath of fresh air." Marilyn's sentiment and good wishes meant a lot, and I've carried her faith in me throughout this undertaking.

Occasionally, family and friends have been puzzled and queried as to why I have chosen to dedicate much time and energy developing two books centering on this unusual group often misunderstood and even persecuted by society. I smile and answer, "I'm not interested in writing a book about Julia Roberts." These eccentric, imperfect women, who dared to walk on the wild side, are also some of the most gorgeous, vivacious, resilient, intelligent, and ethical people anyone would ever want to meet. I don't profess to have familiarity with today's trends in pornographic movie productions, but I have been made well aware there is a vast difference between the caliber of performer and content available today and yesteryear. Without question, my expedition has been incredible, and I believe it has reaffirmed for me that I am bolder than I might have been had I chosen a safer sojourn. It is my hope that I have presented each woman's story respectfully, with dignity, and without agenda.

In this book, I have accentuated twenty-five resplendent women of the golden age of erotic films who worked on both the east and west coasts of the United States between the years 1968-1985. My intention is to escort readers toward a clearer understanding of the beautiful and intrepid females who favored an alternative profession in adult cinema that was cultivated at the apex of the 1960s sexual revolution. By the early 1970s, porno was chic, and performers helmed by artful directors were personified in genuine scripts, supported by costuming and make-up departments in quality film projects that often culminated in red carpet premieres. Several individuals, and particularly women who began working in loops and sexually oriented films prior to the "porno chic" juncture, and/or up until the mid-1980s video boom, became legitimate silver screen stars. To suggest that their chosen path has been comfortable or without debris would be false, for as each unfolding story will reveal, experiences for a female employed in the adult entertainment industry during the generation when it was illegal to participate in the production of sex films, were anything but ordinary.

My interviews with twenty-five incisive female personalities: performers, directors, costumers and scriptwriters, are documented in the following pages. They range in age between forty-six and seventy-six years. Starting with their childhood years and closing with the present day, each woman has communicated her story through honest reflections and multifarious assessments of life and work within the adult motion picture community. Some of the featured women pursued assorted roles during the golden era of X-rated films, while others were occupied in a single capacity. A handful of females presented in this account are still actively involved in a facet of sexual entertainment. Because this book has its lens on women who worked for the erotic film industry, each chapter also contains film highlights.

Only a small (albeit significant) group of women are profiled in this book, but it must be mentioned there are thousands of others now incognito, unable to acknowledge or embrace their past contribution to adult films for fear they will be exposed or fired by employers for having partaken of the freedoms offered in more liberated and anarchistic times. It is why some of the women approached for inclusion in this publication declined the opportunity. For personal reasons, there are also those who have decidedly disavowed themselves from any responsibility or ownership of their former affiliation with the subversive industry. It is important to bear in mind that the women who are not acknowledged throughout this book are no less significant to the genre and era this book covers, as are the ones who are no longer with us.

As the reader journeys through the past and into the present, I encourage you to keep an open mind and a spirit of adventure while willing seeds of judgment to a standstill.

Jill C. Nelson

This Mess
All this surprised me as well.
I didn't plan to ruin my life
Throwing myself at your rocky shore
You bring out the words in me.
To speak my mind, my heart
My truth
I never could hear my own voice
Over the shattering din of other's
You are so quiet that I hear
A poet's voice, sweet and steady,
In my right ear
Please
Give that one lots of attention
During nibble time

— SERENA

Ann Perry
First Lady

Seventy-three year old Ann Perry-Rhine (born Virginia Ann Lindsay) was raised in Spokane, Washington, where she enrolled in a private Catholic school and was on the fast track to becoming a nun. While attending the convent, she met her first husband Ron Myers. Smitten, Ann soon abandoned her liturgical garments and revealed a rebellious streak that would prove to be a dominating trait throughout her life and career. Perry and Myers wed around the time Ann waded into the entertainment pool as a model and dancer before emerging as a Pin-Up Girl, and apparently did a photo layout in a 1961 issue of *Playboy* magazine.

Along with 1960s sexploitation queen, Marsha Jordan, Ann appeared in Nudie Cutie pictures for director Don Davis, but had her sights set on greener pastures. Strong-willed and determined to compete in a man's world, Perry adapted easily as a softcore film actress which eventually positioned her for more coveted roles as a writer, director and producer of hardcore movies ultimately under her own company Evolution Enterprises. Attracted to the illegal nature of the business, Ann was arrested on more than one occasion on morals charges and as the first woman President of the Adult Film Association of America, Perry exercised her status to sway members of the press and strategized methods of bringing a better quality product to fans of adult material.

With the media recognition of two of her productions *Count the Ways* (1976) and *Sweet Savage* (1978), Ann attended the prestigious Cannes Film Festival and continued to create a viable product focused on themed-based sex films that showcased actors' abilities beyond the realm of copulating on camera.

Ann Perry's colorful personal life echoes her non-traditional career in the adult industry. She is the mother of two grown children and has

"I liked owning, producing, directing and writing my own stories because I didn't have anybody to apologize to. I joined the Adult Film Association and I was shooting thirty-five millimeter films. I was the first woman President." ANN PERRY-RHINE

COURTESY OF GREG YEDDING

enjoyed four husbands. In 1978, during the filming of *Sweet Savage*, Perry met and eventually married San Francisco attorney, Joe Rhine, who had represented illustrious individuals such as Timothy Leary and members of the Black Panther Party during the 1970s.

Presently, Ann Perry continues to reside in Southern California, but was unable to participate in an interview for this book due to the progression of Alzheimer's disease. The following pages contain material from interviews Ann gave for filmmaker Cass Paley's *WADD: The Life & Times of John C. Holmes* in 1997, used in conjunction with an interview conducted with her son, Greg Yedding. Yedding graciously agreed to speak with me on behalf of Ann from his home in Arizona, in anticipation that a complete biography will be written about his mother one day.

Nudie Cutie

GREG YEDDING: My mother grew up in Spokane, Washington and lived with her mother and step-dad. I met him only once as a child, and I've since learned she had other siblings which I didn't know of or meet until my

grandmother passed away. I met them at her funeral that we held in Spokane. Most of the information I have acquired about my mother's stepfather is from her half-sisters, Mary and Marjie.

As my mother grew up with her mom and step-dad in Spokane, she attended a Catholic school. While she was there, she met her first husband, Ron Myers. That's where she got the acting name of "Myers," which she used in her early days in the Nudie Cutie movies. Later, COURTESY OF GREG YEDDING

my dad became her second husband. Mom and Ron met at Catholic school where he was studying to become a Jesuit Priest and my mom was planning to become a nun. Then she started becoming a rebel and she and Ron married. Needless to say, Ron didn't end up going into the priesthood, and my mother didn't become a nun.

She had two kids with Ron, her first husband. Chris was her oldest son and he died at six years old of spinal meningitis. I only met him once. My mother also had a daughter, Linda, with Ron, but I don't know where she is at this point. She is older than I am. I had grown up with Linda and I knew her as a child. I did track her down about seventeen years ago but we haven't been able to

COURTESY OF GREG YEDDING

find her. My aunts and I have all been working on locating her. The reason Linda became a recluse is because when she was thirteen while my mom was married to her third husband Don Perry [after my dad], something happened. None of us knows exactly what happened, but my mother disowned her and threw her out of the house. She hasn't talked to Linda since.

In and around 1960-'61 while my mother was still married to her first husband, she started doing modeling, and became a Go-Go dancer in a birdcage for a while in a club. These stories are the things I have found out from talking with family. In 1961, she became a hair model, and then she and my father [Ray Yedding] met in modeling school where my father was a male model. It was a Lou D'Angelo modeling school in Burbank. My mom and dad started dating and she got pregnant with me. I was an unplanned pregnancy and my dad talked her into keeping me. One of her friends worked for a law firm that supposedly drew up the divorce papers for mom and Ron, and then she and my dad got married in Las Vegas.

I asked her once if there were any wedding pictures because I don't recall seeing any and she said, "No, we just got married in Las Vegas." They really did get married but I asked my dad what year he and my mom got divorced and he told me that the year was in

Ann Perry with her mother and father. COURTESY OF GREG YEDDING

1968. She was trying to fight for child support and custody, and the courts wouldn't give it to her because they found out she was still legally married to Ron Myers. They ended up doing what they called "dissolution of the wedding" in 1968. She didn't get alimony, but my dad wanted to be sure that I was taken care of. No matter what private school she sent me, he made sure he paid his half and that I was taken care of.

My mother had also worked for a clothing store in the early sixties called Harris and Frank Clothing, and in 1961-'62 she was employed by another company, Quality Photos, where she had worked with a man by the name of Norman Arnold who ended up becoming my godfather. They did some photo shoots with me — I was the foremost dairy baby in the early 1960s. I was on the side of all of these milk cartons, but I wasn't missing. I was a baby model back then.

In the 1960s mom had used an alias and that name was "Cathy". As "Cathy," she was a Pin-Up Girl, and she was what they used to call a "Lindy Girl" for pens where their tops would come down when you turned the pen upside-down. She was on the lid for Lindy Pens. My aunt Mary had told me that my mom was doing that in the 1960s. I did find some of her Pin-Up pictures where she'd called herself "Cathy". My dad said she did a *Playboy* layout in 1965, but she said she did the layouts in 1961. I've seen the layouts and they are in her garage, but you just can't get into it right now. They are in her portfolio books.

Her father apparently came across the *Playboy* layout. He had known nothing about what she did for a living. I was always told when we went to my grandfather's house to never talk about what my mother did for a living. Her father knew nothing at all until he found her in the layout for *Playboy*. Apparently, she was dressed as "Little Boo Peep," and when you turned the page, she was naked and the sheep was sheared. I've been trying to find it, but I can't. She was also a Playboy Bunny at one time. I don't know if she actually worked in a club. I'm still trying to locate her Playboy bunny costume.

Later, she and my dad ran a mail order company out of the living room of our house. When they started to expand, their friend L.J. Winkler came in to help them and they moved everything to the warehouse. My mom and dad were working together.

"Are you girls a bunch of nudists, or are you just short on clothes?" RUSS MEYER'S *FASTER PUSSYCAT! KILL! KILL!*

ANN PERRY: I believe that it was in 1961 I was in *Playboy* Magazine. Not as a centerfold, but because I had done a movie with a comedian from England who wore magic glasses that made everybody nude. You know, when they first started to do the Nudie Cuties, I made a lot of those. It was in the early sixties. The X-rated films of the time were really Nudie Cuties and it was a time when Russ Meyer was shooting a lot of big-breasted ladies.

Russ Meyer, a German-American former police officer, worked as a still photographer and shot few centerfold layouts for *Playboy* Magazine before becoming a talented cinematographer. Meyer produced his first official Nudie Cutie film *The Immortal Mr. Teas* in 1959. "Teas" created a sensation which unleashed a successive flood of films marked by sexual premise, generally supported by strong female roles emphasized by Meyer's propensity to cast large-breasted women such as Shari Eubanks, Uschi Digart, and later, Kitten Natividad. Hugely successful in his endeavors as a filmmaker, Meyer overwhelmed the imaginations of mostly male consumers and roused wannabes who attempted to craft their own styles and techniques, as they emulated the "King of the Nudies."

Perry recalled the protocol for acting in and shooting early films intimating sex.

When I started in the film business, I worked for [late exploitation producer] Bob Cresse a lot and various other guys that were shooting. I worked up my way up through all the transitions in the business to a little more explicit, as far as being an actress.

In the films, in the beginning, often times you'd be jumping on trampolines or in a swimming pool. Most of it was bare breasts and you couldn't show pubic hair. That was forbidden — very no, no, to show pubic hair. There were certain rules that you had to follow. You couldn't touch a man by the hand. It was interesting. Most of the films were comedies and a lot of the comedians that they used were from England. They were still considered very bad X-rated films at the time and then things eventually progressed. In fact, around that same time, I had a mail order company and I actually got arrested by the FBI for selling film and shipping it across state lines. It was a brochure showing a man and a woman sitting on a bed holding hands, and underneath the picture of the man and woman holding hands, it said, "What do two people do when they fall in love?" Nowadays it would be on TV — probably on the *Disney* channel. It really progressed from there.

As cases were won in court, and as people got more artistic with what they were doing, it sort of segued from your Nudie Cuties into a story line and a plot. Still, the sex wasn't too serious because you couldn't expose the lower part of your body. Men always wore their underwear or their jockey shorts. Otherwise, they could always prove in court that he was nude. They didn't show pubic hair, but they could show women from the rear so if they did a sex scene, for example, the camera was usually behind you and you were sitting on top of the guy. He would have his shorts on.

They weren't loops; they were full length, features; thirty-five millimeter films. As I was saying, they hired a lot of actors and actresses that were in regular Hollywood films. I was in a film with Barry Bostwick [Susan Sarandon's boyfriend Brad in *The Rocky Horror Picture Show*, 1975] one time but these were all still Nudie Cuties. One I did with Diana Dors played all over Europe. They were big in Europe maybe even more so than here in the United States. Some of my friends that were doing films — we would do as many as thirty or forty a year. Many of the producers that were making these films went on later to make general release movies. Francis Ford Coppola did some [adult films] when he first started out.

Twenty-three year old Francis Ford Coppola, an aspiring director and recent graduate of film school, was hired to shoot forty-five minutes of 3-D color footage containing naked beauties to augment the film *Bell-Boy and the Playgirls* (1962) transforming it into a quasi Nudie Cutie contender. The German-produced picture that starred buxom babe, June Wilkinson, revolved around a hapless Bellboy hoping to learn about the mysteries of women by spying on them through the peek hole of a theatre wall. Ann (billed as Ann Myers) played one of the topless models. Likewise, in 1962, Perry (billed as Ann Meyers) portrayed Sally, one of the nude sunbathing school girls ogled upon by Frankenstein, Wolfman, and Dracula in the feature *House on Bare Mountain* directed by mondo, exploitation, sexploitation/ blaxploitation filmmaker Lee Frost, and his partner, producer, and screenwriter Wes Bishop (uncredited). Producer Bob Cresse played one of the leads as Maude Frickert.

Moving Forward

According to Yedding, concurrent with Ann's appearances in some of the early sexploitation films, Perry played a villainess in an episode of the *Batman* TV series and she was the Mercury Cougar woman who appeared in the television ads. By 1967, life started to abruptly change for Greg and his parents.

Nineteen sixty-six was when my mom and dad were still doing the mailing list, and in 1966 or `67 is when they moved it into the warehouse. At that point, my dad was working for a jewelry company, but as I'd mentioned, they got divorced in 1968. I had to go to a foster family for a year while they fought in court over me and mom finally won. She was the type of woman that never really wanted to have kids. It was just the thing to do. She wanted to have kids because everyone else had kids, but she didn't want to have to care for the kids — she would rather someone else take care of us. It was somewhat of a status symbol to have kids. We were always brought up around maids, or houseboys or something like that.

I don't really know what her hobbies and interests were but she did like water skiing and things like that, because there were a lot of photos of us water skiing and snow skiing as kids. She wasn't quite the camper type of girl. I don't think it was her thing, but she went along with it because her girlfriend had kids the same age so we went together to family events. I remember she did like making my Halloween costumes. Inevitably, I got sent away to school so that she could go do her thing. Eventually, my mom was living with Don Davis, the producer whom she had been involved with in several movies. There was an interesting film my mom was in called *Dial a Degenerate* (1969) that was made under Don Davis Productions.

The press-kit for the relatively obscure Don Davis fetish film, *Dial A Degenerate*, that advertised scenes containing "bestiality" in the promotional poster, highlighted Ann Myers in a starring role with an actual release date of 1969 (*IMDb.com* listed the film's release as 1972). "Iann Myers" is credited with writing the original story and screenplay, while curious co-cast members included "John Holmer" and "Frank Mazzone." IMDb also showed early porn starlet Sandy Dempsey as part of the film's team of actors.

While my mom was still appearing in the Nudie Cutie movies, another one of the first films she did for Don Davis was called *The Golden Box* (1970) and it co-starred Marsha Jordan. As a kid, I used to hang around with my mom and Marsha and go to San Diego to The Pussycat Theatres when they were signing autographs. She would take me along, and I would sneak out of the hotel room and I'd go down and watch her signing her 8x10 photographs for people in front of the theaters. I grew up with Marsha and I was told to address her as "Aunt Marsha" so she was my aunt. I think [Marsha] was an exhibitionist.

The Golden Box is a campy, robust adventure starring Marsha Jordan and Ann Perry (as Ann Meyers) playing two former models, Diane and Donna, whose destiny is dramatically altered when their composer friend is killed by the mob. The girls are entrusted to inherit his life's fortune in gold. To claim their inheritance, Diane and Donna must first steal back the book of compositions from their friend's perpetrators and solve a

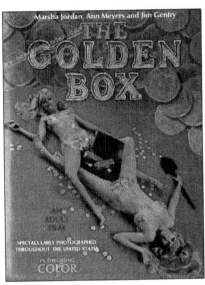

Dial A Degenerate and *The Golden Box.* HOLLYWOOD CINEMA ASSOCIATES

musical riddle concealed within a lyric. With Jordan's knock out curves, and Perry's spry personality, the females (a 1970 sexier version of Lucy Ricardo and Ethel Mertz) decked out in mini-skirts and big blonde wigs, pull out all of the stops in their resolve to stay on task in pursuit of their pot of gold. The feather light film includes full frontal nudity, and a couple of simulated sexual conquests: Jordan beds the bad guy (played by Roger Gentry, the police officer in *The Thing With Two Heads*, 1972) working for the mob and in direct competition with Diane and Donna for the gold bars. The good time girls also engage in some oral antics — sometimes two on one. Gorgeous Barbara Mills joins the cast in a sensual encounter at a marina where Diane and Donna are hiding out from the mob's stool pigeon. It appears Mills is paired with real life husband Frank Mills (billed as Frank Harris, uncredited) as they make love on top of a bunk — humorously revealing afterwards that they are siblings! As dated as this material is, the story is cohesive and brings about some genuine chuckles particularly during the narration sequences provided by both women exhibiting excellent chemistry. Perry and Jordan do a fine job bringing to life a pair of apparent empty-headed blondes, far more resourceful and devious than they let on.

Anecdotes: In a scene where Jordan and Perry enter an adult movie theatre, *Marsha, the Erotic Housewife* (1970), co-starring Ann Perry and Roger Gentry (directed by Don Davis and produced by "Sexploitation King" Harry Novak, one of the most influential early cult film directors) is on the marquee. Additionally, in order to indicate the conclusion of a scene, gold bars spin around rapidly in much the same way that the "Bat" signal rotated quickly designating the next segment in the 1960s *Batman* television series — a distinct reminder of innocent, less cynical times.

> GREG YEDDING: My mother was very much a private woman even though she was outgoing in these movies. Her initial drive was to succeed in business as a woman and she ruled with an iron fist. She wanted to prove to men that a woman could do a man's job and that's what she did. She kept a lot of her personal feelings to herself because she thought it was a weakness. She definitely wasn't going to let that out there. I asked her later on in years after she'd married Joe Rhine why she divorced my dad and she said that he was "too nice". She meant he wasn't a strong, initiative type of man that she thought was going to succeed and make money. What she looked for in a husband was someone who was going to be aggressive and make a lot of money. If they were weak or didn't make money, she moved on.

Hold the Pickle

According to his spouse Helene Terrie, pioneer adult filmmaker Kirdy Stevens, renowned for creating the *Taboo* series, was the first in his league to provide mail order service for hardcore "loops" and sex films directed toward a select client base in the United States starting in 1967. Ann Perry followed suit, and in the interim, she continued to do favors for friends and associates such as Stevens by appearing in their films even though her interests and focus were rapidly progressing to new horizons. Sheer nudity graduated to softcore, and softcore gravitated to hardcore. *The Toy Box* (1971) is an example of a softcore horror film in which Ann had a prominent role. Perry remembered how quickly the business transitioned and she took advantage of opportunities.

The business was changing, and as it changed, I did a lot of films that were semi-horror in nature and they had some nudity. Kirdy Stevens made a few of those films that I was in and it really was fun. I was doing a lot, but it seemed that I was more interested in writing so while I'd be sitting around waiting to go on set, I'd be writing scripts. Then I really got into it and started doing the mail order. I started selling photographs through the mail, and I started shooting sixteen-millimeter movies. The first movie that I shot was called *Peter the Great*, starring a little midget. Again, they weren't hardcore but they were still what you would consider Triple X. They were bad films for the time. This was the first time that they showed a penis or male genitals. They still weren't showing females fully nude. They showed a male and [suddenly] that was all right. In the early days, if accidentally, you got a shot of a man in full nudity, the cameraman would often yell "pickle". That meant that something was showing and they had to reshoot the film. Eventually, it got so that it didn't matter as long as nobody was touching him, and nothing was happening. I shot *Peter the Great* and then I went on to shoot more films in sixteen millimeter. That's how I got involved with the Adult Film Association because I started shooting bigger and better films. I started shooting quite a few sixteen-millimeter movies.

In the beginning, I shot a film called *Doctor I'm Coming* (1970) with John Holmes [Myers is billed as Ann Meers], and I didn't do any hardcore in the film. It could have been edited in later, but I didn't do any hardcore. A lot of times, I got hired to do the dialogue and I didn't mind working with the people doing the hardcore, but I never did the hardcore myself. In *Doctor I'm Coming*, I recall that I was on the phone in a lot in different rooms and the actors were all doing hardcore. Later, I shot John in a couple of sixteen-millimeter films. One was called *Getting it Up* and the other one contained far less plot and more sex that I later shot in thirty-five millimeter. Once I started directing and producing the thirty-five millimeter films, I really didn't often work as an actor anymore. Although there were some people in the business who were friends of mine like Walt Davis [aka David Stephans] that I did work for when I wasn't doing work for anybody else, just because I liked him. I still didn't do any hardcore scenes — whether they added it afterwards or not, I could care less. There was a time when I cared but I didn't care later. I never did hardcore myself [as an actor] in films.

Ann's appearance as an "Abon" girl in director Walt Davis' amusing hardcore feature *Olé* (1971) epitomized her ability to engage with hardcore performers (Gerard Broulard, Judy Angel, John Holmes, Lynn Holmes, Sheldon Lee and Susan Westcott) in an X-rated film without "going all the way". Perry's perky character arrives on the scene delivering products to enhance sexual stimulation just as an orgy is about to break out. She is completely stripped down and spread-eagled beneath various cast members, but the sex is simulated.

It was actually very hard for me when I first began shooting hardcore. I didn't even want to interview a guy to be in a film and look at his penis because I thought that would make him feel bad so I always asked the males to bring photographs. I would interview them and have them read and I'd look at their body with their shorts on, and then I would hire them without looking at their genitals. Be that as it may, it was hard for me in a scene where people were ejaculating and making love to really use hardcore terms, but it worked and I think that I got along with the people that worked for me pretty well. We always got the shots that we needed, while working quickly or whatever.

I shot most of my films in Los Angeles. We had sizable crews working and we just did it. You had to be careful that nobody was on drugs, and that there were no drugs on the set because I wasn't about to take a bust for drugs on the set. We always used to say even if you have to pick the actress up and shake her to see if any fall out of her pockets; we don't want anything on the set. It also makes your shooting a little bit more productive shall we say if nobody is stoned. We were very careful about that and our films were very smooth and went very well.

Changing Partners

While Ann and Don Davis continued to cohabitate, Davis directed a PG (Parental Guidance) film titled *Swamp Girl* (1971) with famed Country and Western singer Ferlin Husky in the principle role as the swamp ranger. Perry is credited as the production assistant and script girl.

GREG YEDDING: While my mom was with Don Davis, there was a movie she did called *Swamp Girl* (1971) that was directed by Don. It was actually one of the Nudie Cutie movies back then.

They put me in this movie. This was in Florida in the Okefenokee swamps. It was about a little girl who was an orphan and grew up in the swamp. Her father was a moonshiner and he died. When the little girl was young and living in the swamp she was supposed to have been kidnapped, so they stuck me in a mailbag and carried me through the swamp. Then the little sidekick guy that was the caretaker where she was living, killed the kidnappers at the swamp so I played a victim in the bag. I was the stunt kid. When they killed the kidnappers, they had to drop me into a rattlesnake pit. I think they had to do the take about five times because they kept dropping me on my head. It was funny.

Greg shared some of the amusing, and sometimes eccentric sides of his mother while on sets, and at home.

When on location there were alligator farms there. [The film's producer] Jack Vaughn's wife and my mom were given baby alligators so she and Jack's wife had a bet whose alligator would live the longest. My mom brought the baby alligator back from Georgia in a sewing basket between her legs on the plane and spoiled this baby alligator. It started barking on the plane and the woman next to her was dying to know what was in her sewing kit. We kept the alligator in a big fish tank in the kitchen. You were supposed to feed it raw hamburger by placing it on the end of a pencil, and then shove it down its throat. One night my mom decided to give it something different and when she later cooked the hamburger, the alligator choked and died.

When we went back to Georgia, I remember sitting in the Marriot hotel and watching my mom play a contestant on *The Dating Game*. She and the guy didn't want to go on the trip together so I don't know what happened there. We just sat in the bedroom taping hundred dollar bills from end to end. When we saw Jack Vaughn and his wife coming into the hotel, we dropped them over the balcony.

They always said that I was like a forty-year old midget. If my mom held a party at the house, I was the bartender. At fifteen, I would make scotch and water for Don Davis.

My mom and I had this thing where we liked to scare each other. Early one morning, I remember I was thirsty and started drinking milk directly out of the container which we weren't allowed to do.

I was drinking milk out of the container and it was a very windy night. My mom with her long, blonde hair was wearing a long, blue chiffon negligee. She had woken up because the wind chimes were too loud, and she wanted to grab the wind chimes so she decided to walk around to the outside of the house. She walked outside and looked into the kitchen window, and saw me drinking milk out of the milk carton. When she knocked on the window, I turned around and the refrigerator light shone on her face and on her light blue negligee. My heart dropped, the milk carton hit the floor, and I started running in space screaming my head off. It was hysterical.

Once again, the seven-year itch incited Perry to sever ties with her current flame and join forces with a new mate. This time her husband was not well liked by her children. Ann, who believed successful men were the catalyst to marital bliss, saw her professional life sustain the momentum it had achieved, while her industrious spirit brought about additional opportunities as Greg explained.

Don Perry would be my mother's next husband after she split with her partner Don Davis. Don Perry owned his own magazine — a money making opportunity. His wife, Patty Gardner, was her best friend. Patty and Don had been married prior to my mother, and they got divorced. My mom got married to Don in 1971. Don was a very abusive step-dad. That's when my sister Linda came to live with us and something happened. This is an assumption from my aunt and family, but we think that something could have happened between Don and Linda, and that's why my mom threw her out of the house. My mom would never talk about it again. Even to this day, she doesn't even know Linda exists. She hasn't seen her or talked to her once since that day. When we talked to Linda, she said, "You'll have to ask mom." She wouldn't talk about it either so it's a dead subject.

We were close. Linda was my older sister. We had a normal type of sibling rivalry. Don's daughter Lisa was living with us, she was older than Linda was. At that point, my mom was trying to boost her career. She was a trophy wife to Don and kids were kind of in the way. I was sent to military school and the girls were sent to private school.

In the 1970s when she was married to Don Perry is when she acquired her production company. The way she got the production company was through someone whose name I've yet to find out, but this individual was being indicted. He didn't want to lose the company so he put my mom's name on the company and then it belonged to her. He was supposed to sign it over to him later, but she kept it and that's how she got into the production part of the business. She called the company Evolution Enterprises.

Evolution Enterprises

As proprietor of Evolution Enterprises and throughout the mid-late 1970s decade, Ann Perry enjoyed her most auspicious and profitable years as a filmmaker. Simultaneously, she also became the first female member of the Adult Film Association of America. Perry knew which side her bread was buttered and played fair while integrating into a field that had formerly been an insulated men's club. By this time, Ann was a seasoned filmmaker but shooting didn't always go according to schedule, especially when the "heat" was on.

ANN PERRY: I was the first person that they had allowed in the Adult Film Association of America [AFAA] that was shooting sixteen millimeter because it used to be sort of a pecking order. Thirty-five millimeter people were way up on top, and sixteen millimeter people were somewhere close to the bottom. Then there were the eight-millimeter people. Forget it. They didn't even speak to them. I joined the Adult Film Association, and then I started taking the money that I was making on the sixteen's that I was shooting, and using that money to make a thirty-five millimeter film. That's how I started into the thirty-five millimeter, directing and producing. I really wanted to direct my own films because I wrote them. I understood what I meant when I wrote a scene and I knew how I wanted it. The other advantage of it was that if there was a problem while we were shooting, I could say "Okay, everybody, take an hour, I'll rewrite the scene," and I would go off and write my own scene and come back and it would work. I understood what it meant from beginning, middle, and end instead of just working on a section at a time. I really had scope of the film.

I was hired to do a film for a producer at Paramount studios one time and he had a partner that hired me to write it and direct it. We went to a sound stage in Hollywood. It was definitely a hardcore film from the front to the back, and they brought a whole bunch of Hollywood people to watch me direct to see how we did it, and to learn how we were doing it — what our camera angles were and how we were lighting and the whole bit. Well, it was very funny. There were two unusual occurrences. One is that I was using a monkey. It was called a Gibbon ape that had belonged to a woman who dated one of the big agents, Hal Guthu. Guthu supplied a lot

COURTESY OF GREG YEDDING

of the X-rated performers in Hollywood. Hal's girlfriend's name was Carol Davidson. Carol had this wonderful ape named Tyler with long arms and long legs so she let me use Tyler in the film. I wrote a crazy hardcore script. It was something like "The Fountain of Youth," and that anybody who drank the semen from the ape would be forever youthful. That was the premise of the film and it was very funny because the ape was a girl not a boy. When we did close up shots of the ape ejaculating into a wine goblet so that the people could drink it, I had to hide a baby bottle nipple in a wig and have the baby bottle nipple sticking out of the reddish-haired wig. On the close up, it looked like Tyler was ejaculating into the glass, and then it would be drunk, and they would remain forever youthful and prolific.

Just about everybody was in this film. Everything went well the first day and all these Hollywood people were sitting around enjoying and voyeuring, as it were, and just having a good time. The second day, there was a rat someplace. Evidently, the rat got the FBI and the cops involved. They came into the sound stage prior to our meeting to start filming and they went into the attic. We came and we set up, and we were shooting, and I was directing. I was shooting this film and giving instructions and all the cops were up in the attic. During our break, they came down and arrested us all. It was funny. I remember one guy was chasing me around a desk and telling me that I couldn't use the phone, and I said, "Yes I can," and I started calling my attorney Stanley Fleishman. I was dialing and running around his desk and the cord was hampering me because we didn't have cordless phones at the time. Finally, I got a hold of Stanley and I said, "Help Stanley, I'm being arrested." He said, "Just don't say anything. Just don't talk to them."

Ultimately, that case became a very big ordeal where Judge Dell ruled oral copulation wasn't illegal between consenting adults. That was our case. That was my case. The name of the producer was Joe Justman and Joe Justman worked for Paramount Studios. We had several court appearances and Joe Justman died during the court appearances. There were many, many actors and actresses, all of whom had their own attorneys, so you can imagine how long this case took to try and get it into court. It never really did get into court, and then Joe died in the middle of all of this. Judge Dell ruled that it was unconstitutional [for charges to be laid] for conspiracy to commit oral copulation which was what I had been charged with because I was the director of the film. I was the conspirator which interestingly, makes that a felony rather than a misdemeanor.

"Conspiracy to commit oral copulation" and other felonies such as "pimping and pandering" during the illegal era of adult filmmaking were charges often employed by authorities to attempt to bring disciplinary measures to those responsible for the production of pornographic movies. Legal eagles like the constitutional attorney, Stanley Fleishman, were often solicited by triple-X producers and affiliates to successfully defend Freedom of Speech and First Amendment Rights.

When you do the act of oral copulation, it's a misdemeanor and you are charged around fifty dollars. That's what a prostitute would be charged if she was caught oral copulating somebody in a car. That's all they were doing. It was very interesting, and that is why the judge was able to declare it unconstitutional because at that time, in the state of California, it was not against the law to have oral sex with a consenting adult. Anyway, that was great and it was a real turning point, except then the police got a little smarter about what they would charge people with when they made arrests.

Counting the Ways

I worked my way through one film called *Teenage Sex Kitten* (1975) that starred Rene Bond which was another softcore film. Not hardcore. As I'd mentioned, people started adding hardcore to films that had initially been shot that weren't hardcore. I think the film became hardcore later. You would shoot your soft version and then you would shoot another version and then use inserts. That was very commonly done. Obviously, it was not as smooth a transition when you were doing that kind of a thing as when we actually started shooting hardcore films.

In *Teenage Sex Kitten*, adult pop cult favorite Rene Bond played a swinger, Debbie, and paid the ultimate price for her free spirit and sexual proclivities. The story starts out innocently enough: along with her best friend Sean and their two boyfriends, Debbie makes plans for a weekend away in Palm Springs — only the group is short on cash. The guys convince the girls to use their sexual wares to help pay for gas and lodgings along the way. After the group arrives in Palm Springs, Debbie runs into trouble with a bar patron for exposing her privates on the dance floor. She is kidnapped and raped by a violent and frustrated misogynist, then beaten, and accidently killed by the kidnapper's overzealous, dim-witted sidekick.

Apart from Bond's overt sex appeal and adorable pixie face, *Teenage Sex Kitten* (with hardcore inserts) is not particularly pretty, and makes one curious as to why Perry (billed under the directorial name "S.B.", aka "Superbitch") wrote and delivered this peculiar and morose story. On the other hand, one of Ann's subsequent films, *Count the Ways*, is quite the opposite in its tone and message.

> I think that the first thirty-five millimeter film that I made was called *Count the Ways* (aka *Let Me Count the Ways*, 1976). It was a romance story and women liked it which was great, as far as I was concerned. There was a little poetry in there and it was handled delicately. It did very well. I kept taking the money that I would make on one film and roll it into the next film.

It is easy to understand how *Count the Ways* with its snatches of flowery poetry spouted by the actors (Tyler Reynolds, Yvonne Green, Justina Lynn, Joey Silvera and Desiree West are all featured), and injections of romantic interludes would appeal to female audiences. The screenplay, written by Perry and set in an academic institution where the professor seduces his impressionable students by reciting Shakespeare and E.B. Browning, has all of the markings of an adult film strategically fashioned with women and couples in mind. That's not to say the feature succeeds in its objective to appeal to a broader audience base apart from classic adult film fans, but one can't discount Perry's attempt to strive for lofty goals. Within the X-rated world, Ann's instincts paid off as *Count the Ways* won an Erotic Film Award and became a successful financial endeavor for Evolution Enterprises.

Greg recalled the immense popularity of the film upon its release and remarked how his mother's clandestine mode of employment occasionally impacted his interpersonal relationships.

> *Count the Ways* (1976) was a big money maker for her. It was her first full feature. She used the name Ann Perry as a director and producer. She still has the ¾-inch videos and has *Count the Ways*, *Teenage Sex Kitten (1975)* and *Sweet Savage* (1978), but as people have distributed them, some of the movies have changed titles. You'd have working titles and then they get changed.

During this time, I wasn't really allowed to have neighbor friends over to the house because you'd never know when they'd be filming or something, or running around. If any of the neighbor kids' parents found out what my mom did for a living, they wouldn't have wanted their kids exposed to it. I had been interviewed on radio while she was doing radio interviews and they would ask her

Family portrait. COURTESY OF GREG YEDDING

about family, and she'd say she had a son. They'd ask where I was and she'd say I was at home. They'd ask how I felt about her career and she'd say, "Why don't you call him and ask him?" Here I am at ten or eleven and they'd call me at the house from the radio program and ask how I felt about my mom's career. I'd say, "It's what she does for work. It puts food on the table and I don't know any different. It is how I grew up." That, to me was a normal life. *The Brady Bunch* [television series] is like a freaky family to me. I just didn't know any different. During the summer vacation as a child, I'd help her in her office and work in her mail order company. I'd be stuffing envelopes and putting adult items in boxes, and sending them off to people.

My mom and Don wanted to travel so we're talking about Vegas every month, and Florida — once in a while, if we weren't in school they would bring us to Hawaii with them. Two or three times a year, we'd go to Vegas with them. My mother's game of choice for gambling was Roulette, and Don's game was Craps. They played Craps and Roulette all the time. What they would do was give us a hundred dollars and send us off to Circus Circus [hotel]. We'd hang out there. We'd always stay at the Riviera Hotel and we'd walk back down the strip to the Riviera and page them over the intercom system. Then they'd meet us and give us another hundred bucks, and we'd go either back to Circus Circus, or we'd go to the bowling alley and bowl every night. We really weren't supervised. We just knew that we had to meet them for breakfast in the morning in the coffee shop and meet out during the day at the pool, and then we'd go see a show. Then they'd give us money and we'd go do our thing.

I had a little more initiative when we'd go to these shows because I was intrigued by people like Norm Crosby, Eydie Gormé, and others. I'd find my way backstage through the kitchen after these shows and I'd go through the dressing rooms and get their autographs. A cute little blonde boy in a suit jacket — man, you can go far. Nobody questioned why this little kid was walking the halls. This is the early seventies, so I was ten or eleven. I still have my autographs of people we met.

My mom wasn't a drinker and she wasn't a smoker; she was a very controlling woman. She was a very cold woman. Like I said, there weren't a lot of physical emotions displayed growing up, but I knew she was fair. She took me away when there were problems from husbands and we'd spend the night in a hotel. She was my mom and I love her to death, but I received physical affection from my father.

Madam President & *Sweet Savage*

ANN PERRY: After I had joined the Adult Film Association and had been shooting thirty-five millimeter films for three, four, five years, I became President of the Adult Film Association. I was the first woman President. I'm pretty sure that I got elected President [of the Adult Film Association] because gentlemen that I had worked for in four or five films: Don Davis, Dave Friedman, and Vince Miranda, got their heads together and made the decision to elect me because I was their buddy. We used to hang practically every evening after we got finished shooting, and they probably thought that they could tell me what to do. Dave would remain Chairman of the Board of Directors and then I, as President, would be great for publicity. It was good press, and it was great for the Women's groups.

The late Dave Friedman, known for producing exploitation and "roughie" pictures, is one of two co-founders of the original Pussycat theatre in the early 1960s located at 7734 Santa Monica Boulevard in West Hollywood, Los Angeles. By 1968, the theatre had expanded to a dozen Pussycat adult movie houses reaching across the state of California. Vince Miranda, in conjunction with his lover George Tate under their company Walnut Properties, bought a fifty percent share of the theatre in 1968 and renovated the façades and furnishings to the tune of one million dollars. After enjoying almost two decades of success, by the mid-1980s, due to diminishing attendance records resulting from the advent of video, the Pussycat theaters were forced to shut down or make the conversion to regular admission movie theatres. At present, only the first and authentic Pussycat theatre remains. In 1985, at the age of fifty-two, Vince Miranda died from cancer complications.

In their way of thinking, they believed they were still controlling the Adult Film Association and now they had a woman, sort of like a figurehead, sticking out there. They should have known better because I have my own mind and I like doing what I like to do. That's why I liked owning, producing, directing and writing my own stories because I didn't have to apologize to anybody. I always figured if I had one that didn't make money, hey, it's my money, so who cares? I mean, I would care, but on the other hand, I wouldn't really feel I had done an injustice to somebody else. I would go along and I was always friendly with a lot of the little producers and the people that were just starting out, and the actors and the actresses. I believe I dealt with them all on my level. We were all filmmakers, as far as I was concerned and I never felt that I was above them. I think that, in a sense, there were a lot of people in the Adult Film Association by then that sort of believed the same way I believed, that it was time that the higher-ups stepped down. I was re-elected for two years so that made three years that I was President of the Association. The important thing was that we wanted the people that were starting out, the little people, to have a chance in the industry, and not just have the industry exist as it had in the past. There were too many rules and regulations.

Around this time, I shot a film called *Sweet Savage* (1979). We were shooting two versions of our movies with the same actors and actresses. I would shoot a version clear through with hardcore scenes, and I would shoot a softcore version with the same people. I'd hire hardcore actors and actresses and that worked real well because my foreign sales at that time were heavily soft core — not much hardcore. It ultimately became a blessing because when cable TV started to buy film, they were buying softcore footage/films and I had all of that. It worked really well.

We shot *Sweet Savage* for almost a month in Arizona which was real different from shooting a day in an apartment when you're shooting a sixteen-millimeter film. We went through a period where people didn't shoot in Los Angeles because the heat was on, so to speak, and you just didn't do that. I always felt you know — I like this business and there is nothing wrong with it, and I'm going to shoot where I like to shoot.

Sweet Savage, another offspring of Evolution Enterprises, is set in the Wild, Wild West, and contained lavish production value evidenced by the exterior sets, costumes, and musical score. "Savage" starred Native American porn actor, Bethanna, as a young woman who falls in love with a white man (John Hollabaugh). The Caucasian male town folk (John Seeman and Jesse Adams) are none too pleased by the cowboy's choice for a mate, so they gang rape the native maiden triggering a small tribal retaliation involving the girl's brother (played by Tyler Reynolds). Incensed, Bethanna's big brother kidnaps the sister (Eileen Welles) of Bethanna's boyfriend and takes her virginity — only to discover he made a mistake and the real perpetrators hadn't yet been caught. Upon realizing the error of his ways, the young native man apologizes to Welles in a letter and teams up with his sister's lover to catch the real bad guys. Carol Connors (in only two segments, although she received top billing) is featured as a busty saloon girl while her real-life husband, Jack Birch, imbibes with Connors in the opening oral scene on a stagecoach. *Sweet Savage* won a prize at the Erotic Film Awards. It deserves an "A" for effort.

You could show a film that would be okay for almost anyone. Again, I always had a problem being convinced that hardcore X-rated material really was bad. I thought that it had a lot of merit and I liked my own films. It was also this time that a couple of the feminists groups here in Los Angeles, one of which is still in existence called NOW, were picketing us. Everybody really kind of benefited from all of that though. We started to get a lot of publicity. We also started getting national publicity and a lot of magazines were calling and wanting to do interviews.

The National Organization for Women (NOW) has been in existence since 1966, with Advocacy for Women's Rights at the heart of the group's fundamental mandate. Since its inception, NOW has grown to over 500,000 members strong, and champions reproductive freedom, lesbian rights, a halting of violence against women, and equality for all.

In the midst of the eye of the firestorm that saw the ranks of various women's groups such as NOW and WAP (Women Against Pornography) vehemently protest an industry that repeatedly produced films containing explicit sexual content, Ann Perry, accompanied by her latest cinematic effort, *Sweet Savage*, proudly attended the Cannes Film Festival. Greg shared in his mother's pride of the success of *Sweet Savage*. Eventually, he was hired to work behind-the-scenes on Ann's productions.

> *Sweet Savage* would be my mother's jewel. I would definitely say that's her golden child. The way they represented *Sweet Savage* (1978) at Cannes was under the title *Sexy Sweet Savage*.
>
> I grew up working in my mom's business and eventually, working for the production company distributing her films and other things. I'd have to go to these film marts where everyone was showing them. We were doing the posters for *Sweet Savage* and hired a photographer named Blasco to do the box covers and magazine posters. The hair and make-up artist didn't show up on set so because I'd gone to a few years of hair school and now I was working in my mom's business, she said, "Greg, you've got to do hair and make-up for these photos."
>
> I said, "I don't know anything about this."
>
> She said, "You know more than anyone else about this." I did the hair and make-up for the posters and Blasco loved what I did and told my mom's company that she needed to send me to professional hair school. I went to Paramount, and I started doing make-up for Paramount and began working on *The Carol Burnett Show* and other shows.
>
> Candida Royalle, Carol Connors, Sharon Mitchell, and Eric Edwards: these are all people that I grew up with and associated with on a daily basis. I grew up in adult world without kids so my

friends were my mom's business associates. My mother hired some interesting people in her movies like Aldo Ray, who had been in all kinds of war movies. I think he played the head villain in *Sweet Savage*. Some of these films were shot in her office. They would have fog machines, and I'd be lacing girls up in corsets and it was great fun. I also did the make-up for *Undercovers* (1982) when she was working.

Perry is billed under the directorial credits in *Undercovers* as Virginia Ann Perry in this funny spy spoof about a high tech device inserted into the vagina of Becky Savage. The mechanism has the power to make men climax in three minutes reducing them to an infantile mental condition. Savage, Sharon Mitchell, and especially Samantha Fox and Bobby Astyr, are terrific in their assigned roles on a quest to harness the appliance with the potential to ruin men and alter world order. Real life companions at the time, award-winning actors Samantha Fox and Bobby Astyr shared in an intensely beautiful love scene complete with a crackling fireplace and appealing set design inducing the tone for a romantic atmosphere and genuine show of eroticism. With meticulous attention paid to scenery, costumes, and makeup, this thoroughly enjoyable caper is one of the best of Ann Perry's collection.

My mother didn't want to make fuck films; she wanted to make love stories, which is evident in her films with candle lighting and costumes. She wanted to make romance movies. A lot of her films came from personal fantasies and she told me once that even the girl-girl scenes came from her own fantasies.

Meanwhile, the tension between her and Don Perry was getting thick back then and Joe Rhine happened to be her attorney. He was a big criminal attorney in San Francisco during the sixties and seventies. Kennedy and Rhine was the name of their law firm. They were a pro bono type law firm back then. Joe was Angela Davis' attorney and Timothy Leary's attorney and The Black Panther coalition. Joe and Kennedy had helped Timothy Leary escape from prison — which was kind of a big deal. There were a lot of other famous clients. Eventually, Michael Kennedy became Ivana Trump's divorce attorney.

The partnership of Kennedy and Rhine also represented porn forerunners Artie and Jim Mitchell back in their prime as the law firm built its unfettered reputation by weaving a diversified tapestry encompassing a radical, anti-establishment clientele. Joseph Rhine, lauded for efficiently and compassionately representing the little guy, and the oppressed, became Ann Perry's fourth husband. Ann and Joe were married for twenty-six years until Rhine's death from heart failure in 2003.

Out of all of my mom's husbands, besides my dad, Joe Rhine was the best. He was awesome. They started dating when she was on the set of *Sweet Savage* (1978) because he was her legal representation. It was filmed here in Arizona. That was one of my first times meeting Joe because I stayed with her while she was divorcing Don Perry. I believe I was thirteen at that time. Don was Jewish and he wanted me to have a bar mitzvah, but it wouldn't have been legal because my mom wasn't Jewish. At that point, they were really fighting so she whipped me away to Arizona. I had gone to school here [in Arizona] in `75, and that's where I met one of Joe's daughters [on set] and we had our own private time in the hotel. They started dating and I eventually learned more about Joe. He was very big with the Farmer's Union, and he was a very well known guy.

Joe and Kennedy decided to dissolve their law firm because Kennedy and his wife wanted to move back East to New York. That's when Kennedy started working for Donald Trump's wife Ivana. He began handling her divorce from Donald. Michael Kennedy didn't want to do pro bono work anymore, but Joe is kind of that down-to-earth, hippie-type dude, and still wanted to do that stuff so he and Bob McDaniels teamed up. They became the law firm of Rhine and McDaniels, and continued doing the pro bono work.

After Joe and my mom started dating and they moved to the Hollywood Hills, I remember that the rental house was down the street from Doc Severinsen. Bob McDaniels had one of the rooms in the house and he was a nudist and a pothead, so he'd be walking around the house nude and stoned all the time.

Meanwhile, Ann's notoriety as a female adult filmmaker continued to make waves as she explained.

A couple of major magazines contacted me and we did interviews, very extensive interviews. I did a big interview for *Playboy* magazine; the Japanese version came out and they took photographs of me and they had a big spread in the Japanese *Playboy* magazine. So all countries were getting interested in what was happening in the United States, X-rated wise. I called up reviewers that reviewed general release films for *Variety* and I actually got people to come out and review my films. I would get screening rooms and serve little goodies. It was done professionally just like the major people

Joe Rhine and Ann Perry. COURTESY OF GREG YEDDING

were doing and so it started to be accepted like that. When we had screenings, we had people from all over. There always had been an interest in our films from the other side. There was always a lot of interest and I think that they saw money. Of course, we always had two or three versions of our films.

Ann's private life was business as usual, as Greg revealed how his mother's wedding to Joe Rhine was one for the record books. One could never guess-who-was-coming-to-dinner in the Perry-Rhine household.

Eventually, she and Joe decided to get married at the house and the Mitchell Brothers were both their best men at the wedding. One of them was the flower girl coming down the stairs throwing rose petals out of a basket. My mom is an avid animal lover and she had this parrot named Flipper at the time. The judge asked if anyone objected to the marriage and everyone was quiet in the background, but you could hear the parrot go, "Oh, no!" They were filming it so you could hear on tape.

On another occasion after they were married, we'd be sitting down for Thanksgiving dinner and there was a new man sitting next to me. After he was introduced as Timothy Leary's son Jack who was wanted for murder, I said, "Okay, just please don't let him pick up the knife."

Just Like Starting Over

Prolific filmmakers such as Ann Perry, who were able to prosper during the golden era boom of erotic movie making, saw the writing on the wall when video and VHS began to dominate the marketplace. Many of the larger studios were able to roll with the changing of the tides but independents such as Perry's Evolution Enterprises decided to cut their losses and seek opportunities elsewhere. Prior to moving out of Los Angeles to Washington, Ann had a couple of decent years left and produced *Ballgame* in 1980 with a star-studded cast headed up by the delightful and sassy, wise-cracking Candida Royalle flanked by ample bodied actresses Lisa DeLeeuew and Connie Peterson. While speaking with Royalle about Ann Perry, Candida shared how she had appreciated that Perry was one of the few directors who allowed Candida to let her own personality to shine through in the role. Royalle acknowledged how the tone of sensuality prevalent in *Ballgame* foreshadowed Royalle's future as a filmmaker emphasizing the female perspective. She is wholly respectful of the wonderful director and person that Ann is. Former Freeway Films director and AFAA co-member, Julia St. Vincent, was a friend of Ann and Joe's and dined regularly with the Rhines and other AFAA cohorts such as Carlos and Maria Tobalina after meetings. St. Vincent recollected Ann had invited her to sing "Take Me Out to the Ballgame" at the AFAA awards show held at the Hollywood Palladium in 1981. The gesture was an effective promo gag fashioned to highlight Ann's latest film offering. When the popular Tobalina film *Casanova II* (starring John Holmes, Jesie St. James and Rhonda Jo Petty) was released in 1982 in which Ann played a TV reporter in a non-sex role, St. Vincent recalled how in keeping with tradition, the closely knit group of AFAA friends celebrated in grand style. Julia's memories of Ann are that she was inclusive, caring, and always a lot of fun.

ANN PERRY: I left the business after I decided that I would like to move from Los Angeles. I should have been smarter and I wasn't, but I thought that I could keep my company here in Hollywood and I could move to Spokane, Washington where I was born and raised. You know what they say; you can't go home again. My whole family was there. My mom was there — everybody. I went up to Spokane by myself and I couldn't believe property values. Things in Los Angeles were starting to get very expensive and I went up there to an area where I was born and raised, and had gone to school where it was like Beverly Hills. I saw this incredible three-story house with an elevator. It looked like it belonged in the heart of Beverly Hills and it was a hundred and twenty-thousand dollars. I made them a low offer and they took it. Afterwards, I called Joe on the phone and I said, "You are not going to believe it. I just bought a house". That's what started it. Poor Joe, bless his heart, he gave up his law practice and moved to Spokane with me. We moved lock, stock and barrel. We sold our house here and I kept my company open in Hollywood. I had my editor here and I took my movieola with me. That tells you how long ago it was; I didn't even have a flatbed, I had a movieola. My editing assistant kept the movieolas that she had down here, and I thought I could keep the momentum going.

Yedding provided a little more insight into Ann's decision to move and set up new operations in Washington.

My mom's mother in Spokane was in a serious fire and burned over ninety percent of her body. She had fallen asleep on the couch with a cigarette, and then they figured out it was an electrical problem with the heater. That's when my mother hung up the production company and she and Joe moved back to Spokane to take care of my grandmother. They were there about seven years and Joe had to pass the state bar exam but they wouldn't allow him in criminal law. He was married to my mom who was involved in porn, so they were living off their savings and decided to buy a movie theater. They bought this very cool old movie theater with the big balcony and big curtains, and turned it into a porn theatre. They would play all of their movies and distributed all of their films there. They started getting raided left and right and strippers would perform on weekends on stage. It was just like the *Rocky Horror*

Picture Show. This is the late 1980s when they ran the Dishman theatre. Other people's movies were coming in too and they began showing them as well.

They tried to close up one night at three in the morning and this one guy wouldn't leave the theater. Joe walked down from the camera booth and discovered the guy had died in the theater right

Left to Right: Joe, Greg and Ann. COURTESY OF GREG YEDDING.

in the chair. They had to call the coroner and it was determined that the guy had been dead for probably over twelve hours. My mother and Joe had to call the guy's wife to pick up the car and she said, "Oh, no, my husband would never be in a porno theater." We wondered what part of the movie he was watching when he died!

Ann's original goal, to keep her feet firmly planted in two states didn't work out quite as she had expected. Her sequel to *Sweet Savage* unfortunately was never completed as the stress and financial burden proved to be too overwhelming.

ANN PERRY: Right before I moved to Spokane, I shot a sequel to *Sweet Savage.* I shot it mainly because the first *Sweet Savage* was doing incredible money in Europe and particularly, in Holland, so they wanted a sequel to *Sweet Savage*. I rented Paramount Studios, the Paramount Ranch, and I hired a lot of people that were shooting general release movies who were in my movie. I also hired the people that were doing hardcore and I mixed them all together, and I shot a sequel to *Sweet Savage*. I moved to Spokane, and then I gave my reels of film to the woman that was doing the editing. I thought that she could do a good job because she had been an assistant editor on a lot of my other projects, but I discovered that it didn't work. When I had my editing facility inside my office, I could walk back and look at what was on the movieola, and I could say, "I don't like this. Change this. Move that". I had such marvelous control because I wrote it and I knew what I wrote. I knew where everything was. I knew the continuity of the film from the beginning to the end. I did take one precaution and that is while I was shooting the thirty-five millimeter I was also shooting video tape. I had all my footage on videotape so that I could look at it, and I could see all my cuts. I could see everything. It still didn't work though because I had to be in Los Angeles. I tried flying back and forth and it became incredibly expensive. I just took all the footage, all the thirty-five millimeter film, and stored it. That was the end of my sequel to *Sweet Savage* and that's how I kind of got out of the business. I finished shooting it, but I never edited it.

An effort has been put forth on the part of friends and associates to get the unreleased sequel to *Sweet Savage* into distribution, in 2012.

GREG YEDDING: You know it's a big stepping-stone for women to make a name for themselves in the adult entertainment industry. I adore and know these women and I respect everything they've done and gone through in their lives. I think my mother is very proud of what she did and what she achieved in the industry. She started something and then the girls just went farther with it. She never regretted it a single day in her life.

Barbara Mills
Eat, Read, Live

2

Barbara Mills (nee Caron) made her erotic film debut in 1968 and has the distinction of never having performed authentic sexual acts with males throughout her brief, but notable career. As a respected sexploitation actress, Barbara reflected on her history in adult pictures with an air of indifference and bemusement. She is known for her mesmeric thespian work in *The Love Garden* (1971) and *Blue Money* (1972), and easily stole the show riding nude horseback in *Sweet Georgia* (1972).

Shortly after turning seventeen, Barbara left her home in Massachusetts and ventured to Venice Beach, California. In the late sixties, she established permanent roots there along with her husband of more than forty years, Frank Mills. Drawn to its bohemian vibe and idiosyncratic lifestyle, Mills flourished in the relaxed beach community and continued to develop her artistic skills while accepting occasional work doing nude modeling and acting. With her long brunette mane and classic appeal, Barbara considered her employment in adult films a stepping-stone which enabled her to pay the bills so she could focus on her primary love, painting. When Mills quit acting after her first child was born in 1972, she was hired to do make-up for occasional adult productions while Frank worked as a camera and lighting man.

With beguiling charm, Barbara fondly reminisced about the cherished friends she met during her years in adult entertainment and valued the charm of the era in which she worked. She believed in doing what was required in order to be happy. Along with Frank, Barbara chartered her life in a way that afforded the couple to embrace several memorable opportunities together. As a woman respectful of all living things, over the years, Barbara fostered her spiritual side and became a non-denominational

"I believed my individualism to be an extension of the sixties revolution. I felt in control of my life. And I had a partner; Frank has been a great life partner." BARBARA CARON MILLS (1951-2010)

COURTESY OF CARLY MILLS

ordained minister. She married five couples on Pomona near Venice Beach before leaving southern California upon her retirement.

In 2009, Barbara and Frank moved to Thailand to be closer to their son Nigel and his family while retaining a close relationship with their daughter Carly, a painter and wardrobe designer residing in Venice Beach. Since leaving the United States, Mills fully immersed herself in Koh Samui's island culture and felt at home within its tropical beauty.

On December 15, 2010, at fifty-nine years old, Barbara Caron Mills passed away peacefully at her "spa" home surrounded by Frank and her loved ones. Following the death of her mother, Barbara's daughter Carly Mills agreed to be interviewed for this book which appears later in this chapter.

I interviewed Barbara Mills in the summer of 2010 while she and Frank visited with Carly in Venice.

She Was Just Seventeen

I grew up in a small town, Oxford, Massachusetts. I had a brother that was two years younger and a sister who was nine years younger. I remember when my parents brought my brother in from the hospital; they hadn't told me they were pregnant and I remember being angry. I was really pissed off. I was a twenty-four month old.

We lost our parents young. Our dad died in 1962 and our mother died in 1969. My dad was in a car accident; he was only thirty-three and it was very sad. He was on his way home from work on a rainy night. I was eleven when my dad died and my mother was useless. I was pretty much a house mommy for a while. I wasn't that good at it. I changed my sister's diapers, but you wouldn't know that today. They had pins back then. It was the time where it wasn't cool to be a widow and it was all couples but my mother had a couple of other widowed friends so they had a little club. They had very little support. It was nothing like they have today. My mother was never able to work after my dad died and my sister was only two. Her heart just wasn't in it. She got Workmen's Compensation through my dad's work and we lived off of that and social security. Seven years later, my mother had a cerebral hemorrhage. Their deaths were both sudden so it kind of put you in a cocoon of shell shock. I'm sad that my parents never got to meet my kids.

I was head cheerleader in high school and co-head cheerleader. My interests were mainly reading, but I was a bookaholic and I enjoyed painting. I started painting in oils when I was about ten.

My friends have suffered from oils, especially as they get older due to the toxins. Over the years, I've switched to acrylic. Acrylics have evolved into a space where you can get any viscosity, any hue you want. I painted at home when I was growing up.

My Uncle Homer really was a role model for me as an artist when I was young. Homer Gunn was his name and he was pretty well known on the East Coast. He's the one who bought me my first set of oils and encouraged me to paint. My Aunt Maxine, a teacher, was also very inspirational and still is to me. I just came back from visiting her.

Homer Gunn, a cubist bronze sculptor, studied at Rhode Island School of Design from 1938-1941 and taught between 1941-1957. He was the resident sculptor at Deerfield Academy in Western Massachusetts from 1957-1969. Due to the abstract form of his impressive collection of work that positions triangles at slight angles yet bears no distinctive definition, Gunn's pieces have been compared to specific works of distinguished conceptual artists such as Picasso and Marcel Duchamp.

I was depressed during my teen years. I used to do murals all over my walls and my mother was okay with it, but I did one painting that was backlit and you know how sixteen year olds are. I had a girl's figure hanging in the doorway. I ended up painting over it, of course.

I had come to visit California on my own when I was seventeen. I thought I was having a nervous breakdown. I had been in high school and I'd always gotten good grades, and my grades had been slipping. Everybody was doing drugs then. It was easy to get pot and I did acid up until maybe 1968, but I was never in love with the stuff. I loved cheerleading and the last thing I did was turn in my basketball cheerleading uniform. I had looked up California in the *World Book Encyclopedia* and came out here. It was February 1968 and I had just turned seventeen. Luckily, I ended up on Venice Beach which at the time and still is, very calm. It was calmer though at that time.

California Dreamin'

Barbara didn't have friends or relatives living in Southern California when she first struck off for the gold coast, but she was able to navigate her way out to the ocean.

I asked the taxi driver to take me to the YWCA. I was alone at the time and it was located at the 6th Street and Hoover in downtown L.A. He said, "Most people go to Hollywood."

I said, "Oh really? I forgot that was near here!" I said, "Just take me to the YWCA and I'll find my way around." The next day I was in for a big surprise because downtown L.A. was horrible at the time. Some guy asked me if I wanted a ride and I said, "Okay, but just drop me at the beach." He dropped me at the beach and he tried to put the moves on me, but I told him I was way too young. I met some people on the beach and they helped me to find an apartment. Apartments were very cheap back then. This apartment was eighty dollars a month.

Venice Beach has always been an artistic community ever since its conception. Being that most of the streets were canals when they first built the city, and then it was the Gay Nineties, and the Roaring Twenties, and bathing beauties and muscle beaches started. It was crazy. There were a lot of poets: Ginsberg and artist Laura Lee Zanghetti lived down here and it evolved, but it has always stayed bohemian. Venice Beach has always been a very comfortable place to live. It's cold sometimes with the wind coming in off of the Pacific, but other than that, it's a good place to be.

Venice Beach, California was founded by tobacco millionaire Abbot Kinney at the turn of the 20th Century and converted into a beach resort town boasting more than two miles of oceanfront property. The beatific canals ensconced within its esthetic neighborhood and modeled after those in Venice, Italy, feature some properties containing gondolas. Topping it off, the canals are offset by the sparkling white coastline shouldering a bevy of athletic and entrepreneurial activity along the boardwalk. In conjunction with San Francisco, in the 1950s, Venice became a haven for the Beat Movement. Since the 1960s youth reform, Venice Beach has grown into an eclectic artistic community where an array of pop figures, artists, and celebrities such as Jim Morrison, Dennis Hopper, Jean-Michel Basquiat, Angelica Huston, Robert Downey Jr., and many others have resided or currently own properties in and amongst the trendy promenade.

I worked at Woolworth's behind the soda fountain. It was horrible. I was just a messed up kid and I knew I had to go back to Massachusetts. I told my mother I wanted to come back. She was worried about me even though she let me go and we decided I was going to go to hairdressing school, so that's what I did. I was back at home until she died in March. At that point, things got crazy. My grandparents were too old to take care of us. We were very close to my grandparents [my mother's parents]. My father's parents died young, when I was a baby, so I never really got to know them. My aunt and uncle were almost at the point of being too old to take care of us at the time, so they hired a housekeeper.

After Barbara's mother passed away, Barbara traveled to New York City where she became involved in modeling and dated an up and coming rock star — a drummer. In 1969, after the better part of a year, Mills debated between a departure to Woodstock or to Los Angeles to become an actor. She decided upon the latter. At the time, Barbara lived with a man who eventually tried to set her up with her future husband, Franklin Mills.

Then I found out I was pregnant. I came back here to California looking for an abortion, actually. Abortion was kind of legal at that point. It wasn't actually legal, but there were some experienced people performing them. I had the abortion because of all of those stories about drugs use and how they can harm the unborn fetus. Two years previously, I'd done drugs; it probably wouldn't have harmed the child, but on top of that, I was in no position to take care of a child anyway. If I had to redo it, I probably would have kept it.

True Love & Sexploitation Films

I met my husband Frank in 1969. Shortly after my mother died, I came out here and met him. He tried to meet me in Massachusetts; he was from Massachusetts too. He had gone back to Massachusetts to his brother's high school reunion. Our mutual friend thought we'd be perfect together so Frank called me on the phone and he sounded so pompous, you know. I didn't want him to come to my dinky little town just to meet me. He did imbue me with ideas and some lofty intentions, but suddenly, he was in California trying to get into the film business. I ended up moving in next door to him three months later. I looked at him and I said, "God damn, he looks like John Lennon." He did then. John Lennon was everybody's favorite Beatle — we had to switch over to the other members of the Beatles when we found out that Lennon was married.

Anyway, Frank and I fell in love then through all of that period. We had our fortieth anniversary in February [2010]. Frank got me work, and he got me an agent. One of his neighbors, I forget her name, got me into modeling. I did quite well strictly modeling and then came the Sexploitation films. It all started when the United States was allowed to show X-rated films, which was in

Barbara and Frank Mills. COURTESY OF CARLY MILLS

and around 1968. That' right when I started. Hal Guthu was my agent's name. He was a sweetheart. The last time I actually saw Hal was in 1972.

Hal Guthu was one of the first agents to represent female and male models and actors during the early days of the softcore film industry in Los Angeles. Guthu's studio was discreetly located on Santa Monica Boulevard in Hollywood where he kept binders containing information on his growing collection of talent and often photographed prospects himself. Hal Guthu died in a rather mysterious fire in 2000. He is widely remembered by those he represented for having integrity and character.

Mills admitted during our interview that her memory is vague about some of the dates and other aspects surrounding her career. The first feature documented in Barbara's filmography is *The Harem Bunch* aka *War And Piece* (directed by cult film director Paul E. Hunt and co-written by Bob Cresse, 1969) in which Barbara recalled using body paint in a mud wrestling scene that didn't come out after the shoot.

Actually, sometimes I can remember things from back then and sometimes I can't. I didn't willingly hold onto any memories. There are some things in my past where I say, "I've got to remember this and I do." It was a job, after all. It wasn't a career move. It wasn't an art form per se. It was a job and it paid well, and it left time for living. I enjoyed the people. It wasn't sexual. I was fierce back then. People were afraid of me! They treated me with a lot of respect.

Unlike many other softcore film actresses who progressed to hardcore once the industry made the conversion, Barbara drew a line in the sand which served to further capture the attention of her grass roots fan base.

The little known 1970 release *Delicato* (aka *Passport to Pleasure*) directed by Nick Philips (aka Nick Millard) is one of Barbara's first endeavors as an actor. Many of the early releases such as this one were billed as Denmark productions in an effort for filmmakers to avoid arrest. *Delicato* featured Barbara (in an uncredited role) in this supposed travelogue adventure along with her best girlfriend at the time, Lynn Harris, in addition to Suzanne Fields and Maria Arnold. Stunningly clad in leather from head to toe (apparently director Millard's trademark), Barbara is portrayed as one of three swinging hippie girls. The film contained simulated lesbian sex and full frontal nudity.

In 1971, Mills and Linda York played lesbian lovers involved in a triangular tryst with Jason York in *The Love Garden* wherein Barbara delivered a remarkable fusion of tenderness and detached cool. Her naturalistic execution, particularly prevalent in her love scenes with York, lends a startlingly tranquil beauty, stirring and delighting the senses in the otherwise average simulated sex film. The respectable outing was produced

COURTESY OF CARLY MILLS

by veteran director Bob Chinn and directed by Mark Haggard. At the time, Chinn had commenced production of the very first adult film series detailing the life and loves of private detective Johnny Wadd, played by John Holmes. A year later, in 1972, Barbara portrayed a young wife and mother in the mainstream flick *Blue Money*, a semi-autobiographical story about a young French Canadian adult film director (Alain Patrick)

COURTESY OF CARLY MILLS

drawn to the forbidden fruits of the industry. *Blue Money* was written and executive produced by Chinn with a relatively healthy sum at the time of thirty-five thousand dollars for the low budget feature.

I wasn't crazy — I was completely nude in my film appearances, but no penetration, no genitalia, and no oral sex. That would have been stupid. If you're going to sell it, you might as well keep your anonymity. They never tried to get me to do more. The filmmakers respected that and you would have to sign a pre-release. There were plenty of others willing to go that way, who got off on it. It was a business. We would talk about vegetable soup on set. I didn't do films for very long either.

The *Class of 74* was a spin-off of *Gabriella, Gabriella* (1972), and that one was released by Crown International. It was bad. It had some decent co-stars and everything, but the script was terrible and the direction was mediocre. *Class of 74* eventually ended up in the Oxford Drive-In in my hometown in Massachusetts! The state finally said, "All right." It didn't have to play in an X-rated theater anymore. I'm having some blocks of memory that is probably quite interesting. I'm just not able to pull out everything.

Although underused, beautiful Barbara Mills is the main attraction in the mildly entertaining feature *Gabriella, Gabriella* (aka *Gabriella* — the original uncut version was never shown theatrically) that is something of a modernized *West Side Story* (1961) except that Mills's character (billed as Gabriella Mills) and her boyfriend (Bob Kresting) prevail at the film's conclusion. Gabriella and Stephen are the subjects of two underground filmmakers with a goal to capture the young couple's pure and undiluted love for one another — something real and pristine within the ugliness and cruelty of the outside world. Mills is utilized mostly as window dressing and has little dialogue, but it's hard to take your eyes off of her sculpted features and chestnut brown tresses. According to Johnny Legend who wrote the storyline, the film's plot was to have been inspired by the late 1960s "peace and love" youth movement, only by 1969, punctuated by the stabbing death at the Rolling Stones concert in Altamont in December of that year, the movement was already in its decline. Directed by Mack Bing and produced by Jack Mattis, *Gabriella, Gabriella* included supporting actress Sondra Currie who was most recently seen in *The Hangover* (2009), and *The Hangover, Part II* (2011). *Gabriella, Gabriella* was re-packaged and re-released under its alternate title, *The Class of 74*, with an "R" rating grossing an impressive four million dollars.

Mills continued accepting work in blue movies during the early seventies and played a seventeen -year old housewife trapped in an abusive marriage to a much older man in Lee Frost's *Chain Gang Women* (1971). The revelatory depiction of incarcerated men working on a chain gang in Georgia during the early 1970s introduces Mills's character as she secretly welcomes escaped cons into her home in hope that the twist of fate will provide her with a ticket to freedom. Once again, Barbara is stunning to observe with her long dark hair and rosy cheeks complementing her porcelain skin. Mills's dialogue is sporadic, but her facial expressions skillfully project the emotions of a woman longing for the subtle touch of a man who can please her physical needs. She is shown naked above the waist in a rape scene, and her bare backside is visible in a subsequent scene where she initiates a lovemaking session with one of the ex-cons.

The film's best bits however, occur in the first half during the interior and exterior prison footage.

I thought *Chain Gang Women* (1971) was funny because it's not my voice. They dubbed it. It was Christmas time and we had plans to go back to Massachusetts to visit our families so it has someone

else's voice and it's funny. They did a poor job with the dubbing. I've done voiceovers too with Dave Friedman. Bob [Chinn] knows him; he's probably dead too — it'll come to me later.

Barbara is referring to David Friedman, the independent pioneer of the Nudie Cutie, movie scene who eventually formulated his own company in the 1950s. Friedman's productions would inevitably include "roughies," a harder, darker-edged variety of sexploitation films often containing violence, S&M, and/or horror themes. Dave Friedman became the third President of the Adult Film Association of America in 1971, and was re-elected four times before becoming Chairman of the Board. He died on February 14, 2011 at eighty-seven years of age.

Sweet Georgia (1972), that film was the one movie where they made me ride on a horse bareback in the nude. I've actually read some of the reviews of my films online. It's funny, I remember I once got a letter from this one guy who had seen some pictures of me in a magazine and wrote, "I just love the photos of you in this magazine. Could you please send me some close-up photos of your feet?" Some people had foot fetishes. I'll admit; I was pretty.

Whether or not she was able to recollect, Mills neglected to mention a film considered one of her best outings, *Matinee Wives* (1970), in which she had an opportunity to show off her competent acting moxie as Linda Devlin, a young, frustrated newlywed. Linda loses her sexual desire for her husband Paul (Stephen Treadwell) and enlists the aid of a friendly neighborhood Madam (Luanne Roberts) who hooks up Linda and her best girlfriend Pat Chandler (Allessanora) with one another's husbands for some hot sweaty sex. Linda lets her inhibitions run wild. Not realizing that their spouses are best friends or that they made love to one another's wives, in the film's paradoxical conclusion, the two men, feeling pompous about their lucky scores, decide to celebrate their sexual prowess by arranging a dinner date so their "lonely, neglected" wives can finally meet.

Panama Red

I stopped working in films in 1972. *Panama Red (*aka *Acapulco Gold* released in 1976) was my last film because I was pregnant. Nigel was born in `72 and I've got a big baby in there. Because of who he was, I thought it was ironically funny that in *Panama Red*

John Holmes was my buddy, patting my pregnant belly and making sure that I was comfortable, taking care of me. He was assistant director on that film.

Panama Red could quite likely be the forerunner to the weed lovers' cult classic *Up in Smoke* (1978) that starred the comedy duo Cheech and Chong. Thin on plot (not pot), but long on cannabis induced ramblings appropriately relatable to anyone who was under thirty in the early 1970s, the non-sex film *Panama Red* doesn't pretend to be about anything other than what the title suggests. Mills plays the very pregnant wife of her male lead, Jim Wingert, who hopes to unload enough dope in time to purchase two one-way tickets to Spain before the birth of the couple's first baby. A parade of familiar faces from late 1960s-1970s west coast adult film fare pop up throughout the picture: Rene Bond, Rick Cassidy, Sandy Dempsey, John Holmes, Alain Patrick, (softcore director) Walt Davis, and a cameo by the film's director Bob Chinn. The original Frank Zappa and Mothers of Invention drummer, Jimmy Carl Black, also makes a rare appearance.

Jim Wingert, an aspiring singer-song writer was solicited by Chinn for the purposes of writing and performing the music in conjunction with his role as the friendly neighborhood marijuana trafficker. Barbara and Frank Mills's Venice Beach home was used for authenticity in some of the film's footage, the very same house in which their daughter Carly resides today. Historically, *Panama Red* is significant to the landscape of the Los Angeles food and beverage industry as scenes were shot at Follow Your Heart (the subject of a new documentary in the works), a natural foods store and restaurant located in Canoga Park which recently celebrated its fortieth anniversary. The owner of the store, Paul Lewin, even had a small part in the feature that was graded one of the top ten "stoner" movies of all time by Toke of the Town.com

A lot of things happened quickly and these shoots were very short. After *Panama Red*, my husband was doing camera work for [director] Alan Colberg and we did some Johnny Wadd films in San Francisco. I was the make-up lady. The film that I remember most is *All Night Long* [directed by Alan Colberg starring Rick Lutz and John Holmes in 1976]. I didn't do the make-up on that one, but Frank did the camera work. They already had a make-up person. He was in his fifties then and had been part of the Max Factor team early on in his life.

John was a funny guy, actually. So was Alan. They all were. [Still photographer and friend] Joel Sussman is still funny. I got along very well with John. We had some yard sales for him. He'd sit there with a stack of *Screw* magazines, and he'd autograph them for people who came to the sale!

One time we were working on a film after Frank had become unionized so he had a different job. I think it was the last shoot I did with Alan and John, up in San Francisco. John had gotten a small dog and he wanted me to go through security before him and distract the people, which wasn't that hard to do when they were all male and I was young. I just chatted my way through and he skipped around the edges with the dog. We all had to leave San Francisco early because there was this big hurricane threat and we had to get home. We got on the plane and we were on a TSA trip, a businessman trip where the seats face each other in some portions. The dog popped out of John's bag and everybody laughed, and the stewardess thought it was so cute. The stewardess was just fawning all over John and she was asking him what he wanted, and then she asked, "What do you do for a living?" The whole plane erupted in laughter. Everybody recognized him but her!

You know, John was very nice to my kids. My kids liked him. One of our other friends, Lynny Harris [early adult starlet, Lynn Harris], had fallen head over heels in love with him and she was heartbroken when she learned he was married. I do have fond memories of John and Bob [Chinn]. I'm going to call Bob up soon.

Eventually, Frank did become a member of the IFC Union. I think it was in 1976, and at that time, I was working as a cocktail waitress. I worked at The Mayfair Music Hall and I waited on a lot of celebrities there. Juliet Prowse, Mae West, and Carey Grant were people I met there. I remember I spilled popcorn in Juliet Prowse's lap! After the kids were born, I ended up going back to college. When my brother died, I went back east for a year with the kids. Afterwards, I came back to California and then I started working for the school system.

Hands On

As a woman who did not choose to make the crossover from softcore to hardcore performing, it is quite possible that in addition to becoming pregnant with her first child in 1972, Barbara felt it was time to close the door on her role as an actress as more explicit sex films began to dominate the adult landscape. Once the change came, there was no turning back. Mills felt fulfilled by her new responsibilities as a mother and continued to find part-time work in different vocations.

I was a teacher's assistant and I attended college. I worked with pre-school children at first, and then I worked with severely handicapped kids — teenagers. The hours weren't good enough and the money wasn't good enough. I also went to work for the grocery industry as a deli-manager and then as a professional cake-decorator. I did enjoy that. When I went into other businesses like the school system, I didn't talk about my past in films. Eventually, everybody got onto Google so those who did, found me. That's okay. As I said, I have gotten e-mails from people a few times, but actually, nobody has ever recognized me personally.

Barbara held her love of art in reserve and proceeded to cultivate her excellent skills in various mediums throughout her years as a parent and while in the work force.

Alan Colberg and his wife Laurie came to some of my art openings. I was a member of the Malibu Art Association for a number of years. I was on the board. We had group shows and it was fun. Some of my paintings are on my face book profile. I like to paint landscapes, people, still life, and food. My daughter and I have been working on some fantasy scenarios, we were out painting late last night. It's a good outlet. Acrylic paints are a great medium. It's safe, it's non-toxic; you can do layers upon layers. You can work fast. It dries quickly. I actually sold a lot of my work just before I retired. It has been a sideline because nobody can actually live by painting alone. That's why I like cake decorating so much. We did all of these custom cake orders. I did paintings on chocolate cake.

Stimulated by a vibrant and conducive environment, Barbara's ingenuity as an artist and creator was heightened. Mill's love of flowers and plants are delicately reflected in her paintings in soft hues and also bold tones. Looking back over the years, Barbara recounted how liberal influences in the world of art, spirituality, and social structures made an imprint upon her and the manner in which she lived. As a result, Mills allocated her acquired wisdom to those fortunate enough to have traversed into her orbit.

I felt my individualism to be an extension of the sixties revolution. I felt in control of my life and I have a partner. Frank has been
a great life partner. He has always backed me up so I didn't feel the
need to press my political views or my religious views that were
practically nil — except that I was a very strong Democrat — on
anybody. I was living in Venice and that was a very individualistic

Carly Mills and Barbara Mills at an art opening. COURTESY OF CARLY MILLS

community. I did feel bad for some of my friends who moved into
less urban areas that had heavily religious or Republican views in
their towns. I invited many of them to come and visit and they did.

Some stayed and had families here, but most of them went back.
Everyone enjoyed the experience of Venice Beach because it was so
unique. Those were some funny days, you know. Venice Beach was
a nude beach for two summers. One year some company flew over
and unloaded a bunch of edible underwear all over Venice Beach.
It was a case of, "I got two strawberries and one vanilla. Do you
want one?" Then there were the malingerers on the side, the guys
who wore beach shorts and knee socks — like peeping Toms. We
didn't care about them. Where I'm living now, Samui, it's a young
society. It's almost a cowboy town. There are no traffic tickets, there
are no parking tickets, and property taxes are low.

Samui Fever

In many ways, Barbara discovered life in Samui was an extension of Venice Beach. Mills and her husband Frank were first introduced to the beautiful island haven through their son Nigel.

A friend of our son's was teaching English in Korea. Teachers used to go down to Samui for a warm holiday because Korea is very cold. It was very inexpensive. The beauty of it is it looks like a tropical island because it used to be a coconut plantation before it became a backpackers' paradise. Now it's more of a spa island. We were working and living here in California until May 2009 and we'd go to Samui for one month out of the year. We retired there last year [2009] so we've only been living there for one year. We bought the house in 2006, so now it's big enough for all of us. It's spread out — every bedroom has its own entrance, its own bathroom. It ambles down the hill. We got very lucky.

It's incredible how affordable it was to build a whole other addition onto the house. We're talking fifteen hundred square feet of addition. The average cost of an American kitchen is around fifty thousand for a remodel. We spent fifty thousand for a huge kitchen/family room, granite counters, step-downs, bath-powder room, and bedroom, and bath suite underneath. That's the difference. Unfortunately, wine over there has a four hundred percent luxury tax — the hotel owners are starting to quack about that now that the new Prime Minister has been approved and all this mess is over in Bangkok — they blew up the Paragon. Where we are, we're relatively isolated. There are about one hundred thousand people tops on this island. High-rises are not allowed. No building higher than a coconut tree. I'm afraid though that people are going to get too homogenously westernized.

I'm going to be sixty. I'm just like a hermit now. I go out to dinner parties and I go out to SOS [Sisters on Samui] meetings on the island, but I'm very happy staying home. I can't work because I have a retirement Visa. I couldn't serve at a public venue because I would be taking a job away from a Thai person. If a certain position is a job that a Thai person can do, they should be able to work at it. They work very hard and they don't make a lot of money. I cook a lot. My son has a catering business so I help him with that. I help him prep. His business is Nigel's Barbeque and Catering. His website is samui-catering.com. My kids are great. Nigel is thirty-seven, and

Carly is thirty-five. Our son's wedding is a special moment in my life, and obviously, the birth of our granddaughter was huge. The first one was born September 13 in Thailand in a moving car! Our anniversary is the same day that Nigel and his wife planned their wedding, so we had a big old party up in the hills of Thailand by the ocean. It is beautiful. I can't wait to get back!

Nigel, Frank, Barbara and Nigel's family and friends in Samui. COURTESY OF CARLY MILLS.

Regrets, I've had (very) few.

You know, things were different a few decades ago. Today you can go to Disneyland and you won't be turned away because you have long hair. I've often thought my own brother should have been born in the cowboy days, in the late 1800s. He died in 1978, in a fire. He just wasn't made for urban life. He listened more than he spoke even when he was a child, but when he spoke, he always nailed it. He was a great judge of character. My sister and I are very close. In fact, she's coming to Thailand on July 1.

Me, I'm too lazy for anything too complicated. I want to eat, live, and read. As far as changing anything about my past, I would have gotten a college degree earlier if the situation had been right and I wouldn't have had an abortion.

When I remember my former work in films, I believe we left behind a free spirit. We weren't condemned for what we did. We were sometimes greatly appreciated for our work. It was interesting. It was an innocent time, it wasn't considered real. The industry is quite different today and it will never go back to what it was. It was a one shot wonder — a small window of time, really.

COURTESY OF CARLY MILLS.

In Memoriam

Shadows are falling and I'm running out of breath
Keep me in your heart for a while
If I leave you, it doesn't mean I love you any less
Keep me in your heart for a while

— WARREN ZEVON

Barbara Mills's untimely death was felt deeply by her family and friends, and by those who cherished the woman who bestowed her gentle gifts of laughter and a sense of timelessness whenever in their presence. Carly Mills described the ceremony held in her mother's memory, and painted an absorbing picture of the last thirty-five years.

My mom was a non-denominational minister and she married five couples in the exact same spot, in Venice Beach, as where we had the memorial. As well, my brother and I were both christened there. They'd had a little ceremony and took pictures. It was interesting because my friend who was at the memorial is also a non-denominational minister and she read a few verses from the

COURTESY OF CARLY MILLS

same book that was my mom's actual copy of *The Prophet.* The energy there was strong, and even some of the couples that my mother had married were at the service. It was just so intense.

We probably had about a hundred people at the memorial. There were also people who couldn't make it to the memorial, but we had about sixty people back at the house. We all stood in a semi-circle and we had the four corners that represented the four elements. It really was incredible. I had no doubt in my mind what I wanted the ceremony to be. Everything I was completely certain of and I believe that's because of her guidance in some way. I was so clear in what I wanted, but then, it turned out even better. Everything about it was so momentous. Not only was it beautiful as planned but we had a bowl of water that was holy water and I bought white rose petals, and everybody went up to her altar and said a blessing or a prayer and put the rose petals and holy water on the altar. When it was time, I called someone from her bloodline which is my aunt and I went to pick up the bowl, and the moment I picked up the bowl we had a show of seagulls fly overhead. It wasn't chaotic or an arrow formation, they just swooped over as I was picking up the bowl. It lasted about a minute. Then we walked down toward the water and we poured the water out, and it was very weird because these dolphins started jumping out of the water. There is no way I could have planned anything like it. This was at Pomona — the ocean front walk at Venice Beach. Straight out from Pomona is where my parents met. My brother and I were born on that street. They'd had over ten different apartments in the sixties on Pomona on the Avenue. We timed the memorial perfectly to the sunset just as it was going down.

The picture of me and my mother together is really weird because during the service when I believe the minister was reading, my friend just happened to be standing there on the other side of the semi-circle and took a picture of me in front of the photo of my mother — that is my reflection in the photo. It wasn't planned or anything.

Escape to Passion

Barbara had always made motherhood her first priority, but as her children grew older and became inquisitive about their mother's past work in films, Mills began to slowly divulge.

CARLY MILLS: To be honest, for years and years, my mom was embarrassed of that time in her life and of that work. She really took measures so that my brother and I wouldn't know about it. It was only times when people would visit they would be more relaxed and have a bit of wine that these stories would pop up. When I became a teenager, I really started to wonder what was going on with all of this. As a young adult, I started looking stuff up on the computer and then I found that she had a fan page and there were these people writing really nice things about her. One of the things said was that she hadn't progressed to hardcore, which is partly why they were so enamored with her. Then we talked about it, and I told her, "Look, it's innocent and it's cute. You have a cult following of people who are really into this. It's something you should be proud of." She started to embrace it after that.

We knew that she was a model, and we knew she'd been in a couple of movies as an actress. I know she took us to a movie once and she wore big glasses. It was one of her later movies where they had just edited in material from previous movies. You know how they pick all of these old films and splice bits together. We walked out and she told us the story about it. Yeah, we'd seen all of these glamorous photos of her, but we hadn't known she had such a huge body of work. I've recently been collecting the posters for her films and *Escape to Passion* (1970) is one that I own. It sounds like it could be a good one.

Barbara (as Barbara Caron) had more than a few speaking lines in *Escape to Passion* where she played Audrey, the wife of Jason (Sebastian Figg), a Roy Orbison impersonator. Jason's ball-busted buddy Leo (Leo Schumaker) attempts to emulate his bad guy cinema idols by robbing a bank. After a shoot out with police Leo, his girl, and another crony plan to hide out at Audrey and Jason's pad. When they land in on the couple, an orgy is in full swing. Leo is incredulous that his overweight boss is in the middle of the party, and grotesquely covered in gooey Crisco oil while naked Audrey and a girlfriend take turns gliding across his stomach like a water slide. Sensing things will go from bad to worse, Audrey begins to cozy up to Leo, his pal, and his girl, in hope that one of them will take her along with them before the cops arrive on the scene and haul everyone off to jail. In the role of Audrey, Barbara is frisky, and as always, she is equipped with a naturalistic essence and sensual, classic appeal.

CARLY MILLS: I really believe that the key to all of this is these women like my mother were glamorous and they were edgy, and they were doing things that people considered questionable at the time. It's interesting because everybody was unique. They all came from all different walks of life. They were trying to get by, that was the major point. They weren't trying to be an actor. If a

Barbara with Carly and Nigel in the 1970s. COURTESY OF CARLY MILLS.

person has done something they're proud of or not proud of, you have to own yourself.

When my mom gave birth to my brother is when she started doing makeup on John Holmes's sets. — She stopped acting, and then when she had me she stopped completely because she had two kids and it was too hard to work with both of us. My brother was always on set with my parents and he remembers a lot more than I did. I was probably only two or three years old.

She was a stay at home mom so she took care of us, and she also took every single art class she could at Santa Monica College. I used to go with her to the art classes in whatever medium she was working in. I would have a coloring book and she would be using either charcoal or watercolor paints. She took a nude sketching or painting class and I used to go with her to that. It was my first experience with nudity when I was five years old. My parents never told me there was anything wrong with my body or anyone else's body. I never had any of those sexual fears or that it was wrong. They made sure that I was okay with it myself and not to be embarrassed about it.

Her first job was at an art store and then she got a job as a teacher in a Special Ed class. She was teaching Special Ed students — people with Down syndrome and other things. She also ran a daycare for a long time in the school system and worked in the school system for many years. When she went back to school to become a teacher, she ended up working in the food industry. She did deli-management and then she went into cake decorating. When she graduated from college to become a teacher, she was already making the amount that a teacher would make. My mom never took the final test that was required to become a teacher. You know, she really had wanted to become a teacher, but her insurance was better in the food industry and she was now doing the cake decorating which she really liked because of the artistic part of that. There wasn't any real reason for her to make the big move. Even when she retired, she was making cakes in Thailand although I've heard that it's more difficult because it's too hot there for the icing but she was doing it. She painted when she was there too. I photographed all of her paintings when I was last there because I want to put together a website of her artwork.

Carly and her mother enjoyed many common interests apart from their shared enthusiasm for painting and self-expression through art. When I visited Carly in July 2011 at her mother and father's former Venice Beach residence, it was like stepping into a time warp to more carefree, spirited days. The house is immediately inviting with wonderful art pieces created by both Barbara and Carly covering much of the naturally lit wall space within the home. The reverent sixties aura still lingers in the air like a ghost, and the outside garden is dotted with flowerbeds and herbs along the path, with little clay sculptures peeking out from behind clusters of cacti.

With coffee mugs in our hands, we sat down in Carly's living area surrounded by several guitars and microphones as she continued to describe life with and without her mother.

My mom was just so goofy. She liked to read Tarot cards. I read Tarot cards, but that was her big thing. I think she used it as an excuse to sit around and have girl time or talk about life or anything that interested us. It was our time to communicate about what was going on. So we would do that all of the time and we'd turn on our music. We painted together, too with our music playing. I always like to think about that. Even when I visited my parents in Thailand, she asked me if I'd brought my Tarot cards. I had forgotten — they'd been on the table at home so I didn't bring them. I ended up going to a bookstore and bought Tarot cards and they were easier to use. I always did the readings. That was when she had been in the hospital, so we never got to do a reading after I got her the Tarot cards, but I used them the other day and I got the best reading I'd had in years and years. I guess she had helped with that.

I had lived with my parents for quite a few years. My brother moved out early, but I would move out, live with a boyfriend for a year and come home. I lived with them for twenty-nine years, and I'm only in my thirties, so they were my friends. I really liked to hang out with my parents. One of the things I really miss about my mom is that my dad would put on music, and me and my mom would dance together. I could still do it by myself and feel as if she's there, but I really think about that. Dancing with my mom, she really loved that.

She was very spiritual. We were raised in a Pagan type fashion. I never went to church ever, I don't recall. At Christmas, she would talk about the winter solstice and things like that. We really had a non-traditional upbringing. My mom was very spiritual, and my dad, too.

Love Hurts

The reason I'm still single is because I have never seen anything that resembles the way my dad looks at my mom. It's the most beautiful thing you've ever seen. He gets this joy in his eyes. It's a real intensity. He sees her as if she's eighteen all the time. It's extremely difficult for him since she's been gone. He's not as communicative as my mom was. I would always talk to my mom, and my dad would talk through her, but now I talk to him almost every other day. He's doing better than I would expect really. I can only imagine how hard it is for him with her gone.

My dad didn't come to the memorial in Venice Beach, but he has remained in Thailand. The whole Buddhist ceremony is difficult and they do cremation and have an open casket. I don't think he was ready to face any more grief. It's just too sad for him to be here and be present for the memorial. She had about one hundred people at the memorial in Thailand. It started three days after she died. That would never happen in L.A. — it was just amazing, the outpour of people.

Her death from Hepatitis C is somewhat of a bone of contention for all of us. When they came home in May [2010], they had all their tests. My dad has little things he has to go to the doctor for and they had their annual check-ups. They would take a test for the liver and get the numbers back. She went to have all of her tests and she told us that everything was fine, that all of her numbers were normal, but I actually wonder about that because the doctor had not gotten back to her before they left for Thailand. I had said to her "Make sure you call him." I never heard anything back from her. Either she didn't call, or she thought he would call her if there was something wrong, or she was fine and it just happened very quickly. I don't know how long these types of things take. They were living a healthy life in Thailand. When they found out they had Hepatitis C they stopped drinking, but they might have a little glass of wine at a party.

In August 1999, *The New England Journal of Medicine* reported five million people living in the United States infected with Hepatitis C (HCV) believed to be one of the greatest public health threats in this century including the contraction of HIV. Eighty-five percent of people exposed to the virus will contract Hepatitis C in its chronic form, and twenty-five percent will eventually die from cirrhosis or liver cancer.

My dad has Hepatitis C too, but his numbers are fine. They believe it's from a blood transfusion that my dad had. He had several major surgeries throughout his life, and apparently, donated blood for Hepatitis C. The blood was tested only up until 1992. If it can only be transferred by blood, at some point, he and my mother must have transferred blood having been married and together every day for forty years. I had no idea that it could happen so suddenly. They didn't even know how extreme it was. My mom and dad had talked when they found out that her liver was starting to fail. This was after she went to the hospital in Thailand, and they were talking about whether or not they should tell us before Christmas, so they obviously didn't know it was so severe because my mom thought it would be better to wait until after Christmas.

She died on December 15 [2010]. She talked about having a stomachache and had heartburn, but that was about it. As a family, we're happy that she didn't have to suffer. She had hated doctors and hospitals; they made her uncomfortable. If she had to go, that was the best way, I think.

A Different Drummer

My mom seemed very satisfied in her life. When I think about the list of accomplishments she's had in her life, serving on the board of the Malibu Artist's Association and all of these things that she has done, it's a huge list.

There is one thing we found after she died. She used to hide Christmas presents all over the house and every year she'd forget some and come out in July and say, "Oh, I found another Christmas gift!" It was my job to look all over the house after she died and find them. We found that she bought herself a drum. She had been talking about wanting to learn to drum bongo drums. One of her best friends plays the drum and she was really into the drum circle, so she bought herself a drum and had been planning on learning it. We all got drums for Christmas because of it.

One of the things she asked me when she came into my room the night before she went into the hospital — I had played the guitar for her and she'd never heard me before, and she came into my room and was giving me a back rub. We were talking, and she asked me if I thought I would ever have children. I said, "You know, Mom, I'm not going to have kids. I don't really want children." I've been through a couple of big break-ups this past year, and she asked me if I thought I'd start dating again, and wondered about the direction my life was going to be taking. She already has one grandchild. I wish I would have told her that I was going to have kids because she would have maybe stayed longer or something. I think she knew. I've been telling her for the last ten years that I didn't want to have kids, but sometimes I change my mind when I meet a nice guy. My mother always told me how gratifying having children is and talked about carrying on the maternal line, mother to mother. She wore a wedding ring that was from her great-great grandmother from the 1800s, and when she died, it was going to be my ring, from mother to mother, to mother, to mother, or from mother to daughter. She was interested in keeping that line alive so I feel bad that I didn't tell her I wanted children.

It's funny. I ran across a picture yesterday. She was sitting in a sports car with her hair curled like Goldilocks with a racecar driver. She's sitting there topless in the racecar. She looks so sweet and innocent with her autograph.

COURTESY OF CARLY MILLS

I think of my mother as everything. She'll never be just one thing. She's a mother, a daughter, an artist, a creator. My dad calls her a "savior for the lost and stranded". There is no way I can pinpoint her life or soul; she's everything. It's the nature of people; none of us can be boxed in. We may choose to show a different side, or different mood, and people know us in different ways, but you can't discount one thing for the other. We had a very close relationship. My family was close, and everybody I've talked to are amazed because a lot of families don't get along. We're family, but we're also friends.

The day before they left for Thailand, my mom and dad were sitting in the backyard in the matching white wicker chairs, and my friend was over and she was playing the guitar for them. My mom had this smile of bliss; this real inner calm and peacefulness, and then I looked over at my dad and he looked all sad and pouty. His head was down and he had a tear in his eye, but she was so ready to go and then they danced. They danced together, and it was just so beautiful. I can't tell you how many times I had to tell them to go get a room. They were always so lovey-dovey. I don't know how people do that. We're all very lucky.

She had wanted to go to Thailand for so long, and she practically had to force my dad to go, but she created her happy place and that's her legacy really. She retired three months before they left so that's two years ago. She always sounded so happy and calm when I talked to her on the phone.

When I arrived there before Christmas, my brother had picked me up from the airport, and when I got back to the house, I was excited to see my parents because it had seemed like such a long time. I really missed them and I wanted a hug. I got inside and my dad ran up the stairs and gave me a big hug, and I saw my mom on the patio downstairs. She was just smiling and I walked down there. It was so funny because she said, "Oh Carly, I was just so happy to see you that I didn't feel the need to run over there. I didn't feel anything urgent about it. I am calm because we're all here together."

Final Thoughts

It's so weird to talk about her in the past tense. I still try to say, "My mom says," instead of, "My mom said." On her birthday, her sister and I are going to go on a boat to actually sprinkle the ashes. Her sister is in Ventura. I am especially close with her after my parents moved. We spend holidays together and she comes over often. I've always considered Lisa like my sister. She's more of a sister to me than an aunt. My mom pretty much raised her. She was actually in one of the films as background, or an extra with my mother when she was around fifteen.

I haven't seen any of my mother's films. I'd like to see *Panama Red* especially because it sounds like it was kind of cheeky and funny. My brother was born in August of 1972, so if my mom's about eight months pregnant in it, it would have been filmed that summer. A friend of my mom's called us one night to tell us that *Chain Gang Women* was on TV so I have an idea about that one. There is this whole resurgence of the Cult-Drive Inn classics which is kind of fascinating. It really made her world to know that her films had affected people, because as I'd said, she'd been ashamed of it in the past, and she became comfortable with it and embraced it. It was a part of her that she could finally feel whole about again, and not keep parts of herself away.

Looking back on it, there were so many prophetic moments. Looking at it unconsciously, she was completely fulfilled and maybe that's why she didn't need to live any longer. It feels that way to me in so many ways. They say "Only the good die young." She was loved and she was happy.

3

Georgina Spelvin
The Angel in Miss Spelvin

Georgina Spelvin has accepted that her stage name derived from "George Spelvin," the pseudonym used in American theatre by an actor seeking anonymity, will always be synonymous with her blue screen alter ego Justine Jones, the lead character in director Gerard Damiano's unforgettable adult classic *The Devil in Miss Jones* (1973). As the eloquent and introspective matriarch of the adult golden era of superstars, Spelvin continues to create enchanting moments through her verbal dexterity, her intellect, her indelible humor and wisdom. Today, she makes it all seem relatively easy, but her life has been anything but simple.

Born Shelley Graham, the daughter of a geologist who also served as Captain in the army, the Texas native moved frequently as a young girl forever adapting to new environments. While struggling to establish a place amid her peers, Spelvin found she was out of step with the latest fashion trends and often felt an outsider. As a result, she followed her own set of rules as a transient student. While residing in Tyler, Texas, Georgina joined a summer ballet camp and discovered her *raison d'être*; she grew enamored of the graceful theatrical expression and responded to the required discipline of dance. With her high school diploma in hand, Spelvin was lured by the bright lights of New York City along with the ambition of a career on Broadway. For more than a decade, Georgina danced in chorus lines and was involved in reputable theatrical productions. Eventually, as the eldest member of a commune of starving artists, Spelvin actively sought employment for the group which coincidentally landed her a role in a hardcore film production. It became a seminal point in her life. Similar parts followed, and Spelvin was suddenly in great demand for mature roles requiring sensuality and a keen ability to personify dramatic characters with flair, depth, and experience, as the

"I was actually thrilled to do an entire role and build a character and everything which is what I had set out in life to do. When it turned out to be a hardcore film, in the midst of shooting, I was not about to walk off the set. I just went right ahead and did the scene as it seemed to me it should be done." GEORGINA SPELVIN

COURTESY OF GEORGINA SPELVIN

scope of her filmography and awards for her work reveals. As Georgina's star continued to ascend, so did her penchant for alcohol. Inevitably, the bottom fell out of her world, but she has been effectively rebuilding ever since.

After leaving the acting profession behind, for several years Georgina was employed as a desktop publisher for the L.A. County Medical Association's bi-weekly magazine. In 2005, Spelvin was interviewed for the documentary *Inside Deep Throat* and had an anticipated cameo role in the remake of *The Devil in Miss Jones* (2005) with Savannah Samson reprising the Justine Jones character. More recently, Georgina's priorities have shifted to writing. Her first book, *The Devil Made Me Do it*, was published in 2008 to very favorable notices. Plans for a second book are in the works as is the audio version for "Devil" which Georgina painstakingly recorded herself. Today, at seventy-five years old, Spelvin is happily married to her true love, and recently celebrated more than thirty years of sobriety — an achievement she considers monumental.

I interviewed Georgina Spelvin in the fall of 2009 by e-mail, and over the telephone in November 2010.

Doodlebug Daughter

I was christened "Shelley". It was my mother's name and her mother before her, so I just wanted my own name. People think my name is short for Michelle, but the name "Chele" was made up when I was a pretentious teenager.

My early years were spent in the back of a Ford coup for the most part. I was always the new kid on the block. It isn't uncommon these days, but rare in the thirties. Dad was a graduate of Texas A & M College, so when the war broke out he went into the army as a First Lieutenant. He was soon promoted to Captain — then to Major, when he was assigned to be the Provost Marshall at Fort Howze, in Gainesville, Texas. This is sort of like a Chief of Police. It meant he welcomed all the celebrities that came to the base to entertain the troops. Mom and I would be introduced, and I had been kissed by Bob Hope, Gene Autry, and numerous other lesser names before I was seven.

Daddy was a Doodle bugger, a geologist that went around drilling holes in the ground in order to set off charges of dynamite in them which made little wiggly lines on a seismograph printout much the way a small earthquake would. These told the

Humble Oil Company — later Esso, later Exxon — all the spawn of Standard Oil of New Jersey where to drill for oil. There's a small bug called a "doodle bug," common to that part of the world—East Texas, Louisiana, and Oklahoma that backs itself into the sandy dirt to escape predators. When they do that, they kick up little puffs of dirt, rather like the cloud over a drill that's pulling one of those cores, hence "Doodle bugger". The crew doing this work would be moved to a new location frequently.

Whenever we landed in a new town, mother would locate a good market, the library and nearby church. Any denomination would do — it was just needed to get me out of the house on Sunday mornings. Her parents had both been English teachers. Their home was in the quaint Gulf Coast town of Victoria. I was left to spend many pleasant days with my grandparents while my parents settled into the new apartment, trailer, or once even a tent. Grandmother's house was filled with books. I don't remember learning to read. I was amazed when I got into public school and found that not everyone could. Bored to tears through most of my early school days, I escaped by getting a lot of colds, bronchitis, tonsillitis, and so on. I was allowed to stay home in bed and read. Mother never allowed school to interrupt my education. I was treated to my first sight of a ballet dancer at about the age of three and determined that I would become one. Twenty-three years later, I finally admitted that I simply had not been issued the needed equipment for such an ambition. By then, I was flying high on Broadway so it didn't matter so much anymore. Nothing grabs my gonads quite like a perfect pas de deux. Sigh.

I have a younger brother, ten years younger. My mother and father fought like cats and dogs, but they stayed together to the end. When my mother died, it just took the absolute inside out of my dad's heart. He hung on for another two and a half years, but that was it — growing up, I thought, "Oh my goodness, these two people hate each other." There was one time when they even discussed possibly getting a divorce, and I thought it would have been so glamorous. I would have loved it if they'd gotten a divorce, and then mother would take me to New York where I want to go anyway to be a ballet dancer. Of course, that didn't happen.

As a kid, we were moved into many neighborhoods which presented a new dynamic. I was always the outsider. If everyone in school was wearing ballerina skirts and little ballet shoes, I would talk my mother into buying me those, and then we would move, and everyone would be wearing skinny pencils skirts and loafers. We didn't have a lot of money so buying new clothes every two weeks was out of the question.

When I was living in a little town called Tyler, there was a teacher in Dallas a hundred miles to the west who had actually been in a ballet company — his name was Nikita Talin [Talin had danced with Ballet Russe de Monte Carlo]. We were all in utter complete worshipful awe of this man, and he was an incredible character. He would drive over to Tyler on Saturdays to hold what were called Master Classes. The senior students from all of the various schools in town — there were about three in all — would gather and take these Master Classes and he would hold a summer camp situation in Dallas, two or three classes a day. It was very concentrated work. This was the first true ballet I had encountered. Up until that point, I had done "point step, turn around with your hands in the air" ballet that had been taught to me at the local schools. I even had one teacher who had taught shuffle step in ballet class. For those who have ever taken dancing lessons, you'll know what I'm referring to.

COURTESY OF GEORGINA SPELVIN

This was outside of school. I was very lucky, in the fourth grade, I got to go to the school that was the teacher lab for the education programs at the University of Texas and we lived near the campus. They had orchestra in fourth grade. You could pick up a horn, and sit and toot, and they had incredible art classes, and drama, and all of the good stuff along with the reading and writing and arithmetic. At the age of eight or nine I knew that whatever happened in my life, dancing, and hopefully, singing one day, although I was never very good at it, and being on a stage some way or another, had to be.

The public school system in Texas, and the school systems all over the place have completely abandoned an important part of education, it seems. If you do not get it outside of school, you're just not introduced to it. That's why the music today sounds like somebody pushed a garbage can down the stairs. Where are their heads? The best way to count is by music. You'll learn far more math studying music than you will in a math class. Although I was never into the graphic arts that much, what little bit of schooling I did get in that area became totally invaluable when I was trying to make a living, and I got into computer graphics. I loved art, but I'm not good at it. With a computer, you don't have to be.

I was a very curious child and I played doctor and explored a lot. The actual encounter with a male penis came along in the seventh grade, I believe. He was an older man in the eighth grade, and we went out double dating with his best friend and his best friend's girlfriend who had been a couple for a long time. This was a small town in east Texas. It was very rural. They were practically a married couple and we were double dating with them, and they were getting it on in the front seat, so I really couldn't figure out a way to say "no". I thought, "Oh, well, you know, it's going to happen someday so why not?" and it was not as glorious as everything I'd read by a long shot, and it hurt. It took a long time to figure out how to do it right. Even with all the exploration, I didn't really appreciate sex until I was married for a while, to tell you the truth. Now I'm beginning to find it quite nice. — Never give up.

I was always just a little weird. I never quite fit in. When I'd figured out the dynamic, we'd move again. I naturally fell into the persona of the outsider, the one girl who, because we would move, didn't really worry about my reputation. As soon as I was old enough to fit into the category, I kind of became the class whore in each town. I was very sexually promiscuous, and this doesn't fit in well with the standards of a small Texas town. The nice girls didn't and the nice girls hung out together, and I wasn't one of the nice girls. I didn't let it bother me because I was going to be a ballerina, and leave them all behind soon anyway. My associations, my close friendships which endure to this day, were ballet students who were not the locals.

We'd been in one town for the whole time just as my mother grew up in one small town. Her younger sister was considered "promiscuous" by local standards. She'd gotten pregnant by an officer in the air force during WWII. I can remember in about 1946 when I was around ten years old, she advised me to be very careful with boys and "just never let them do what they want to do to you, or you'll end up paying for it in the long run." I didn't understand what she was talking about at the time, but later, it clicked: "Oh right, she got pregnant and had to get married." It was talked about in my family during my whole youth, but here was a case where my aunt had lived in one town her whole life and got pregnant. Not having lived in one town my whole life, I don't know what I'd do, but it definitely made a difference in her life.

As Georgina reflected upon her indiscriminate teen years, she shared details that came to light regarding family secrets once she opened up her life in a cathartic measure through the release of her book.

I've learned some family history just recently, just in the last few years in getting to know my cousins because I didn't during the time that I was living away from home, and doing disgraceful things like kicking my feet over my head and fucking people on screen. In my dotage, I've reconnected with a lot of my family. A lot of that came about because of the book. I've been able to rekindle friendships. I think that in some cases, and in the case of this particular cousin, for the first time they sort of heard my side of it. I was the one who ran off to New York and then did terrible things. As we were talking, and she was talking about her mother who had to get married — of course, in those days it was very sub rosa that her father had been terribly abusive, physically abusive. She was terrified of him and that he was going to beat her mother to death some day. This was totally news to me. I had no idea. They were just always the nicest, grandest couple in the world, but there was a side that I had never suspected. This came out after the book had come out, and my cousin had come to visit her grandchildren and such, and said, "Let's get together for lunch." We did, and then subsequently, had gotten together a couple of times and talked about family history which I never really knew anything about.

Broadway Bound

Convinced New York was calling her name; Georgina continued her school studies and didn't become a permanent fixture in the city that never sleeps until she'd taken care of important business back home.

Dancing was the big thing for me. I had stars in my eyes. I recently saw the film *Black Swan* (2010) and it's not a terribly good film; my husband hated it, but it certainly is a very accurate picture of the ballet world. That was my ambition as a child up until the time I went to New York. I had finished my high school in Dallas, and came back and transferred my credits back to Tyler so I could graduate there, and so my dad could come and see me actually walk across the stage and get a diploma. That was very important to him. My going to New York to try to have a career as a dancer was predicated by my getting that diploma. I wasn't going anywhere until I did that.

When I graduated from high school, that next summer I got a job in a chorus in a musical at the Dallas State Fair. At that time, they did a series of the musical comedies from New York, and usually imported the stars, if possible. The chorus was hired locally and we would rehearse the numbers ahead of time. We would do the smaller roles. The chorus would be done locally, and then the stars would come and fit into the show. We got to do things like *Brigadoon* with Van Johnson; they were not big name stars that have lasted to this day, but they were big names at the time. Van Johnson was such a sweetheart, and Edie Adams was doing *Wonderful Town* that I did. She was married to Ernie Kovacs at the time. He had come in to be with her while she was there for those two weeks. It was my first taste of real showbiz.

Brigadoon, a musical, is the story of a Scottish town appearing mysteriously every one hundred years. *Wonderful Town*, another musical with a score composed by Leonard Bernstein, is based upon a 1940 play by Fields and Chodorov centering on a collection of books written by Ruth McKenney titled *My Sister Eileen*.

At the end of that season, one of the dancers, a ballet dancer at the same school taught by Nikita Talin who had had the school in Dallas [Academy of Dance Music Theatre], chose a boy Jerry [Jerome] as his lead male dancer. It was hard to find boys willing to do ballet, so if you find one and you're a ballet teacher, you do everything you can to hang onto him so you've got partners for all of the girls. Jerome had been living in the back of the studio when I had lived with the teachers who had an apartment across the street so that I could study every day and go to school.

Jerome and I got an apartment together in New York at the end of the season in Dallas. That was my way to get to New York. He and I were friends forever. He was the first gay person I ever met and I don't know what's happened to him. I haven't heard from him in months. He hasn't answered any of my letters and I'm afraid he may have died and nobody's told me. He's lived in Hawaii for years and years. He sent me a CD that had been made of his batique art process. He would go out and gather the mosses, the herbs, the flowers, and he made his own colors and created these batique hangings with batique cloths. He washed them in the streams you know, and he has this wonderful video. He sent me a video with hundreds of slides and no note of explanation or anything. They just arrived in the mail and I wrote him back to let him know that I had received them. I didn't know if there was something special he had wanted me to do with them or hang them. I never heard from him, but I got an answer back from someone saying that he had been working for the city for years in Honolulu and something or other occurred. All of a sudden, the city was suing him for thousands of dollars saying that he had not paid the amount of rent that he was supposed to in the city owned apartment where he had lived for thirty years. It sounded like he was going to be out in the street, so I don't know what happened to him. I think he wanted his art to be someplace safe because he was possibly literally thrown right out on the street. As I say, this is about six months ago and I haven't heard from him since. We were friends and roommates for so many years. Nineteen fifty-four is the season that we were together in Dallas for the musicals, and then we came to New York and had an apartment together. We shared apartments and everything was terribly flexible during those years. It's a big hole in my life right now not knowing what's happened to Jerome.

Spelvin was eighteen years old in 1954 when she filled in as a replacement for a can-can girl at the infamous Latin Quarter Supper Club once located between Broadway and Seventh Street on 47th Avenue, also known as Times Square. At the photo shoot prior to her dancing debut, Georgina suited up with a veil barely obscuring one of her breasts. The portrait, considered at the time to be risqué, hung in the lobby of the club for several years until it finally closed.

I went to auditions and got into industrial shows, and got in the chorus of the Latin Quarter which was great fun. My friends from there surfaced when I was doing the book and I got to spend some time together with them out here. One of my friends has since passed away. That's what happens when you get to be seventy-five years old, you see, people start to die.

Spelvin was hired as the lead dancer in the chorus for choreographer, Bob Fosse, in the musical production *The Pajama Game* reflecting on labor issues in a pajama factory. Starting its run in 1955, the break was Georgina's first real shot at Broadway. Spelvin's mother who toted her young daughter around for years from one dance studio to another, and had sewn all of Georgina's costumes, did not miss her daughter's opening on the Broadway stage. Playing the secretary Gladys Hotchkiss (Carol Haney was cast in the original role; her understudy was Shirley McLaine) to Myron "Old Man" Hasler (Ralph Dunn), Spelvin awed the enthusiastic audience with her snappy footwork in the show stopping dance number "Steam Heat." After opening night, young Georgina, along with her mother, cast members and friends, dined at the infamous Sardi's restaurant adjacent to the theatre. In her memoir, Spelvin said one of her most satisfying moments was when Vincent Sardi himself sent over a celebratory bottle of champagne to

Georgina dancing "Steam Heat" in *The Pajama Game*. COURTESY OF GEORGINA SPELVIN

her table — a sure sign that she had arrived. When the show closed in New York in 1957, Georgina toured South Africa with it.

After a quickie marriage in 1957 to a young British actor, Christopher, followed by a quickie divorce a few months later, Spelvin soon fell in love again. Eventually, she was involved in a long-term romance with a married stage manager, Ian. Ian, who later became a producer, hired Georgina to star in a summer stock reverie of *Damn Yankees*.

In 1960 while working as a choreographer in Las Vegas, Georgina met up with Hollywood star Sammy Davis Jr. and his "Rat Pack" cronies consisting of Frank Sinatra, Dean Martin, Peter Lawford and Joey Bishop.

The actors all appeared in several films together in the 1960s and were in town shooting *Ocean's Eleven* (1960). Spelvin became a personal guest of the fellows while they made several appearances at the Sands Hotel. She even joined them in a benefit show for a local Children's Hospital.

Georgina first met Davis Jr. in 1954 when she was a chorus dancer for summer stock, and asked for his autograph before he became world

Georgina is pictured to Dean Martin's far right in the blonde bob hairstyle and black skirt and sweater. COURTESY OF GEORGINA SPELVIN

famous. As a young hoofer herself, Spelvin marveled at Sammy's amazing tap dancing abilities, and provided Davis Jr. and his pals with the names of a few restaurants that would serve people of color during the 1950s. Subsequently, Spelvin received an invitation from Davis Jr. to join them for dinner which she accepted.

In a Pickle

Georgina has other distinguished accomplishments in her portfolio throughout her early years in New York: She danced in the chorus line for *Guys and Dolls* (1963), and according to her autobiography, Spelvin was Shirley MacLaine's dance double and stand-in for the New York scenes of *Sweet Charity* (1969) directed by Bob Fosse. During down time, Spelvin continued seeking work as a dancer and actor, on stage and in film. Meanwhile, as the swinging sixties wound down, Georgina was about to take centre stage in a new cultural phenomenon.

Two Broadway shows do not quite qualify as solid credits, but I had faced the fact that I was not destined for stardom and was earnestly pursuing the crafts of filmmaking, and doing what I could to protest the war in Viet Nam. We were trying to live as a commune dubbed "The Pickle Factory," and we were a group of people eager to be a part of the film world. In order to make films we were trying to get along. We were starving, we being the group of film crazies that lived communally in a warehouse in Greenwich Village. While trying to make a living as a film editor, chance landed me a part in a film that turned out to be a porno. The rent was due. Being sort of the senior member of the club, I looked through the trade papers which I was familiar with from my days of being a dancer, and actually getting to do a couple of real movies: *Hello Dolly* (1969) and *Sweet Charity* (1969), specifically — and so grabbed anything that was starting production of any kind of film. I would call and say we had equipment to rent, people to work, we could scout locations, and we could handle commissary craft services if any help was needed. Doing this was how I got asked to work on a film. I don't really know the name of it anymore, but it was a quick tits and ass film, not a hardcore film. It might have been 1971 or 1972.

According to Wikipedia, Georgina actually surfaced in her very first film in 1957 titled *The Twilight Girls* (aka *Les collégiennes*) — a lesbian story wherein Spelvin appeared topless, and actress Catherine Deneuve is featured in her debut role. *Sex by Advertisement* (1968) was Spelvin's first (uncredited) part in a sexually oriented film, a quasi-Sex Ed production in which she played Dr. Joanne Ridgefield. The minor stint was followed up by a similar (uncredited) part in the softcore flick *Career Bed* (1969) featuring Georgina as a mother who pushes her young daughter into showbiz.

Just a few months before I did *Devil and Miss Jones* (1973) I was gathering up guys to play sailors, and I knew somebody who had a boat in a marina in Long Island so I arranged for the location for them. I don't think I did craft services, I believe it was a send-out kind of a shoot.

The Beau Buchanan film *High Priestess of Sexual Witchcraft* (1973) paired Spelvin with New York porn actor Marc Stevens as the Priest. It was the beginning of a beautiful friendship.

> On that film set, I met Marc Stevens who was the funniest, sweetest guy I had ever met who wasn't totally a fag. He'd sent me to see Harry Reems who was Gerard Damiano's assistant director. They needed a cook. One of the guys working as one of the crew came over and handed me a script of a film that he was going to shoot that week. He was looking for somebody to play a mother, a mature actress, and I got the job.

The late Gerard Damiano, a former hairstylist from the Bronx turned prominent adult film director, demonstrated a flair for double entendre within his story telling and was one of the few pioneers of X-rated features to treat his material seriously. Hot on the heels of his success with *Deep Throat* (1972), Damiano was primed to take an exceptional talent such as Spelvin under his employ when he set about to cast his next meaty picture, *The Devil in Miss Jones*, in 1973.

> Jerry [Damiano] had me read for the role of Justine Jones and decided that even though my tits were small, I could act so that's how that got started. I didn't really realize at the time it was a hardcore film. I knew it was obviously a sexy film, but I'd never seen a hardcore film. I'd seen some hardcore footage before because I'd worked as a film editor a lot, but I didn't know anything about *the* business. It was a job, it paid some money, and we needed money. I ended up fornicating before a camera because I was too embarrassed at my naiveté to run away when I found out that's what it was.

The Devil in Miss Jones

In 1973, when *The Devil in Miss Jones* held its worldwide opening in Toronto, Canada, no cost was spared by director Gerard Damiano. Georgina Spelvin luxuriated in a suite in one of Toronto's classiest hotels. She was treated to fine dining, champagne and caviar while cavorting with the press and the public who lined up in droves to watch the much-hyped film. Warned beforehand by her New York comrades "Toronto can be quite chilly in August," (Toronto is rarely anything but hot and humid in

August with temperatures usually hovering around the mid-high 80s) and armed with a five hundred dollar spending allowance, Spelvin selected a wardrobe that would hopefully suit all occasions including a pair of platform shoes. Georgina stated in her book that the travel expenses for her trip to the Canadian premiere far exceeded the amount she was paid to star in the film.

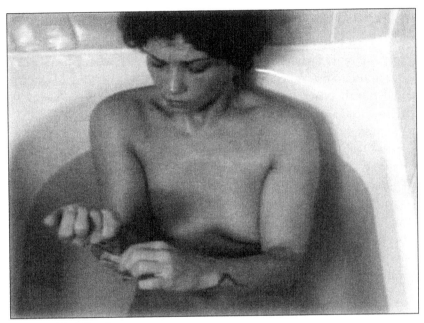

The Devil in Miss Jones. VCX

After the success of the Toronto premiere "Devil" made the rounds to New York and other major cities, and was reviewed by the late Judith Crist, founding film critic for *New York Magazine* after the *Herald Tribune* folded. Crist gave Spelvin kudos for her dazzling performance as Justine Jones, though her review for the film itself was tepid. *Newsweek* also covered the film and lauded Spelvin a "remarkably talented actress." Highly regarded movie critic Roger Ebert gave the film a three star rating out of four and wrote of Spelvin's performance: "there burns in her soul the spark of an artist, and she is not only the best, but possibly the only actress in the hard-core field. By that, I mean when she's on the screen, her body and actions aren't the only reasons we're watching her. Alone among porno stars, she never seems exploited."

"Devil" was one of three films to garner the new term "porno chic," which included Damiano's *Deep Throat* and the Mitchell Brother's *Behind the Green Door,* both released in 1972. While Spelvin's performance and the film continued to amass glowing notices across the United States, Georgina breathed a sigh of relief after she received a congratulatory telephone call from her younger brother. The actress was worried he might not understand.

Spelvin clarified her reasons about her choice to do the film.

There was this stuff call FILM back in those dark ages. Tape was later. I felt glad to have a job. I was actually thrilled to do an entire role and build a character and everything which is what I had set out in life to do. When it turned out to be a hardcore film, in the midst of shooting, I was not about to walk off the set; I just went right ahead and did the scene as it seemed to me it should be done. We thought, "Oh boy, we're in the movies. They want us to actually fuck. Okay." It's not as if it was something we didn't do everyday anyway. That's more or less how it came about. We weren't people who went out and said, "I want to be paid to have sex." We would have been out on the street if that had been the initial idea. We were actors, and if the scene called for you to cry you may require the help of a few eye drops to get you going, but you would really cry — that's called acting. Being the sort of person who was always willing to live and let live the porno world was just another branch of the business of show, as far as I was concerned.

The Devil in Miss Jones is the second film I did which involved explicit sex. The script was intriguing, and again, I had originally met Jerry through Marc Stevens with the idea in mind of doing craft services for the shoot. It was a weekend shoot; they were just shooting fuck films. Jerry, after having done *Deep Throat,* wanted to do more. His idea was that sex films could have more meaning and a message so he wrote *The Devil in Miss Jones,* and directed it, and did a lot of the editing, and put the music together for it and helped me in the kitchen. I was also doing craft services.

Easily eclipsing several other films of the early adult genre and era, *The Devil in Miss Jones,* a most impressive picture, is sustained by a foreboding musical score. Superbly, Spelvin plays mid-thirties virgin, Justine Jones, who takes her own life by slashing her wrists in a bathtub, and comes face-to-face with the Devil's wingman. He grants her one last request for a brief reprieve from an eternity in hell so that she may return to earth and experience her greatest wish, one of the "seven deadliest sins." Because Justine's desire is sexual in nature, she is paired with a teacher (Harry Reems) who helps break down her inhibitive barriers so that she may partake of the forbidden fruit with an unmarked slate. Commanded by her tutor to hold a rubber anal plug inside of her rectum prior to embarking upon oral, vaginal, and anal sex with him, Justine experiences an orgasm of epic proportions. Miss Jones goes on to enjoy girl-on-girl action with actress Claire Lumiere captured in tender splendor before taking on two men (featuring Spelvin's good friend Marc Stevens), and subsequently, a hose, and some fruit — followed by the infamous arousing rendezvous with a slithering pet snake.

Apart from Georgina's incredible breadth as an actor, her final scene with Damiano provides the ultimate thrill as the two are sequestered in an infinite life sentence, locked together in a cell/hell consumed by their own anxieties, fears and desires — never to be quelled. Throughout her performance, Georgina carries herself with grace and sophistication which is quite remarkable considering the sensitive nature of some of the sexual activities in which she takes part.

It was very much like, "Let's get together and do a show in Daddy's barn." It had that feel that everybody was working together toward an actual end. The fact that it was a sex film was because that's what it was. That's what they gave him the money to do. If it had been a film about baseball, we'd have been out there playing baseball. It was a film about sex, so we were in the barn doing sex. Still, there was this incredible feeling that I hadn't really experienced since the days of doing summer stock which was that everybody had a specific role to play, whether it was coiling cable, or fixing the casserole, or adjusting the lights, or picking up the trash and keeping the place clean. We were all together in this remote location somewhere — in either New Jersey or New York.

Doing the film was an adventure that everyone was equally invested in and I thoroughly enjoyed that aspect of it. There was a great deal of camaraderie and it was just a lot of fun. We were laughing and scratching, and having a good time. I honestly thought no one would ever know I had done such a scandalous thing as fornicate in front of a camera. I had no idea I would have to create the character of "Georgina Spelvin," and live with it for forty years. Later, I had to go before the Grand Jury and explain that I was not taken across state line for immoral purposes, but I don't know if I was taken across state line. I certainly wasn't taken across state line against my will.

Spelvin appeared in court in Memphis, Tennessee for her involvement in *The Devil in Miss Jones* and was not required to serve any time. The authorities had no grounds to prove she'd distributed the film across state lines which she hadn't. Georgina's co-star, Harry Reems, wasn't so lucky. One of the most recognized male stars of the golden age, Reems (born Herbie Streicher) assimilated into adult films as a starving artist/part-time cab driver, much the same way his young contemporaries had. Reems made a big splash while creating controversy in the hit picture *Deep Throat* the year before "Devil" was released. After an arrest in New York in 1974, Reems was indicted in Memphis, Tennessee in 1975 for conspiracy to transport obscene material across state lines. In 1976, he was convicted in conjunction with four production companies and eleven other people. On an appeal that was facilitated by renowned attorney Alan Dershowitz, Reems's conviction was overturned in April 1977. Eventually, after being granted a new trial, the charges were dropped. During the trial, Reems was supported by eminent Hollywood actors Warren Beatty and Jack Nicholson.

Georgina happily worked with Reems again in 1974 when the two were hired for *Wet Rainbow*.

One thing that's not mentioned in my book is when Herbie Streicher and I were doing *Wet Rainbow* (1974). We'd just finished doing some rather down and dirty, quick, get it done sex and we were looking forward to our scenes coming up that were much more dramatic and not just "let's get the cum shot, fellas". We had this scene where we were supposed to get in an argument in a taxicab or something. I think it was Herbie's idea. He said, "Let's show them how good we are. Let's really get into an argument and just shake them to their boots that we're not going to finish this film."

I said, "Okay, let's do that." We got into this spitting fight, and we looked like we were going to tear each other's throats out and the director was just almost in tears, he was just shaking. I didn't learn until many years later that the guy who was directing the film had sunk his life savings into the movie, and unfortunately, the distribution people just screwed him royally. He did get his money back, but he never made any money off of it. At this moment, we'd had the crew and everyone else ready to pack up and leave the set. They thought they'd never get the love scenes between these two characters. Then we finally cracked each other up to the point that we laughed and I don't think the director ever quite forgave us. It was a nasty thing to do. Talk about regret. I regret doing that. It was fun though to have the affirmation to show everybody that we could really do it.

Harry was, like the rest of us, an out of work actor, and we had several mutual friends in the business beyond the porn business. He was a very good actor and still is. We've kept in touch and e-mailed

COURTESY OF WORTH MENTIONING PUBLIC RELATIONS

back and forth for a while and we've talked on the phone a few times. He said, "You know, I'm not going to be able to keep up e-mail with you because I've got so much arthritis in my fingers."

I said, "Oh, I'm so sorry to hear that."

It's interesting; I simply don't watch myself on screen. It's not because of the sex, it's just that I've never been able to not watch myself without saying "Why the fuck did you do that?" I'm always a bit embarrassed to see myself on screen, porno or not. I'm always awful. It's either what I'm saying or the way I look. I'm very critical so it's agony to watch anything I've ever done; that's why I like stage work — you don't have to look at it later. Nobody likes to look at our own warts.

Peccadilloes

Despite her newfound fame with "Devil," and offers for an experienced actor on the bargaining table, Spelvin continued to be paid the going rate for female erotic performers at the time: one hundred dollars per day. In her book, Georgina credited Annette Haven for being one of the first women in porn to demand and receive more and believes Haven helped to change the status quo which eventually allocated more money and opportunities for women working in sex films.

Spelvin recalled how well into her career she met fellow porno chic star, Linda Lovelace (of *Deep Throat* fame), for the first time on a television show. Coldly, Lovelace turned her back after Spelvin introduced herself. Marilyn Chambers on the other hand, was much friendlier and instigated a meeting between Spelvin and Sammy Davis Jr. The song and dance man had become friendly with Marilyn through her husband Chuck Traynor (formerly married to Linda Lovelace). Chambers was astonished to learn Spelvin had already met Davis Jr. several years earlier and the two stars were reacquainted.

During the early 1970s while her fame was on the incline, Georgina became involved in a mutually tender relationship with her best girlfriend, Claire Lumiere, who sometimes performed along with Spelvin in acclaimed adult features including *The Devil in Miss Jones*. Claire had been a part of the "Pickle Factory" commune and, like Spelvin, was often hired to provide craft services on set as a sideline. When the affair ended, Georgina packed Claire off on a bus to Florida where Claire planned to resume her academic studies. Three months later, Claire returned to Spelvin's life and the two moved to California. Shortly afterwards, Claire and Spelvin parted ways. Spelvin spoke of her mother's reaction upon learning of her daughter's employment during the years when she and Claire were still involved.

I was not close to my mother really, as I grew up. I was during the dancing and that whole area, but as I tried to kind of show in the book with selective pieces of conversation between us, I was totally uncomfortable with her about sex. I'd never had close girlfriends in my life because of moving around a lot. At one time, I remember I was standing at the sink during a visit home and I, at the time, was in this relationship with Claire which is a peculiar thing to me. She's known mostly as Claire. I always talk about her as Claire and I don't reveal her real name because she's trying to overcome those peccadilloes of her youth. She's very straight-laced and has converted to certain viewpoints I'd shunned so as a youngster. Anyway, I was home visiting and mother turned to me at one point and said, "Well, I don't know. Maybe it was the water in Jasper. Your cousin became a lesbian and you're a nymphomaniac."

I said, "I'm not a nymphomaniac." Really, I'm not. I was trying to be good humored about the whole thing.

There will always be a negative stigma attached to women and sexuality as long as we are totally confused about our sexuality as human beings. I don't really see that going away in my lifetime. I have my own prejudices. I look askance at people working the streets and at the same time say to myself, "Hey, you're the one who says you shouldn't be judgmental." My instinct is, whether it's a natural instinct put there by God or whether it's manufactured: civilization says if you're going to have a stable community you have to have females who reproduce, and you have to be able to know who your children are. That means if you reproduce you only have sex with one person. Their lord and master or whatever, reproduces the children he can recognize as his own, and therefore, passes property on to them. Civilization is based on property ownership, and property ownership requires identification of lineage which means that anything that doesn't contribute to that, or slanted into that slot of activity in civilization, is superfluous. When I say "superfluous" that's not entirely true because obviously prostitution is needed, otherwise it wouldn't exist. People say, "Of course there have to be whores," but you don't want your daughter to be one. It's hardly anything new. During Belle Époque, women were beautiful enough, or smart enough or lucky enough to have had a sponsor to be paid by only one man outside of their marriage. The heroines and stars of their day were not an unattractive little girl sucking dicks on the street corner of town to get money to eat, scorned and probably always will be. Even when we're living in self-contained spacecrafts there will be that element somewhere.

Hitting the Mark

Throughout the bulk of the early to mid-seventies, Spelvin's film work encompassed leading roles illustrated in pictures such as the 1973 grindhouse extravaganza *The Erotic Memoirs of a Male Chauvinist Pig* (released by Video-X-Pix in 2010) and also accepted minor, but significant parts. She played the hooker in the magnificent Radley Metzger feature *The Private Afternoons of Pamela Mann* (1974) starring Barbara Bourbon and Darby Lloyd Rains, and starred and worked in costuming for the1974 mainstream exploitation film *Girls for Rent* (aka *I Spit on Your Corpse*). Georgina continued to develop a reputation as a sought after character actor in several other adult-oriented projects.

In 1975 Spelvin gave an arresting performance in esteemed director Robert McCallum's first hardcore picture *3:00 A.M.* which featured a scene with Claire Lumiere in a small supporting role. Born Gary Graver, McCallum had previously collaborated closely with Orson Welles on *An Evening with Orson Welles*: a six-part series developed for Sears Department store, in addition to other worthwhile projects. Moving fluidly between mainstream and adult film/television worlds as a first class cinematographer and director, Graver used the handle "Robert McCallum" when directing sex films.

3:00A.M. stars Georgina as Kate, a woman secretly in lust with her brother-in-law Mark (Frank Mauro) while residing at the home of her sister Elaine (Rhonda Gallard) and their family. One evening at precisely 3:00 a.m., Kate accidentally kills Mark after a lover's quarrel on his sailboat. Devastated by her loss and frightened that her sister, niece and nephew Stacey and Ronnie (Clair Dia and Charles Hooper) will find out what she's done, Kate tries to atone for the drowning mishap by tending to the psychological needs of the family. One by one, they begin to act out their grief through aberrant sexual behavior. Lonely and suicidal, Elaine finds herself in the arms of an unknown lover while her teenage son Ronnie embarks upon an affair with the family's neighbor Vicki (Sharon Thorpe who is exquisite as the seductress). Later, pent-up sexual tension is consummated between siblings Ronnie and Stacey, yet Kate's conduct is the most extreme. While taking a shower one afternoon, she is ravished by a complete stranger (Claire Lumiere) who makes a surprise appearance. Later, after tucking in her young niece, "Aunt Kate" violates Stacey during her slumber. Engulfed by her guilt over the events of the previous few days, Kate departs from the family home leaving behind a cassette recording describing her role in Mark's death. In a semi-comatose state, she walks

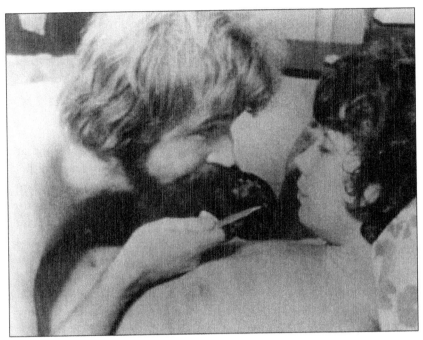

Male Chauvinist Pig. VIDEO-X-PIX

out toward the ocean to meet her own fate. Although the film itself is at times choppy, poorly lit and slow-paced, Spelvin's performance as the other woman emotionally paralyzed over bringing about the sudden death of her lover, and the impact on his family, is disarming and exact.

Throughout a pilgrimage of exposure in the medium of adult films, it seemed apparent by the mid-seventies that Spelvin had found her calling. I wondered at this point if Georgina believed her chosen vocation supported or opposed the omnipresent feminist movement in full swing at the time she was at the height of her film career.

If someone offers me a certain compensation for a particular job of work, I do that job to the best of my ability. If they did NOT pay me the amount they said they would, I would feel exploited. I've never had that happen. If standing up for one's rights and demanding respect as a female human being is being a feminist, then I suppose I am one. I don't understand why one has to be a feminist in order to stand up for your rights. Rights should be granted to everyone and the sex of the person involved shouldn't be a consideration. At one time women did have to get together and say, "Hey, we're people too. We're human beings and we should have a say in the government." If men should have a say in the government then we should have a say in the government. I've encountered so many feminists who were anti-porn that probably made me hesitant to join the club and become a card-carrying member of some sort.

"You Gotta Have a Gimmick"

By the mid-1970s, Georgina's reliance on alcohol became a dominating force in her daily existence and began to compromise facets of her life. After making a permanent move to California and continuing film appearances, Spelvin was invited to parlay her "Miss Jones" persona into a stage act as she embarked upon a supplemental career as a stripper. Her new friend and confidante, Dee, was assigned the task of costumer and dresser for Spelvin's burlesque shows where she was hired as a headlining act accompanied by a friendly snake. Georgina incorporated select musical numbers from *The Devil in Miss Jones* into her stage show and removed her clothes while dancing to the famous burlesque number "The Stripper."

Spelvin admitted in her book that the booze helped her to get through the peeler performances which she felt, by comparison, were a demotion from performing sex on camera within the intimacy of a smaller group of spectators. Georgina made a habit of getting clean whenever film work was available, but the trend would not continue. In 1976, Spelvin sobered up and worked to get into respectable physical condition in order to prepare for the New York production *Take-Off* released in 1978, a big budget feature directed by Armand Weston in which she assumed the part of a Roaring Twenties socialite. Spelvin and Wade Nichols (aka Dennis Parker) a bisexual actor who debuted in the 1975 film *Boynapped* and who also played Police Chief Derek Malloy on the soap opera *Edge of Night*, assumed the leads in the triple-X adaptation concerning perennial youth. Based upon the book *The Picture of Dorian Gray* (1890), by acclaimed writer and poet Oscar Wilde, the sensational epic, *Take-Off*, is set in the present day (late-1970s) at the home of Darrin Blue (Wade Nichols).

During Blue's summer afternoon party, one of his guests, Linda (Leslie Bovee), enjoys a sexual conquest with a hot Texan by the name of Roy (Eric Edwards as Rob Everett). Afterwards, they discover an old black and white reel to reel depicting a handsome man and his aristocrat girlfriend making love during a picnic. Upon returning to the party, Linda is introduced to Blue who takes her for an afternoon drive and begins to share a story about

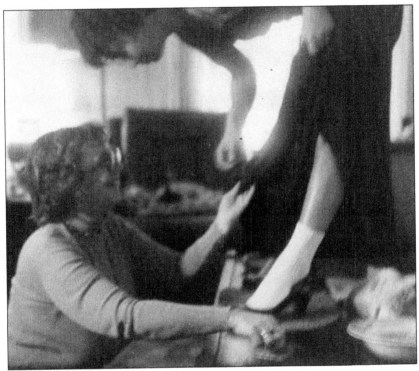

Georgina and her friend Dee. COURTESY OF GEORGINA SPELVIN

the old film reel. The viewer is suddenly swept back in time to the 1920s and reintroduced to blue-eyed Blue, frolicking with his sophisticated lady friend Henrietta Wilde (Georgina Spelvin). It is made clear Henrietta is the same woman previously shown in the black and white film, and the intricacies of the tale begin to unfold within the story through flashbacks: We learn that Henrietta believes youth, beauty, and pleasure are the most important essentials in life. Wilde confides to Blue, that at her own request, her chauffeur secretly filmed their lovemaking session. She invites him to observe his own specimen of physical elegance so that he too will understand the importance of eternally preserving one's prime of life. Darrin can't help but marvel at his own embodiment of human excellence and he is convinced Henrietta's philosophy is correct. When Wilde eventually disappears from his life, Blue gains not only a substantial inheritance, but also a lifetime of youth — he is forever twenty-five yet, his image captured on eight-millimeter film will deteriorate gracefully and naturally.

Take-Off proceeds to move through several decades chronologically as Blue learns through his own introspection, and during his many encoun-

Take-Off. VIDEO-X-PIX

ters with some notorious historical characters: John Dillinger, Virginia Slimms, Jean Harlot, and the not so notorious, that perpetual youthfulness is an illusion and a curse. When Blue eventually experiences the free spirited 1960s, he begins to feel alienated and craves the sentimental romantic he once was. Suddenly, Blue is transported back to present day. Darrin finishes sharing his story with Linda and they culminate their afternoon with a sexual romp that inevitably brings things full circle.

Enough praise cannot be bestowed upon this enormously entertaining and intelligent undertaking that is truly a presentation where sex (as good as it is in this film) takes a back seat to the fundamental plot. Georgina and Wade Nichols are positively outstanding in their corresponding roles as the grand Gatsby-esque, carefree couple. All of the supporting talent (Annette Haven is wonderful as Virginia Slimm) including the non-sex players, are invaluable and integral arteries to the central story. For her fine work, Spelvin racked up another Best Supporting Actress at the 1978 AFAA awards.

When *Take-Off* wrapped, Georgina went from sipping champagne with the cast and crew to drinking alone from a paper bag near a New York pier three days later. She was barely recognizable when her old friend Marc Stevens noticed her and got her into the County Rehab for a two-week stay. Spelvin said she remained sober for one year following her assignment in the spin and dry cycle. When she reluctantly made a return to the bump and grind circuit after an unsuccessful turn in a musical comedy, she hit the bottle again. Thus began the painful and slow process of recovery and relapse. Georgina shared the history of her drinking and the details of an intervention on her behalf.

> I was sipping beer as a baby and finishing up the dregs of everybody's drinks at parties. My dad was in the army so he and my mother had parties quite frequently. I wasn't drinking all the time, but the lure of alcohol was there from the beginning. My sobriety date is November 11, 1981. It wasn't my doing. I'm not to be congratulated. AA is the one to be congratulated. AA works.
>
> My friends, and an almost former husband — the guy I was with for over ten years although we never actually got married — in the book he's identified as Ian. He is a very talented writer and works for one of the big studios out here. These friends who were letting me crash at their house while I was bouncing around the burlesque circuit drinking myself into oblivion — called Ian and said, "We've got to have an intervention or Chele's going to die". He called my mother and my mother flew out from Texas. I had come home from one of my burlesque gigs one night and here the living room was filled with the friends I was staying with: Ian and my mother, and some other people who were mutual friends to enter this intervention. They sort of said, "Look you're going to kill yourself. Please go do it fast and stop this. It's very inconvenient to all of us." That's what got me on the sobriety track.

After the initial intervention attempt misfired and Spelvin reverted to her old habits, Georgina's mother, determined to help her daughter remain sober, traveled to Atlantic City with Georgina where she was booked to strip at a club for one week. Each morning began with a few slugs of vodka doled out by her mother to stave off nausea and tremors so that Spelvin could perform her act, which generally began with the simulation of a few tantalizing scenes from *The Devil in Miss Jones*. After her floor routine, Spelvin entered into a Q & A with the audience, cleverly and humorously staying a few steps ahead of the queries while leaving her admirers laughing. Once her obligation was fulfilled, Georgina returned to Tyler with her mother, and spent the week drying out under the watchful eyes of both parents.

Social drinking is a part of civilization. To get it into the alcoholic brain which is already debilitated from alcohol that some people can drink and some cannot, and you're one of those who can't — is a real challenge. I've got matching chips from AA that could probably line a room. I don't think I've met anyone who has managed to get through quitting alcohol on the first injection. You know, I started smoking again when I went to the AA meeting. If you've been a smoker and you're in an atmosphere where everybody is smoking, it's hard not to because you're smoking anyway. You're sitting there inhaling it; you may as well be enjoying it.

The Show Must Go On

Director Bob Chinn always hoped he'd have an opportunity to direct Georgina Spelvin. He saw his dream culminate when the Los Angeles based adult company, Freeway Films, went into production with the seventh installment of the popular Johnny Wadd franchise, *The Jade Pussycat* in 1977. Spelvin was hired to play detective Wadd's sly and sultry foe as Chinn described in his following comments.

For the Johnny Wadd film *Jade Pussycat (1977)*, I was extremely fortunate in being able to cast Georgina Spelvin in the role of the dangerous villain Alexandra. I had seen her in *The Devil in Miss Jones* and loved her performance.

Working with Georgina was a real delight. It was simply wonderful to work with a real actress for a change. One who was capable of taking direction, and then turn around and really do something with it. Unfortunately, during the shoot she and John didn't always get along. Both had very strong personalities which tended, at times, to clash, making for some very tense moments on the set. I think there was probably some professional jealousy on the part of John at being upstaged by Georgina, but both were professional enough to get the job done, and no one would know it from the result.

Forty-one year old Spelvin and Holmes shared the screen during a pivotal moment in *The Jade Pussycat* when private dick Johnny Wadd (with an invaluable jade piece in his possession) discovers he's met his match in the ultra-sophisticated Alexandra (Spelvin). He must decide how to outsmart her before resolving his case. Spelvin is at her delicious best while stroking Holmes's crotch as she growls, "I've heard a great deal about you…"

Georgina Spelvin and John Holmes in *The Jade Pussycat.* I-CANDY

With eyes fixated on her face, Wadd slowly retorts, "Like what?"

During the interchange that follows, the film's speed is accelerated creating the effect of a campy Chaplinesque sequence, and the two are suddenly in fast forward mode, preparing the hideaway bed for love. Afterwards, Alexandra knocks Wadd out cold with the base of a lamp and makes off with what she believes are the coveted goods. Holmes, who is not usually recognized for his ability as an actor, demonstrated better than average acting chops in his scenes with Spelvin possibly because her presence and expertise positively influenced their pairing, resulting in a solid, understated performance.

Georgina confided that she wasn't at her best when she and Holmes's characters traded barbs during drinks prior to their sex scene together, yet the exchange turned out to be one of the most salient and engrossing moments in the engaging noir film.

I have to confess that during that film I was in very bad shape. I was drinking, and although I wasn't drunk at that particular moment, a drunk is not an attractive person under any circumstances. I really don't remember very much about it. I think I remember something about opening up a couch bed in a hotel room. I said, "Can we try to make this funny?" I hoped it was. I remember Bob as being just the gentlest, most patient, wonderful director. He made it as easy and as palatable as possible, but I just was not in good shape. It's the great embarrassment of my life to tell you the truth, but we live, we learn, we hope. There's no point unless you peel it all back.

Once again, putting her battle with the bottle on the back burner, in 1979 Georgina starred in *The Dancers* with her good friend and actor Richard Pacheco (aka Howie Gordon, one-time *Playgirl* Magazine's "Man of the Year"). Pacheco, who made his first official adult film appearance in the Bob Chinn picture *The Candy Stripers* (1978) became one of the most preferred male performers of the erotic golden era. He is a multi-award winning actor, producer, and director.

Spelvin recalled how casual and at ease Pacheco and his wife were about the whole business when the couple brought their infant son Bobby to the set.

This is a kid on the set in [Pacheco's wife] Jeremy's arms the day that Howie and I did our scene in the big old brass bed for *The Dancers* (1979). I met her, and here I was going to be having sex with someone whose wife is in the room with their infant in her arms. She was so charming and she said, "This is what he does and he's very good at it." I said, "Well, that's wonderful!" We became good friends and I've had lovely times with them at their home in Berkeley the last couple of years, which is really one of the plusses of finally sitting down and writing the damn book.

Directed by Anthony Spinelli (aka Samuel Weinstein), *The Dancers* highlights the sexual activities of three male strippers (Richard Pacheco, Randy West and Joey Silvera). Dubbed The Dreams, their bombastic manager (John Leslie) books his act in a small town where he and the guys engage in liaisons with various females. By chance, Catherine (Spelvin), a well-off bookish spinster meets and falls in love with Jonathon (Pacheco), one of the dancers with aspirations of becoming an actor. In a sweet and touching scene, Georgina and Pacheco each deliver a dramatic interpretation of the opening lyrics of the 1961 popular song "Cupid," written and performed by Sam Cooke. Pacheco's interpretation is robust and stirring while Spelvin's locution is expressed with a quiet eloquence, matching their passionate love scene that is ushered in with gentle foreplay. In 1981, a Best Actress award was granted by the AFAA to Spelvin for her skillful, subtle performance.

Georgina appeared in a handful more hardcore movies before her anticipated retirement at age forty-seven. Before she did, once again, she and Bob Chinn teamed up to make *Tropic of Desire* (1983) marking Georgina's final year employed as a pornographic actor. Chinn summarized his second encounter with Spelvin.

> I got to work with Georgina again on *Tropic of Desire* in which she played Frances, the lesbian madam of the legendary Pink Flamingo, a popular bordello in Hawaii during World War II. This time we got to know each other much better. I hadn't realized before that aside from acting she had worked in virtually all aspects of the film industry, and I gained a new respect for her and her abilities. She helped me a lot during the production of that film with her personal support and wise suggestions. I will always be eternally grateful to her for enriching those two films with her presence.

Prior to her retreat from sex films, the loss of both parents within a couple of years of one another became the catalyst for Georgina to finally strive to remain dry.

> It took my mother's death. After mother died, I really started going to meetings. After mother died, somebody had to take care of my dad and I couldn't do that and drink. Mother, I'm sure, knew it. I don't believe she committed suicide, but I'm sure at one point she decided, "Well if I stick around, you're never going to get sober" so she knew I would have to. I'm going to confront her with that when we get together again. My mother and I had each other's number all the way down the line, but we tiptoed around it. We were very considerate of each other, I think. That was the basis of family relations.
>
> I haven't attended meetings since I came back from Tyler. I tried going to a couple of meetings, but I think it was the third one I went to at this little church that is right down the hill from our house, and one of the people there literally went over the table and attacked somebody on the other side. It was just a little too rowdy for me. I

thought I would find a different group and I just never found another one. I'd already had about three years under my belt at that point and I did intend to find another meeting, but I just never got around to it. Believe me, if I ever felt a need to pick up another drink today I'd find an AA meeting. You never get over it. If you're a diabetic, you're a diabetic. If you're an alcoholic, you're an alcoholic. Alcoholism is a disease that totally takes control of your life. Everything you do or don't do can be blamed on it which is actually rather convenient.

Staying Afloat

After her mother's unexpected passing, Georgina picked up the pieces where her mother left off. She joined her mother's card club, took her mother's place in the Tyler church choir, and decided to enroll in several college classes where she ended up returning to her theatrical roots and appeared in a couple of small productions. After the death of her father, Spelvin returned to California, and once again, won a role in a local play. She met the man who would soon become her friend, lover, and third husband. Today the two reside in a Hollywood home almost directly underneath the Hollywood sign fulfilling a long time dream.

When my mother and dad died and I came back to California to live, my first husband, Christopher, who was still my best friend, phoned me one day and said "I need a ride out to a theatre". They wanted him to read with people. Maureen, his third wife and estranged from at that point, had just had his little MG car impounded. He owned her some back child support money. He was without wheels and wanted me to drive him over to North Hollywood. I went with him to this play reading and while I was there the director asked me to read a role. I was offered the role of a religious spouting female who — well, it was never quite established whether she was a prostitute or not. She obviously had a sideline that kept her going.

The play was *The Hostage*, and in this play, a gentleman was playing the role of Rio Rita, this screaming queen character. [John] was excellent in the role and as we talked during the day, I discovered that he belonged to the same health club that I did. It proved to be sort of the watering hole for the Hollywood gay crowd, so I assumed he was gay and we became good friends. Later, he showed up at a picnic with a gorgeous blonde bombshell. His cousin had escorted me to this picnic and I said to him "I thought your cousin was gay?" The cousin I was with almost drowned in the hot tub laughing. I then realized he wasn't gay, and the poor dear didn't have a chance after that. Neither one of us had children. When I look around the world today, I am frankly glad. It's getting very difficult to grow up and to have a life.

Steven Guttenberg and Georgina Spelvin in a publicity photo for *Police Academy*.

Spelvin's primary source of income for two decades after re-establishing herself in Los Angeles was derived from work as a desktop publisher for the L.A. Medical County Association. Occasionally, she continued to accept straight acting opportunities on the side. Georgina's most enjoyable experience was joining the cast as a supporting player in the *Police Academy* (1984) films that starred Steve Guttenberg, Kim Cattrall, and Bubba Smith. The first movie was filmed in Toronto.

I've been to Toronto three times, twice doing the *Police Academy* movies, which were just so wonderful, and once because I had a job working in North Tonawanda. It was just great fun to run over to Canada. I love Canadian people; they're everything American people should be.

I LOVED being in *Police Academy* with Bubba Smith. I'll never forgive myself for turning down his invitation to dinner. I was *so* terrified someone would think I was a guaranteed lay that I cut myself off from friendships that were probably being offered with no ulterior motives at all. I was bent out of shape and sort of would walk into situations where I thought, "Oh, everybody knows what I do and most people don't particularly approve of it."

I was very defensive, which was just stupid; it was just very stupid. Why would they have called me to do the film in the first place if they'd had an issue with it? It wasn't only because of having done the sex films; I was always terribly intimidated by those that I admired. In the ballet world, to be in the same class with Melissa Aiden, I couldn't do anything. I just stood there paralyzed watching her.

In 1989, Georgina played the part of a Bette Davis-type sexually abusive mother in the mainstream movie *Bad Blood* (directed by Chuck Vincent) featuring Veronica Hart and Randy Spears, in addition to Hollywood "B" actors Linda Blair and Troy Donahue. She also made appearances in several TV programs including *Dream On* and *The Lost World*.

Since leaving the acting world behind, Spelvin is appreciative of small pleasures.

I'm starting to enter into what is considered the pie chart years. I seem to have the constitution of an iron bucket of which I am entirely grateful. I'm just real lucky in that department. I go to the gym every day — well, John goes to the gym, I actually go to the spa. I garden as much as I absolutely have to so that I enjoy looking at it. I'm not one of those people absolutely thrilled over a new species, or someone who knows the names of everything. I know the name of nothing. I like flowers. In fact, I'm looking out the window right now — we had a good rain last night into the morning, and when it rains in California, it's dancing in the street time.

I wish I could really sing. I couldn't compare with Edith Piaf singing, "No Regrets," that's for sure, but why in the world should anybody have regrets when we can't do anything about it. There are moments when somebody reminds me of something I did or said, and I think, "Oh god, what a stupid thing to have said." I regret that I did it, that I was that stupid and so forth, but not to the point where I think, "Oh, god, what a terrible person I was and must still be for having done that." No. We all just go along grabbing any log that comes close enough to keep us above water. By the same token, of course, I am rather reticent to censor anybody else for anything another person does. We are the people we have become because of everything that happened to us. It just isn't possible to change who we are so what's the point of speculating? Yes, examine your life. If you don't like what happens due to something you've done, don't do it again.

The Devil Made Her Do It

In 2005, Georgina was interviewed for the documentary *Inside Deep Throat*. That same year when former performer turned adult film director Paul Thomas (born Philip Toubus aka "PT") invited Georgina to do a cameo in the remake of *The Devil and Miss Jones*, she was reluctant to participate. Spelvin had reprised her role as the sexually frustrated Justine Jones in *The Devil in Miss Jones, Part II* (directed by Henri Pachard/Ron Sullivan) in 1983, and she didn't feel the need for a three-peat. PT's persistence paid off, however, and Georgina was hired to play a bathroom attendant in two scenes in the Vivid video *The New Devil in Miss Jones* (2005) starring Samantha Samson in the title role and Jenna Jameson as "Miss Devlin." Dick Smothers Jr., son of Comedy King Dick Smothers, surprised some people when he also performed in the big budget production. Spelvin couldn't help but enjoy the camaraderie on set and made a new lifelong friend in Penny Antine (aka Raven Touchstone) who wrote the script and worked as a costumer.

Within the last five years, Georgina graciously accepted an honor extended by Bill Margold and company to be inducted into the annual "Legends of Erotica" in Las Vegas where wryly, she etched in cement: "Don't do it!"

In the summer of 2011, Georgina was one of Penny Antine's guests at a luncheon Antine hosted in her home during my trip to California. A woman of small stature with grey hair swept back into a ponytail opened the door. It didn't take me longer than a few seconds to realize it was the spunky, quick-witted Ms. Spelvin herself. Within the small group that also included Veronica Hart/Jane Hamilton, Spelvin regaled us with a hilarious story about two raccoons that had recently broken into her home and set up housekeeping. At one point, she jumped to her feet to simulate the furry creatures washing their faces and brushing their teeth in her bathroom leaving us all in stitches. After lunch, Penny led us to her guesthouse stuffed to the rafters with costumes from various movie sets she'd worked on. Georgina obliged my request by holding up the maid uniform she'd worn in the recent remake of "Devil."

Penny and I were separated at birth. I only met her six years ago when Paul Thomas talked me into doing a walk-on in his remake of *The Devil in Miss Jones*. She not only wrote the script, but also did wardrobe for the shoot. We met. We bonded. I loved 'em all, really. I never had a negative experience with any director or fellow actor whilst plying the scurrilous trade. Nor did I ever have a bad experience with any producers.

Jane Hamilton is another great lady. I think I did only one film with Jane, but bonded with her as well even though we were not in touch much after I left the business. [Spelvin and Hart actually appeared together in the film *Urban Cowgirls* in 1982, prior to *Bad Blood* 1989.] However, she married a fantastic guy I had had a severe crush on back before I got involved in porn. When she told me they were getting hitched, I almost dropped my uppers. Naturally, we became even closer friends. Michael ["Iron Mike", Hamilton's late husband] went on to that great motorcycle rally in the sky last year. Jane stays very busy, but we e-mail each other frequently. I adore e-mail; it's my new window on the world, I just love e-mail.

Gloria Leonard is another of my frequent email-pals as is [holistic sexologist] Barbara Carrellas. Gloria is one of the most courageous, intelligent, charming, and delightful women I have ever met. Annie [Sprinkle] was invaluable in my efforts to get a book on the market and I just adore her. Her pal Veronica Vera is another sweetheart I've come to know recently. We met at Jerry Damiano's eightieth birthday party. Marilyn [Chambers] was always wonderful to me. When she was married to Chuck Traynor, they hosted me at their Las Vegas spread once. I never understood why he has such a bad rep. He was always a perfect gentleman whenever I saw him. Gosh, who else? I know I'm forgetting a lot of folks. I've met more ladies of the trade since I've gone "public" again in my efforts to sell this damn book.

The first time I met Juliet Anderson was when I was doing some readings, and trying to sell my book up in San Francisco a couple of years ago. We met through Howie Gordon, who again, is a swell guy and what a writer he is. His son is doing a one-man show called *Debbie Does My Dad* and I can't wait to see this. He's going to bring it to L.A. I think his show might be opening tonight [November 20, 2010] at the Centre for Sex and Culture in San Francisco. I'm hoping they're going to get a venue here so I can see it. I'm hearing that it's hysterical.

Georgina models the maid costume she wore for her role in *The Devil in Miss Jones, Part II.*

Debbie Does My Dad is about growing up as the son of the golden age adult performer, Richard Pacheco/Howie Gordon.

The idea of making a film with sex in it during the golden era was totally overrun by showing sex only wall to wall. That's what people were buying and still are. I know zilch about the adult film industry of today. I haven't been active in "the trade" for thirty years. I've never enjoyed watching porn so I've seen very little of it, old or new. I'm not a historian, but if the recent interest in "The Golden age of Porn" is any indication, we women must have left a mark. I don't think I'm a household name in that many households so it's not impacted my life at all, but I'm sure *The Devil in Miss Jones* is the one for which I shall be remembered, as long as I am remembered.

"We Ain't Giving up Nothing!" *THE PAJAMA GAME*

Since the completion of her memoir, Georgina discovered a whole new trajectory has opened up for her as she keeps busy with work on her second book project, and writes a monthly blog that can be viewed at Georgina's World.com. Spelvin put the finishing touches on recording *The Devil Made Me Do It*, which will soon be available as an audio book. "Devil" recently became available for Kindle e-readers. When we spoke, Georgina shared the process of writing and the assemblage of the e-book and audio formats.

Until I wrote the book, life was just a dream — "sha boom, sha boom". Now, I find myself back in the saddle with all the interviews. I ain't complaining; mind you — e-mail, readings, and the gawdamn book keeping I have to do for the various governments that must get their cut of the action.

I love writing. Always have. I'm trying to find time to work on *Goin' Down in Flames* — a new book that I promised myself I would have finished by Christmas. I can't give up my mornings at the gym nor my lunches with my adorable better half, and the [*The New York Times*] Sudoku and crossword every day after the gym. In spite of my best intentions, I often see something in the garden that just must be done before I can sit down at the computer and write — and when I do finally open up the darling little box, well, I have to check the e-mail first, and then it's time for supper — the news — and bed.

I have been working on the new book insofar as occasionally. I have stacks and stacks of notes and files and files. It's going to be harder to pull this one together by a long shot. I'll get to the writing part again someday. Really, I will. With the first one when I finally sat down and said, "Okay, there has to be some kind of structure to this thing" so chronology is the easiest.

COURTESY OF GEORGINA SPELVIN

What I have been doing is recording the first book and it has been quite an experience. It's been wonderful and I'm sorry it's done. I've just been having so much fun doing it, and re-reading it, and revisiting the work because I would remember some little incident or whatever and find it in the book, and use it for these readings that I felt would be interesting to a particular audience. Other than that, I hadn't read the book.

[*Devil Made Me Do It*] will be available as an audio book. When the producer, a guy by the name of Sam Caldwell who lives in Shreveport, Louisiana first approached me about it, he wanted me to come to Shreveport and do it there and he would put me up. I said, "No, I can't leave home for three or four weeks, I just can't." He sent me a microphone and a tripod and said, "Let's try it and see what happens." This place is so noisy and we're right on the street and we have cars and planes going by, and there was construction at the top of the hill. I started getting up at four o'clock in the morning when it's quiet and from four to six am it was quiet enough that I could record. I did that for nearly three months I guess, and it's all done, except there will be several re-dos, I'm sure.

At first I thought, "Oh god, what a chore." I was very reluctant, and then when I got everything set up and started reading it I was totally charmed. I thought to myself, "Hey, you know, this is pretty good!"

With that feeling percolating through me, I couldn't wait to get up and get to it every morning. I'd wake up and see the clock and it would say three-thirty, and I thought, "Great, I can snooze for another half hour." Then I'd wake up again and look at the clock and say, "Oh god! It's four fifteen!" I'd get up and get my things set up and get my tea and sit down. I'd rehearse into the microphone and get comfortable and I'd lay down two or three pages at a time. The poor man has an editing job ahead of him like no other I can imagine, but he seems very pleased with what he's getting, so I leave it in his hands.

This is a self-published book and I've actually made money. It's amazing. Amazon automatically deposits in my account and then sends me a notice every week or so notifying me of my commissions. "Sam the Man" who is redoing my site, who is the same man who is producing the audio recording, will tell me that my hits to my website go up every week. I find it amazing that that many people are looking at my site. I didn't really try too hard to find a publisher because at the time of my book's release, the whole publishing industry seemed to be falling apart and I didn't know how to deal with all of that, so I saw no reason why I couldn't self publish. I knew how to put a book together. I did all of the typesetting and everything myself, and simply sent files to Lulu.com, but I didn't know that I would be required to market the thing, and I didn't know what that was all about. That part of it has taken up more of my time than I ever expected it would. It doesn't matter what you've written, the world will not be knocking at your door so you have to stand up and sell the suckers.

Before we wrapped up our interview, I asked Georgina to describe her "Kodak" moment. She added a few funny and heartfelt parting thoughts.

The night I went on in the lead dance role of Gladys Hotchkiss in the musical *The Pajama Game*: When I took my solo bow, the audience gave me a standing ovation. Wait, there's more. The rest of the cast gave me a big hand. It's hard to top a moment like that.

Learn to type. Oh yes, this is for everyone — MOISTURIZE DAILY — ALL over. Just reaching everywhere is good exercise.

Four things in my life keep me standing: My husband John, who I adore, my sobriety, my friends and my garden.

Marilyn Chambers
Girl Next Door goes
Behind the Green Door

4

Of all the female stars to resonate with aficionados of the golden era of adult, Marilyn Chambers towers above the rest. Legendary for her unbridled, acrobatic sexual eccentricities onscreen, Chambers' early years offer a glimpse of her potential as a maven in her field.

Born in Providence, Rhode Island in 1952, Marilyn Ann Briggs came from good stock. Her father worked as an advertising executive, and her mother was employed as a nurse. Along with her brother and sister, Marilyn's family eventually settled in Westport, Connecticut where she was exposed to the finer things in life. Chambers was actively involved in gymnastics and trained as a junior Olympic diver as a young teenage girl. She was also known to have been extremely fond of the male persuasion, and in her senior year, Marilyn was Homecoming Queen. Although not particularly interested in pursuing a career as an academic, with her wholesome good looks and natural orientation as an actress, at seventeen, Marilyn traveled to New York and enlisted with the Wilhelmina Talent Agency where she was promptly sent on auditions for commercial and film work. Effortlessly, Chambers won a small role as Robert Klein's girlfriend in *The Owl and the Pussycat* (1970), a Barbara Streisand vehicle that also co-starred reputable actor George Segal. During this period, Marilyn was photographed for the now infamous Ivory Snow soapbox advertisement that surfaced just as her career as an adult performer emerged after she agreed to appear in *Behind the Green Door* (1972) for brothers Artie and Jim Mitchell. When the pair made an offer for her to star in their production and engage in real sex on camera, Chambers flatly turned them down, but reconsidered when they agreed to pay her an impressive sum of money for her efforts.

"I had a great time. It was the time of my life. You know, we had people standing for three blocks waiting for an autograph. Adoring fans who really enjoyed my work and who made me feel like a little princess. I felt it was my job to work hard and make my fans proud."

MARILYN CHAMBERS (1952-2009)

"Green Door," which showcased Marilyn engaged in sex with African American porn star Johnny Keyes, did big box office business and Marilyn enjoyed overnight stardom. Chambers soon followed up with another Mitchell brothers' endeavor, *Resurrection of Eve*, released in 1973. Suffice to say, her fresh-faced image as the girl-next-door touting boxes of Ivory Soap was squashed once her alter ego was discovered.

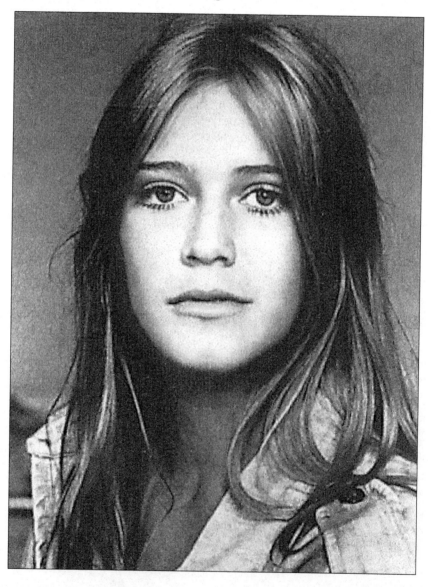

After imbibing in a smorgasbord of perks reserved for those with epic stature, Marilyn was selective about ensuing roles, and along with her entrepreneurial husband and manager, Chuck Traynor, she maintained an aura of mystery while giving her fans just enough to keep them coming back for more. Chambers' film career reached a climactic point in 1980 with the release of *Insatiable*, where she once again proved herself an actor, and performed for the first time with her male counterpart in legendary status, John Holmes.

In recent years, Chambers worked in a varied range of professions. An ardent advocate for animals in need of TLC, she remained connected on the fringe of the adult business and was a popular attraction at Horror Conventions. While married to her third husband, Chambers realized her most important role in life when she became a mother for the first time to daughter McKenna, now twenty-one. Conveying her strong maternal instincts to family, friends, and acquaintances, Marilyn greatly valued the precious unity that she and McKenna shared as mother and daughter. Sadly, their time together was cut short when Chambers passed away suddenly on April 12, 2009 from a cerebral hemorrhage and aneurysm, only weeks before her fifty-seventh birthday.

In 2011, Marilyn Chambers' biopic filmmaker Valerie Gobos spoke with me about Ms. Chambers in order to contribute to this portrait. McKenna Taylor also shared memories about her legendary mother. I talked with Marilyn Chambers in June 2007.

The Owl and the Pussycat

The Owl and the Pussycat went to sea
    in a beautiful pea green boat.
They took some honey, and plenty of money,
    Wrapped up in a five pound note.
The Owl looked up to the stars above,
    and sang to a small guitar,
'O lovely Pussy! O Pussy my love,
    what a beautiful Pussy you are,
      you are,
        you are!
What a beautiful Pussy you are!

— EDWARD LEAR

VALERIE GOBOS: Marilyn was born in Providence, Rhode Island and was raised in Massachusetts. She had a brother and a sister. She was a sophisticated girl, which is something you can't take out of her. She came from a very good family on the east coast. Her mom was a nurse and her dad was an advertising executive in Massachusetts. I think she was popular in school. She loved the boys. She was more of an athlete, and I believe she was also a Homecoming Queen. She was definitely more interested in singing, and dancing, and acting, and modeling, versus being an intellect. There were no problems within the family dynamic. When she did start to model and got into that field, her dad really did not want her to do it. He tried to discourage her because he was involved in the business as an advertiser. He was exposed to actors and models, and he didn't encourage it, but she really loved it.

Marilyn had loved Sophia Loren. She mentioned that in her book [*Marilyn Chambers: My Story*, 1975]. It was Ann Margaret and Sophia Loren — those two were her favorites. Of course, growing up in the 1960s, Ann Margaret was so popular and to Marilyn, one of the most glamorous, sexual women was Sophia Loren.

When Marilyn first started to model, she put her portfolio together. After she was finished with her schooling, she would take a train into New York. She'd registered with Wilhelmina Talent Agency. It was a modeling agency and she started to model. She was more of a commercial model, not high fashion, which was the old girl-next-door type of thing. She had done hair commercials. In the audio for *Still Insatiable* (1999), she talked about where she did a couple of hair commercials, and a couple of modeling jobs. The similarities are ironic. I did the exact same thing probably at the exact same time.

Marilyn started exploring acting when she registered with the talent agencies. She was dating a boy who had gotten a bit part in *The Owl and the Pussycat* (1970) and he said to her, "Would you like to come with me on set to see what a movie is all about?"

She said, "Yeah." It's just like a fairytale story because when she was on the set of *The Owl and the Pussycat* she had her portfolio with her and somebody said, "Are you an actress?"

She said, "Yes."

They told her, "They're holding auditions upstairs. Would you like to audition?"

She said, "Sure," and she got the part of Barney's girlfriend in *The Owl and the Pussycat*. It was quite easy for her.

In a poignant example of art foreshadowing life, seventeen-year old Marilyn (credited as Evelyn Lang) played the girlfriend of Robert Klein's supporting character Barney in the comedic film about an enigmatic, aspiring actress (Streisand) who provides occasional sexual favors on the side, and moves in with a neurotic writer (George Segal). Although Marilyn's role is minor, *The Owl and the Pussycat* has a winning formula and concentrates on the funny antics that transpire throughout the unlikely arrangement as the two leads are polar opposites in their educational backgrounds and mannerisms.

Barbara Streisand, who Marilyn thought was a real witch on the set, did not want to go to Los Angeles to promote the film so the producer sent Marilyn and another actress to L.A. She had never been out west before, so they sent the two of them to promote the film and that's when she fell in love with L.A. Then someone suggested that she would love San Francisco and she went up there. When Marilyn went up to San Francisco, she realized there weren't a lot of acting jobs going on there, and so she worked in a Health Food restaurant and danced. I think she started doing topless dancing but she didn't talk very much about it. It could have been bottomless and topless, but it was definitely topless. Being so athletic, she was comfortable with her body, and of course, during the late 1960s/early seventies everyone was taking their bras off, and going around and getting crazy, so she had heard about this audition. She had read about it and she thought it was a "bowling" film, but it was a "balling" film. In her interviews and in her own words they had said to her, "Are you willing to take your clothes off?"

She said, "No problem."

Then they said, "You'll have to have sex on camera."

She said, "Absolutely not." She left. That's when they called her. Before this, she had gotten the Ivory Soap job. Years later, it ended up on the shelves. They hadn't released it right away, but when they did, it was in sync with *Behind the Green Door*.

Behind the Green Door

While working as a model, Marilyn was photographed holding an infant for an advertisement to be used on the front cover of the now infamous Ivory Snow soapbox for Proctor and Gamble. One year prior to making her adult film debut in Artie and Jim Mitchell's *Behind the Green Door* (1972), Marilyn appeared nude in Sean S. Cunningham's film *Together* (1971), but the part did not immediately lead to straight roles as she'd hoped. Chambers said that when the Mitchell brothers offered her the lead in *Behind the Green Door* she asked for an exorbitant salary in addition to a percentage of the film's gross.

> I did that because I didn't want to do the film. I thought, "Okay, I'm really going to give them something they're going to say 'no' to." I said, "I'm from New York. Don't you know who I am? I'm not going to do that!" They were cool guys and they were very foxy, very sly, you know. They had their shit together for a short period. I loved the Mitchell brothers. I loved Art and Jim and still do today. They're like brothers. They gave me the opportunity to do something and I thought, "Okay, I'll do a couple of films for them and then I'll get out of it, and I'll be able to do stuff in Hollywood." I agreed [to do the film] and I got a percentage [of the film's gross] for approximately ten years, and then it was over. That part of the contract I forgot to look at.

"Green Door" builds methodically as the story is described by two men in a diner providing an eyewitness account of a specific sexual event during flashback mode. Marilyn Chambers, known in the film only as Gloria, travels down the lonely northern leg of the infamous 101 coastal highway alone. After checking into a hotel, she orders a beer on the patio a few hours prior to being kidnapped by two men (Artie and Jim Mitchell) and whisked away to a private club. Blindfolded at first, Gloria doesn't appear to be drugged, but she is strangely serenely calm when approached by a female who reassures the beauty dressed in a striking black evening gown (accessorized only by a pair of white pearl earrings) that she will not be harmed in any way. Gloria falls immediately into a hypnotic trance under the woman's caring words, and is guided through a green door onto a stage. In short order, she becomes a sacrificial sex offering for the expectant group of select guests wearing masquerade masks and costumes. The audience is informed that Gloria will not be harmed, only "ravished" and "loved" in a way she has never before experienced. They are told that she won't remember a single moment of the event afterwards. Six female attendants appear on stage, and proceed to undress and make love to Gloria, their tongues and fingers wander upon and inside of her orifices as they warm her up for the evening's entree. The sudden appearance of African American porn star, Johnny Keyes, donning tribal paint and wearing white crotch-less tights, creates a hush throughout the room as he makes his way across the stage toward the overripe Gloria. Keyes picks up where the women have left off, and penetrates Gloria with machismo exuberance, making intense eye contact with his luscious partner until they both reach a spellbinding orgasm. The spectators become increasingly

Behind the Green Door, COURTESY OF MITCHELL BROTHERS FILM GROUP

aroused by their lovemaking, and eventually, while Gloria performs oral action to three grateful males, the masturbatory circus is completed by a mass climax.

What is most astonishing about *Behind the Green Door* is the fact that Chambers does not utter one word of dialogue, yet she is mesmerizing as the sensuous Goddess, pleasured beyond her will, as she becomes an

Marilyn Chambers and Johnny Keyes. COURTESY OF MITCHELL BROTHERS FILM GROUP

abstract emblem of erotic power. "Green Door" is artful at times throughout its presentation and also contains some special effects, but it is the volatile, taboo Chambers/Keyes sex scene that leaves its sticky mark considering that interracial pairings were sparse and relegated mostly to loops during the early golden era years.

MARILYN CHAMBERS: When *Behind the Green Door* came out, I heard a rumor that my dad's friends took him to a place where they were showing *Behind the Green Door* and didn't tell him. It's funny, because my parents and I never sat down and talked about my career. I told my parents about the film. I was up front with them, but for me, sex, drugs and rock and roll in the late 1960s and early seventies was "I don't care what you think. You're not going to tell me what to do." They just kind of had to ride out the storm and then we became very close. My dad was always kind of secretly proud of me. One of my uncles would take me to see all his old cronies and he was totally proud of me. My dad's brother would say, "Here's Marilyn Chambers. She's my niece."

Despite the culture of sexual and societal liberation cultivated during the 1960s youth movement and enveloped throughout the United States and environs, entering sex films as a performer or in any other capacity in the early 1970s was strongly censured.

VALERIE GOBOS: Marilyn was so sexual. She really loved sex and she really enjoyed it, and she was a feisty, sexual young girl. She said that sex was such a turn on for her and it was even more of a turn on when the camera was rolling. She loved it, and it really excited her, which is typical of all actors. They love it when the camera is on them. I never heard her say anything about her dreading it or not liking it. She talked about how it was very physically challenging to stay in a position for a long period until they got the shot, but she was an athlete so she was in great shape, and she was strong physically. I think so many women in the straight world are romantics, and so there is that fine line, is it making love or having sex? Women in adult are just having sex and pleasing others. It's much different from the typical woman who is more about, "I love him. He loves me." The focus is different. Another thing Marilyn said that I think is interesting and I like is that when she did go out to Hollywood, she found that all of these actresses were sleeping their way to the top, and that Hollywood was so corrupt with these producers and directors saying, "If you want the part, you have to sleep with me." She decided when she made a decision to get into adult films, that if she had to have sex to become a star, at least she was picking and choosing with whom she would have sex.

I think the first woman she had sex with looked like Sophia Loren and she talked about this woman in her book. She had gone on an audition and the woman was there and had said, "Hey, you're really cute. Do you want to come over to my house and meet my boyfriend?" They ended up doing a three-way. It is something nice she talks about in her book.

Marilyn preferred to become a star having sex on screen instead of doing it only to get a small part, and then move on only to be used and abused. She would rather be in control. She was good at it. I think so when I watch her films. She really had star qualities, for sure. She was lovely. She was trained, she was buttoned-up, and she thought she could crossover. Of course, later throughout the years like so many others, she found out that once you go over there you can't come back again.

Marilyn articulated her opinions and her experiences regarding the implications of her decision to star in *Behind the Green Door*. Like with any other career choice, there are good days and bad days.

You certainly have to be an exhibitionist as an actor, but in porn films, it has to be to an extreme. [It's] like "Look at me!" You know I was a junior Olympic diver. I was a gymnast. I did all kinds of things and it was always like, "Look at me, Mom and Dad! Look! Look!" You know how a little kid goes "Mommy! Mommy! Look at me!" I always wanted to be reassured that I was wanted, and that I was doing well. I went way overboard and provided a lot of embarrassment to my parents, of course.

I never considered myself a prostitute, which was always the big controversy. In the old days, it was like "You're a prostitute because you take money for sex." No. I have a contract and I actually get paid before. It was difficult to decipher when I was younger. It was always like, "Whoa, am I a prostitute? Let's set parameters here.

It's an interesting thing. For a very long time I've been obsessed with wanting to write a book or doing a documentary about why people go into the porn business and is there a type of person. Why did they do it? What was their childhood like? If you were getting your master's in psychology, this would be a great thesis. I have had a lot of questions about my own life, but I had a great childhood. Something interjected in there though, to propel me in that direction whether it was outside forces or inner stuff. There are so many women that it would be very interesting to explore — and guys too. Why or what is the type of person who is able to do this? What drives them to this? It's a very similar background. It's a pattern. It would be interesting, but it wouldn't be pretty. It's a definite downer. Most of the time, they either wind up loaded on drugs killing themselves or they wind up in terrible marriages,

1980s recreation of Ivory Snow promo. PHOTOGRAPHY BY KENJI

broke. If you look at the volume of people who pass through the adult film world, if you look at the statistics of people there are very few, a very small percentage that are still okay and around. You have to get through it and be a survivor. I'm a survivor.

A lot of the women who are getting into porn today, I don't want to say they're bubble-headed dopes, but look at the statistics, not real good. In the old days, if a girl was going to do a couple of porn films, she was doing it to get herself through law school or whatever, to create a life for herself afterwards. It wasn't something she was going to be considering for her career. For me, it was considering a career in mainstream, thinking it was a steppingstone because I was looking at stuff like *Last Tango in Paris* (1972) and this type of a thing, which would have certainly told me that it was a possibility there was a transition that could be done. I was considered for a lot of other things, but when *Behind the Green Door* came out, it was like, "Oh yeah! Alright, okay." The pendulum was moving forward, and then all of a sudden, it would swing backwards because everyone went nuts and [later] there was the Meese Commission, and so on.

According to some reports, Artie and Jim Mitchell, the two porntrepreneurs and co-owners of the O'Farrell X-rated movie house that opened in 1969 at 895 O'Farrell Street in San Francisco's Tenderloin district, picked up on the resemblance between Chambers and the popular film and television actress at the time, Cybil Shepherd. Cleverly, they used Marilyn's likeness as a promotional angle for "Green Door" as it dovetailed neatly with the arrival of the new Ivory Soap box that featured blonde, wholesome looking Chambers posing with an infant. In an effort to avoid scandal, Proctor and Gamble quickly terminated Marilyn upon discovering her extra-curricular employment while the Mitchells seized the controversy to further boost ticket sales when *Behind the Green Door* was released. The cumulative gross for the picture is estimated to be $25 million and was made on a $60,000 budget. Alternate images (such as the one on the previous page) depicting Marilyn holding the Ivory Snow box have been used repeatedly to encourage sales of Chambers' films and memorabilia. Chambers herself was well aware of the financial benefits of capitalizing on the paradoxical Ivory Snow image.

In 1973, the Mitchell brothers parlayed the success of *Behind the Green Door* recasting their fresh new starlet who delivered an above average acting performance, in *Resurrection of Eve*. *Resurrection of Eve* (aka *The*

Mitchell Brothers Resurrection of Eve) is a subliminal porn takeoff on the *Three Faces of Eve* (1957) starring Joanne Woodward, only Eve in the Mitchell's story doesn't suffer from Multiple Personality Disorder — although one could argue that her husband does.

Resurrection of Eve is told in three phases with two young actresses playing the part of Eve during her formative years. In the first act, Eve

Publicity photo for *Resurrection of Eve.* COURTESY OF MITCHELL BROTHERS FILM GROUP

(Nancy Weich) is sexually abused by an "uncle" before the age of thirteen in a very disturbing manner. In the second act, Eve (Mimi Morgan) survives a horrendous car crash that results after an argument with her boyfriend Frank (Matthew Armon) who accuses her of sleeping with a black male boxer (Johnny Keyes as himself). Eve undergoes complete reconstructive surgery to her face, and Frank (forever the cad) is all of a sudden smitten by his hot "new girlfriend." After Eve marries Frank, he decides he needs more spice in his life and imposes his will upon Eve to accompany him to orgy parties so that they can swing. Eve is unwilling and uninterested, but slowly she comes around, and eventually, reunites with her old friend Keyes. Frank, the chauvinist boor that he is, isn't too happy about it.

Taking into consideration *Resurrection of Eve* was made in the early part of the seventies decade when women explored their sexuality well beyond the borders of what was previously considered appropriate, it is evident when watching this picture that females still had a long way to go in order to achieve equality inside and outside of the bedroom. Had the storyline focused upon Eve's pleasure center and "coming out" as the title suggested, rather than Eve as the repressed and subservient partner to her husband and his requests for the majority of the film, the conclusion would have been more satisfying. One redemptive highlight is the presence of beautiful Marilyn Chambers whose sparkle and smile almost make up for any deficits and the underlying message of sexism. In 1975, the Mitchells released *Inside Marilyn Chambers* consisting of footages from previous collaborations between the two parties.

Chuck Traynor & Superstardom

VALERIE GOBOS: Marilyn was dancing at the O'Farrell Club, which paralleled *Green Door*. It was during the time she was working with the Mitchell Brothers and she loved them. I'm not quite sure which dates she was dancing and doing her films, but I think she was doing them hand in hand because busloads of people would show up at the theatre to see her.

The O'Farrell Theatre served as a movie house and as a venue for striptease acts and live sex shows since it first opened in the late 1960s. Famous adult film stars that had appeared on stage or performed private sex shows over the years in addition to Marilyn Chambers (who according to Chambers was the theater's largest drawing card) included John Holmes,

Annette Haven, Amber Lynn, Nina Hartley and Erica Boyer. The historic O'Farrell Theatre is currently in operation today as an adult emporium.

Despite its worldwide reputation for nonconformity that the sexually diverse city of Francisco has become known, during the time of Chambers' popularity, the Mitchell brothers were charged with obscenity more than once. They fought for their First Amendment rights in court and won. Chambers once recounted how on two occasions in the 1980s she was arrested for lewd conduct and for prostitution while headlining a show at the O'Farrell Theatre. She remarked that the awestruck police officers treated her well, and requested she sign autographs for them as a memento of having had the magnetic star as their special guest in the San Francisco jailhouse.

Valerie Gobos emphasized the magnitude of Marilyn's marketability.

Marilyn also went to Cannes Film Festival. I remember seeing footage of her at Cannes and I'm not sure what she was doing there if it was *Green Door* or what it was, but my goodness, to be able to be recognized at Cannes Film Festival — she really was a starlet. When Chuck Traynor took her on to manage her; that was his goal he had said to turn her into a starlet with the limos and the fur coats and really make her as glamorous as she could possibly be. He had done the same thing with Linda Lovelace as well. He was just ending his relationship with Linda Lovelace when he met Marilyn.

Behind the Green Door screened at the Cannes Film Festival in 1972. It was extremely well received. In an era where the new phenomenon of porno chic was welcomed at the World-class event, budding celebrities in the sexual film world schmoozed with their Hollywood equivalents, and Marilyn was on top of her game.

In 1975, when Chambers was introduced to her second husband Chuck Traynor (former spouse and manager of porn star Linda Lovelace) she was enchanted. Initially, the union served both parties well as Chambers believed Traynor would be an influential player whose Hollywood connections and experience would expedite her goal of progressing toward mainstream stardom. Traynor was obviously drawn to Marilyn's star quality, and expected that his own standing within the entertainment community would be heightened. It is no secret to those familiar with Chuck Traynor's reputation, he had been much maligned by Linda Lovelace in her 1980 memoir *Ordeal*. Likewise, staunch anti-porn feminists, the press, and the adult community also criticized Traynor for his apparent brutal physical and emotional abuse of Lovelace during the years they were married and while acting as her manager. Lovelace's allegations of violence, threats using weapons, sexual abuse and torment on the set of *Deep Throat* and throughout her turbulent relationship with Traynor have been well documented. Some elements of Lovelace's claims against Traynor have also been challenged over the years as to their authenticity. Fellow former performers

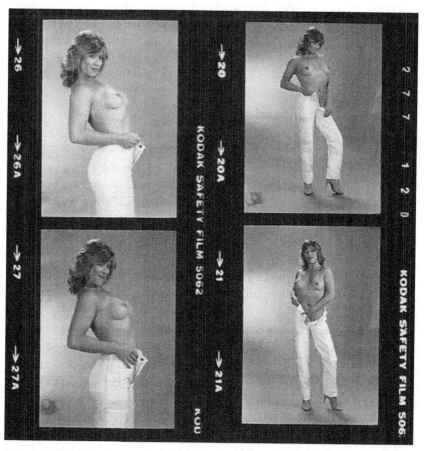

PHOTOGRAPHY BY KENJI

(including Chambers) and those who were present on the set of *Deep Throat* have contested Lovelace's charges against Traynor (that he held a gun to her head during filming) and disbelieve accusations that Traynor coerced Linda to commit specific sexual acts on camera. Conversely, in recent years, another performer who was present on the set of *Deep Throat* has come forward to say she witnessed sounds of Traynor beating Lovelace in a hotel room while on location for filming. Incidentally, there is no love lost between the adult industry and Lovelace who denounced the industry after she left films (and divorced Traynor) after joining an alliance with anti-pornography feminist activists in an attempt to blame the pornographic movie business for the mistreatment and exploitation of women. Joined by ardent supporters such as the late Andrea Dworkin, Gloria Steinem, and Catherine McKinnon, Lovelace and the group cited Linda's assertions of Traynor's dominant and reprehensible actions on set and beatings metered out to Lovelace while they were still married, as evidence for their plight. Unfortunately, Lovelace became a sacrificial lamb during the anti-porn campaign. She was discarded by the same group that had adopted her as their so-called spokesperson once she was no longer integral to their mandate. In her 1986 book titled *Out of Bondage*, Lovelace focused on her life after 1974, but reaffirmed her stance she was threatened by her former husband to perform sex acts on camera.

Tragically, Linda Boreman died on April 22, 2002 at age fifty-three after her involvement in a serious automobile accident just three months before Traynor's death. Ironically, April 22 also happens to be Marilyn Chambers' birthday. In a thoughtful and caring gesture, Marilyn donated money toward a liver transplant for Lovelace prior to her removal from life support while still in hospital.

Throughout the years while she was married to Traynor, and after their divorce in 1985, Chambers did not speak in a disparaging way about Chuck or make public claims of physical or sexual abuse during their involvement. Privately however, Marilyn discussed the true nature of the relationship with few trusted friends. Co-workers and business affiliates who crossed paths with the couple recalled Traynor as controlling and territorial. It is believed Traynor wrote portions of Marilyn's (now out of print) autobiography *Marilyn Chambers: My Story*. When we spoke in 2007, Marilyn outlined how Traynor had uniquely managed her career.

Chuck and I didn't socialize with people that I did films with — instead he kind of tried to make me be above that — whether that was good or not. Obviously, it was good, because he always wanted to create a fantasy where I was kind of untouchable to the people that I was around, but on the screen, very touchable. When I would meet my fans, I was very touchable. The people that we worked with, we didn't really socialize too much with them because then they would know too much about me and find out I was a real normal person. Any star, like Scarlett Johanson, you don't know anything about her. She is a mystery and a fantasy. That's why guys want her because they don't know that she farts and that she is a regular person. She is a complete fantasy and that's what a movie star should always be. Chuck told me, "Always give people what they don't expect." That was his best advice to me.

That movie *Boogie Nights* (1997), I absolutely don't get it. It wasn't anything that I knew. I couldn't really deal with it at all. Maybe that was what the porn business was, but I was with Chuck Traynor.

During the early years of their relationship, Marilyn and Traynor associated with major Hollywood personalities and retained close ties with "A" list entertainers such as Sammy Davis Jr., among others. While she and Traynor were an item Chambers embraced opportunities to dance and perform as a singer in Las Vegas nightclubs, in addition to headlining at the O'Farrell Theatre in San Francisco. She even cut a single, "Benihana," a pop/ disco tune. The number, produced by Roulette Records, didn't achieve the kind of success on the pop charts Marilyn hoped, but the song eventually paved the way for her to showcase her better-than-average vocals in films. All the while, Chambers continued to read for mainstream movie roles.

I did many different auditions for Hollywood and it became a case of "Yeah, we really want you, but the producer's wife —" There were about three films where I was just about ready to sign the contract and they even had the money up front. Once they even had an announcement in *Variety*, it was a film with Rip Torn when he was young and still good-looking. *Variety* printed "Congratulations to Marilyn Chambers for doing *City Blues*." Rip Torn was co-starring and Norman Mailer had written the [1976] script. We were even in rehearsals. Nicolas Ray was the director. He had done *Rebel without a Cause* [1955]. We met at my apartment with Nicolas Ray, Rip Torn, me, Norm Mailer and we did the whole thing. We were rehearsing and then Nicolas Ray went off the deep-end on cocaine [in 1976], and he died in 1979 and that was the end. That's the story of my life! I'm never going to win the lottery. That kind of shit kept happening to me throughout my life. It's bad luck, I guess.

Rabid

In 1976, Marilyn's luck changed when she was hired to star in the Hollywood film *Rabid* (1977) directed by David Cronenberg. The Canadian director scheduled the shoot for Montreal where Marilyn arrived on location with Chuck Traynor in tow. In the 1992 book, *Cronenberg on Cronenberg*, David Cronenberg recalled Marilyn fondly and relayed the process of having worked with the star and her husband.

"[Producer] Ivan [Reitman] just said, "It would be really great for us if you like Marilyn Chambers for this movie, because her name means something, we can afford her and she wants to do a straight movie. But if you think she's bad, we'll forget it." I think what she had to sell was the girl next door, who fucks eight guys at once. She's the cheerleader; she's the one everybody wanted to fuck at high school. She does it, right there on screen. I've never to this day seen one of her hardcore movies, but I saw a softcore movie she did and she was incredibly sweet and unspoiled.

When I met her, she was a lot harder than I had hoped. She had plucked eyebrows and her hair was very pre-Farrah Fawcett. She had been doing Las Vegas. Chuck Traynor, her husband/manager, was not my favorite kind of guy — very tough. They were both into trading gold-plated revolvers with Sammy Davis Jr., that kind of thing. It's a world totally foreign to me; not one I'll ever get to know too well. Chuck was very protective of Marilyn, and very supportive of the movie. Marilyn herself was very shrewd and sharp, and worked hard. She'd obviously had some rough times since that first little movie that I saw of hers. She was a real trouper, and invented her own version of Method acting. When she had to cry it wasn't a problem, because Chuck would say, 'Remember when Fluffy died?' — Fluffy was her cat — and then she'd cry.

I thought she had real talent, and expected her to go on and do other straight movies. She went back. I don't know if it was Chuck, or that the industry still wouldn't accept her."

Cronenberg is known for trippy, fascinating Sci-Fi films, often containing strong sexual overtones including *Videodrome* (1983), *The Fly* (1986), *Naked Lunch* (1991), and *Crash* (1996). The director apparently hired Marilyn as his leading lady in his second feature after his first choice, Sissy Spacek, was scratched because of her strong Southern accent. *Rabid* featured Marilyn as Rose, a tortured young woman injured in a serious motorcycle accident. Upon receiving skin grafting, Rose is transformed into a blood thirsting vampire. An organ resembling a phallic symbol is tucked beneath her armpit and utilized as a kind of syringe enabling her to extract blood from her victims. The wounded morph into zombies and converge on the city creating mass hysteria.

Marilyn clearly demonstrated pure acting moments on screen in a career best performance, pleasantly surprising movie audiences familiar and unfamiliar with her previous film work. The cult production succeeded in creating a new fan base for Chambers in the Horror genre.

The inscription reads "Joel (Remember the armpit?) (Love You) Love & Kisses, Marilyn Chambers, XXX" COURTESY OF JOEL SUSSMAN

Still photographer Joel Sussman was hired for the filming of *Rabid* and recalled Chuck Traynor made his presence known on set by behaving in a domineering manner. During filming, it was suggested Marilyn pose nude in order to help promote the picture, but Traynor argued because *Rabid* wasn't a sex film, nude photos would not be permitted. Sussman took Marilyn aside reminding her that generally studios hired their own publicity teams to determine decisions regarding the promotion of a movie rather than managers. Sussman remembered Marilyn as a delightful person to work with and contended she was very affable on a personal level. Chambers wrote the personal inscription (pictured above) on a t-shirt Sussman has kept as a fond memento of his interaction with the gregarious superstar.

Insatiable

In 1979, two years after the release of *Rabid*, and while Chambers' star still shone brightly, Marilyn made two more short adult movies for Artie and Jim Mitchell: *Never a Tender Moment* and *Beyond de Sade*. Both films contained all-girl erotic scenes and showcased new starlet, Erica Boyer, in a supporting role.

Comparatively speaking, Chambers acted in very few pornographic films during the 1970s decade, yet her legendary status and carefully crafted career path made her an elite celebrity and one who was also known to folks unfamiliar with sex films — a genuine litmus test of stardom.

Valerie Gobos explained the reasons for Marilyn's staying power.

It's interesting because Marilyn really was a good actress, singer, dancer, and model. I don't believe any of the other performers were as multi-talented. She was a great athlete, so you have someone with star qualities. Seka, I think she's wonderful. Seka is exceptionally good at what she does and what she has done with her career. I love her and I love the way she's been able to hold her head high and remain strong and out there in a classy, sophisticated way. I don't think she really has the Hollywood star quality that Marilyn had. The difference is that Marilyn is a Hollywood star, not just a porn star. She was a star in the entertainment industry. Thousands of others make adult movies, but Marilyn is someone that had star quality, just like any other star. When you look at anyone who is a star and you try to analyze what makes a star a star, you can't really define it, either a person has star quality or they don't. I think she'd like that, too. I really do believe that Marilyn was a star. I think that even if people in the public did not approve of pornography, they still thought of Marilyn Chambers as a star. So many people would gasp and say, "Oh, Marilyn Chambers! She was the Ivory Soap girl!" If I look at many of the adult performers that I'm familiar with now, I see Marilyn as a star. I see her and I see John Holmes. I don't see anyone else that achieved that level of star quality.

In 1980, the two larger than life legendaries in the adult sphere, Marilyn Chambers and John Holmes, combined their talents and marquee drawing power in *Insatiable*, a big budget feature that Marilyn, along with producers and many fans, believed was her most successful and sensually provocative blue screen effort. Saving the "pièce de resistance" for optimal effect, Holmes does not appear on screen with Marilyn until the final scene. The Bogey and Bacall of their profession and generation, Chambers and Holmes appeared together in three major releases between 1980 and 1983. Marilyn described her first meeting with Holmes, and recollected what it was like to have vaginal, oral, and anal sex for the first time with her well-endowed male counterpart.

Let me say that back when I was doing what I was doing, the biggest deal was having John Holmes. I had seen him and I'd seen films with him, but I thought, "Oh god". I didn't find him attractive, but his big dick was fascinating. I mean, I like big dicks, but that's ridiculous. That's an oddity. That's Ripley's Believe it or Not. The biggest thing was taking that up your ass. That was like a gangbang with about fifty-thousand guys. You can't do it, you can't deep throat him; you can't take it up your ass.

In the old days, you'd go to the movie theatre and John Holmes' dick took up the whole screen! People don't go to movie theaters any more so it's totally obsolete even talking about that. You know, the porn business has done a great disservice to the men of the world, making them feel inadequate. It's a disservice because guys think, "Oh, my god, I have to have a twelve inch dick to satisfy my woman." Not true. Obviously, the male participation is a dominant force in the adult film industry. They're the long lasting, no pun intended, persons, and they've stuck around. It is not about their face — their schlong is what's important. Nowadays, where do you go? There is nothing that hasn't been done before; now it's becoming a circus act where this is not real life. This is just ridiculous.

In *Insatiable*, I did the last scene in the movie with John, and I remember Stu Segall, the director — well, he called himself Godfrey Daniels at the time — we were shooting this film in San Francisco or something. It's funny, because my mind starts to get a little foggy here like, "Was it *Insatiable 1* or was it *Insatiable II*?"

Stu says, "We're going to go pick John up at the airport in San Francisco."

I said, "Okay great." I'm not sure if another person was there, but we got into the car and we drove to the airport, and we picked up John Holmes. I was so totally nervous. I'd heard so much about him. I was not afraid, but just totally shy like, "Oh my god." He and I were sitting in the back seat and we were talking, and I was just kind of looking at him in awe, going, "God, this guy is really smart." He really is reasonably articulate. I don't know now if he told me he was married, but I know he told me that he had a sheep farm. In any other context, it would be like, "Oh yeah! That makes sense." He said that he was just kind of a country boy, and he was doing all of this so that he could live a normal life. He was so not the John Holmes that I thought he was going to be. He didn't come marching up going, "Hey! Move over bitch!" He was a meek, kind of gentle man. I thought, "Oh, okay, is he going to be able to take control here in the scene?"

He was like, "Don't worry about it." He said, "You'll never be able to deep throat me or take it up your ass."

I said, "Oh really?" We had a bet going. Let me tell you, it was difficult because at that time John was doing a lot of cocaine, although he wasn't flipping out or anything in the car. I mean, we all were. What can I say? I never did it when I actually had to do a scene in a movie or be on stage. I saved it for later because I always wanted to be the real me. I might have had a couple of drinks occasionally, to loosen up. It wasn't as if I was out of my mind, which really kind of blew my mind. Later on, people were shooting heroin, which I couldn't believe. That's so unsexy. That never appealed to me, ever.

When John and I actually were getting ready to do the scene, it took forever. He was in the bathroom. He was doing coke, like a gram up each nostril. I remember he had a straw, and it was like, "Come on, John, let's go." I remember it was hot. It was a black room where we had to have this black stuff all around and all the other guys were ready. John came out and he couldn't get it up. It was like a big floppy old worm. What he would do is hold it at the base and try to squeeze some of the blood into the head. We really had a difficult time with that. He never really got totally hard, but I think we faked it enough to make it look real. It was real; it just took forever. We were exhausted. Of course, he said, "I'm sorry, I'm sorry..." He just wanted to get it done and move onto the next snort, or whatever. At that point, in John's life he was sick of movies, and women, and having to do this for a living. Obviously, he was escaping into drugs for that reason.

I was never worried about him. The professional mode kicked in. When they say, "action," that's when your mind control kicks in and you are in a different dimension. You are involved in something where you know millions and millions of people are going to be seeing this, and it's just a weird feeling. You need to make this so sexy because you're not going to have another chance. People are [also] going to be seeing this, many, many years from now and thinking, "That was hot!" The film is very erotic. I think that we did what we were supposed to do and I think, as professionals, we accomplished our job. I think we did a good job. Apparently, people liked it because they bought the movie. You're going to fuel interest, and gossip and controversy with someone like John Holmes and me as to what kind of persons we really were.

In *Insatiable*, Chambers portrayed the beautiful, sexy Sandra Chase, a wealthy model/actress whose parents are killed in an automobile accident. During a trip to London, Sandra vows she'll live life to the fullest and decides to explore her sexual desires which are plentiful. The first of these is a hot Jacuzzi encounter with the pretty and uninhibited Renee (Serena). The two women are sweet and evocative in their lovemaking, reminding fans of vintage material there truly were beautiful women during the golden era, equipped with full bush, and natural breasts (and in Serena's case, unshaved underarms). In the following segment, Sandra flashes back to a memory involving the family gardener Nick (David Morris) who took her virginity on the pool table (considered by some viewers to be rape, although Chambers' character is more than willing) in an extremely erotic scene that almost steals the show. (Chambers had since stated that the scene with Morris is one of her most sensual and authentic performances.) Sandra's next encounter is with Richard Pacheco portraying an actor. He assists her on a deserted highway after her car breaks down, and is delighted to receive much more than he bargained for in the way of a blowjob for his Good Samaritan efforts. In the subsequent scene, John Leslie makes an endearing appearance as Roger Adams slated to be Sandra's co-star in her upcoming film venture. Adams is invited to dine with Sandra and her assistant, Flo, played by popular 1970s star Jesie St. James. As Sandra overhears Flo's cries of passion while she and Adams engage in coitus on the patio (conveniently located just outside of Sandra's bedroom window) she masturbates gleefully on her bed while conjuring up an impressive list of fantasy lovers in her mind's eye for inspiration. Moments later, a familiar, elongated member emerges from the shadows, as a surprisingly sexy John Holmes arrives in time to bring the film to a fitting crescendo. John caresses Chambers gently while planting tender kisses on her face and mouth. Taking command of the fantasy, he moves her into position and buries his face between her thighs before penetrating each of her chambers. When Holmes finally climaxes upon her tummy, Sandra faces the camera and pleads almost in anguish, "More...I want more."

Insatiable is one of the premiere films of its genre with a healthy production budget, vibrant cinematography, reliable acting, and entertaining musical numbers performed in part, by Marilyn herself. In a humorous nod to her days as the Ivory Soap girl, early on in the film, Chambers opens a closet to retrieve a robe and a box of Ivory soap is shown on the top shelf.

In 1984, Marilyn reprised her role as Sandra Chase in the sequel to *Insatiable* titled *Insatiable II* with Juliet Anderson, Jamie Gillis and Paul Thomas. Although the film contained some exceptional performers, it proved a tough act to follow the success of its predecessor as Marilyn explained.

Insatiable was my favorite film. I looked the best. I felt the best. I felt the sexiest. It was like the prime of my life right there. That was a time where you saw me being totally sexual, everything was great. Everything was going my way and I just felt sexy, and I felt happy. I wasn't into drugs and alcohol. We partied, but that wasn't my life. I love that film, but the problem with the film industry is that they got so into, "Let's make it a story for women, so women will watch." Then they went overboard and the films had too much story and too much talking, and these people can't act. Then it evolved into vignettes. There's a beginning — a

middle and an end. There's not this big long story that you have
to sit through. The tape is worn out in certain sex scenes. That's
what they want to see. The filmmakers went from stag films to
loops to *Behind the Green Door*, which was very experimental, to
an *Insatiable* type thing — back to almost loops, which were sort
of like vignettes [as in] *Marilyn Chambers' Private Fantasies*; five
fantasies in one film.

Fantasies & Reality

When VHS came out that was a huge turning point. Because
then people started shooting on video. You could be the straightest,
staunchest person in the world but this is a person's human nature.
They are curious about sex. Everybody has sexual fantasies. The
older I get, I believe you don't want to have those fantasies, a private thing you do in your own home or behind closed doors unless
you're a swinger — Everybody doesn't have to know what your
sexual fantasies are. We are different people in this world. We are
different people when we go to work. In a straight job, around the
water cooler, you can't say, "Oh yeah, we did this and that," because
it's going to haunt you. Our generation, we just wanted to be free
and live the way we wanted to, but that's not how life works.

Marilyn Chambers Private Fantasies [*Part 1*] is very well orchestrated and it has a gymnastic feel. I can't remember when we did
the gym scene in *Private Fantasies*, I think it was the same time we
were doing *Insatiable* because we shot *Marilyn Chambers' Private
Fantasies, Part One* [released in 1983] at the same time.

Marilyn Chambers' Private Fantasies is interpreted through several
montages, two of which are clips from an earlier film, *Spirit of Seventy
Sex* (1976), that don't feature Chambers.

A few moments after well-toned Marilyn introduces the first vignette
in "Fantasies," she is appropriately seated inside of a fitness club, dressed
in a fitted leotard. While confiding she'd like to have sex on all of the
equipment, she proceeds to demonstrate her amazing physical agility by
turning a few cartwheels and doing a couple of headstands and flips. The
camera pans over to John Holmes hitting a punching bag. When he turns
around, Marilyn is positioned at his feet. They share a lingering open
mouth kiss before he bends her sinewy body backward over the bench
and begins deep cunnilingus while she talks dirty to him. From that point

on, the two stars reposition themselves on various pieces of equipment in order to experience all forms of penetration until reaching a climax.

The fifth segment features Marilyn in a shrouded gothic bowling alley. Introducing Ashley Welles and Jane Lindsay: both women are dressed in dark cloaks and move slowly toward the squatting Chambers. They disrobe and Marilyn takes them on in a sensuous *ménage a trois*, which includes anal licking, spanking, and nipple biting. Chambers is anything but bashful and lies across Welles's back in order to give Lindsay easier access to her orifices with her hands and fingers. In turn, she extends the favor to Welles and Lindsay.

In the final sixth segment, Marilyn enters a soda shop wearing pigtails and dressed in a cheerleader uniform. Immediately, she begins to tease the shop owner and patron played by Michael Morrison and (early male performer) Mike Ranger sporting a porno "stache". With very little effort, they convince Chambers to show them her cheerleading moves until she is on her hands and knees on the counter naked. The guys go to work on Marilyn, who seems to enjoy every bit of the attention — even the insertion of the cherry into her cherry. Marilyn then works Ranger and Morrison over (she impressively deep throats Morrison) while Ranger gets her in the behind as she begs for more.

Between the years 1983-1987, Chambers starred in five more installments of *Marilyn Chambers Private Fantasies* distributed by Caballero, showcasing her with a number of male luminaries including Harry Reems and Richard Pacheco. The recurring series also depicted Marilyn opposite some of the newcomers of the 1980s decade in the way of Christy Canyon, Sheri St. Clair, Tom Byron, Jerry Butler, Billy Dee and Buck Adams. Due to the success of their two previous onscreen trysts together, in 1983, Chambers and Holmes teamed up together again.

> John went to jail, he came out, and we did the *Up 'N' Coming* (1983) movie. I remember sitting in a room with John, and he was kind of waiting for his scene. He'd become this person who had become way more introverted. All of a sudden, his intellectual side had sprung out.

In *Up 'N' Coming* Marilyn starred as Cassie Harland, a rising songstress who sleeps her way to the top of the country and western circuit. The multi-talented Harland wages war against a diva she had once emulated, the washed-up alcoholic, Althea Anderson, played very convincingly by the terrific sexy bombshell Lisa DeLeeuw. Anderson knows her days are numbered, but refuses to go down without a fight and the two women (Chambers and DeLeeuw supplied their own vocals throughout) contend for top spot in this big-budget production centering on the two competitors. Marilyn efficiently demonstrates her physicality in various sexual encounters including a funny scene with Richard Pacheco as a radio personality, and with Savage who is very good in the role as Harland's hard-boiled studio exec Jimmy King. The story builds toward a climax that eventually pairs Harland with country music's legendary outlaw — fresh out of jail, Charlie Strayhorn (John Holmes in a cameo role that is tailor-made). Smitten when she gets a load of Strayhorn's pleasure package, Cassie and Strayhorn get into it as they entangle themselves within a slew of veteran performers during the requisite orgy scene at the conclusion.

Although a little harder looking around the edges compared to how she appeared in *Insatiable* three years earlier, Marilyn is remarkable in all facets of her performances in and out of bed, in addition to her vocal capacity. Chambers performs the film's title song lending a personal touch. The Special DVD Edition of *Up 'N' Coming* includes an audio commentary provided by Gloria Leonard, and offers a Marilyn Chambers "photos" section and "cast bio."

Having worked again with John Holmes immediately following his release from jail for contempt after a first-degree murder acquittal, Marilyn commented how drug abuse can radically alter a person's personality while noting corresponding factors between Holmes and Jim Mitchell.

I can't remember what the story is, but I don't think John did rat because that's why he went to jail. He didn't tell on anybody because he thought, "You know, I'll just go to jail and do my time." I admire that. What he was involved in was not a good thing, but that's what drugs do. That kind of shit happens. He was similar to Jim Mitchell after Art was murdered. I visited Jim in San Quentin. Robert De Niro wanted to do a film based on Jim and Art's life. He was interested in doing the life story of the Mitchell Brothers but he wanted to do it below the belt, he didn't want to do it above the waist. He wanted to do the whole thing. He flew me up to San Quentin to see Jim and Jim said, "You know what? I don't give a shit about who's doing a movie about it. I don't care if it's Robert De Niro or God. I am not telling anything about anything." He said, "This was a major tragedy and it was a mistake. It's a tragedy I will never talk about." The film was never done correctly.

In February 1991, Jim Mitchell drove to his brother's house armed with a .22 rifle in response to family and friends' concerns about Artie's exacerbated battle with alcohol and cocaine. During his visit, Jim fatally shot Artie and was charged with voluntary manslaughter. (Marilyn was one of many guests in attendance who spoke at Artie's funeral.) The details about what transpired during the confrontation between Jim and Artie were re-enacted during Mitchell's trial, in which Jim was represented by pro bono attorney (and old friend) Michael Kennedy, former partner of Joe Rhine. Mitchell served three years of a six-year sentence in San Quentin Penitentiary. After his release from prison, Jim resumed his role as owner and manager of the O'Farrell Theatre and created a fund in Artie's name with proceeds going to a local drug rehabilitation centre and to the San Francisco Fire Department. In 2000, *Rated-X*, a cable television film presentation revealing the rise and fall of the two brothers was made in Toronto with Hollywood actors (and brothers) Charlie Sheen and (director) Emilio Estevez portraying Jim and Artie Mitchell. Tracy Huston played the part of Marilyn Chambers.

Jim Mitchell died of a heart attack at his home in Sonoma County in July 2007, in his sixty-fourth year.

MARILYN CHAMBERS: When people get addicted to anything, everything goes in the shitter. They want that drug. No matter whom you step on in your way, you'll do it. There's a reason why people become addicted. They don't like who they are. They don't want to look at who they are, or what is at the root of the problem of why they are who they are. They may have been molested or no one cared about them, or someone that they'd loved left them for someone else, whatever.

Marilyn's Brightest Light

In 1985 Marilyn and Chuck Traynor parted ways, and toward the latter part of the eighties, Marilyn began to scale back on film roles. It is worth noting that Chambers was a guest on *Live with Regis and Kathy Lee*, along with Hulk Hogan in May 1989, another endorsement of her ability to crossover as a pop culture figure.

During the years when she performed at Las Vegas Night clubs, Marilyn met the man who is believed to have been her greatest romance, Bobby de Piece. Little is known about de Piece, a likely pseudonym. Due to unfortunate circumstances, the two were not be able to share their lives together as Valerie Gobos explained.

Bobby de Piece was said to be the love of Marilyn's life. He worked at a lot of strip clubs in Vegas. There was a problem one night when he escorted somebody outside. A fight broke out and someone ended up getting killed. Bobby wound up taking the heat on that. In 2010, he was released from jail. I was recently contacted because somebody, apparently, is doing Bobby's life story.

Marilyn in gauze. COURTESY OF MITCHELL BROTHERS FILM GROUP

I don't know exactly, but before Marilyn died, Marilyn and Bobby had started writing letters to each other. It was kind of nice that Marilyn was able to put closure on that. I think Bobby has a young daughter who is married at this point. The incident happened earlier on.

According to Marilyn, one of her greatest regrets concerned her love life.

You know, I chose men who were violent and very sexy, but I could never choose the proper mate. That doesn't go for the last guy that I had my child with, but we had our problems. There's drugs, there's alcohol; there's all kinds of stuff involved in any relationship that I've ever had. When you're in the sex business, when your sexual libido is heightened constantly and that's all you think about and that diminishes, it is like "Oh, my god. Who am I? Who would want me?" And then when men do go out with me as soon as they find out after so many dates who I am, it's like, "Forget it." It's way too intimidating. I've never met a guy who is like, "Okay. That's cool." Seka, I think, has met a guy who makes her happy. He accepts her for who she is and they have a good relationship.

My career has been phenomenal, but in retrospect, I'm not sure I would do it again. It's been great but it's really provided a very big stigma. It's a stinky stigma and lasts forever, unfortunately. It's something that's always going to be out there and no matter what you want to do, if you want to do mainstream, or if you want to go back into the woodwork and just be a normal person, you can't. I'll tell you one of the most difficult things is having a relationship with a man. I'll be a spinster to the day I die. I don't know if I want to be married, but I'd like to have a relationship with somebody. Again, do I want that? I've lived alone for so long, I am my own person and I don't need a guy. Years ago, I needed somebody. I was very needy. I was looking for daddy. I think most of the chicks in the porn business are looking for a daddy figure. Something is definitely lacking. They were either molested, or abused, or not paid attention to.

As her own career as an X-rated entertainer continued to wind down, Marilyn met and married her third husband William (Billy) Taylor. She gave birth to her first and only child, McKenna Marie Taylor, born on May 13, 1991. The birth of McKenna was clearly a landmark in Marilyn's personal life. Chambers and Billy Taylor divorced in 1994, but as she looked toward the future and reflected upon her past, Marilyn always spoke with love whenever her daughter's name was mentioned, even if she was unable to find a suitable mate.

Marilyn with Billy and McKenna Taylor, 1990s. COURTESY OF MCKENNA TAYLOR

The best thing that's ever happened to me is my daughter. To be a mom is the best thing in the world. You know, that's all I ever really wanted to do after I had finished doing films. When I met my last husband, I just fell madly in love with him and our goal was to have a house, a home, and a family. That's what I really wanted to do. I did it for a while, and then other things got in the way where it just didn't work out. I still do have my daughter and I still do have a great relationship with him, the dad. That's because I was very intent on making it work. You have to work together.

You know, it's the kind of thing where she's now sixteen and when the empty nest syndrome comes, I don't know what I'm going do! I'll probably go up and be near my sister back east. I have a brother and sister who are still there. My sister is back in Washington State so I'll probably move closer to her. Right here, I'm alone. I don't spend the holidays really with anybody. I don't. I want to be with my family. My sister has her sons and her grandchildren, and she's a great cook. I'm a good cook myself. You know, at her house, we cook and we have all the family and we have parties. That's what I would like to do.

VALERIE GOBOS: I do think Marilyn was lonely during her later years and I think she would have loved to have found her soul mate at the end. McKenna, her daughter, had said that Marilyn really did love her dad. Yet, it's kind of unclear as to why they got divorced. He has since passed away. He died the same year she did, so I wasn't able to interview him. McKenna was living with her father before he passed away. He had a big house. She liked the fact that he had the big home, but she and Marilyn were together all the time and they were very close. The father was in and out of rehab, so maybe McKenna wanted to be close to him for that reason. She lost both parents in one year.

McKenna Taylor is a bright, twenty-one year old woman currently working on an undergraduate degree in psychology at a California University. The fact she lost both her parents tragically, before the age of eighteen has not discouraged or jaded the sweet and vibrant Taylor. With her head on straight, McKenna is surrounded by a supportive network of extended family and friends. When McKenna was invited to contribute to this book, she provided another shade of Marilyn Chambers Taylor, the nurturer and immortal celebrity from a daughter's point of view.

MCKENNA TAYLOR: My mother wanted to be the best mother she could be. I really do believe that was her goal in life, and she accomplished it from day one.

My mom and I loved to cook, watch movies together, dance, sing, and cuddle with our pets. Her hobbies also included gardening, and most importantly, she liked to help people in need. She

Marilyn and McKenna Taylor. COURTESY OF MCKENNA TAYLOR

rescued animals off street corners and would talk on the phone for hours with friends if they needed her.

Some of my fondest memories of my mother are our cooking shows. My mother was the best cook. I would be her little helper with cooking dinner, and she would go over absolutely everything she was doing so I could learn. Whenever I made any kind of meal for myself, the first person I would call would be my mother. She would be so proud of me for taking her advice and making a great meal on my own. Another memory of my mother that I will never get out of my head is of us dancing and singing together. We would be in the car and turn up the music so loud, and just dance and sing a lot. Of course, there is also my mother's laugh. I could hear my mother laugh a mile away. Her laugh and smile lit up a room as soon as she entered it.

My mother was very open about the adult industry and told me a lot about it when I was old enough. At first, I was obviously in shock and a little bit embarrassed until I got older. Once I was able to understand her past and really get to know it, I was able to embrace it and love it because she did. My mother would tell me stories about her life and I enjoyed it so much. I am still so proud of her for the accomplishments and hardships she overcame.

Talking about her career, I think a moment that brought my mother great happiness and pride was when she was given the keys to San Francisco. I recently visited San Francisco and was lucky enough to be able to stop by the O'Farrell Theater. The very first room on the right, which is a sitting room, has posters and memorabilia of my mother's. I talked to a very nice man [Ted McIlvenna, President of the Institute for Advanced Study of Human Sexuality in San Francisco] who has been working there for over thirty years, and we talked about what an amazing person my mother really was, not to just me, but to so many others.

San Francisco was my mother's Hollywood. Getting the keys to the place which gave her the big "break," must have been thrilling and a mirror image of how much she was able to influence not only people, but also, an entire city.

Still Insatiable

By the mid 1990s, and sporadically throughout the new millennium, Marilyn, as sexy as ever, resurrected her adult film career by appearing in special select performances. *Still Insatiable* (1998) directed by Jane Hamilton (Veronica Hart), paired Ron Jeremy, with Chambers, and is probably the film she is most remembered for during her comeback. Two other significant features made within the last ten years of her life are *Dark Chambers* (2000), and *Edgeplay* (2001) directed by Jane Hamilton.

At forty-six years of age, Marilyn is a little rounder around the midsection than in previous film projects and her face definitely shows signs of seasoning, but Chambers reaffirmed in *Still Insatiable* why she is hailed the paramount female star of her era. Marilyn is a California Senator on a mission to permanently ban pornographic material while covertly, in an effort to gain a better understanding of the films she is hoping to eradicate, she screens a movie, and becomes turned on. This leads to a succession of provocative coital circumstances, not only involving Marilyn, but also people under her employ who go out of their way to satiate the Senator. The well-preserved Chambers' reemergence as a porn star is hot and magnetic as ever, both in her masturbatory scene (where she positively glowed), and with her fellow performers: Julian, Julian St. Jox, Mr. Marcus, Julie Ashton, and Kylie Ireland. Marilyn has not lost her libido as she participated excitedly in a group sex scene, joined Julian for an anal scene, and shared a double dildo with the girls. Predictably, the Senator reevaluates her stance on censorship in the film's conclusion.

MARILYN CHAMBERS: My parents both passed away within five months of each other in 2000. [A few years before], I was doing an appearance in Seattle or something, and I was staying with my mother and my sister was over. I was getting ready to go and my mom said, "I can't imagine why anybody would want your autograph?" My mother was one of those kinds of people, a very independent Leo. My sister would say, "But Mom, she's a famous porn star, are you kidding?"

My mother was just, "I don't want to hear it. I don't want to know." They would come and see me occasionally. I did some straight plays when I was in Las Vegas and she came and saw those. When I was doing a nightclub act, she came to see me at the Empire State building with my dad. They had tried to participate, but it was difficult for them. As a mom, and as a middle-aged person, I totally understand that.

In accordance with most actors who work occasionally, during the years leading up to her own death, Marilyn was able to support herself through mainstream employment options and managed to juggle the two personas up until the end, as Valerie Gobos described.

She was working at the car dealership selling cars. In fact, until recently, they still had her voice on the voice mail when you called the dealership. They all really loved her there, and I guess it was kind of hard when they had to finally take it off.

I believe she had also gone to get her assistant nursing degree at some point. She was very much an advocate for animals. She loved dogs and cats, and animals. Until her last day, she was involved with Horror films. I think the last project she had done was the voice-over for *Porndogs: The Adventures of Sadie* (2009), and it went into DVD. I interviewed the director [Greg Blatman] of that film in San Francisco and they had Sadie there; Marilyn was going to play the voice of the dog. It's a great interview. We have her in the recording studio, but she did crossover into Horror and the guys who were involved in that became very close and were devastated by her passing. She would do these conventions and show up, and sign autographs for the Horror film circuit similar to Seka and some of the others.

It's unfortunate, because even to this day if you Google Marilyn's name or go online you can see so many other people making money off of Marilyn Chambers. Marilyn Chambers didn't make near that amount of money off of herself in her later years: the compilation scenes, and photos, and the merchandising. I think that out of respect to McKenna, her daughter, this is something really to address now.

Marilyn knew she was a star, and she would have liked to have been a different type of star, but I don't feel that she one hundred percent regretted it. I think she knew that and that's maybe what was frustrating for her was looking back on her life with not a lot of money, and not making a lot of good decisions because she knew who she was and what she even could have been. I think she switched gears like all women do, and again, becoming a mother became the most important thing to her in her life.

Not many people are aware that in her later years Marilyn also donated her time counseling young people about the dangers of drug abuse. Chambers expressed her feelings on the subject of lament.

The difference between the adult industry today and back then is we shot films; we put stuff on film. Not that many movies were made, and plus, you had to go to a movie theatre. The other thing was we had a lot of controversy. We had the church; we had the Republicans. We had the John Birchers. We had situations where people got up and they were soap boxing and denounced it. It is an entirely different era of women being funneled into the industry today. They can't do anything else or they've been told by some Svengali guy, "I'll make you a star." They think they're going to be the next Jenna Jameson, the chicks of today, or making millions and millions of dollars. With people like me paving the way, that's wonderful, but if you start at eighteen, you're done by the age of twenty. Some of these girls do approximately eighty films a year! They're totally overexposed. It's like "We're done with you. Next."

As for me, I have to get through this life. It's either screw the day that I got into this and be a totally bitter, resentful woman who's just furious because everyone's making money off of me, or I can say I

Marilyn with Kay Parker. COURTESY OF WORTH MENTIONING PUBLIC RELATIONS

have to move on. I can equate it with someone who worked for me who stole all of my jewelry; every single bit of it that I had been collecting since my early twenties — everything; items that had been given to me by Sammy Davis, and others. It took me about fifteen years to not hate these people. They were never arrested, but everybody knows they did it. It's the kind of thing where it just engulfed me. It's very difficult to let go. You can also parallel it to what was stolen from me by being a porn star, my adulthood. You know, from the years eighteen to forty. It was stolen from me, but I allowed it. I did it. I own up to it and I did make a lot of money. I had three husbands who also enjoyed my money.

Life is too short to be bitter and angry and hateful. It's not worth it. There are a lot of people who are making a lot of money off of me right now. I spent almost six years in court in Las Vegas trying to do this and that and the other thing and with the internet today, the amount of people that sell my stuff, and take little things from other films and make other films. When you call them and say, "cease and desist" they go, "Fuck you. Sue us." I'm sorry, I don't have half a million bucks to sue. Even then, you're probably not going to win so the disadvantage of being an adult film star is that you better be really, really smart and have a great attorney, and own every single piece of merchandise that you do before you do it. Because if you don't you will be screwed in the end, and you will be taken advantage of and thrown to the dogs. If you don't care, great, but if you do care — it's cause and effect. I mean, I have other things that I do that require my time. I have projects going, and honestly, at age fifty-five I thought I'd be retired but guess what? Not happening! When it's over, it's over. I had always envisioned myself saying "Thank you and good night," when I was about thirty-two and that would be the end of it. It doesn't work like that.

Thank You and Good Night

As I mentioned in my introduction, I had hoped to meet for dinner with Marilyn in Santa Monica when I visited Los Angeles in July 2007. Unfortunately, Marilyn had to cancel out last minute. I remember sitting in the cab speeding down the freeway toward West Hollywood to visit family when I received her call, and afterwards, informing my astonished driver that Marilyn Chambers had been on the phone. He smiled and said. "Everybody knows Marilyn Chambers".

In addition to the documentary and feature film retrospective on the horizon, there is also a Marilyn Chambers biography in the works.

VALERIE GOBOS: Right now, my company, Gobos Film & Entertainment, is producing a full-length documentary on the life of Marilyn Chambers and life after porn. I am also pitching a feature film to the studios. I'm hoping to reach not only the adult world, but also the public about Marilyn's life. It is also about the subject of sex, a subject which I think everyone finds to be interesting. Maybe we can bring that out a little bit more into the general market. All I know is that I fell into this, and I knew that I had to do it.

MCKENNA TAYLOR: I would like people to recognize that yes, my mother was an adult film star and was damn good at it, but she was also an amazing woman and mother. She had an amazing heart. She was a shining star, on and off the camera. I miss and love her dearly.

Classic Marilyn. COURTESY OF MITCHELL BROTHERS FILM GROUP

MARILYN CHAMBERS: I was Marilyn Chambers seven days a week at all times. When people met me, that's the person I was. I wasn't just Mar. I was Marilyn Chambers, and then as I got older, I had to become me. It was real difficult to make that transition into what I really was. Everybody goes through the "Who am I?" and discovering yourself, but mine came a little bit later and after coming off of a very big run. You know, it's difficult to be that person twenty-four hours a day, seven days a week, and come down off of that and be somebody else. That's what I found very difficult.

I really want to get it out there to the public to let them know when I was involved in my career I had a great time. It was the time of my life. You know, we had people standing for three blocks waiting for an autograph. Adoring fans who really enjoyed my work and who made me feel like a little princess. I felt it was my job to work hard and make my fans proud. I really do think that's the true meaning of a star, if you can be a complete fantasy.

Roberta Findlay
New York City Woman

5

Roberta Findlay inferred her life has consisted of a series of random acts, and that she moved whichever way the wind happened to blow without a specific direction or objective in mind. It would be a challenge to attempt to contradict the dogged and refreshingly blunt Findlay, who is the first female cinematographer in America, and maneuvered a twenty pound, thirty-five millimeter camera on her small frame to boot.

Born to Hungarian immigrants in 1948, Findlay, also known as "the human tripod" to those in the cinema world, was raised in the Bronx and is the youngest of three children. At around age four, Roberta began to play classical piano which she continued to do exceptionally well over the next twelve years. Her father and mother presumed that their believed prodigy would surely gain fame and fortune as a world class, concert pianist, but at age sixteen, while attending New York City College in the mid-1960s, Roberta met her husband Michael Findlay. An avid vintage movie buff and budding filmmaker, Findlay was ten years Roberta's senior. After becoming an arranger and accompanist for Michael's silent film screenings, Roberta and Michael soon took their act to local coffee houses in the East Village. Michael also commenced to direct his own cult, sexploitation films centering upon the subjects of rape, torture, and bondage. The offerings often featured Roberta in small acting roles where she was usually billed as Anna Riva. The Findlay team explored simulated sexual extremes in several enterprises, and created a stir of controversy for too much realism when their biker-themed picture *Snuff* (released in 1976), shot in Argentina in the early seventies, was refurbished with a fatal five-minute ending that was not a part of the original footage.

In the early 1970s, Roberta took the reins and proposed to write, direct, shoot, produce and compose scores for softcore ventures: *The Altar of Lust*

"I made it a rule, an absolute rule for all of the films that no women were allowed on the crew except for make-up. The technical crew: cameraman, gaffer, grip and sound — I never hired a woman. I don't like women."

ROBERTA FINDLAY

(1971) featuring Harry Reems, and *Rosebud* (1972) starring Jamie Gillis and Darby Lloyd Rains.

Roberta left Michael in the mid-seventies for another companion — by that time she was considered a virtuoso camera operator with a flair for lighting technique. She accepted the capital offered to produce, direct and shoot her own films. At first, Findlay continued in the trend of shooting softcore, but couldn't resist the temptation to progress to hardcore when it became evident there was greater financial gain — even though she felt ambivalent about directing sex scenes. Findlay often used aliases (to the tune of Robert Norman) for some of her X-rated films that ranged from moody to humorous with a dash of panache. Two of the movies in which Roberta was involved were notoriously busted: *Anyone But My Husband* (1975) and *Honeysuckle Rose* (1979).

During her hardcore film career, Findlay teamed up with recording studio owner, the late Walter Sear, and ultimately produced more than thirty titles before video arrived and the demand for adult theatrical releases diminished. Findlay and Sear transitioned to the Horror genre, which generally depicted fright/slasher premises exhibited in two of their popular titles: *Tenement* (1985) and *Blood Sisters* (1987).

For more than fourteen years, Findlay (who is also fluent in French) has presided over Sear Sound, a prestigious Manhattan recording studio that Walter helmed over forty years ago. The studio attracts many distinguished musical greats from all over the world such as Sir Paul McCartney, Norah Jones, Eric Clapton, Sting, Bob Dylan and David Bowie. Niche artists: Scissor Sisters, Yoko Ono, Rufus Wainwright, and Deathcab for Cutie have all recorded there.

In their latter years together, Roberta and Walter enjoyed making annual pilgrimages to Europe and were ardent opera fans. Now that Walter is gone, Roberta finds herself tuning into the Turner Network to watch some of her favorite classic directors. She is not a fan of modern technology and prefers to communicate by landline telephones and snail mail.

Roberta Findlay rarely grants interviews, and still isn't certain why she agreed to talk about her life and career in November 2010 for this book, but I'm glad she did.

The Pianist

I was born in the Bronx, which is a part of New York. I was a child in a slum and it was a war zone even when I was a kid.

Actually, it was a Jewish neighborhood when I was a very small child, and as I grew older, it became a war zone.

I have a brother and sister much older than me. We had a nuclear family. Nobody got divorced or anything. My parents were, in essence, peasants from Hungary. In those days, everybody worked including me as soon as I was able to. My mother worked as a clerk and sometimes a bookkeeper, and my father was a drycleaner. They worked very hard as people did then. It was a hardscrabble life. We were near the Bronx zoo, so that was exciting!

I had a happy childhood and I started playing the piano when I was four or five-years-old, which became the constant in my life for about twelve years.

When I attended public school, in those days, it was grades one through six. I skipped the fourth grade actually, and then in junior high school, I skipped the eighth grade. I was in special classes. Unfortunately, I was about fifteen when I finished high school, so at fifteen, I entered The City College of New York [CCNY], which, at that time was a very good school — not its music department, but it was considered a fine Engineering school. I went to college and graduated from City [College] at age nineteen — nineteen and a half. At one time, you were able to go to City College or you'd go to Queens or to Hunter, but I went to City, I don't know why.

I was in City College during the late sixties, and then the year after I graduated, it became open enrollment. That was the end of the city colleges in New York. The system fell apart, and eventually, they became remedial schools. When I was there, it was free. There was a yearly fee of maybe fifty dollars or something, but they were free. Yet, it was very difficult to get into the city schools. You needed a high mark on the SATS [Scholastic Assessment Tests]. They had SATS then, and City College was actually the hardest to get into. I studied music, which is a totally useless occupation and pastime.

At the age of seventeen, I had no concept of what it is to live or what one does with one's life. My parents thought that I would be a great concert pianist. Unfortunately, I'm very dexterous and I can play very quickly, so they thought that's what I would be: a world famous pianist that had come out of poverty or misery or whatever. The dexterity was a fake; it was a façade, actually. It didn't make me a very great pianist, but I'm fast. I don't play anymore. It's not that I didn't like it, but it came to me when I was about nine or ten that I could never be a world-class pianist. It was silly — out of the question. My parents didn't know Liberace from Horowitz. Civilian people don't know. They would say, "Doesn't she play beautifully?" I continued in music. I didn't even take education courses so I couldn't teach anything — not that I would.

I met my husband [Michael Findlay] when I was at school, but I was too young to get married at sixteen, and then finally, we were married when I was eighteen. I was unconscious. I didn't think. I'm not very emotionally grounded. I just do what comes along. I was sort of in love for a few weeks and he wanted to get married. His parents insisted, and my parents thought the world had ended — that marriage would end my career. My career had ended long before that. We got married and I was a teenage bride. My husband was ten years older than I was. I'd say he was a lapsed Catholic. Actually, he was studying to become a Priest and went to Catholic school here, to Cathedral University in New York, and then gave that up and matriculated to City College, which is where I met him. Interestingly, he was a film nut and was all about old films. He ran a program at the school that showed silent films and he needed a pianist to accompany the silent films. I volunteered and I was paid a little here and there. I always worked at the school and at the office. I worked as an accompanist for the Gilbert and Sullivan Society. I was living at home, of course. I'd never seen a silent film. I could have cared less, but I think we started with *Birth of a Nation* (1915) — what a nerve! I improvised a score based on all of the music I'd studied. I didn't make up anything; these were just pieces that were famous compositions. I didn't know what I was doing.

I played for about twenty-five films during that year. The music department was on my case that it was demeaning, and I was giving a bad name and reputation to the music department. They wanted me to stop. Martinets, is what they were, dogmatic martinets. They were refugees, actually, from Germany, and they ran the department. They didn't find it cute or endearing. I kept playing. It was challenging and interesting, and then we ran a program in the East Village after we got out of school for silent films at a coffee house. I played again. This is the mid-late 1960s.

Grindhouse Theatre

Early into their careers, Michael was approached to refine the surrealistic S&M drug movie *Judas City* (later released as *Satan's Bed*). After the picture was sold, sex scenes were incorporated into the short feature. Roberta made a brief appearance herself in the revamped film as a young woman (billed as Anna Riva) bound to a pool table. She is also listed in the credits as a lighting technician.

There was a film made in the mid-1960s in which we were not originally involved. The film was a very bad movie called *Judas City* that they had been trying to sell for years. Nobody would buy it because it was so terrible. Finally, my husband met somebody — I don't know who he was at the time. I was a kid, but they bought the picture years later after it was made, in 1970, or something. My husband was asked to fix it up to make it into a sex picture. It was black and white — it was terrible. Afterwards, my husband went on to make a series of awful softcore porn films. I didn't work with him — I know all of the websites say the two of us worked together. I think I'm even in a couple of them. I was in a couple of them.

Roberta appeared in select early softcore films using the stage name Anna Riva under the direction of her husband Michael. She wrote screenplays, provided narration, and taught herself the ropes of cinematography through an organic process. Michael (sometimes billed as actor Robert West) interjected himself into his own "grindhouse" productions (a term derived from the now defunct burlesque theatres on New York's 42nd Street, before the conversion to adult movie houses where striptease acts were also known as "bump and grind" shows) that typified 1960s sexploitation pictures.

Michael (aka "Julian Marsh" when in the director's chair: Roberta had fancied Warner Baxter who'd played the character Julian Marsh in the 1933 award-winning film *42nd Street*. She suggested the stage name for her husband) was one of an eclectic group of filmmakers on the east coast during the mid-late 1960s whose artistic eccentricities transcended cinematic landscapes by uniquely combining sexuality, violence, gore, and S&M motifs. Michael's first exploitation film was *Body of a Female* (1965), which incorporated the appearance of legendary Pin-Up girl, Bettie Page. Roberta had a minor debut role in the film as the Cuban stripper, Cindy. She is billed as Anna Riva.

Michael Findlay's *Take Me Naked*, listed as a 1966 release, unveiled a very young and partially naked Roberta Findlay in a surreal and oddly compelling study blurring eloquence with the perverse. A delusional alcoholic/Peeping Tom overtakes and murders the teenage Elaine (Findlay) after a succession of sexually suggestive sequences engaging the victim in an intimated lesbian tryst. Shrouded within a narrated overlay, a female and male take turns reading erotic poetry written by Pierre Louÿs, even during the bizarre necrophilia segment.

Sold as a double feature with *Take Me Naked* through Something Weird Video, Michael Findlay's *A Thousand Pleasures* (1968) is a similar

Take Me Naked.

tale of misogyny and mayhem in which Michael portrays a man who murders his wife (Roberta Findlay) to infinitely silence her incessant badgering. "Peculiar" is a befitting word to describe the nature of much of Michael Findlay's work, and although his craft might not necessarily appeal to mainstream movie goers, at the very least, one could argue that Findlay's films dramatically and concisely mirror the nefarious cavities of the human mind.

Three cornerstone films directed by Michael Findlay, who had a starring role in each, are commonly known as *The Flesh Trilogy*. They consist of *The Touch of Her Flesh* (1967), followed by sequels *The Curse of Her Flesh* (1968), and *The Kiss of Her Flesh* (1968). The "Trilogy" series is characterized by fetish acts and exaggerated violence, generally directed toward strippers and prostitutes carried out in deviant, gory fashion predating the slasher/horror flicks that gained an enormous cult following in the

1970s. Roberta is credited in all three productions as cinematographer. She also provided voiceovers.

Michael made a series of demented — crazy — they're psychotic movies. I mean, he should have been locked up. He took out his frustrations or whatever, in the films. It's a good thing he never

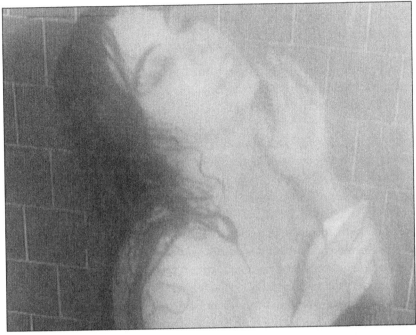

Roberta Findlay.

killed anybody. It was all about murdering women — that was his fantasy or desire or something, but he wasn't like that at all. He was a sweet gentle soul. I grew to hate him, but it had nothing to do with the work. We were together for about seven years, I guess.

I thought he was the only one who was that demented. He made about a dozen titles of that nature, but he was generally the director/cameraman. Somehow, through osmosis I learned how to shoot. He didn't teach me and I wasn't particularly interested, but I started making cheap movies in New York for distributors that were hardcore. They were soft core in the beginning — somehow I learned how to shoot and edit. I don't know how it came about. I just seemed to know. It was for money. I had no skills. I didn't know what to do with myself. I should have gone to a normal type of job or something, but I never did — it sort of fell into my lap. I'm a better cameraman than I am a pianist. A couple of the distributors said to me, "Hey, do you want to make a film?" Of course, one of them was my boyfriend so he said, "I'll give you a few thousand dollars so you can make a film."

Findlay is referring to former film distributor and producer, Allan Shackleton, who became her collaborator after she eventually left Michael during the early 1970s.

I made a few for him early on. I guess they were soft core. *Rosebud* (released in1972) was one. *The Altar of Lust* (released in 1971), that was the second one.

The Altar of Lust (1971) showcased Harry Reems in a co-starring role just one year before he became famous for portraying a physician aiding a young woman (Linda Lovelace) with an abnormality in Gerard Damiano's *Deep Throat*. *The Altar of Lust* is the story of Viveca (Erotica Lantern), a blonde patient seeking the advice of a psychiatrist Dr. Rogers (played by adult film director Fred Lincoln in appearance only). Vivica wishes to understand her newly awakened erogenous desires and responses toward men and to women. The limited feature is an effective representation of a "roughie," as it embroiders the semblance of sexual tenderness and innocence between Lantern and Reems, within the tougher fabric of domination subsequent to a rape scene that opened the film. Roberta wrote the screenplay and acted as narrator (as Viveca) throughout, piecing together the allegory, while Michael Findlay (uncredited) supplied narration for Dr. Rogers.

Snuffed out by an Angel

It was in 1973 or 1974 that we went to Argentina and shot *Snuff* (1976). Michael was the director, and he appeared in the thing. I was the cameraman. It was the first film I actually shot. It was a hand held, thirty-five — the film itself was based on the Manson gang. I shot it and it was all dubbed. There was no sound at all because everybody spoke Spanish and it was supposed to be an American film. I also directed the lighting, which my husband really didn't know much about. The only things I shot outside of thirty-five millimeter were some things I filmed in sixteen for PBS [Public Broadcasting System], believe it or not. Everything I shot was thirty-five. You could shoot in sixteen, but you'd have to blow the negative up into thirty-five to make prints to show in theatres. It was fabulously expensive.

At the time of its release more than thirty-five years ago, *Snuff* (originally titled *Slaughter*), centering on a tough female biker gang, was considered one of the more controversial cult pictures in contemporary film as it was hyped to contain an actual murder or "snuff" content on camera. Compared to today's world of hi-tech wizardry, the scene in *Snuff* depicting the homicide of a young woman, is dubious and obviously faked, yet various self-interest groups protested the graphic content of the film when it played in New York theatres. The debate continues today about the authenticity of the "snuff" genre, in general. That being said, it is unanimously agreed Michael Findlay was a guru in the sphere of filmmaking.

Michael's interests actually lay in optics and the science of optics. After I left, he developed a 3-D system that was patented by his benefactor. — It is the system now being used. It's a portable, two lens, filming system that was a huge set-up for three cameras and was used in the 1950s by Hollywood. You had three cameras to shoot 3-D, which is the same portable system Michael had developed. I had nothing to do with it, but it's used today. I don't know who owns the patent now.

Michael was actually killed taking this device, the prototype, to Cannes Film Festival. He was on the roof of the Pan Am building in New York to take a helicopter to the airport. I don't know why because he was terrified of flying, but the helicopter fell apart and killed a bunch of people on the roof and on the street. He was sort of cut in half by a rotor of the plane. He never got on the helicopter.

Michael Findlay passed away on May 16, 1977.

I had run away with another guy and Michael was devastated. He was a mess. What could I do? I was a very flighty and ungrounded creature. I do whatever sort of comes along. I worked as a filmmaker for the distributor who was my boyfriend. Towards the end, I made a film called *Angel #9* (1974), and I think when it was resold, it was re-titled *Angel on Fire*. It was hardcore. When he saw it he said, "Oh my god, I'll be arrested" which is ridiculous because this was long after *Deep Throat*.

Roberta Findlay wrote, directed, produced, and edited (under the name "Anna Riva") *Angel on Fire* combining entertainment value with ethereal set designs and a hefty slice of retribution. Released in 1976, *Angel on Fire* is the story of Steven, an abusive, egocentric boyfriend who gets run over by a van. After a brief stopover in heaven, Steven is returned to earth as a woman renamed Stephanie (Darby Lloyd Rains) by the lovely Angel #9 (Jennifer Jordan). While dwelling in a feminine body, "Stephanie" is about to experience heartache and the sensitivities of being female, when "she" falls in love with Jeff (Jamie Gillis) a photographer and self-serving misogynist. When they first meet, Jeff gives Stephanie the royal treatment, but changes gears when he grows tired of her and begins to indiscreetly screw other women. He becomes abusive and downright mean after Stephanie informs him she's pregnant — a ploy designed to snag Jeff for keeps, but backfires once he correctly surmises Stephanie purposely stopped taking contraceptives. Jeff shouts, "I

Angel on Fire. TVX HOME VIDEO

don't care if you raise it yourself or get an abortion, but get the fuck out my life!" and means it. Stunned, and a little too co-dependent for her own good, Steven/Stephanie gets a taste of his own medicine and finds it hard to swallow (pun intended) the same treatment in female form that he doled out when he was male. Finally, Stephanie reaches her breaking point and is returned to heaven; restored as Steven and rewarded for his/her painful enlightenment by Angel #9. In the closing frame, the two heavenly beings proceed to celebrate the carnal benefits of celestial freedom. Eric Edwards co-stars as Angel #10, and Marc Stevens is the first of Stephanie's earthly sexual conquests.

They really weren't busting that many films at that time, although I've made a few films that have been busted. [Shackleton] got scared so he sold *Angel on Fire*. Then I took up with another guy, and that was the end of him.

Human Tripod

Findlay said the final straw with Allan Shackleton (who passed away at age forty from heart problems) occurred when he refused to pay her for a film she'd shot for him. After Shackleton socked her in the eye, Roberta's attorney informed Shackleton that if he paid Findlay the twelve thousand dollars he owed her to make the picture she would drop the battery charges. Ironically, Roberta hadn't actually brought charges against Shackleton, but her attorney correctly ascertained a threat would be an effective way to strong arm Shackelton into making good on his promise, which he did.

As a filmmaker, Findlay seemed to hit her stride when she connected with her eventual lifelong partner, Walter Sear. Prior to Findley's break up with Shackleton, she and Walter met in Shackleton's office where Walter handed her his business card. Sensing an obvious connection between Findlay and Sear, Shackleton took Walter's card and tore it up, but Roberta had memorized his address and telephone number. Although Sear was legally married the thirty years that he and Findlay were a couple, he did not divorce his wife, and he and Roberta maintained their own residences. After their meeting, Findlay and Sear began producing a succession of hardcore movies — many of which incorporated humorous scenarios and considerable dialogue. On more than one occasion, the couple hired actors that would garner them the greatest financial return on their investments while shooting several scenes for different films simultaneously, much to the chagrin of some of the hired talent. Findlay became very adept as a cameraman and confidently extended her intrinsic talents wherever she was needed.

Cameras are heavy, even the old Arriflex which is what we used. It's called the "wild camera" and you couldn't tape sound with it at that time. Loaded with film, it weighed about twenty pounds, I guess. I'm not very big physically so when I shot with a hand held camera, I looked like a tripod because I couldn't move the damn thing was so heavy. Then we graduated to heavier cameras — to thirty-five — to forty- pound cameras that you could hardly balance. In the horror films we used a heavier camera [a Panaflex], which was better balanced, but with all of the handhelds, I was like a tripod. I could barely hold a camera, but because I could, it saved us a lot of money. Instead of setting up elaborate shots and so on, I could just move. I was a human tripod — everybody knew about that.

I got used to it, but after some years, I developed a lump on my breast where the motor sat right on that spot. I went to the surgeon and they said they'd have to remove the lump. I knew exactly what it was, and of course, I was right. It was a cyst, a lump, but it had grown there because of the camera motor. They took it out and there was nothing there. I'd break every camera cable because they were not meant for females. Every camera cable motor would hit the side of a woman's breast, so the cable motor would get bent. As I was shooting, I'd be bending it and it would break.

We could make movies very, very cheaply because we did all of the work. Walter Sear, whose name is on the studio Sear Sound — the two of us did all of the post-production at the old studio. I was the cameraman, director, producer, editor, and he was the Prop Manager. All of it was done by us. It didn't cost anything. We bought film stock and hired the actors. I enjoyed shooting dialogue scenes.

I was in the editing room with the old movieolas on a picture that I made with two guys that was actually good. It was cheap and it was called *Fantasex* (1976). It made a lot of money in this country, but I cleverly sold out before it was released. I wrote and edited that one and directed it. It was kind of unique. I think it was made around 1978. I don't know — it's all a great blur. I directed the scenes through the camera. I wandered around holding a thirty-five millimeter camera.

Fantasex is indeed a creative, atypical production. As employees of a publisher of dirty novels, the sex obsessed, but timid Bernard (Jeffrey Hurst) and his secret, equally shy admirer Jane (Terri Hall) voyage through several fantastical episodes together exploring their sexual desires unrestrained and free. Cleverly, the tale continually blurs the bridge between reality and delusion utilizing unique costumes and sets, as it adeptly demonstrates the crossover from the concrete into the surreal.

Several other films identified by Findlay's trademark for blending comicality and sex were produced in close proximity to one another, and starred some of the well known classic adult stars of the era. *Anyone, but My Husband* (1975), *Sweet, Sweet Freedom* (aka *Hot Nurses*, 1976), *Sweet Punkin' I Love You* (1976), *Dear Pam* (1976), and *New York City Woman* (1980) all contained strokes of wit and humor. C. J. Laing (who often played a lost soul seeking sexual treats), Eric Edwards, John Holmes, Jennifer Jordan, Tony Perez, Darby Lloyd Raines, Crystal Sync, and

Marlene Willoughby were cast repeatedly — in part, because Findlay would shoot many storylines simultaneously.

Sweet Sweet Freedom is set in a hospital in arrears, whose patients are dying before they can pay their bills. With its *National Lampoon* style of humor, this film manages to elicit several laughs, in what seems a parody of porn films, which means the trade off is that the sex scenes are more tepid than hot. Slim Pickens and Sweet Freedom band perform during a celebratory orgy at the film's finale.

Sweet Punkin' I love You show- cases C. J. Laing as lowly servant Punkin' Peel aspiring for greener pastures. She marries her wealthy older boss David Creen-Smith (Marlow Ferguson); only the groom has a heart attack on their wed- ding night. Grief stricken, Punkin' orchestrates an orgy party with the help of her assistant Dixon Cocks (Jeffrey Hurst). In the film's closing minutes, Punkin' expertly admin- isters TLC to the organs of three men (Tony "The Hook" Perez, John Holmes, and Jeffrey Hurst) in a sala- cious four-way scene. Once again, Slim Pickens and the boys close out the bash.

Fantasex.

We could never raise money ever for anything. Walter would downplay and denigrate the film business and I'd say, "Would you stop that? No one's ever going to give us money for something they can't make a dime on."

Eric Edwards got incensed because we had a habit of saving money to shoot two or three films at the same time with differ- ent scripts, of course, but the location and the actors were there. We'd use those actors in the same location for different films. He refused to continue to screw or whatever when he realized he was reading scenes from different scripts. I guess it was two films, so he felt he should be paid twice. I think that I told him to shut up and do his job. I probably gave him an extra twenty bucks or something!

In the finest of these cumulative outings, the relatively highbrow comedy *Dear Pam*, stars Crystal Sync as Pam Slanders (porn's answer to former columnist Ann Landers), a woman of high morality and virtue who holds the fate of her readers within the grip of her pen. When Slanders breaks confidentiality with Harry Phallus (Eric Edwards) one of her loyal readers because she is appalled by his confessions of promiscuity, Slanders defames his character (and his member) publicly. Joined by two British cohorts Richard Grandik (John Holmes), Barton Fartblow (Tony Perez), and a female supporter (Jennifer Jordan), Slanders is determined to get to the base of Phallus' "indecent" sexual behavior, but instead, exposes her true colors as a latent nymphomaniac. Slim Pickens band cranks out the tunes once again during the closing frame as an orgy ensues including the entire cast and company.

We always had very elaborate scripts and I paid a lot of attention to the non-sex scenes. I had no moral compunctions about any of this stuff, but I just found the whole thing disgusting — shooting sex scenes! I probably shot fifty hardcore films and we owned twenty-six of them, but I was always disgusted by the sex scenes so I'd say, "Okay, everybody screw." That would be it.

By the mid-late 1970s, we were shooting theatrical releases and Holmes said to me, "What are you, a dialogue freak?" He took the script and threw it. He made up the stuff as he went along, and he was actually very funny. He was amusing. He was kind of personable. Walter and I didn't know he was on drugs. We were so square and so dull. We didn't know anything about that. I've never had any drugs. I like Jack Daniels.

New York City Woman (1980) was my idea. It's a free film. We'd shot Holmes probably in five pictures and we had a fair amount of outtakes, so I took all the outtakes. There are a thousand cuts in that film, which is a lot — and we shot Holmes reading his memoirs in *New York City Woman*. *Anyone But My Husband*, Tony Perez had been in which got busted and I took all of the outtakes and put them in *New York City Woman*.

With a catchy rock number for the title song, *New York City Woman* resourcefully incorporated multiple scenes from *Sweet, Sweet Freedom* and *Sweet Punkin', I Love You*, in conjunction with outtakes from *Anyone But My Husband* to design a new story built around the life of porn star John Holmes playing himself. Holmes decidedly takes a leave of absence from adult movies in search of the one woman who can satisfy his sexual appetite. Most of the newly embedded scenes are shot on a rooftop in New York where Holmes chronicles his sex life on tape in a funny, self-mocking manner, stressing the point that the woman of his dreams must be equipped to deep throat him and more. The film also features C. J. Laing, Tony Perez, and Eric Edwards (from earlier footage).

Anyone But My Husband is a film I'd made for another distributor and that was really rough. It was made in the late 1970s. I made that, and it was busted all over the country. I was the cameraman. I wasn't busted on that one, but my friend produced it.

Anyone But My Husband (1975) starred C. J. Laing as a newlywed Nora Pelman enticed into having an affair after she is neglected by her husband (Robert Kerman, aka R. Bolla). Eric Edwards supplies another fine performance as one of Nora's dalliances, but the film's most scintillating and controversial ingredient is the three-way fisting scene that takes place while Nora bathes with pals Tony Perez and Deanna Darby lending a hand. In 1970s porn, fisting scenes were guaranteed to attract attention from law enforcement officials, as was the case when *Anyone But My Husband* debuted as a theatrical release.

A Taste of Honey – Do Not Pass Go

The second bust was with Jack Bravman during the filming of *Honeysuckle Rose* (1979). Actually, both of the busts were with him. The year was probably around 1979. It was a bad arrest in Point Pleasant, New Jersey, and we were shooting at night in a closed shopping mall in a Beauty Parlor. Serena, Samantha Fox, Eric Edwards, and John Holmes were all on that shoot and we were all arrested. They'd covered the windows and such, but there was a crack in the window and the security guards looked in and said, "Oh, my god, look at John Holmes doing that terrible thing!" The police came in and busted us, and Walter said, "Do you have a warrant?" And no, they didn't.

At gunpoint, he said, "We're not leaving."

They said, "Oh yeah?"

Walter said, "No, we're not leaving, you have no warrant." We left and they didn't have a warrant.

Honeysuckle Rose (Findlay is billed as Robert W. Brinar) features Serena and John Holmes as a poor young farm couple, Sam and Kate, hoping to hit pay dirt with their race horse Honeysuckle Rose. Rosie eventually comes through with flying colors. In the interim Kate and Sam become disenchanted with one another and seek sexual refuge with other partners outside of their marriage. Samantha Fox, Herschel Savage, Bobby Astyr, and Carter Stevens all portray willing conquests.

Because Findlay had a habit of shooting scenes for several films concurrently, the scene that was captured in the beauty parlor aforementioned by Roberta in her description of the bust, does not appear in the final production of *Honeysuckle Rose*. However, the similarly titled *Honey Throat* (1980) directed approximately the same time by Findlay's friend John Christopher, is also set in a beauty parlor. Eric Edwards, Arcadia Lake (Edwards' girlfriend at the time), Samantha Fox, Serena, and John Holmes all round out the cast. Roberta Findlay is listed in the credits as cinematographer.

We lost quite a lot of footage at the bottom of a well. It's where Jack hid the film. The lab tried to peel the film off and got a lot of the footage, but a lot of it was lost. I was unloading the film stock at the time from the cameras and putting it into film cans. Holmes said, "Expose the film." He said, "Take the film out of the camera and expose it so it doesn't exist." I couldn't do it. I'd shot all day and I just couldn't do it.

The police conducted the bust all incorrectly. They searched the car and they had no warrant for that at all. They took money from the glove compartment because Jack's an idiot and left money in the glove compartment. They also busted the camera — they ripped out the film that was in the camera — that was part of the settlement too, because they broke the camera.

John got out of jail first and was signing autographs for the police. According, not just to Walter, but also to the guys, they kept all the men in one cell and the women in another cell — Holmes was terrified because we were in the county courthouse jail that was filled with murderers and convicts. The women were moved into a closed wing, so we weren't exposed to anybody else, it was just us. The guys were in with convicts and Holmes was terrified of being raped or killed or whatever, so he hung onto Walter and said, "Protect me! Protect me! I'm scared!" The crew all surrounded him and wouldn't let anybody near him, but he was a real baby. Anyway, the upshot was that Walter, being the tenacious, stubborn, pseudo lawyer sued the police and won. It was tried in Point Pleasant. The reward was very, very small but we won the case. The judge threw the case out at the arraignment because they had violated six amendments. It was a bad arrest.

To add an amusing postscript to the story, Roberta admitted that during the arraignment she entered the ladies' room and very quietly tore up the signed releases into tiny pieces and flushed them down the toilet to destroy any remaining evidence.

Like many of her fellow adult directors, actors, and producers, Findlay adopted different pseudonyms while working in the illegal business in addition to "Anna Riva," which she generally used when acting and shooting early on. To further confuse things, "Anna Riva" is also the pen name of the occult writer Dorothy Spencer (1923-2005).

Over the years, queries and discrepancies have arisen regarding names adopted by Findlay and her colleagues. According to Roberta, "Harold Hindgrind" was actually Walter Sear. J. Angel Martine was Jack Bravman, while "John Christopher" was the pseudonym used by an associate director Roberta often worked with. Christopher was well liked. He was also one of the very first people in the adult industry to have contracted HIV, and died in the early 1980s from the disease. Most commonly, if she wasn't billed as herself, Findlay was credited as "Robert Norman" when directing, and sometimes editing pictures such as *Anyone but My Husband*.

Seen and Not Heard

"Women who seek to be equal with men lack ambition." TIMOTHY LEARY

Despite Roberta Findlay's small stature and physique, her ability behind the camera won her respect and deference by the all male crews. With a cagey glint in her eye, Findlay is clearly the exception to the rule, and makes no bones about the fact she isn't a fan of "hiring women to do a man's job."

I made it a rule, an absolute rule for all of the films that no women were allowed on the crew except for make-up. The technical crew: cameraman, gaffer, grip, and sound — I never hired a woman. There are a couple of reasons for that. I don't like women; that's one reason. I can't stand women and children. Women are annoying and get in the way and they talk too much. Those days were long before digital, video, and small cameras and so forth. Women were not physically and are not physically capable of doing the technical work that's required.

I remember one day the grip had to do something else, I don't recall what it was, but he sent in a woman to replace him. We're dealing now with feeder cable which is very, very heavy. It goes from the box to the lamps and it is two inches in diameter. It's a rubber cable and it's very heavy to carry that stuff. Walter, my partner said, "Oh no, she mustn't do that, it's too heavy." Then he ran and he was filling in for her. She really couldn't carry this stuff. I said, "Well, that's crazy. Women can't do this physically."

During the early 1980s, I worked on a film that had nothing to do with sex pictures. I was hired to be the cameraman on the film [*The Waiting Room*] that was never released. It was made by the granddaughter of Jack Warner. She was a very rich girl and she hired me as the cameraman. It was an all woman crew. That was her idea. She wanted to show the world that a group of women could technically and physically make a film. I think we shot for a month, but after a while I said, "Karen, this is crazy. The women can't move a dolly from the floor onto the stage. They physically can't pick it up. Let me hire some of my guys." She had to relent. I thought it was a nutty idea but she paid very well. It was a psychological drama or a study, but I don't think she made another movie. She hired me as a cameraman based on a sex picture that she'd watched.

A sex picture we made that's rather interesting is *Mystique* (1980) with Georgina Spelvin and Samantha Fox. I got carried away with a poem by Paul Valéry. That'll show you. It had a score by Gustav Mahler and it's very arty. It's ridiculous, but it's interesting in my opinion. This was sort of an arty sex picture and it played at the Pussycat Theatre, which was a chain in California. It was the biggest sale that you could make. The man who booked the films said, "What is this, the fucking opera?"

I said, "No, no. There's no resemblance there to operatic form." That's what he thought, that it was orchestral symphonic music. It wasn't much of a sex picture, but it was arty.

The Tiffany Minx (1981), an excellent crime thriller, is another one of Findlay's most inventive sex films released toward the end of the golden era. With a clever assortment of plot twists and exceptional performances throughout, this little gem is undoubtedly a career high for Findlay in the adult genre. A wealthy heiress, Jessica Grover (Crystal Sync) is a pawn in a game of cat and mouse when she kills a home invader (Carter Stevens) with a pair of scissors in self-defense after he rapes her. Feigning concern for her safety and mental welfare after the incident, Jessica's adulterous husband Paul (Jeffrey Hurst) insists they rent a house at the beach so she can put the ugly incident out of her mind. Jessica notices Paul has grown close to Anne (Marlene Willoughby), allegedly helping him to close a shady business deal and finds herself distracted from her concerns when she becomes friendly with a couple Pinky (Jennifer Jordan), and her gigolo boyfriend Matt (R.Bolla). While marooned at the beach house, Jessica senses her money-grabbing husband is devising ways to drive her over the edge when bloody pairs of scissors randomly appear at various locations. At the expense of hurting Pinky's feelings, Jessica retreats in her budding relationship with Matt, while Matt has his own designs on Jessica's fortune.

The Tiffany Minx. GOURMET VIDEO

Without giving away the revelatory conclusion, *The Tiffany Minx* accomplishes in every category where other erotic films edge close, but don't make the mark. Stalwart acting, impeccable timing, tantalizing sex, an excellent soundtrack and cinematography, in conjunction with a top-notch screenplay, qualifies this picture a purebred of X-rated features. Candida Royalle also makes an appearance, as does Samantha Fox in the opening scene adding her indelible personal touch. The marvelous Robert Kerman (R. Bolla) is typically golden in the sex mystery.

Samantha Fox stands out in my mind when I think back to our films. I kind of liked her; she was sort of strange. I haven't seen these people in twenty or thirty years. She was an inveterate liar, I think. She'd make stuff up just for fun, but I found her to be interesting. She was prettier than most of the New York crowd, anyway. Bobby Astyr was her boyfriend actually, and he was a nice fellow.

In Findlay's personal experience, there are distinctive aptitudes between the American east and west coasts caliber of actor. The performers Roberta hired from the east coast were more serious in their approach to the material. In her recollection, they didn't often require enhancements (one might say courage) in the way of alcohol or drugs in order to copulate before the camera. Findlay recalled that the talent brought in from the west coast liked to imbibe in drugs particularly, and engaged in an overall lighter party atmosphere on set.

We imported Amber Lynn from California. She was a trip; she was very funny. Paul Thomas we imported from L.A., and then there was "The Germ," Jamie Gillis from New York. He considered himself a — I don't know what it meant, a Columbia University Professor. He actually fancied himself a professor, but I honestly don't know what that meant. He tried to affect a kind of professorial accent and he carried a pipe, and was generally weird. I would say he was just in style, and what I intimated about him was that he was the most insecure of them all. Why I thought that, I don't know, but here he was a nice Jewish boy...

In keeping with her unwillingness to hire women to fulfill roles other than in the acting and make-up departments, Findlay was open to bringing in reputable male counterparts to assist on her sets when she faced the occasional conundrum about supervising sex scenes.

I had the bright idea, I said, "Walter, we're just no good at directing sex scenes. We're just no good at it." He didn't object so I hired Ron Sullivan. I think I gave him his pseudonym "Henri Pachard". I thought on *Mascara* (1984) we'd get really well directed sex scenes. I'd known Ron Sullivan for years. He was good directing sex scenes. He was enthusiastic and knew what to do, but he was kind of a dope and he had no concept of how to put a film together. He was a director and I hired him, but I'd say, "Ron, what's your next camera position?" The camera was a blimp camera and needed to sit on a head on a dolly, and it was pointing at the power supply which is a big piece of electronic equipment sitting there. He said something like, "Now it's perfect."

I said, "Ron, the camera is just sitting there out of the way." I said, "Look, it's pointing into a piece of equipment."

He said, "No, it's perfect. It's perfect." After that, I didn't even ask him. I just moved to the next scene and operated the camera myself.

I was a great stickler for hierarchy. We hired him to direct and even though he was an employee, we had to listen to his direction. Walter said, "No, we're going to lose our money if this clown keeps on going." As long as the cameraman took care of the set-ups then he was fine.

Ron actually had a certain touch, he really did. He was innovative in working with actors if you can call them actors. He did some things in a unique way. He was inventive, not technically, but he'd come up with some interesting ideas. He had some talent. It's just that technically, he didn't know anything. As far as editing was concerned, I was obsessed with editing. I wanted to make sure that all of the cuts matched unlike today's world, which has been influenced by MTV where you don't see matching cuts.

Cecil Howard, that's another funny one. He's listed as director on *Fantasex* but he didn't direct it, I did. I gave him that name. Howard Winters was a friend of mine and still is. We made a couple of pictures with him. *Justine* is ours. *Justine: A Matter of Innocence* (1980) if you can believe that, and *Platinum Paradise* (1981) which he owned. *The Playgirl* (1983) was one of our pictures with Veronica Hart that was kind of sweet story about writers' block. Under my desk, there is a giant bag full of stills from all of the films, all of the sex films. They're color slides.

All that *Glitters*, is not gold

Glitter (1985) is not bad. That was Shauna Grant. Again, we had outtakes from a couple of films that we shot her in before she died. It's said that someone killed her — okay. No pretty girl would put a shotgun in her mouth, but I have no idea. This shows you my moral ethical code. After she died, I filmed somewhat of a documentary. I pretended it was real and that it was something of homage to her, but it wasn't. I just put it together figuring we could make some money from it. Joyce James, who was sort of respected for writing for dirty magazines, believed this was an honest attempt to make a documentary, so she did all the on camera narration to tie the thing together. I don't even remember it.

Shauna Grant (born Colleen Marie Applegate) was found dead in Palm Springs on March 23, 1984 due to a self-inflicted rifle wound to the head, just two months before her twenty-first birthday. There has been much speculation of foul play surrounding Grant's death relating to her forty-four year old boyfriend at the time, Jack "Jake" Ehrlich, who had allegedly been Grant's primary cocaine supplier. (Grant had taken an overdose of pills a couple of years prior to her suicide). At the time of Grant's death, Ehrlich was serving a five-year sentence for cocaine trafficking, and had apparently terminated his relationship with Grant over the telephone from the jailhouse.

Some industry insiders believed Findlay's final adult submission, *Glitter*, effectively ended her association with the pornographic movie business as the feature resulted in some disgruntled campers when it was perceived Findlay's intentions to make the Shauna Grant picture were less than compassionate. Not that Roberta or her entrepreneurial constitution was disconcerted by the industry's reaction to her efforts — quite the opposite. Along with her partner, Walter Sear, Findlay deviated into the Horror genre. Times were changing anyway as the shift to video preceded the legalization of the production of adult movies by a few years in California which served to completely reconfigure the art of presenting sex on film.

Glitter.

I left the field and was glad to get out. I was happy if I never saw another sex picture again. It is true that most of the world doesn't respect people who make pornography. It's not a dignified thing to do. I'd gotten into the Horror genre after the sex films. I stopped making hardcore in the mid-eighties purely for monetary reasons. Video came out and adult theatres were running video so they would rent a cassette or buy a cassette. It wiped out the whole domestic theatrical part of the industry. We made a lot of money theatrically, and then all the small video companies could sell video, of course. Caballero bought all our films and paid very well. Most companies eventually went down the drain or they were bought by other larger companies. In Europe too, they were swallowed up by other companies. We switched over to making horror pictures.

Horror Show

Just as Findlay had done while working in the "dirty picture" business, as she referred to it, Roberta applied the same policies and principles when making the crossover to horror flicks. Her instincts as a filmmaker and businessperson were timely.

The crews got bigger and bigger as we got into horror films — we had fifteen guys or whatever. The horror films are okay; there's no sex in them. *Prime Evil* is owned by Crown. You can see the stuff on Netflix. I made up all of the titles.

Tenement and *The Oracle*: the first two of Findlay's horror pictures, were filmed in 1985 and became successful financial ventures prompting Findlay and Sear to produce more films in the Horror genre. *Blood Sisters* (1987) and *Prime Evil* (1989) followed the two original releases. That's not to say Findlay believed she created great art.

Set in the Bronx, *Tenement* focuses on the survival tactics of several ethnically diversified tenants after their residence is overtaken by a vicious gang. The film aims for shock value and excels as several gruesome and macabre scenes pepper the feature. The 2004 DVD release of *Tenement* contains several bonus tracks including a director's commentary and interview footage with Findlay. Roberta recollected that when she read the script she was reminded of her childhood years in the Bronx, and said that many of the situations depicted in the film: gang war activity, junkies, prostitution, and occasional heated conflicts between tenants, were characteristic of her former neighborhood. Findlay believed her movie told a moral tale of good overcoming evil, and expressed that when the film screened in New York theatres, audiences rooted for the underdog (the tenants) as they put their differences aside and banded together in order to reclaim their homes. The picture received an "X" rating when it was released in 1985 for its graphic violence.

In *Blood Sisters*, seven big-haired "eighties" girls are required to remain overnight in a haunted house as part of their initiation into a college sorority. Unbeknownst to the girls, some of the guys booby-trapped the house prior to their overnight visit to add a little more spice to their stay. Before settling in for the evening, the ringleader of the sisterhood, Linda (Amy Brentano), informs the girls the house is indeed haunted. Thirteen years before, the house was a brothel wherein all of the residents were killed. (This is illustrated in the opening sequence when a boy returns home to his mother at their house of ill repute after being called names by a girl he had invited to show him her privates.) Undeterred by her warning, the girls follow Linda's instructions to go on a scavenger hunt and plan to meet back in the main room of the house along with their findings. Apparitions (both visual and audio) are witnessed by a few of the overnight guests. One by one, four of the girls are hunted down and killed in typical gory fashion by someone dressed in a white gown and heels. The remaining few females are scared right down to their boots, but fear doesn't prevent them from taking one last look around the dimly lit manse for their missing friends. The psycho killer confesses his insanity in the final scene while wielding a knife over the chest of Linda. After promising he won't hurt her, he spares no one. Moral of the story: It's unwise to leave a crying baby unattended.

In the 2004 DVD release, Roberta Findlay was interviewed briefly about *Blood Sisters*, in addition to one of the actors, Elizabeth Rose. Compared to the sex films Findlay shot in the seventies and early 1980s, *Blood Sisters* contains a couple of sanitized simulated sex scenes, but enough bare breasts and innuendo to trigger the hormones of teenage boys. Findlay explained because she is obsessed with photography, she paid particular attention to the lighting of the picture and described how the last scene of the film — "the money shot" — was the one that required the largest financial investment. Walter Sear had even crafted a special dolly dubbed the "Wally dolly" in order for Roberta to have optimum camera accessibility throughout filming. For his part, in addition to production and editing, all of the original music was performed by Sear and Michael Litovsky on a Kurzweil 250.

A Man's Woman

Regardless of her impressive list of credentials as a female cinematographer and director, Roberta doesn't indulge herself with the notion that she is a pioneer or a trailblazer, as a woman or otherwise.

I am unique in that there weren't many women doing this kind of thing, but a pioneer is someone with a conscious effort trying to make a breakthrough and I was not. A pioneer is someone setting out to do something new and innovative that's never been done before. I found myself in this field and I never got out. It never occurred to me to think, "Oh, oh, I'm a woman. Are they going to respect me?" It never occurred to me to think about it and I never did. If you know your job and you know what you're doing, then there isn't any discrimination, or sexism or anything like that. I never experienced it. I never ran into it ever and I worked on other films apart from sex pictures with other crews and never had a problem. I just didn't think of it. I figure that in every field, and in any field, if the woman knows what she's doing in that field there will be respect and the guys will listen to her. The guys always listened to me and there was never a problem. Okay, the grips used to carry me around and put me on the dolly and stuff…

I did join the cameraman's union in New York which was 644 IATSE. It was the first union. They accepted me based on a reel of film I put together minus the sex scenes, just based on the photography. That was good. I had two sponsors that were in the real world. I then got busted in New York, the first time, and they asked me to withdraw. I did, and I was ashamed. Who knows what would have happened? The dues were enormous.

Feminists, they used to annoy me. I found the whole thing very tiresome. I didn't see it. Again, I've never had any experience of hostility or anything like that. The only thing that is slightly relatable is in the studio. I am aware that because we have many foreign clients in our studio they would rather not deal with me which is customary protocol in their countries — Germans, particularly, and the Japanese in the beginning, but not anymore. The Germans and South American men are the same, but we don't have many South American clients. The men from Spain are fine.

Once again, it's the story of my life. I became a studio manager about twelve years ago, I guess. That's all because I didn't have anything else to do. We had stopped making films and Walter said, "Why don't you be the studio manager?"

Sear Sound, New York, New York

The name of our recording studio is Sear Sound and it is in Walter's name. The studio has been in business for about forty years now. He had another studio about two blocks away but we've been here about twenty years. The groups that come in here, some of them, you might have heard of. We have lots and lots of rock groups. Yoko did her last album here, and Bob Dylan and Paul McCartney have been here. Norah Jones did her two albums here and many famous people. Roberta Flack is doing her album here right now actually. I can never think of the names of the groups, but Lou Reed did his two albums here. He's in next weekend. We tend to get older people here. Sony Japan is here all of the time; it's their New York studio. Tom Waits, Bryan Adams and Rufus Wainwright have all been here.

The website is *SearSound.com* and you can read a list of all of the artists who have recorded here over the years, and all of the artists who have recorded here in the last six months. There's also a page with famous producers and people like that. All of the information is on the website and the engineers who look on the website can see the equipment lists. We have three studios actually, if you count the mastering room and they're working all of the time.

Within the industry, there is a distinction. We have very old equipment. It's analog; it's not digital equipment. This is now being sought by many freelance engineers in the field. It's now all digital recording and you need hard drives. A lot of these rock groups are going back to tape. Rufus Wainwright and Sonic Youth did a bunch of albums here. They're all going back to tape, so we have all of that equipment here that Walter kept in pristine condition. We also have all of the digital equipment for the rest. We have the Beatles' old machines from Abbey Road studios. Walter bought out the basement. Actually, he didn't buy it; they gave the stuff away. They were throwing out the old ¼-inch machines and he took all of these machines and reconverted them into ½-inch machines. In fact, we have one 1 inch, machine. The Beatles recorded on these machines.

I don't know much about the Beatles except Paul McCartney was here at the studio a few years ago. I barely recognized who he was. Yoko did her last album here about a year ago. It was recorded here by our engineer. This is actually the studio they were recording during the time when Lennon was killed — they had actually worked here. It used to be called The Hit Factory many years ago. This is the studio where *Double Fantasy* was recorded in 1980. We weren't here at that time — the original Hit Factory closed.

Walter was, and is, still quite famous in his field. It's a very narrow niche field that I don't expect civilians outside of the field to know anything about, but in the field, he's known as "The Godfather" of recording studios of analog. He's very, very famous and well respected.

Walter died on April 29 of this year [2010], so I'm here alone. It's not that much to do. I take care of everything. We have a crew of men, of course, who do the sessions, and engineers, and the techs. They were here before he died and they continue on doing sessions. I knew nothing, zero, zip, or could care less about sound when I started becoming a manager, but I learned everything. There I am again. Sometimes we're booked months ahead and sometimes not. It's not like the old days.

Sear Sound, New York.

The music industry has now fallen apart just like the film business because of the internet, and all of the free stuff, so the labels are not spending the sums they used to spend. We'd get young rock groups who would come in for a month, two months, and the labels would just pay. The studios will eventually close. Most of them have in New York. All of the big studios like us — this is a big studio — have gone bankrupt. There is only a handful left. This is a unique place, which has nothing to do with me. It sort of comes full circle. Sean Lennon did his last two albums here. Julian [Lennon] has been here a couple of times.

In April of 2011, my husband and I visited Roberta Findlay at Sear Sound in New York City, located at 353 West 48th Street. Upon stepping into the studio located on the sixth floor of the building, we were greeted by stark reminders of Findlay's former life as a filmmaker, as two large mounted posters of *Blood Sisters* and *Prime Evil* loom large in the visitor's lounge. Beneath her desk lies a tattered paper bag chocked full of film stills from adult productions that obviously haven't seen the light of day in many years. In person, Roberta is funny, humble, and self-deprecating; you can't help but like her.

Findlay took us on a tour of the three studios within the premises that are adorned with wood and oriental carpets lending a homey, warm ambience and hippie vibe to the retro environment. Sting departed just one hour before our arrival, but his keyboard and sheet music were ready and waiting for his return on the following Monday. The smallest studio inside the spacious setting is where Yoko Ono prefers to record. The hallway next to the waiting area contains photos and sketches, cartoons and scribbles by many of the studio's famous guests. Sean Lennon's black ink depiction of Walter is remarkably accurate and reminiscent of his own father's lithographic art.

During our tour, Roberta showed us the original Moog synthesizer designed by Dr. Robert Moog that gained worldwide popularity amongst the rock and pop world during the late 1960s and seventies after its debut at the Monterey Pop Festival in 1967. Walter, an engineer and inventor, had been Moog's partner. It was Sear and not Moog, who implemented the keyboard for the synthesizer enabling the instrument to be played.

D'Angelo was here for ten months! How about that? I don't think it's finished yet. Virgin Records is paying the bill so we were delighted. Ritchie Havens has also been here — he recorded his last album here. We do an awful lot of jazz albums with jazz musicians. As a youth, I assiduously avoided all of this noise. I liked what I played and I only played classical music.

Two Road Together

Findlay reiterated that Walter was very well liked and appreciated by the clientele at Sear Sound. In a thoughtful gesture, when Walter was in the hospital for a short duration after falling ill, Yoko Ono, one of his most ardent admirers, sent bunches of flowers not only to wish Walter a speedy recovery, but she also sent flowers to Sear's nurses and aids to ensure he would receive the best care. Unfortunately, after making a brief recovery, Walter passed away. Since Walter's death, Roberta has spent a good portion of time alone and at the studio. It is more than evident she admired and respected the genius that was her late partner. Although she would never admit it, Roberta and Walter were equals.

Having never owned a driver's permit after a negative experience that arose years ago when Michael had tried to teach her to drive, Roberta walks several blocks to and from work, and takes cabs around the expansive city that has always been her home. Last fall, she went on a Panama cruise with friends, and in the winter of 2012, she and pals went on a Caribbean cruise. Findlay enjoyed herself, but life isn't the same without Walter. She accepts that she will not meet another man like him, and isn't interested in trying. In addition to sharing many common interests, Roberta and Walter enjoyed dining together daily and they were political junkies.

Walter and I used to go to concerts regularly, and to the opera. We always chose our own operas and saw six or eight operas a year. The last opera I had tickets for but I didn't go. The season ends at the end of May. I still do travel but it's lonely. Walter and I traveled to a great many places in the world. Generally, we'd go to Europe at least once a year. In 2010, we traveled to Italy on our own personal little tour.

I don't do much of anything. I read and do the crossword puzzle. I look at old films. That's about it. People think I like horror films and crummy old obscure films and that's not true at all. I'm a great fan of American directors from the 1930s, the forties and fifties. My favorite directors are William Wyler, Billy Wilder, John Ford, and John Sturges. I enjoy them and watch them over again. We have Turner Classic movies and that's all I watch. Billy Wilder's films are tremendous to me. He was innovative and a *pioneer*. Wilder went through the MGM system. His films are all big and expensive like *Wuthering Heights* (1939).

Walter and I were happy. We fought, of course, but I forget those times. He would just clam up. He was what you call passive-aggressive. The argument would just end. I couldn't fight! I wish I could remember everything more so that I wouldn't be so unhappy, but I can't. I only remember the good stuff, but there was plenty of bad stuff. Walter was a stubborn mule of a man. It either had to be his way or not at all, but that was okay. He was very special.

6

Jody Maxwell
Portrait

As an erotic film star, Jody Maxwell is renowned not only for her acting talents, but for a specific specialty, one she was able to perfect during a relationship with a boyfriend while majoring in speech and theatre at college. Her unique gift involves singing and performing oral sex simultaneously — no small feat for those who might consider giving it a try. More importantly perhaps, is the Kansas City, Missouri native's awareness of her competence, confidence, and self worth; characteristics in which she credits her family for providing a solid foundation, particularly after surviving a psychologically devastating experience at age ten.

Jody's father and grandfather were prominent attorneys. Her mother's craft was providing accident victims and WWII veterans with artificial human eyes, a delicate procedure that required a great deal of skill and concentration. Although her parents eventually separated, Jody acknowledged that their social conscience as well respected community leaders made an impact on her choice to become a forward thinking individual.

A straight "A" student who won "Miss Buick," Maxwell maintained a scholarship at private girls' school, and had the honor of graduating with the highest achievements and awards in the area of speech and literary competitions and meets in the hundred-year history of the school. She enjoyed a large group of friends and became involved in sports and politics before embarking in theater and speech studies at the University of Missouri. At nineteen, Jody's mother was tragically killed in an automobile accident leaving a void she worked hard to overcome.

Prior to graduating from university, Jody attended a lecture given by *Deep Throat* director Gerard Damiano, and was invited to have dinner with him and several guests following the symposium. Impressed by her remarkable facial bone structure, raw beauty, and stage background, Damiano

"I feel that being in adult films was empowering, but maybe even more than that it was emancipating. Now, if those two things are a form of feminism I guess it could be called that. I found making adult films liberating. I found the industry liberating." JODY MAXWELL

COURTESY OF JODY MAXWELL

offered Maxwell a starring role in his next picture. He was taken aback when Jody informed him she first wanted to seek her father's permission who had become county prosecutor. Her father examined Damiano's offer scrupulously, and after giving it his stamp of approval, Jody was on her way to New York City to do a screen test for the lead role in *Portrait* (1974).

As a discerning hardcore, film actor, Maxwell's credits are limited as she often turned down roles in order to keep her options open for non-adult film work. In the 1980s, Jody cleverly created her own brand of softcore sex show, incorporating a stand-up routine that encouraged audience participation. Throughout her film and stage career, Jody also had monthly columns in *Escapade, Capers*, and *Cheri* magazines, and wrote feature stories for them as well. During her post-adult film career, Maxwell contributed pieces to sexually oriented magazines such as *High Society* and *Adult Cinema Review*, and worked as a phone sex operator as herself with an elite company. The details of which are included in her 2004 book *My Private Calls*. Maxwell has also been employed as a substitute teacher. Her inherent desire to encourage youths to strive for excellence has been her mandate.

Currently, Jody is re-developing her memoir and working on an erotic novel while sidelining as an editor for a publishing house. Presently living in the Northern California area with her second husband of more than twenty years, Jody is an exceptional bowler, she loves to read, and duly supports her home- town Kansas City Chiefs and Royals.

I interviewed Jody Maxwell in the spring of 2010.

Corn Fed Redhead

I was born and raised in Kansas City, Missouri. I was a Mid-Western corn-fed girl all the way. Corn is a big crop in Missouri, but I'm totally a city girl. My father was a prominent attorney, and my mother was mostly a homemaker, although she did have a career. In all of the time I've done interviews I've never told anybody that she worked with artificial human eyes; she fitted them in people's heads. This was for people who had lost their eyes due to accidents such as during fireworks, and so on. There was a great demand for this procedure after WWII. My mother had learned how to do this long before I was a gleam in her eye and before my parents had met. She was introduced to two German men situated in the Chicago area and they taught her this profession. Not many people could perform the technique adequately, and my mother was excellent at it. We'd be at home having dinner and she'd receive a telephone call that someone had lost an artificial eye in a summertime party or something like that, and she'd have to leave.

The two men who had taught her were actually glassblowers and they learned the profession in Germany. They came to America and because they had done glass blowing, they were able to match the eyes perfectly. You couldn't tell the difference. The eye would actually move in the socket and everything. She would usually only work one day a week running the Kansas City office for them as people would heal from surgery in between. They were based in Chicago. My mother would take care of patients. The rest of the time, she was a homemaker. Former professional football player, Fred Arbanas, was one of her patients; he had an artificial eye.

My mother was also actively involved in a lot of volunteer work, and she was involved in charity work. It was a great love of hers. Both of my parents were the founders of the Missouri Safety Council and they were both heavily into charities, organizations, and helping people. They served the Chamber of Commerce and they were both on boards. That's the kind of background they had, and that's how I was raised, to be exposed to things like that. Because I was an only child, my family did a lot of activities together. We took trips and we did social things together.

On one such trip, during a family vacation to Banff, Alberta, in Canada when Jody was about twelve years old, she was introduced to Walt Disney and his wife who (figuratively) kidnapped her for the entire day. Once it got close to dinnertime and Jody still hadn't shown up, her parents were set to call the Mounties when Disney and his wife returned with Jody in tow. She remembers the experience as one of the best of her childhood days.

My parents demonstrated affection toward one another. Now, my father was a handsome man, something of a Casanova type guy. He subscribed to *Playboy* and he would show me *Playboy* interviews. *Playboy* magazine had a reputation for excellent stories, so I grew up reading *Playboy* because of the pieces in there. Sometimes I would take an article out and use it for school. Our home was open that way, but we didn't really discuss sex per se. Overall, I'd say that my father was more open-minded than my mother was. My parents and I frequently interacted together, but later, when I got into my teens, I wanted to go my own way. I was a typical teenager. I'd say we were pretty much a well-rounded family.

Jody's near picture perfect family life was sadly disrupted when she became the victim of two perpetrators who robbed her of her innocence one summer day in a brutal and vicious manner. She hadn't yet reached puberty. Through her adult eyes, Jody's ability to accept the incident for what it was is truly admirable.

I got raped when I was ten by two high school boys. If you want to consider that a loss of virginity, I guess, you could, technically. It was bad. That incident has become a nightmare problem for me. I came from intelligent people and because I had a wonderful dad, I was smart enough to realize that those boys were not the norm. I was ten, and I knew that. I did not turn against boys or men because of that experience. I had a boyfriend in grade school at that point who had been my boyfriend since I was four years old, and he was wonderful. I always had a boyfriend; I don't think I was ever without a boyfriend in my entire life. It was an emotional experience, and it still hurts. I understood that, in general, boys are not that way. I survived it in other words. Girls and women need to realize there are a lot of bad apples out there, but there are also a lot of wonderful men. Bitches are out there, and there are a lot of wonderful women. We are made up of all kinds of different people, and there are bad people in all walks of life. You just have to accept people. The one thing I am going to do when I write my memoir is name those two people because I've never done that. I'm going to save it for my book. They both turned out to have great careers and they never had to pay the price for what they did. It's a very complicated story that I don't want to go into right now. They say that after an experience such as that one occurs your grades are supposed to fall. I was devastated — it happened in the summertime, but my grades did not fall. Over the years, I had to compartmentalize what happened in order to survive it. I was not going to let it ruin my life.

Eventually, I won a four-year scholarship to my high school. It was a scholastic scholarship, so I had to maintain an A average in order to keep my scholarship. I went to St. Teresa's Academy that was a private girl's school. I was active in a lot of different organizations while I was there. I was a class officer and I have a list of organizations documented in my yearbook that is a couple of inches long.

I feel I did have a wide range of friends. I had my favorites, obviously, a close group of friends. A couple of gals and I used to be called "The Three Musketeers". I also had another group of girlfriends I used to run around with quite a bit, too. We had a number of slumber parties, and I was first attendant Homecoming Queen, which means that I was first runner up. I received a crown too — this was at Rockhurst High School, an all boys' Jesuit school. I won a dancing contest when I was in school. I had lots of friends,

but I also had buddies who were guy friends. They would call me for advice about their love lives; they always wanted my advice. It's been that way my entire life. People come to me for advice, whether I can give it or not. I also participated in something called Mock United Nations during my junior and senior high school years. We drew for countries. I actually participated two years. My first year I drew a small African country I knew nothing about, but by the time we began I knew EVERYTHING about it; the country was Dahomey [part of West Africa, now known as the Republic of Benin]. The second year, my jewel, I got the United States and that was so wonderful! We became the United Nations. It was a thrilling experience. In college, I participated in MISL [Missouri Intercollegiate State Legislature]. We got to take over the legislative branches of government for several days. It was wonderful.

By the way, I would be remiss if I didn't add something about my parents: as beautiful a marriage and as close as they were, my father left me, and my mother on the first day of my junior year in high school. He had fallen for some gal. He broke my mother's heart and mine as well. He returned home Easter weekend. It was very shocking to everybody because no two people were closer than my parents were. They did everything together. I was always daddy's girl.

When I graduated from high school, I had the highest number of points and awards, and certificates that the school had ever seen from all the speech leagues in the greater Kansas City area, covering areas of Missouri and Kansas. My honors and awards, and overall points that have never been surpassed were in the field of speech. This is the oldest private school west of Mississippi, so the school was over a hundred years old at that point. I was accepted at every college to which I applied. I didn't get turned down anywhere. I didn't go to the university, USC. I was planning on attending just because my father suddenly said to me, "Oh, by the way, you can't take your car in your freshman year." My father had given me a

COURTESY OF JODY MAXWELL

brand new convertible for my sixteenth birthday. I honestly don't have what might be considered a typical porn background.

I got married after my first year of college at age eighteen and a half. Maxwell became my married name. My father had said, "Why don't you wait another year and I'll get you a sailboat?" I decided not to wait. I love sailing — I should have taken the sailboat.

Jody remained distracted with academia and friendships after her marriage to Jim Maxwell, but another tragic set of circumstances supervened.

My mother was killed in an automobile accident in Colorado when I was only nineteen. It was very sad. My parents were separated when my mother died in the accident. She was a passenger and it was bad. Everybody in both cars had been killed. Four people died that day. It was a rough time for me that year and very traumatic too. I am not sure you ever get over a violent death of a family member like that. Anyway, I lost my mom then.

I had a little girl, but she was born prematurely, and she passed away. This wasn't too long after my mother had died. After I married Jim Maxwell, my father fell for another gal and left home again. Eventually, my father remarried, and I have three stepbrothers, and later, a half sister.

When I went to college, I majored in theatre and speech and I starred in plays. *Rhinoceros* was the first. I believe that speech was probably my greatest love. I was a member of the Speech League and I continued heavy involvement in public speaking. I did that and I entered all kinds of competitions. I also enjoyed my involvement in politics. I did have political aspirations but my grandfather said, "Please don't." My grandfather [who sat on special council for United States Government] and I were very close. This was my father's father. When he ended up passing on, it was on the national news. My grandfather had prosecuted Tom Pendergast in Kansas City. There was a lot of that kind of thing going on back then; it was a certain era. Pendergast was a bad guy.

Tom Pendergast reigned as a political "boss" over Kansas City and Jackson County, Missouri, while giving employment to workers during the Great Depression. Pendergast, a drinker and gambler, was also instrumental in strategizing the election of key politicians when he managed to manufacture an abundance of false votes in the 1936 election. Specifically, Pendergast's efforts tipped the scales to influence the favorable outcome of the election of Harry S. Truman (who eventually became the thirty-third President of the United States) when Truman became judge of the County Court of the eastern district of Jackson County, Missouri.

In his 1948 book, *Missouri Waltz, The Inside Story of the Pendergast Machine by the Man Who Smashed It*, Maurice Milligan, the DA of Kansas City and investigator of fraud cases pertaining to political elections, wrote extensively about the intricacies of the Pendergast trial, and how he was able to effectively bring about a guilty conviction. Also worth noting is that during the Democratic primary, Truman defeated John J. Cochran and Tuck Milligan, the brother of the federal prosecutor Maurice Milligan. Pendergast, whose case was built on a $750,000 insurance scam, pled guilty to charges of tax evasion during a period of ten years from

1927-1937. He was fined $10,000 and sentenced to federal prison for fifteen months.

Damiano Calling

Gerard Damiano came to my university because he was speaking there, in Kansas City. That's how we met. It was my last semester in college. I was President of the local chapter of Zeta Phi Eta, National Professional Communications Fraternity for Women. I was involved in Republican politics, which is how we were intro-

duced. Anyway, a friend of mine had introduced me to Damiano. I was going to do a story for their publication. We were introduced, and then Damiano started asking me questions. He told me I was pretty and he loved my facial structure. "Beautiful," is actually the word he used. I told him that I was majoring in theatre and speech and was in a play at the time. His eyes got huge and he asked me to have dinner with him that night. I hesitated, but then he said we were going to have dinner with all of these other people who

COURTESY OF JODY MAXWELL

owned the Chelsea theatre in Kansas City. There was going to be a dinner party at Jaspers. This was an excellent gourmet Italian restaurant that is famous. I thought, "That sounds pretty harmless, I can drive there." I agreed to have dinner with him and I picked him up at his hotel. We all went to dinner and during our meal he said, "How would you feel about starring in my next film?"

Damiano said that I could replace Linda Lovelace. He wanted to give me a name and I said, "Did you give Linda Lovelace her name, Jerry?"

He said, "Yes".

I said, "I don't think I want you picking out my name." I wanted a name that sounded like a normal All-American gal because that's what I was. I may be sexy, sensual and erotic, but I wanted to be

America's sweetheart, that was my attitude. He said, "Okay, well think about it." I had not intended to use the name "Maxwell".

At that point, my father had become a county prosecutor and my mom had already passed away. I told him I had wanted to check in with my father to make sure he didn't have a problem with it. Damiano knew my father was a prosecutor and he said, "Am I going to be safe?" He had told me he'd get back to me after graduation, so he called and said, "Have you thought about a name yet?" This was three months since we'd met, he had asked me to do a screen test and I said, "Well, let me talk it over with my father." My father had known about Damiano because he'd read about him in *Playboy*. My father thought about it; my stepmother is a former *Playboy* Bunny. Anyway, he said that if I wanted to do it to go for it. I know he'd seen some adult films. He made sure that Damiano knew where I was at all times, and everything was on the up and up. I absolutely had his blessing.

This was in 1974. You know, I wouldn't even have considered his offer but I just happened to read in *Playboy* the month before, an article called "King of Porn". It was a great article on Damiano and about how excellent he was and he was the best in the field and a man of class. That influenced me tremendously. If I had not read that story I probably wouldn't have been interested. At the time, I knew zero about porn. I had grown up in Kansas City and I had not seen it. I had no idea what the films had in them — I only knew what people had told me. I had seen *I Am Curious Yellow* (1967) and that's about it. It was an erotic film.

I had a legitimate screen test, and then I went home and talked to my dad again, and made a decision after giving him a copy of the contract. After that, I went to New York to film the movie.

I was college president of the Young Republicans at that time, and I was Vice-Chairman of the Jackson County Young Republicans. I also sat on the Board of Directors of the Missouri Young Republicans, and was still in office when I made *Portrait* (1974). Damiano, who was not enthralled with Republicans, used to say I was "unique" in the world of porn. The people in erotica were very tolerant of my background, although not one of them ever agreed with the Republicans. At the time, it was understandable.

Damiano called me one day while I was at school and asked me to call him back right away, that he needed my professional name NOW! He said he had an interview with *The New York Times* and he was going to tout his new star, so he needed my name. I had made him promise *not* to use any name without my permission. Anyway, I didn't get home until that evening. I called him immediately, but no answer. I called him again at the crack of dawn the next day, but I was too late. He had done the interview. I asked him what name he used for me, and he replied that he used my real name, as he had no other choice since he made a promise to me. I groaned, I'm sure, and asked if I couldn't give him a name then. I remember his reply to this day, "Jody, once *The New York Times* publishes your name you're stuck with it forever!" He said it was too late and I was going to be using the All-American, girl-next-door type of name after all. Anyway, that's how I ended up using my married name, which I kept after our divorce for a couple of reasons, one being that we had a daughter together. My father tried to talk me into taking my name back, but I didn't.

Jim Maxwell and I had split up by the time I did my first film for Damiano. My ex was not too happy I'd used my married name as he was now out of law school and had started practicing law. His parents — as opposite as night and day from mine — were kind of freaking out. Eventually, he got used to the idea and found out he got more gals himself because of who I was. It has actually enhanced his love life! Jim and I have been mostly on good terms over the years.

Playing the Flute

Gerard Damiano hired Jody Maxwell specifically for his 1974 production *Portrait* wherein Jody played a young woman in distress at her psychiatrist's office. Her character suffers from a multiple personality disorder although it is not certain what the origins of her emotional difficulties are or whether she, in fact, suffers from any malady at all. Jamie Gillis, Rita Davis, Alan Marlow and Maxwell all appeared in uncredited roles.

Film critic, Roger Ebert spoke briefly with director Gerard Damiano and Jody Maxwell about *Portrait* in July 1974, just a few months prior to its release. Ebert described Maxwell as a "pneumatic beauty," and was told by Damiano that although Jody was the only "whole woman" in the story, her various personalities included a young woman, a teenager, and a hooker. For unknown reasons, *Portrait* is not available through conventional means and it is doubtful many original copies are in existence today.

Based upon the little information known about the film, *Portrait* would be a great candidate for restoration and revitalization.

I could never forget *Portrait*. I'm the only female in the film, except for one segment that was added later. One other gal is in the film. It had Jamie Gillis, Alan Logan, David Christopher and

COURTESY OF JODY MAXWELL

Rita Davis who died of a drug overdose in the late 1980s, I think. I heard about it second hand.

Jamie Gillis took my film virginity. In my particular case, Damiano paid Jamie to be on set and to be around me for about three days. Not to have sex, not to act, not to do anything but get comfortable. I didn't ask for that, but he offered me that. I had a world premiere for *Portrait* in Philadelphia. We had a red carpet ceremony and everything. It was quite the big deal. I did interviews for television, radio, and newspapers with top columnists. It was really quite exciting.

Larry Flynt interviewed me [in the May 1975 issue of *Hustler* magazine titled "Jody Maxwell: Conversation with the Queen of Fellatio" by Larry Flynt] personally after the film's release. I'm the only interview he has ever done. I'd done some things on film that had never been done before and he was amazed. They were things that I'd done in my private life before I'd met Damiano. I wasn't having oral sex before I was with the guy I married. It was a couple of months before my eighteenth birthday before I had oral sex. Then, when I met this other fellow that I got involved with after Jim Maxwell and I broke up, I started swinging. We got swinging together and I sort of created a unique talent. I could sing and suck at the same time so they called me the "singing cocksucker". I always said I was a frustrated singer, that was my whole problem, but that was kind of a joke. It was Christmas time and a guy that I'd been going with; we'd had too much champagne. I always believed that sex should be fun and if you have a romance going on, you should have fun. It doesn't have to be serious all of the time. I don't know why, too much champagne I guess, but I just burst into *Jingle Bells* while blowing him. His reaction was so phenomenal! Here's a man I'd been going with for quite a while and he was quite used to my tongue and mouth, and suddenly, he was losing control, but he was laughing at the same time. Well, that just encouraged me to do more.

Remember, speech was one of my majors. I do open my mouth when I talk. I don't like to talk with lips half closed. I discovered it was quite fun, and the reaction, as I said, was phenomenal. We used to swing with this other married couple, so I demonstrated it for them and they just totally freaked out. All of these people were just amazed. The other guy's wife said, "Could you please teach me how to do that?" I started teaching her how to do this. She wasn't doing it as well as I was, but she was having fun trying. Her husband responded the very same way. He said, "My god, that feels so incredibly good." Talk about a contradiction. It amazed me as much as it amazed them, trust me.

Actually, I sung in two of my movies, *Portrait* and *SOS* (aka *Screw on the Screen*, 1975). *SOS* is now digitized. I play myself, "Jody, the singing cocksucker from Missouri". Because I was able to do it, I was the first person who was able to suck two guys at the same time. I figured out how to do it when Chuck [my boyfriend] and I were swinging. This was not something I developed for porn; this was my private love life. It just happened to end up in porn. Damiano was surprised and thrilled to know that I had a special talent and wasn't aware of this before he'd hired me for *Portrait*. I wasn't trying to put Linda Lovelace to shame. I was just doing my own thing. I did do double penetration as well. I was actually one of the very first actresses to do a double penetration scene. I also changed songs in the Damiano film. It was one of my first sex scenes and I got a little bit nervous. I was afraid I'd forget the words of the song so I changed it on him. It was okay. It worked beautifully. I had a repertoire of songs.

When I'd had oral sex with two men, literally, at the same time in *Portrait*, Damiano told me it had never been done successfully by anyone in mainstream erotica before. I told him I could do it, so he allowed me to direct the scene. To make it work though, the men must not have any hang-ups about their penises touching! They definitely do touch in this scenario. Damiano had me in every single scene in the movie. That was another first for a feature in the world of erotica.

I was kind of amazed when I saw myself on the screen. I'd actually made a straight film that a lot of people don't know about, preceding *Portrait*. I'd made two. I had a small role in a 1970 movie called *The Other Side of Madness* [aka *The Helter Skelter Murders*]. It was a docudrama of Sharon Tate's killing. Then I made a science fiction film so I'd seen myself on screen before, but of course, seeing yourself naked on screen was a lot different. It was kind of shocking to me not in a bad way, but obviously, somewhere along the way, I figured out I must be something of an exhibitionist. I'd have to be comfortable even doing this. There are those who are not exhibitionists who are not comfortable doing this like the late Terri Hall who I'd worked with in *Gums* (1976), *The Devil Inside*

Her (1977), and *Unwilling Lovers* (1977). I don't think Terri was an exhibitionist and I think she was very uncomfortable. Even in theatre, you'd have to have that capability. Some film people can be total introverts and not be exhibitionists.

The term "exhibitionist" is broadly used throughout this book to describe a specific personality type drawn towards the expression of what many consider extreme sexual or uninhibited behavior. One of several clinical psychiatric definitions for "exhibitionism" is as follows: "sexual gratification, above and beyond the sexual act itself that is achieved by risky public sexual activity and/or bodily exposure."

Jody contended that she contorted her body in a most unusual way in order to accomplish a rare performance concluding with a triple penetration scene for the satanic themed film *The Devil inside Her* (1977) opposite Rod Dumont and two other male performers. Set in the 1800s, as a mid-west farm girl, Maxwell's character, Hope Hammond, conjures up Satan incarnate in a fit of jealousy over her sister's (Terri Hall) suitor when their devoutly religious father forbids the girls (he cruelly beats Hall) from participating in physical contact with males. As a result, all hell breaks loose (pun intended) as Satan possesses various family members and forces them to have sex with one another — and with him. Despite the insidious nature of certain portions of the film (that also featured Annie Sprinkle), Jody's distinct personal style as an actor is most effective, and she is clearly an attractive and inspiring performer.

I did a triple penetration, which was definitely the hardest thing I've ever done. It was a little bit painful. Rod Dumont, who played the devil, got me warmed up to make me able to do it. They told me I didn't have to do it. The producer asked the director if I would consider doing it. I thought about it and I said, "Well, I'll try it." I've always been known for being tight. That turns people on too. Rod showed me how good his tongue was and that helped. It was twice as difficult to do because I was on a picnic table outside in the middle of the Poconos. It was very, very difficult. It had to be slow and easy. I had to be really well lubricated because it was challenging. I think what's important about a scene like that one is that if I enjoy it, people are going to enjoy it and that helped me a lot. My biggest problem in my own mind, and I told the director [Zebedy Colt] this was how to justify a [cum] shot. In real life, men aren't usually spurting all over here and there. I wondered why men would want to see that, and then I talked to a lot of men and they said they got off on it. I don't know why they do. I thought it would be more interesting if I agreed to do a scene like that. If I had a choice, I let the directors direct.

Prior to filming *The Devil Inside Her*, Maxwell portrayed an artist in the engrossing Video-X-Pix noir adult picture *Expose Me Lovely* (1976), the story of a hard-boiled New York City detective Harry "Frosty" Night (Ras Kean). Night finds himself in a hospital with his face in bandages and virtually no recollection of how he ended up there. Slowly, he retraces the last few days of his life and recalls that a woman (Catharine Burgess) had hired him to find her missing brother Keith Spencer. While following shreds of clues as to the brother's whereabouts, Frosty interviews the last people to have seen him and pays a surprise visit to Terry Lawford (Maxwell) who recently painted a naked portrait of Spencer. With distinguishing red hair and impeccable diction, Jody seems right at home as the eccentric artist with a penchant for painting nudes. When Lawford suggests that Night remove his clothes, the scene flashes forward to the two enjoying quite a furious work out in bed as Maxwell literally blows on and inhales Kean's penis. The scene is memorable and surpasses much of the other sexual action in the picture. As Frosty's ex-wife, actor Jennifer Welles is eloquent and beautiful in her manner, and radiant in her sex scene with Kean. She imparts key information leading to the eventual surprise ending involving the transsexual performer Eve Adams. (Adams appeared earlier in the film, along with the wonderful character actor Bobby Astyr in a segment foreshadowing the story's conclusion.) Annie Sprinkle (as Annie Sprinkles) pops up in an orgy scenario prefaced by an exotic, erotic dance ritual performed by two female cast members. Overall, *Expose Me Lovely* (inspired by the 1928 foreign film *Lady of the Lake*) contains a grimy and subdued undercurrent with a score that perfectly complements the material. This is a noble achievement in its genre on the part of the film's director and writer Armand Weston.

In addition to *Expose Me Lovely*, Maxwell is proud of her involvement in three superb Video-X-Pix releases: *Satisfiers of Alpha Blue* (1980), *A Girl's Best Friend* (1981), and *Outlaw Ladies* (1981). According to Jody, the Damiano production *Satisfiers of Alpha Blue* is one of her most significant pictures containing exceptionally hot scenes: double insertion, anal, and a not to be missed sucking interlude with Lysa Thatcher and Hillary Summers. *A Girls Best Friend* is the first time Maxwell worked with Ron Jeremy.

In *A Girls Best Friend* (1981), I had a sex scene with Ron Jeremy and I was on my hands and knees. I had on this beautiful lingerie and a silk dress that they bought for me. [Director] Ron Sullivan never spared any expense. Anyway, I had on a designer garter belt, and bra and panties, and I got on my hands and knees and he pulled my panties down to my knees. He was eating me and he fucked me,

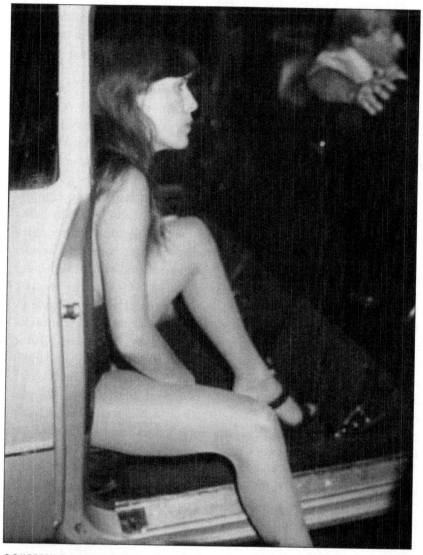

COURTESY OF JODY MAXWELL

and at the point where he was supposed to cum, Ron pulled out and came on my ass. Instead of leaving it like that, he pulled my panties up over [the cum], and started rubbing it into the silk panties. That was erotic and it felt erotic. It was a real turn on because it was different, and it was interesting. Instead of "Wham, bam, you're done." I think that Ron Sullivan made cum shots interesting. Many of the films from that era were erotic. I get turned on watching John Leslie. He was just a very sexy person.

In *Outlaw Ladies* (1981), there's a scene with me, and Samantha Fox, and Joey Silvera that has been rated one of the top twenty-five sex scenes of all time by [late adult historian and critic] Jim Holliday and other places. Samantha takes my hair and she tells me to stick out my tongue and not move. Joey comes on my tongue without me flinching, and I'll tell you that it was hard to do. Again, it was extremely erotic but very hard to do.

Outlaw Ladies is an exposé of the private sex lives and cravings of six women, defined by distinctive imagery as one vignette links to another. The film opens with Jody Maxwell in the primary role as Barbara. Married to Victor (R. Bolla), the sexually unfulfilled socialite learns how to seek and utilize her tendencies toward dominance and submission through guidance provided by her girlfriends, Evelyn and Abbey (Samantha Fox and Juliet Anderson). When Abbey visits for afternoon tea, Barbara introduces her to a young boy toy (Ron Hudd) for Abbey to play with while Barbara quietly observes and eventually assists by inserting a dildo into Abbey's behind upon request. We are also introduced to model and actor Cassie (Marlene Willoughby) who presents herself to the public as the model of femininity yet she engages in some sensual exploration of her own with Abbey's husband Harland (Bobby Astyr). Cassie carries herself with decorum and poise as she sweetly describes what they are doing in bed.

A young novice attorney Deidre (Veronica Hart) employed by Barbara's husband Victor, enjoys some kinky fun on the side when an artist Eddie (John Leslie) playfully teaches her how to take his member up her rectum for the first time. Merle Michaels plays the role of Felicia, an insecure friend of Victor's who works diligently to perform fellatio to his liking, in hope for expert cunnilingus in exchange — with success.

In the aforementioned scene, Maxwell and Samantha Fox (Evelyn) are in perfect sync while taking charge over the masculine looking Joey Silvera, as the women assume control, and alternately defer to one another through the erotic passage. Barbara achieves ultimate sexual satisfaction when Silvera unloads upon her stationary tongue. The rather complex storyline directed by Henry Pachard (Ron Sullivan), is a vehicle for some of the best talent in the industry. All of the characters aid and abet one another in this sophisticated sexual pilgrimage that becomes a metaphor for a deeper understanding of self. Maxwell brings a rich quality to the role resulting in texture and depth of character. Undoubtedly, this is one of her premium outings.

Also released in 1981, which boasts Jody Maxwell amongst other stellar cast members is reputable director Cecil Howard's *Neon Nights* — one of the last true classics of the vintage era.

> I feel I was very fussy in my choices of movies that all are significant works for various reasons. However, although some of my movies certainly were superior in quality and story line and I really love, I think my first movie *Portrait* was the most significant. I made history of sorts in the world of erotica with that movie. I sang a song, lyrics and all, while having oral sex. That certainly had never been done. As I'd said, it was not a gimmick either. Going beyond *Deep Throat* where the situational humor is with the audience, I introduced true erotica with humor actually included in it. I honestly believe in sex, and lovemaking can be hot, and passionate, and totally sexy, and have humor in it too. This was and is my personal belief. I showed that a person can make love, and it can be fun and funny, and wonderfully hot all at the same time. My great love — and people can tell — is that I loved to get off on camera. I did and I would. I never faked an orgasm ever in my life. Most of them fake it, trust me.

That's Entertainment!

With thirteen sex films under her belt, Maxwell's filmography is miniscule in comparison to many of her colleagues. Jody's background in theatre and speech proved to be a dynamic asset when she developed a one-woman entertainment show attraction initiated at Show World in New York, appealing not only to fans, but also to the very curious. Adept at streamlining her sexual propensities to cater to the growing demands of adult audiences, Maxwell occasionally modified her program to satisfy a mixed clientele. Astoundingly, she was able to accomplish this without performing live sex.

I was the first erotic star to do a stage show that was not stripping, and who did NOT have an initial background of stripping. I was approached by [former sex club] Show World in New York City to do anything I pleased on stage. With my creative mind and some helpful suggestions from [stripper] Honeysuckle Divine, I created a very sexy standup comedy act that also showed what

COURTESY OF JODY MAXWELL

a particular audience wanted to see. It was completely different from any show to which audiences had previously been exposed. Our shows repeatedly sold out, and more and more women came as the word got out. Frequently, their men would bring them. It was funny, sexy, interactive, and sometimes educational too. I had a legitimate theater background so I used those talents combined with my sexual abilities and talents. I was the pioneer for Annie Sprinkle and many other erotic stars who took the stage. I feel my stage work was significant because it opened another venue for the stars.

I opened up in Show World, in New York, and perfected my act as I went along. I was the very first one to venture into that field. It was a one-woman show. Of course, Show World had hardcore sex, but I had my gown cut a strategic way because I wasn't a stripper, and I was not a dancer of that kind. I'm not a clumsy dancer, but I'm clumsy, in general, and I didn't want to go out and make a fool of myself. I was talked into this by the Show World people so I knew they wanted T&A. I would walk out on stage in these sexy costumes and I would expose myself, and I would show them the sweet pussy they all wanted to see. I happened to have a well-endowed clit, and it would jump. A jumping clit was almost too much for them. I would show my boobs and shake them, and I'd occasionally get close to the guys in the front row, but that would be it. Thank god, I was quick-witted.

I would have a card-sized table with a few chairs out there and I would invite a male up on stage. I'd take questions from the audience and I would tell jokes, and I'd talk about the profession, but I kept it entertaining. I would give them whatever they wanted to see, but it was never usually more than just for a moment. The management shook their heads. They couldn't figure out how come they were selling out because this wasn't hardcore sex. We were doing a straight show. The men in the audience would think they were going to get their cocks sucked, but that's not what happened. Instead, I sucked on their finger. I would sing a song on their finger. They would get so turned on; it was amazing. People just loved it. They'd come back and bring women with them.

Eventually, it was suggested that I put a bowl of water on the table and suggest that the guy sit on the table. Then I was able to wash a man's hand because I didn't know where his hand had been. It was an excellent idea, so I started doing that. They thought they'd get to wash me and figured they'd get to do all kinds of things to me, which they didn't get to do. It got more interesting as time progressed. About the third time I did this, a guy asked me how the bowl of water would be used. He said, "What do you want me to do, sit in it?" Everyone thought it was hilarious, but afterwards, I got thinking about it. I thought, "I'm going to get a guy to sit in a bowl of water." I ran that past management and they said, "There is no way any self-respecting guy in New York City is going to sit in a bowl of water for you, or for anybody else, Jody. I'm sorry, you're good, but you're not that good."

I said, "You wanna make a bet?"

The next show I had I asked the guy to sit in a bowl of water and you know what? He did. He didn't actually take off his pants but he sat in a bowl of water. He had slacks on and the audience just about died. I had trouble not breaking up, but I gave all of the appropriate looks. I've been told that I have impeccable timing, so it came off very well. I would expose a breast, or sometimes I would have them identify parts of the body. I had the men wash their hands, and I would suck and sing on a finger while he was sitting in a bowl full of water. Most of the time, I'd ask the guy to drop his drawers and they would do it!

I brought this show all over different parts of the country. The police would come in occasionally to see what I was doing and they'd love it! They'd come back that night in plain clothing and bring their wives. I was actually demonstrating how to suck cock. I'd say that the best way to learn how to suck was to do it on your finger. Women would start to come in, and sometimes, I'd get married couples or people who were going together would come in. A gal would come up and suck on one of the guy's fingers while I worked on the other hand. I would teach them how to do it, literally, while they were up on stage. It was a very unique show.

This show that I did was probably quite tame compared to hardcore sex shows that would take place right on stage. My show was about entertainment. It was hot, and I made it a learning experience. It was great fun. I was quick-witted enough. We took questions from the audience and I always involved them into the show, which was probably a smart thing to do. When you can do that, it doesn't matter if it's R-rated, or a comedy, or drama. When you incorporate the audience, you'll have a successful show. Things became funnier as time progressed because the men would take their pants off, and eventually, they'd take their underwear off too. Sometimes I'd be sucking on somebody's finger and suddenly you'd see this cock pop up!

Simultaneously, I also began working for *Cheri* as a writer and some other magazines including *Hustler*. The reason I did all these things at the same time is because somebody who was in the business, not an actor, but someone who was close to me that had known the adult industry far better than I did said, "Don't take every film offered. Don't become overexposed because you don't want to become jaded." I regret turning down some films. I turned down some projects that became good X-rated movies. My idea, initially, was that I had wanted to make regular Hollywood movies. In order to achieve that, the less X-rated, the better. That's what I was told so I did everything. Because of the kind of films I made, and because of the type of shows I did and the writing I've done, I've managed to have lasting power. The editor at *Hustler* said to me, "You left us wanting more." That's how you should do it.

As she heeded the advice of her friend, Maxwell sharpened her writing skills and found work as a columnist for several adult magazines compris-

Jody and actor Warren Beatty. COURTESY OF JODY MAXWELL

ing of *Escapade, Capers, Partner* and *Adult Cinema Review*. In turn, Jody was able to thrive as an adult celebrity, but she didn't neglect her roots as a young politicized woman who advocated the importance of supporting future leaders and staying abreast of topical issues. *Maxwell* maximized her title and time as a young delegate representing Missouri at a National Young Republican Convention in Chicago which, according to her, involved a lot of work, a lot of partying, no sleep, and an abundance of X-rated activities. During her employment as a reporter for *Cheri* magazines, Maxwell made a point of covering Democratic and Republican Conventions as a feature storywriter. She fraternized with the likes of fellow political activists such as Warren Beatty when Presidential Democratic candidate Jimmy Carter ran against incumbent Republican President Gerald Ford. Maxwell was even an invited guest at the White House, and once attended a party hosted by President Nixon's daughters.

Over the years, Jody has grown disillusioned with what she perceives is a hypocrisy of the origins of the Republican Party mandate.

Unfortunately, for a party claiming to believe in fundamental individual freedoms, they certainly want to control our lives when it comes to sex and related fields. Now, many of these current high profile people who call themselves Republicans have bastardized the party and turned it into more of a fundamentalist, ultra-conservative party using the name "Republican" as the umbrella for them to gather to give them power and influence. I feel that this is no longer the party of Lincoln or of my grandfather.

Sex Tales

Determined to perpetually reinvent her image to keep things current, Maxwell made another transitory move in the 1980s when she joined Personal Services Club and functioned as a phone sex specialist. Jody remained a club member for twelve years titillating affiliates and fans with sassy sexy talk documented in her book *My Private Calls* (2004). Adapting from one end of the adult pool to another was a seamless passage.

It was not that difficult, in part, because I started doing erotic calls while I was still involved with everything else. I looked upon it as another gig. As a trained, legitimate actor, this was more acting, simply a different kind. The fact I was playing myself, "Jody Maxwell, erotic film star," made it a kind of a two-edged sword. I didn't have to create some fictional person that more often is the case with phone sex people handling the calls. They can be whoever the caller wants them to be, but they constantly have to create new personas. In my case, while I could be a fictional personality, I was still Jody. The callers knew it. So in that sense, it was limiting. On the other hand, the great majority of my callers were fans; they were very positive and nice. A high percentage simply wanted to talk with me, not have phone sex. However, my actual sexy calls were often a whole lot of oral sex, but certainly not all, by any means, of course. I understand that, knowing who I am, but sometimes it made it harder to branch out to other scenarios that I would have liked to have done more often to increase its freshness to me. I did have every possible kind of call, but the greatest emphasis was oral sex. A lot of times I would be asked to sing some song like "How

Much is that Doggie in the Window," and my wonderful fans would get off on my phone warbling. That would always amuse me in a good way. The brain is a wonderful and fascinating sex organ. Some fans would hear me say "hello" and they were finished. It truly amazed me!

Totaling the amount of years she spent as an adult entertainer, I asked Jody if she ever experienced any undue backlash as a star of sex films or as a phone sex celebrity.

Early in my career, I did a radio interview in my hometown. I was very naïve about what the public reaction might be, but because I was in my hometown, I figured I'd be safe. I was supposed to go to the studio but I was sick. I had a bad case of the flu, so I called and asked if we could do it over the telephone. I didn't know the host. I didn't check him out. I just agreed to do the show and didn't realize I was setting myself up. It was horrific; I learned a lot from that experience, trust me. People kept calling me and saying terrible things.

I did have a couple of bad experiences, but I've compartmentalized anything negative. The negative connotations had absolutely nothing to do with me getting into porn, nothing. Yes, admittedly, I've had terrible nightmare problems from a couple of experiences, but again, it had nothing to do with me getting into this field. I didn't seek out this particular career path; it sought me out. Remember, I'd thought about it for a while. All I agreed to in the beginning is that I would talk to my dad about it. I told Damiano that I'd get back to him.

You know, my uncles probably had a little tougher time dealing with my career, but my aunts were great, especially my mother's older sister. We were very close. She was a professional seamstress and helped me a lot with my stage costumes.

In every single X-rated film that I made, if I didn't want to work with a particular guy, I didn't have to work with him. It is quite different today. When I was inducted into the Erotica Hall of Fame in 2006, I also did a story for *Hustler* about what is going on today. I interviewed a lot of today's girls and everything is so strange. This one girl told me that she decided she can make more money from doing "ass-fucking" scenes than anything else. I asked her if she ever does any acting and she said, "Oh no. They call me when they want me to do an anal scene." She's a "star". To me, that's not really

being a star. It's what we used to call a "body". No lines except for
things like, "Oh! That feels so good," or, "Do it to me!" Anyway, she
said she's treated like a superstar.

What's nice about the piece that *Hustler* did on me is how they
described me, and our era: "That's when stars were really stars." I
thought that was nice. Today, the industry is dull and they all look
alike. I know that Bill [Margold] is concerned because many of the
golden age stars have passed away and that's very upsetting. Bill's
right, of course.

Liberation

I laugh because I think that, personally, according to my own
experiences in the other world separate from the adult industry,
women have been more exploited. I'm referring to the working
world. In porn, generally, what you see is what you get, relatively
speaking. Hundreds of thousands of cases of women have had to
sleep their way to the top. People joke about the casting couch but
it does exist.

Years ago, I actually did a blaxploitation movie [exploitation
films designed for an urban black audience] called *Bucktown* [1975,
directed by Arthur Marks featuring the late Thalmus Rasulala, a
brilliant black straight actor and one of the stars of the television
mini-series *Roots*] for a wonderful director who had made the *Perry
Mason* series. The cast was terrific. I really enjoyed them. I was
treated with respect by everybody. I played a topless dancer. It was
during the film shoot I became acquainted with someone connected to that movie who I felt was the old "casting couch" routine
type of individual. He said, "If you do this and that for me, I can
make you this, that, and the other." It was so stereotypical, like a
line from a "B" grade movie.

I never thought of myself as a feminist in the true sense of the
word. I might even have been offended at one time to hear that
word used to describe me, but I was/am more offended to be called
or implied subservient to men or a lesser person because I am a
female. I feel that being in adult films was empowering, but maybe
even more than that it was emancipating. Now if those two things
are a form of feminism, I guess I could be labeled as a feminist. I
found making adult films liberating. I found the industry liberating.
I pretty well got along with everybody. I tried to choose carefully

what I made, and my reasons were varied for my choices. There
were fewer games played by people in the biz than people dealing
with and living so-called "normal" lives. I'm proud of the work that
I did in the industry. There were perks too, of course. I met a lot of
Hollywood people who treated me as an equal and with respect. I
know that's not true of all of the stars.

COURTESY OF JODY MAXWELL

"Empowered" is a term frequently and carefully used by some of the relatively unscathed female veterans to accurately represent the positive components of having worked in the erotic movie industry. To be fair, obviously not all female or male performers necessarily agree that participation in sex films for mass audience consumption worldwide is a self-esteem booster, or that it can't negatively impact the lives of many sex performers short or long term. All things being equal, working as an entertainer in any capacity can have detrimental and salutary consequences.

I think people like Candida Royalle, Juliet Anderson, Samantha Fox, myself, Annie Sprinkle, Jane Hamilton and Sharon Mitchell — the industry controlled her for a while before she was able to control it — I feel that all of these people are somewhat empowered by their experiences in the adult industry. Too often people think we're all runaway kids, taken advantage of by those pretty mean old men. It's just not the case. We all were paid well, obviously, and I was well paid. Most of the directors and producers, they're not trying to sleep with you, they're trying to make a buck. Why blow it by sleeping with you? If you go to work at an office, before you know it, inevitably someone is trying to sleep with you. This goes on in all sorts of careers. It happens far too often. In this industry, you're allowed to have a say if you want to sleep with someone, or if you don't, on camera. I guess in a way, we're all feminists. Feminism in today's world, I think, is confusing for young girls.

In 1983, Jody married her current husband who has remained outside of the adult entertainment industry. In 2012, the couple is still happily ensconced. In Maxwell's spare time, she exercises her other well-honed physical gift as a skilled bowler competing in tournaments for both winter and summer leagues.

After I got married again in the early eighties, I did my phone sex, and when I left, I started teaching school. At present, I'm substituting. California does tight checks. It's funny I haven't been confronted because they know me by my married name now. I did all of my paperwork legally. I gave them all my names: my married name, my maiden name, and my so-called "porn" name.

In everything I've done, I have always treated the people I encounter with respect so I've been treated with respect back. I think that's a great part of my life.

Candida Royalle
Femme

As the eldest daughter of a professional jazz musician who played with composer and band leader, Raymond Scott, Candida Royalle spent many of her childhood years in Brooklyn, New York, and relocated to Queens after her father remarried. Born with natural artistic ability, Royalle aspired to be a fashion illustrator and studied at the prestigious and culturally diverse High School of Art and Design in Manhattan. She later attended Parsons School of Design and the City University of New York where she enrolled in Beat Generation Poetry studies and became involved in the women's movement. Drawn to the counterculture of the late 1960s, Royalle traveled to San Francisco's Haight-Ashbury district and melded with political activists and avant-garde performers. In 1975, after a period of singing in jazz clubs and selling her art, Candida began freelancing as an actor in the adult entertainment industry for extra funds.

Despite having appeared in less than fifty hardcore movies throughout her short career as a performer, Royalle's vivacious manner, coupled with her pretty face and alluring physical attributes made her a popular item among adult fans. Her fondest memories as a performer are roles she accepted in some of the campy, light-hearted, hardcore films such as *Hard Soap, Hard Soap* (1977) and *Hot and Saucy Pizza Girls* (1979) directed by Bob Chinn. Along with some of her contemporaries such as Serena and Annette Haven, Royalle also appeared in Blake Edward's international hit film, *10* (1979) starring Dudley Moore.

When the 1980s arrived, along with HIV, Royalle did some soul searching and decided her talents would be better served in the area of production and directing. The conversion from motion pictures to video provided an ideal opportunity for Royalle to launch Femme Productions in 1984, an entrepreneurial venture developing adult movies for women

"When I made my choice to start into production, it was a great way to embrace my name and everything I had done and just say, 'You know what? I'm not going to run for it. I'm going to take my fame and do something I'm proud of.'" CANDIDA ROYALLE

PHOTO COURTESY OF CANDIDA ROYALLE

and couples with concentration on female centric erotica. As the very first woman in a male dominated industry to have founded her own production company catering to both genders, Royalle is proud of Femme's staying power. In recent years, Femme's lines have expanded to include the availability of an ergonomic, erotic product, Natural Contours, designed with the sensitivities of women in mind. Additionally, the company gives generously by donating proceeds from sales of a specially crafted massage device, Petite Pink Ribbon, to Breast Cancer Action *(BCAction.org)*.

Broadening her extensive range of talents, Royalle, who still resides on the east coast, penned a bestselling, sex advice book titled *How to Tell a Naked Man What to Do* in 2006.

I spoke with Candida Royalle in the winter of 2010.

There was a Girl

I grew up in the greater New York area in every borough except Staten Island. I spent the first few years of my life in a very pretty section of Brooklyn called Carroll Gardens where I later lived again. My father's side of the family was part of a large wave of Italian immigrants who settled in Brooklyn. Italians were big on settling roots and those homes are still in the family.

When my father remarried, we moved to Astoria, Queens, an affordable area where a lot of young couples moved to start families. It was an ethnically diverse section of New York, a mix of working and middle class families and I was happy there. My mother, wanting us to live in a "nicer" area, pushed to make a move up to a very pretty section at the northern tip of the Bronx called Riverdale. This was a much more upscale part of New York, and the fact that my dad, who made his living as a professional jazz drummer, could afford this with the help of my mother's income as well, is quite impressive.

Being an artistically gifted child, I went to the high school of Art & Design in Manhattan. They have a system that still exists in the greater New York area whereby any student [residing in NYC] can attend so long as they pass the artistic requirements and maintain a good academic record. I felt very fortunate to have gotten such a cultural education that enabled me to develop my talents. I later went on to attend one of the premier art colleges: Parsons School of Design, also in Manhattan.

I know that there are people who were fortunate enough to have had very stable, happy homes — I think I was well loved but there was a lot of instability. My original birth mother left when I was eighteen months old. My father was a very complicated, difficult man who spent more time on his music than he did with the family. He was nine years older than my mother was and she was really quite something — she had had three of us by the time she was twenty-one. My mother was a very pretty girl from St. Louis, Missouri, who started young. She was half-Cherokee, and half Scottish, Irish, and British. She gave birth to me at home, natural childbirth, which was almost unheard of in 1950. He was considerably older, and I think that she probably found it difficult to be left alone with three small children all the time, including nights, which is when musicians work and when he was home, he wasn't one who could easily communicate. He was a loner who just wanted to practice his music. She tried to leave him a few times and he would always come after her and take us all home. The last time, he finally took only my sister and me home. My half-brother was from a previous marriage.

My father expressed sadness later on in his life when we talked about it because he had loved my half-brother a lot. While he couldn't very well take him from her, he didn't feel he could leave my sister and me with her. She was a young woman with three children, and while he would have supported us, he feared she would take us back to St Louis and he'd never see us or be able to check up on us. I think that it was a very difficult thing for him to have taken us from her and he apologized to me for that later on. I look back at that now as a grown woman, and I can only imagine the turmoil and the difficulty they both went through. He took us home to his mother, my grandmother, in Carroll Gardens. We went to Grandma's and that was a good thing because she was very loving and affectionate. We had a lot of relatives, aunts and uncles and cousins, but it was also unstable for me. At that age, you need to know Mommy is there and I used to call my different aunts "Mommy". It was particularly difficult when my grandmother got ill and my sister and I were farmed out to different relatives, even foster homes a couple of times. This was particularly traumatic for me.

My father wanted to find another wife. He was a jazz musician through and through. He did not do the conventional fatherly things and he really needed a woman to help raise his daughters. My stepmother came along and she fell in love with my sister and me — especially me. We really bonded and I needed a mother.

When I was four and a half, he remarried and we all moved to Astoria, Queens. The stability was good, but my parents didn't have a loving marriage and they lived a fast life. They both worked in top nightclubs and hotels — he was in the house band at the Waldorf Astoria, and Tavern on the Green where they had actually met. They were responsible; there was always food on the table, but they lived hard and there was too much alcohol, too much fighting, and it was an extremely challenging childhood. On the one hand, I was loved and I took part in all the traditional hallmarks of a good middle class childhood for that time. I was a Brownie and a Girl Scout and I took dance lessons, and I had a lot of friends. I was actually a very good kid. I wasn't difficult; I was sweet and really didn't get into trouble, but it was not a particularly happy home life. It got worse over the years. Luckily, we spent a lot of time — weekends and holidays at my grandmother's in Brooklyn, being with all the relatives and cousins — that was a good refuge for my sister and me.

I understand that my mother came to see us a couple of times, but she probably went back to St. Louis. My assumption was always that for a woman to give up her children that way she probably needed to put a wall around her heart and that was it. It was certainly fodder for therapy for me. Over the years, my sister and I made a few feeble attempts, once the internet was around, to find her. I know that if I gave someone the information some investigation could be done to find her or my half-brother if they're still alive, but for some reason, I've not had a great impetus to do it. I think there's probably some resentment. She would certainly be able to find us because we still have our family name. I think there's also some fear. There were times, especially after I got involved with the adult industry where I thought, "What would she think of me?" "Would she judge me?" How horrible would that be? I don't know what she would be like. I don't know what my half-brother would be like. I've kind of accepted it, and I think that I've accepted my stepmother for being my mother and that was it. Of course, I'm curious, and I would have loved to have heard from her mouth how she could just walk away from two baby girls. Again, she was young — she was only twenty-two years old at the time, and I know what I was like at twenty-two. It'd be horrible to be saddled with three children and with a husband that you don't want to live with. I don't know what I would do in that situation.

I was very creative as a child. Both my sister and I were drawing as soon as we could hold a pencil. We were also both musically inclined, like our father, and even my stepmother was a great singer so we sang a lot. I was always singing, and dancing, and performing, and I spent a lot of time alone so I really learned how to entertain myself. I used to go up to my grandmother's bedroom where she had a closet full of beautiful dresses and petticoats from when she was a young woman and had loved to dance. I can still see myself putting on all her clothes and petticoats and dancing before the mirror or at home, putting on records and singing along. We used to do the typical thing: puppet shows for the neighborhood kids. My sister and I loved animals. We were brought up with a real respect for life. My father would bring injured animals home when we were little so we got an early education. I used to have tanks with chameleons, and turtles, and frogs, and I'd create different environments for them. I loved drawing glamorous women wearing beautiful gowns. I had tons of cutout dolls so it was easy to draw the clothes and cut them out. I had a Barbie doll with a red bouffant hairdo and a fabulous wardrobe with a glamorous career. She and a handsome boyfriend named Ken, of course, and a sports car! My sister and I had a globe that we would spin and wherever our fingers landed would be where our Barbie dolls would go on their next trip. The funny thing is it said a lot about the kind of person I wanted to be. My Barbie was a career woman with a great wardrobe, and a handsome boyfriend, and a penchant for traveling. Essentially, that's who I became.

Verve

I began dance training when I was ten and danced and sang in school choruses and shows, so I had a lot of things that I loved to do. I was never bored and never without plenty of ways to entertain myself. I always had a lot of girlfriends that I hung out with, and while I remained quite innocent until the age of eighteen, I loved boys and was quite the little flirt.

I would say that my [paternal] grandmother was, in some ways, a role model for me. She was brought here from Italy at the age of two — I think it was in 1900. Like so many young women in those days, she longed to be a schoolteacher. She was a very gifted self-taught pianist. When she was very young, a music teacher begged her father to let her give my grandmother free lessons but he wouldn't. He pulled her out of school in the sixth grade to help support their large family. I believe she never forgave him for that. She was a very smart young woman with many gifts who was forced to become a milliner in a factory. This left her with a lot of bitterness, but the amazing thing was that she learned how to invest in the stock market and accumulated an impressive portfolio of stocks and bonds. Ultimately, she owned and bought her own home in what became a prestigious area now known as Carroll Gardens, in Brooklyn. My parents, on the other hand, were clueless about investing and saving for the future. It was definitely my grandmother who was my role model in terms of being a financially independent woman and learning how to invest and take care of myself.

My grandmother also had a tremendous effect on me in terms of the delight she took in music and dancing. She had a great collection of 78's along with her old 78 player, and she'd put them on and dance for us and dance for me and my friends and showed us the old dance steps. She'd play the piano and get us to sing with her. At night, she would put on the TV and watch old black and white movies from the thirties, forties, and fifties, and my sister and I would stay up late watching them with her. She didn't care if we sat up and watched movies late into the night since it was always weekends or holidays when we didn't have to get up for school. I was brought up on a diet of glamorous women who sang, and danced, and looked fabulous, and had great wardrobes. To this day, I love those old movies! What a spirit my grandmother had!

On the other hand, because my dad was so independent minded — he always taught us to think for ourselves — I eventually developed a taste for people who dared to be different, and to be who they are and not feel the need to conform; people who didn't follow the rules just because someone told you to. I remember dressing up at the age of thirteen like a beatnik as my Halloween costume. It was adorable. I was a skinny little thing and completely flat chested. I dressed all in black and had this little short, bobbed haircut. I wanted to be one of those people who spoke for themselves and dared to live by their own rules. Apparently, that really stuck. I would say I didn't have any exact role models, but I admired people who thought for themselves and lived life on their own terms.

As a young, budding, artistic female, Candida received affirmation of her prodigious skills when she later was accepted at Art College. Parsons

School of Design in New York City continues to enjoy global recognition as a leader and trendsetter in the world of innovative art, fashion and design.

I went to Parsons School of Design, one of the foremost private art colleges right in Manhattan for a year until I lost interest in becoming a fashion illustrator. Then I moved out on my own. I

COURTESY OF CANDIDA ROYALLE

worked for a year to support myself until I found a way to go back to college and attended CCNY [City College of New York] for about a year and a half. I majored in psychology and minored in art. CCNY's campus is actually in Harlem, and has some amazing professors. I studied poetry while I was there with one of the original Beat Poets, Joel Oppenheimer.

I was very fortunate to grow up and be educated in New York City. We have a system here that allows students to audition for specialized high schools in the arts and sciences. It doesn't matter whether or not your family has money. Talent, good grades, and a commitment to your art is all that is required. I loved my years at Art & Design, and going to high school right in the heart of Manhattan. I got into the women's movement in college. That was a big turning point for me.

Conversely, as a late bloomer, and as an attractive teenage girl, Candida was ill prepared for the onslaught of attention she received from males of all ages which serendipitously happened to coincide with the second wave of feminist ideology.

I was a late developer and a very skinny little girl — I didn't even need a bra until I was nearly fourteen. I so wanted to be shapely, but by the time I started blossoming in to a curvaceous little thing the whole "Twiggy" look came in to style, and suddenly, it was all the rage to be skinny and flat chested! I eventually became this very pretty, shapely girl, but suddenly, all of these grown men started coming on to me! They see a beautiful, young, blossoming, sixteen, seventeen or eighteen-year old girl walking down the street and these guys just lost it. I had so many men coming on to me and trying to get over on me. Finally, the guy that I worked part-time for in an exclusive Manhattan tennis club, a former Olympic champion from Hungary, assaulted me in his office. I had to threaten to scream in order to get him to let go of me and I had to leave the job. Things like this were starting to happen left and right. My boss I had worked for in this up and coming company called Ticketron before I went back to college, demanded that I kiss him goodnight every night. In those days, we didn't have laws against that kind of thing so I felt kind of like, "Oh, I guess I have to kiss him every day in order to keep my job!" All of these experiences politicized me. I became a staunch feminist at nineteen.

The feminist movement was wonderful. It gave my life tremendous depth and meaning. I learned an awful lot and I've always gotten along great with women, so this was a very big part of my formative years. When I was twenty-one, I left New York City and went to San Francisco. I got in with a group of very avant-garde San Francisco people, many of whom were part of the big gay rights movement that was happening in the early seventies.

I had gone to San Francisco about a year before with my first boyfriend — we were there for just a few days and I fell in love with it. That had to have been about 1969. I always knew I wanted to come back and I was really fed up with New York, I didn't want to be in New York any more so I went to the house that my [former boyfriend] was staying at, even though he and I had broken up by then. It was a house in Haight-Ashbury and I really clicked with them. I felt that I had arrived. I was "home". It was everything you'd heard about. It was a blend of hippies, freaks, gay rights activists, and avant-garde performers — a real hybrid. It was wonderful — a lot of drug experimentation I have to say, but that's what was going on then: free concerts in Golden Gate Park and lots of dancing so it was a wonderful, creative, joyful period. I started performing with some of the original Cockettes, and Angels of Light and it was wonderful.

The Cockettes, a group of performance artists with a psychedelic slant were founded in the late 1960s by George Harris Jr. (aka Hibiscus) and based in the North Beach district of San Francisco. Because of creative differences, the Cockettes divided into two troupes by the early 1970s: the Cockettes and the Angels of Light — the latter of the two did not charge admission to patrons.

We were part of a truly unique sub-culture that's only beginning to be recorded in books and documentaries. A scene that, like so many culture-shifting movements, was born of inspiration and transcendence, but eventually burnt itself out on too many drugs that numbed rather than inspired.

Starving Artist

I started doing avant-garde theater and singing in jazz clubs and all of the training I'd done with my dance and my art, I started using in free style ways now. I was selling art in galleries and I was performing, but not making a lot of money. It wasn't about money or "materialism" back then.

The way I got into the adult industry is that I needed to make extra money. We would put on shows and never charge admission; we did it for the love of it. I needed to start making some money obviously, and I answered an ad for nude modeling. I'd gone to art schools and drawn from nude models for years though I was always very shy about taking my clothes off publicly. The agent asked me if I wanted to be in an adult movie and I was horrified! I hadn't even seen one and I stormed out of his office. My boyfriend at the time, a musician, decided that it sounded like a great way to make money, and he went and auditioned. He was so cute that he got the lead role in a big Anthony Spinelli feature called *Cry for Cindy* (1976). The movie opens with him on a motorcycle with the girl [Amber

Hunt] who played "Cindy" on the back. I thought, "I'm going to go visit him on the set and check out what this is like". Like most people, I thought it was a sleazy industry, but I went there and I really had my head turned around. The people in the cast were beautiful; it was a large and professional crew. There were scripts. Anthony Spinelli was a doll. Auditions to get into these top tier adult movies were not easy, and the money for a struggling young artist was great. That's what really drew me in.

The late Anthony Spinelli (Samuel Weinstein, aka Sam Weston), one of the masterful, adult film directors of the porno chic era, is the brother of Hollywood character actor Jack Weston. Spinelli is known for producing quality X-rated features with character development and evolved plots. *Cry for Cindy* starred two of the most talented male actors of the golden age, John Leslie and John Seeman opposite Amber Hunt in the lead female role.

By the mid-1970s, imaginative filmmakers eager to jump into the burgeoning adult market were inspired and encouraged by the immense success of the trio of hit films: Gerard Damiano's *Deep Throat* (1972) and *The Devil and Miss Jones* (1973), and Jim and Artie Mitchell's *Behind the Green Door* (1972).

I did actually try two loops in one day to see if I could handle it. Fortunately, the actor that I was set up with was very sweet and kind. The woman that I was set up with for the other one was completely disinterested so that was not such a great experience. The guy who was shooting the loops was everything you might presume about someone making adult movies. I mean, he was nice, but he was just sketchy and I look back and I wonder, "Oh, my god, how did I go on in front of him?" The money was great. He had actually been known for creating those light shows they ran behind the big rock concerts. He also made features — so yeah, it was *The Analist* (1975). I don't really like to talk about it because it was not a good experience for me and I don't like to give the movie any promotion.

I wish that I had refused [certain aspects of performing]. I definitely got facials in some of those films and I should have refused. I went along with some of that stuff — I mean, you had to, to be in those movies — that's what you had to do. It was not easy.

I think that, in general, it's not easy to see yourself on film. Even mainstream actors will often say that. Of course, when I went through the process of doing a lot of work on myself and making sure that I was comfortable with having been in movies, it was confrontational. I still had to go through my process of coming to terms with my choices. Once I did that, which was during the 1980s, I took out some movies and looked at them. I had done so much work on myself and thoroughly explored my feelings about having been in the movies that it was okay. It was fine to watch. In fact, I distinctly remember feeling like one would feel if you looked at pictures of your children because it was so removed by then. I was much older so I would look at it and think, "Oh, look how pretty I was back then!" What I marveled at is that I didn't know how pretty I was. It was a good lesson because it was something that said to me, appreciate who you are now because twenty years from now, you're going to look back on the "you" now and think, "Oh, what an attractive woman."

There is a prevailing presumption by anti-porn feminist groups such as NOW (National Organization for Women) who made this statement in 1980: "sadomasochism and pornography constituted violence, not sex, and were inherently dangerous," that women didn't and don't have the option to make their own choices and had marginal input once they agreed to appear in a sex film. As far back as the late 1960s when hardcore loops became popular as a mail order item, generally, a mutual agreement and contract existed between the actor and the agent/production company as to what acts would be required of the performer once the cameras started to roll. Suffice to say, that doesn't mean agents, producers, and directors didn't sometimes push for more ultimately leaving the decision up to the performer. Ironically, in many respects, the work was far less demanding for women during Royalle's era when the production of adult films was still illegal than it is today with many restrictions in place.

In those days, it wasn't the same as today. You didn't get paid for sex acts. You got paid a day's wages. It changed because once they started shooting on video they began cramming so many scenes into one day, the performers had to charge for each sexual performance in order to protect from being overworked. Back when I was in movies, you would do one scene or at the absolute most, two scenes a day. Back then, there were lists of what you would and would not do. It wasn't as if you were going to get more money for one or the other. It was sort of like a contract. You would audition for the movie, and you would get a deal memo stipulating how many days you would work and how much you'd be paid. They would also hand you a sheet of paper with a list of various types of sex acts, and you'd check off what you would and would not do. I'm sure there were probably some girls who did feel railroaded, but [it boiled down to] how strong you were and what your level of self-esteem was.

I had one experience very early in my career in a movie for Alex de Renzy. Of course, he's very well known. I got hired for a big party scene and I hadn't been in very many movies yet. I didn't get into adult movies because I liked having sex on camera, I got into them because I liked performing, and I liked dressing up, and getting made up, and it was good money.

I went to do this two-day shoot [at night] and there was a lot of stuff going on in it. There was supposed to be this wild party, and it was really quite a production. Alex de Renzy was known for big, outrageous movies. It was about this huge Albino [Ken Turner] — this very nasty guy who would beat up prostitutes. They threw this big party to get back at him. The script called for the girls to get him drunk and they were supposed to do all of these things to him. At a certain point, they started handing out beers to all of the actresses. I've never liked the taste of beer and I didn't take any. Finally, they said, "You have to drink something," so I asked "Why?" That's when I found out that all the girls were supposed to degrade him by standing over him and urinating on him. I immediately went into my rebel-rousing feminist ways — I was always the leader and I'd get all of my girlfriends involved politically! I gathered everyone around and I said, "Look, I am not going to do this. I never agreed to this. None who doesn't want to do this should be pushed into doing it. We should stand together." I should say that only about four women in all ended up willing to do it. de Renzy was very angry with me and said, "You'll never work for me again" — which I didn't, but that was fine with me. They'd really tried to push me. He was so incensed that I would stand up to him and not do what he said.

Royalle is referring to is *Femmes de Sade* (1976) which encompassed a lengthy list of actors (many uncredited) including John Leslie, Joey Silvera, Lesllie Bovee, Annette Haven, Linda Wong, and Desiree West — to list only a small cluster of names. Ken Turner, a giant of a man who played the perpetrator in the story, was urinated on and possibly defecated on during the scene that Candida described.

Six years earlier, in 1970, de Renzy's groundbreaking movie *Pornography in Denmark* paved the way for aspiring directors and financiers of controversial sexual-themed films to take the necessary risks involved to produce pornographic material that was illegal to make, but not to purvey. Denmark is the first country in the world to have lifted their ban on pornography in 1967 which compelled de Renzy to travel to Copenhagen in 1969 where he attended the world's first adult oriented trade show, "Sex '69."

Royalle, who is certainly not a prude by any stretch of the imagination, preferred to participate in adult films on the west coast that were more comical in nature in contrast to some of the edgier and often darker features that were being produced on the east coast during the 1970s.

"Hot & Saucy"

I would say my fondest memories as an actor are when I did some of the silly movies for Bob Chinn and producer Richard Aldrich like [*Hot & Saucy*] *Pizza Girls* (1979) and *Hard Soap, Hard Soap* (1977). They were great guys and very sweet. As environments go those were some of the nicest, especially *Pizza Girls* where we all had so much fun learning how to skate board around the parking lot of the motel we were staying at during the shoot.

Candida Royalle and her real-life best girlfriend, Laurien Dominique, appeared alongside onscreen pals Christine de Schaffer and ditzy bombshell Desiree Cousteau in the comedy *Hot & Saucy Pizza Girls*. The film is enjoyable fun and frolic. It follows the pizza delivery girls through the steep, windy streets of San Francisco as they skateboard their way into the bedrooms of lonely horny men and women looking for a little extra topping. After much prodding by the cast, even director Bob Chinn was part of the ensemble cast in a non-sex role as Holmes's cohort in the dough making business at Shakey's Pizza Parlor, while Paul Thomas and Richard Pacheco teamed up as business partners of a rival take-out restaurant conniving to steal business away from the thriving Shakey's. Adult actor, John Seeman, is funny as a private investigator hoping to put Shakey's out of business, and in the process, falls head over heels in love with Cousteau's character, Ann *Chovie*.

Royalle often worked with the most popular talent during her years as an actor which occasionally meant those with the biggest egos would dominate the sets. While attending a script rehearsal for *Hard Soap, Hard Soap* Candida recalled that John Holmes "made eyes" at her from across the table. The rehearsal was the first time she'd met the legendary star, and Candida was flattered by his attraction to her. Shortly afterward, Holmes took Royalle by the hand and led her into a tiny room where he made love to her while the rest of the cast and crew remained outside.

John Holmes wasn't one of my favorites to work with really because of his emotional problems. He really was a nice guy. He was sensitive to me, you know, but he made the set unpleasant sometimes throwing his weight around and being the prima donna. You end up making it difficult for everyone. Since becoming a director, I tell you, he wouldn't have lasted with me. I don't care how big of a name someone is. Even what he did with me was rude while making everyone wait outside! That's terrible! It really was. Of course, we were just doing a day of rehearsals, we weren't ready to shoot, but still it wasn't nice.

In the hilarious send up *Hard Soap, Hard Soap*, a satire of the seventies soap opera *Mary Hartman, Mary Hartman*, Royalle and Dominique team up as scheming girlfriends, Linda Lou and Penny Holmes in their attempt to resolve the sexual hang-ups experienced by their families and their community. Linda and Penny extend libidinous services to those with the greatest needs including the mailman and the custodian. They even help a blind woman to regain her sight in the most unusual way as the film builds toward a fitting slippery-wet finish. The rest of the cast list is filled out by Paul Thomas, John Holmes, Joey Silvera, Jon Martin, John Seeman and Joan Devlon.

Proactively, Candida furnished her life with lasting friendships formed during her early years in the industry. She gives kudos to her tight band of friends who constitute Club 90 — a small group of elite women that toiled as pioneers throughout the early days of erotic filmmaking. Royalle still communicates with the girls on a regular basis through telephone and e-mail.

I've made wonderful friends in the industry, very, very close friends, many of whom I'm still close with like Veronica Hart and Annie Sprinkle, Veronica Vera, and Gloria Leonard — all of whom make up the support group that we formed almost thirty years ago.

Of course, I don't see her often, but also Samantha Fox, and I'm still very close to Merle Michaels. It's funny that I have to try to come up with their stage names that I hardly ever call them.

John Leslie was wonderful. We had a little affair and he took me under his wing when I started out as an actress. We always held one another in high esteem. He directed one of the few adult movies I

Candida with Mike Ranger in *Hot Rackets*. CAL-VISTA

really liked called *Dog Walker* (1993), a very well done film. Sadly, he passed away from a heart attack this past year [2010]. He was much loved in the industry.

John Leslie, one of the most admired leading men and directors to have worked during the golden era, was a mesmerizing presence and performer who appeared in more than three hundred movies during his tenure as an adult film actor. Royalle also spoke affectionately about Jon Martin, another one of her favorite male co-stars.

Jon Martin played my husband in *Hot Rackets* (1979), and he was the other actor I dated for a while. I generally didn't date actors from the industry, but he and John were the exceptions. I ran into him a few years ago in Manhattan and we had a very nice visit.

Hot Rackets is a humorous story about a day in the life of a wealthy couple (Royalle and Jon Martin). The two uncover various ways to spice up their sex lives at the local tennis club where nudity and sexual favors are offered as membership amenities. Many familiar faces pop up in highlighted scenes: Rhonda Jo Petty and Mike Ranger portray Royalle and Martin's best friends and engage in some steamy sex while the club masseuse/oral queen, played by Laurien Dominique, encourages Candida to experiment in some girl/girl exploration. A blonde seventies main-stay, Cris Cassidy, in the role of Royalle's housekeeper and Turk Lyon as the chauffeur, partake in a memorable sticky encounter in a greenhouse. Desiree Cousteau (billed as Desiree Clearbranch) is her cute bubble-headed self, as she is tag teamed by Martin and Ranger in a Jacuzzi. What is striking about *Hot Rackets*, which could pass as a mainstream picture without the sex (true of many of the features of the seventies decade) is the playful and innocent flavor of the storyline and sexual situations. Royalle, always a joy to watch, has impeccable timing creating a perfect bookend to her fun-loving, extroverted personality.

Candida remembered a few more of her former associates.

The other one I'd say I enjoyed working for was Henri Pachard who has since passed away. He was lovely. I did *October Silk* (1980) for him and he was a doll. Even Ronnie, Ron Jeremy. I didn't actually perform sexually with him, but I played his sister in *Fascination* (1981). You know, he was very sweet. I even met his parents in Queens, way back when we worked together, must have been 1980. You know who else was very nice to work with was Jack Wrangler. He was so professional. I worked with him in my last movie; a beautiful period piece called *Blue Magic* (1982) that I wrote and had a starring role. It was directed by Larry Revene and produced by my ex-husband Per Sjostedt. I really wanted Jack as the lead because of his professional acting and comedic skills. He also passed away, not long ago. He had married the famous singer, Margaret Whiting, and returned to directing and producing theatre in New York. Sadly, he was still young and thriving.

Blue Magic starred Candida as an alluring woman with a mysterious past spanning hundreds of years. Upon inviting several couples into her gothic mansion for a dinner engagement, the group soon finds itself involved in an erotic adventure far surpassing the light banter preceding the sexual experimentation. The orgasmic evening inevitably and dramatically alters the lives (possibly eternally) of all participants.

Empowered...to a fault

Thoughtfully, Candida addressed questions regarding preconceived ideas and generalizations regarding women working within a primarily male governed environment.

There's no black and white way to respond to it. I think that, on the one hand, the industry probably does have more of a tendency to attract young women who have a fractured sense of themselves or who have been overly sexualized as children, or who have been given the impression that their true value is in their sexuality. Because it is something that is still scorned upon in our society, if you go into something that will bring scorn, it makes one wonder why someone would do that to oneself. On the other hand, I would balance that out by saying not every girl does come from a traumatized, abused, sexualized background. That has to be said first. Then I would point out that the statistics that I recall state that a full third of the female population of the United States has been sexually assaulted or abused or are victims of incest. That's what they figure. That's the entire population, that's not the adult industry, that's the big picture. So, that said, I think that we as a society have a vested interest in making sure that women don't see performing sexually for public consumption as a viable and respectable option to follow.

One of the underpinnings of our society has traditionally been the family unit, and it was always believed that one of the ways to ensure that we have a family unit is to make sure that one parent stays home and is the truly functioning parent. Society had decided that parent needs to be the woman so that the father can know who his heir is. If women become too sexually evolved and empowered even to the point where they're performing sexually for public consumption, then you really are sending a message to young girls that this is okay. Really, what they mean to say to girls is, "No, no, no...To be a viable choice is marriage and motherhood. To be a respectable citizen you must remain virtuous and not fall into certain pitfalls and do certain things." For girls to follow this path, they have to be punished somehow, or else it is seen as an okay thing to do.

According to the Crisis Intervention Centre that reports one out
of every three women nation-wide are sexually assaulted in a lifetime,
Royalle's statistics are accurate. Of all of the countries who track these
findings, the United States reported the highest incidences of rape. In
contrast, thirty-three percent of all males are sexually assaulted, either as
a child, or an adult.

> I think that most of our culture still doesn't accept [sexual per-
> forming] as a choice for women, and we're conditioned to believe it.
> I think it helps to uphold a certain underpinning, a structure of our
> society. It pretty much started with Western Religion and the Church.
> Prior to that, there were certainly cultures and societies that were
> more open sexually. Women were allowed to be highly sexual and
> they were still respected, prostitutes and women who taught sex —
> that this was not a bad thing. It was a very different kind of culture.

While it is true that many conventional religions do not always recognize or welcome females as sexual human beings or encourage women to
embrace their own sexuality, several cultures are not accepting and have
never been accepting of women who do not adhere to traditional roles
and expectations intrinsic to the practices and etiquettes of a specific
country or group. It is well documented that select countries and cultures
ostracize women and even brutalize them using extreme methods in the
way of physical torture and worse as a means of punishment for innocent
displays of affection as simple as hand-holding or revealing a portion of
the face or body in public. Western civilization might not condone women
in pornography or pornographic material in general, but a relative plateau
of tolerance does exist.

> I think that pornography itself is a reflection of how we have
> perverted our sexuality and for the most part, what would be
> described as "male" pornography makes sex look rather dirty, and
> mechanical and loveless. I think it's a reflection of what we've done
> to our sexuality through positioning it as something dangerous and
> bad, needing to be controlled and suppressed. I spent all of those
> years looking into my soul and trying to look objectively at having
> been in movies, and whether or not this was good or bad — was
> this bad for society? I had to flesh it out for myself and I couldn't
> live with this burning question in my mind. "Oh, my god, did I take
> part in something horrible?" I don't think it was, but I don't think

we'll see in our lifetime a society that doesn't condemn it even while millions of people consume it.

I was an okay porn star, but I was definitely not one of the more monumental ones just because I always had a little shyness. There was always some conflict about doing it. I certainly wasn't like Jenna [Jameson] who came into this wanting to be the biggest porn star.

COURTESY OF CANDIDA ROYALLE

I remember thinking, "Ah, no one is going to see these things". I had thought that they'll go into some vault eventually and collect dust somewhere. It's interesting that the guy [mentioned earlier] with all of the loops, lost all those loops in a big fire. I thought, "Oh boy, talk about karma!" He was one of the ones who tried to take advantage of the girls. I think that definitely my most significant work is as a director. There's no doubt about that.

Femme Productions

Candida set her talents in front of the camera aside in the 1980s when the AIDS crisis adhered itself like an unsightly scab to the adult entertainment medium. Royalle took bold steps in 1984 when she decided she could improve upon the current formula of sex films by appealing to the desires of female audiences and couples as opposed to catering specifically to the traditional trench coat crowd. The timing was optimum as the conception of video, an unexpected meeting through a friend, and the encouragement of family helped Royalle's idea to become a reality.

I think a number of things came together to make this the right thing to do. I had gone into therapy to understand why I did what I did. After much reading and exploring, and looking at it through a historical perspective as well as my own personal perspective, I decided there was nothing wrong with performing sexually with others for others to view, and enjoy, and learn from. I felt that the pornography that existed reflected a society that had great conflict about sexuality and above all, there was no woman's voice. We were not getting a whole lot out of looking at these films other than easy jerk-off material. That is fine in and of itself but there could be so much more. Of course, that got me to thinking that it would be interesting to create movies that had a woman's voice that actually had good information, and that people could actually learn something. I knew there would be some people who would love movies that are more intelligent with more craft and artistry. At the same time, women were starting to become more curious because of the feminist movement. We had received permission to explore our sexuality and quite significant: home video and cable television were introduced in to the culture. This really gave people a place to view and explore these movies and their fantasies at home. They could now look at them within the safety of their own home. I saw this all come together and I thought that it was a viable market that the industry was ignoring.

In my own personal life, I was married at that point for a period of four years to a great guy and we had a nice life together. I had been working by writing articles — a number of different articles for different magazines — mostly men's entertainment magazines.

COURTESY OF CANDIDA ROYALLE

I was doing gossip columns for *High Society* and I did a funny expose for *High Times* magazine of which I am most proud. I was in my very early thirties by this time and I always wanted to have my own career and be able to take care of myself. I had given up on the idea of performing on stage singing, because I had developed stage fright for some reason and I was looking for something that was a reliable career choice like a business. It had to be creative. I thought I'd be a good person to create adult movies from a woman's perspective because I had experience in the adult industry. There are directors that would have loved to explore eroticism, particularly back then. They wouldn't touch it because it would ruin their career. I had nothing to lose. I already had a big scarlet letter on me.

At the same time, through an incredible series of coincidences, I was called out of the blue by this woman named Lauren Niemi, who had come to town from the mid-west. She was a photographer and she had this idea that she wanted to create erotic rock videos from a woman's point of view. This was when rock videos were all the rage. An old friend of mine that I had lost touch with for fifteen years who I had just run into on the street sent Lauren my way after hearing her pitch the idea to someone in the office where she was working. Lauren came to see me and we had a total meeting of minds. That same day, my in-laws had been visiting and were packing and getting ready to go back home to Sweden and my father-in-law overheard Lauren and I talking. At that point, they were in the production and distribution business in Europe and had started the first major video distribution company in Sweden. They had made their fortune producing Spaghetti Westerns in Italy. They had also invested in some of the bigger adult movies like *Roommates* (1981), *Games Women Play* (1981) and *Blue Magic* (1982) which was the last movie in which I had both written and starred.

When they got back to Sweden, my father-in-law called. He'd been saying for the last year that I should direct and he said that if I could find distribution, he would invest in Lauren's and my production company. He said it was a brilliant idea — to do these movies with class. I thought, "Well, this is clearly meant to be." We formed our company right then and there: Femme Productions. In February 1984, we registered our company name. We wanted something that said "woman" and I came up with "Femme," which is of course, French for "woman".

We shot our first movie, *Femme* (1984), in April and then two more *Urban Heat* (1984) and *Christine's Secret* (1986) that summer. *Christine's Secret*, where we finessed our trademarks of pairing up actual lovers and shooting with as much existing light as possible rather than using harsh lighting, went on to win five awards from the New York Adult Critics Association including "Women's Favorite Erotic Scene". I went to the three biggest adult distribution companies — they didn't have to put up any production money, just the cost of distribution. They all kind of patted me on the head and said, "Nice idea, Candida, but women aren't interested in this sort of thing."

My former partner [Lauren] and I — We're an interesting case study because I credit her with equal responsibility for the initial launch of Femme Productions. Her coming into my life really gave me the impetus to do this. She came up with the solution I was looking for when I had pondered, "How do you turn an adult movie into something that appeals to women?" I didn't want to make up some big old soap opera plot and then surround it with the same old formulaic mechanical sex because what really needed to change was the sexual depiction; the erotic component. How do you create believable stories with people who don't have a lot of acting skills?

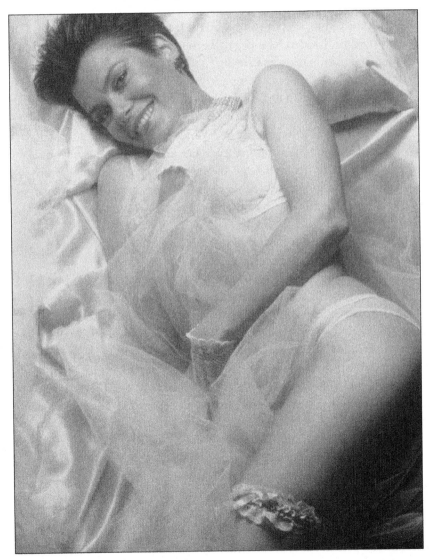

How do you keep it simple while also engaging the viewer? When she came up with the idea to do an entire erotic rock video, I said, "This is the perfect solution."

We went our own separate ways after about a year. She was getting married. I think her husband was pressuring her to stop making sex movies and I think she had some conflicts with my husband and me. My husband was the assistant director and kept on eye on the entire production, keeping an eye on his father's investment. He was a bit hard on Lauren who began as the director while I produced. While it was our vision and she had a photographer's eye which was lovely, she and I were both completely inexperienced in terms of running a set on our own and my husband could be a fierce taskmaster.

After going our separate ways, I continued on my path. We've stayed in touch and have remained somewhat close. She did a little bit of video work after that, but later, became a stay-at-home mom home schooling her two sons. We've gone off in two completely opposite directions. She will say to me, "Look at me. I'm a stay at home mom. I wonder what might have been in store for me. You went ahead and did all this".

I'll say, "Gee, you have this stable, wonderful home life and a husband. You still love each other and you have two sons. I never had children and I wonder what it would have been like if I had." You always wonder, but in the end, we each did what we chose to do. She helped create something very special and unique and shares in that legacy, but her life today is very fulfilling and interesting for her in another whole way.

I'm very proud of Femme. I knew it was going to be big. You just know in your gut when something is right, and I did it as a very pro-woman thing because the films I'd been in did not celebrate female sexuality. They used us and paraded us up there to get off on, but they didn't give us any sort of voice. I wanted to give something back to women, and I wanted to create movies that women could look at and feel good about sexually.

Femme (1984), the first picture produced by Femme Productions in which Royalle is credited as a writer, producer, and director starred Rhonda Jo Petty in the title role and co-starred Jerry Butler. Shot in rock video style that is surprisingly crisp, the film has a classic eighties texture with lots of big hair, exaggerated make-up and tasteful lingerie. The sex scenes are framed as six one-act fantasies patenting Royalle's vision for what she believed women wished to experience in an erotic movie. Petty and Butler, two of the most attractive and famous performers of their respective eras, occasionally appear to be going through the motions which is a little disconcerting, considering that at the time *Femme* was filmed, Petty was not in a good emotional space. On the other hand, Sharon Kane is healthy in her appearance and clearly enjoys her sexual

PHOTOGRAPHY BY ARNE SVENSON

interaction with her partner (Klaus Multia) as she envisions making love with a soap opera star in the sensitive exchange. Tish Ambrose, who began her career in the early 1980s, and gay star George Payne (Payne also acted in a good percentage of heterosexual adult films) are also part of the ensemble cast. A twentieth year special edition of *Femme* was released in 2004. Commentary and insights into the transitioning years of the adult business are provided by Royalle.

> I worked on a lot of stuff in therapy — I also wanted to get back in touch with my original, lovely, and pure sexuality and passion that I felt I had come into the world with. That often gets spoiled by society and religion. I discovered how much guilt and shame I had about sex, and I wanted to put something out there that celebrated women's sexuality. Especially back then, women didn't look at those movies and feel sexy. I wanted to create something that made them feel sexy and good about it.

Leilani

Former adult film actor, director, and writer, Howie Gordon, contributed the following introduction and two photographs to this next section in his dedication to the late adult film star, and dear friend of Candida Royalle and many others, Laurien Dominique. Dominique is lovingly remembered by her nickname, Leilani (aka Lailani), meaning "heavenly." Gordon recently completed writing his memoir titled *Hindsight*, a journal of his own experiences in the industry under the stage name Richard Pacheco.

> This image of Leilani (on page 253) is very flapperesque to me. It harkens back to the wild days of the Roaring twenties. There is a hardness in her face; a smoldering mistrust that bespeaks the difficult life of the farm girl who had come to the Big City to become a dancer or a showgirl and now already has been used and passed around by some bruising men. It's aged her. She's older than her face and beyond her own innocence. She could use the sense of humor of a Carole Lombard to arm herself for the struggle. She could use the kindness and affection of a true lover before ever being asked to surrender her body again. It was a random moment on a rooftop. It was young people playing tough. Using their sex, using their bodies just like the grownups that they would one day become." — Howie Gordon, Berkeley, 2011

In 1986, Femme released Royalle's most personal piece, *Three Daughters*. The erotic Harlequin romance feature set during spring break features Gloria Leonard in her final acting appearance as the mother of three daughters about to navigate their own sexuality. In a bittersweet tribute to her beloved best girlfriend who passed away tragically prior to the film's completion, Royalle dedicated *Three Daughters* to Laurien Dominque (listed in the credits as Lailani Detgen).

Candida agreed to share memories of Laurien for this chapter.

Laurien was like a sweet ethereal little beauty. She was a very bright, very smart, and gifted young girl. I met her when she came to San Francisco at the age of fifteen. She grew up as Laurie Ann Detgen in the mid-west. I think she was from Illinois and had a very sad home life. Her mother wasn't well. I think her mother ended up in a mental institution, although a lot of women ended up in that situation back then when they probably just needed some good therapy. Her father raised her and her brother until he remarried — it was kind of your typical nightmare situation where his new wife got pregnant with a child, and the two former kids were moved into the

Laurien Dominique. PHOTOGRAPHY BY HOWIE GORDON

basement. Who knows, maybe it was a nice, furnished basement, but from the stories Leilani told, they weren't treated well. That certainly was how she remembered it anyway. The fact that she was allowed to leave home at fifteen doesn't sound like they cared a whole lot about what happened to her. A lot of young kids like Leilani ended up in Haight-Ashbury. The streets were lined with beautiful old Victorian row houses, and there were flats that were inhabited by groups of kids who came to San Francisco from all over the states.

She lived in one down the block from where I shared a flat with a bunch of transplants from New York. Ours was an infamous, colorful house of artists and performers including Jorge Socarras, who performed under the name Jorge Havana and later went on to form the progressive rock group Indoor Life, and Joe Merlino who worked and performed under the name Joe Morocco. We had a lot of "orphans" pass through and Leilani became a beloved member of our "family". We were all orphans really, and although I was only about twenty-two years old myself, I became her big sister. We all took her under our wing and she began performing with us. She and I sang together, she would do the melody and I would do the harmony. We had these wonderful smoky voices that blended beautifully. We all performed together in avant-garde theatre groups created with some of the original Cockettes, like Scrumbly Koldewin, and Martin Worman, and Pristine Condition. One of the funniest groups Leilani and I were in was an all girls group called White Trash Boom Boom with Dolores [Delux] Deluce.

After my boyfriend, Danny Isley, who was a musician and one of the original Cockettes began performing in a few adult movies under the name Danny Leighton, Leilani decided to follow him into the business. I followed the two of them in to the business! It was a great way for all of us to make some money so we could continue to spend the majority of our time doing our art and free performances.

Leilani was a heavenly little beauty who believed in the existence of other realities and other worlds. Life was difficult for her. I think her happiest time was when she went to Hawaii and she came back with the name Leilani. She was always looking for a way out through science fiction, or experimentation with drugs. I guess we all were looking for ways to escape in those days. I think Leilani was never meant to be here for very long…and eventually, she found her way out.

I was living back in New York and I was married, and three years in to making movies for my studio Femme Productions. I had flown out to San Francisco to do the *Phil Donahue Show* when he was touring the country, and here I was being squired around in a limo and my husband and I went to see her and it was shocking. Her face was sunken in so that she looked like a much, much older woman and she was begging us to buy her a drink. This was after she had been warned by the doctor so it was clear to me that she didn't want to live. The contrast between where each of our lives had taken us felt sad and tragic to me, she had been so gifted and had had so much promise. She was all laughter and telling me, "Girlfriend, it's so good to see you."

Alcoholism killed Leilani, and malnourishment. She was so thin — she really didn't eat much and she ended up in the hospital with a distended liver. Her doctor had told her that if she continued to drink she was going to die. Leilani died from a brain embolism, which is essentially a stroke. She was twenty-nine but far older than her years. And I remember I came back to New York, and I was writing the script for *Three Daughters,* and the very last line

"Girlfriends," Leilani and Candida. PHOTOGRAPHY BY HOWIE GORDON

of the script is Heather, the lead, telling her best friend on the phone, "I'm going to miss you, girlfriend". That was my call out to Leilani. She died while I was writing the script and I dedicated *Three Daughters* to her. To this day, I can't watch the end of that movie without tearing up.

What I will always remember when I think of Leilani is a very delicate ethereal flower with a silky warm voice, translucent, green eyes, and a seductive smile that let you know she was in on the joke of life and only stopping by on her way to a far more magical place.

Deep Inside Porn Stars

I didn't grow up saying, "Oh, I want to be a porn star!" On the one hand, I thought there was nothing wrong with it. I was a part of a culture that was exploring sexuality wildly, and openly, but on the other hand, I know that if I'd had better self-esteem and more belief in my talents and abilities, I would never have gotten into adult movies. My parents left me in New York after my first year of college and moved to Florida so they could try and save their marriage — which, by the way, they never could. Feeling lost and disinterested after two and a half years of college, I moved to San Francisco, along with so many other young people from all over the country who were searching for their own identities while rejecting the rules we all experienced growing up. We rejected materialism, marriage, and all the other social structures we felt restricted people from truly enjoying life. We experimented with sex, and drugs, and many of my friends lost their young lives to too much of a good thing.

In hindsight, I came to believe that had my parents played a more active role in my life at that time, watching more carefully what I was up to, and insisting that I at least finish college before taking off for the other side of the country, I probably wouldn't have made those choices. In our culture, you don't make the decision to appear in adult movies without realizing on some level that you're closing a lot of doors behind you. It's not easy breaking a taboo. It's with you forever. Certainly, I've wondered about what my life would be like if I'd chosen something else. I excelled at what I did. I was supposed to be a fashion illustrator. It's a good thing I didn't. I don't think that there *are* fashion illustrators anymore! How could I not occasionally wonder what would life have been like if I'd chosen a less controversial career?

Just before I started Femme Productions, *Playgirl Magazine*, back when it was still taken a bit more seriously decided to do a piece on some of the top porn stars. The writer who was commissioned to do it brought five of us together. They set up an elaborate photo session where we were dressed up as Victorian ladies at tea and the article was called, "How to make a thousand dollars a day".

"Deep Inside Porn Stars," *Playgirl* Magazine.

It featured me and Veronica Hart, Kelly Nichols, Tiffany Clark, and Annie Sprinkle. Between the time that we each spent being interviewed and photographed, we all gave generously of our time. I recall the writer came over and spent all day talking to me, as I was right on the cusp of starting Femme Productions. I was in a good space — I was ready to trail-blaze. She got a lot of stuff out of me and out of all of us — we were all very interesting women with fascinating and unique stories to tell. Yet, when the article came out, it was focused almost entirely on Tiffany Clark who was probably, it would be safe to say, the least fortunate among us. She had a history of abuse and I don't mean to be cruel because she was a very sweet girl, but she fit all the stereotypes. It was clear that she was the focus because it made for sensational reading. Fair and balanced, it was not. I was furious and I wrote a scathing letter. It was not nice.

I would do it differently today, but I used to be very hot tem-pered. I hadn't yet learned how to temper my words. They did print part of [my letter]. During the interview she had asked for my advice on how to give a good blowjob, so in the letter I outed her for this, writing something to the effect of, "next time go see a sex therapist instead of wasting my time looking for free sex advice". Naturally, they printed that part! As disappointing as it was this was, it became the turning point at which the media and the culture started to perk up and pay attention to who we were, as women and as human beings.

The performance we did, "Deep inside Porn Stars," really blew the lid off. This was our legacy: do not categorize us in to the same old stereotypes: victim, whore, women without a future. We're far more complex than that. We have goals. We have college degrees and careers. We have families, husbands, and children. We have businesses and we own our own homes. You may be uncomfortable with that but that's who we are.

The Club 90 group was essentially born out of necessity when several friends gathered together to plan a baby shower for Veronica Hart in 1983, and began to open a dialogue about their association with the adult indus-try as women. Club 90 served as a haven whereby each member could air personal feelings, experiences, and grievances without the possibility of external judgment or condemnation. The women took a symbolic vow that all conversations would be strictly confidential. Through Femme Productions, Candida was able to encourage members of Club 90 to actively devise a new and different brand of pornography, personally designed to reflect individual dynamics, strengths, and capacities. All of the women in Club 90 have directed films under Femme's umbrella. "Deep inside Porn Stars" became an original theatrical piece that was the genesis of the collaboration between Club 90 and the feminist art group, Carnival Knowledge. Stage material was adopted from actual intimate conversations that had taken place within the group.

Adult movies are out there for all to see. You will be judged for it and people's opinions will definitely take into account what you've done for the rest of your life. I have friends who have made the choice to try and keep their porn careers a secret from their families, their future husbands, and it only ends in disaster. That's why when I made my choice to create Femme productions, it was a great way to embrace my name and everything I had done and just say, "You know what? I'm not going to run from it. I'm going to reclaim my name and recognition and do something I'm proud of with it." Back when I was an actress, the assumption was that women didn't get in to pornography unless they were hookers or victims of some form of abuse, or had no other options. No one wrote about us, no one talked about us, no one really thought about us. We were still seen as an enigma, as tragic and unfortunate. I would say that another thing I'm proud of in terms of a legacy is that we changed how women in the industry are viewed.

Head Held High

I've always hung around with interesting, creative people who have never been judgmental of me. I would say that about my men too. I've never picked abusive men. My father wasn't an easy man, he had his own set of problems, but he wasn't a physically abusive father. There are things that I'm not willing to share about my home life and my father that are deeply personal. I may talk about them in my own book one day.

I've sacrificed pieces of my life. I have very little relationship with the Italian side of my family any longer, a whole piece of my family that was a major part of my life when I was growing up. Before I left for San Francisco, I had already showed signs of becoming different. I had become a woman's libber and part of the hippie culture, which they didn't approve of so I didn't stay in touch with them once I left New York and lived in California for eight years. Italians don't forgive easily and I think they felt betrayed. They probably heard something about my lifestyle, which would have naturally been shocking for hard-working, middle-class Italians. When I came back to New York, except for a few, most of them were not comfortable or interested in reconnecting with me. It was actually mutual. I found I had little to say to them. While it sometimes makes me sad to think about the huge family I lost, I accept it as an unavoidable consequence of choosing to break the rules and live according to my own beliefs.

While certain members of her family distanced themselves once Candida's profession became known, other relatives were surprised to find out about their famous cousin after the *Playgirl* magazine piece was published. Several of Royalle's first cousins accepted her with open arms and no judgment, which became the beginning of an even closer relationship. Similarly, Candida and her sister have made their bond a priority.

My sister is my love. My sister is probably my greatest grounding force in my life at this point. I have the feeling she'd say the same thing about me even though she has a son. He's living his own life now and in terms of a grounding force, she relies on me for emotional support more than she would on her son. She was a single mom, so she doesn't have a husband to rely upon. She lives out in California so we don't see each other more than a couple of times a year but when we do, it's just precious. I love her dearly. We've had a lot of things we had to work through because of the complicated childhood that we shared. Even though we were close as little girls, it just seemed inevitable that when you have parents who had tremendous conflicts with each other and with their own lives, they often take it out on their kids and end up — not necessarily consciously — but they end up playing the kids off of one another. She acted out by having a life-long weight problem. She was a beautiful girl, but she would often take the position that I was the lucky one, and I was the pretty one, and I was thin, which of course, invalidated all of the things that I was going through. I wasn't allowed to have problems and feel sad and insecure. There was a lot of stuff to work through which we finally did in our thirties. We had some fierce confrontations and amazing breakthroughs because we chose, each of us, to work through our issues with one another because we knew we were all we had when it came to family. We were determined to have a good, loving relationship. One thing that helped was that we're very similar in terms of our political views — remarkably similar actually, and we're both very analytical. It's great. When we get together, it's somewhat like two peas in a pod. The older we've gotten, the closer we've gotten. We even sound alike and laugh alike — if we're both on the telephone, you can't tell who's who. It's kind of spooky. We've melded into one another. You know how people look like their pets. That's how we are!

My father was definitely a troubled man and I had to come to terms over the years that, in some ways, he bore a lot of responsibility for me going into the business. I came to understand that part of the reason I went in to the porn business was my need to feel loved by my father: the unrelenting search — in all the wrong places — for the good daddy. Once my sister and I reached puberty, he withdrew any affection for us. I believe he was afraid of his own feelings toward us. After my sister left home and my parents barely spoke to each other, and probably never touched each other, my father took a lot of his anger out on me by being highly critical and unsupportive of me as I began to formulate my own ideas, political and otherwise. For having such a sweet, pretty daughter who never got into any trouble and showed tremendous talents and gifts, he stopped showing any appreciation, rarely came to my dance performances, or spent any time with me.

I've had to redevelop my self-respect and I've had to look things right in the face and dig up all of the stuff that I felt uncertain about, and the stuff that was sort of niggling at me and making me feel like "Oooh, should I be ashamed of what I did?" I looked at it head on. I took out the worst and the scariest and ugliest things in my soul and looked them in the face and not just with the industry, but other mistakes I have made. You have to find a way to forgive yourself and understand yourself. Then you can move on.

In June 2012, Royalle's hometown New York City became the meeting place for the first official reunion in fifteen years of the Club 90 group. The women came from across the United States and beyond for a joyful celebration: a wedding union for one of their own, former porn actor and writer Veronica Vera. As it happened, I was in New York City with a girlfriend during the same weekend. Graciously, Candida extended the invitation to join her and a few friends on a small boat parked in the

marina located at the W. 79th St. boat basin in Manhattan. It was wonderful to finally meet in person after having spoken with Candida on a few
occasions over the past five years. Royalle is petite, bright, and lovely, like
precious shimmering light. She welcomed us into the fold as the group
passed around bread and cheese, cherries, grapes, sparkling water and
wine. It was a delight to be included in such rare and wonderful company.

Candida Royalle. PHOTOGRAPHY BY PEGGY GIROUX

I worry about all of the young women coming into the adult industry now, and not having the wherewithal to go into therapy. I'm sorry, you can't do something that's this controversial and taboo without having some conflict about it, and in some way, it stays with people for the rest of your life. Even though we know that there's nothing wrong with what we did, a lot of people are going to judge you for it. If I had the wherewithal and the inclination, I would start some kind of place for women to come and get counseling because they're going to need it. It's not as if I'd be telling them, "You're a sick person" or "you're a bad person". Just talk about it and make sure you're okay with it because it's the only way to stand up to people's judgments. You've got to have self-respect, self-love, and self-understanding.

8

Gloria Leonard
The Grand Damndest
of them All

Gloria Leonard is considered by her contemporaries as the highly esteemed "Grand Dame" of the golden era of erotic films. Now in her seventy-second year, Gloria still possesses razor sharp wit, intimidating intelligence, beauty and savvy. Leonard's verbal dissertation about her life, career, and the world around her is often delivered with delicious, acerbic humor that would make Leonard's teenage mentor, comedian and satirist, Lenny Bruce, smile in his grave.

As the youngest of four children, the New York native was just five when her siblings all left the family roost. During her elementary and high school years, Leonard excelled at her studies, but was prone to haunting jazz clubs or hanging with pals at the Mosholu Parkway across the road from her school. Some of those in her eclectic group of comrades went on to become famous personalities in the television, film, and fashion worlds.

Bored with the college scene after a short stint, Gloria decided to put her writing skills into effect and landed jobs with various PR agencies in New York. One of her roles was comprised of composing liner notes for Elektra Records when they were still a start-up company. Leonard's adept work aptitude afforded her several employment opportunities outside of the Big Apple as well. In the 1970s, she served as assistant production manager for a small film company based in Puerto Rico. Eventually, she returned to New York where she graduated to Wall Street for a short term as a registered rep for a brokerage firm.

Disillusionment with high finance in the mid-seventies, along with the realities of single parenthood, brought about a new direction in

"I am somebody who was at the forefront of what was considered as a rebellious and radical industry that is now quite commonplace. I feel we championed free speech and freedom for people to do what they want and to watch what they want." GLORIA LEONARD

PHOTOGRAPHY BY KENNETH BREWSTER

Leonard's professional life when she applied for a production job on a Radley Metzger (Henri Paris) film and wound up cast as a supporting character in *The Opening of Misty Beethoven* (1975). The exceptional feature, nourished by Leonard's debut performance became one of the most highly touted films of the adult genus. Gloria is one of the first X-rated stars to have achieved international stardom when she filmed multiple features in France in the late 1970s.

Since her start in adult pictures, Leonard has been lauded as an ardent advocate for First Amendment rights. She has gone toe to toe with fervent, anti-porn feminists such as Andrea Dworkin, and participated in lively public debates during guest appearances at colleges and universities across the United States. Leonard's diverse credits, apart from acting and directing, include publisher of *High Society* magazine for fourteen years. In 1983, she developed the concept for phone sex lines and won a Supreme Court ruling over the controversy of the lines on behalf of *High Society*. The bonafide powerhouse, who also served as President of the Free Speech Coalition for two terms, has literally received every accolade possible in the erotic entertainment genre.

In contrast to her past, Gloria lives a quiet lifestyle today and recently returned to Hawaii after spending a couple of years in Florida. She remains close to her daughter and granddaughter, and continues her weekly e-mail communication with her pals in Club 90.

I spoke with Gloria Leonard in March of 2010.

Earth Angel

I grew up in The Bronx in a very normal — for that time — environment. I am a first generation American, both of my parents came from Europe. My father was self-made. We lived at a time before cell phones, GPS, and internet. Ours was the kind of neighborhood where you would leave in the morning and play all day with your friends, and come home in time for dinner. No one ever looked over her shoulder with any kind of fear. It was a very innocent time.

I was a very good student; I think I was about an "A" student. Other than starting to smoke at fifteen — that was the most dastardly of any deeds that would be considered a bad girl kind of thing — of course sneaking a lipstick tube under my jacket and then taking it off when I came back home — it was definitely another time.

It's interesting; somebody just sent me a link [Google maps] that enables you to find any address with 360-degree photos, so I actually was able to look at the building that I spent the first eighteen years of my life. I even found my bedroom window. It's totally awesome. I hit two or three other places I've lived too and it's kind of sentimental.

Although I had three siblings, I was a change-of-life baby. I don't know if that term is still applicable today. My mother was well into her forties when I was born at a time when that was considered very scandalous as opposed to now a days where it's sort of chic and divine to have a child in your forties. As a result, although I had siblings, by the time I was five they were all married and gone and out of the house. My two sisters were not in my life once they moved out and started their own families; they sort of forgot about having a kid sister. Any role models that I had were made up in my mind because there wasn't a specific person I can honestly tell you that was anything of a mentor deliberate or otherwise. I just sort of floated around. I was in a state of inertia for a couple of years.

My father was a very cold, sort of impervious guy who made no bones about letting me and everybody else know that he was pissed-off about having to be a father all over again, and regrettably, would often introduce me as his mistake. My mom was far more sensitive and motherly, but I think they were just weary, at that point, of raising children. You have to bear in mind that I became a teenager in the 1950s when everything in society was changing. You know, rock and roll music, and hairstyles and clothing styles, and my parents were hard pressed to understand all of the dynamics that were going on in the world. Why I wasn't the doting daughter — my other two sisters married the first guys they dated and went off and had children. I knew that was not going to be my fate, at least not immediately.

As a young teenager, we used to hang out; it was like a living room. We called it "The Parkway" which was actually Mosholu Parkway in The Bronx. It was right across from our school which was Junior High School 80 — I don't know what it's called now. We'd go and do our homework, have some dinner and dash back out there. Many years later, there was a piece in *New York Magazine* about us and it was called "The Parkway All-Stars". It seems to have produced this gaggle of over-achievers. For example, I went to school with Robert Klein. Gary and Penny Marshall were part of the crowd. My friend, Herb Nanas, went on to Hollywood and became the manager to Sylvester Stallone, Rosanne Barr, Gary Busey and Albert Brooks. Interestingly enough, two of America's leading fashion designers also came from our neighborhood. One was Calvin Klein and the other one became Ralph Lauren, but I knew him when he was Ralph Lifshitz.

The June 1982 *New York Magazine* article titled "The Parkway All-Stars Come Home" commemorated the reunion of approximately fifteen hundred members (many had grown up between the 1920s and fifties decades) of the clan, several of whom had gone on to become newsworthy public figures. On May 30, 1982, Gloria Leonard stepped out of a limousine flanked by a group of centerfold girls passing around matchbooks and visors bearing the name *High Society*, the erotic news and pictorial magazine Leonard published. Along with her comrades, Gloria clamored to purchase one of the "I love Mosholu Parkway" t-shirts that were sold to reunion attendees. According to the *New York Magazine* piece, in the 1950s, Leonard was one of a tough gaggle of girlfriends named "Earth Angels" branded after the song "Earth Angel," recorded by The Penguins in 1954. The girls were identified by their matching club jackets and pedal pushers.

I think we were extremely funny, bright, and inquisitive, and I think there was some kind of magical dust in the air that sort of imbued us with this knowledge that we were at the crest of a kind of a turning point, in terms of not following in the footsteps of our parents.

Fortune Smiles on the Brave

I was a huge jazz buff even long before rock 'n roll became rock 'n roll. I was underage, but I would lie to my parents and tell them that I was going to the Night Centre at the local school, and instead I would jump on the "D" train and get off at 52nd street and I haunted all of the old jazz clubs. I have the distinction of having seen people like Billy Holliday, Charlie Parker, and Stan Getz. There was no carding in those days and because I was tall, no one ever questioned my age. I was pretty much a jazz-nick who fell into the likes of Lenny Bruce. In fact, if ever there was a mentor that could be considered such, as far as I'm concerned, it would be Lenny Bruce.

I literally was a groupie. I followed him from gig to gig, essentially, because he was so honest. Bruce verbalized all of the shit that people talked about or whispered about, but didn't have the balls to openly discuss. Of course, the thing that went off in my mind was, "Wow, here's a guy who really thinks a lot like I do, and has the chutzpah to get out there and talk about it." Aside from him being a so-called comic, he really was more of a philosopher as far as I was concerned. I wrote and produced a film for Candida for her Femme line and I dedicated it to Lenny Bruce. The name of the film that I directed for her was called *Fortune Smiles* (1988). To this day, it is lauded, according to Candida, by some very highly respected, influential groups of people including the American Society of Educators and Therapists, heads of Universities and psychologists. The piece that I did, in particular, seems to have stood the test of time. I'd say it was a couple of years into her Femme line. Candida gave each of us an opportunity to write and direct a film for Femme Productions.

Fortune Smiles, directed and presented by Leonard, appeared in the 1988 Femme video production *Sensual Escape* in which Gloria guides the audience through the tribulations of a young dating couple about to embark on an impassioned journey together toward carnal heights. Nina Hartley and award-winning actor Richard Pacheco (in his first comeback appearance in adult films) are featured in the principal roles.

Anyway, after finishing school I stayed with my sister who had five children for a while on the west coast before I got a job and lived in my own apartment. I was off on my own at a very young age, at least for that time. I was also a virgin until I was eighteen and a half which, by today's standards, I guess, would be middle age. I really did not like L.A., although this was the late 1950s. Coming from Manhattan and New York City where you could jump on a bus, or a taxi, or a subway, the requirement of having to drive miles to get anywhere was really a turn-off and I returned to New York probably about a year and a half later. I attended college for one semester and was thoroughly bored. I felt that I knew more than the other students did and I bailed on that whole deal. I enjoyed being in the workplace. I was a decent writer, and subsequently, wound up working for a couple of different PR firms in New York where my writing skills were put to good use in the form of press releases and writing liner notes. I worked for a small record company. This was at the very beginning when they were on 14th Street and they had about a thousand square feet. It was really the beginning of the beginning.

In addition to wanting to write, I thought I might, if things went my way, consider modeling or acting — I'm 5'9". That was pretty much it. I had a number of office jobs which included the ability to be creative in terms of writing skills, and I had some very funny accounts that I wrote about that, of course, sometimes made big news. For example, during one of my PR jobs, one of our clients was a place in Upstate New York called Black Watch Farms. Their claim to fame was that they produced and sired prize-winning Aberdeen Angus cattle. It turned out that this one bull named Lindirtis Evulse had been purchased for about a million dollars and had been underwritten by Lloyds of London. Poor old Lindirtis couldn't get it up. He was taken to the University of Alabama, somewhere in the south, where a team of surgeons tried to correct his problem. Amusingly, that year, *Esquire* magazine–they used to do an edition once a year called "Dubious Achievements Awards" and Lindirtis made the cover. That experience was one of a number of different clients that made the job fun.

Leonard's personal achievements are anything but dubious. In addition to being on the ground floor of the now famous Elektra Entertainment Group (founded in 1950 as Elektra Records) where she had been employed as a copywriter, Gloria apparently also worked for Johnny Carson's publicist, and later, kept in step with the big boys on Wall Street.

Many years later in the 1960s, I worked for a brokerage firm. At that time, I was the only female at a brokerage place with about forty guys. Ultimately, I got my certificate to be a registered rep and handled several transactions myself. I was there for about two or three years. I wasn't crazy about it because everything that you do down there and every sentence that you speak, is about dollars and money. I found it very unfulfilling to talk about dollars all of the time, especially when they weren't mine! It was very dry.

I had lived in Puerto Rico for a couple of years and I had a job as the assistant production manager for a small film company called United Hemisphere Productions, in San Juan. They actually had the plum contract of Hunt-Wesson where they did the TV commercials for Hunt-Wesson products. They'd take the commercials that were filmed in America, use a Spanish speaking cast and reshoot them. We also did a feature film, the name of which eludes me. It was my responsibility as an assistant production manager when we were shooting day for night, to make sure the streetlights were on, and that lunch was there, and a lot of little jillions of details. When I came back to New York, essentially, I was hoping to get a job in a similar situation. However, it didn't happen that way so I resorted to my secretarial skills and did a nine-to-five thing working for a large accounting firm which, of course, has now been shut down in shame. That was the Arthur Anderson Company.

Arthur Anderson Company, based in Chicago and formerly one of five prestigious American accounting firms, received a guilty conviction for offenses relating to the auditing of Enron, the Texas energy corporation charged with overinflating the company's success and assets by falsifying financial records. Enron was unsuccessful it its efforts to file for bankruptcy in 2001. Although the guilty conviction was later overturned by the Supreme Court of the United States, Arthur Anderson LLP currently maintains a low profile and functions as a shadow of its former self due to the scandal that tarnished the company's reputation.

It was during the time that I was holding these office jobs that I became aware of the adult business — in and around 1974-1975. By that time, I was in my thirties, hardly a time when one considers becoming a sex symbol.

I've been married three times. I've outlived two of the three and I don't know anything about where the third one is. I had a teenage daughter who was about thirteen or so when I got into the business. I learned that in a couple of hours I could earn what it took me more than a week to earn sitting behind a desk. I actually went up for a job thinking I would get a job in production, and it was Radley Metzger — nom du porn, Henry Paris who made *The Opening of Misty Beethoven* (1975) which is still considered a classic in that genre. Being a bit of a Svengali that he is, instead of working on the film, I ended up being in the film which was my first film.

The Opening of Misty Beethoven

Leonard's database reveals that one year prior to her reputable appearance in *The Opening of Misty Beethoven* she was part of an ensemble cast in a movie titled *Executive Secretary* (1974). In conjunction with *The Opening of Misty Beethoven*, Metzger's earlier film, *The Private Afternoons of Pamela Mann* (1974) starring Barbara Bourbon, is also deemed one of his most triumphant hardcore motion pictures.

> Jamie Gillis is the one who got me connected to Radley. I did one or two loops and I met Jamie on the set, and somehow, unbeknownst to me, he had told Radley about me. Recently, after Jamie died, I spoke to Radley and we were commiserating about Jamie. I learned that the reason Jamie recommended me is because apparently, he had a girlfriend at the time that was supposedly committed to the role that I wound up doing but pooped out. She backed out of it at the last minute and I guess Radley said to Jamie, "You'd better find somebody else."

The Opening of Misty Beethoven is the porn adaptation of the George Bernard Shaw play *Pygmalion* starring Jamie Gillis as Dr. Seymour Love, a sexologist who grooms a young hooker Misty Beethoven (Constance Money), into a sex-pert. Commissioned by Dr. Love to transform males with sexual shortcomings into super-studs, Misty's ultimate conquest is put to the test when she comes between Dr. Love's two friends (Gloria Leonard and Ras Kean) in a ménage a trois, taking full charge in her provision of sexual gratification for the couple manifested in dominant-submissive fashion. With confidence, Ms. Beethoven is successful in all of the challenges on her list creating a sensation across Europe which increases Dr. Love's bankability in his field. The young protégé recognizes Dr. Love is empowered by her triumphs, and soon realizes that her role in his success is negated and even mocked by him. Misty tricks Love into engaging in sex with her, and suddenly, the redistribution of power is turned over to Beethoven. Misty is elevated to teacher status while Love is relegated to the dunce chair bound in leather and handcuffs.

Allegedly set in Paris, Rome, and New York City, with its wry tone and clever script, this excellent Radley Metzger feature's original musical score was composed by Elephant's Memory band, the same group that had backed John Lennon on his first few solo records in the early 1970s. Defined by its expansive locations, sizeable production values, and solid acting turns by Gillis, Money, and Leonard (a standout supporting role in her first official feature), not surprisingly, *The Opening of Misty Beethoven* received high praise and accolades at the time of its 1976 release winning Best Actor (Jamie Gillis), Best Director, and Best Picture awards by the AFAA (Adult Film Association of America). *The Opening of Misty Beethoven* is also one of the first films to be inducted into the XRCO Hall of Fame. Standing the test of time, the picture continues to trump most of the other classic adult productions in every category. In 2004, a remake was released, *Misty Beethoven: The Musical,* directed by Jane Hamilton. Video-X-Pix has plans to restore the original picture to near high definition quality for Blu Ray in 2012.

> *Misty Beethoven* is funny, it's risqué; it's witty. Radley was just a brilliant filmmaker and we shot it at a very professional sound stage. Shooting *Misty Beethoven* was also very difficult because I was really naïve. I didn't know what the protocol is for behavior on a porn set. In the beginning, I was more concerned with, "Do I look fat? Are my stretch marks showing? Are my feet dirty?" that sort of thing, instead of throwing myself into the work, and especially being thrown in the midst of women ten years my junior. I had a child — they didn't. Juliet Anderson had started shortly before I did, but she wasn't a mom either.

Indeed, Leonard was a seasoned thirty-five year old woman when she accepted the opportunity to appear in the highbrow pornographic film, and was assigned a meaty role. Suffice to say, her maturity was an asset rather than a deterrent. As a single parent who believed in the virtue of honesty, Gloria had conferred with her teenage daughter before proceeding forward with the standing offer.

> I actually discussed my decision to work in adult films with my daughter prior to doing it. I explained that just the way there are movies with comedy, and with action, and horror movies, there are also movies with sex. I told her that I was contemplating performing in one and she was very supportive and encouraging. Occasionally, a few years down the line there would be somebody at school who would make some sort of an unpleasant comment to her, but she was tough, she let it roll. She, of course, enjoyed the perks and the benefits. We got to travel and not have to struggle as much. You must remember too, that I have never received a dime in child

support. If I didn't work, we didn't eat. So yes, I was motivated by the profit, but I was also motivated by it as sort of a political statement because I was so anti-censorship. I thought this was a good spit-in-the-eye to all of the tight-assed people.

I thought that everybody operated the way that Radley had. Unfortunately, I came to learn down the line that a lot of them were just schlockmeisters. The whole idea of film requires a great deal of skill. You need a lighting person, you need a decent camera operator, you need a sound person; you need wardrobe and so on. In my opinion, the advent of video spiraled the quality of adult material down the tube because every putz with a video camera can be a producer. The overall experience of having worked on the set of a sex film is dependent upon the cast, crew, and the people calling the shots. In many instances, the whole is often greater than the sum of the parts.

You could work on one film and have a good feeling that it was really going to be worthwhile. There were films that were hard conditions with schlocky guys. One of whom had a penchant for jumping into a sex scene when a guy was losing his hard-on. They would just shoot the penetration part and you'd always recognize him because he had a freckle on the side of his dick. It was Leonard Kirtman. I don't know if that was his nom de porn, but I think so; there was an individual who used the name "Carter Stevens" who was another schlocky guy. He's probably living off the blood of young girls.

I liked working with John Leslie, Tom Byron, Rob Everett [Eric Edwards], Richard Bolla [Robert Kerman], and Paul Thomas. One of the other guys whom I liked working with and he's passed on, is Bobby Astyr, an anagram for "Satyr". He was very short, and for comedic value often times directors would pair me up with him because he was short and I was so tall. My favorite joke then was, "He's so short that I'm the kind of girl he has to go up on." He was very sweet, and it was very sad when he died.

French Kissing

From 1975 and into the years that followed, Leonard continued to solidify her omnipresent position in the erotic motion picture business. In 1978, she co-directed her first solo effort along with director Joe Sarno who generally gave recognition to the star of the picture. *All About Gloria*

Leonard showcased the stunning brunette as a sex columnist about to launch her own magazine while reminiscing about past sexual highlights with several lovers. With a *Mary Tyler Moore* inspired theme song, the storyline purports to be based upon Leonard's own memoirs and personal experiences in bed. At the outset, *All About Gloria Leonard* establishes Gloria as one busy lady. Appearing in seven of nine sequences, her sexual activities range from seducing the office boy Horace (nicknamed, "Horse" for good reason) to pretending to be a call girl so she can find out what it's like to be paid for sexual favors. An inventive *ménage a trios*/sausage fest sequence is also incorporated into the story: Gloria surprises three gangsters (featuring R. Bolla) playing craps in the alley and supplies the men with royal oral treatment. The final scene of the film contains porn impresarios Jamie Gillis and Marc Stevens uniquely portraying themselves as porn stars. First, Leonard interviews the two men for her magazine. After making an inquiry as to who is the superior stud, Gloria finds out for herself and participates in a double penetration scenario (generally, in the 1970s "double penetration" implied vaginal and anal penetration simultaneously with two male partners, while the modern definition of the term describes two penises in one orifice) in her only anal scene. Leonard's eventual second husband, Bobby Hollander, is also in one of the montages making love to a young redhead with a well formed behind while Gloria gets turned on as a voyeur. Leggy Leonard easily carries *All About Gloria Leonard* with style, smarts, and charisma in this special screening experience.

In the fall of 1978, after being temporarily laid up with minor surgery, Leonard was hired to co-star with John Holmes in a trio of pictures directed by Carlos DeSantos scheduled to be filmed in France. Up until that point, very few adult movies were equipped with production budgets bulky enough to shoot internationally. The two leading stars, Leonard and Holmes, had not crossed paths prior to the France shoot because of their living on opposite coasts. The first two features *Extreme Close-Up* (1979) and the 1981 release *Johnny Does Paris* were filmed in Paris during the beginning of their sojourn, prior to traveling to an extravagant Chateau situated on the coast of Brittany where the cast and crew wrapped up with *La Belle et le Bête* (unreleased).

The first time that John Holmes and I actually met was when we got to France in the late 1970s to shoot three films. We shot the first week to ten days in Paris, and then we moved to this fabulous 16th Century Chateau on the North West coast of France in

Brittany, in a little town called Quimper which is spelled Q-u-i-m-p-e-r. Of course, John being the hillbilly that he was pronounced it "Kwimper." He would have his diva moments and I told him that the set wasn't big enough for two prima donnas. You know, for the most part, once you got to know him he was gentle and he was sweet, but he also could be very isolated and kind of sketchy. He drank quite a bit when we were on location. Scotch, I think, was his beverage of choice.

We got out to this beautiful 16th Century Chateau and we were not only shooting there but we were also staying there. I think it also did double duty as a hotel at some point. It was magnificent and everything was winding and stone stairwells and very impressive. The film was partially financed by the French government. There was some kind of a system back in those days that you could make a film in France, and if you utilized at least half of the cast and crew who were native French people, the government would underwrite a portion of the effort. We got out to the Chateau and about the second or third day of shooting one of the French girls came down with the clap. The producer sat down and tried to figure out all of the possible cross-contamination of crew sleeping with actresses and so on. It turned out that about twenty of us were possibly at risk. They found an old country doctor, and so as not to cause too much of a scene, we went in discreet little clusters of threes and fours to the doctor. In France, they don't inject you with anything, but they give you the medicine and the hypodermic needle, and you're left to your own devices through a pharmacy or a nurse to actually inject it. John, being the fabulous bullshit artist that he was told us that he had at one time worked as an attendant on an ambulance. It's hard to separate the wheat from the chaff.

Holmes had actually worked as an ambulance driver as a young newlywed in the mid-1960s while posing for nude photo layouts and participating in related adult work.

John volunteered to do the injections so there I am in this grandiose bedroom with a fireplace. I'm on the bed, and I'm lying there with my ass in the air and he's about to inject me. I'm thinking to myself, "this could be the only case in history where the man who possibly infected me with the disease is also injecting me with the cure." It was funny. You know, I have a box here of cards and letters that he had written to me over the years. He also sent me a gorgeous, fluted, silver drinking straw that is stamped Tiffany and Co. which of course, related to the use of cocaine back in those days. He sent me all of the pictures he had taken of both of us. Later, he wound up robbing my house. He didn't leave anything worth more than two dollars. He even took the toaster! I never saw him again and shortly after that was the Wonderland murders.

A couple of years after France, Gloria married late adult film director Bobby Hollander and re-located to Southern California. She and John rekindled their friendship at a time when Holmes had become heavily involved in crack cocaine. One day after John generously shared some freebase with Gloria, Hollander, and a female friend in Gloria and Hollander's Los Angeles home, an eyewitness claimed that someone fitting Holmes's description was allegedly seen driving a van away from the residence after it had been burglarized.

When I was with *High Society* Magazine, John had agreed to do a pictorial layout with just the two of us because we had never done anything like that. We were at the photographer's studio and he would hide in the dressing room. We couldn't get him the fuck out of there. He'd be in there for an hour or two at a time, and when he did come out, all of his cuticles were bleeding from probably chewing them or cutting them. He was so wired, you know.

High Society Feminism

According to Leonard's filmography, it would appear she made over forty films not including non-sex roles. Due to the profusion of films and loops turned out during Gloria's years in the business not to mention the fact that the content was illegal, at a certain point, it would be difficult to track the number of scenes, films, and titles. Therefore, it is understandable many former performers wouldn't have an accurate recollection of their own data.

I was in the business from 1975-76 until the early 1980s. I really only made about thirty films, but because they sliced and diced so much, there are many compilations out there. I don't know how many there are, and then, there were quite a few I did that were non-sex roles. They needed somebody who could actually act. Back in the day acting was actually a certain criteria. You know, it's funny, some girls like me at the time, loved the dialogue. You can give me somebody else's also; I didn't care. Whereas, somebody like Annie [Sprinkle] was terrified of speaking. Give her all the sex in the world to do and she was fine, but if she had to speak a line, she was just frozen.

I never ever perceived my work as being exploited. Nobody ever held a gun to my head to do these movies. This was all a matter of our own free will and choice. Contrary to the stereotypical perceptions out there, nobody was ever drugged and dragged off of the streets. The only person whom I ever hated was Linda Lovelace because even in her book (*Ordeal*, 1980), and when she spoke publicly, she would always bring up the fact that a gun was held to her head when they were making *Deep Throat* (1972). What she would neglect to include was that the gun was not held by anybody involved with the actual production, rather than by her boyfriend [Chuck Traynor], a lousy choice in men that she made. That always pissed me off that she wasn't totally forthcoming about the circumstances. Marilyn Chambers was a very honest gal, whereas Linda adopted this kind of "I'm a victim," and "poor me," and wound up having all of these hardcore, humorless feminists supporting her.

Marked with potent intellect and a natural predilection for politics, Leonard discovered she was in her element as an educator staunchly opposed to censorship. Gloria firmly believed in defending an individual's right to decide what is best for her or his own body.

I earned quite a good living by the way specifically in the eighties, literally speaking at dozens of colleges and universities very often debating the so-called, "feminists". My thinking was if the bottom line of the feminist movement is for women to be able to choose whatever they want to do without any repercussions, well, shit, that's what I'm doing. You should be cheering me on, not wagging your fingers at me.

Leonard's speaking engagements were not limited to the college and university circuit. On several occasions, she was a special guest on trendy television talk shows of the 1980s with illustrious hosts: Larry King, Oprah Winfrey, Geraldo Rivera, and Maury Povich. Not to be outdone by his competition, Gloria was invited to spar with the popular self-proclaimed "King of all media," shock jock radio host, Howard Stern. No matter where or what the venue, Leonard was prepared to present her case astutely and articulately, often leaving her adversaries in the dust. Most significantly, Gloria Leonard was instrumental in fostering change and encouraging naysayers to think outside of the box.

Sometimes it would start out where the female contingent would be opposed to me, but in the long run, at the end I always garnered more positive feedback than negative. People would come over and talk to me, and say, "You know you really changed the way I think." I would always inject a little levity. I was a very good speaker and could string more than two sentences together. Then, of course, at some point, lesbians started producing very hardcore pornography, at which time, feminists would have no basis for their argument any longer because they were turning out stuff equally the same in content that the men were doing. I'm a chartered member of a group called Feminists for Free Expression and I've been acknowledged by the American Film Institute at an event called Women in Film.

The mandate for Feminists for Free Expression (FFE) an organization founded in 1992, is to ensure individuals have a right to view, hear, and produce material of their choosing freely and without censorship or interference from the state "for her own protection." Presently, Candida Royalle and retired porn actor Veronica Vera are on the Board of Directors of FFE. Before the birth of the 1980s "sex-positive" feminist movement, early pioneers such as American sex educator, artist, and author of *Sex For One,* Betty Dobson, referred to the sexual enlightenment of both genders as the "pro-sex" feminist movement and has been an inspirational influence and role model for women and like-minded thinkers. Dobson embraces sexuality in its most basic form and views the politicization of sex as negative, sexless, and a restriction of the act itself.

As a member of FFE, Leonard's speaking appointments often overlapped with her primary function as publisher of *High Society* magazine.

I was with *High Society* for fourteen years. I was the publisher of *High Society.* I didn't really transition into the position, the transition came along when I was still doing films and I continued doing films while I was at *High Society.* Not many, but a few. I wasn't just a figurehead. I would go out on the road and meet with wholesale agencies to try to get better placement on the racks. I oversaw almost all of the centerfold shoots and I wrote the lion's share of copy and a column. I was really a working publisher. They got far more for their money than I'm sure they anticipated. That's another situation where I got dumped with no severance, no bonus — because I was a schmuck who didn't have anything in writing to cover my ass. It was all on a hand shake, and after fourteen years, they felt that they needed somebody younger. Carl Ruderman, the guy who owned the magazine, was a major prick.

While on Leonard's watch as its publisher, *High Society* was one of the preeminent selling magazines in the adult emporium and is reputed

for publishing naked photos of "A" ranked Hollywood celebrities such as Barbara Streisand, Ann Margaret, and Margot Kidder — all of whom attempted to sue the magazine. Never one to refrain from turning it up a notch, in 1983, Gloria created the concept of telephone sex lines and in joining forces with *High Society*, won a controversial case pertaining to the sex lines before the Supreme Court.

Leonard ended her career as a performer in 1984, but continued on a remarkable pace in her professional life. She and Bobby Hollander divorced, and not surprisingly, Gloria found the time to host two television programs: *The Leonard Report: For Adults Only*, and *Gloria Leonard's Hot Shopper Hour*. Leonard effectively fulfilled every conceivable capacity one could achieve as a woman and an individualist. Gloria was the female personification of the Free Speech Movement and First Amendment Rights. If that wasn't enough, Leonard decidedly took on another major position with the Adult Film Association of America (AFAA).

I have been the head of three different organizations whose incarnations changed as the sex industry changed. My appointment as Administrative Director of the Adult Film Association came later [from 1989-1992]. I was President of the Adult Film Association of America which then morphed into the Adult Film and Video Association of America, which subsequently was supplanted by Adult Video Association. Then, and finally, the association transformed into the Free Speech Coalition of which I served two terms as President. I gave it up in the early part of the nineties.

Bill Margold, a long time friend of Leonard's and former director of the volatile Free Speech Coalition has often debated with the organization over various contentious issues. Margold is a firm proponent of increasing the current legal working age for a sex performer from eighteen to twenty-one. One of his signature quotes precisely addressed the hypocrisy surrounding censorship (or "common-sense-or-ship" as Margold referred to it) that is typical of the Ratings Board: "If you cut a tit off, you'll get an 'R' Rating. If you kiss it, you'll get an "X"" To this day Leonard continues to reap respect and adulation from industry friends such as Margold.

I hear from Bill Margold occasionally. We e-mail each other every so often. He calls me "Mommy". He's a bear. I saved his can a couple of times, too. The Free Speech Coalition wanted to dump him and I wouldn't hear of it.

Smoke and Mirrors

"The difference between erotica and
pornography is the lighting." GLORIA LEONARD

After exhibiting proficiency in all opportunities presented in the erotic-oriented business and reaching beyond the borders of the industry as an advisor rethinking the women's movement in innovative and unrestricted ways, Gloria has earned the right to observe and analyze the meaning and implications of the legacy she and her relatively small group of fellow renegades left behind.

We were lucky in our generation. The downside of that however, was back in the day when you made a film, it showed for a week or two at some theater and then, boom, it was gone and the next one came in. No one anticipated the advent of VCRs and DVDs and the internet. We really got fucked all the way around literally, and figuratively, in terms of finance. We had no coverage, no medical and no union. In fact, for a brief period there was some kind of attempt by some of the performers to try to organize a union. It was very quickly shutdown by the powers that be. As far as careers go and travel, I've been somewhat adventurous and was willing to try lots of different things. I've lived in a number of places, having been born and raised in New York City. I've lived in Hawaii, I've lived in California, I've lived in Puerto Rico; I'm now living in Florida.

Working in the adult industry has given me an opportunity to meet people that I would otherwise never have met. It's given me an opportunity to travel to places that otherwise I might never have had the opportunity to visit. It has given me a platform from which to espouse my political views. Bearing in mind that here I was raising a child single-handedly without benefit of child support or anything else — working my tail off to put a roof over our heads and food on the table — this was before the term "Women's Lib" ever existed, I was doing this.

When we were in films, you had a day rate, you got paid and it didn't matter if you had one sex scene or three sex scenes, you were expected to perform for a flat rate. You could always ask up front for more money and if you weren't happy with it, bye-bye.

However, nowadays, the pay system is by the scene. To me it's like video prostitution — it's like being paid by the hour. It's a whole other world.

Nowadays, pornographic material is so readily available and so common on the internet and on DVDs and pay per view, and on cell phones, that it has become an integral part of the cultural landscape that people accept and are not nearly as shocked by anymore. I don't know if society has become desensitized, but they've become more accepting of it as a form of entertainment. Everybody has a sex life. Whether you choose to be celibate or not, you are a sexual being, regardless.

I am somebody who was at the forefront of what was considered as a rebellious and radical industry that is now quite commonplace. I feel that we championed free speech and freedom for people to do what they want and to watch what they want. There is some material out there that is somewhat reprehensible and that I take issue with; nevertheless, it is still covered by the First Amendment.

I think, essentially, you really need to have your head screwed on real well before committing to this business. Once your image is committed to either film or video, it's forever honey. There's no going back and erasing it. I don't think we went into this with the idea that we'd become tough. That's the reality of it all. Unless you're prepared to deal with the fall-out and any repercussions, don't do it. I think that by and large, the women that you are dealing with from the so-called golden age are succinct about expressing their experiences and the aftermath, and they know what's what. Without stereotyping or generalizing, I don't think that the girls who are presently in the business have any grasp of the topics that we've covered here today.

You know, I'm on all of the quotation sites and this is what I'd said: "The difference between erotica and pornography is the lighting." It's attributed to me and I used it once in an interview several years ago, and somehow it got plucked from there. I'm in between George Bernard Shaw and Albert Einstein. It's really true because dim lighting, or some kind of coverage where you think you're seeing something, but then, you're not really sure and then you bump it up a couple of "F" stops and it's the same thing in a harsh light — it's suddenly pornography. Film has a depth of field that is totally different from the flatness of video.

Feminists opposed to the existence of pornography as a form of entertainment at the expense of the alleged exploitation of women, have also expressed opinions about the differences between pornography and erotica — women Leonard faced off against when she was still a participant in the adult business as its unofficial spokesperson. Feminist, activist, and journalist Gloria Steinem once wrote, "Pornography is about dominance.

Erotica is about mutuality." Apart from the flawed observation that (all) pornography is tantamount to dominance, Steinem's statement causes one to question whether "erotica" can also be about dominance between consenting partners. The late feminist Andrea Dworkin's definition blurred the two terms: "Erotica is simply high class pornography; better produced; better conceived; better executed; better packaged; designed for a better class of consumer."

Perhaps a more precise description of the term "pornography" is a quote derived from the Hollywood film *First Monday in October* (1981) in which Walter Matthau's character Justice Dan Snow said "One man's pornography is another man's poetry." In short, the absolute definition of the word "pornography" is rather ambiguous and specific to any given individual and her/his own personal interpretation.

Back in days of film, my barometer used to be if you removed all of the hardcore sex scenes, would you still have something worth watching. A lot of the old films, you'd have something worth watching. It's kind of ironic, the very first adult material was what they called "stag" films and they were shot on eight millimeter and there was usually no sound and it would make the rounds every Friday night at some dude's house who had a projector. Here we are, flash forward, where technology has amped up and anything is possible, but the content is, in my opinion, back to square one. It's just gratuitous sex for no rhyme or reason. You know it's interesting, you see all of these so-called Hollywood starlets whether it's Paris Hilton or Kim Kardashian, and John Edwards who all had or have videos out there of themselves having sex, and for some reason it doesn't seem to impugn upon their existence or their profile. They're still considered the same as ever. There isn't that dastardly, "Oh horrors. What did you do?" It's very much a part of the cultural landscape.

It was interesting when I did the college talks, particularly seeing the responses from people who were so adamantly opposed to it, afterwards being softened by it having a human face. I applaud you for taking on a topic that in many circles is frowned upon.

"Gloria Leonard is not just a Porn Star" JAMIE GILLIS

Along with William Margold, Gloria Leonard was inducted in cement into the Hustler Hall of Fame in front of the Hustler store in 2002. Larry Flynt was unable to be present as he was under the weather at the time, but his daughter, Theresa Flynt, spoke candidly on his behalf. With tears in her eyes, Flynt reiterated her father's sentiment that Gloria Leonard was the female counterpart to her father. Leonard was clearly moved by Theresa Flynt's heartfelt words and by the induction ceremony itself, as was Bill Margold who stated his greatest honor was to be inducted into the Hustler Hall of Fame alongside his special friend, "Miss Gloria Leonard." Of all of the males, she befriended and revered in the business, Leonard had great affection for the former adult thespian, Jamie Gillis.

Nowadays, I'm divorced from the actual industry itself. I only hear things through the grapevine. The most recent and sad piece of news of course, is the passing of Jamie Gillis [on February 19, 2010]. Jamie and I remained good friends over the years. I recently was dumping stuff from my computer and found a whole bunch of e-mails that we had shared. During one of my trips to New York about three years ago, I had dinner with Jamie and his long time companion, the Restaurateur, Zarela. He was a very interesting and terrific guy. He was mischievous and incredibly intelligent, funny, hot, and smart. He could spout poetry and Shakespeare; he spoke fluent French, and he knew a lot about the world around him. He didn't rest on his porn laurels.

I've taken Jamie's death very hard. It's been harder for me than any of the other deaths that have occurred over the years. I think some of it has to do with the fact that nobody knew he was ill. Not only did nobody know he was ill, but poor Zarela had to carry that on her shoulders. You know I guess we all sort of thought of him as invincible and that he was impervious to these kinds of things. Melanoma is usually associated with skin cancer and yet, he had it internally.

Jamie inducted me into the Las Vegas "Legends Hall of Fame". He stood behind my chair and of course, predictably, extolled my virtues, but the thing that he said which actually brought me to sobbing tears is this: "Babe Ruth was not just a baseball player. Frank Sinatra was not just a singer, and Gloria Leonard is not just a Porn Star." That, for me, is my Kodak moment. It was very, very touching.

I wrote a piece about Jamie to be read at The Beverly Cinema in California that Bill Margold asked me to do and I used that in there. My tagline following the quote was, "And Jamie Gillis was not just some guy who showed up to fuck." There was an elegant air about him, even in the most tawdry of settings. I said, "You were a force to be reckoned with. Of course, we will all miss you." Since I had mentioned his knowledge of French earlier on in the piece, my closing words were, "Adieu, Mon Ami." He was very worldly. Jamie was one of my favorite guys in the business.

In the early part of the 1990s, Leonard uprooted and moved to Hawaii, but returned to Los Angeles in 1998 to work for a private Los Angeles company that distributed adult material. Gloria is no longer affiliated with the pornographic entertainment industry, but she has graciously given her time to a few high profile film projects during the latter part of the 1990s and in the new millennium. Prior to returning to Hawaii, Leonard participated in an on-camera interview for Cass Paley's award-winning documentary *Wadd: The Life & Times of John C. Holmes* (1998), and she joined director Julia St. Vincent to provide commentary for the

2001 DVD re-release of the revolutionary 1981 film *Exhausted: John C. Holmes, The Real Story*, along with Bob Chinn. Gloria and Marilyn Chambers jointly supplied insightful commentary tract for the Special 30th Anniversary Edition of *Insatiable* released in 2010. In spring 2012, Leonard provided a full length commentary for the soft version of the Video-X-Pix Special 2 disc re-release of "Misty Beethoven".

AFAA Awards. COURTESY OF WORTH MENTIONING PUBLIC RELATIONS

Autumn of Life

Everyone extols the virtues of Facebook. I am not a member of any social network because to me, e-mail is fine. Between you and me, if I were to list my real name, which is what I would do if I were using Facebook and you were to Google it, there would always be a link to Gloria Leonard. I have a small circle of genuine friends who I, of course, have revealed myself to, but you know, my neighbors don't know.

The whole Club 90 group sprung from Annie [Sprinkle] and me while planning a baby shower for Jane Hamilton's [Veronica Hart] first child. I verbalized something to Annie that I guess she construed as something negative about the business, as it likely was. We used to be fearful of talking down about the business for fear of not getting work. She expressed a desire to return to being Ellen Steinberg [Sprinkle's birth name]. You know, "Ellen Steinberg wears sensible shoes. Annie Sprinkle wears four inch stilettos." "Ellen Steinberg is chubby. Annie Sprinkle is curvy." She went through this whole litany of this duality, and it then occurred to me that maybe there was a need for women in this business to have a safe environment in which to discuss very personal issues. That was how Club 90 was born and, of course, our one Commandment was that nothing we ever discussed there could be revealed outside. It was called Club 90 because that was the numerical address of one of the people whose home we used for a lot of the meetings.

We've been pals for over thirty years and we connect on almost a daily basis. It's a real sisterhood and it's a great, not only support system, but you're dealing with people who have gone through the same experiences as you have. You know, appearing on film, sexually, isn't like anything else. You can't compare it to prostitution or anything else. It has its own set of foibles and repercussions.

The one thing I would change is to probably have been savvy in terms of business and finance. I was somewhat naïve in terms of what my worth was, given the scope of what was ultimately earned using my likeness and my appearances. The truth of the matter is, in the long run, here I am and I'm in my late sixties and I am struggling, financially. I'm looking into a reverse mortgage because I was just cut off of one credit card and my limit lowered on another. My bills far outstrip any income I have, so it is kind of sad that after fourteen years with a magazine, and in the business, and all of the money that was made off my likeness and my tuchas, that I'm struggling. It seems that all five of us in Club 90 are struggling. We commiserate online about it all the time about how fucked up it is that this stage in our lives we're sweating nickels and dimes.

About a year ago, I moved from Hawaii to Florida. I still have my house in Hawaii which I have rented out to a very nice gal, but my daughter and granddaughter live here. My granddaughter is fourteen and I was feeling like I wanted to be near them. I was in my late sixties and who knows; nobody knows how much time we have left on this planet. I just felt that I needed to spend more close time with the little family that I do have. My life today pretty much revolves around my daughter and my granddaughter, and my friends. I'm in Sarasota, which is on the Gulf side. It's across the state on the Gulf of Mexico side and it is a gorgeous location. We're not all in New York anymore. Candice [Candida Royalle] is on Long Island. Veronica Vera is the one hold out in Manhattan. Jane lives in L.A. [now in Las Vegas]. Annie is in the San Francisco area, and here I am, another old Jew living in Florida, just what they needed.

Last year (2011), Leonard returned to her home in Hawaii. However, early in June 2012, Gloria flew to New York City to attend the wedding of Veronica Vera and reconnect with her Club 90 group of girlfriends, many of whom had not seen one another in fifteen years. Several of the women, including Annie Sprinkle, Jane Hamilton and their friend Kat Sunlove, also participated on a panel at the Museum of Sex a couple of nights following the wedding. While Gloria was in town, she joined the gathering organized by Candida Royalle on a small vessel docked at the West 79th Street boat basin marina on Manhattan's Upper West Side. Since Candida had suggested I plan to come on board during my visit to New York, I happened to be sitting in the sunshine with my friend and her daughter-in-law, when suddenly, I noticed Gloria hurrying along the dock toward the boat. I hadn't known for certain she would be there that late afternoon and was pleased to meet in person as we conversed and joked over a couple of glasses of Cabernet. Leonard is extremely affable and very funny. She has the soul of a comedian and a memory like an elephant.

I do some writing. I'm actually working on my book which has taken me far too long to get motivated to do. About a month or so ago, a very dear friend of mine in New York, who had nothing to do with the adult business — we were just neighbors and have remained really good friends thirty years later — has a girlfriend considerably younger who is a TV commercial producer and has done other production projects. She apparently won in some kind of a contest, ten hours of studio time at a major studio in New York. She was commiserating with my girlfriend on how to use this

Gloria Leonard.

studio time. My girlfriend started telling her about me, and my life, and she was just immediately hooked. I've been spending days upon days answering pages and pages of single-spaced questions, and lining up people for on-camera interviews that are willing to talk about me. I'm also going to make a west coast trip to talk to some of my west coast friends. We're all doing this on a whim and a prayer. Who knows, maybe something will come of it and maybe nothing will come of it, but it seems like a worthwhile thing to tackle.

I'm going up to New York in May to do some of the on-camera stuff. I'm paying my own airfare. They're coming down here in two days to go through a dozen or more boxes that have been languishing in my daughter's garage. You know, I'm not that ego driven. I never did the scrapbook thing. This gal seems very savvy. She sees it with a number of different platforms like maybe for a web episode, maybe for a film festival, and so on. So right now, I'm looking into, along with a lawyer, the whole intellectual property thing.

Presently, Leonard's legacy is on ice. In the interim, Gloria continues to document her life in autobiographical format in the event she plans to publish one day.

All of my awards that I've won over the years are somehow in those boxes. I don't remember what all of them are anymore. I know it sounds rather braggadocio, but only so many awards one could win in the adult industry and I've won pretty much all of them and then some.

9

Rhonda Jo Petty
Roller Girl

Rhonda Jo Petty might not have achieved the status of elite female performer as some of her contemporaries like Seka and Ginger Lynn, but she has clearly etched out a place as one of the sexiest and most provocative "B" females of the golden era. A Chatsworth, California native, Rhonda Jo gained notoriety as a Farrah Fawcett clone during the promotion of her first starring role in *Disco Lady* (1978) because of the remarkable resemblance she bore to her Hollywood counterpart. Petty quickly magnetized a cult fan base that appreciated her inclination for the raunchier rape and fisting scenes which became synonymous with her name after her second adult feature *Little Orphan Dusty* (1978).

During her tumultuous developmental years, Petty and her younger sister were subjected to an abusive father who had an affinity for dirt bikes, multitudes of drugs, and a brief association with Charles Manson and his devotees at Spahn Ranch in Chatsworth. Prior to her parents' separation, Rhonda raised goats and discovered a love for horses and Equestrian riding, a hobby that provided shelter from her stormy home environment. After several episodes of truancy from school and a thirty-day stint in Juvenile Hall, Petty moved in with a boyfriend and decided to try her hand at nude modeling which led to her foray into X-rated movies. Fearful of her father's reaction after opting to use her real name in *Little Orphan Dusty*, Rhonda Jo went into hiding for almost two years.

Throughout her career, Petty ingested drugs in all shapes and sizes, and engaged in several volatile relationships including an affair with a Hells Angel biker from Palm Springs. Despite her reckless lifestyle off camera, Rhonda Jo approached her roles with a conscientious and professional attitude recognizing that her work in adult entertainment was a job, not unlike any other form of employment. Petty believes it is she

"I wouldn't change my life for the world. I'm grateful to be alive today because I should really be dead. I've experienced a life that most people could never say that they have. It's made me who I am. It has been a hell of a ride." RHONDA JO PETTY

PHOTO COURTESY OF RHONDA JO PETTY

who inspired the "Roller Girl" character personified by Heather Graham in P.T. Anderson's *Boogie Nights* (1997), and not the late porn actress Shauna Grant after showing off her prowess on roller skates in films *Sex Rink* (1979) and *The Champ* (released in 1980).

Emotionally derailed due to alcohol and drug addiction by the late 1980s, since her retirement from the industry, Petty has wrestled with her share of demons. In recent years, she has worked on making peace with her past and forgiving her father. Today, they share a precarious and delicate relationship, but Rhonda still feels the lingering effects of a traumatic childhood.

Rhonda Jo resides on three acres of land in Riverside, California, along with her two adult children, a couple of dogs, several horses and some chickens. As she grapples to put it all in perspective, Petty is proud of her reputation as a pioneer, and remains one of the industry's most note-worthy and personable feature female stars. On April 12, 2012, Petty was inducted into the XRCO Hall of Fame.

I interviewed Rhonda Jo Petty in the fall of 2009 and early winter of 2010.

San Fernando Valley

I was born in North Hollywood in 1955. My parents were eighteen years old when they met, and nineteen when they had me. They'd met at a party in the San Fernando Valley. Back in those days, you got married — to get an abortion was underground. They got married and had me. My father was a very angry young man and my mother was a passive, sweet, mousy type of woman. She would give you the shirt off of her back — just the sweetest thing in the world, but my dad had issues.

My childhood was like a black hole. It was horrible and there was lot of physical abuse. I mean, hardly a day went by when my father didn't beat me, and my sister. My sister is two years younger than I was. I got the brunt of it because I was the older one. My mom stayed with this man and she was scared to death. He would threaten her life and he'd beat her.

After I was born, they lived in an apartment for a while and my mom told a friend of mine a story that I didn't even know until a few years ago. After I came home from the hospital, if I cried, my dad would stick me in the closet and wouldn't allow my mom to get me. The first time I do remember, I was about three years old, and we lived in a little house in San Fernando right outside of Van Nuys. My dad was a construction worker and he was a plasterer. He was a hard worker and he did well. I remember one day my mom standing in the kitchen. She was stirring something in a bowl, and she was crying and crying. She was there all day long; it seemed to me. I went into the kitchen and I said, "Mom, why are you crying?" She wouldn't answer me.

Television was a big thing then and my dad bought a TV. I recall the house and the neighborhood because a Mexican family lived next to us and they had lots of kids. Even when I was three and

four, I'd go next door and they would feed me. I always loved to go next door. I don't remember my dad being around too much then. I can't place what my bedroom looked like, or my parents' bedroom — I can only remember the rest of the house. I don't know if something happened there, I just blacked out.

When I was five years old, we moved to Van Nuys and we lived right next to the Van Nuys Drive-In. In fact, I think that's still there today. I remember going to the elementary school there, but the house in Van Nuys

COURTESY OF RHONDA JO PETTY

is when all of the abuse really went on and my mom's life was being threatened. One time, my dad beat her and cut her face and she went to my grandmother [my dad's mother]. My grandmother told her, "You need to go home, Joan, and you don't tell anybody about this." Back in those days, they didn't have help for women who were abused.

There were three boys in my dad's family and they were from Canada. They are Norwegian, but they lived in the western part of Canada in Saskatchewan and my grandmother's parents [my father's mother] owned a big wheat farm there. They started a town, Hanley, and owned the Red and White store and they also owned a trucking company. My grandmother's family was pretty well to do. I don't know too much history on my grandfather's [my father's father] side except that he was a very kind, gentle man. I loved him to death. My grandmother was the one who was screwed up. I've seen pictures of my dad tied up in high chairs and there are toys tied to it, and I heard stories of her keeping leashes on them and tying them to doorknobs. I'm sure she beat them; she would beat me with a wooden spoon. She was a very uptight, skinny little thing that always wanted to know where you were going, what you were doing, and very controlling. She could be a bitch, so I really believe that my dad and his brothers were abused by her. She had a very saucy mouth. Something happened to my father for him to have become so abusive and sadistic.

My relationship with my father today is totally different. He has mellowed, and today he is trying to have a relationship with me, but those sixteen years with him were a nightmare. He has called me at times and told me how sorry he is that he wasn't there for me, even when I was little, and that he feels bad about everything. My sister has talked to him about what happened, but I never really have. You know, I've had to go through all of this and tried to get to a point where I just appreciate the relationship that I have with him today. What happened in the past is the past. I can't change that. It is sad what I had to go through — I could tell horror stories of what he did. He was very sadistic. He would kill animals in front of me. He would beat me with chains and just do horrendous things.

Escape Route

When I was nine, we moved to Canoga Park. The Valley was very cliquey compared to where my husband who grew up in Pennsylvania in a little town called Tars. My dad knew a lot of people in the movie industry, the legit movie industry, so I knew people who were drivers, make-up artists and wranglers.

I fell in love with one of my dad's friends, Harold Bates, who was so good to me. He was a wrangler and I loved horses. He wrangled out animals for the movies — mostly horses. In Van Nuys at that time, they had a ranch where they'd house all the movie horses. They had a white Stallion named King Cotton that they used in a movie, and the Hollywood TV show horse, Fury, was there. Harold Bates would take me to that ranch a lot and he'd pick out a horse for me to ride. He was wonderful to me and I looked up to him. He was a great guy.

I have been a horse freak for as long as I can remember. My mom would buy me those Breyer statues of horses which I still have from back then. I would dive into my horse fantasies with my Breyer horses and that's how I would escape. I wanted a horse so bad. When we moved to Canoga Park, my mom finally bought me one around age twelve. We boarded it down the street. The Eppers family lived across the street. Jeannie Epper was the stuntwoman for *Wonder Woman*. We used to play with her kids so I grew up with her kids but she was flippin' crazy. That woman was wild. She'd get pissed at her husband, get on her horse, and go down to the bar and ride the horse into the bar! They were all drinkers and partiers and they were crazy. All of her kids ended up going into stunts. Jeannie Epper recently received a [Taurus] Lifetime Achievement Award because she was the first stuntwoman in films. I was around all of those people.

Jeannie Epper, whose film and television appearances include *Romancing the Stone* (1984), *Armageddon* (1998), *Wonder Woman*, and *Charlie's Angels*, is the first woman to receive the prestigious Taurus award for over two hundred appearances in a fifty-year career span. The 2004 award-winning documentary *Double Dare* chronicles Epper's life and career.

Around that same time, my father did drugs very heavily. He was a very high functioning addict. He did speed for a long time. Back in those days, they did those double-cross bennies, and he'd go to work with a jar full of bennies and feed them to his crew and they'd get the work done. There were uppers and downers, and so I was around drugs a lot because of my father. He smoked marijuana; he took drugs but he was never a big drinker. My dad hung around with a gang of motorcycle guys, and was sort of in a motorcycle club called The Scramblers. They were the first club that started dirt bike racing. Back then, they used to race BSAs [Birmingham Small Arms Company] and Triumphs, and they started the dirt bike races which later turned into Motocross. My dad was very out there and people loved him. He had a great personality. He knew lots of people; he worked hard and made good money.

My dad had me on motorcycles from the time I was five years old — dirt bikes. I knew a lot of the motorcycle racers including some of the big guys like Jim Pomeroy. I used to know all the big wigs because my dad was pretty well known in that industry. That's what everybody was doing in the Valley, riding dirt bikes, or this or that. I rode motorcycles and dirt bikes for years.

I started doing drugs when I was just twelve years old. I would be dragged to parties out in Malibu where they'd put mescaline

Teenage Rhonda Jo with her father. COURTESY OF RHONDA JO PETTY

in the punch and people would be all fucked up. Cheech [Marin] lived next door to one of the places we used to go. My younger friend and I would be on the beach and he'd be smoking pot. He had two black dogs and they had bandanas around their necks. The other kids and I couldn't sneak any drugs from the party so we'd go down to the beach and smoke pot with him. My uncle [mother's brother] did drugs, but not my mom. She drank and smoked in the very beginning, but when I was around five years old, she went back to her religion which was Mormon. She dragged me to the Mormon Church, but by the time I was twelve years old, as I said, I was doing heavy drugs. Pot was not a big thing for me, but the downers around then like the Pink Ladies, the F-80s, and the F-40s — those are all downers. I started taking acid when I was around thirteen or fourteen years old.

Recreational use of psychoactive drugs gained in popularity particularly among teenagers during the mid-late 1960s. Ingested primarily for mind-altering purposes, regular use of psychedelic substances during adolescent years can have detrimental immediate and long term effects as the physical and psychological components of an individual's constitution have not yet developed. Each person's reaction to the influence of chemicals within the system is independent of another's.

Between the ages of twelve and thirteen, in an abusive family situation with a mother who couldn't help me, my grandfather [my dad's father] became this big teddy bear in my life. My grandmother watched me a lot, and she loved me because she always wanted a girl and I was the first girl born. During the years when I was a baby and on she would watch me because my mother became a hairdresser, so she took care of me when my mother worked until I was around seven years old. I became very attached to my grandfather; he was the one who saved me. When he came over to our house, he'd always say, "Leave Rhonda alone". He was my whole world and he passed away when I was around thirteen. That devastated me because I felt as if he abandoned me into this situation. It's crazy. You would think that somebody would notice the bruises or something, either my uncles or someone in my family, but it was just not discussed back then. After my grandfather died, I just sort of gave up because there was no one around to save me. A lot of my dad's friends were using too and were abusive parents, so I really grew up thinking that all of that was normal. That's what surrounded me.

I thought my father was going to kill me. I did not think I'd make it past eighteen. After my parents divorced, my mom wasn't really around but I lived with her. She had met another man and got married, but I don't know where she was. I was using drugs and still riding my motorcycles, still getting in trouble and not really going to school. I remember she bitched and yelled at me. My dad was in another relationship. He got married to a woman who had three kids. I'm very close to his new wife. I have always had a good relationship with her.

Helter Skelter

I got kicked out of junior high four times for drugs and would be sent back and forth between different junior high schools. My dad beat the shit out of me every time; believe me. He was livid. The first time I was busted in junior high, I had taken some downers and I ended up passing out in class. When I woke up, everybody was gone except for the teacher sitting at her desk. She said, "Rhonda?"

I said, "Oh shit." I took off running into my locker — I don't know why except that I was really messed up and had taken too many downers. Next thing I know, the principal is in my face, the teacher is there and there's security. They dragged me into the office and they called my mother. I'll never forget the principal sitting there with a pencil telling me to follow the pencil with my eyes. They called the police and they kicked me out. It was on my father's birthday. My mom came to the school, and picked me up and brought me home. She paced back and forth in the living room and kept saying, "Your father's going to kill you." It was at that point that I couldn't take it anymore. This was going to be a big beating. I thought, "I don't care anymore."

That was the day that I disconnected and I cut my head off from my body. I mentally just disconnected. It's funny, down the road when I did films I was able to do that. It is disassociation. You know, I was a self-injurer and I didn't even know what that was then but I would burn myself. I was in so much emotional pain that the oven in our house had a lip on the top and it would get very hot. I wore bangs and I would pull my bangs up, I don't know how I ever figured this out, or what made me do it but I would sit there and burn my forehead on that oven. I would do that a lot. I'm surprised I don't have scars on my forehead. Generally, I've been diagnosed as bi-polar stage one.

Based upon the information known about self-harming; it is the process of inflicting pain upon oneself which generally occurs in the form of cutting, burning, scratching and head banging. Injurers often exhibit acts of self-mutilation in order to relieve feelings of stress, depression, self-loathing and failure. Individuals who demonstrate this form of masochistic behavior are often recipients of psychological, physical, and sexual abuse, and can be excessive users of various substances.

I was thirteen when I had sex for the first time and it was with my sister's boyfriend, but she wasn't really going out with him anymore. His name was Blair Burnbahm. I had quite a few girlfriends. We stayed together all the way through. We were close in high school. One was Wendy Gregory and the other one was Cindy

Lang. The three of us were tight for years. My girlfriend, Wendy, was going out with Blair's brother and she got pregnant by him. She was only fifteen and her mother was dying of cancer. Wendy and Cindy were my best friends and we got into so much trouble together. We all had horses so we'd ride horses together. The three of us used to go ride at Spahn's ranch.

COURTESY OF RHONDA JO PETTY

When my parents got divorced, we moved to Chatsworth. That's where the porn industry is now, in the San Fernando Valley, way up in the north end in the hills. It's kind of a real rural area. You could have horses then but not so much anymore. My mom got an acre. I was in 4-H. I had bred and raised goats from the time that I was twelve and I used to show my goats at the L.A. County Fairground for a few years. My girlfriend Cindy's mom had a ranch not that far from us that was really at the bottom of the hill where Spahn's ranch was. My other girlfriend lived down the street so we'd usually go riding at Spahn's ranch. His place was like a studio that resembled an old western town, and he had an area where he would board horses. They shot a lot of westerns out there because it had a lot of large rocks and woods, and it is horse country. We'd hang out there and help with the horses, and it was just a place for us to go. Old man Spahn was nice and we weren't any trouble, but I remember when Charles Manson moved in there. He always scared the shit out of me. He never said anything to me and never approached me, but he would catch my eye, or he'd be looking at me as I rode past him. He had a pet crow and it sat on his shoulder. As time went on, more and more hippies showed up. I was only around thirteen. I remember some of my girlfriends' older sisters and brothers were going in and out of there because there were drugs available. I think if I'd been a little older, sixteen or seventeen, Manson would have approached me. Mostly it was the older kids who were hanging out there.

Spahn ranch is a five hundred acre spread located just above Chatsworth, California. Over the years, it was used as a set for films and television programs requiring a western flavor. The sprawling rural desert property was purchased by dairy farmer George Spahn in 1948, and later, became a hideout for Charles Manson and his "Family" of devotees. Allegedly, old man Spahn benefitted from the sexual services provided by Manson's female members in exchange for free lodging, although Spahn was actually blind and unaware of the extent of the nefarious activities taking place at the ranch.

The infamous murderous rampage carried out by members of the Family occurring in 1969 resulted in the deaths of seven people including movie star Sharon Tate. Although he was not present during the killings, Manson orchestrated the murders, and he and several members (another male and four females) were convicted of First Degree murder on all counts. Out of curiosity, Rhonda and a childhood boyfriend visited the house in Benedict Canyon where the pregnant Sharon Tate had lived along with her husband, French-Polish director, Roman Polanski. (In 1977, Polanski was arrested for sexual assault of a thirteen-year old girl and indicted on six charges including rape. Polanski pled not guilty to all charges and agreed to an eventual plea bargain.) The residence was located up the street from Rhonda's friend's mother's home. Years later, when Petty began working in adult entertainment and was scheduled to do a layout for *Playboy* Magazine, Sharon Tate's sister, Deborah, was the make-up artist hired to apply Rhonda's make-up. During the course of conversation, Deborah informed Rhonda that if Manson were ever to be released, he would not live to see the light of day. Manson continues a lifetime incarceration in maximum security at Corcoran State Prison in California.

As time went on, they were living in the rocks and running around naked and they were doing acid — it was just getting more packed up there. My mom's brother ended up living there for a couple of months; he was a speed freak. He and my dad were good friends, but they've had a rough relationship.

Up in Chatsworth, people lived in the hills and the knolls, and everybody knew who the drug dealers were. There were rock bands that lived up in that area, and somehow, my uncle met Manson and he got dragged up there. My dad told me that he went up there one time to get some drugs. He pulled up in a brand new green Cadillac and asked for drugs. Apparently, Manson came out and got upset with my uncle for bringing my dad there. He considered my dad a "pig" because he had money and drove a brand new car. He was "the establishment," so I guess my dad got chased off. Manson was upset and kicked my uncle out. My uncle eventually moved in with us and I remember him having to withdraw from speed.

I really didn't attend the last couple of years of high school. My attitude was that I didn't give a fuck. I hardened myself against the world and I went all out doing heavy drugs. I had dirt bikes and I had a beautiful new truck that my dad had bought for me when I was sixteen — that's something he did do for me — he bought me things. I drove that thing around like a wild person. Back in those days, everybody would tail gate up and down Van Nuys Boulevard, hundreds and hundreds of kids. I'd get in trouble over there all the time, and I'd end up with tickets, like twenty or something. When I turned eighteen, my dad found out about the tickets and he made me go turn myself in. I went to court and the judge pleaded with me to do a repayment plan and said, "Rhonda, you don't want to do jail time." He even pulled me into his office. I was just, "Fuck everybody." He was offering to do anything to avoid sending me to jail but I was just, "Fuck you guys. I'm not paying it."

I had a very bad attitude so I got sent to jail. I was sentenced to thirty days in Cybil Brand [L.A. Women's County Jail], but I only ended up spending twelve or fifteen days for good behavior, and then they let me out. My dad and mom came down to see me. My mom was crying and my dad was laughing. Cybil Brand was bad. They threw me in with all the prostitutes and all of the girls coming off of heroin. All of the dykes and the lesbian girls were in a different section and they scared the shit out of me. They were trying to smoke toothpaste and do whatever they could do to get high. You know, I had to play tough to make it through that. I'm a tough cookie.

Disco Lady

When I was eighteen, I met this guy and I moved in with him. His name was Tim Lagoy. He lived in the Valley and we moved around to a couple of different apartments. Within about six months, I was thinking about modeling. I got a photographer who took pictures of me with clothes on — I'm only 5'2", but they turned out nice. I was looking in the newspaper one day and saw that World Modeling Agency needed models on Van Nuys Boulevard, so I went down there and met Jim South. He's still around. I found out that it was for nude modeling. I thought, "What the hell? I'm a free spirit." He started telling me how much money I could make. Jim South really was the big agent back then. I'd like to take a moment to give a pat on the back to Bill Margold who was also an agent, because he's done work on the history of the industry and he tries to keep things alive. I'm very supportive of him.

Dallas, Texas native, and former Insurance salesman Jim South (James Marvin Souter) is a well-known talent scout and recruiter for the adult entertainment industry. South opened World Modeling Talent Agency in Sherman Oaks, California in 1976. In addition to Rhonda Jo Petty, he is credited for helping launch the careers of many prestigious stars such as Ginger Lynn, Christy Canyon, and Shauna Grant. After her introduction to Jim South, Rhonda Jo quickly became a sought after ticket.

You know, in the home, my dad made jokes with my mother and he would tell sex jokes, nothing explicit, but he would always joke about sex. In our home, sex was very open. Sex wasn't a dirty thing in our house. My dad would grab my mom's boobs or grab her butt in front of us and joke about sex. I think my dad raised me with a healthy attitude towards sex; that is another good thing he did give me. My dad was a character and he liked to tell jokes, and when he was in a good mood, he'd tease about it so sex was okay.

Anyway, Jim took some Polaroid photos of me, and the next thing you know, he started calling me. I began getting covers of magazines because I was the new hot item. Whenever they have a hot girl come in there, everybody wants you. I was making money hand over fist doing magazines. I was on the cover of *Cheri* magazine and *High Society*. They start you off with the magazines and then they approach you about doing the loops — I would say about six months after I started. You know if I ran the place,

that's probably how I would do it too. You'd see that if a girl was okay with nude modeling, you're going to approach her about doing films.

I was getting around a little bit and getting to know some of the girls. Of course, my boyfriend was having a rough time with it. He was very physically abusive. I ended up doing a shoot with him for a hardcore magazine. To tell you the truth, I vaguely remember doing it with him, and in the end he never really liked what I did and it did cause problems between us. Even though he caved in and did that shoot with me the one time. In fact, my husband found that shoot on the internet — somebody uploaded the pictures, so I have those.

At one point Jim South approached me about doing hardcore, and of course back then, there were a lot of hardcore shoots for magazines. I was nervous and I was scared in the beginning. I really don't remember the first loop that I did. The first time I had a girl-girl scene on a loop, I was very nervous about it. When I did *Disco Lady*, I was okay with the process by that time. I don't remember now who had approached me to do *Disco Lady* (1978). Bob Chinn was the director of that film which was the first feature I ever did. It was a thirty-five millimeter movie.

Bob Chinn is a sweetheart. He's a very gentle, nice man. He was always very professional and good. He was never rude. I really love Bob. It's funny, Bob always stayed out of the drugs and all of that. He didn't really socialize much with a lot of those people. I always wondered what he was doing in that business. He just didn't seem to be the right type of character.

When I walked off the set of *Disco Lady*, they asked me what name I had wanted to use. I was already using my real name without a problem. My family didn't know yet. I turned around and said to them, "Use my real name. I don't care." Little did I know; I was just trying to make a buck. My real name *is* Rhonda Jo Petty. My gay friends call me "Rhonda Jo," but that's my real name. My dad wanted to slit my throat for using my real name in films.

Director Bob Chinn recalled that his friend and stuntman, Jerry Wade, introduced Chinn to Rhonda Jo Petty one day by exclaiming, "Get a load of those zyzycks!" Wade's comment was in reference to Petty's ample breasts. The two men invited Rhonda to play the lead in an upcoming movie titled *Disco Lady*. Rhonda did not profess to possess acting skills, but she was able to pull off a reasonable performance in a role that didn't demand a great deal of experience in the acting department. Her uninhibited sexuality encouraged the film's cameraman, an Israeli immigrant by the name of Jaacov Jaacovi, to offer Petty a starring role within a storyline he had proposed for a jointly directed film project (with Chinn) called *Little Orphan Dusty* (1978). Billed as the "Farrah Fawcett of Porn" Rhonda's long, feathered blonde locks framing her fine facial bone structure created a remarkable resemblance to 1970s *Charlie's Angels* television star Farrah Fawcett. The marketing hype associated with the risqué venture that widely advertised taboo fisting and rape scenes, caused Petty's star to ascend. Subsequently, the film was busted in theatre after theatre, but the negative publicity generated curiosity which translated to box office success. At that point, there was no turning back. Rhonda would soon learn to assert herself in the work place. To date, Petty has watched only a very few of her movies.

Little Orphan Rhonda

After *Disco Lady*, Bob had me come and do *Little Orphan Dusty* and that's when I met John [Holmes]. *Little Orphan Dusty* (1978) was scary for me because of John Holmes. I was very nervous about meeting him and working with him. At first, he didn't like me.

Rhonda Jo Petty and John Holmes in *Little Orphan Dusty.* vcx

About the second day or so, we sat down next to each other and then I opened up. We were sitting on the stairs inside of the house at the beach where we were filming, and we just started talking. We became very good friends after that.

He knew I was nervous; he knew I was scared about the big thing between his legs and he was so gentle with me. He was so good with me. He took his time because he knew that I was nervous. You will hear a lot of girls say that about John. John had a way with women. He would massage your back — he was a little bit like Ron Jeremy. He'd play around with you and sweet talk you, and he just had a way with women. John was such a sweetheart. I believe though that he was also a pathological liar and he made up millions of stories, but he would pull you in. He'd take your cigarettes and say, "Give me those cigarettes. You're not smoking those cigarettes," and he'd put them in that briefcase of his. Then, I later found out, goddammit, that he smoked too! Oh, my god, he was a character, a real character — a little bit of a con artist and very, very colorful. Anyway, it all really started for me when I made *Little Orphan Dusty*. I didn't know it was going to go big. I figured nobody would ever see it. I used my real name again, and soon it came out who I was because the film was advertised in the newspapers and at The Pussycat Theater. That's when my dad found out.

Rhonda Jo Petty played waif Dusty (Petty is completely shaved) as the film tracks the sexual and emotional experiences of the wayward girl. After running away from an orphanage, Dusty is raped by a motorcycle gang and left naked and unconscious in the Southern California hills. She is discovered by a local artist Frankie (Holmes) who takes her under his wing. Following a few orgy parties at Frankie's, and some ugly confrontations with the biker gang ringleader, Dusty discovers that she's pregnant. Realizing he is in love with her, Frankie swears off all other women and proposes to Dusty. The two misfits marry before one final altercation with the gang members.

Little Orphan Dusty contains three fisting scenes and two rape scenes. One is a gang rape so for those who prefer violent free porn, this film is not for you. These types of depictions are illegal in contemporary X-rated movies, and even at the time, they were against the law.

During the shoot, Petty felt that Jaacov Jaacovi was insensitive and that he and his wife at the time, newcomer Svetlana (aka Svetlana Marsh) were controlling and cruel. Bob Chinn, who assumed a joint directorial role in the project, stated that Petty's stamina, energy, and co-operation made it possible for the challenging two-day film production on a meager budget, to be completed without any glitches.

Jaacov Jaacovi was intimidating. I was scared to death and he wanted that first scene in the film to be a rape scene where I am raped by a motorcycle gang. It was very hard to do. You know, I was very naïve, but now that I look back on it, I see exactly where Jaacovi was going. His whole reason for doing what he did was because he wanted to cause controversy for the film's release. We were on the set, and at first he wanted me to do the fisting scene with a guy and I said, "Oh no. No. Their hands are huge. Are you kidding me?" He finally talked me into doing it with a girl with a ton of Vaseline, and yes, it hurt. I let him intimidate me because of where I came from. That was a rough one to get through, but good old Rhonda…I have another fisting scene by myself, and then the one with John. I look back on it and I ask myself, "How did I ever let [Jaacovi] talk me into doing that?" The fisting scene with John was faked pretty much, because there was no way I was doing a man. I know that they had to make sure the angle was right — we faked that. I don't think I could have done that — the girl was hard enough.

When my dad found out about the film, he said he would break my legs and my arms. He was pissed! At that time, I really had little contact with him. They didn't know where I lived, and I didn't speak to my father again for I don't know how many years. I said, I didn't expect the movie to come out and I got scared. This is where some craziness really started happening in my life. I was living in Van Nuys at the time in an apartment with a girlfriend. I had a little VW and I was on the freeway, and this guy drove up alongside of me and he kept pointing at me to get off. My off ramp was coming so I got off and he followed me all the way to my apartment building. He got out and he said, "You look so familiar." I ended up inviting him into my apartment. He had cocaine. We started talking and it turned out that he was involved in the X-rated business. His name is Ruby Gottesman. He's still in the business today. He started seeing me, and at that time anybody that had cocaine, I would hang out. We started a connection and it was afterwards that my dad had called me. I was very scared and I told Ruby about it. He said, "Rhonda, let me get you a place at the beach and we'll hide you. I'll take care of you, and you'll never have to work again." At that point, I was scared shitless. My entire family was going to find out. Then, the film started getting busted all over the United States because of the fist-fuck scenes that were in it.

We found a place on Manhattan Beach in a house they had split down the middle into a studio. It was so cute. It had glass all the way up with high ceilings. I was right on the strand with a big porch with a cute little kitchen, a garage, and I had my own backyard. I think it was only three hundred or six hundred dollars a month. He put me in there and he paid the bills. He was married and had kids. I was young and naïve and I never really figured out what it was exactly that he did in the porn business. He came in and out of my place and showed up about twice a week. He would leave me vials of cocaine because he was a huge cokehead.

Time went on and nobody knew where I was — not my family, and not my friends. I was on the run and hiding out. I wasn't expecting this big hoopla with the film coming out and theatres getting busted. Here, I'd been going along quietly, and now, all of a sudden, I was splashed all over the place.

There was lot of drugs and I'd go on these trips with Ruby to Hawaii and everywhere. On one flight, he brought a vial of five grams of cocaine. I took it into the bathroom, and by accident, I snorted a huge amount and I almost blew my brains out. After a period, Ruby called me and said, "Rhonda, I'm not going to be able to come around for a while." It turned out that the FBI was looking for him because he was a pirater. He was pirating these movies in the black market. I thought, "Oh shit!" I was totally dependent on him and suddenly, he's not showing up.

Rhonda Jo's Sugar Daddy, Rubin "Ruby" Gottesman, former owner of X-Citement Video, was eventually arrested and sentenced to ten years in prison for duplicating X-rated movies. In 1987, Gottesman was charged with distributing videotapes of Traci Lords made while she was underage. Gottesman was sentenced to one year in jail.

I remember I went eight days without eating. During this time, there were neighbors next door to me. They were a little older than I was but they were big partiers.

With Gottesman gone AWOL, Petty was soon introduced to a new boyfriend.

I had met a guy through them that was a member of the Hell's Angels from Palm Springs. I really thought he was cute and started seeing him–this went on for a while. He had his own private little plane and he would come to my house at least twice a month with large amounts of cocaine while Ruby lay low. Ruby didn't really care that I was seeing the Hells Angel guy anyway. I can't remember his name now, but he was maybe 5'6" with blonde hair, and very cute. He also had a bodyguard with him who was about six feet. They would start to cook the cocaine at my house to make rocks out of it.

You know, Ruby had disappeared from my life during this time so one day I called the friend of the Hell's Angel, the bodyguard, even though I had a lot of pride. I didn't tell him that I was starving, but I'd told him things were bad and that I was frightened. He flew in, picked me up, and we flew back to Palm Springs. When we got off of the plane, he didn't take me to his friend's house. Instead, he sat me down and said, "Rhonda, I've got something to tell you." He'd said that the Hell's Angel guy I was dating was married, and on top of that, the bodyguard wanted me to go to bed with him! I freaked, I just freaked and I refused. He had somebody pick me up and drive me back to my place at Manhattan Beach.

I had another friend at the beach who was a Jewish guy which is what led me back into the business. He came over one day and saw what dire straits I was in and he said, "Rhonda, you need to go back to work. Let me help you. I'll help you get a big contract and I'll help you get big money." This is when Julia [St. Vincent] and her uncle Armand [Atamian, owner of Freeway Films] entered the picture. I had done some work for Armand before. Phone calls went back and forth, and this Jewish friend of mine took over the calls and said, "Let's go to Las Vegas". We went to Las Vegas and he got us a room. We were sitting around the pool one day and he started making a deal with Armand over the phone. He played my agent and I got fifteen thousand dollars for two films and a boob job.

Welcomed back into the fold with open arms, Petty was hired to play the lead in two movies for Freeway Films. Petty and Armand's niece (and second in command) Julia St. Vincent discovered many commonalities between them even though they worked on opposite ends of the porn spectrum. Rhonda Jo often stayed at St. Vincent's Hollywood apartment where she could unwind and occasionally partake in seasonal traditional celebrations such as Thanksgiving dinner with St. Vincent and friends.

My breasts were huge, but at that point, they were sagging. I wanted a reduction so Armand agreed to pay for that. I got fifteen thousand dollars and a thirty-five hundred dollar breast reduction. People will notice in my films after that. You can see my scars, but I went to a phenomenal plastic surgeon. We tried to cover them up a lot with make-up, but you can see them especially during the first year after it was done. Eventually, the redness went away.

The two films that I was hired to make for Armand were *Sweet Captive* (1980) and *Sweet Dreams Suzan* (1980). We shot those films back-to-back in two weeks and they were on thirty-five millimeter film. In one of the scenes at the end of two weeks, I couldn't even walk I was so coked out. They had to prop me up in a chair.

I loved Armand. Armand was like an uncle to me. He treated me so well. I loved him. I would go over to his house and I would have dinner over there. I had a good relationship with him — he was a very kind man. Julia and I became good buddies.

COURTESY OF RHONDA JO PETTY

California Girls, also released in 1980, is a compilation fashioned from a series of loops. Not a great picture by any standards, it enabled Petty to strut her stuff as a primo Roller Queen/hustler on the Venice Beach boardwalk where she effortlessly skated circles around co-stars John Holmes and Tiffany Clark. Filmed at the height of the disco era, Rhonda's impressive "hell on wheels" roller derby performance obviously made an impression on *Boogie Nights* director Paul Thomas Anderson, as is evidenced by the integration of the "Roller Girl" character played by Heather Graham, in the 1997 film.

The jury seems to be divided when polled about the accuracy quotient regarding the popular film *Boogie Nights* which had the partial effect of rendering the pornographic film industry into an acceptable commodity. Many golden agers believe the feature to be a true portrayal, while others don't. Petty's feelings are somewhere in the middle, but she doesn't dismiss the likeness between "Roller Girl" and herself. It is said that imitation is the sincerest form of flattery.

Boogie Nights is corny. They got the outline of everything that happened, but then they made it corny. I saw the Amber Wave [Julianne Moore] character as Gloria [Leonard] and Bobby Hollander in the Burt Reynolds role. Gloria was like our mother because she was older than the rest of us. Roller Girl was supposed to be me. The wife [played by Nina Hartley] who was in the sex scenes was Bill Margold's ex-wife, Drea. She used to do that to him where she had sex with men. I'd really like to see the real thing done one day.

Girls and Boys Club

I always had a good reputation for showing up on time. I was always a good worker and there was never a problem. I did pride myself on that. I always suited up and showed up. No matter how sick and fucked up I was I always suited up. Work and money motivated me. I got very good at it — the lighting and the angles. I knew what they needed. My dad instilled good work ethics in me.

I think that a lot of the girls came from abusive backgrounds. We didn't really talk about that then, but down the road, I found out. I always felt when I was working that a lot of the girls were there to prove their sexuality. It would just be the biggest turn-off to me. I couldn't stand it — they weren't the big names. Some of them were really screwed up. They just couldn't wait to work and they loved it, and they were just idiots in my eyes. I didn't like people who weren't professional. They were there to get fucked and prove what a good fuck they were and, "Look at me!" They would walk around and spread their legs — even when they weren't working! I just hated that. Most of the bigger names were all professional. I saw it as a job and you were there to work.

I didn't like working with any men who walked in that I didn't know. There were a lot of times that I would refuse to work with guys, if it wasn't Paul Thomas or Eric Edwards or Ron [Jeremy]. If I didn't like them and they seemed funky, I wouldn't work with them. I never did. I never screwed anybody that I can think of, off the set.

John Leslie and Eric Edwards — they were great guys, nice guys. Ron Jeremy really was a character. I always got a kick out of him, and I liked Ron, but he would drive me crazy. He'd come in the dressing room and expect me to bend over for him. Annette Haven had her nose in the air, and Marilyn Chambers. You'd be in the bathroom with some of them at the awards shows and they wouldn't even acknowledge you. The rest of us all got along great. We had fun together, we partied together — Sharon Mitchell and Vanessa Del Rio, Kandi Barbour, and me. The last I heard and this was years ago, is that Kandi Barbour became a prostitute and was living in a little tiny rented room in New York.

Kandi Barbour, a popular 1970s adult film starlet, was found dead on a street in San Francisco on January 26, 2012. According to Wikipedia, Barbour was fifty-five years old, homeless, and had been living on the streets.

I always got along with Sharon Mitchell. We did a few movies together, but I don't think we ever worked together in a sex scene. The majority of the girls I got along with — we were all doing the same thing.

I felt very in control. Once I had made a name for myself, I could say what I would and what I would not do. I could say, "No, I'm not working with him, and no, you're not putting a "cum shot on my face." I view myself as a person who has her own opinion and who has had her own experiences. This is who I am. I took a serious approach to the business and I liked the money. I think another reason that I got into the business is because of my attitude. My parents were not there for me at all. I feel like I got dropped off at the end of the world. By the time I left the house, they didn't give a shit if I went to college. There were no offers like, "Oh, Rhonda, what are you going to do with your life?"

I thought to myself, "Fuck my dad. I'll show him. I can take care of myself." That was my attitude back then, and it wasn't real healthy, but it drove me to show him that I could take care of myself and I didn't need him. I think that I did what I did because I was abused as a child. All I was doing was continuing the abuse. That's how I look at it.

During the era when I worked, it was a big party and the people became my family. These directors and producers, they felt like family. Everyone would watch out for one another and you'd go over to their house and have dinner. It was a tight circle. A small, intense community that was all underground. I started working for Bobby Hollander and Gloria Leonard at Gourmet Video, and I would party with them a lot. I would also party with Bobby when Gloria wasn't around. He did Quaaludes and cocaine.

In and amidst the perpetual party atmosphere, Rhonda continued to appear in films. A couple of the movies she is most proud of were produced toward the end of her twelve year run as an adult performer.

I enjoyed making *Country Comfort (1981)* which I think was VCX. They took us to Paul Getty's ranch to make that film. They had found this little cabin and they went to Western Costume and got us these dresses from the Western days. They spent some money on that film and it had Georgina Spelvin in it. I love her; she was great, and she really took me under her wing. That's a cute little movie and I'm pretty well known for it.

The western feature *Country Comfort* starred Rhonda Jo Petty (as Beth), Georgina Spelvin (as Martha), Drea (as Clara), and a young actor Ginger (as Sarina, not to be confused with Ginger Lynn) as four southern rural women trying to make ends meet at the end of the Civil War. Life for the females takes an interesting turn when stud Tom (Randy West) arrives at the ranch to deliver the news that Martha's husband and son (Beth's spouse) were killed during battle. Beth, who has been having her libidinous way with the farm hand Marsh (played by Tommy La Roc) in her husband's absence, is suddenly relieved of guilt for her betrayal and becomes engaged. Meanwhile, Momma Bear Martha hires Tom to help Marsh with chores around the spread and he finds his way into her heart.

Another great film was *Baby Cakes* [released in 1982]. The people that produced that became a part of my life for a while. They'd have me over for dinner and I met the producer's younger sister Pandora. *Baby Cakes* is one of my best films that might still be available to buy.

Baby Cakes, an Essex production chronicles the adventures of three girlfriends on a four hundred mile bicycle trip down the California coastal road 101. The northern California location was particularly cold while donning skimpy costumes, especially in Big Sur where most of the filming occurred, but Rhonda Jo described this project which included Randy West, Mike Horner, and Billy Dee, as an easy flowing experience that allowed for her and the others to leisurely bicycle their way along the picturesque California shores. Petty's ease and comfort with the material and setting, is likely why her performance is natural and realistic.

I was in the adult industry for about eleven-twelve years from 1974-1986. The last film that I made was *Satisfactions* which was in 1983. *Satisfaction* is a great film and it did really well. It got great reviews. I looked good on the cover — there's a big box cover of me. I still have the red shoes that I'm wearing in that film. I did a scene where I'm on a construction site with three guys, and from what everybody tells me, it was a great sex scene. I think it even got "Best Sex Scene" that year. You can still get it, but you know I've never seen it. I have it here but I need to watch it one day.

Rhonda Jo's hot scene with three construction workers played by Ron Jeremy, Herschel Savage, and Danny Weirdman in Robert McCallum's cleverly crafted *Satisfactions* definitely gets the juices flowing, especially when Petty is initially paired with Savage. Dressed in a white mini-skirt, red stilettos, and thin panties, Rhonda Jo (as Connie, the boss's daughter) ascends a stepladder taunting Savage who is positioned at the bottom looking up her skirt. Tired of her cock teasing, Savage roughly grabs Connie from the ladder and plants a hard kiss on her mouth. Turned on, Connie asks for more and Savage is only too willing to "satisfy" her needs as the two get down and dirty, and are eventually joined by Jeremy and Weirdman for a foursome.

It is a recognized fact that at the zenith of porn's golden era during the mid-late 1970s and into the early 1980s, celebrity adult performers such as Marilyn Chambers, Georgina Spelvin, Seka, Rhonda Jo Petty, and many others often attracted the attention of mainstream Hollywood admirers. Max Baer who played the handsome, dim-witted "Jethro Bodine" in the 1960s TV series *The Beverly Hillbillies* (and later became a producer and

Rhonda Jo with Max Baer. COURTESY OF RHONDA JO PETTY

entrepreneur) was a familiar face amongst the X-rated crowd and often attended adult shows in Las Vegas near his home. Petty's initial encounter with Baer started with a simple phone call one evening more than twenty years ago placed by Max and his cohort, Academy Award-nominated actor Nick Nolte. Max and Rhonda began a closely-knit telephone friendship that lasted until 2004. Baer once sent Rhonda a medical prescription and flowers when she was ill, and visited Petty faithfully at the Adult Entertainment Shows in Las Vegas whenever she appeared.

On the Road Again

As is often the expectation and standard among many women who work in films as sex performers, eventually they take their merchandise on the road where they are hired to appear as feature dancers — not unlike rock bands that tour to publicize their latest musical offering. Most will agree that the lure of big money is attractive, but as Rhonda Jo explained, stripping from city to city takes its toll in more ways than one after a few years.

At a certain point, you could only make so many films. I was growing tired of making films and it was just time to go on the road with them and promote them. The last six to eight years before I quit, I was doing performances all over the United States and Canada, where the money was good. After you got popular, the nightclubs wanted you to come and be their main attraction, but you had to do a strip tease show. It started to be the thing where we'd go to the strip clubs and we would become headliners. After the show, I would spend five — ten minutes on the microphone answering questions. It was good money. That was very popular back then, and from what I hear, it is today too. It's just easy good money, and you are out there promoting your films. I was pulling in eight to ten thousand dollars a week, and then after each show, I'd do Polaroid photos and sign them — that was another thousand — two thousand dollars a week. I did that for eight years and I then would shoot a movie here and there. I did make some in between and did some magazine shoots, and I was just all over the place. A lot of us did because the money was difficult to turn down.

I did a lot of shows in Windsor, Ontario, and I appeared once in Vancouver and in Toronto one time. I loved Toronto. The bar was very small but I loved the shopping there. There was a club in Windsor called Jason's and there was the Million Dollar Saloon.

When I started, there was one club in Chicago with the burlesque strippers. I remember one lady, Dixie Dew, a burlesque stripper, used to help me with costumes. We porn stars were moving into their territory, but I got to meet these old burlesque queens. Back in those days, they didn't have implants; they would get silicone injections in their butts and their boobs, and when they got older, they'd all these lumps because of their injections. Dixie Dew had a lumpy butt by the time she was old.

The shows were half hour each and ran from noon to midnight. I'd fly into a Holiday Inn, and I did so many of them it got to the point where I wouldn't know where I was. I would work solid for two months. I'd work six days a week and five shows a day. On Sunday, I would fly to my next gig. It was very lonely on the road.

I had an agent and he would book the shows for me. This was from the late seventies until the day I quit, which was in 1986. I started in the business in 1974, and I quit the business in 1986 — almost at the end.

It's a good thing that I was a hard worker and I liked money and doing these appearances at first. I'd fly in and out of New York where

Rhonda Jo and her friend, Brian. COURTESY OF RHONDA JO PETTY

I lived for six years and partially in Massachusetts too, because I had a boyfriend living there. I went out with him on and off for six years. He was very verbally and physically abusive. The day he threw my dog down the stairs was the day I ended that relationship.

It was a very lonely life but I had a gay friend, Brian, who would go on a lot of trips with me. He was sort of my entourage and a very close friend. I lived with him a lot in New York and he would go with me a lot to these gigs, all over the United States and Canada. He acted as a bodyguard, but again, it was lonely because I lived in dressing rooms and it was a lot of isolation. It was tough, and I find today that I like to isolate because I lived in such isolation for so many years — living in those dressing rooms and hiding away from everybody. If you came out, they would bombard you. You had to be careful if you went out about who followed you. I sat in dressing rooms for eight years. If I had time off, I'd go down to Florida and live it up. A lot of my money went to cocaine and clothes, and I had a car. I didn't even really have a home base because I was all over the place, and when I did come home, I'd spend some time with my friend Brian at his house or with an old stripper that I knew. One time I did have a house for a year at upstate New York, but for me to have a place — I was just never home much. I lived on the road. When I got off work, I might fly back down to Massachusetts, or stay in a hotel, or go to Florida or to the Bahamas, and take a break.

I have a President's pin. It's from when [George] Bush senior was Vice-President. Every single city I went, there would be advertisements in the paper stating I'd be appearing at a certain club. When I was in Kentucky and at the Kentucky Derby, I made an appearance at a club there and these men appeared in black suits. They gave me an invitation and a President pin and asked me to come to a party. They dropped off the box and the President's pin, and when I lifted the lid of the box, inside of it was a note that had the Ramada Inn written on it, along with the room number. This was in 1983, I think. Vice-President Bush had wanted me to go to his hotel room. I never went! I couldn't get off work to go but he sent two guys in black suits to the club where I was working. I still have the pin and the box. This stuff is on my bar — I protect it. Bush senior portrays himself as this self-righteous, holy, religious person, and here he wanted me to show up at his hotel room.

In 1985, I had a nervous breakdown in Dayton, Ohio. I was at a point where I was overworked and I was an alcoholic, and my stomach was so bad that I developed ulcers. I was living on Maalox, milk, and vodka. It was getting very bad for me; I had a nervous breakdown at a hotel in Dayton.

The last night I was working there, a guy came up to me and said he had cocaine and friends and invited me to go out with him. I went out and I blacked out. The next memory I have I was stuck in my hotel room, and all of my acrylic nails were melted. I was trying to smoke a cigarette lighter. They were trying to take it away from me, and I was waking up out of this blackout going, "What happened?" They told me I was trying to kill myself. They said, "You tried to light yourself on fire. You tried to jump out of a window. We've been sitting here with you all night." I ended up going back with the same guy to his house a couple of days before flying home and he started to say, "Oh, I love you. You need to quit the business. I have money," and on and on. He scared me and I got the fuck out of there as quick as I could. I was experiencing a nervous breakdown at that point, and I flew back to Boston where

my manager was. I was so bad I could barely talk, and I ran to the bathroom in the back of the bar that my manager had owned. He sent me to the psych ward and that started a trend of going in and out of hospitals for two years, in and out of psych wards. Back then, rehab was just starting to happen. It was a nightmare.

Emotionally, I was a wreck. All of those years I was using, and now I wasn't using. The emotions I had shoved down inside of me were coming up. During that time, my manager was trying to get me to go here and there, and I just couldn't do it. I couldn't do it sober. After two years of trying, we both agreed — that was it, I was done. That's when I moved back to my family's house in California. I went and lived with my sister.

I went to beauty school for manicuring and I got my license and did that for a while. It was extremely hard for me. Then I met my husband who was a friend of my sister's husband. They had worked in business together and they introduced us.

Horses lend us the Wings we Lack

At first, I wanted nothing to do with men. I had been so jaded and so hurt, but he just kept coming and coming. I finally went out on a date with him and after two years, we got married. He had no problem with my past at all. Even to this day, he's always going on the internet to buy up my stuff and see what's for sale — posters and so on. I don't want to say he's supportive of it, but he's fine with it. In fact, he's got bigger eyes for it than I do. Sometimes, I couldn't give a shit where I came from but he thinks it's great and wonderful.

I got pregnant after going out with him for two years. We had just moved to this place where we are now — this big place with three acres. I had his two older kids that I was taking care of and we had wanted to get horses. We got this place and we started getting into horses, and I just started getting into raising kids. I was pregnant and had a baby, and then I had another baby, so I was just living the American life and all the pornography was behind me. I was a mom and I was a wife, and we started showing horses. That has turned my whole life around.

Alcohol and drug addicts and their families understand relapse is part of recovery. For Rhonda Jo, the road to sobriety is one well traveled. With the ongoing support and love of her family and children, Petty's commitment to staying on the wagon is sincere. Rhonda Jo has been working on her sobriety for most of her adult life. At the time of this interview, Petty and her husband were still together. As of March 2012, after more than twenty years of marriage, Rhonda Jo and her husband have parted company.

I'm very grateful that I have two wonderful kids; they are MacKensie and Brock. MacKensie is almost twenty-one and Brock is nineteen. They are such good kids. They both live at home. McKensie recently started doing hair and modeling, and Brock is going to community college right now. They've known since they were teenagers who I was.

Rhonda's son Brock recently made the Dean's list.

They've been through it with me too. I've had bouts where I started drinking again — I've had a couple of years here and a couple of years there, and they've always stood by me. They've always been supportive of me. I've been sober now for five years. There was a time when I'd had fourteen years of sobriety behind me.

My mom is the sweetest thing in the world. She has never judged me; she is very religious. She's always been supportive of me and had an open door. My dad was angry in the beginning, of course, but nowadays he'll make comments that surprise me. One time he said, "Oh, Rhonda, me and Uncle Bobby were on the internet and I told Bobby you were in *Debbie Does Dallas* (1978). Weren't you in that movie?" It blew me away because it has been something we don't discuss. Here he was coming off as if he was a little bit proud of me. He knows that I made it big in the industry and he's made a couple of comments here and there to let me know.

It's been a very rough life, and you know, even to this day, I feel like I've had to hide in the closet a lot because my dad is still alive and what he did to me while growing up was horrific. I'm not allowed to talk about it. It seems like I'm waiting for the day for my dad to die so that I can finally talk about it. He had cancer this year, and this sounds terrible, but the day my father dies is the day I will feel free. It's tough because my dad has changed tremendously, and I know he feels bad, but the relationship we have today is good. He's always calling me and telling me "I love you," but then I think, "Where was that when I was little?" I love my dad but I have to say I resent that I'm supposed to pretend that everything was great and wonderful. I'm just not allowed to talk about it so I feel I have a dirty secret. He tells me he is sorry for the past, even though we don't get into what happened. I think he has erased a lot, and he's glad I got out of porn and got married and had kids. That's when he started getting involved again in my life. He and my husband are close. It's just like everything's great, and nothing ever happened. I hate it that I'm in this closet. That's what I'm working on right now. I'm walking through what happened, and I'm learning how it had affected me. I need to deal with all that shit. I don't know how I've lived through it all, I really don't. I should have been dead a million times and for some reason I'm here. I am currently going to counseling.

By the time I was seventeen, nobody was there for me and I was out on the streets. I feel like I almost didn't have a choice — I fell into it. It just was what it was. I really ran away, and I wasn't in touch with my family and I got a new family, which were the porn people. The porn directors were good to me. They treated me well. Well, I thought they did because there were bowls of cocaine and Quaaludes and, "Come to our house, Rhonda. You're great and we love you. You're wonderful." Even though there were drugs around, they treated me really well. They'd treat me like a daughter. I'd never had that before. I got more out of them then I ever did from my family, but I'm not saying that doing pornography is the right way to go, especially nowadays, no.

So, you wanna be a Porn Star?

Rhonda Jo maintains friendships with few people from her days in the business. She has gained perspective from the positive aspects of her experiences as she witnessed the transformation — for better or worse that has taken place since she left. While visiting her ranch in Riverside County on a hot summer's day in July 2011, Rhonda Jo took me on a tour of her sprawling down home spread fully equipped with a horse stable, swimming pool, tennis court, a stretch limo in the driveway, and her favorite pet, a rather large and cuddly bulldog. I met her son, Brock, and her daughter, McKensie.

Rhonda Jo is unassuming, unpretentious, and kind. She opened up her home and her life as we sat sipping lemonade on her colorful outdoor patio and talked easily. Now, at fifty-six, "Soccer Mom," Petty spoke candidly about the good ole days — and the not so good.

I stay in touch with Ronnie [Jeremy] and I'm very close with Johnny Keyes. He comes down, and stays with us and cooks for us. He and my husband are the best of friends. They talk all the time. He's more of a character than Ron Jeremy is. He lives up in Washington and he's a jazz singer now. Johnny is godfather to my kids, and his son is very close to my daughter — they text each other all the time.

It was a small family of us. Nowadays, all of the girls want to be a porn star. Back then, it was looked down on. It was degrading; there were just a few of us who were doing it; maybe twenty girls. It was a very tight family and everybody knew everybody. Even though we had the girls back then who were trying to prove their sexuality — they were in and out of there, but the real ones like Seka, and Vanessa del Rio, and all of those girls, we were family back then and we were the only girls who would do that. It's a god-damn meat market now. They eat you up and spit you out.

I believe that the adult industry exploits women. Any woman that goes and does porn, I don't care what you say they are being exploited. To me, that's just the way the world is. The business has gotten so reckless. I talked to Ginger Lynn a few years ago when

Rhonda Jo and Johnny Keyes. COURTESY OF RHONDA JO PETTY

she was doing talk radio for Playboy, and she told me that she couldn't believe the girls who came in to do interviews for the show. She said, "Girls are stitched from here to there and wearing pads." What they make the girls do these days is horrendous. It's not the same as it was when I was working. Now, everyone wants to be a porn star — in our time, you didn't tell anybody!

When my kids started going to high school, and since porn has become more mainstream, other kids would say, "Oh, I want to be a porn star." Word got around school because up where I live there are a few kids around. I was always home and these kids always came to my house. I've seen them all grow up. My kids have had positive and negative experiences, but they have always supported me. There have been times when they've even been proud about it around some kids, but they've experienced both kinds of reactions. What has shocked me the most during the last ten years is how acceptable pornography has become. I can't believe the stuff that they have on TV now. I was watching Bravo last night at 11:00pm and they now have advertisements for the adult channels. They show girls in bathing suits and they are advertising the porn channels — satellite.

Rhonda and her best friend.

Today, I'm very moralistic. It's funny because I shock my psychologist. He said, "I can't believe that someone like you, who did what you did, would become as moralistic as what you are, Rhonda."

I don't worry about people judging me. If I did, it would drive me crazy. I've always been very private, and have always been careful about who I have around me. Even after being married for twenty years, I only allow friends into my home who I know don't judge me and I feel comfortable around. If people show up and I'm not comfortable around them — you're not coming in my house. The only friends that I allow are people who accept me and don't judge me. I don't need to be judged because I know why I did what I did.

I've had to deal with the bad side of it and the good side of it, but I'm fine with it today. I'm almost proud of it because at least I did make a name for myself and I have a real good reputation in the business. They finally put me in the Hall of Fame. I wouldn't change it for the world because it's a part of my past and a part of who I am. I've seen a lot, and I've met so many people and traveled all over the country. I've done that whole drug scene — I really lived it! I've experienced a life that most people could never say that they have. It's made me who I am. It has been a hell of a ride.

10.
Serena
Tiny Dancer

Affectionately dubbed the "the last Flower Child" by friend and adult film historian, Bill Margold, the statuesque strawberry blonde, Serena, plays coy about how old she was when she made her debut in a sexually explicit movie. Quite possibly, her first film was *Massage Parlor Wife* (1975); some databases list the release as early as 1971. Serena's appearances in adult pictures reveal a delightful display of free spirited, perennial youth encapsulated by sexually charged, unrestrained performances that are marked, but not exclusively, by BDSM, double penetration, and rape scenes. Serena has said there was a time in her life when the only "real sex" she had was on camera.

Contemplative at heart, Serena, a Southern California born Karen Black/Mia Farrow hybrid, developed a sensibility to the human condition by osmosis, through the painful process of adolescence and teen years due to a misdiagnosed mental health condition. When she entered adult movies and during the era in which she worked, Serena was convicted about changing minds regarding sexual taboos and the right to personal freedom. Money was not the motivator, for Serena it was the opportunity to rally against conventionalism, and spread the word about sexual liberty toward an attainable paradise where people could be free to manifest their fantasies in demonstrative symbolic expression. At the zenith of her career as a pornographic film celebrity, Serena was able to communicate her exhibitionistic tendencies in front of the camera and throughout her red-hot relationship with golden age legend, the late dark knight of porn, Jamie Gillis.

Within a filmography spanning more than ten years, Serena's appearances include the memorable and erotic hot tub segment shared with Marilyn Chambers in *Insatiable* (1980), in addition to a very brief

"Getting into baring my body was no 'moral' choice. I was completely at ease in my nakedness. Nudes were in abundance in etchings and prints about the house. They were a part of my mother's collection. The figures on the walls of my childhood are nude women by the seashore in the moonlight." SERENA

PHOTOGRAPHY BY JOEL SUSSMAN

appearance in the Hollywood blockbuster *10* (1979) starring Dudley Moore and Bo Derek. *Teenage Cruisers* (1977), one of Serena's most popular films, is a cult fan favorite frequently on the marquee at the New Beverly Theatre in Los Angeles. Serena readily admits she enjoyed the glory days of porn and being a starlet, but also recognizes she wore "Serena" as a mask which enabled her to release the uninhibited, carnal style that is consistent in her film facade.

Today she has not strayed far from her hippie roots and philosophies. Serena is soulful and works as an artist in multiple mediums depending upon inspiration and the season. Some of her unique pieces are on display at the Erotic Heritage Museum in Las Vegas and at the Institute for Advanced Study of Human Sexuality in San Francisco. When Serena is not designing art, she cherishes time spent with her soul mate and her beloved family.

I interviewed Serena in the spring of 2010.

Serene, Serena

I grew up in a wonderful town. I would still be living there except that the smog drove me out. It was in the foothills, right up against the San Gabriel Mountains: the Angeles National Park with lots of oak trees. I was born under an oak tree. That's the family story. Dad was at his second job, he had worked the night shift and Mom decided to have a hot fudge sundae at four a.m. Mom was home with my older brother and he called dad at work and said that my mother had to have a hot fudge sundae. He'd better come home because my mother was having the baby. My brother held the flashlight and I popped out in my dad's arms. He had pulled over under an oak tree because there were no sidewalks then; it was a very rural place. There was a plaque placed on the tree in a small ceremony.

My real name is Serena. The nurse told my mom that I should be Carla, but Mom didn't like that. She thought she made it up because she'd had such a serene birth. My dad literally pulled the car over and they had me with barely a grunt. The hospital only charged us half. They cut the cord, and I was allowed in my mother's bed being "contaminated". Babies born in hospitals in those days would normally be put in the nursery away from their mother. I would say I'm the middle child, but there were two older than I am. There is a gap between the two sets of siblings in my family, but there is a strong link because we all adore mother.

My parents had incredible taste in houses, and we moved around to different homes and knocked out walls, and changed them around and then we'd resell. Then we'd go to another house and turn it into our dream house. We would do that as a hobby. One of the houses was in Mount Oak Park; it's still there. It's a private park. It's huge, just acres and acres. There were eight or ten houses in it. It was wild and I kind of grew up there in one of the houses.

My mother went to the temple which was at the very top of the mountain. It's called the Ananda Ashrama founded by Swami Paramananda. Vedanta teaches to respect all religions and it's a type of religion but there is Jesus, Krishna, Mohammed; they are all there in the chapel. All of the idols are there. The teachers there were primarily Sisters from India: that was kind of the influence of my life.

First Communion. COURTESY OF SERENA

My father was a Polish Catholic from Chicago, and he and I would go to the Polish Church downtown in Los Angeles where they only spoke Polish and Latin, so I got these two different things and it was wonderful visually.

Vedanta's philosophies are taught by the Vedas. The texts constitute the most ancient spiritual scriptures of India. Contrary to Christianity's practices, Vedanta's premise is not founded upon the desire or need to be saved. Rather, the faith teaches that we are never lost, but in ignorance of our true selves only to be reclaimed through a journey for self-knowledge.

Early Influences

My parents were very interesting people. We would go to museums a lot and my mother read constantly. My father is a hero of WWII and a hero in his life. He was born in Chicago, learning English as a second language. He worked two jobs and worked his way up from severe poverty. He went to night school. He had worked his way up in the county, from loading trucks on the docks and kept taking test after test in order to better himself. He reached the top job from the most labor intensive: head of transportation for everything that moved, literally, from airplanes to trains to buses, everything in Los Angeles County. He would be an amazing character study — he is a real everyday hero.

My mother was a server, but in her youth, she worked for Hollywood studios — Paramount. She had experience in the offices. Her father was also involved with movies in that he was one of the very first artists that painted "one sheets" for theatres. They used to be painted by hand! That's what he did for a living. He'd be down in the basement of a theater painting posters for the next movie coming out. There is a fabulous book out [*Now Playing*, 2007, by Anthony Slide] about those artists that did the movie posters; it's about the art and history of movies. I love movies. If only we'd kept one of his posters! Ephemera like this cannot only be worth something in dollars, but even more sentimentally. My grandfather's name was David Carlos Leberman. As Jews, we had to drop the "I". I am close to my ZaZa — that is grandfather in Polish. My Busha, his wife, was the love of my formative years because she was also an artist and a poet.

We had an incredibly connected, happy family. I was daddy's little girl until I had a younger sister, and unfortunately, it probably was at that time that my bi-polar disease flared up. From the time she was born until the last two years, we didn't really know each other. I didn't really remember her. I have complete amnesia of any evil doing to her. Lately, I've been spending a lot of time with her and we'll have coffee. She'll just look me in the eye and say, "You don't even want to know. You were so mean to me. You were so awful."

I'll look at her and say, "What are you talking about? I love you, you're my sister." I had been in some kind of a rage because I was daddy's little girl. I had horrible jealousy; it was just rage, rage, and hate. The mania of being bi-polar has me seeing a red haze over everything and my gut eats itself, burning. Unfortunately, I had that jealousy with men later in life — it's one of the issues that I need to work on. Everybody has something. It took years being misdiagnosed as a teenager for me to get any medication for my disease and still it must be monitored closely. I want to be the one to say you know, "If you love me let me go," so I have got to learn that.

As a child and before her bi-polar condition manifested itself in extreme behavior, Serena found solace and freedom in her expansive surroundings. Along with a girlfriend, she developed a reciprocal rapport with nature and animals.

Mountain Oaks Park is the place that I've always considered home, even in the many houses we moved around in, even now. There was my next-door neighbor, Leah, from this wonderful, big family. She was my age and where we lived was the kind of place where we could get lost. We found an old pomegranate tree from years back that had been abandoned, an old orchard, and we would play in that and in chicken coops up in the mountain. We'd hear coyotes late at night. It was rustic for a suburb, but it was because of its location. I had one oak tree that I would play horse on.

I remember coloring with Leah and insisting that the sky could be yellow or something. She'd go between the lines and I'd think that was horrible! I'd climb out my bedroom window during my daily naptime and go gnash on dog biscuits. Leah had a big bag of dog bones on her deck and we'd sit there and munch on those — it would be wonderful. She was the only close friend that I consider I've ever had. I still connect with her. I also had another friend, a best friend, in junior high. I remember she collected Barbie dolls. Then we got the brilliant idea from a TV movie to run away together. We were busted and thrown in Juvie [Juvenile] Hall and our parents separated us. That's all I remember of her. That was quick lived.

I got good grades. The second grade, my math went down because my father got "crippled" in an accident at work. That took up most of my childhood where he was in a cast, wheelchairs, canes, and braces. He had several surgeries on his knees and painkillers became my dad's life and everybody's life in my family. I feel my break with the mathematical side of my brain was justified in my child's mind. After my father, Daddy, was taken down in those pre-PC days, he would fight the rest of his life with severe body issues. He was taken by hospitals, surgeries, heart attacks, pain, painkillers and therapy. This memory is totally linked in my brain with the letting go of the side of my brain that is the logical half. I've been living my life on this lobe, thus the label "artist."

"Art brut" — Dubuffet said he was trying to get back to the real art — the only quality art, which is that of childhood; it is the moment I am able to pinpoint when I decided to follow the path of the Artist.

I always tell this story and I swear it's true. The first painting I ever sold was at age four years old. I was in Hawaii and we were sitting at a sushi bar, and my dad was bragging to the next guy at the sushi bar because my dad talked to everybody. Mom always would say, "Your dad never met a stranger". He was bragging about his little girl because she could work with chopsticks. I'd learned to eat with chopsticks before I could use a fork. I was eating sushi with the chopsticks and we were examining this artwork I had just done in the last two days. Anyway, the guy that my dad had been talking to bought it. It was great and I think I got four dollars. I don't think I've ever painted a watercolor as good, because the scene of it is still in my mind.

Serena's early educators also stand out firmly in her mind as influential role models that commanded attention, but who were nurturers and conditioners.

In third grade, I had a wonderful teacher named Mrs. Kimble and she had sort of a goose chin. She was old, and flabby, and charming, and looked like something from another age. She reminded me of Dame Margaret Rutherford playing Jane Marple [in one of author Agatha Christie's novels]. She taught me the love of reading, so I really became a reader and won all of the prizes in contests that determined how many books you could read. You would receive a book for winning and I'd always get these good books. Mrs. Kimbel in the third grade was like a mother, I mean, she was that important to me. My mother understood that. Mrs. Kimble was third grade and Miss Tucker was fourth. I've got to give these women credit. Miss Tucker was quite tall and looked like Eleanor Roosevelt and had very strict sort of body language, but she loved Mexico and the *romantic* Mexico. Miss Tucker loved all of the wonderful, beautiful things about Mexico and really got that into my blood. I love Southern California and Mexico too, that whole culture. That became very important in my life. My folks oozed romance with each other; they were soul mates, so I got the concept.

My sixth grade teacher was Miss Schwab. If we were quiet at the end of the day, she would read to us; it was so cool. We were in sixth grade, but it was like being regressed and having your mother read to you. You felt like a big person, but cradled. She was reading us *The Lion, The Witch and The Wardrobe* [1950, by C. S. Lewis]. That was elementary school. I'm proud to have kept up very good grades in those formative years I attended formal schooling. My idols were my teachers, and my Daddy, who sang every song to me. I wasn't close to Mom [at that time] because of her deafness which was later corrected.

Though she respected and admired her mother, Serena sometimes sensed a competitive rivalry, and believes they shared many common personality traits.

My mother was very wise in understanding people's space. I remember I had a boyfriend that I was convinced my mother was in love with. I think it was true, but mother was able to just be a mother and be in love with a man in her mind. It wasn't sexual; it was just like loving a movie star. You can truly love George Clooney or whoever your idol happens to be. It was kind of interesting because I was a teenager having sex, and having the hots for this guy and I knew that about my mother. I could see inside that she had a secret life in there. I think that was the first time I saw my mother as a woman. We're just both so psychic. I mean she would have psychic thoughts that would protect the family. One year of violent rain storms the river flooded and you couldn't drive in or out of Mountain Oaks Park. Mom and I were home and her new baby was asleep in her crib. You couldn't hear much for the howling of the wind. Mom jumped up extremely suddenly, and ran into the crib room to get my sister. The hill behind that room was giving way to the pressure of a mudslide. I think we're both just in tune that way. I'm very much in love with my mother, and luckily, am now able to let her know. I just came back from visiting her in Las Vegas.

The Tiny Dancer

Ballerina, you must have seen her, dancing in the sand
And now she's in me, always in me, tiny dancer in my hand.

— ELTON JOHN AND BERNIE TAUPIN

The Catholic Church in downtown L.A. was fabulous and ornate. There was much ritual to it. That is actually the place where I found another one of my idols which was [Mother] Mary, who was always on the right side of the altar. Well, stage left. She comes up a lot in my art. A series of six-foot tall paintings I did are called *The*

Big Women: each is an archetype; she is one. The mother and child; it's a beautiful image. I had a wonderful time nursing and holding my own baby, it was one of the highest moments of my life. The frosting was holding my child and nursing her in my rocking chair.

The theme song of my life might be *Tiny Dancer* by Elton John [and Bernie Taupin]. I grew up adoring Rudolf Nureyev. My parents'

COURTESY OF SERENA

first date was going to the movie *The Red Shoes* [1948]. As a girl, I was in all kinds of lessons, dance lessons, TV acting, theatre lessons, and singing lessons. I had 8 x 10s done and did auditions. There was a time in my life to learn my art and to use up all my excess energy. Forget the Soccer Moms of today, I got driven all over L.A. County. I remember sticking to a real mentor in my life whose name is LaVon. She was my modern ballet teacher. It turns out that my partner, my love, my soul mate: his aunt is named LaVon, and I'd never heard that name before. He and I share all kinds of little coincidences which are proof of the rule: ultimately, everything is a coincidence. I took lessons with LaVon for many years — I loved her, I love "the dance". It was probably into the teens that I had done most of the lessons, but I have recital pictures of myself at age seven when I studied under LaVon. She ended up marrying a man who was a big, strapping, tall man. He would put a leotard on and come to the recitals and dance, and he was the only man. It was funny to most of the other girls, but it was wonderful to me to see a man there.

Once Serena reached her teen years, her fragmented self began to spiral out of control. Sexual activity brought a reprieve from her mental and physical pain, but Serena's anguished emotional state led her into hospitals for psychiatric assessment and behavioral management.

I had terrible teenage years where I was very abusive and hated [my mother] because of my bi-polar condition. I really had a tough, teenage hormonal trauma. Everybody goes through it, but I had it very bad where I was dragged into several mental institutions in a straightjacket. I had a very hard time with my menstrual periods; endometriosis left me screaming into the pillow for a week a month and that only got worse working in the Industry. My uterus never should have tried to take on so many strangers, but my mania had an itch that sex seemed to quell. I took all that pain out specifically, on my mother; I was so angry at; "the mother". Now, after having been medicated and I'm fine, I'm that much more appreciative of her.

Endometriosis afflicts more than six million girls and women in North America. The chronic condition is characterized by the absence of tissue that normally lines the uterus. Instead, the tissue is located upon the ovaries or in the area between the vagina and rectum, and can cause pain before or during menstruation and during sexual intercourse.

Interestingly, I am a "Four" on the Enneagram, a fascinating study of personality types.

The Enneagram is a personality trait test reputed to have validity relating to mystic theories based upon nine different scales. The abbreviated definition of Serena's number, a "Four," is as follows: "Fours" are self-aware,

Protecting our Freedom. COURTESY OF WORTH MENTIONING PUBLIC RELATIONS

sensitive, and reserved. They are emotionally honest, creative, and personal, but "Fours" can be moody and self-conscious. Withholding themselves from others due to feelings of vulnerability and deficiency, "Fours" feel contempt and are derisive of ordinary ways of living. "Fours" typically have problems with melancholy, self-indulgence, and self-pity. At their best inspired and highly creative, a "Four" is able to renew oneself and transform life experiences.

Junior high was probably too much sex, drugs, and rock and roll. I had a year of high school in Lake Tahoe and that was too much sex, drugs, and rock and roll. I went back to junior college later in my life. I really don't consider myself a high school graduate and I'm proud of that. That's just the path I took.

Precious and Few

During one of Serena's first employment opportunities, she met Thomas Blaquelord, who became her first husband. She also made a contact who introduced to her the notion of better paying options. Serena and Blaquelord eventually eased their way into films together.

Unfortunately, it was my first blind date I think, when I got hooked up with my first husband who was not a good find. We had a combative few years; it was nothing more than that. My husband and I were together as a couple and I got discovered working the counter at Bob's Big Boy, which is a tradition in our family. My mother met my father at Bob's when she was a waitress in Bob's Big Boy. It's a southern California chain with the best restaurant training, just terrific. Everything was all laid out for you. They gave the world these wonderful waitresses. Bob's was known for the niceness of their servers and the great food, so we were proud to work there. I dream about it so often I can actually taste the food in my dreams. Bob's Big Boy is now a landmark. Recently, I went to an event in L.A. with Bill Margold and he gave me a driver that was from Guam. The first place I wanted to go was Bob's Big Boy; it's exactly the same as it was except it no longer has a drive-thru, and there was a long line on the street of about forty people to get in! It's just a coffee shop but it's the best.

Anyway, I was working at the counter and this guy came in by the name of Ray Sebastian Jr. His father was Ray Sebastian

who was a make-up artist for the early legitimate Hollywood
movies. Ray Sebastian Jr. tried to pick me up, and he laughed
and said, "I'm for real — you could make more money doing
something else." He pointed out the window and he was driving
an ambulance. I laughed because my boyfriend, who I was with
before I married the father of my child, was named Rick Lipp.

COURTESY OF WORTH MENTIONING PUBLIC RELATIONS

He was an *organ*ist and at the time I was with him, he worked for the band *Climax:* their hit was "Precious and Few". Rick had this hearse that the band had used to move their equipment around until they upgraded to a band bus and roadies. I went to a prom gig with them. It was the only prom I ever went to and I was with the band! Rick gave the hearse to us as our wedding gift. I was married in black velvet and got the hearse. We were married on paper. Our relationship was about fighting each other. This is in the 1970s. I saw him recently at Christmas [2009] and every atom in his body is pure hate for Serena. He's so bloated and red from alcoholism and it's as if this is the only thing keeping him alive. It's so laughable and sad — as if I cared. Seeing him really allowed me to let it go.

Nuptials for Serena and Blaquelord were merely a precaution and formality for the young couple who had both started working in movies and were fearful about possible persecution and prosecution for their illegal involvement.

Ray Sebastian Jr. is the one who connected me to my first agent, Hal Guthu. My husband and I were both in a movie called *Sexual Ecstasy of the Macumba* (1974) directed by Carlos Tobalina . There was the gorgeous Egyptian theater in downtown Los Angeles and Tobalina needed to keep making movies so that people would keep on coming. He made these cheap, X-Rated movies and showed them at this glorious, gorgeous theater. An X-rated movie was something to see in those days and people would go because they were shown at this beautiful theater.

The Egyptian Theatre on Hollywood Boulevard in Los Angeles was built in 1922 by Sid Grauman and Charles E. Toberman. It is admired by visitors for its intricate ornate Egyptian style architectural design. The Egyptian housed the world premiere of *Robin Hood* in 1938. Grauman and Toberman were also responsible for constructing the El Capitan and Chinese theatres located in the same vicinity.

I did not do hardcore at that time, but when the film opened, it was apparent they had spliced in hardcore footage. I had only agreed to do softcore up until that point. I was afraid of the law, it was scary and we had the vice knocking on our door. At that point, L.A. cops were pigs, and they were always in your business. It seemed like every time we were driving we got pulled over. Here I am with a guy, who has hair down to his waist, and we're driving around in a hearse and they really didn't like that. We got busted and we married so that we wouldn't have to testify against one another in court.

Bill Margold and Serena, 2012.

Serena admitted the probability of she and her husband testifying against one another in court was next to nil, but in 1974 while it was still illegal to participate in the production of adult-oriented movies, she was naïve and unwilling to risk going to jail.

I got my second agent on my own, which was just down the block. That is how I met Bill Margold. Bill Margold ran the office. Bill is a true historian and he and I are spiritually linked in many, many ways. He'll be typing my name in his computer and I'll call him. Anyway, Bill and I are brother and sister — not blood. I really consider him my brother. I'm as close to him like a sibling as anyone could.

Renowned Adult film historian, William Margold, has worked in all capacities of the adult film industry in the areas of performing, script writing, film critique, and directing since joining the brother and sister-hood in 1973 when he started in the genre as an agent.

At the time, it was called Pretty Girl [Modeling Agency] which led to different kinds of photography. I kind of got known for bondage photography for a while because they used to call me "The New Bettie Page". I did them all — the centerfolds, and covers, and spreads. I didn't do *Playboy* at first because I am not the busty girl next door. I eventually ended up being in *Playboy* three times in "Sex in Cinema," and they saw I was perfect for their new magazine they were promoting: *Oui* magazine. I was still living at home with my parents and I did a layout for *Oui* owned by *Playboy*. We were living on a wonderful property with big oak trees and there was a renter living on the premises who was a nice young man. He brought the *Oui* to my dad and said, "Whoa man, this is really cool. She's gorgeous. Look at your daughter!" That kind of ended my life with my parents for many, many years. That was it. I didn't see them for a long time until the mid-eighties. A good ten years — I had many adventures and I made all of those movies in that period.

Serena on the Silver Screen

I think I was a spy in my first hardcore film. It was a feature, but I believe it was probably in the courtroom when I actually first saw myself on screen. I know I've seen a lot of my movies on video. I remember seeing enormous billboards of myself and thinking how striking that was. They were advertisements and the posters covered walls of construction areas in Manhattan.

Getting into baring my body was no "moral" choice. I was completely at ease in my nakedness. Nudes were in abundance in etchings and prints about the house. They were a part of my mother's collection. The figures on the walls of my childhood are nude women by the seashore in the moonlight. Having modeled for my father who was a phenomenal photographer and he raised a professional photographer [Daniel Gray], I was completely natural in front of a still camera.

For the first time, Serena divulged what it was like to be a temple housing an overabundance of sexual energy and how she was unequipped to harness that kind of potent power. In a kind of masochistic response to the force, physical discomfort became a side effect of some of her onscreen liaisons.

I know that I have a lot of power: "Every man and every woman is a star". I used to write that out when autographing. Unfortunately, because I didn't have a lot of control over that power, it had a lot of control over me. It did make me almost insatiable as far as my sexual drive. Luckily, for all, most of my sexual drive was on camera. That's a double edge for me because I hurt myself

COURTESY OF WORTH MENTIONING PUBLIC RELATIONS

physically, but it also prolonged me getting more balance. I had balance as far as my brain chemistry, but I got a bruised cervix and had a lot of problems. People were very, very rough on me — I'm sure accidently, most of the time. Foreign objects were inserted into me that weren't flesh and that is horrible. As long as John Holmes was, he never hurt me. As long as his cock was, he wasn't into raping my pussy.

A lot of it was the director's fault. I've wanted to talk about this. In most of my movies, I feel that I'm not acting in a script because I'm a certain character. I'm not being an actress. I'm just being a whore for the director so that he can get off. It's usually the director or the producer whoever is standing there saying, "Say, fuck me! Say, fuck me!"

I don't want to say, "Fuck me." They are very aggressive during most of the love making scenes unfortunately, where it was an intrusion. I never liked that about the movies.

PHOTOGRAPHY BY JOEL SUSSMAN

On the other side of the coin, Serena also recalled high caliber artists who worked in her circle and cited still photographer Joel Sussman as someone whom she revered for his impeccable eye and proficiency. As has been noted, Sussman captured some of the stunning images of Serena featured in this chapter.

Joel Sussman was an archetypical, big time, legitimate, thirty-five millimeter film still photographer. He could have been doing big movies at the studios. I always got that from him, that he was a total professional. I admire that.

One of the true times when I was being myself is in a movie called *Olympic Fever* (1979) which is actually quite a good movie — I must recommend it. I've enjoyed watching that one as a full feature film. There's one point in it where I'm doing my Monkey laugh. I didn't know it was my monkey laugh; it's just me having a good time in bed evidently. I'm happily and joyfully laughing. The last time I saw this movie was with Bill Margold and he said that when they play it at the theater, it's just like *Rocky Horror Picture Show* (1975). Everybody does the Monkey laugh.

Serena (as Janet) and Laurie Smith (as Kristin) play two swimmers part of an American team contending for Olympic Gold in Philip Marshak's *Olympic Fever*, a refreshingly funny and light-hearted take on the manipulation and antics behind-the-scenes during Olympic competition. The stakes are high, and under the guidance of coach Rod (Bill Margold), Janet and Kristen, along with their teammates (Candida Royalle, Connie Peterson, Hillary Summers, and Vicki Glick), strive to give their all in hopes of attaining the coveted title. Sinister forces are at play, however, as former, United States Olympian, Kenneth Swift (Paul Thomas) has joined the Russian judges (Ron Jeremy and Seka) in an effort to sabotage star swimmer Kristin along with her chances for a gold medal. First, they must determine how Kristin is able to sustain record -breaking times. When Ken isn't able to obtain the secret information from his girlfriend, Janet, or from Kristin herself, he and the Russians decide to kidnap, drug, and whip Kristin, rendering her incompetent for the competition on the following day. In the nick of time, Janet catches wind of her two-timing boyfriend's plot. With the aid of Coach Rod (Margold appears to be driving his beloved "Bear Mobile" van — he and Serena come across as comfortable old friends) the two locate the hideaway where Ken and the Russian coaches are holding Kristin. Fisticuffs ensue and on the following day of the competition, Kristin reveals the secret to her success as she extracts some lucky elixir from Coach Rod's rod, just minutes before she and Janet are due in the pool.

Paul Thomas makes a perfect bad guy, in tandem with Ron Jeremy's valiant attempt at a Russian accent, but the highlight of *Olypmic Gold* is Serena who shows off her innate flair as an actress and is at her sultry best. A pleasure to watch, Serena's effervescent presence magically transforms the material from a porn cliché to an entertaining adult feature worth watching.

> I worked with Ron Jeremy [Hedgehog] in *Olympic Fever*. It's funny because as sweet as he is, I met him in a rape scene in the Bronx [before *Olympic Fever*]. It was so scary, I was a California girl and he had never been out of Manhattan, which was mind blowing. They took me to the Bronx, and had Ron Jeremy and a couple of other guys in black leather, rape me in an elevator which was claustrophobic enough. It was the scariest thing; if you really want to scare yourself, that's one of the predicaments you'd put yourself in. I was quite scared of him for a long time, but I'm sure he's just a nice man. He's always very sweet to me whenever I run into him at functions. Actually, around the same time as *Olympic Fever*, I did a 3-D movie, *Blonde Emmanuel* (1977), which is also still shown in theaters. *Teenage Cruisers* (1977) is fun too. There's only about five of them that I think are good.

Also known as: *Disco Dolls in Hot Skin, Blonde Emmanuelle* stars two of the most attractive adult performers of the era, Serena and Mike Ranger, heading up the stable of actors in this campy film that manages to weave a believable plot within the fabric of the 3-D psychedelic adventure. Chick (Ranger) and Emmanuelle (Serena) become starry-eyed lovers upon their first meeting. They attempt to consummate their burning passion, but Chick can't maintain an erection long enough to get the job done. As nightclub manager — Chick inevitably dodges hopeful dames in his wake, and decides to talk to a shrink about his shrinkage.

There are some entertaining and fun gags throughout this zany flick. At one point, Harry Balls (Bill Margold) teams up with Chick to convert the nightclub into a brothel. Hilarity follows as Balls keeps the cops at bay, while Pat Manning grows a pair of her own balls in her appearance as a domanitrix, and Serena and Lesllie Bovee enjoy a little girl-on-girl delight. The film's shocking ending foreshadows a page right out of John Wayne Bobbitt's book.

With the tagline, "They'll strip your gears and pop your clutch!" *Teenage Cruisers* (aka *Cruising for Sex*) has one of the best soundtracks of 1970s adult flicks containing a good number of rock and roll and rockabilly tunes spanning three decades. The story jumps all over the place however, as local DJ Mambo Reaves (played by one of the screenwriters, Johnny Legend) fills the airwaves with nonsensical ramblings while various characters cruise the streets in search of sexcapades. People seem to interconnect through random experiences, and unrelated sexual groupings pepper the story.

Big-breasted Babsy Beaudine (Christine deShaffer) has escaped from an asylum, and kidnaps a high school teacher (Bill Margold) who becomes her sex slave. Serena, who is deserving of a better script, gives a first-rate performance as a woman who longs to make out with her long time boy-friend, Johnny, and imagines him covering her from head to toe with his load as if it's from a can of silly string. Handsome Rick "the Bod" Cassidy appears from out of nowhere (likely a clip from another endeavor) in a hot sex scene with a very willing partner. Out of the blue, two women compete in a topless, bake-off contest while the next scene hints at bestiality as a beautiful woman becomes aroused while brushing her donkey. *Teenage Cruisers* makes a valiant attempt to achieve the cool factor and works well as a cult sex film, but lacks clarity and continuity. Still, it's jam-packed with lots of action and decent sex. Of course, it also has Serena.

Blonde Pussy & the Beast

In California, pretty much I had fun with everybody. When I first started working in the Bay area, [former pornographic actor and director] John Seeman was around and he was very gentle. This was all before Jamie, who was the worst/best influence.

When I first got into films it was because I was a hippie, and like Alfred Kinsey, believed that people should be out fucking in the streets, walking around naked and on the grounds of Berkeley, California, and whatever. Since I've moved to Northern California, it's too cold up here to always be doing that. In the northern part of the state, it was pretty laid back and I was making films for all of the right reasons. Bill always calls me the "Last Flower Child".

During the 1970s, Serena was often invited to parties hosted by vari-ous Hollywood celebrities. She remembers how she and fellow starlet, Constance Money, were once guests at the Playboy Mansion. Serena was Warren Beatty's date and Money was paired with Hugh Heffner. The two couples wound up in Hefner's bedroom having sex, but the men ingested so much cocaine they were unable to achieve an orgasm which Serena didn't particularly like. She described the experience as painful for the women and said, "The drug made the men hard, but they weren't able to climax," due to "coke dick" — a term associated with the side effects of excessive cocaine ingestion. Despite the technical difficulties, a good time was had by all.

Serena and Jamie Gillis. PHOTOGRAPHY BY JOEL SUSSMAN

I want to thank Ron Jeremy — he gave a mini interview to the *National Enquirer* about how Warren Beatty and I had gone out. It was a very sweet little article about Warren Beatty and me. I always talk about that first night.

At the same party, Constance talked about Jamie Gillis to Serena (Money and Gillis had both starred in *The Opening of Misty Beethoven* in 1976). At that point, she and Jamie had not yet met, but the Columbia University grad that became a highly regarded adult thespian intrigued her. Serena and Jamie Gillis eventually became a consummate couple in a long and involved complex relationship while making films together.

In 1978, Serena and real-life lover Jamie Gillis, co-starred in *People*, a Gerard Damino docu-film considered a precursor to today's trend of "Reality" or "Gonzo" porn. Serena and Gillis, always unpredictable, exciting, and forever daring, made classic adult film history as two of the most sexually deviant, delicious stars of the era. In addition to Gillis, Serena reflected upon some of her favorite people in the business.

> I enjoyed working with [director] Gerard Damiano. Unfortunately, at that time, you would get flown to Chicago and there would be some money put together for what they called a movie. If they could afford you, you'd go, even if it was just for somebody's basement or something. Those "one day wonders." As for actors, of course, there was Jamie, but on the west coast, I liked John Nuzzo [John Leslie] a lot. Holmes is in a class of his own. Bill [Margold] calls John "The King," and to anyone who is really in the business, there will only be one King like Elvis. When I first started, I was doing films with Georgina Spelvin and she was sweet.

The same year *People* was released Serena appeared with Gillis in Robert McCallum's *The Ecstasy Girls* (1979) in which she played twin sisters Nancy and Diane Church. The twins, along with their two siblings (Lesllie Bovee and Laurien Dominique) and Aunt Madeline (Georgina Spelvin), are in line to inherit their grandfather's fortune. Unbeknownst to them, a devious uncle, J.C. Church (portrayed by the multi-talented character actor, John Alderman, aka Frank Hollowell), hopes to alter the natural course of the inheritance by exposing the girls' sexual wantonness. Knowing his dying father is concerned about the virtues of his granddaughters, Church hires an out of work actor (and escort to the rising stars) Jerry Martin (Jamie Gillis) to film the sisters and their aunt during the heat of passion. His hope is that once the footage is exposed to his father (Richard Norris), the fortune will be left solely to J.C. Martin is paid one hundred thousand dollars up front, and he recruits a couple of buddies and burgeoning filmmakers (John Leslie and Paul Thomas as hilarious sidekicks) to help seduce the sisters and film the action.

The action is definitely hot from the outset of this feature as Gillis and the rarely seen actor Nancy Suiter (who has achieved cult status based upon few appearances) are part of an intense threesome, while Aunt Madeline and C.J. watch from the hallway. Soon to follow, are Gillis and Nancy (the edgier twin) who engage in a great S&M game of cat and mouse. Nancy banishes Jerry/Gillis behind bars where she toys with him and taunts his penis until he breaks free and punishes her in a mini torture chamber.

Serena is exceptional in her interchange with Gillis as she methodically brings him to the edge like an elastic band, and then snaps him back to the corner. When Gillis (as Jerry) turns the tables and becomes the dominant, Serena is equally as effective as she fearfully obeys his every command while intimating that his requests are not part of the game. Jerry finally climaxes, and it is revealed he sensed what Nancy

Ecstasy Girls. CABALLERO CLASSIC. PHOTOGRAPHY BY JOEL SUSSMAN

wanted all along and gave it to her. Later, when Jerry and Diane (the reserved, well-mannered twin) are paired together for a picnic in the rain, their sex scene is tender and loving — a complete paradox to the earlier sexual rendezvous in leather with Nancy. With Desiree Cousteau added for good measure and honorable acting turns from all involved, *The Ecstasy Girls* finds a perfect balance between eroticism and smart dialogue, with competent pacing between the sex and non-sex scenes. By far, *The Ecstasy Girls* is one of the supreme offerings of late 1970s adult entertainment.

It was a fun time when I was with Jamie Gillis. He didn't fly and we would travel from California to New York where he lived, and go back and forth across the country on the train and have adventures. We'd be three and a half days on the train, with lots of pussy running around for Jamie to drag back to our den. We would have a lot of fun. We were sexual creatures. When I was with Jamie, we were on the prowl for practically anything that moved. That's a time in my life where he really was "The Beast," and I "Blonde Pussy". I had flown in from California as this golden angel with a one-week gig. I stayed for two years as a natural born New Yorker. My accent was so thick that in a couple of months people thought I was a local. I loved the role; I loved acting the part. His tenement was between Times Square and Hell's Kitchen and the Restaurant District. Paradise for him, he could walk to the sleazy area of which he was King and get some pussy; eat, and call out the window back at home to the Puerto Rican transvestites on the corner. Jamie and I had this period together, where we were just together fucking through the disco era. Fucking leaning up against walls in dark Clubs; fucking en orgy at Plato's Retreat. It was a period of time that was very hot — sizzling hot, a short part.

The well-known New York sex club Plato's Retreat catered to porn stars, swingers, celebrities, and socialites during the 1970s and up until 1985. Gillis is known to have been a fixture at the club during the peak of its popularity. Formerly located in the Ansonia Hotel on the Upper West Side of Manhattan, Plato's was closed down by Mayor Ed Koch in response to the outbreak of AIDS before relocating to Fort Lauderdale, Florida. In 2006, Plato's Retreat 2/The Slammer re-opened and now functions as a Men's club.

Serena and Gillis continued living and working together, and in 1979, Serena turned in a tender performance as a Southern Belle in the Philip Marshak release *Dracula Sucks* (aka *Lust at First Bite*), the X-rated counterpart to Bram Stoker's brilliant horror drama, *Dracula*. Jamie Gillis is eerily astonishing as Count Dracula as he proposes to seduce the women (Serena and Annette Haven) while visiting the mansion adjacent to his. Matching Gillis on screen in her sensuality and versatility, Serena, as Lucy Webster, captures the imagination of viewers as she haltingly encapsulates the charm and innocence of a Southern girl unaware of the powers of the Count's crafty ways. When Gillis finally consumes Serena, their chemistry is at its hottest as they make love with an intuitive ferocity. *Dracula Sucks* is an intriguing incarnation of the original story, and generates some great sex with the help of the esteemed lineup: John Leslie, John Holmes, Mike Ranger, Kay Parker, Annette Haven, Seka, Paul Thomas, Pat Manning, Bill Margold, and Nancy Hoffman — all tip top in distinctive roles.

Instrument of Lust

When asked if she had a voice when it came to choosing to work with a particular actor or performing a specific sex act on camera, Serena outlined the rules within the parameters of the adult entertainment business and its cast of participants and personalities.

It would depend upon the film and the director. Probably the producer who wrote the checks would have the last word. You wouldn't want to argue with anybody. Of course, you wouldn't stomp off the set. Some women would play diva and play those games. I was always the "can't we just get along" type. I would always try to adjust whatever body part of mine wasn't comfortable to some level of comfort. That would be the trick for me. A lot of the uncomfortable feelings came from the fact that strangers would be getting together, and that's not all that hot because they don't necessarily fit together well. Maybe it's a turn on to watch, but they are not the right people necessarily, without a lot of K-Y jelly lubricant.

One scene that did not require K-Y jelly is the erotic Jacuzzi encounter showcasing Marilyn Chambers and Serena together in *Insatiable* (1980). With her short-cropped, copper hair, Serena, breathtakingly beautiful and at the height of her sexual prowess, brings a playful attitude and genuinely sensual approach to her lovemaking with Chambers within a story about one woman's vow to indulge in life's sexual appetizers after her parents are killed in an automobile accident. It is believed there is cut footage of a fisting scene between Serena and Marilyn Chambers that was purposely edited out of the film because of risk of arrest.

Two years prior to making *Insatiable*, Serena had given birth to a daughter, Lucy Sky Diamond, named after the young girl in the 1967 Lennon and McCartney song "Lucy in the Sky with Diamonds." When Serena lived in Paris in the summer of 1979, her two-year old daughter had gotten gum in her hair. Serena sat in the tub with Lucy to cut the gum out, and then proceeded to cut her own hair short so that her little girl would stop crying. When she returned to the United States, Serena arrived on the *Insatiable* shoot literally by helicopter (as is shown in the film) sporting a becoming pixie coiffe.

Understanding there were many commonalities between people working within the sex industry, Serena respected a person's unique view of oneself and acknowledged her own individuality. She believes she and her generation of erotic performers were on an elevated platform.

> I went all over the country booked as a "Star of the Silver Screen" with a stage show. The clubs can be very, very depressing, populated with depressed men. Gross, gross, gross. These are people with not much else to do in front of mirrors applying layer after layer of make-up for hours and hours through the thickest cigarette smog ever, gossiping. No boss is there to tell them to do anything, they sit and gossip and grouse. All they talk about is family dysfunction and being exploited and all that stuff. It *is* true: but their own depressed energy is *keeping* it true for them. It had nothing to do with my case whatsoever, I am of The Dance, and swirl magick in my movements.
>
> I want to say that all of those girls in Vegas with fake boobs have allowed themselves to be exploited, but they seem to feel at peace with their decision. Looking the same as the next Barbie cutout seems to be a style. "The Industry" opened up that whole mindset after I'd retired. My industry was different: first story, then sex. Body type wasn't that important.
>
> I was an active feminist in the eighties, marching on Washington, and wearing all white during the marches, and oh, I had fun. It was with the women *and* men. I visited the women's art history museum, which is art only by women. It's a marble building, but you walk and the entire rotunda ceiling is pink marble. It's gorgeous! It's so wild with beautiful paintings. A painting I was working on through that decade is twelve feet tall by nearly thirty feet long called "Women under Discussion". On it are almost life size women dancers.

In light of her experiences as a renegade female adult performer who pushed the limits to extremes even within her particular vocation, Serena related what the tandem of feminism and sexuality represented to her, as an inclusive designation.

> I think it is to be completely one self. To just express one self, no matter what that is. That would be the definition about being a man, too. In the eighties, it was about gender and it needed to be. I remember being the spokesperson for Doc Johnson, waving my hand at the vibrator. That was one of my little gigs when I lived in the Valley. It was a strange, fun time.

I'm glad to have lived through the sexual revolution. I missed AIDS by minutes. I've learned a lot because it was such a different life than other people live. Whatever the view of your world is, you just need to take and learn from it. Life itself is masturbation. It is masturbating the Self, if you will. I've learned it's really, really good to have an orgasm, and you should do it every day somehow.

You should laugh, and have some kind of absolute bliss in your life. You should take responsibility for that and not depend upon anybody else to give you that. You should just do it for yourself or ring a bell! You owe it to yourself and you owe it to the world. If everybody just did that for themselves, and took care of themselves, and got out of everybody else's business, the world would be happy and at peace.

Everybody has regrets. The worst thing to have is regret, but it's like guilt — it's useless and it doesn't do you any good. It eats you up inside. I wish I would have had more acting training and better scripts to play, but most all the sex was at least interesting: some dull and sweaty; some champagne and cocaine — the drug of choice at that time — created some honest, giggly, fun sex with familiar bodies mostly. Days on the set were "hurry up and wait".

We had a shared film lingo with the grips, ADs and fluffers (!) that wove us into a family of sorts. I crocheted the world's second longest scarf — it had no end — in the long hours of lighting setups. The heat under the lamps that were used then could be scalding hot — performing in a crowd: the light creating a fire in the surrounding darkness of the soundstage, the cave. Sex could be like that when I was the instrument of lust. The object: my pussy, the entryway to happiness. I hoped to give this to the people that saw me through the flickering in the darkness of their theatre. In my personal time off the set, I was reading philosophy and studying Tarot, and putting together a sort of White Magick of my own.

Aftermath

I like to think I am in part responsible for the openness and freedom of speech we have today. My older sister has seen my films and supports my decision, and my other siblings are sexually positive because of the times we grew up. I've always been bi-polar and I've always been a loner, so I live a lifestyle like a hermit. I'm able to talk to my [younger] sister now. I don't have any girlfriends. Actually, my childhood friend Leah and I send each other Christmas cards and I did see her when I was in the hospital in a coma. As soon as I came out of the coma, she was there, so I know she is with me. That's one of the only times I've seen her in all my life. It's okay because I have this connection with my best friend.

In the fall of 2001, Serena experienced an altercation with a fixed object during an impulsive act of desperation. She suffered extensive injuries to her body from the fall that transpired, and was hospitalized and in a coma for one month. Today, Serena regards the event as a life-altering opportunity.

I was torn between two men and I threw myself out a plate glass window and down a mountain. It was self-inflicted. I guess I wanted to go bye-bye — I couldn't seem to keep anybody happy. I couldn't stand it anymore — so much pressure. It was a very interesting experience. I think that was really the only time I got that close. I've never *thought* of myself as suicidal, but I get extremely manic and then I'm depressed.

The pain my body has suffered has made me a lot more compassionate of others. You need to "get taken down a notch" by life sometimes, you know, to see who's really in charge. It was really a good experience. Death is nothing to be afraid of; I looked straight in its eye. Of course, I came back kicking and screaming I might say, but granted, a lot of peace. It wasn't like, "Oh, I have a second

COURTESY OF SERENA

chance now." Knowledge was given to me, but working through years of rehabilitation was the price I've paid. It manifested in me as having a lot more control of my life and a lot more true happiness. The fact is that the path of my life has always been on certain levels, and now I'm on a different level. I like who I am. My solid upbringing with such interesting people as parents got

Serena. COURTESY OF SERENA

me through the wild years when I was young, gorgeous and doing movies, living in Hollywood and The Valley, and being part of the porn scene. My kid sister who went through Pre-Med, but considers me "the smart one," has the paperwork on my IQ testing. I have an embarrassingly high IQ, and, like all mad "artists," I've made my way as best I could.

"Goddess" equals Peace, Love & Happiness

It was a very special time, and this group of women that are included in this book — we were all very special and we were special as a group, as a community of artists. Like the Hudson River school of porn. I still have the taste of glamour that it gave me and I've actually started to appreciate it more because at that time I was treated with stardom and deference, which is delightful and delicious. You can eat it up, and as a young woman, that's the good part. That's why you put on lipstick and wear high heels. You can get back to that if you look in the mirror every day and like what you see. I felt I was an instrument of the message Peace, Love and Happiness. I still do.

I just got back from a month of playing with my daughter and her two kids and my mom and my sister in Las Vegas. It was fabulous. I couldn't have had more fun. It was just great. I had a big sewing area there and I got to go out to dinner with everybody; I got to ride on Ferris Wheels. I was there for a Christmas party, a New Year's party, Christmas day, Martin Luther King day, my sister's birthday — a Capricorn kid — and my birthday, on January 20, right on the cusp of Aquarius. I have a good relationship with my granddaughter who I adore. I just finished making her a quilt. We are on the same wavelength, because I like to be six and blissfully happy and that's how she is. What could be better? I'm a sexy grandma and I'm very happy.

What I do in the winter rain, I live on the top of a mountain in the redwood trees and look out on the redwood trees, play with my little bird and draw Marilyn Monroe. I'm obsessively drawing Marilyn Monroe this year, obsessively on purpose, finding out for myself why people make an image, an idol. I am drawing the Marilyn face that Andy Warhol did in a photograph. I'm doing that piece my way. I want a hundred of them, one hundred different ways. It's that face over again, but each time, it will be Marilyn twinkling at you, just a little different. She comes alive and it's fascinating to do. I just fall into her honey and when I feel a swoon, I know she has come alive under my hands.

When it clears up and becomes spring, I do the garden — that's out by the coast, and I play with my horses. Then when it becomes

PHOTOGRAPHY BY PAUL JOHNSTON

summer, I've got to start sculpting; that's my schedule. I sculpt into the fall and then I'm firing and glazing. That was my routine last year and it worked really well. A lot of my pieces went to my family — I took a piece for everyone, but I sell enough. I sculpt phalluses, and goddesses, and eroticism and yard art.

When I found the other half of me, my soul mate, words poured forth, and for the first year of knowing him, I did nothing but love him and write poetry. It's the juice, it's just like the river; it goes where it goes.

The closing poem is an example of Serena's talent for articulating the written word in this symbolic gesture of love and desire for her partner.

Sex

My toes standing on the tops of your feet;
You hold me suspended as if I weigh nothing.
All my body pressing into you;
Sweat the sweet and sour sauce of lovemaking
Tangy and sharp, salty;
Your breath on my ear hot,
A trade wind bringing your gifts;
A hollow box echoing, the moans in your chest
When I find what you need.
Hips leading, I slide the length of you –
My hands move around you
Hold you
Hold your bones
Your body
Your breath;
Hold the life that is in my embrace
I circle you and I am pierced by you
There is nothing else.
Lust our only boundary
Lust has no conscience
No memory and no allegiance.

Annie Sprinkle
Global Goddess

Annie Sprinkle's list of professional and lifetime achievements beginning with her chosen field in prostitution, burlesque, and erotic entertainment where she still reigns as the buxom, golden shower Queen — and presently as a Ph.D. sexologist-activist, eco-sexual conceptual performance artist, lecturer and writer is staggering and a tribute to her dedication to her craft and her devotion to the environment. To quote one of Sprinkle's artist friends, Kembra Pfahler, the pleasantly curvaceous Annie prefers not to "yesturbate," and constantly propels forward with a third eye on the future as she conscientiously teaches about the indelible fusion between sex and ecology.

Since leaving her work as a prostitute/sex performer, Sprinkle has reinvented herself many times while remaining true to her heart and her passion for sexualized issues. She is the ultimate alpha female of her era and continues to swath paths in new territories exemplifying what it is to be a feminist: a term that is once again in favor and credibly articulates Annie's modus operandi.

The eldest of four, Annie Sprinkle (now her legal name) was born Ellen Steinberg in Philadelphia, Pennsylvania in 1954. The family migrated to Southern California where they settled into a life of normal domesticity. Annie happily participated in family gatherings or outings to musicals, the movies, and various activities. Sprinkle's father supported his brood as a social worker and would eventually become a professor at USC (University of Southern California). Annie's parents were politically progressive and active members of the Unitarian Church; they extolled the virtues of their belief system to their children. When she was thirteen, the family moved to Panama in Central America. While earning her high school diploma, Sprinkle dabbled in various hallucinogenic drugs — to

"I was in mainstream adult entertainment for twenty years. I've been in alternative sexually oriented art and film for almost as long. Theater, visual art, performance art, writing, but still almost all sex related. I feel like my best is yet to come in the Eco-sex movement I'm helping to co-create." ANNIE SPRINKLE

COURTESY OF *ANNIESPRINKLE.ORG*

which she attributes the expansion of her psychological, sexual, and spiritual peripheries.

In Tucson, Arizona in 1973, Sprinkle began working at a theatre where she was introduced to her first X-rated film, *Deep Throat* (1972), when it played at the twenty-four hour movie house. Annie found the film to be an exhilarating event coinciding with the coming out of her introverted shell. Charmed by *Deep Throat* creator and director, Gerard Damiano, Annie and Damiano kindled a meaningful romance and long time friendship.

While studying filmmaking at Kirtman Studios in Manhattan, Sprinkle (who later studied photography) decided she was better versed in the act of performing oral sex than the girls she observed on screen and made her hardcore feature film induction in *Seduction* (1974) followed by *Teenage Deviate* (1975). Annie soon became known for alternative mainstream porn showcasing her superior and playful abilities in the art of fetishism. Her famed original erotic piece, *Deep Inside Annie Sprinkle* (1981), was one of the largest grossing pornographic films in the early 1980s. In 1999, the educational and explicit DVD Annie Sprinkle's *Herstory of Porn* provided audiences with over one hundred clips from Annie's inspiring filmography, ranging from her maturation years to present day. Sprinkle also helped to launch Club 90, an exclusive group of women characterized by their careers in porn during the golden age. In 1992, Sprinkle received her Ph.D. in Human Sexuality from the Institute for the Advanced Study of Sexuality.

The sex industry continues to shape shift in the new millennium, and Annie Sprinkle, in conjunction with her life partner Beth Stephens (a tenured Professor at Santa Cruz University), remains steadfast and true to herself and to our universe. With a caring and concerned heart, Sprinkle celebrates and promotes the symbiotic relationship between eroticism and the world as its Eco-Sexy Spokesperson, Friend, Mother, Sister, Daughter, Lover, and Philosopher.

I spoke with Annie Sprinkle in February and in March 2010.

Gypsy Dreams

I was born in Philadelphia, Pennsylvania in 1954. At the age of five years old, I moved to Los Angeles with my family. We went to Granada Hills in the San Fernando Valley, a suburb of Los Angeles. I didn't like it very much but we had a swimming pool in our back yard and I loved swimming. That's partly why I chose the last name "Sprinkle".

I was the oldest of four kids so by the time I was five there were three more kids, which was a bit tough. I was expected to tie my own shoes and feed myself, but couldn't so I grew to be a little insecure. My mother was busy with other kids. That's about the worst thing that happened during my childhood. That's actually not too bad. In fact, my parents read us stories a lot and we went camping, and we did a lot of family activities. My mom taught English as a second language once we got older. She was one of the best in L.A., and my dad was a social worker and later became a college professor. My mom is still alive.

I have Russian and Polish Jewish blood; my grandmother spoke Yiddish. We were culinary Jews and ate the right food for the right holidays. My parents were always very political and anti-war, and pro-civil rights. My parents were Unitarians and I was raised Unitarian. They were Liberal intellectuals. A lot of famous Americans that worked on the Constitution were Unitarians. It was about believing what you are drawn to believe. You can be Jewish, and also be Unitarian or Christian and be Unitarian. It is a very open-minded concept. You can be very religious or you can be an Atheist. My parents are pretty much Humanists.

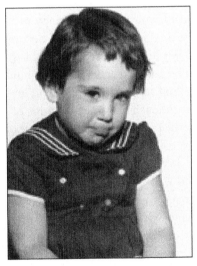

COURTESY OF *ANNIESPRINKLE.ORG*

Predicated upon the belief that God is "one," the practice of the Unitarian faith is rooted in Christian theology with origins in Transylvania and Poland dating back to 1540. Unitarian devotees denounce the Christian belief of the "Trinity" that symbolizes and unifies God with Jesus (the Son) and the Holy Ghost as a single unit or that Jesus is the incarnation of God.

I was very shy, very shy. I preferred staying in my room doing art projects. I liked to paint by number, and I did ceramics and ballet and tap, and I was a Girl Scout. Actually, I was a Blue Jay, which was a Camp Fire Girl. I was so shy, you know, I think my mom was kind of tough on me but I was never physically abused. Once I had my hand slapped for reaching into the cookie jar. That was it. I was never sexually abused. My dad was working a lot.

My parents were not sex negative, but they weren't very open about sex either. They left a few books lying around on the shelf like *The Kinsey Reports* [*Sexual Behavior in the Human Male*, 1948, and *Sexual Behavior in the Human Female*, 1953] and the *Joy of Sex* [1972] which they figured we would find when we were ready. They didn't talk to us about sex. At the Unitarian church we were shown films of babies being born; the church is well known for having sex education and they are sex positive, in general. I had that healthy influence. Essentially, I think I was raised to be political. Sex is political. Other than that, no one ever could have predicted the life path I would take, especially me.

As a child I thought I'd become an art teacher. When I decided to get into porn at eighteen, I thought, "Well, I guess I won't get to be an art teacher." Who would hire me once I did porn? I was willing to risk it to follow my muse. Interestingly, now I do sometimes teach art and I do a lot of college lecture gigs *because* I did porn! I am invited to lecture about once or twice a month. I love the college atmosphere.

I come from creative roots. My grandfather was a portrait painter and a commercial artist. Dad was a tap dancer, playwright, and a singer. There were many times when we would all gather around the piano, which Mom played. My family went to a lot of museums and we traveled a lot, so my parents were very supportive of the arts and we went to the theatre and saw many movies together. My family all loved musicals. The movie *Gypsy* (1962) was a family favorite, and also *West Side Story* (1961) and *Damn Yankees* (1958). Musical theater had a major influence on me. Especially *Gypsy*, which was about a stripper. It's a great film with Natalie Wood.

Gypsy was originally a smash Broadway musical with Ethel Merman in the title role of Rose Hovick, the domineering stage mother of renowned burlesque performer Gypsy Rose Lee. To achieve success vicariously, Hovick drags her two young daughters, Louise and June, across country in a desperate attempt to secure the girls bookings in various Vaudeville houses. When the girls became too mature to pass as children (and June marries a dancer), at the encouragement of her mother, the shy and lesser talented Louise auditions to strip at a mediocre burlesque theatre and discovers a new and thriving career: thus creating the stage name, "Gypsy Rose Lee." With original music and lyrics composed by Jule Styne and Stephen Sondheim, the musical was adapted from Gypsy Rose Lee's own memoirs and made into a feature film in 1962 starring Natalie Wood (who did her own singing) in the feature role of Gypsy. Rosalind Russell took over the reins as "Mama Rose."

Annie Sprinkle didn't grow up with an overbearing mother who pushed her into stardom, but not unlike Gypsy Rose Lee, as a painfully introverted girl, Annie was a dormant flower waiting to be nourished.

Of course, I loved the Beatles and I can tell you a sad story. When I was twelve, my girlfriends and I got tickets to the Beatles at the Hollywood Bowl, but the day of the concert, I was so terrified that I couldn't cry or scream just right — I was so excruciatingly shy and was afraid I wouldn't be cool enough, so I told them that I didn't want to go. It's crazy, huh? John was always my favorite Beatle.

At thirteen, we moved to Panama in Central America and I went to high school in Panama. At fourteen, I did my first LSD, psychedelic mushrooms and marijuana, and that kind of cracked me open and I learned about altered states. That was during the late sixties and happened to be what millions of people did back then. When I was seventeen, we stayed in a house with friends of my parents, Dr. Vern and Bonnie Bullough R.N. They were famous Sexologists who wrote dozens of books about sexuality. They had a huge sex book library. They made an impression on me in that I learned people could study sex, and not have to hide the fact.

The late Dr. Vern Leroy Bullough, a Ph.D. Dean, lecturer and scholar, wrote several books and editorials on sexuality and diverse practices on the subjects of prostitution, feminism, and medieval medicine. In recent years, Bullough broadened his readership with writings on the history of the nursing profession within the context of the medical community. Bullough earned his Bachelor's degree in Nursing at California State University in 1981 though he never practiced. As a sexual activist, Dr. Bullough became a lifelong advocate and supporter of gay, racial, and feminist groups. Bullough's spouse, the late Bonnie Bullough who came from meager beginnings, achieved a Master's of Science degree in Nursing, and later became a nurse practitioner before her appointment as Professor at California State University. Along with her husband, Bonnie Bullough gave over one hundred lectures on human sexuality and co-wrote and edited more than thirty books. The Bulloughs were Humanists (the philosophy and/or practice centering on human values) and belonged to the Unitarian church.

I happily let go of my virginity at seventeen when we got back to California. In 1973, I moved to an artist commune in Oracle, Arizona with my first boyfriend. A few months after I gave up my virginity with him, I moved to Tucson and I had sex with fifty guys over the next six months. I automatically began to document my sex life. It was just a little list of names with some notes really, but I thought I should write down their names at least, for some reason. Then I became a hippie in Tucson for years, where I eventually worked in a porno movie theatre selling popcorn. In Tucson, Arizona *Deep Throat* (1972) was playing. It was around 1973. I'd never seen a porn movie before and I didn't even know they existed. I got a job selling popcorn at the Plaza Cinema. After work one night, I went to see *Deep Throat* and I was totally shocked and amazed. I loved it! Wow, I had no idea that there were movies that showed actual sex. I had a thought of sex as something so intensely private even though I had become quite promiscuous. *Deep Throat* was a lovely film. It was very funny and it had great music. Linda Lovelace was wonderful and a marvel.

Deep Throat featured Linda Lovelace as a sexually frustrated housewife on a quest to have an orgasm. Her therapist (played by Harry Reems) enlightens her to the fact that her clitoris is located inside of her throat. In order to experience a climax, Lovelace must first learn to perfect her oral technique by "deep throating" males, resulting in immense sexual pleasure and satisfaction for both parties. Buxom Carol Connors (mother of Hollywood actor Thora Birch) who later enjoyed success in adult pictures such as *The Erotic Adventures of Candy* (1978), *Candy Goes to Hollywood* (1979) and (director) Ann Perry's *Sweet Savage* (1979) played Reems' nurse. Interestingly, the term "deep throat" is the pseudonym given to the informant Mark Felt who provided *The Washington Post* writers Bob Woodward and Carl Bernstein information about President Nixon and his government's involvement in what became known as "Watergate" in 1972. In 1974, Woodward and Bernstein published *All the President's Men* about the scandal which became an award-winning film in 1976. Felt's identity was revealed thirty-one years after President Nixon's resignation.

The Plaza Cinema was open twenty-four hours a day so guys would come in and talk to me in the middle of the night. They gave me lots of attention. I loved to flirt with them. Then the police busted the theater for showing porn and *Deep Throat* went on trial for obscenity. I was subpoenaed to be a witness in the trial, to appear in court, and I met Gerard Damiano in the witness waiting

COURTESY OF *ANNIESPRINKLE.ORG*

room. Linda Lovelace was also there. In the seventies, you would get arrested if you got caught making porn. No one quite knew if it was legal or illegal. Thanks to all the *Deep Throat* court cases porn [eventually] became legal.

Damiano was a lovely Italian man. I asked him to teach me to "deep throat". We became lovers for a year and a half. I was eighteen and he was forty-five, and we stayed friends. I went to Florida for his eightieth birthday. He died a month later in the fall of 2008. He lives on in my heart and my clit.

Between the time the Plaza was busted and the court case, I had ended up working in a little desert massage parlor. I worked there for three months before I realized I was doing prostitution and not merely being a horny masseuse. Prostitution really fit my needs at the time. I could have gone to college like all my friends, but instead I went on a big adventure.

Besprinkled

Damiano really didn't get me into porn. He didn't want me to become involved in films. I was already working in prostitution, so he had helped me to get a job in a massage parlor in New York through Al Goldstein who was the publisher of *Screw* magazine at that time. I liked it; it was a nice job. I really liked the work and was very happy doing it, but I wanted to learn filmmaking so I got a job several days a week apprenticing filmmaking at Kirt Studios. Leonard Kirtman had a big loft film studio in the West 20s, in Manhattan and they would crank out several hardcore feature films a month — mostly "one day wonders." I was the script girl, sheet changer. I fluffed for a few films and suddenly realized, "I can give a better blow job than that". I fluffed for Harry Reems once when he couldn't get it up. Eventually, Kirtman asked me to do a film and I said, "Okay".

Leonard Kirtman, founder of International Film Industries (aka Kirt Film Studios) worked as a taxi driver before producing Nudie and low budget Horror films in the late 1960s-1970s. By the mid-1970s, Kirtman graduated to making hardcore productions. In 1977, Kirtman proclaimed he would no longer be affiliated with pornography, and instead, made films that were R-rated. Eventually, Kirtman reverted to the hardcore market.

I remember the first time I saw myself as a centerfold. It was the first or second issue of *Cheri* Magazine. It was a national magazine, but it was all over Manhattan on newsstands. Before the internet, there were lots and lots of Men's magazines. I remember getting the issue I was in and thinking to myself, "Oh my god." I'd never seen a magazine with such a big, gaping, pink pussy before. It filled half the centerfold. Up until that time, the newsstand magazines were more like *Playboy*. It was kind of a big deal at the time. I was excited. It was like, "Wow." I remember observing how my pussy looked even though I'd already seen it on film, but I didn't notice it as much somehow as I did in the magazine. The magazine was available right on the corner where anyone had access to it, as opposed to having to go into a theater to see a porn movie. Nowadays, it's no biggie to be in porn. In the seventies, there weren't very many people in porn. There was a lot more stigma back then.

In much the same way that 1970s and eighties pop culture musician David Bowie created a medley of alternative personas such as "Ziggy Stardust" and "The Thin White Duke" to reflect various stages in his life and musical career, young Ellen Steinberg invented an identifiable moniker, "Annie Sprinkle," reflective of a specific porn genre.

When I had to pick a name, the word "Sprinkle" popped into my head and I just really resonated with it. I really enjoyed golden showers, spit, cum, waterfalls, swimming pools, hot tubs and the beach — anything wet. Still do! When I first saw myself on the big screen, I was very excited. I was very proud of myself being a shy wallflower and all. I went straight into hardcore. Later, I did about six "B" movies and dozens of documentaries. Eventually, I would pioneer several new film genres: edu-porn, gonzo, post-porn, art porn, feminist porn…In the seventies, the people in porn were all about filmmaking. They almost all aspired to do Hollywood type films. Porn emulated mainstream movies. Today, it's very different. Porn became its own genre.

Annie Sprinkle was twenty years old in her feature debut within an interracial group sex sequence in a film titled *Seduction* (released in 1974) along with Jamie Gillis and Andrea True, the former porn star turned Pop Artist with the 1976 signature hit, "More, More, More". True passed away from undisclosed causes in November 2011.

In 1975, Sprinkle surfaced in various productions: *Too Hot to Handle*, *Teenage Masseuse*, and *Affairs of Janice*. During her youthful years in the business, Annie Sprinkle's name became analogous with some of the fetish facets of the genre, specifically "golden showers," the act of urinating upon or being urinated on during or after the act of sex, as is evidenced in Sprinkle's starring role in the Video-X-Pix vehicle *Teenage Deviate* also released in 1975.

Billed as Annie "Sprinkles," Annie's sweet demeanor renders endurable the rudimentary but intriguing *Teenage Deviate* (written and directed by Ralph Ell and produced by Leonard Kirtman), about a naive young woman gone astray in New York City. When the film opens, Ella (Annie) is seated in her psychiatrist's office chomping on chewing gum while reminiscing about the sexual details of her previously sheltered life. Ella attempts to gain a clearer understanding of her severed relationship with her mother. With great fondness, she describes her first sexual experience with a blonde boy (Ras Kean) one afternoon in the backyard of her home. In her description, the boy spanked Ella repeatedly (and hard) on the backside during intercourse, resulting in a golden shower as Ella lightly urinated on her friend prior to his climax. Ella expressed to her shrink the fervor of her mother's anger when she happened upon her naked daughter and her lover, prompting the doctor to probe Ella further about her experimental love life and how it affected her feelings about herself and her mother.

In order to gain independence, Ella explained how she'd traveled to stay with her cousin Audrey (Nikki Hilton) in New York City. Audrey had been keeping her louse of a boyfriend Hank (Ed Marshall) in beer and cigarettes while Audrey turned as many as eight tricks a day. Ella fell in love with Hank and shared that the two had an affair behind Audrey's back. While Audrey was out on the street, Hank manipulated Ella into blowing him and his buddies by reminding her if she truly loved him, "freebies" are expected. As a seeker of genuine love and affection in all the iniquitous places, Ella told the doctor she obliged the creeps and discovered there are worse things in life.

Quickly, Audrey learns what is going on under her nose and she and Ella become embroiled in a scrap. Audrey tosses Ella out of the tiny apartment, and tearfully, Ella calls her mother only to be verbally berated again (a scene that is poorly filmed as one can clearly tell that the individual playing Ella's mother is not on the telephone, or even female!). Undaunted, Ella tries her hand at romance once again. This time, her Romeo (Helgar Pedrini) is married — a fact that doesn't come to light until after the lout takes her to a cheap motel for even cheaper sex.

Annie as Ella possesses a sweet and lovely essence in her core that inevitably gets her into trouble with the people in her life who attempt to take advantage of her good nature and intentions. *Teenage Deviate* was released in 1975, but Annie believed it may have been filmed in 1973.

COURTESY OF *ANNIESPRINKLE.ORG*

I started out doing very mainstream, vanilla, hardcore porn, but after a few years, I became kinky. I was the girl who liked all kinds of fetishes and unusual fantasies. I was only too happy to do the S&M scenes, the interracial scenes, golden showers, and most movies back then had a "rape" scene. A few directors could be manipulative and would try to get a porn actress to push herself, but that was the

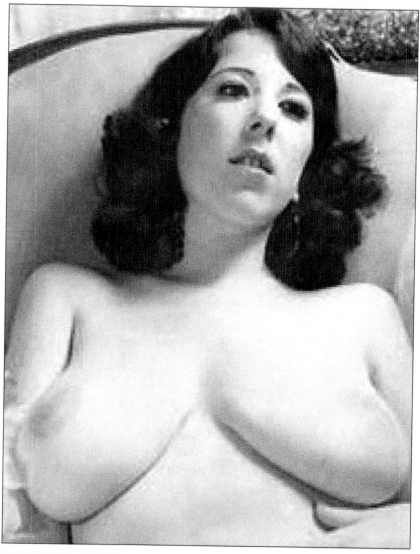

COURTESY OF *ANNIESPRINKLE.ORG*

same as any acting or theater job. Overall, I had good experiences. I had only a few bad days, but what job don't you have occasional bad days?

I worked a whole bunch with Bobby Astyr. He was a lovely Jewish guy, funny and sweet. Most of the New York porn actors were Jewish guys in the old days. I'm not sure why, maybe the Catholic boys had more shame. There weren't that many Jewish women interestingly. I might have been the only one! Of course, a lot of the producers and directors were Jewish too, just as they are in mainstream Hollywood.

Bobby Astyr (born Robert H. Charles) was born in New York in 1937 to Jewish parents, and made over one hundred and forty film appearances until his death from cancer in 2002. During his years in the business, Astyr tried to help many of his addicted and alcoholic porn friends. He was one of Sprinkle's frequent co-stars with whom she participated in various porn proclivities exhibited in films such as *Satan Was a Lady* (1975) directed by Doris Wishman (as Kenyon Wintel). Annie (as Anny Sands) plays the promiscuous sister of a soon-to-be-bride. In the first of two scenes with Bobby Astyr (as Bobby Astyn), Sprinkle is bound in leather wrist and ankle cuffs while she (with nary a trace of public hair) and Astyr enjoy oral and vaginal copulation. The scene is accompanied by a buoyant musical score which, in tandem with Annie's bubbly personality, depicts the hardcore landscape as loose, fun, and pleasurable.

Sprinkle definitely worked with her fair share of porn's rogues.

Porn star Marc '10 ½' Stevens was my close friend and lived down the hall from me at 90 Lexington Ave in New York. He was actually gay, but straight for pay. We worked together a few times. I had a bit of a crush on Jamie Gillis and Harry Reems. They both had a bit of a mean streak, but I liked that at the time. I was rather masochistic, so I found bad boys hot up until a certain point. When I developed more self-esteem, I became less interested because I just perceived them as a bit mean.

I actually never worked on the west coast the entire time I did films even though I'm from the San Fernando Valley where I grew up which is now the porn capitol of the world. The porn capital was New York City in the old days.

Vanguards & Revelations

Key guiding lights stirred the young insubordinate with the activist spirit making a vital impact on the impressionable, open-minded Sprinkle during her developing years as a sex worker.

Xaviera Hollander, "The Happy Hooker" was an influence on my life. I read her book [*The Happy Hooker: My Own Story*, 1971] early on. Another big influence was Margo St. James. She started the American Prostitutes Rights Movement. In 1975, I joined her non-profit organization: COYOTE [Call off Your Old Tired Ethics]. She had printed this little newspaper *Coyote Howls* about decriminalizing prostitution and I thought, "What a concept." Working in prostitution was and still is illegal.

Before COYOTE, St. James was married to Paul Avery, the former *San Francisco Chronicle* journalist targeted by the "Zodiac" killer in the early 1970s. St. James is the initiator of the forerunner group WHO (Whores, Housewives and Others). As a frequent lecturer and attendee at multiple international women's conferences St. James opposed state control over the sexual practices of its citizens, and was credited with decriminalizing prostitution in the state of Rhode Island. However, in an example of a return to the pre-sexual liberation era, the law was reinstated in 2009. Presently, prostitution is still illegal in the United States with the exception of some sections of Nevada. Working legally in sex films in the state of California didn't occur until 1988 thanks to the Hal "Freeman" decision detailed in some of the later chapters. In a comparison between sister countries, in March 2012 laws banning prostitution in Ontario, Canada were struck down opening the door for prostitutes to work legally in brothels or "bawdy houses". The federal government has plans to appeal.

Other great influences for me would be Martin Luther King and Gandhi. Later, when I crossed over into the art world, artist Linda Montano was a guiding force and a huge inspiration. She taught me that life could be art.

Prominent feminist and performance artist Linda Montano personified the motto: "art is life." For the past five decades, Montano has explored the intrinsic connection between life and art through the creative process of staging living art ceremonies. She conducts workshops designed to heighten and intensify an individual's spiritual experience in relation to one's life.

I also was influenced by Rajneesh, the "sex guru" through his books and through his disciples, especially Jwala who was my Tantra teacher and friend.

Sprinkle's major mentors and influences are often closer to home. Annie is enriched by the rapport and presence equitably shared by women of the same accord.

Another huge influence on me in my life was my porn star support group, Club 90. We started as a group of eight women and then went to five of us as Sharon Mitchell and Kelly Nichols moved to California, and Sue Nero dropped out. We met for ten-plus years in New York City, then as some of us left Manhattan, we made our meetings virtual, but we get together whenever we can. We have been meeting since the mid 1980s. They are my best friends: Veronica Vera, Veronica Hart, Candida Royalle and Gloria Leonard. We were all porn stars and we formed the first porn star support group where we would go around in a circle and share our thoughts, feelings, dreams, dramas and process. Our chemistry among the five of us has been phenomenal. One day it would make a great Hollywood feature film like the Bette Midler film *Beaches* (1988) or something like that. We still stay in contact by e-mail at least once a week. We are very close. We'd like to have a reunion sometime soon. We've been "meeting" now for twenty-six years or so.

As mentioned in chapters 7 and 8, Annie Sprinkle and the original Club 90 members joined in June 2012 in New York City for the nuptials of their colleague Veronica Vera. Since the reunion, Sprinkle announced on her Facebook profile there are currently two documentaries in the works about Club 90.

A lot of the women who were in porn in New York at that time got out of the business, but all of us from Club 90 are still working in an area of sexuality, fully on our own terms except that Gloria is retired. Most of us were innovators of new ideas, products, services, and genres. I think that some people are cut out to be in the sex industry and some aren't. I was middle class and had a lot of options. I chose sex work over other kinds of work. There are very poor women who don't have the choices I had and are not doing sex work because they want to. That's very different. Sex worker activists say "Outlaw Poverty, not Prostitution." As far as my personal experiences working in porn go, I had a good time and am very proud of my past.

I think that how we are raised has a lot to do with how we experience sex work. For me, it really did build my self-esteem. I'm a creative kind of person and being a sex worker is a very creative job when done with creativity. In general, my parents supported me. After about ten years or so in sex industry, they realized it wasn't just a passing phase. They were supportive of the things I wanted to do. They didn't necessarily like it; they were worried about me, but they did support me in doing what I wanted to do. I wasn't forced into anything or on drugs or alcohol. That is in the imagination of anti-porn feminists. I have noticed that if you have a drug and or alcohol problem that can make it a lot harder. I tried all the drugs, but never had a drug problem.

A lot of people have some connection with the porn or sex industry in their pasts. It's funny because we're in San Francisco I can't tell you how many old women come up to me and say, "I used to be a dancer at…" I say, "Really?" You'd never know they were a dancer by looking at them, but a lot of people probably don't think I look like I could have been a dancer or porn star, for that matter. One time a girlfriend and I went to visit her son. Her son happened to have a girlfriend who looked just like a porn star. She had this *Debbie Does Dallas* (1978) kind of porn star look with big boobies, and a little, teeny body and blonde hair. I just got the funniest feeling walking around with her that people would be thinking she's the porn star, but in reality, I was the porn star.

I think that a lot of people are jealous when other people are having more sexy fun than they are. So they like to judge porn stars as bad people, but they are actually envious. I know, because sometimes I'm that way! I admit it. I can catch myself being judgmental too, occasionally. Then I acknowledge that I did the same stupid shit, the same stuff, and I had a good time doing it. I don't think people would cop to that necessarily, but I think it's there. It takes balls so to speak, to do something that certain people look down on; I think it's like any job. I could never know what it's like to be in the army. I don't really have that experience. I could look down on people in the army if I let myself because I wonder how they can do that. How can they sign up to participate in war? I know some people do it because they are poor and they need education, but it's still kind of a mystery to me. I suppose I'm glad there are some people who like to go to war. Maybe that's a good thing. I suppose that sometimes war is necessary, but I'd rather be a lover than a fighter. I'm sure that I'm a total mystery to some people. They can't imagine doing the things that I've done.

Deep Inside Annie Sprinkle

Admirably, Sprinkle has never allowed her gender to interfere or dissuade her from aspiring to her many endeavors as a woman, a prostitute, a porn star, burlesque performer, feminist, activist or Sex-ecologist. Cultivated as a pure child of the sixties, Annie readily embraced the revolution against conformity and espoused many of the issues and concerns relating to the Women's Movement. As an original however, Sprinkle effectively fine-tuned components of the feminist agenda to fit her own needs and purposes that are perpetually burgeoning.

I would love to see women have equal rights and equal opportunities. I'd like to see women in equally represented positions of power. I spoke at a feminist class at the university a couple of days ago and the teacher was talking about how they stopped using the term "feminism" and started using some other term. I believe it was, "Women's Issues" or something. I love the word 'feminism'. Many universities are bringing the word back because it's a very important part of our culture and history. We need to acknowledge the importance of it. I wasn't a feminist until I went to college and learned the true meaning of the word. My parents were both feminists. Mom once protested the Rolling Stones *Black and Blue* (1976) album cover. I figured I probably wasn't a feminist because I didn't like censorship.

Some folks truly can't believe that I actually had a good time and liked and chose my work. As I mentioned, I was never a drug addict or an alcoholic. I was more on the co-dependent side. I experimented with drugs and I really got a lot out of those transcendental experiences. As a teenager in high school during the late sixties, we were doing LSD and I had some bad trips. I was not prepared, but I have no regrets. I think it was a good experience. If you learn, you win. It's important to make mistakes, especially with sex. How else will you learn?

When I look back to my best work in sex films, *Deep Inside Annie Sprinkle* (1981) is kind of a classic. It just got re-mastered and came

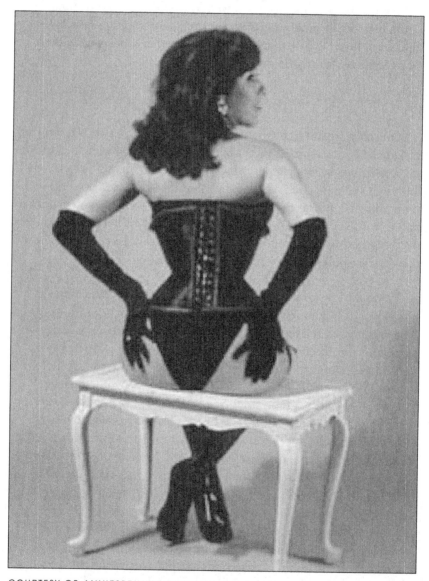

COURTESY OF *ANNIESPRINKLE.ORG*

out with a beautiful three DVD set with booklet that is super great. It's a nice collector item from the golden age of porn.

1981 was a seminal year for Annie Sprinkle with the release of *Deep Inside Annie Sprinkle*, the second highest-ranking adult film of 1982 behind *Insatiable*. The New York production, a joint directorial venture between Joe Sarno and Annie who was paid an impressive ten thousand dollars, was filmed during the first week of December in 1980. Guided by Sprinkle's creative and personal touch, the feature is an intimate portrait of the porn star's private sexual life with friends, lovers, and strangers.

Deep Inside Annie Sprinkle introduces Annie in the opening segment seated at a piano. Sexily outfitted to feature her abundant bosom, Annie is a radiant picture of health and well-being. She begins to share photos of herself: in the first picture, she is a child surrounded by a visibly happy family unit; the second image shows a typical teenage girl alone; and in the third, Annie is flanked by a group of girlfriends. Sprinkle begins to detail an overview of her young life and ascension into the taboo world of erotic work and describes some of her hottest desires as she segues into the subject of her fantasies.

Annie's first fantasy: making it with two guys is actualized as two buff male attendants (Roger Ram and early 1980s Video-X-Pix regular Bobby Soccie) make an appearance. The three proceed to sample fruit from one another's assets prior to a simultaneous double blowjob endeavor uncommonly carried out in Triple X films at that time. Next, Annie brings breast fetishist Sassy into her boudoir for some funky girl time. They are joined by a preppy looking (and slim) Ron Jeremy. Sassy hangs back a little after Jeremy arrives. According to the liner notes for the 2009 Special DVD edition of the film, Sassy retreated because of Jeremy's apparent body odor. Undeterred by a little human scent, Annie digs into her scene with Jeremy causing "The Hedgehog" to expel his load with great vocal effects. Following, is probably the most provocative scene in the film as Annie cozies up to performer Marc Valentine and explores his buttocks. She fingers him, and they provide mutual analingus (a rare act in heterosexual films during the era) prompting an excitable outcome that (according to Annie) left Sprinkle with a sore anus by the termination of their coupling.

In the surrounding footage, Annie claims her most memorable and enjoyable sexual encounter is with first time adult actor and Annie's former real life lover Mal O'Ree. They are featured in a controversial golden shower scene now considered legendary. (The performance was absent from most of the original copies because of potential peril with law authorities, but has since been reinstated for the 2009 re-release.) Until the initial release of this title, golden shower scenes were infrequent and existed mostly on eight-millimeter loops.

The balance of the sexual rendezvous within *Deep Inside Annie* Sprinkle continues in the tradition of shock value, but delectable Annie manages to keep things in a comfortable zone for the viewer mostly because of her natural attraction to sex and its spectacular possibilities. Not to be missed is her genuine solo multiple orgasm number coupled with an ejaculation, brought about with the aid of an extraordinary vibrator — the female act was especially scarce at this particular period in the history of adult productions, making it even more enthralling. The scene is anchored by a naughty live sex-capade show in which a few male attendees (Jack Teague, Mike Filene, and Michael Gaunt) join Sprinkle for a public display of affection at a New York theatre while one of her previous films (Sarno's *Slippery When Wet*, Video-X-Pix) plays on the big screen. Afterwards, an all female orgy is on the menu concluding with a beautiful daisy chain configuration enacted by all of the women in the vista including Lisa Be, Heather Gordon (aka Heather Young/Colleen Anderson), Barbara Miller, and Lee Starr. Following up, Annie dons her photographer's cap and instructs a young model (Bunny Hatton) on the finer points of exuding sensuality. With the help of a male friend (Buddy Hatton, Bunny's husband), the three make love.

The tone of the decisive finish is fittingly established by Sprinkle once again as she prepares the audience for what is about to unfold. While revealing that one of her favorite sexual experiences is intimacy with someone whom she greatly cares for, Ron Hudd is brought in for this special scene. Evocatively presented with tender kisses, things are sweetened by slow hand foreplay, promising a fulfilling and exciting end. Apparently, Annie felt that her encounter with Hudd didn't quite translate the message of love she had hoped for, but to the naked eye, the lack of emotion is merely a blip on the radar screen.

The 2009 Video-X-Pix uncut collector's edition is an essential acquisition for fans of the genre featuring three disks including a full commentary with Sprinkle, a Q & A with Sprinkle, two bonus scenes, and a twenty-four page pictorial booklet with liner notes by adult film historian Benson Hurst. To sum it up, *Deep Inside Annie Sprinkle* is a consummate, no-holds-barred submission supple and devoid of artificiality. Obviously, Sprinkle was turned on by the acts of promiscuity and sexual play. Authenticity is Annie's forte.

The "Great Dying"

Thank god I was never brutally attacked or a victim of a brutal rape or of a real crime. That would be another story — if I was at the wrong place at the wrong time or the right time, whatever. I've been very, very lucky. I just heard about a friend who was attacked about ten years ago, some guy tried to kill her. She was a dancer and he followed her home and forced his way into her house, and he tried to kill her. It turned out that he had killed two other women. She hit him with a barbell on the head and fought him off. She was too hard to kill. You know, once something like that happens you might be sorry you did something, but I've been so, so lucky.

My friend [the late-porn star] Marc Stevens used to live down the hall from me. He was doing angel dust and crack, and I saw him become totally paranoid, and crazy and desperate. He became a drug dealer and he got so fucked up. Then he got AIDS and eventually died a miserable, lonely death with all his dealers around with guns and his windows blackened. This was right down the hall from me. It was very, very sad, but also very scary for me too.

Marc Stevens began his porn career in the early 1970s. Regarded by his fellow actors and industry friends as Marc "10 ½" Stevens due to his exceptional physical endowment, after struggling to overcome an addiction to drugs, Stevens passed away in 1989 from AIDS.

One night somebody climbed around on the balcony and I woke up, and some guy had his hands on my ankles; he was feeling my ankles up. That was probably the scariest thing that has happened in my life. I said, "Excuse me. Could you please leave?" He left. It turned out that he was a friend of Marc's and he was into drugs. He just liked to crawl around on the balconies when he was high. Apparently, a week or two later he drove right into a brick wall and was seriously injured.

Marc was never public about having AIDS. He went the way of John Holmes really, with drugs. This was during the mid-1980s.

Sprinkle earned a BFA in photography from the School of Visual Arts in 1986 and often created erotic imagery. Annie's close friend Veronica Vera, one time Wall Street trader and former porn star known primarily for her work in Gerard Damiano's 1982 film *Consenting Adults* (a story

Sprinkle and Vera conceptualized) concentrates her efforts on writing about sexuality issues. More recently, as "Miss Vera," Veronica operates a cross dressing finishing School for "boys who want to become girls." A few years prior to his death from AIDS in 1988 (just one year before Marc Stevens), Annie and Veronica spent an afternoon together with their industry friend John Holmes while on assignment.

PHOTOGRAPHY BY ANNIE SPRINKLE

A few of my photos are in Cass's [Paley] film *WADD* [*The Life & Times of John C. Holmes*, 1998]. They are photos that I took of John Holmes, just a few casual shots. My dear friend Veronica Vera, a writer, was interviewing him and I went along and just took some photos of him standing at a freeway entrance. He was holding a briefcase. The reason I took a picture of him carrying a briefcase is because he was really into being a businessman at that time. He had started his own business [Penguin Productions], so the story was about "John Holmes: Businessman". We both went out to lunch with John. He was sweet as pie. He was a darling. I was quite charmed.

You know the 1980s was a different time for AIDS. I would have sex with people who had AIDS or who were HIV positive. I would already be having sex with them, and when AIDS hit we didn't really know how it was transmitted. I just assumed I had it because I was already having sex with someone who did. There were no tests at first and people didn't get tested really, so it was quite a different time than it is now. Now, it's unforgiveable. I always say my hemorrhoids saved my life because I didn't have a lot of anal sex. If I'd been having a lot of anal sex, I'd be dead. One of the best presents I ever got from [my partner] Beth was when she got me onto her health insurance plan. Then, I got a hemorrhoid operation. That's love…getting your lover a new anus!

Unprotected anal sex is considered the riskiest form of sexual interaction between two or more partners, as the rectum and sphincter are highly susceptible regions.

After AIDS hit, I did a lot of spiritual stuff, and learning and exploring the healing arts. Learning about orgasmic breathing was pivotal for me. Learning the "fire breath orgasm" from Harley Swiftdeer changed the way I experienced sex forever.

Teacher, healer, and martial artist Harry Swiftdeer of the Deer Tribe modified the art of the "Fire Breath Orgasm." The term has since been redefined as the "energy" orgasm that is a profound mind, body, and soul experience which helps to eradicate pent up anxiety, emotions, and stress that can compromise an individual's ability to let go in order to attain a total and fulfilling orgasmic experience. It is believed the Fire Breath Orgasm generates enough energy to sustain a person for extended periods. The technique is an interesting practice as it illustrates a defined synergy between sex, humanity, and the cosmos.

Everything has worked out pretty well. If I died tomorrow, I'd die very happy. I've already had a full life. If I had gotten AIDS and died in my thirties, I would have been really bummed. After the "Great Dying," the waves of death, everything after that was gravy. It's a miracle that I didn't get AIDS.

Post-Porn Modernist

During the epoch of AIDS and its relationship with the adult industry, as Annie's filmography shows, she continued to make occasional appearances in videos, but there arose a great need to validate and make her work more meaningful. It was at this stage Sprinkle felt a new sense of self, beginning to cocoon. Her alter ego "Anya" emerged. "Anya" is defined as an introspective peacemaker — a wise, spiritual, eco-centered persona rather than the more egocentric "Annie" — the self-described narcissist, porn star/people pleaser. Anya was a way for Annie to resurrect and bridge the gap between Ellen and Annie as she moved fluidly toward an

COURTESY OF *ANNIESPRINKLE.ORG*

authentic frontier as a Post-Porn Modernist. One of the tangibles distinguishing Annie Sprinkle from her female associates in terms of how her past has influenced her present is that Annie is constantly unfolding and in motion. Everything is a learning experience.

Were there a few missed opportunities for me? Maybe — I would have taken more financial courses in my twenties so I would have been better at money management, although I wouldn't have been interested. Money has never been that big a motivating factor, but it sometimes has been an aphrodisiac of sorts. My mom made me take typing in high school even though I didn't want to do it. I wish she'd said, "You're going to need this financial course. You're going to need to know how to balance your check book." Of course, now it's even more complicated with the computer. It's hard to get the banks to send you a statement on paper nowadays.

Because my dad was a Professor of the University Southern California (USC), I had an opportunity to go to USC for free to get a good college degree. Instead, I went to the School of Visual Arts (SVA) in Manhattan so that I could live in New York City. It was a private college and I had to do a lot of burlesque to pay for it all because I paid for most of it myself. The USC degree might have been more beneficial, but I didn't value college education as much as life experience. Now, I really value a good college education more than I did back then. Again, I had a great education at SVA too.

I'm proud of all of the prostitution. I really enjoyed that very much. I had over three thousand clients. When I stopped enjoying it, I got out, but it was an exciting and satisfying experience for twenty years. Sometimes I'm still tempted to go back into prostitution! As far as porn, I have no regrets at all.

One missed opportunity was when I did my first one-woman show "Post-Porn Modernist" in the late 1980s. It was very controversial and I became part of the debate about the government funding of art and the NEA [National Endowment for the Arts]. I didn't get a grant, but The Kitchen where I performed, had. My show was debated on the Senate floor. It's in the Congressional Record. That attempt at censorship really launched my career, but I was uneducated about the issues. I was so used to being censored and controversial. I didn't understand the significance of the arts censorship issues. I got calls from news shows, and *Larry King* and

I was getting a lot of attention. I didn't do it, because I didn't know how to debate the issues. That was a missed opportunity, but that's okay. I generally don't like doing TV shows, but they are such good exposure. That's often what counts in business these days, but not to me.

"Post-Porn Modernism," an offshoot of the expression "Post-Modernism," is a term with a broad definition. It generally applies to the spectrum of literature, art, philosophy, architecture and is probably best described as a "personal truth" as it denies the absolution of existing principles as finite, challenging the idea that one size fits all with respect to how we perceive "reality." Annie's original Post-Porn Modernist show contained accounts of her many personal experiences before and during her work as a prostitute and in porn. The event also incorporated intimate nudity and explicit acts with some interactive audience participation.

A Post-Porn Modernist makes sexually explicit media that is more arty, conceptual, experimental, political, and/or humorous than mainstream porn imagery. It often has a critical sensibility and while it usually contains some hardcore sex, it is not focused on being "erotic." Post-Porn Modernism is the genre a Post-Porn Modernist works in currently and more popularly called "Post-Porn" for short. Today, numerous American and European artists, performance groups and some pornographers define their work as Post-Porn such as Charles Gatewood, Post Op, Carole Queen, Orgia, Girls Who Like Porno, Tina Butcher [aka Madison Young], Tristan Taormino, Sadie Lune, María Llopis and Del LaGrace Volcano.

Tristan Taormino, probably the most well known of the group referenced by Sprinkle in the above quote was born in 1971 and has several articles, books, and a few sex films (in which she participated) under her belt. As a feminist pornographer, author, columnist, and sex educator — like Annie, Taormino has established herself as one of the world's foremost authorities and keynote speakers on the subject of human sexuality and its diversities.

I'm kind of the mother or grandmother as it were of Post-Porn. I'm very proud of that. I also helped pioneer other genres of sexually explicit films. I did some varieties of "gonzo" porn before it was called gonzo porn, in films like *Consenting Adults* (1983) with Gerard Damiano. I did feminist porn early on and then educational porn, and now eco-sex-porn, so I'm still going. I love pioneering new genres of explicit material and making bridges from porn to art and back again.

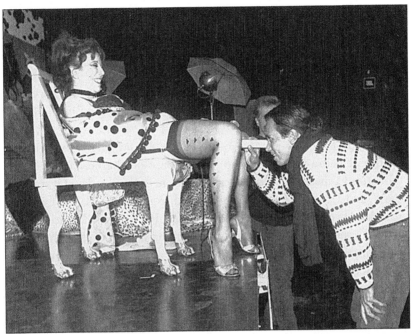

Public Cervix Announcement. COURTESY OF *ANNIESPRINKLE.ORG*

One of Sprinkle's most popular art pieces in the relatively new class of Post-Porn Modernism is her "Public Cervix Announcement" theatrical performance in which she sat spread-eagled on a stage (sans panties) and invited audience members to inspect her cervix using a speculum and flashlight. The event incorporated a clever slogan "Cervix with a smile" attached to an image of a happy face sporting two eyes and a hole in place of a mouth. The purpose of the piece was to break down barriers and fears surrounding the naked human physique while inviting guests to celebrate the female body.

In 1990, Annie's documentary-style film *Linda/Les and Annie* illustrated an affair with boyfriend Les Nichols who was born female (as Linda), and through the advent of modern medical advancements underwent surgery to obtain male genitalia. In her usual upbeat and idiosyncratic manner, Sprinkle divulged the intimacies of her first sexual experience with Linda as Les throughout the feature.

After having sex with three thousand-plus men, I felt like it was time for a change. I had a couple of relationships with transsexuals: a female to male, and a male to female. I think of myself as what I call "Metamorphosexual" — always in a state of change.

A few years later, Sprinkle was ready for an environmental change.

For twenty years, I lived and worked in Manhattan — in prostitution and mainstream porn, then transitioned into the art world doing art projects about my life in sex. In 1994, I left the Big Apple and made my way back to California to be closer to my family. I was ready to move out of New York. I had a longing to be near nature. I had a girlfriend who had a house on the beach and at that time, I just needed the ocean. We were in Scotland and it was cold, and I said, "I feel so disconnected from nature." I had lived on the eleventh floor and she said, "Well, it's winter, I'll take you to my house in the summer." I started going to the beach with her in Long Island and then I knew I had to move and get out of the city, and be near the beach and beauty. At that point, the city was very predictable and nature was this exotic adventure. I moved to live on the beach. I had lived in cities all my life. Being in nature suddenly was so much more exciting. Now I live in San Francisco which I call the "Clitoris" of the USA. It's small and electric. Two blocks from our house is a great hill that is a park and feels like being out in nature.

It seems perfectly fitting with Annie's love and respect for all things natural, green, and erotic, she would find herself residing in a city nestled on the beautiful San Francisco bay welcoming and even encouraging of eccentricities. For those who believe in karma Annie is a living example of a person who can't be knocked out. When the chips were down after a devastating life experience, Sprinkle concocted a big batch of lemonade and decided to get her Ph.D. She also got back in spades.

I'm very lucky. I have wonderful friends that I've had for years and years that I adore. About thirteen years ago, I was living on a beautiful houseboat in Sausalito. When I was out on the road, my house sitter accidentally burnt the place down. I lost most everything I owned, my two cats died, and it was pretty disorienting. Without asking for any help, people started doing benefits for me all over the world. There were about twenty benefits. People started sending me all this money to help me get back on my feet. It was the most beautiful experience. I'm so glad I got to experience so much love. It was intensely physical, like sex, but a different flavor. I took the money, and went and got my Ph.D. I was so touched by all the people who wanted to help me from the porn community to the BDSM community to the porn fans to the art folks to the spiritual communities I had connected with. It was deeply touching and life changing. I realized the importance of community and of love.

I really have been blessed to have been part of a wonderful community of women who created a sex-positive, slut-positive, porn-positive movement. Not all porn is something to be positive about, that's for sure. The freedom to make it and to see it is precious. Sure, a lot of the women in porn had some self- esteem issues, but what group of women didn't? It's a bit better now. With Club 90, we showed that we can be slutty, we can be raunchy, and we can still be smart, powerful, integral, successful and interesting women. Certainly, as a whole — pun intended — the porn stars of the seventies and eighties helped pioneer a new kind of pornography: "The Golden Age of Porn." Before that, it was very much the male bastion — they were mostly eight-millimeter loops.

I was recently at the memorial service for Jamie Gillis here and I was nostalgic for the old days, but at the same time, I was glad that I don't have to do that again.

For Annie's legions of fans, Sprinkle's decision to stretch beyond the confines of sex films probably felt like the end of too much of a good thing. To this day, Annie and all aspects of her vintage work will infinitely remain entwined. She presides over the golden age era with a dominant voice and presence, and is indubitably one of the classic legendary females.

I'm the "Golden shower Queen". I'm the "Golden shower Goddess". I've been in alternative sexually oriented art for almost as long as I did films. Theater, visual art, performance art, writing, but still almost all sex related.

Herstory of Porn

Derived from an expansive collection encompassing twenty years in the making, Annie's authoritative piece *Annie Sprinkle's Herstory of Porn* (1999) resonates with many fans of the erotic medium. Based upon a theatrical performance Sprinkle did by the same name showcasing montages extracted from her massive body of work, *Herstory of Porn* encapsulates Sprinkle's infinite status as the spiritual and artistic "Green" Goddess of the present age.

> Some of my older films are just god-awful. The older films are more of a crapshoot. I don't do mainstream porn movies now, but I still sell some of my old porn films on my website *anniesprinkle.org.* I definitely still do some sexually oriented media. For example, for five years I did a theater piece *Annie Sprinkle's Herstory of Porn* where I performed live together with some clips from my old porn movies. I made a video of that show. It's available at *Anniesprinkle.org. Herstory of Porn* (1999) has clips from twenty-five years of my sex life, the best and the worst.

Herstory of Porn is nothing short of luxury for the senses and contains three special disks. Annie Sprinkle graces the opening sequence with a backdrop resembling a movie house. Decked out in her customary porn star glitz and glam, Sprinkle greets the audience with her trademark sparkling, capricious personality that adult fans have grown to expect and admire. Annie invites the audience to accompany her on a journey through her "herstory of porn" beginning with a tongue-in-cheek commentary about Sprinkle's novice years in adult entertainment initialized by loops in 1973 (she appeared in approximately fifty in total) and eventually, feature productions, many of which were grind-house in nature.

Annie's 1970s experiential performances are comprehensive and assorted: hippie-dippy porn, horror porn, disco porn, S&M, genital piercings, "investigational" porn comprising of vaginal sausage insertion (as an example), fisting, anal beads, tampon envy, little persons, and last but not least, the infamous golden shower. Sprinkle conceded that once she established herself as the girl who was willing to try anything — mainstream adult film directors were no longer interested in hiring her. The star explained that although she generally enjoyed her work overall, occasionally, situations arose on set that were uncomfortable. Annie cited the film *The Devil Inside Her* (1977) as an example of an experience where she was overcome by the film's extreme improvisational aspect while playing a young woman besieged and raped by a group of men.

The second section of "Herstory" focuses on the 1980s. It is marked by Sprinkle's transition toward experimental, enviro-sexual frontiers spanning into her Post Porn Modernist years and beyond. Sprinkle revealed how in 1984 her life took on a different course when she met Jamal, a tantric sex guru who taught her how to unify energy, sexuality, and spirituality in order to achieve a more intensive and meaningful orgasm. Armed with this newfound knowledge, Annie proceeded to direct her own film for Femme Productions titled *Rite of Passage* which incorporated some of the techniques gleaned from her relations with Jamal.

In 1990, Annie experienced another awakening of sorts when she reconnected with her childhood passion for inventive undertakings personified by her performance in the arty porn film *War is Menstrual Envy* (1992). Sprinkle also collaborated with Canadian filmmaker Cynthia Roberts to create Docu-porn, which inevitably opened the door for Annie's Post Porn Modernist chapter. At this stage of her life and career, Annie became a lesbian and believed the inauguration of several Post Porn Modernist pieces would gain her entry and acceptance into the gay and lesbian community — it did. *Sluts and Goddesses* (1998) touted as the cornerstone of Sprinkles' milieu, is a "Goddess-in-the-making" workshop. In other words, the video excerpt is an instruction on how one becomes a slut/goddess in several easy steps. A few highlights of this practicum are shown, and it certainly appears to be outrageous, exotic fun. Simultaneous to the "Sluts and Goddesses" phase was Annie's decision to bond once again with nature. Subsequent scenes reveal Annie unplugged as she "medibates" beneath a cascading waterfall, followed by the release of emotion and the sanctity of prayer.

In the final segment of *Herstory of Porn*, Annie teaches viewers how to make their own porn. She weaves together a vibrant and fascinating mermaid story signifying the passing of the torch from one Goddess to another and dies a symbolic death.

The two bonus disks are also educational and enlightening. The first is a fifteen-minute highlight reel from Annie's "Post Porn Modernist" show filmed live at The Kitchen in New York City. The passages play like a mini version of *Herstory of Porn* as Annie walks the audience through the various stages of her career (including a snippet from her now famous "Public Cervix Announcement"), but with a more informal and interactive focus. A resonating element from her signature show is Sprinkle's stark appearance on stage dressed down in a dressing gown without make up. Drawing comparisons between her fundamental self, "Ellen Steinberg," and her public persona, "Annie Sprinkle," Annie proclaims:

"Ellen Steinberg is shy."

"Annie Sprinkle is an exhibitionist."

"Ellen Steinberg is fat."

"Annie Sprinkle is voluptuous."

"Ellen Steinberg wears sensible shoes."

"Annie Sprinkle wears spike heels."

When the self-assessment concludes, Annie confides to the audience: "I'll tell you something you might not know...Ellen Steinberg *is* Annie Sprinkle..." "Now I'll tell you an even bigger secret..." "Annie Sprinkle *is* Ellen Steinberg."

The third disk on the DVD collection is a discussion between Annie and sexologist, Jeff Fletcher, about the advancement of eight-millimeter loops between the 1950s up until 1985. The two explain what the shorts represented for society in terms of sexuality, morality, politics, education, and liberation. As various loops flash across the screen including some familiar faces such as Mai Lin and Sharon Kane, Annie comments about the purity and simplicity of the performers and performances during the primitive years of adult filmmaking, and draws parallels to the contemporary era.

There are definitely more options for sex workers today. There are so many ways to do things and reasons to do things. I love to do career counseling with sex workers who are in transition and do it quite often. There is not really "one size fits all" kind of advice I give. It's about "What do you need and want, and how do you go about getting it?" I find myself asking advice from young people such as "How do I do Facebook?" and "How do I twitter?" So much of it now is about the computer and marketing.

If you want to do a book, that's one thing, but you have to really be able to market a book now. Young people know that. I used to know how to write a good press release, and put it in the mail and put a stamp on the envelope. Now, you've got to know how to do search words and buttons, and social networking constantly. I love to come up with names for new businesses, help brainstorm titles, publicity stunts, actions and ideas. I love to collaborate with others.

I have a friend who had an idea about doing the first burlesque film festival and I thought, "God, yeah, you have to do that. Why don't you call so and so and do it this way or that way?" Giving advice or suggestions really depends upon the individual project or person. Today, a lot of my work is collaborative — most all. Then again, so was making porn films. It's a group effort; group fun, actually.

If I have a legacy, it's probably creating the genre called "Post-Porn". I like to think of myself sort of as the "Yoko Ono of Porn" and making porn more spiritual and conceptual. I guess I'm kind of still creating this idea of Post-Porn. I've always been a great admirer of Yoko Ono. She has long been a huge inspiration to me. I love her work and I adore the art and activism John and Yoko did together. I'm on Yoko's Twitter feed and she consistently delights and amazes me.

One would be remiss not to mention some of Sprinkle's additional alternative and symbolic one-woman performance art conceptions as they further demonstrate her talent for educating the public how to adopt eroticism and sensuality into an individual's life in a fun and non-invasive manner. In addition to her "Public Cervix Announcement," Annie also devised "The Legend of the Ancient Sacred Prostitute" incorporating a magical masturbation ceremony during her act. Other theatrical pieces include "Peace in Bed-In" which took place within four major cities. "Peace in Bed-In" is a sex educational statement emulating the work for world peace first manifested in Montreal in 1969 by John Lennon and conceptual artist Yoko Ono.

Numerous other events have been conceived by Annie over the years to convey the marriage of sex, peace, and enlightenment detailed on her website anniesprinkle.org. Sprinkle continues to lecture and pen articles and has been the editor of various magazines. Annie is also the author of several publications similarly themed to her films and art expressions: *Dr Sprinkle's Spectacular Sex — Makeover Your Love Life* (2005), *Annie Sprinkle, Post-Porn Modernist: My 25 Years as a Multi-Media Whore* (1998), and the 2006 publication *Hardcore from the Heart: The Pleasures, Profits and Politics of Sex in Performance (Critical Performances)*. There is a graphic comic book and other interesting dissertations underscoring her seemingly tireless work in the area of sexology, not to mention, a selection of sexually oriented self-help videos. Without a doubt, Annie is most definitely the Queen of all multi-media, and she knows how to work it. With a sense of humor, Sprinkle prefers to keep her focus on the here and now.

I'd rather talk about today. Like my artist friend Kembra Pfahler said, "I don't like to yesturbate." I do like to masturbate!

Eco-sexuals: Annie and Beth & Bob

For the past ten years, I have been with a wonderful woman Elizabeth Stephens. Beth is an academic. Beth is a West Virginia girl. She's an artist as well as a tenured art professor at University of California in Santa Cruz. She's also a graduate student and getting

Annie, Bob and Beth. COURTESY OF *ANNIESPRINKLE.ORG*

her Ph.D. We live in Bernal Heights, [San Francisco] along with our dog Bob. Beth has wonderful academic friends and I have wonderful porn star and whore friends. Our parties are so much fun because academics and sex workers are a great mix. They're so different. I'm with the love of my life.

I'm crazy about her. I never expected to have a good, healthy, mutually satisfying relationship. I was never that interested in relationships, just having lots of different kinds of lovers. I treasure love. I've really found a life partner so that's been very satisfying. I didn't even know I was looking for someone. We have been lovers and collaborators for ten years. We work together, so we're together almost every single minute of every day. Most days, I feel like the luckiest girl alive. It's been an amazing journey.

On January 14, 2007, Sprinkle and Stephens officially tied the knot in a non-traditional wedding ceremony on the west coast of Canada.

She was interested in ecology and I was interested in sexology. Then we got excited about the combination of both and it works out nicely. Beth and I have done some experimental sexually explicit art projects. We call it "Eco-sexuality." I don't feel like I stopped doing anything; I've just changed what I do. As I changed, the work changed. The audience changes and my reasons for doing things change. Thank goodness, things change. In the beginning, it was filmmaking and sex, and then of course, it all turned to video. Now it is ecology and sexuality. Beth and I have a new theater piece called "Dirty Sexecology — 25 Ways to Make Love with the Earth". In it, Beth sings a song while I do a ballet striptease to a Yo-Yo Ma piece at the same time. At the end, we get naked, and we get in these two big breast-shaped piles of dirt and have sex. It's very dirty. It's about loving the Earth. I feel like my best is yet to come in the Eco-sex Movement I'm helping to co-create.

Sprinkle and Stephens are a team generating innovative and improved ways of enlightening inhabitants of a vulnerable planet. They teach that a greener mindset can be sexy and even erotic with the right attitude. In 2005, the pair made a commitment to devote seven years to projects signifying love which is part of their "Love Art Laboratory." Their recent collaborative piece titled "Dirty Sexecology — 25 Ways to Make Love with the Earth" might seem preposterous to some, but even skeptics can't deny the two women are consciousness-raising with ingenious buzzwords like "Eco-sexual" as they challenge the population to protect and provide nourishment to the earth. Sprinkle and Stephens have even written their own version of "Commandments" for those to adapt into their daily lives if they wish to comply. As part of the ongoing celebration of earth, Annie and Beth have staged a series of weddings as a metaphor, symbolizing a special and treasured union with various elements of the planet: the sky, sea and soil.

We have done some very cool, eco-sexual wedding performances. In the last one we did, "White Wedding to the Snow". Ninety people helped create the wedding. We did it in this huge cathedral and four hundred people came. During our vows, we got rings made of ice; then we got penis-sized icicles and we consummated our marriage with the snow by inserting them in each other.

Afterwards, we lifted our wedding dresses, and put our pussies into the snow and kissed. It was hot and cold both! It's not your usual live sex show, but it is live sex on stage.

Since Annie and Beth launched their Love Art Laboratory project, the weddings have clearly become the centerpiece of related art projects. Each one constitutes a uniquely crafted idea — such as their first marriage to the earth. Specific fabrics and colored hues are worn by the couple and their guests, mirroring the seven chakras recognized in Buddhism and Hinduism traditions and employed in modern yoga practices.

White wedding in Ottawa, Canada. COURTESY OF *ANNIESPRINKLE.ORG*

We have had eleven big performance art weddings. Eight have had environmental themes. First, we married the earth, then we married the sky, and there was another one where we married the sea. We have also married the moon and the Appalachian Mountains. In March 2011 [in Ottawa, Canada], we married the Snow. When we went to Vienna [in 2010], we had sold out one hundred and seventy seats. The audience was very enthusiastic. We'd worked on the show, and it had gotten better since we did it the first time in Boston so we had a great crowd, and it got good reviews — it's a process. We are doing a second Eco-sex Symposium this summer [2011]. A lot of people resonate with our concept of Earth as Lover. You can make love with the earth through the senses. We're actually quite emotionally connected on an energetic level at least with nature. We don't really know for sure how much the earth feels our love; maybe they're just symbolic gestures, but we feel connected and in love with nature.

Earth Mother, Lover, Mate and Friend

I have always been aware of various nature fetishes like dendrophilia, which is the erotic love of trees. People have sex in trees, or with trees, or hug trees. I also like wind play, fire play, and airplay using breath or the wind from motorcycles. I love getting pounded by waterfalls. I find it incredibly ecstatic. A certain hotel in Vegas has a pool with a waterfall that you can stand under. I go to that hotel and stand under the waterfall just to get high.

I am an Eco-sexual, Sex-ecologist. "Eco-sexual" was a dating term people would use to describe the fact that they were interested in "eco" things. Beth and I have usurped the term to describe actually being lovers with nature. In addition to eco-sex weddings, we're doing eco-sex walking tours; we made an eco-sex bumper sticker, we have an eco-sexual theater piece. We've created some fun charts and graphs which explain eco-sex. They're on our web site: loveartlab.org. Also at: sexecology.org. It was recently re-launched on Valentine's Day 2012. We're not really inventing anything; we're repackaging it.

As Annie conceded, the brand of Sex-ecology practiced by she and Beth isn't an original tenet. "Pagan" is translated from the words "country dweller," often used to describe a non-Christian. In ancient civilizations such as Greece or Rome, a pagan worshipped many Gods, and believed a specific deity was associated with various facets and spirits contained in nature: a God or Goddess of the sky or of the natural world. Later, people connected spirit Gods and Goddesses to their various occupations. Also considered a fertility religion, the feminine component of the Pagan faith is traditionally revered and exalted. Sprinkle and Stephens have effectively improvised the primitive practice, modernizing it to fit their mandate as a means to engage people in a unified and positive way.

Eco-sexuality is truly about exploring the places where sexology and ecology intersect. Beth and I are switching up the metaphor from Earth as Mother, to Earth as Lover. We are trying to make the environmental movement more sexy, fun, and diverse. We're trying to create a whole new sexual identity and area of research and sex education. We're really having fun, and it's satisfying to do something that's much bigger than I am. It feels important. I'm recreating myself as an environmental activist, and having a blast. Green is sexy!

Annie Sprinkle in Toronto.

Early in January 2011, on a cold, snowy afternoon, Annie was scheduled to present her "Eco-Sexy" lecture at the University of Toronto. I booked off work and drove downtown against traffic to the campus where I hoped to have an opportunity to chat with Annie prior to sitting in on her presentation. About a half hour before her lecture, we relaxed in the teacher's lounge drinking herbal tea and nibbling homemade Canadian maple fudge while Annie organized her power point presentation. She showed me various photos she planned to use spanning her life and career. I marveled that she hadn't yet finessed her speech prior to her trip to Toronto, but she reassured me she liked to "change things up." A few minutes after 3:00pm, Annie was introduced to a packed house of students enrolled in a Sexual Diversity course. Described by the Master of Ceremonies as a "prostitute, porn star, and sexual intellectual," Sprinkle took the stage, enthusiastically entertaining the captive audience as she utilized sensual imagery on a screen depicting environmental intimacy. Fond embraces between flowers and foliage in lush forests were juxtaposed with more erotic nature photographs suggesting the presence of genitalia. While educating the students about the many ways in which the world can be cherished as a sexy, precocious, precious companion, Annie competently conveyed the message that everyone can become better caretakers of one another and of the earth once our "E" spot is identified.

Eco-sexuality is sensual or spiritual and it can be very emotional too. Beth and I actually made breast cancer fun. I was diagnosed with it six years ago. It wasn't bad at all. We dressed up in costumes for chemo and made art projects out of the experience. I've been all healed and in great health now. You know, we both got chubby for a while. We travel a whole lot for our work — internationally. I get tired of traveling, but the work entices me. We were traveling all of the time and doing stressful work so we both gained some weight. Even that was an interesting experience that I don't really regret. We both just lost fifty pounds. It wasn't too bad losing it either, we were ready.

How many husbands or wives would be okay with the history that I've had? Beth's very cool about it. She's up there on stage having sex with me. Here she is a fully tenured professor. She's really a wonderful artist, she's so sex positive and she has got balls. Not actual ones, but she is a perfect, perfect mate. Porn stars lives don't all have tragic endings.

12

Sex "Kitten" Natividad

Brazen, buxom and brassy, "Kitten" Natividad, former burlesque queen, Pin-Up girl, and adult film actress, has delighted in arousing male sexual fantasies for four decades.

Born in Mexico in 1948 to a teenage bride, Francesca Isabelle Natividad was three years old when her parents divorced. Before the age of ten, Francesca and her mother immigrated to El Paso, Texas where they settled in with her new stepfather. Natividad adapted easily to her congenial surroundings and dutifully assisted with her younger siblings. While engaged in secondary school studies, a relative hooked the young teenager up to keep house for actor Stella Stevens in Hollywood for summer work where Natividad flourished. After graduating from grade twelve, Francesca was hired as a key punch operator but quickly became unfulfilled by the monotony of her work. At the advice of a friend, she decided to audition as a Go-Go dancer, and ultimately became an exotic dancer, a profession she found to be gratifying and profitable. During her early years as a stripper, Natividad adopted the stage name "Kitten".

While married to her second husband, Kitten was introduced to sexploitation director, Russ Meyer. She became a star prodigy after her provocative debut as an orator in the cult classic *Up!* (1976). *Beneath the Valley of the Ultra-Vixons* (1977) followed as did a lengthy relationship with Meyer, and subsequently, several breast augmentation surgeries that provided Kitten with a forty-four inch chest.

Once well established in the entertainment industry, Natividad appealed to a greater male audience potential in mostly softcore appearances in blue screen features. She also tantalized audiences as a sensuous busty hellcat in several mainstream projects, and accepted roles in

"I consider myself a liberated woman. I still like men, and I like to take care of them. As far as respect, I believe people have certain roles to uphold, and that applies to both sexes. I will tell you that I am very proud to be a female. I like to show my tits and show off my ass."

FRANCESCA NATIVIDAD

COURTESY OF *KITTENCLUB.COM*

hardcore sex films in order to increase her stage value after earning a name for herself in various Gentlemen's clubs in California and Nevada. Flaunting her stuff with self-assurance and flair, Kitten is also famous for her trademark champagne bath repertoire as part of her stage show. Her notoriety as a large breasted beauty often presented unusual fringe benefits: in 1985, Natividad was invited to entertain Oscar winner Sean Penn and guests during Penn's bachelor party on the eve of his marriage to Madonna.

Although plagued by alcohol and drug addiction for many years, Kitten adheres strictly to her sobriety regimen today and faithfully attends Alcoholics Anonymous. After three husbands and several relationships, at age sixty-four, Natividad is happy to be single and content to have her pets as loyal companions. She is the proprietor of multiple apartment houses in Los Angeles, and remains selective about the people whom she chooses for tenants.

When her long time lover and friend, Russ Meyer, was diagnosed with dementia, Kitten acted as a caregiver for him until his death in 2004. Natividad regards Meyer as a trusted advisor, and an enigmatic personality within what she considers an unimaginable life.

I interviewed Francesca Natividad in March 2010.

Humble Beginnings

I was born in Ciudad, Juarez, Mexico. My mother was very young when she had me. I think she got married at fourteen because she got pregnant with me. My father was a very tall and handsome man. I was born, and then they were divorced around three years later and my grandmother took care of me. I had a wonderful childhood because I was spoiled rotten by her. Both of my grandmothers spoiled me. They would dress me up, so I always wanted to dress up and be the center of attention.

My mother remarried a Mexican who was American citizen and we moved to El Paso, Texas where I became an American citizen, but that didn't happen until I was about nine years old. I didn't speak English when I moved there but they wanted to put me in the fourth grade. I refused and I said, "Put me in second grade." I went into second grade and I learned English in one month.

My mother went on to have other children and my stepfather was working and going to college. He became an engineer later on; he was a wonderful man. I took care of my younger siblings, made the dinner and so on, but I was also very good in school. I was very smart.

It was a normal childhood. My mother started working at the same time my father worked and went to college. I came home from school, did homework and made the dinner — there were no hobbies. I did like to put on the radio and dance around the house doing housework. My childhood was definitely not the life that kids have today. I was very responsible as a child. I can't say anything terrible about my childhood. I don't feel bad about my childhood because it taught me one thing: I didn't want any children when I grew up. I remember those two a.m. feedings. My mother would go to work so she called on me — I'm the oldest one — to go get the baby and change his diaper; give him his bottle. I thought, "Is this what I have to look forward to?" Not for me. I'm from the era of baby boomers and we are different from other generations. We started doing things differently and we behaved differently.

As a teenager, I loved the way Bridget Bardot looked. I wish I looked like her, and I loved Natalie Wood. Honestly, I get bored talking about the beginnings of my life because it's so long ago and there aren't any big highlights. I had no tits and I was a very skinny girl. I wasn't boy crazy or anything, but I was into being the popular one — the clown. I enjoyed it a lot because I got attention.

I fell in love with my first boyfriend, and being from a Catholic family, I had to take my sister along on my dates. She's the one who was born after me — she hated going on dates with me. My sister was always a chaperone and if I went to the Drive-In, I had to take the whole family. Occasionally, my boyfriend and I would take cover because it was cold, and we would do heavy petting. I think graduation night was my first time alone with him and we did it. It was not good because it happened too fast. I actually think he was already shooting before he got it in. It was a disaster, but you know what? There was the always next night! It got better and better every time.

For a young girl originally from Mexico, Kitten had few difficulties adjusting to life American style. As a teenager in the mid-1960s, she was ecstatic to land a plumb, summer employment position with one of Hollywood's hottest and most desirable celebrities.

On my vacation from high school during my junior year, my uncle got me a job working as a maid and a cook for actress Stella Stevens. I loved it. She's my hero. She was a wonderful, wonderful person and I loved her and her kid. After graduation, I came back to work again with her. It wasn't going to be forever, but I enjoyed working for them. She wasn't married at all. She was beautiful and she lived with a guy who was the owner of some nightclub that was very hot. When I went back to school, I was the hit of the entire school because I had lived with a movie star. It was just wonderful!

Stella Stevens, a sex siren and Pin-Up girl in her own right, had posed for *Playboy* in 1960 before becoming a Hollywood actress. Stevens landed roles in some of the popular comedic films of the decade such as *Girls! Girls! Girls!* (1962) cast opposite Elvis Presley, and won parts in other trendy productions. In many ways, Stevens and Kitten were kindred spirits.

I graduated from high school in El Paso. My other grandmother was living here in Los Angeles and I came to visit her and fell in love with [Los Angeles]. I said, "This is where I want to live the rest of my life." I already knew, and I knew what I had wanted in my life — not as a teenage girl, but when I first came to this city. After graduation, I went to key punch school, and then I got my diploma and I got a job as a key punch operator. My god — was that fucking boring! Jesus! I fell asleep at the key punch machine.

Blessed with a shapely figure and effusive personality, Natividad decidedly took a page out of her former employer's book and set her sights on becoming an entertainer. In the beginning, a detour or two presented some competition with her career aspirations.

A friend of mine that lived across from where I lived had a sister who was a dancer. She told me how much money she made, and I thought, "Oh, my god, I've got to get that job!" and I did. It was hard because I didn't want to leave my job as a key punch operator because I had benefits, but I was probably there for about a year before I got into dancing. When I first started dancing I was single, and eventually, I gave it up because I got married. The first time I got married, I was around twenty-one. He was way older than I was. When I met him, I was nineteen and he was around sixty-four. He was a Russian guy with a big cock, and then later, after I got married to him I missed dancing. He told me that if I went back to dancing it was over. After nine months, we annulled it. That was fine with me.

Altogether, I've had three husbands, and I've kept one of my married names because when I used to stay at the hotels I would

COURTESY OF *KITTENCLUB.COM*

have guys knocking at my door. They'd see "Kitten Natividad," or "Francesca," and the hotel would give them my room number, so that wasn't good. My fans don't know my real name.

At the ripe age of twenty-one, Francesca, who assumed the stage name "Kitten" apparently as a nod to the demure side of her demeanor, received the first of many silicone injections for breast enhancement surgery in Tijuana, Mexico — a procedure believed to have been a rite of passage for topless dancing, particularly during Natividad's prime years. Armed with her twin forty-four cannons, Kitten commanded top dollar as a crowd pleaser for patrons of burlesque nightclubs populating the dance circuit in the late-1960s-early 1970s. She and other plucky beauties worked it out as headliners in the infamous Classic Cat on Sunset Boulevard.

My reason for getting into stripping and adult entertainment is that I really enjoyed the attention. It was my decision to get into it, and into the dancing. It was also for the money. I have to tell you that money is at the top on my list — and the men. You do meet a lot of guys, of course. My heart, my everything belonged to dancing and stripping. I was a stripper first. The reason I initially got into porn is because it would reach out to more men. I did the layouts to make a name for myself.

Going *Up!* With Russ Meyer

I was already married when I met Russ [Meyer] and I was working at the Classic Cat. At the time, he had the movie *Supervixons* (1975) out and the star of his movie, Shari Eubank, was working at the club. She was a beautiful girl, a very sweet girl from Illinois. They told him that he should come and check me out because I was the kind of woman he liked for his films. He came by while he was working on another film called *UP!* He said, "You're so hot looking, I want to put you in that film no matter what."

Prior to fortuitously locking horns with cult filmmaker, Russ Meyer who would undoubtedly impact her life's path, Natividad was briefly seen in a club scene in an uncredited bit part as a Go-Go dancer in the 1972 straight film *The New Centurions* starring George C. Scott.

By the time Kitten and sexploitation sultan Russ Meyer were introduced in the mid-1970s, Meyer had spent almost two decades smothered
in cleavage. Rather famously, he launched the careers of far more than
his share of amply endowed women in campy, satire-laden, sexy features
usually depicting strong, indomitable women beginning with his first
venture into filmmaking with *The Immoral Mr. Teas* (1959). For almost

COURTESY OF *KITTENCLUB.COM*

twenty years a compendium of hits and misses followed, partly comprised of *Vixen!* (1968), *Beyond the Valley of the Dolls* (a 1970 release written by film critic Roger Ebert, not to be confused with the original 1967 movie *The Valley of the Dolls* starring Patty Duke and Sharon Tate), and *Supervixons* (1975). Meyer's stellar line-up of big-breasted (and more often than not, au natural) protégés encompassed Babette Bardot, Shari Eubank, Uschi Digart, Tura Satana, and Kitten Natividad to name only a handful — definitely in the literal sense.

> He hired me as a narrator and that's how it started. After that, he kept asking me out and I said, "I can't go to dinner, I'm married," and then finally, I don't know how it happened, it just happened. We started dating each other. I eventually had to make a decision to leave my second husband, but I didn't have any regrets because he was too much of a control freak. He has passed on already. It's all very complicated.

Developed from a script written by Meyer and Roger Ebert (under an alias), the feature film *Up!*, is appropriately suited under the "extremely bizarre" category for exploitation film fans. Consistent with most Russ Meyer pictures, the outrageous storyline is laced with metaphors, and exists primarily to showcase beautiful, large-breasted vixons frolicking nude in tranquil outdoor settings. In an effort to explain the sequences of events, characters, and multiple convoluted plots throughout the bewildering tale that is actually a murder mystery, naked Natividad keenly provides cryptic narration in mannerly fashion as "The Greek Chorus" while various scenarios are depicted. Bisexuality, fetishes, and various softcore sexual situations add flavor throughout, and are supported by a wide array of musical accompaniment. Raven De La Croix, Edward Schaff (in the role of former Nazi Adolf Schwartz, a parody of Hitler), and Candy Samples (as Mary Gavin) are featured.

> When I started with Russ Meyer — those were not pornographic movies. He was not a pornographer. It was T & A, baby. They were nude films, period. A lot of the mainstream films made today with the big stars, they look like they're fucking each other. They don't call it porn though. It's a movie, which is not that different.

Hollywood has come precariously close to showing genuine sex acts in recent decades, but no cigar — or "pickle" to be more precise. Examples of mainstream pictures containing one or more simulated sex scenes in the past forty years are directors Bernardo Bertolucci's *Last Tango in Paris* (1972), Adrian Lyne's *Nine ½ Weeks* (1986), Alan Parker's *Angel Heart* (1987), James Toback's *Two Girls and a Guy* (1997), and Stanley Kubrick's *Eyes Wide Shut* (1999). An illustration of an exception to the rule is Vincent Gallo's indie film *Brown Bunny* (2003). Shot in sixteen millimeter and

COURTESY OF *KITTENCLUB.COM*

blown up to thirty-five, "Bunny" made waves at the Cannes Film Festival because it contained an explicit scene featuring oral sex followed by an orgasm. However, *Brown Bunny* was largely panned by audiences and film critics alike. Roger Ebert, who later gave the re-edited version "thumbs up," initially had said "Bunny" was the "worst film" ever screened at Cannes which led to a verbal war between Ebert and Gallo. Despite the fact the feature itself is not considered to be on par as a Cannes competitor, the inclusion of the controversial sex scene was a rather bold stroke by Gallo to break free from the status quo.

Russ Meyer did not do porn films. I love him to death. He's dead now, but I have to come to his defense. Later, I did some Triple-X films, but Russ would be rolling in his grave because he could not compete with porn.

Meyer's reasons for remaining in the shallow end of the porn pool are blunt and to the point. He said, (a) "I don't want to do business with the mob," and (b) "I don't find what goes on below the waist to be that visual."

He was my old man on and off for ten years. I wanted to marry him. He's the one I should have married. We had our own residences, but Russ paid my rent and he lived with me at my place. In other words, he had his own place, but I wouldn't live there because it looked like a factory. He worked out of there. I didn't want to sleep there and so we lived and ate in my house, and then he'd go to work at his house. The only furniture that he had was a dining room table and a bed. The rest was all equipment for his movies and cutting rooms and screening rooms, and it was like a big warehouse. His work was his tunnel vision. He lived, breathed it, and slept it. I only did two films for him. *Beneath the Valley of the Ultra-Vixens* (1977) was his last film; he never did another movie after that.

Beneath the Valley of the Ultra-Vixens is indeed Russ Meyer's last official classic film co-starring Candy Samples. Uschi Digart provides narration in addition to Meyer. Written by Meyer and Roger Ebert and directed by Meyer, the hero in the *Beneath the Valley of the Ultra-Vixens* is Lamar (Ken Kerr) with a fixation on entering his wife Lavonia (Natividad) through the back door. Lavonia's disgusted reaction to her husband's misfire(s) creates a domino effect of circumstances and the appearance of more top-heavy women, each one serving to teach Lamar to satisfy his woman through more conventional (vaginal) means. Fortunately, for the couple, the story has a happy ending as Lamar sees the error of his ways and converts to the missionary method of pleasuring Lavonia.

Considered by critics to be less than stellar work, Meyer's swan song, *Beneath the Valley of the Ultra-Vixens* (apparently, a commentary on Meyer's own homophobic predisposition), has redeeming qualities mostly in the way of its star, Kitten Natividad, who is in virtually every scene doing what she does best — playing a luscious, over-sexualized, busty dish. In 2001, Meyer produced one final effort, *Pandora Peaks*, starring model, stripper, and pornographic actress Pandora Peaks.

After *Ultra-Vixens*, I kept doing layouts and I was on the road. I did some hardcore films that were an hour long with fucking and sucking — that was in the 1980s. I forget sometimes though. You know, one time a guy said to me, "We did a hardcore film together." I said, "We did?" I didn't even remember fucking some guys! I don't remember their names. I don't know, honey. Hardcore wasn't a big part of my life. I wasn't a real hardcore chick. I don't even remember the directors' names. I was like a walking Zombie back then.

Cup of Coffee in Hardcore

Natividad's contribution to the 1970s-1980s hardcore market was mostly limited to nude, softcore/simulated sex scenes and the casual girl-on-girl interlude as seen in the 1983 film *Bodacious Ta Tas* with Patty Plenty. Kitten was also known to do the occasional "beaver" (spread-eagled) scene or provide complementary faux oral action. Generally, the stripper turned actress was hired for big breast exposure.

John Holmes and the All-Star Sex Queens (1980) is an example of a straight softcore production showcasing Natividad, along with fellow ample-breasted beauties Uschi Digart, Candy Samples, and Kelly Stewart. After auditioning for casting director (Holmes) the three chesty females take turns frolicking in the sack with "The King," but without actual penetration. Natividad related that once the camera stopped rolling, she and Holmes enjoyed a little nookie and shared toots of cocaine; one of the habits she developed once her film career began.

> John Holmes was very charming. I had a crush on him and we had sex off-camera. It wasn't that I was forced to have sex with him or got paid to have sex with him. It was because we wanted to. It was good and he was a gentleman, but he preferred eating pussy. He didn't like fucking. He said he had no feeling in his cock. He just didn't like to fuck. He said that the blood flow made it heavy, but I really enjoyed it.

While scouting some of the work in Natividad's filmography, it seems likely her first feature hardcore production involving actual anal penetration was at age forty-two. In the 1991 film *40, The Hard Way* Kitten participated in an anal performance with James Lewis and Sasha Gabor. Other hardcore inserts interspersed within her unusual film career are sporadic as Video on Demand and online hardcore distributors reveal. Natividad explained how the shift from softcore to hardcore transpired.

What happened along the way and it's very easy after ten years of working in bars every single day, six days a week — I ended up becoming an alcoholic and a drug addict. I'm sixty-two now; that happened when I was about thirty. I didn't really care for alcohol and drugs, but I did it because I was so fucking bored after a while and I found out that when I'd drink it was all wonderful. That was around the time when I first met Russ Meyer and he was a big alcoholic. None of my other husbands drank.

When I went into porn, I was in bad shape. I was a lush by that time. When I quit, I didn't miss it at all, and now, I don't drink either. I went through a phase and now it's over. When I stopped drinking my life got back on track and I'm doing okay. Sometimes my friends will ask me to have a drink and I think why should I get started again? One might lead to two, and that might lead to more. I don't want that. I do go to AA to remind me not to drink. I've enjoyed my life whether it was bad or good. Sometimes I didn't know it was bad!

Pornography films can be done in one day. I only did something like five films [with penetration] in all — it wasn't a career. I did a little here and there. Some girls have done hundreds of movies. No matter what I did, it became big because I already had a name, but that's about it.

Kitten downplayed her hardcore sex appearances during our interview, and rightfully so since they are indeed few and far between — but available. Other titles containing Natividad engaged in anal penetration mode are *Private Fantasies 4* (1991) opposite Nick East, and *Titillation 3* (1991) with Marc Wallice (seven years before Sharon Mitchell and AIM confirmed Wallice was HIV positive). Rounding things out with a masturbation scene is one of Natividad's recent appearances in *Busty Mature Vixens 5* (2008).

The commercially successful *Kitten Natividad Collection* (released in 2006 by Alpha Blue Archives) is an assemblage of various segments encompassing some of the star's best softcore work in addition to showcasing the infamous "champagne" number lifted from her stage act. The collection includes one hardcore piece and a glamorous choreographed striptease routine for a pair of bar patrons (Ron Jeremy and a friend). Coy Kitten demonstrates every inch of her assets with class and impeccable style — a true testament to her roots in burlesque and as an experienced Pin-Up model. Natividad acknowledged working in adult movies sometimes had its benefits.

You know, Bettie Page was very hot in the fifties and I was hot as a Pin-Up in the seventies. At one time, there were plans in the works to do a book on me, but then they decided not to because they felt that the Pin-Ups of the seventies were not that interesting. That really hurt my feelings. That was also the era where we were taking porn very seriously; we thought we were big time Hollywood. We had scripts and everybody had tons of lines — they were cornball films but they were kind of cute. They don't make them like that now. It's just fucking, but we used to have actual scripts and would be required to learn all of these lines. I loved it! We got big time money.

A lot of girls just don't last in the business. They might be dysfunctional or they are just overnighters. On the other hand, some of them who did have a horrible life were able to make themselves stars. I am so proud of Jenna Jameson. She's worth forty-five million dollars or something and she's very smart. You know, one of the strippers I danced with came from a wealthy family and she was given everything and people would say, "Why is she a stripper, she comes from a great family?"

I'd turn around and say, "Hey! I come from a great family and I'm doing this!" You get my drift. What's more is that she stripped because she loved dancing and enjoyed it. I'd say the people who were exploited never made it to stardom. They were not stars. To be star material you had to have a little bit of a brain or somebody that had a brain pushing you. Anybody can get into that business, but you don't necessarily become a star — a little bit of talent helps too. You have to be smart to have survived in this business, period. Oh, my god. Particularly, when you're older and you're still pretty much on top of the game and still worth your price.

Premium Price for Bodacious Ta Tas

Later, I eventually got into mainstream films. I did *The Best Little Whorehouse in Texas* (1982), and I did *Another 48 Hours* (1990), and *My Tutor* (1983). They were all mainstream films. I was also in *The Gong Show* (1980) movie. If people go to my website [www.kittenclub.com], they'll see I did hundreds of movies, but only about five of them were porn.

During the early 1970s, Natividad also made an appearance on creator Chuck Barris's *The Dating Game* as one of the eligible bachelorettes. In the 1980s, she was hired to virtually play herself in the comical spoofs *Airplane* (1980), and *Airplane II* (1982) with Lloyd Bridges and Leslie Nielson. Kitten followed up with a brief cameo in *Night Patrol* (1984) starring Linda Blair and Andrew Dice Clay. In 1984, fans caught her dancing in the opening of Mitch Ryder's music video cover of Prince's composition "When You Were Mine."

COURTESY OF *KITTENCLUB.COM*

Despite her work assignments away from the muted lighting distinctive in burlesque lounges and nightclubs, Kitten has proved you can take an exotic dancer out of the limelight, but you can't take the diva out of the girl.

I consider myself a liberated woman. I still like men, and I like to take care of them. As far as respect, I believe people have certain roles to uphold, and that applies to both sexes. I will tell you that I am very proud to be a female. I like to show my tits and show off my ass. I like the high heels and I like being a female. I enjoy it, and I like being a cock teaser. Once a cock teaser, always a cock teaser. I actually like doing everything, but that's why I especially liked stripping. I just LOVED turning men on.

Knowing I am from Canada, Natividad teased notwithstanding the lack of expected amenities at certain Canadian hotels, performing as a headliner in various Ontario cities actually wasn't that bad…honest.

I stripped for three decades throughout the seventies, eighties, and nineties. After a while, I just wanted to stop. I toured everywhere including Japan, but after a while, you get tired of packing your shit. One day, you say to yourself, "This is crap. I don't like this anymore." Especially in Canada, they put you into some shitty hotels where there wouldn't be any hot water. I'd have to go to the girl's room next door and ask if I could shower. I stripped in Mississauga, Ottawa, Windsor, and Niagara Falls. I loved it and I loved that Canadian beer! I had a lot of fans and made a lot of money there. Let me tell you, come pay day, the Canadian government took a lot off my pay in taxes. I gave them thousands of dollars, but I also got to dance in some places that were in the countryside. It was fun; it was wonderful. I do love Canada!

I've always believed to be the best that you can, and be clever with your costumes and music and movement. Enjoy, and you'll go far. It shows when you're enjoying yourself, and if you're up on stage, everyone will enjoy your show. When I was stripping, I could tell if someone wanted to be there or not. You would see the disgust that they had for stripping in their eyes and on their faces and I'd think, "Why the fuck is she up there?"

Something that I feel very good about is there were only four girls with big tits. There was myself, Candy Samples, Uschi Digart, and Kelly Everett. We were the ones where the photographers would say, "Your boobs are too big. Don't you know that most women don't have big boobs?" We said, "We have to get men to like them and then women will get big boobs." We were the ones who started the big boob trend. Russ Meyer never liked the phony ones, and then toward the end he even liked the phony ones better. He

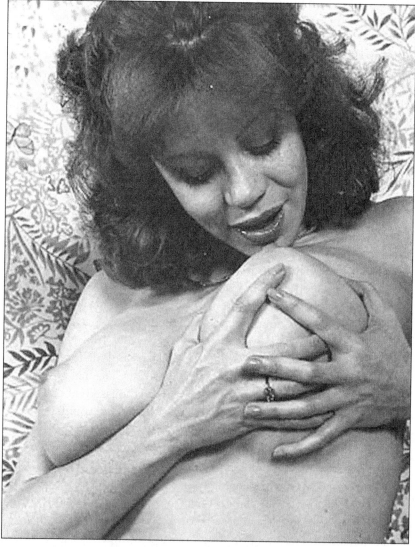

COURTESY OF *KITTENCLUB.COM*

would love it today. Everybody went to my films or bought my films because they wanted to see my big tits. That's my claim to fame.

Natividad's breast augmentation procedures were a blessing for her career and later, a curse when she was diagnosed with cancer. Kitten endured a double mastectomy surgery in 1999, and continues to remain cancer free today. Formally introduced in 1961-62 and commonly used for years as a breast enlargement application, silicone began to create health risks. In 1992, silicone implant sales temporarily ceased because of a lack of sufficient studies on long-term effects. Silicone appliances utilized for implants today are now in their fifth generation cycle and are believed to have a very low incident rate of leakage or shell rupture. Buyer Beware.

I had silicone injections which caused my breast cancer. I had gone to Mexico years ago where they had given me industrial silicone instead of pharmaceutical silicone. It was just like fucking gasoline. Some of my friends have died from it because it eventually travelled to their lungs. I've had reconstruction surgery and everything's fine. I've got big breasts again. At the same time, if I didn't have breasts I'd be good to go anyway. I'm very lucky and I'm making the best of my life so I have got to do well.

Kitten has lost more than a few friends along her journey and some have chosen to age gracefully. Most recently in February 2011, Japanese born Tura Santana, a kick-ass, cult film hero and stunt queen who starred in the 1965 Meyer flick *Faster Pussycat! Kill! Kill!*, died from heart failure at seventy-two years old. Former Meyer babes and adult feature notables Candy Samples and Ushi Digart have opted to live privately and without a lot of fanfare in Palm Springs. Unlike some of her girlfriends, Natividad is one of the fortunate ones. Kitten is respectful of her quality of life and selective about the people with whom she chooses to fraternize. Financial freedom is integral to her years of semi-retirement.

I don't want to be in a relationship now because it's nice not being in one. I have a dog and four cats, and when I open the door, they're all waiting for me. I'm thinking "Oh no! Leave me alone! I've got to go to the bathroom!" I love my animals though and that's the important thing. I'm also very particular about whom I fuck, especially in this day and age. I didn't particularly go for the pretty boys. I go for somebody who is interesting and wonderful and who is crazier about me than I am about them. I do have an active sex life today; everything's good. I'm in a good place. I really don't think I want to get married because I have so much to lose. If anyone wants to be with me, I have to have concerns about someone wanting to go after my two apartment buildings unless he's got more money than I have! I'm not interested in sharing and I'll just let him know right off the bat.

Real Love

During our interview, Natividad was boisterous, vivacious and funny — characteristics one might expect from a gutsy woman worshipped for her hourglass figure. Not only is she an unforgettable presence in movies, but Kitten's ribald dance routines captured on smoky stages across two countries and throughout three decades are legendary. When speaking of Russ Meyer however, Natividad candidly communicated the details of his last few years. Tenacious until the end, Meyer completed his own autobiography: *A Clean Breast: The Life and Loves of Russ Meyer* (3 Volume Set, 2000). Meyer was also able to finish off other enterprising endeavors despite being plagued by Alzheimer's. He eventually died of pneumonia in 2004. A shrewd businessman who owned the rights to almost all of his movies, Meyer bequeathed his entire fortune to research.

He did the book. He did a documentary for *Playboy* and photography. He really had dementia in the end. I would say to him, "God, what is wrong with you?" People can hide it for many years. I think that's the reason he would start several projects and never finish anything. That wasn't how he normally was. I knew something was wrong because I also went on to work for him as a secretary, and then I took care of him when he had his Alzheimer's until he got very bad. When he got so bad that he lost control of his bowels, I was the one who cleaned him up. That was a result of the dementia and his alcoholism. He was never put in a home. He had male caregivers come 24/7. It cost him ten thousand a month to live where he was. I was friends with him and his girlfriend — we became friends after so many years of being together. Then, when I had breast cancer, he financed my medical bills.

He was probably worth eight million dollars when he died. He had a lot of money, but it all went to cancer research [at Memorial Sloan-Kettering Cancer Centre]. You know his estate will still be raking in big bucks, but his secretary had power of attorney for his company and she hates all of us, although she doesn't mind the money that benefits her. She thinks it's awful what we did, but the "dirty money," she loves.

Russ was marvelous — he was my dear friend for life.

Kitten's Nine Lives

The two apartment buildings I own in Hollywood today I run with an iron fist. Not that I'm prejudiced, but I mostly rent to gay girls. You can't have horn dogs around here.

Since officially leaving show business, in recent years, Natividad earned a tidy income as a phone-sex specialist combined with invitations for special appearances, feature articles, and occasional minor roles in low-budget pictures.

Years after first noticing her in the driver's seat of Russ Meyer's Mercedes, director Adam Rifkin hired Natividad to play Ruby in *Night of the Golden Eagle*, a 2005 film noir (that also included Ron Jeremy) about two criminals determined to go straight, but without success.

Along with several X-rated friends, Kitten was a welcome guest celebrity in *Pornstar Pets* (2005) joined by her pit bulldog and three cats. In 2009, Natividad and Tura Santana were both seen in *Sugar Box*, a tawdry little story centered in a Women's prison. Kitten was also one of several former Pin-Up girls to be spotlighted in a 2006 *Playboy* magazine pictorial "History of Bikinis."

Natividad's website shows a short of the burlesque queen from a few years ago, on stage dressed in a plunging back, sparkling evening gown entertaining fans while in the midst of a seductive dance number. As recently as June 2011, Natividad, along with some of her pals, shared her wares at the Orleans Hotel and Casino in Las Vegas for a Russ Meyer tribute.

I stay in touch with some of the women that I worked with for Russ Meyer and my stripper friends, but none from the porn industry. Occasionally, I'll see Sharon Mitchell and she's a very nice person. Sometimes, I'll see Nina Hartley but she won't even say hello to me. Does she think she's hot shit, or what?

I can't really hide. All of the information about me is on the internet and it's everywhere. I'm not making my money doing movies anymore so it's sort of forgotten. When I meet up with my neighbors, we talk about other things, not about my career. They treat me very normal. I've been living here for fifteen years. They kind of know who I am but I'm always doing my gardening. I don't throw wild parties and they haven't seen me drunk because I've been clean and sober for ten years. I don't make excuses for the person I am and I don't brag about myself either.

COURTESY OF *KITTENCLUB.COM*

I enjoy my friends a lot, and I enjoy hopping on a plane and visiting them, and sitting up and talking. I love to go to the movies with friends or I go out shopping, and if there isn't anything I want to buy, I'll just go to a movie. It's great. I'd love to live anywhere as long as I am happy. When I visit my girlfriends in West Virginia, I love it there, and I want to live there, or Palm Springs or wherever I travel. I get to go visit them and enjoy those cities.

I would love my legacy to be that I was someone who really enjoyed men. I did it for men. I did it for them, baby. I've got all these diamonds and apartment buildings and I owe it all to men! Whatever has happened in my life is fine because I'm in a good place now. I've got my shit together.

13

Miss
Sharon Mitchell

Sharon Mitchell was the only child adopted from a Catholic orphanage by a police officer and his wife living in rural New Jersey in the mid-1950s. Although Sharon's year of birth shows 1956 on various internet sites, according to her, the actual birth year is 1958 making her an underage seventeen-year old when she first worked in adult movies.

Celebrated by classic porn fans for her tough, campy, androgynous persona and daring on-camera predilections, Sharon's childhood years were stamped with feelings of insecurity and confusion about her own sexuality and place in the world. Before the age of ten, Mitchell's mother and father divorced prompting her mother to assume a position as assistant administrator of a hospital for the criminally insane. Her Hungarian grandmother was assigned the duty of co-raising the clever and auspicious child. To this day, Sharon claims her grandmother championed her independence, and imparted pearls of wisdom to her young charge.

Frustrated by her mother's controlling ways and feelings of neglect brought on by her alcoholic father's absence in her life, Sharon abruptly married at seventeen, but had the marriage annulled six months later. Never one to be bound by conventionality, Mitchell arrived on the New York scene in the mid-seventies, while still a teen. She signed on with the Dorothy Palmer Agency and began to fine-tune her acting skills doing bit parts in TV commercials, soap operas, and the occasional film. Sharon also studied contemporary dance with the Martha Graham Dance Company.

One of her earliest appearances in an adult feature is a minor role in a scene from *That Lady from Rio* (1976) starring Vanessa del Rio. Mitchell easily adapted to prominent parts, such as her starring role in *The Violation of Claudia* (1977) opposite Jamie Gillis. Sharon continued building her portfolio, alternating between porn and mainstream work. Eventually, she

"It was kind of the best way to say fuck you to the Catholic Church and to the orphanage, and all of the nuns and all that nonsense, and to my parents at the same time. I was an anarchist, so it was a way to cause trouble and mayhem." SHARON MITCHELL

developed a well-earned rough reputation appearing in BDSM movies and/or assuming dominatrix or "butch" roles coinciding with a publicized needle addiction to heroin.

After working with two generations of performers and sustaining a stalker attack in 1996, "Mitch," as she is more commonly known by friends and colleagues, eventually cleaned up her act. She was granted an honorary doctorate in Human Sexuality from the Institute for the Advanced Study of Human Sexuality in San Francisco. In 1998, Mitchell became the director of AIM (Adult Industry Medical Healthcare Foundation), a much needed non-profit organization based in Los Angeles that expedited on site STD and HIV testing in addition to providing counseling for adult performers. In 2008, AIM was harshly criticized for its alleged failure to comply with principles and guidelines outlined by California law concerning patient Health and Safety. Mitchell released a statement in December of 2010 claiming AIM had been wrongfully attacked and was the target of a conspiracy campaign waged by AIDS Healthcare Foundation (AHF) and the L.A. County of Public Health (LACPH).

In May 2011, after succumbing to the mounting pressures exerted upon the organization by AHF along with a pending lawsuit from a former performer for breach of patient confidentiality, AIM closed its doors claiming financial hardship.

In November of 2010, just six months prior to AIM's closure, Sharon Mitchell spoke with me from her home in Northern California.

Daddy's Girl

I was born in 1958. It says 1956 in my bio because I lied when I first got into adult entertainment. I was adopted from a Catholic Orphanage and I grew up in New Jersey in a very rural area on a farm. My uncle's farm was very close by.

My dad was a police officer. My mother and dad got divorced when I was very young and my mother eventually went on to become the Assistant Administrator of a very large state hospital for the criminally insane. It was interesting growing up in rural New Jersey. I've just always been one of those people that even as a child I felt I never fit in anywhere, but wanted to fit in everywhere. My parents doted on me to a certain extent but I wouldn't say I was too spoiled or anything.

I was out of diapers young and walking very quickly. I learned how to read very, very, young. I was extremely bright and I won some kind of contest when I was four years old for reading books. Other kids used to pick on me for being adopted. It was kind of confusing because my family always celebrated the day that they adopted me it was such a big deal. I always wondered if it was a big deal or if it was a curse. It just didn't make that much difference to me.

Interestingly, the Catholic Church, I believe, was the second largest white baby dealer in the United States during the 1950s and they would charge ten thousand dollars for a white baby. They had all of these terms and conditions: you'd have to put the child through the Catholic school and donate lots of money until the child reached a certain age. There were other [alternative] adoption agencies, but apparently, you'd have to wait about ten years to get a white baby. For some reason, my parents wanted a white baby because it was the fifties, I don't know. Now I don't think anybody gives a shit because we're almost all the same color anyway, but back then, I guess if you aligned with the Catholic Church and you were willing to donate a specific sum and promise that you'd convert if you were not already a member — I think my mother had been Protestant. She had to change over to the Catholic Religion and my parents had to send me to Parochial school until I received the Sacrament of Confirmation which is when I was twelve or thirteen. They had to donate a tremendous amount of money to the local parish.

Every single month a nun would come around until I was about nine years old. You never knew when she was going to come, day or night. If they did not sufficiently believe a child was being cared for properly, they would take you back and reboot you out to somebody else.

Prior to the development of oral contraceptives in 1960, during the 1950s through to the early 1970s, unmarried, pregnant Caucasian American girls and women were encouraged and often pressured to place their babies up for adoption rather than choosing abortion or keeping the infant after giving birth. According to historian Rickie Sollinger, author of *Wake up Little Suzie* (and at least one other scholarly book centering on the era of "baby scooping"), unwed mothers were generally considered undesirable as parents because of supposed "lack of self-control." Therefore, many unwed females felt they had to capitulate to societal expectations and the belief that married women were better equipped to raise children. Sharon Mitchell has never felt compelled to seek out her birth parents, but she has often wondered about her family genealogy and medical history.

Just recently, there has been a health issue come up, and in that issue, I've found that I'm very rare — less than four percent of the population type of gene. I'm a very rare type. I was going over the results and the research you know how you do. I thought, "Wow, if I'm less than four percent of the population and there's something like eight billion people, back when there were only three billion people there must have been less than one percent of this type." My [birth] parents might be dead now. I'm almost fifty-three years old, but it would be interesting to know now where they came from for that reason.

When my adoptive parents divorced, I was between the ages of five and seven and we had to move around a lot because of our financial situation and financial issues. After my mom had to go to work, her mother started living with us and looked after me and quite often our other cousin, the only other kid in the family at that time who was adopted. He was adopted from the same place I was so we kind of fit in pretty well, the two of us. We were like brother and sister. Then we kind of got pulled away by the red neck side of the family.

My grandmother was very wise in a lot of old world ways because she came from Hungary and she had a tremendous amount of knowledge of herbs and sex and everything from stockings to having babies. She was just a world of knowledge and she was always perfectly okay with who I was and perfectly okay with telling me who she was. She was wonderful.

There was always something about me that people didn't really like — I'm not exaggerating. There was something about me that made everyone uneasy and people were not very nice to me. They would break my toys. Our family business was a roadside grocery stand because we were part of a large farming community and I'd often work in the fields. When I became ten or eleven, I started working at the stand. I remember someone kicked me for putting their bags in their trunk or something or my cousins would accuse me of stealing. There was always something.

I used to idolize my dad but my dad was away a lot. He had remarried. He was very handsome. He had advanced quite a bit in the community. He was the president of this and president of that. He was an alcoholic and travelled a lot, and just seemed to have it all going for him. I kind of idolized him and when I would go out with him, he would drink so I started drinking at a very young age. About ten years old.

My mother was extremely possessive and overbearing so all I wanted to do was get the heck away from her. I just had to get out of there; I had to go. I don't know where I had to go, but I had to go. She had obsessive overbearing control issues. She over-disciplined and things like that so that feeling of having to get out, I feel had me really rush through my childhood. There's not a whole hell of a lot that I remember of it.

When I was very, very young I wanted to be a fireman, and I wanted to be a bride, just because of the dress. I never had any ideals of being a bride; I just liked the dress. My aunt had made me a wedding dress to play with when I was young.

A couple of teachers were somewhat influential along the way. I think a science and a math teacher. Oddly enough, I wasn't very good at either subject. Well, I was reasonably good at science and I wasn't very good at math, but I excelled in everything else. For some odd reason my mind had difficulty grasping certain mathematics. When I got older, I really had a hard time with mathematics and I have no idea why. I also had liked the Beatles you know, but I really didn't have any mentors. I had a lot of friends. I always had a lot of friends, but again, when I went through adolescence I just didn't feel I fit in anywhere. I wanted to fit in so I was on the basketball team and I was on the cheerleading squad. I was smoking pot behind the school so I was doing a little bit of everything. I was always looking for something to sort of fill those dead spots. I liked attention a lot. I relied upon my sense of humor quite a bit until I found sex. I was having sex at twelve or thirteen years old. It was with my girlfriend, a neighbor down the street, and then, eventually, with one of her brothers. It was kind of a small town.

Walking on the Wild Side

Sharon's exposure to alcohol before she was thirteen through her father's introduction led to self-medicating, and eventually she experimented with various pills, pot, and several other mild-altering substances.

As Mitchell moved from her teens into adulthood there wasn't anything she wasn't willing to try at least once — including marriage. Unafraid to diversify and assert her independence eventually expanded to include Sharon's immersion into sex films.

As a teenager, I got into my mother's painkillers for her back. I was taking them all through high school: Darvon and Darvocet, things like that, along with alcohol and marijuana, and the occasional acid trip. Heroin was a prevalent drug in the city when I was growing up, but out where we were, I think it was a little hard to find. You'd have to go into a real shitty neighborhood in one of the coastal towns like Asbury Park or something. To find heroin you'd have to really go out of your way. If it had been around, I'd have been happy to participate in whatever.

I got married at seventeen [to Larry Kipp] to get out of the house. He was a local guy who was a couple of years older than I was. We were married for six months and then I left. I got the marriage annulled. However, I was legally emancipated. I could do whatever I wanted to do and went to New York on my own. I started working with Dorothy Palmer Agency, and Dorothy Palmer would book me on soap operas. Over the next seven years, I did a tremendous amount of bit parts in movies; talking parts in television and commercials. I did a lot of that while I was doing the adult entertainment. I was also a back-up singer, primarily in a band. I did a little bit of singing and a little bit of percussion. I did some back up for The New York Dolls and The Heartbreakers — a lot of famous punk rock bands. Actually, we used to go to The Factory with Andy Warhol — I used to work in a lot of Andy's movies as well as porn. I've known Legs McNeil [author of *The Other Hollywood: The Uncensored Oral History of the Porn Film Industry,* 2005] since I was seventeen years old and we're old friends. We used to be in a rock band together. When he came out to California, he really needed some help and I helped him hook into the porn business. I think his book came out pretty good. The mobster aspect of it was accurate. Anyway, I was also working on a number of different things in New York City. I had quite a bit of formal training in New York and at the School of Visual Arts. Then, at age eighteen years old, I went to the Drama School of London for six months. I kind of didn't settle in with porn full time until around 1978.

The Internet Adult Film database (Iafd) lists Sharon's very first hard-core on camera appearance in a 1975 film titled *Lisa Meets Mr. Big* with Marlene Willoughby and other lesser known actors.

I think my first adult movie was a low budget one before I did a film called *Joy* (released in 1977). I also did *That Lady from Rio* (1976).

COURTESY OF WORTH MENTIONING PUBLIC RELATIONS

Of course, it was starring Vanessa del Rio. That's when there was a lot of money around and the budgets were very high. It paid extremely well and they had lots of special effects and costumes and all kinds of things that they don't have in adult entertainment these days. I really liked Vanessa and I really liked the ladies that were in the industry. I seemed to really fit in with them. They were kind to me. They were nice to me; they were funny. I really feel like I fit in there.

I did one of my first scenes with Jamie [Gillis], and another young man [Russ Carlson] in Vanessa del Rio's film *That Lady from Rio*. The director was trying to talk me into a double penetration or something and I had never even fucking heard of it you know. Jamie was like, "This girl just walked on the set. She has no idea." I remember him arguing with the guy about that and he just kept saying, "You know what? Just listen to me. I'll take care of you for a couple of months." He could see that someone could have taken advantage of me. From that day forward, I worked with him in tons of films. He always watched out for me and he was always a sweetheart and never judged me. We lived together from time to time and with other folks and we shared apartments.

One of my favorite actors was a guy named Bobby Astyr. He was an incredibly funny, funny man. He was a very, very talented trumpet player and drummer. He was a character actor because of his height; he was very short. He passed away from cancer about twenty years ago, I think. I did my first scene with him [in *That Lady from Rio*] and I remember the director was Shaun Costello. I was sitting on Bobby, and Shaun said, "Say something dirty." I didn't know how to say something dirty; I'm a fucking Catholic girl from New Jersey, so I go, "Ohh...ahhh...ahhh..."

He said, "No, no, you have to say something dirty, you know." I was sitting on Bobby in kind of reverse cowgirl position and I said to Bobby, "Oh, baby, come in my hand." I jumped off his cock and put my hand out behind me and he actually jacked off in my hand. I quickly learned how to talk dirty. It's usually about the action where it feels good or where you want it to go. I didn't really know how. There is a little park at the end of my street in Manhattan, where one of the actors wrote: "The cum in my hand" park.

That Lady from Rio (1976) is an action film where Sharon (with striking white streaks in her brunette hair) acts as one of Vanessa del Rio's trusted associates of a slave trading operation that selects and supplies girls for bordellos worldwide. Sharon certainly had her *hand* full in more ways than one in her rousing athletic scene with Bobby Astyr that almost pales in comparison to her double penetration scene with Jamie Gillis and Russ Carlson. In this case, two penises are inserted into the vagina with Mitchell positioned on top of Russ Carlson and in front of Gillis while assuming a doggie style pose.

I loved Jamie [Gillis]. Jamie was like the perverted father I always wanted to have. Again, he was someone who looked out for me a lot the first couple of years. Jamie represented nothing but pure love for me: absolute, unequivocal, pure love.

Violation of Claudia with Jamie might have come out in 1977, but it was made in 1975.

Skin Flicks

If it is true that Sharon Mitchell's actual date of birth is 1958 as opposed to her official birth date of 1956, she would have been seventeen years old during the production of *Violation of Claudia*. In the 1977 release, Mitchell fills out the starring role as Claudia, a young neglected wife of a business executive living in New York. Disregarding age of consent for a moment, Sharon confidently brought a moderate level of maturity, poise, and conviction to the part while giving one the impression of a woman nurtured to become a refined sophisticate. Married to an older man Jason (Don Peterson) who doesn't appear to notice his charming young wife, Claudia fills the void in her life busying herself with private lessons and the trivial affairs partaken by the upper crust. One morning during her tennis lesson, she and her instructor Kip (Jamie Gillis) meet one another's gaze while in the midst of Kip's follow-through demonstration. They have lunch and Kips senses sadness conveyed in Claudia's large brown eyes. When asked what is troubling her, Claudia confides with some trepidation that her husband doesn't have time for her and she feels alone. Realizing he might snag another vulnerable victim for personal purposes, Kip suggests he could offer Claudia employment to join his concubine of women. In other words, Kip is a pimp and would like Claudia to hook for him. Shocked and insulted, Claudia politely thanks Kip, but is clearly not interested in prostituting herself. After making a quick exit, Claudia keeps her appointment with her masseuse who allows Kip to step in for him without Claudia's knowledge as she lies face down on her tummy. She protests the slight of hands, but Kip begins to touch Claudia in places that haven't been caressed or stirred in a long while. She no longer resists his invasion, rather, Claudia responds eagerly, and eventually opens her mouth welcoming his climax upon her face. A few days later, Jason leaves town for a business trip. Claudia gives the housekeeper a few days off and picks up a young athletic male (Victor Hines) hitching a ride. She brings him back to her abode for

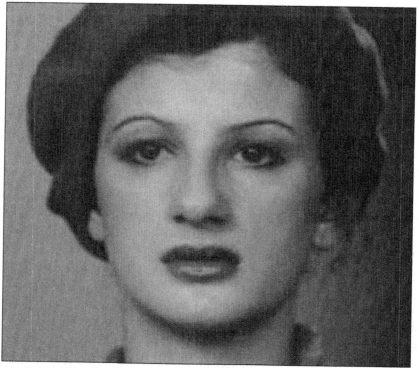

Violation of Claudia. COURTESY OF VIDEO-X-PIX

sex and siesta. At sixteen, the boy is not about to turn down a romantic overture from an attractive and determined woman ten years his senior. Their sex is delicate and slow in the modestly lit space, properly underscored by the crackling logs on the fireplace in behind. Primed by the adulterous act, in the following scene Claudia reconsiders Kip's initial invitation. Her first client is a prominent Senator (Waldo Short) with a propensity to dress his naked dates in whipped cream, cherries and chocolate sauce. Claudia isn't sure about the Senator's partiality at first, but lets her guard down and actually enjoys her participation in his food fetish. After finishing him off with a chocolate dipped blowjob, Claudia is soon en route to meet another customer. The next gentleman, dressed rather flamboyantly, comes equipped with a plastic sheet. When Claudia inquires what he plans to do with it, the flowery fellow quips, "I'm going to sprinkle you with my fairy dust." Not wanting any part in being urinated upon, Claudia rushes home and suddenly senses someone is in the house. Apprehensively, she climbs the stairs toward the master bedroom. Upon opening the bedroom door, Claudia is astonished to find her husband providing anal pleasure to a male friend (two guesses as to who the strange bedfellow might be) as the camera freeze frames her startled face at close range.

The Violation of Claudia directed by William Lustig (as Billy Bagg) also boasts the talents of the delightful Jean Silver (as Long Jeanie Silver) in a dream sequence, and Crystal Sync as one of Kip's other escorts. The show is owned, however, by Sharon Mitchell's galvanizing execution of the dejected young New Yorker in a loveless marriage.

> There was another movie [*Waterpower*, 1976] where Jamie played a shell-shocked veteran from Vietnam. He was stalking me and there was this big, big stunt. I had never done a stunt before where I had to get shot. I had to sort of unhook myself from these electrical things and fall into the pool at the same time. I look back at that and think, "Oh, my god".

Waterpower (1976) is a relatively dark and ominous film set in New York directed by Shaun Costello (although there has been some discussion about who actually assumed directorial duties). Jamie Gillis stars as Burt, a Vietnam vet and deeply disturbed man who becomes obsessed with cleansing women of their dirty minds and sexual ambitions by breaking into their homes, raping them, and administering enemas by force. Mitchell appears early on as Eve, an employee of the "House of Eden" managed by the "Madam" of the brothel (played by Gloria Leonard). Burt pays ten dollars for Eve's generous services and gets off quickly, but becomes inquisitive about other "specialty" selections on the menu of the house, and witnesses an enema procedure through an observatory window. (Eric Edwards and Marlene Willoughby act as the physician and nurse orchestrating the technique to "Pamela" played by Long Jean Silver.) Burt becomes excited and consumed by what he witnesses, thus leading him on a perverse rampage throughout Manhattan.

The storyline is loosely based upon the story of Michael H. Kenyon, the Illinois "enema bandit," who terrorized students during the 1960s and seventies by employing the exact same tactics demonstrated in the film.

Costello has admitted *Waterpower* was his version of *Taxi Driver* (1976) in tone and psychotic obsession with Gillis adeptly mimicking Robert De Niro's brilliant portrayal of Travis Bickle.

Gerard Damiano is listed in the credits as the director, producer, and presenter, although it is believed at the time of the film's release, Damiano's name was attached in an effort to boost sales. Reportedly, *Waterpower* was financed by the Gambino crime family. There exists a cut and an uncut version of the film containing additional explicit footage. Sharon Mitchell does not perform a stunt in the VOD version of this film as she had stated, so it is possible the scene was a part of the cut footage.

As far as acting goes, I'd say anything I did with Gerard Damiano I am proud of because he was a perfectionist and he would rehearse us. These were deep, deep plots. Even the *Dracula* movies were deep plots and someone would always commit suicide at the end which I just loved — yeah, anything by Gerard Damiano. The only actress I know of who was involved with him off screen was Paula Morton. Paula was in the movies and those two fell in love immediately.

Mitchell granted tremendous justice to a generous role in a fascinating Damiano tableau exploring the business side of the 1970s porn industry. As the porno superstar Susan in *Skin Flicks* (1978), Sharon beautifully communicates the dichotomy between the sex performer — completely unrestrained on screen, and the human being behind-the-scenes — yearning for real love in a sound relationship. Susan falls for her director Harry (Tony Hudson), a talented artist and caretaker of the girls on his watch. Harry impels a mobster financier Al (a tremendous cameo by Damiano) for time and budget extensions so that he can produce a quality film. Al isn't interested in anything but "fucking and sucking" Angrily, he threatens the film "better get finished on time" — or else. Things become increasingly complicated when Norman (Jamie Gillis) enters the picture and is enamored of Susan. When she snubs him at a party, he decides he'll "fix the bitch's wagon," and plots revenge on her. Meanwhile, Harry is working fastidiously at finishing his picture and the heat is on, only he can't come up with a suitable ending.

As one might have guessed, Gillis' presence in the film doesn't go to waste and when we flash on to the next scene, Norman has Susan at his disposal. He threatens her with a knife, cuts her undergarments, and forces her to admit she wants him to fuck her which he proceeds to do. Believably fearful as she begs for her safe release and life, Susan knows she must capitulate to Norman's sexual demands. The final frames of the picture cleverly leave the viewer with a spine tingling reaction perplexed as to whether Harry actually used Susan as bait in order to capture a sense of realism in film.

There was a ton of money around in porn and I made up my mind that I was just going to stay working regardless of the type

COURTESY OF WORTH MENTIONING PUBLIC RELATIONS

of work there was. There were two things I knew I didn't want to do: one of them was prostitution and the other one was working as a waitress. I wanted to do fucking avoid those two things. I was getting a lot of work as well. There wasn't enough money to become a fulltime mainstream actress. I would have done it sure but back then, porn was kind of a rotten thing to do. You had to walk into a theatre to watch porn because it wasn't on TV back then; it wasn't even on videotape. It was really, really a shocking thing to do porn which was part of the appeal for me. It was kind of the best way to say fuck you to the Catholic Church and to the orphanage and all of the nuns, and all that nonsense, and to my parents at the same time. I was an anarchist, so it was a way to cause trouble and mayhem. It's very funny, because at the same time I always maintained this sort of code of honor that I wouldn't do certain things and I wouldn't work for less than this, and so on and so forth. Those things got difficult to maintain especially toward the end when the industry was changing and I was doing drugs and things like that, but I managed to not cross that line.

It's interesting. My mother's side knew, but they didn't want to talk about it. I remember one Easter I came in wearing hot pants. They were these bright green hot pants with purple patches and stuff, and we were all sitting down and one of my uncles started screaming and yelling because I was in *Hustler* magazine that month. My grandmother stood up, and put her hands down on the table and said to my uncle "Well, if you weren't jacking off to the fucking magazine you wouldn't have found your damn fucking niece in there! Now, can we drop this fucking discussion?" No one ever said another word about it on my mother's side of the family. It was very funny.

Before I got fully into the business, my mom and my dad had wanted to meet everyone I was working with so I actually had a little picnic. I invited Herschel Savage and Gloria Leonard, and my mom and dad met them. They were great. They loved them, and of course, my dad really liked it because I was like his buddy like the son he never had, you know. That was very cool to him. He said, "As long as you're doing what you want to do." He was good with it. My mom just never brought it up. They certainly appreciated all of the expensive gifts and stuff, but I don't think they appreciated where it came from.

We really looked out for each other. I used to babysit for Gloria Leonard. John Leslie, Jamie Gillis, Eric Edwards [Rob Everett], John

Holmes, and Herschel Savage as well — those guys were just sort of my big brothers. We were the core of the industry. We were the Air Corps, the Marines, the fucking Navy, and everything else. We were it.

During interviews, Mitchell generally makes a point of underscoring the Mob component, particularly during the golden era of the erotic

COURTESY OF WORTH MENTIONING PUBLIC RELATIONS

movie industry stressing that organized crime controlled a significant portion of film production and distribution through financial means. Our interview was no different.

Back then, there was the Mafia and the movie theatres. The Mob hired all of the wonderful directors to direct us and they made sure we were very talented. They made sure we looked good and they made sure we were well rehearsed. All of us back then were very good actors and actresses who most of the time were doing something off Broadway. We were all trained in show business in general, as actors, dancers, singers, or whatever. We were all multi-talented and there were probably not more than thirty-three of us — that was the core. You know, everyone was very into portraying these characters that we portrayed. If we didn't have a character, I don't think half the people that were in porn could survive today. We couldn't just turn the camera off because we really got into these roles and rehearsals, and costumes. I really loved that part of it and I miss that whole period of it all. Having said that, I didn't shit where I ate primarily, and I didn't date a lot of people in the industry. The first girl I think I dated in the industry was [former porn actress] Ming Toy. Ming Toy and I were very good friends and lovers for a while, and then we both discovered that we were dating the same guy. The guy was someone I had dated, believe it or not, in high school. So the three of us kind of lived together for a while, but I used to primarily like the rock and roll bad boys.

When some of us lived in Greenwich Village, we had this wacky gynecologist who lived at the end of my street — I lived on Downing Street. She had been in a concentration camp and had obviously survived the war. She was a serious gynecologist with a very severe German accent and we would come in every once in a while, if we had something. It wasn't often, but I think once we got scabies or something — none of us ever knew what that was, but I think it was from a film we'd worked on. Our hands and feet started itching, and we just didn't know what to do and she said in her thick accent, "Stop fucking for a living!" I remember one time when she gave me a pap smear I saw her tattoo of having been in the concentration camp — it was very interesting, but she was always reprimanding us and she was just great. She was one of the few nonjudgmental people because usually it was, "What's a nice girl like you?"

"Mitch"

An undeniable characteristic that attracted and sustained erotic film fans lodged in Sharon Mitchell's camp is her androgynous appeal in tandem with her adventurous "soft butch" lesbian inclinations on camera specifically in the area of cunnilingus. The more comfortable "Mitch" (as she came to be known) became in the sex game, the more outrageous and daring were her professional and personal personas. In straight roles that were more prevalent in her novice years as a performer, or bi, "Mitch" clearly came into her own.

When I was younger, I would play the sweet heroine parts. As I got my chops up as an actress, and as a showbiz person my talents shone through, but also my bisexuality came out big time. Porn was able to kind of hone that and make me feel that was not an issue because I couldn't for the fucking life of me — you take a kid from the middle of New Jersey on a fucking farm — I'd wonder, "Am I gay? Am I straight?" I mean, I didn't know and I agonized over that for a long time. Then when I got into porn films, it was like, "Oh, I'm just sexual." It didn't take me long to cut my hair after that!

I was one the first girls [in sex films] to chop my hair off. I was also one of the first to start to coif their pubic hair — I would do that for all of the girls. This wasn't as much about shaving; it was more about trimming everything so that it wouldn't look like a lawn mower would have to do the job. I couldn't go on the road and fit into a lot of these costumes and it just bothered me when stuff was poking out the side.

A lot of the guys back then were gay too or bisexual. Wade Nichols [aka Dennis Parker] and I worked together, but there were not that many women he could work with. He could kind of flip me over, you know. Wade was just a doll. He was so handsome. He was like the Errol Flynn of porn. He was New York based and part of the first wave of people to get HIV. He was just a great guy. In addition to porn, we also worked on [the soap opera series] *The Edge of Night* together. We had done this movie called *Captain Lust and the Pirate Women* (1977) and he played the Errol Flynn role. He looked just like Errol Flynn and I played Sweet Anne, the heroine, and he rescued me. It was just a wonderful swashbuckler movie. We shot on a replica of "Nina the Pinta," and "The Santa Maria" [named after explorer Christopher Columbus's original three ships] that they got on a loan. He was just a sweet, sweet guy. At around this same time when we were paired on this soap opera, he was playing a cop and I was playing a private nurse, which is the role that I played on *Edge of Night*. We just looked at each other and we laughed — it was just this gigantic private joke that we had. We just had the fucking giggles all day long. We could not complete a

COURTESY OF WORTH MENTIONING PUBLIC RELATIONS

take to save our lives. It was an inside joke because we had just been fucking on a boat in the Atlantic ocean a few weeks ago, and here we are in front of the cameras at NBC, it was really fun.

I also did other mainstream things like *Tootsie* (1982) and a couple of other films like *Cruising* (1980), but for a few exceptions, I was doing porn. In *Tootsie*, I was in a restaurant scene with Terri Garr, and I said, "Pass the salt." I played a boy, a kid in *Cruising* who says to Al Pacino, "Oh, you're from the Bronx, I'm from the Bronx." It's funny because a casting director who was a very good friend of mine — I used to get high with his secretary, she was one of the few people I ever got high with — he would put me in anything he could and when the guy got sick I happened to be working as an extra that day. He said, "Mitch can play this part!" The kid who originally had that line got sick. Louis said, "Yeah, Mitch can play the part of a guy, really. Just put a wife-beater on her, she'll be okay!"

Adult film roles were plentiful for Sharon and she worked hard to put forth her best effort when actualizing a character even in films with less than robust scripts. As the 1970s edged closer toward the eighties decade of social and economic change, Mitchell's warts began to surface. Sharon Mitchell's heroin addiction has been well documented over the years and is almost as legendary as the star herself. As a former needle junkie, Sharon is completely open about discussing the influence of drugs in her life, and how she graduated to mainlining heroin after spending most of her adulthood ingesting practically every chemical available. Although she has finally put it down for good, Mitchell ascertained "H" was the ideal remedy for the weariness and isolation she'd come to feel as a porn star, and inevitably as a stripper by the early 1980s.

You know people always ask me, "Was it heroin that drew you into porn?" It really wasn't about one or the other. It's just that I was experimenting with drugs ever since I could probably walk. I had been working every night literally, so when cocaine came along it kind of helped me stay awake. Heroin was the perfect drug for me, and the good thing about it I was very careful, thank god. I never shared a needle and I was so secretive, I didn't want anyone to know. There was nothing like heroin. There's nothing that can compare to it before and very little since. It was something that took away any kind of anxiety or pain that was emotional or physical, or any type of chaos going in inside of my head — any type of feeling that I didn't fit in. When I found that to go with the cocaine, I eventually dropped the cocaine.

I became lonely for two reasons: I was a career porn star and that's what I was. Pretty much everything legitimate had dropped off. I did a lot of adult films, but I would go out on the road dancing because you just can't do that to your body. You can't work in

COURTESY OF WORTH MENTIONING PUBLIC RELATIONS

porn every day for months at a time. It's exhausting and it's just not healthy. I'd go out on the road for a while, and give myself a break and come back. The burlesque gave me a nice porthole to rest my other body parts and just stay toned and stay in good shape and obtain a fan base — all that good stuff. When I started stripping, I think I was one of the first strippers on tour that had been in porn. I featured when I was in New York City at one of those legendary burlesque theatres when they still had a fucking band. I co-featured with [renowned burlesque stripper] Tempest Storm for Christ-sakes. The dance training that I had was [American dancer and choreographer] Martha Graham. Martha Graham and [modern dancer] Isadora Duncan had always been idols growing up as a child. I got into it almost as soon as I hit New York, just taking classes. I think I did a six-month tour at one point. I had become very good at dancing. Anyway, when I was a stripper it was very funny because they had that bump and grind thing, and I just didn't have the fucking body. I didn't know how to dance in high heels because I hadn't really learned, so it was really kind of difficult to do what they were doing. I remember one of them came up to me and said, "You know kid, it's not really about doing exactly what we do. If you have your own style it's all about how you take your clothes off." She really gave me the go ahead, and taught me the art of burlesque and strip tease, and how to make a twenty-five minute feature show a show, using gimmicks and gags and dance steps. She really taught me that. I was able to go out on the road probably for about eighteen years, I'd say. Today, doing porn is a stepping-stone toward prostitution as it used to be for women who wanted to get into the feature stripping business.

While juggling porn with feature dancing and other activities, Mitch's drug habit, although well concealed at first, strained her relationships with the close dependable friends she fostered in the business. In denial, she kept herself distanced from the group by multi-tasking. Sharon continued using heroin well into the eighties, and for a large portion of the nineties decades. I queried Mitchell about the famed Club 90 group and wondered why she was not a lasting member of the core infrastructure of girlfriends, with whom she had come to trust and admire.

You know my favorite female co-stars are all of my best friends Veronica Hart, Kelly Nichols, Samantha Fox, Vanessa del Rio, Marlene Willoughby, Long Jean Silver, and Candida Royalle. I've always loved Candice. She's the most intellectual one out of the gang, and Gloria Leonard, of course. We were all very good friends, very close pals. Annie Sprinkle is my friend and neighbor to this day — she lives in the next Valley.

There's a reason I wasn't a part of Club 90, I think. No one ever said it but there was a reason, there was a distinct reason. There was a bit of time there toward the end of New York I was on the road a lot and I was going back and forth to San Francisco quite a bit. I had also started directing a little bit here and there, and they were two hundred and fifty thousand dollar budgets. [Former adult actor and director] Fred Lincoln would help me. He was just great and he was also a wonderful mentor for me growing up in the industry but drugs became extremely prevalent.

I'd gotten into the drug scene very quick and I think it made them all nervous. This is probably in the late 1970s-early 1980s. I think I left New York for good in 1982- `83. It's kind of cloudy though because there are an awful lot of drugs. I don't think anyone knew really that I made such a gigantic transition from the cocaine to the heroin. I'd lost a lot of weight and I believe it became kind of apparent that they were extremely worried about me. I kind of hid from them socially. I was embarrassed, and I think somebody mentioned something to me. I don't remember who it was, it might have been Annie, it might have been Gloria, I don't remember, but then I felt very upset.

I eventually put the weight back on and I realized that I had to be very careful because my body was what I was selling, and I did look like shit. That became the beginning of really building a persona around my career and around my drug addiction. I kind of created this persona of "Miss Sharon Mitchell," and took care of everything — any havoc that I wreaked the night before, staying up all night or going into a bad neighborhood to cop drugs and maybe getting into a little bit of trouble, I could fix with a connection or money or whatever. I really kind of grew into protecting myself, but it was extremely, extremely lonely.

One thing leads to another

By the mid-1980s, it was obvious to everyone involved in the pornographic picture industry the conversion from shooting sex on film to videotape was highly successful, and immediately began to yield massive profits despite what many believed was inferior quality. Most of all, the video trend enabled consumers to enjoy pornographic films privately within the comfort of their own homes. After adult theaters were forced to close down, video stores sprung up and flourished as special designated "adult" sections were located generally toward the back of the stores, often behind a curtain segregating mainstream movies from X-rated.

PHOTOGRAPHY BY KENJI

In 1982, Mitchell unfastened her masculine side again in *Every Which Way She Can* as Randy Often, the ass-kicking cowgirl befitted with short hair, a bandana, a studded leather belt and skin-tight designer jeans. Mitch appeared to be right at home as a tough talking chick who lays down the ground rules to Herschel Savage prior to making out in his car. When accosted by wannabe bikers (Paul Thomas and Joey Silvera) after the fact, Randy gives in to a little head but then outsmarts the wise guys when she flashes a blade. Serena adds spice to the lean plot by performing a great strip tease routine followed by some full saddle gyrating down at the local watering hole.

Leading up to 1988, the atmosphere in the city of Los Angeles was as hot as ever as zealous vice-cops re-doubled their attempts to bust adult movie producers and actors while studios and performers continued taking risks. Mitch's obstinate nature and loathing for authority and the system won out as laws preventing the production of sex films in the State of California were about to change.

I was in Los Angeles in the late eighties and video had boomed. Everything had almost completely switched over from film to video. We were still shooting film style with reasonably large budgets, and we were still making money hand over first. Most of the time, we were flying back and forth from Los Angeles to San Francisco, and either working in a studio there or in a house or somewhere on the outskirts. We started getting lazy and instead of taking the whole crew and meeting in a parking lot and having to take a big truck all the way up to the mountains or flying everyone there, we all started to work in the hills of Malibu. There are a lot of mansions there and they were kind of hard to get to so why not? We started doing that, it was very clandestine and believe it or not, they actually had a Task Force. Can you imagine watching porn and pursuing shoots? It was actually quite funny, but [detective Lloyd Martin] was a real character and he was determined to get something on someone. It was very close to the time when [director] Hal Freeman had just been arrested and things were kind of hot, but we were taking a chance.

I was working for the Zane brothers on the east coast. I'm not going to get into their history because I think they're still alive and working, but they were producing this particular movie. I forget who the director was, but I remember the guy who owned the house was a very wealthy actor or producer, and he was a very good-looking guy. He had a big house, a boat — you name it and of course, he loved all the girls around. I think it was called *Backside to the Future* (1986) and Erica Boyer and I were in a bathtub. We were taken on that shoot and all of us were held in jail — all of the actors, and there were about eleven of us there. Randy West and I were the only two who didn't turn state's evidence. I was sick as

a dog because I had a huge fucking habit. They wanted us to testify that the Zane brothers were panderers. I said, "Wait a second, wouldn't that make this a prostitution situation?" Then there was the obscenity issue to go along with it.

Based upon information notated on *lukeisback.com* the Zane brothers of Sicilian ancestry were founded by Charles Zicari (Chuck Zane) and his Uncle Dominic Zicari. The Zanes first emerged as porn producers in 1983, and eventually formed Zane Entertainment. Allegedly, Dominic Zicari was responsible for bringing adult bookstores and peep shows to western New York, where he owned and operated more than forty locations. Dominic was charged over one hundred and fifty times for selling obscene material and was convicted. In a few short years, the Zane Brothers whose films were considered by many to be subpar even by industry standards, declared bankruptcy for the first time after the company was taken over by Chuck Zane (at Dominic's insistence) following the bust of their joint venture *Backside to the Future*, the first of two installments. In 1998, Zane Entertainment helmed by brothers, Matt and Mark Zane, repackaged themselves as "gonzo" specialists attracting a chic and more contemporary demographic. Zane Entertainment began to sign on new stars under contract such as Sunset Thomas.

This had been the second time I had been arrested for obscenity. I had won the first time I had been arrested in New York. I just was not going to sign it so I kicked dope in jail; it was awful, but what the fuck was I going to do? I just did not agree. I just couldn't. There was no way I was going to walk around with anything on record saying — first of all, that I was doing something obscene, and second of all, I was doing something that wasn't of my choice — that I was being pandered out to do. I wasn't signing it, I said, "Fuck that." I didn't give a shit. License or no license, I didn't care what the end of this all meant. To me, it had a very strong meaning to my being and who I was, and I was just not going to fucking agree to that.

Thank god, we held out because Randy and I were the only two — I think we stayed in jail for about two weeks. Because we held out, we won. The whole situation was overturned and then the motion picture and television business started allowing insurance and life insurance for adult entertainment to be shot in Los Angeles County.

In August 1988, the California Supreme Court overturned pornographer Harold Freeman's conviction for pandering (hiring actors to work in a pornographic film production) several years after the original adult oriented movie titled *Caught From Behind* (1983) was busted. The court ultimately interpreted that Freeman's conviction was an infringement of First Amendment right to freedom of speech. Following the overturned conviction, the state of California unsuccessfully appealed to the United States Supreme Court. Justice Sandra Day O'Connor ruled that the California Supreme Court's judgment was founded on an independent and adequate basis of state law therefore bringing about the effective legalization of hardcore pornography in the state of California, known today as the "Freeman Decision."

Following *Backside to the Future*, in 1983, Sharon won the CAFA (California Adult Film Award) Best Actress Award for *Sexcapades*. Directed by Henri Pachard, *Sexcapades* regards a fledging director who accepts an offer to direct a porn film against his wife's wishes. That same year, Sharon won Best Supporting Actress for *Night Hunger* (1983), a Damiano directed erotic thriller with Eric Edwards, Sharon Kane, Jerry Butler, Honey Wilder, and Laurien Dominique. In 1984, Mitchell won the AFAA award for Best Actress in *Sexcapades*.

"You can't please everyone, so you've got to please yourself." RICK NELSON

According to her filmography, Sharon Mitchell's career as a director began in 1980 and concluded in 1997 including twenty-nine titles. One of her noteworthy directorial efforts is *Be Careful What You Wish For* (1994) starring Veronica Hart, Kelly Nichols, and Sharon Kane.

> I was never a very good director. I never really liked it that much. I directed and produced about forty films and some videos. I just didn't like it and I wasn't very good at it. You know you're never any good at anything you don't like, but I needed money so I did it. I had a good job and obviously made money, but I just didn't like it.

Despite her impartiality about directing, Mitchell recalled that she and her female colleagues felt a sense of endowment of power as unified women working in a sexually oriented industry.

You know, we thought we were feminists. When the feminist movement came out, we thought "my god, aren't we fabulous, we're ahead of our fucking time." We were not only taking control of our sexuality, but in the big part of our world, we thought, "Aren't we special." And all of a sudden, boom, people like Andrea Dworkin, and all of these cranky people who probably hadn't had a fucking

COURTESY OF WORTH MENTIONING PUBLIC RELATIONS

orgasm in a hundred years, started coming after us. They were leading women in the feminist movement, and within that movement, they actually created a subculture called Women against Porn [WOP]. They'd pick on us and so on, but we thought we were feminists. We thought we were the definition and the height and example of that. We formed something called Feminists for Free Expression (FFE). Gloria [Leonard] and one of us have always kept it going. There was always an invitation to go on TV or radio to debate them. They thought we were fucking stupid, I guess. You get someone like Gloria back then who is just going to run rings around anybody; I don't care who or what the fuck you are. She's just so bright, but they targeted her because she was the first female editor of a men's magazine [*High Society*].

Three of the original founding members of Feminists for Free Expression are author, professor and ACLU President Nadine Strossen; former performer, director and author Candida Royalle; past President Dr. Marcia Pally, also an author, professor and teacher who works and writes in Berlin for six months out of every year.

They targeted Gloria and we would go — a few of us. Sometimes, it'd be me and Gloria and Candice or it would be Janie [Hamilton] and Kelly [Nichols] and Gloria. We would go and if it was actually a TV show or a radio show, they would never show up, they were such chicken shits. I know that Gloria had a back and forth debate with them, but I believe it was years later. When the movement was that hot bed of controversy, we were so surprised. You couldn't be any more surprised than we were.

Sharon readily welcomed controversy and contended she felt supercharged and empowered when critics of the adult community were appalled and outraged.

I was in Boston and I did something [I think was] called the *Nun's Bad Habit* [title and year of release are unknown]. It was with Herschel Savage and I played the nun. I was standing next to a candle which turned into a penis candle. Then the candle turned into Herschel Savage as this Jewish angel, and it was so controversial. People were throwing stones at me. Of course, coming from the Catholic background I was first in line, "I'll do that part!" There were people throwing stones at me and calling me names and so on and so forth, and I just thought, "God, there's something in them that this particular thing just pisses them off". It always goes back to the porn roots and that I've come out of there and made myself something. It's almost as if they think, "You don't deserve that," or that we all deserve AIDS. We represent something that really, really gets under their skin because an individual never gets ticked off about something unless he or she has a part in it.

We know that we are nice people, probably some of the nicest fucking people you'll ever come across. We've raised each other's kids and we've loaned each other money. We've been pals all these years. We've made our living; we didn't hurt anybody. We're not a bunch of fucking gangsters. We've evolved through a very tough period to struggle for what normalcy means to us. Whatever that means individually or collectively to us, and those of us who have survived it — you can't find a better group of people.

AIMing to Please

In March 1996, Sharon Mitchell was viciously attacked by a man just outside of her apartment after completing her stage act in a strip club. Reports stated the unknown assailant pushed Mitchell inside of her residence, broke her nose, crushed her larynx and raped her. Sharon managed to reach for a ten-pound dumb bell and knocked the man out cold. It wasn't until later when she realized that the man, an avid fan of her work, heckled her earlier at a club where she had been working. Sharon has publically stated that the rape attack was a pivotal point in her life and cited the incident as the reason for her decision to redeem herself and remain drug free. She enrolled in school and received her doctorate in Human Sexuality.

In May 1998, Adult Industry Medical Healthcare Foundation (AIM) was founded in Los Angeles as a non-profit facility. Sharon Mitchell proactively and efficiently took on the role of director in response to the threat of AIDS and HIV in the adult community. Regularly, AIM tested more than one thousand sex performers every thirty days for the detection of HIV and other sexually transmitted diseases, and built itself a reputation as a reliable and safe health clinic.

In 2004, five sex performers were informed by AIM they had contracted HIV. At least three of the cases (one of which was Canadian newcomer Lara Roxx) were traced to male porn star Darren James who apparently contracted HIV while working in Brazil that same year.

James tested positive in April of 2004, and was the first veteran actor to have contracted HIV since Tony Montana's positive diagnosis in 1999. Mitchell and AIM called for an immediate work stoppage so that all performers could be tested at least three times over the course of a two-month period and cleared prior to returning to work. The quarantine lasted for sixty days.

Sharon Mitchell at the former AIM offices. COURTESY OF HUSTLER VIDEO

Five years later, in 2009, the Los Angeles Public Health Department stated there were sixteen unreported cases of HIV within the adult community. AIM responded the cases were individuals not currently working in sex films, but seeking employment as adult performers. In October 2010, AIM reported a current performer had tested positive for HIV and came under scrutiny by the AIDS Healthcare Foundation. The individual's name was not released to the public, but Vivid Entertainment and Wicked Pictures (the latter being the only adult production company known to practice condom use) temporarily halted production. It was later revealed the HIV infected performer's name was Derrick Burts who had worked in straight and gay pornography.

In May 2011, AIM closed its offices declaring bankruptcy following a private lawsuit that resulted after AIM's database was believed to have been stolen and used to compile actual names and personal information of over 15,000 performers (including HIV status) on a site called Porn

Wikileaks (started by an embittered former performer). Porn Wikileaks has since been removed from the web.

The following portion of Sharon Mitchell's interview was conducted in the summer of 2007, in person, on the premises of AIM's principle office in Sherman Oaks, California. Sharon stated she was generally in the office three days a week. In light of the recent ruling in Cal-OSHA's (California Occupational Safety & Health Administration) favor for mandatory provision of condoms for sex performers by adult production companies, Sharon's 2007 commentary on HIV and testing methods exercised by AIM prior to its closure is relevant.

When I first started AIM in 1998, the average length of a career of a young lady entering at that time if she was pretty and/or motivated was between three and five years. Now it's approximately three to six months with eighteen months being the longest. There's no money in it anymore. There is nothing to discuss. Their clothes are already off. It is like "yesterday I had three dicks in my ass." I don't think I had anal sex the whole time I was in movies.

John Holmes [1988 death from AIDS] made me aware that there was HIV in the industry, and that's clearly something that everybody didn't want to look at. I didn't even want to look at it even being an addict. I thought this is a reality now and I'm just going to have to suck it up.

I was getting tested every three months and I remember because I was a heroin addict, I was going to a methadone clinic of course, and getting my HIV test. I was asking people at the methadone clinic "Would you test my friends from the porn business for free on the county being that they'll be my partner?"

They said "sure," so I would send people to the methadone clinic to get tested.

If John hadn't been positive, I don't think I would have gotten that awareness or the wherewithal to really look at AIDS because that's something that's just been, even to this day, it's indestructible — the amount of denial that's in the adult entertainment industry when it comes to HIV and STDs. People just don't think that they're going to get it because they see so little of it, and they don't realize just how much of it we do see.

Usually, when people contract HIV, they contract it outside of the industry. That's been my experience running this place, but I've only been doing testimony on the industry for the last ten years. It seems like a lifetime, but before that, very few people were getting tested. I mean, even when John came out and said "I'm positive," and so on and so forth, I started to get tested on a regular basis and I started to ask people for tests, but not everybody did. At that time, these tests were not detecting [HIV] at six weeks, and seven weeks, and twelve weeks. The strains back then were so much stronger and just the sheer fact that the few people who had it had such a strong strain of AIDS. I remember junkies dropping like flies, down on the lower East Side.

They were dealing with the ELISA methodology [then], which is the antibody. The antibody can take any healthy, young person probably beyond six weeks now. [Back then] people could have been infected for maybe twelve weeks before they found out because the ELISA antibodies weren't as accurate as they are now. Sometimes people could go up to six months and it would go undetected so someone could have had it and it not even come up on a test. They could have had it a week after the first six-month period when it was negative. You never know. So that's why when we use window periods — that's why we use a totally different method of testing. We use PCR-DNA, an early detection method here that can tell just ten days after exposure. If someone is positive, we're able to get them and their partners and put them aside. We're able to make sure that not many people get it. We can't guarantee that no one's going to get it, but we can guarantee that we're going to catch it very quickly.

While developing *John Holmes: A Life Measured in Inches* (2008) my writing partner Jennifer Sugar conducted extensive research involving tracking symptoms after initial exposure to HIV, early HIV detection, and the differences between the ELISA and PCR-DNA testing methods. The following information is excerpted from our book.

"In as little as four weeks after HIV infection occurs, some people may have symptoms, although many people are asymptomatic for as many as eight to ten years, or even more. Symptoms are flu-like: fever, swollen lymph nodes, as well as joint, muscle pain, and a red splotchy rash can spread over the body in two to three days after the fever develops. These symptoms of acute HIV infection tend to last about two weeks and then the feeling subsides. Early ELISA tests likely required close to six months in order to show antibodies, so a negative test did not necessarily equate to negative HIV status, but today, negative results from an ELISA are very reliable. Tests that rely on HIV antibodies such as ELISA, have shown to be the most reliable testing methods."

We can't keep HIV out of the industry. It's impossible. We try you know, but we see between ten and twenty people that want to come in the industry every month and have HIV and if no one tested them or looked at their tests, and we weren't here...

It's a totally different industry now than it was back then. You've got where you're testing two-thousand people a month, five

hundred of them are new, you know, five hundred come and go —
about one-thousand stay around for anywhere from six months to
three years. It's a high transient industry. Back then, it was like three
hundred of us on both coasts. Certain people have dropped out like
Darren James. There have just been people who have dropped out
and you knew that they had HIV. Some people said, "I've got HIV,
and I've got to go," and some didn't, they just dropped out. It's very
easy to fall of the face of the earth in this business and we'll never
find you again, you know. God knows if they did, or who they were,
or what happened.

As one of the first pioneers to organize AIDS testing, Sharon Mitchell
well recognized the urgent need for awareness and education of sexually transmitted diseases, and believed that, in general, studios should be
fiscally responsible for ensuring the health and safety of all performers.

I think we should be paying for an entire battery of tests including pap smears. Everything that we recommend in our newcomer
packet should be paid for by the company, and I think that since
they're not going to use condoms these things need to be continuously monitored even more than they are now. If people aren't going
to use condoms they should choose this test every two weeks or
every ten days, and they should really tighten all the eclipse periods and window periods so that there is less of a chance of anyone
getting anything. The way it is now one individual works for forty
companies and one company doesn't want to take the responsibility
of paying for it, and they want to put all that responsibility on the
actor. They're doing the minimum with what they can do — what
they can afford — and so we're looked at as a necessary evil. Then,
they could always use condoms, god forbid. What the fuck is that
about? For Christ's sake, we offer condoms — you can't even see
these things [in movies].

On January 24, 2012, The Los Angeles Times reported that L.A. Mayor
Antonio Villaraigosa signed a binding law stating that porn performers
must wear condoms while working in areas requiring a city state permit. The
law requiring condom use among porn actors is believed to be the first in
the nation by local government. While the AIDS Healthcare Foundation
regards the law a victory, some production companies are concerned about
financial losses and believe movies depicting the application of condoms

don't sell as well and that several performers prefer not to use synthetics, particularly during extensive shoots. Companies have threatened to move production outside of city ordinances to continue production. According to the *L.A. Times* report, the new law does not apply to filming on certified sound stages that don't require permits. Presently, in addition to Los Angeles County, shooting hardcore material is legal only in the state of New Hampshire therefore compromising outside considerations for now. Adult historian William Margold believes rather than imposing condom use for all sexual scenarios in adult productions, STD testing should be stepped up to twice monthly, and intravenous drug testing should be implemented in movie productions in exchange for condom free oral sex, mandatory condom use for anal sex, and arbitrary consideration for vaginal activity. In May 2012, *L.A. Weekly News* reported the L.A. Council's chief administrative officer requested a ninety-day extension by the city to determine how exactly to enforce new laws requiring condom use at on-location porn sites. Furthermore, the LAPD and the L.A. Fire Department do not have the inspection skills, or manpower necessary to implement the mandate.

During our interview, Mitchell believed the application of condoms would be a win-win for everyone.

> They say, "We'll sell more without a condom." Why? There's still that theory that people want to see what they can't do. No one lives without a condom in real life so they want to view people at risk or whatever. It probably would take a survey to find out the reason why. I mean, I used condoms most of the time from when I started testing. I would work with people that I knew continuously. If I worked with someone that I didn't know that well, I would always use condoms. Even I was condom optional until about the last three years that I worked. If I knew someone, and I knew that person was getting tested, I would forgo the condom. I worked with Marc Wallice once without a condom while he was positive. For the most part, the last few years, I used condoms all the time.

Fifty-two year old Marc Wallice tested positive for HIV in 1996 and contaminated several women with the virus after allegedly concealing his positive status from the industry for a two- year period.

> When I started this whole process, when I founded AIM — he [Wallice] was the guy that gave six women HIV. I had discovered that I had worked with him right about the time that he had gotten

HIV. I'd probably been exposed so many times to the virus and built up some tolerance, but I don't know. They say people build up a resistance to these things. There are also theories that if you go back to Eastern European ancestry and your family history has had the bubonic plague, that that insulates some. Who knows?

My theory is the public are going to watch porno one way or the other — you make it, they're going to buy it. If there's a condom, they're still going to buy it.

14.
Kay Parker
The Conduit

Born and raised in Britain post World War II, Kay Parker's memories of her first four years in Birmingham are at times grim. As an asthmatic sufferer, Parker welcomed the occasional reprieve when her father, a Navy man, brought his family to the lush islands of Malta (meaning "honey sweet" because of its diverse bee population) where he was stationed on two occasions during her school days. The change in environment and mild climate not only improved her health, but it infused Kay with optimism and hope, traits that have remained with her to this day.

At age twenty-one, Parker transplanted to New Mexico, "The Land of Enchantment," where she was hired to work in an upscale boutique in Santa Fe. Although Kay had excelled during previous work experience as an au pair in Germany and was fluent in the German language, she was ready to broaden her horizons. After remaining in New Mexico for a year, Parker eventually found herself living in San Francisco at the height of the sixties revolution. She continued to expand her employment options which included managing a small rock band. During her free time, Kay delighted in absorbing Indian and Japanese cultures and cuisine while studying acting. When the opportunity arose through her friend, the late adult film thespian and director John Leslie, to appear in a non-sex role in an erotic movie directed by Robert McCallum, Parker accepted the invitation after much deliberation. In 1976 at age thirty-two, the curvaceous, natural beauty appeared in her first scene depicting sex, and later gained notoriety for portraying a woman who embarked upon a sexual relationship with her adult son in *Taboo* (1980). Kay believes her sensitive approach to the subject of incest in a highly acclaimed performance was an empowering experience that has helped to facilitate immense personal spiritual growth and development. She does not subscribe to coincidence

"Who I am at this point in my life is a spiritual mentor. The career was a piece of my past that brought me to this point with wisdom and understanding." KAY PARKER

PHOTOGRAPHY BY KENJI

or accidents. Her 2001 autobiography titled *Taboo: Sacred, Don't Touch: An Autobiographical Journey Spanning Six Thousand Years* is written in an easy flowing and convicted prose as Parker shares with readers the joys of her esoteric and extraordinary live(s).

In her present role as a teacher, counselor, and metaphysical guide, Kay Parker has a heightened awareness of serendipitous moments which have proven to bring enlightenment and clarity to her journey and to the lives of others with remarkable precision. With grace and dignity, Parker apperceives her present state of being as an integral step progressing toward a continuum of harmonious peace, a devout calm with God, and with the universe.

I interviewed Kay Parker in November 2009.

True Brit

I grew up in Birmingham which is in northern England, and during that time, it was just after WWII. I was born in 1944. It was very grey and miserable. I actually don't remember anything before the age of four. I think that's always an indicator that things were a little grey.

The earliest memory I have is of a dollhouse that my father had made me. He was actually a very talented woodworker and he was very artistic although he never developed that. My earliest memory is of that dollhouse, a beautiful dollhouse, and it actually had a little flushing toilet in it.

My father was in the navy so when I was four or four and a half we were stationed overseas on the island of Malta in the Mediterranean. We actually spent two tours there. We went there twice during my childhood which was a Godsend for me because it was so beautiful there at that time. My childhood was interesting because I experienced that diversity of the greenness of England and then the Mediterranean. It was just beautiful with beautiful waters. We got to live fairly well when we were overseas because my father had what was called an overseas allowance so we had a little more money. We didn't stay on the military base. We always lived in the towns such as they were. It was very interesting; it was a nice time. When we would go back to England, my health would deteriorate. I had asthma as child.

I wasn't happy being in England because it was just too difficult. My father coming from the war, he'd had a very specific traumatic experience where his ship was blown up and it went down; he was one of a handful of survivors — these were the experiences that were never spoken about. One of the terrible things about war is that for the most part, men never get to recover from it. My dad never really recovered and my family took the brunt of his pain. My father would fly off into rages and there was physical abuse,

although we didn't call it that in those days. If you spoke out of line, you got slapped. There were times when he would fly into a rage and one particular time, he turned on my brother who was six years younger than I was. I thought he was going to kill him so I intervened. I jumped in between and said, "Hit me instead". It didn't happen all the time, but you had to walk on pins and needles.

COURTESY OF KAY PARKER

My mother was a stay-at-home mom. Women in those days, under those circumstances, didn't go out to work. I'm the middle of three and I have an older sister, and there *is* such a thing as the "middle child syndrome". The middle child tends to want to be the peacemaker. That was absolutely me because I am that person in terms of what I call the archetype that we manifest our gifts. Mine is what I call the idealistic peacemaker so I was doing that even as a child. I couldn't quite figure my parents out. I've always said that when you finally resolve your relationship with your parents, you're done.

In Britain, it was interesting because our school had been an army barracks and it was remodeled into a school. The school system in England is different than it is America, but I don't remember too much about school in the early years at all. When we were in Malta, it was very different, obviously. There were always one or two friends around but I didn't hang out with cliques or anything like that — I was kind of a loner. It's tough on kids when you move around a lot.

In the English school system there's an examination that children take at the age of eleven years old and it's called the eleven plus.

If you pass, you have the option of going to either grammar school which is college prep basically, or technical school. If you don't pass you go to what they call a secondary modern school or a basic high school, and you're out by fifteen or sixteen. Surprise, surprise, I passed the eleven plus and I went to grammar school. I was the first in my family actually, to do that. Then we went back to Malta just after I had started in grammar school and they were studying a different syllabus. Our school was dealing with the Oxford and the others were dealing with the Cambridge. By the time I got back to Malta, they'd gone back to the other syllabus so it was one of those situations where I would have had to have recapped two years. I opted out.

I read a lot as a kid; that was my main hobby. I also had a hobby when I was growing up that involved cutting out pictures of film stars in any magazines that I could get my hands on. I would meticulously paste them in my scrapbooks, and frequently, I would pick Hollywood couples and put them on one page; they would each have a page. Janet Leigh, Tony Curtis, Rock Hudson, Doris Day, I loved, of course, and I loved Hollywood musicals. They were lifesavers for me especially when we were in Malta. On the Naval base, they showed films and a lot of them were Hollywood musicals. Of course, those were the days of the old Hollywood musicals. They were fantastic. What was curious about the scrapbooks is that they were tucked away in my parents' attic in their home in Kent, and years later, I think it was back in the mid-1980s, my mother revealed to me that they had come across them and they had burned them. Not maliciously — they were just cleaning out. My mother said, "I didn't think you'd like them dear. I didn't think you'd want to keep them," and I went "What?" You know, in a funny kind of way, looking at it from a metaphysical kind of perspective, maybe by burning them it allowed them to go beyond the physical in a positive way.

I had no aspirations at all, really. We weren't taught to have dreams and to aspire or to have high goals. We weren't supposed to do that. It wasn't part of the cultural upbringing. I didn't have parents who said to me, "You know, honey, whatever you want to do, you can do if you set your mind to it." I think there was still so much recovery from the war. It was all they could do really, to survive. You know after the war we used to have food rations — I do remember that. You couldn't have more than your quota.

I had a role model who was a friend of my mother's. Actually, later on we became friends because we were more on par intellectually and mentally. This woman had raised two daughters and went back to school herself. She ended up working in the penal system in England. In fact, she ended up working in Maidstone Prison which was a big prison in England. She was able to establish programs for the inmates and these were heavy-duty fellows. I remember that she would arrange an evening where people could come from the outside world and interact with them. It was called "rehabilitation" which was so smart as far as I'm concerned. I remember sitting in a room with these guys, this was maybe in the late-1970s, and having a conversation with one of the great train-robbers. One of the men who had been involved in that was there and I remember speaking to him. You know, these guys were kind of withdrawn, but they were approachable to some degree. I was so impressed with her. She did something that I thought was extraordinary in terms of setting up those programs in the prison. There is very little, if any kind of rehabilitation, for men. I have a friend who is a judge on the east coast and we talk about these kinds of things all the time. It's just shocking that there are so few programs and so many men incarcerated. What a great thing to do and I aspired to sort of be like her. She was an amazing role model for me because she went beyond the norm.

Recently, she and her husband actually came to stay with me. They now live in Australia, but I cannot communicate with her because there is still a way of dealing with the world that I call very British. There is skepticism. It's almost like a subtle anger. Whenever we talk, she never asks how I am. It's more about money and prestige, and practical, linear stuff. Even though it is her way of caring, I can't respond on that level. Not too long ago she sent me what can only be described as a personal greeting and I thought, "Oh well, it's there somewhere."

I left school at fifteen and a half. I was very surprised actually, that my parents allowed me to do that, but they didn't resist. The first job I got was in a hairdressing salon. Things were very different in those days of course and it was a salon in a town near where we lived where only the "better wives" went. You just couldn't walk in off the street to get an appointment. It was definitely for the upper class. There was a perfumery downstairs, and then upstairs, was the hairdressing salon. The women who ran it were so rigid, they were much like the teachers I'd had at school! It was okay, because I thought that at least I'd get some training and they did send their girls to London to study cosmetology. After about three months, my father made me quit because I used to come home smelling of perfume. He just didn't like it. After that, I worked in a stationary store, and then I took a job in London in another store just to get out and spread my wings a little bit. There were several jobs. I remember working in an English teahouse and I did baking for a few months. Finally, when I was just about to turn eighteen, I left England with a friend, and went to Europe and hitchhiked around Europe.

The Accidental Tourist

We were on the road about five weeks or so. We didn't have much money at all but. In fact, my father drove us to the train station — this is kind of profound — as we were leaving, because he could not tell me he loved me, he thrust a small amount of money into my hand. It wasn't much at all and he kind of grumbled "Take care of yourself, you'll be back in six weeks, mark my words". He was expressing what I would later come to understand as jealousy of my freedom. He couldn't speak honestly about his feelings, so that was the way he expressed whatever it was he was expressing.

Six weeks later, we were in Germany and my traveling companion's money was stolen when we were youth hostelling. She wired her parents and her parents immediately wired back and said, "Come home. We're sending a ticket, come home." I stayed. There was no way I was going back and giving my father the satisfaction of his words coming true. I couldn't do that. That was my motivating force to keep going actually, so it served me in the long run.

I had gotten a job with an American family as a maid. I had met a boy of course and he had taken me back to his family. They were so sweet to me and kind of set me on my feet. I helped them out domestically for about nine months and then I said, "That's it. I didn't come here to be a maid. I'll get a job as an au pair."

I ended up living in Germany for two and a half years. I worked and learned the language which had been a dream. I did have an aspiration of learning to speak another language. Within four months or so, I was fluent. I got a job with an amazing family in

Munich and learned how to speak German from the kids. They had three children and my job was to simply help with the kids, do a little cooking and a little ironing, and that was it. I got to live-in, in their beautiful home and I loved them dearly. It was just so blissful for me. The family was involved in the world of theatre and opera. My employer was a wonderful, wonderful woman who had been an opera singer and had dropped out to raise her family. She was very funny and very entertaining, and incredibly generous. I will forever be grateful to her — she was a beautiful woman. She was a Cancerian. I have a lot of Cancerian women in my life, including my sister.

It is perhaps not surprising Kay is drawn to individuals born under the Cancer sign given her own nurturing and strong loving nature. For those who put stock in astrological charts, it is interesting to make comparisons. Common personality traits associated with Cancerians are typically caretaking characteristics, particularly when it involves familial ties. Known as the sign of the crab, Cancers also possess an external "face" and often present an air of over confidence sometimes bordering on conceit when in truth they are masking feelings of inferiority. Those born under the Cancer sign are known to retreat when challenged, yet their emotional well-being depends upon a connection and camaraderie as a social animal.

That was the second year I was in Germany, and then my father became ill. I went back to England for a couple of months and stayed to help because he was so incapacitated, and they had just moved into a new home. My brother and I actually did a lot of work in the garden and around the house. Then there was a point when there was a tremendous scene where my father attacked my mother and I knew it was because of me — there was something about me that often seemed to arouse anger in my father. I came to understand through my relatives that he was just simply jealous of me. He loved me — at his funeral, one of my dear aunts said to me, "Your father was so proud of you." Of course, I bawled like a baby because he never said it to me. I finally got to understand that and see why he was so enraged, but so much of it had to do with the war as far as I'm concerned. Certainly, before that, he was mad at his dad. A lot of the work I do today is helping people to understand what we take on from our families and the family tree and all that we inherit when we come in. There is a reason for that in terms of our soul overlay. Its purpose is to give us our human experiences, but after a while, we need to say, "Okay, thank you very much!"

Post-traumatic stress disorder is the contemporary term to describe the presence of extreme anxiety due to an experience of severe trauma. It can include anything from personal threat of death, to sexual, psychological, and physical abuse. People categorized with PTSD often endure flashbacks or dreams that replay the stimulus causing chronic symptoms of panic, fear, and an overall inability to function in a methodical and controlled manner. Anger, paranoia, irrational thought patterns and episodes of violence which Kay described in association with her father as a survivor of WWII are consistent with the condition that afflicts many Vietnam War veterans and survivors of abuse.

The day after my twenty-first birthday, I left again and went back to Germany. I didn't really know where else to go. It was one of those very dramatic turns of events. I had to leave and I just got on a train and went back to Germany to the people that I knew there. I started to work at a German department store because my German was good enough. After about three months, my American friends, the family that I had worked for originally said, "How would you like to go to the States?" They could tell that I was kind of in limbo and I said, "Well, I don't know. I suppose."

I didn't really have any dreams of doing that. Anyway, within a matter of weeks, I had a green card and I came over at the end of 1965. I ended up traveling with a family to New Mexico. They call it the "Land of Enchantment," and it is. It is so unlike any other state in the United States. It's like a country unto itself. It's beautiful and there is a lot of American Indian culture there.

"California, I'm coming home. Oh, will you take me as I am?" JONI MITCHELL

It's always so interesting to me where destiny takes you. There's definitely a path laid out. The second day I was there I got a job working for a French woman who had a boutique in the middle of the courtyard of the La Fonda hotel, in Santa Fe. The La Fonda is perhaps the oldest hotel in Santa Fe. It was right in the middle of the town in the plaza. It was interesting. I think the woman hired me on the spot actually; it was called Suzette International. What I came to discover about this location is that it was just an amazing little place. It wasn't just a little boutique. It had a back room with racks and racks of clothing. A client would come in and sit down and be served demitasse which was coffee in a little cup. They would tell you what they were looking for, in clothing. Then you would go into a back room and bring out these items.

COURTESY OF KAY PARKER

At that time, Suzette had a daughter who was my age in boarding school in Europe, so I kind of became somewhat of a surrogate daughter to her. I stayed in her house sometimes to take care of her dogs when she was away in Paris working on her lines. She carried different lines like The Villager line, and I would model the clothing for her clients. I'd just stand there, not actually walking. It was an amazing experience because she catered to a lot of famous people who came through Santa Fe or who lived in New Mexico. She designed clothing for them. I met Greer Garson and there were members of the original King family who were oil millionaires. They had discovered oil, and the TV series, *The Beverly Hillbillies*, was based loosely on their experiences. There were a couple of sisters and one of them used to come in with the most amazing cowboy boots. I couldn't believe the colorfulness of these characters so it was an incredible experience.

I was only there a year because at that time, there weren't many young people in Santa Fe. There was a lot of old money there in the hills. The kids used to go to school in Colorado; the Colorado University, in Boulder. After a year, I decided that I would sort of follow the boys back to school and see what would happen, just to move on. I went to Boulder and found out later that it was a very mystical place. Boulder has a lot of spiritual energy. There are certain centers around the country that people tend to vacillate. I found out later on when I arrived in L.A. that many people I knew had been in Boulder around that time including a man [Aaron] who has probably had the most influence on my life. He was my teacher and friend and we were involved in spiritual work together. He was there at that time also, but we didn't know each other.

Parker's dearly loved friend Aaron passed away in November of 2010.

I stayed in Boulder for about a year and then I got pregnant. I was just so, so naïve and so wet-behind-the-ears, as it were. I couldn't keep it so with the help of a friend, I was able to get an abortion and then it was time for me to move on again. I got on a Greyhound bus and headed for San Francisco. This was the flower-child era. I didn't know that, but I found out when I got there. Sex, drugs, and rock and roll, I was right in the middle of it. It was great. I was in San Francisco from about 1968-1978.

I had so many diverse experiences in San Francisco. The first job I got was working for Wells Fargo Bank, and then a year later, I found myself working for a company called India Imports. I've always been attracted to all things Indian and Japanese, actually. I started to be aware of past lives and why the connections. The job of working in a store led me to managing stores by the way, and I was with them for a few years and did a lot of work for them. It was really quite amazing because it put me in touch with the Indian Culture. At the same time, we were all smoking dope and I was involved in all these diverse experiences. It was also about that time I started to understand more about myself and who I was, and to recognize some of my talents. People started to call me, "Momma Kay" because I had a nurturing personality. They always knew that mine was a shoulder that they could count on.

Talking Dirty

I met John Leslie. How we met is a secret and we decided a long time ago that we would not divulge that, so I honor that. It was just one of those fluky things. We met and we started talking and we agreed that we were both actors. I had no idea what he acted in, but I would soon find out! Most of my friends at that time were in the music business because I was living in Marin County, which was north of the Golden Gate Bridge. It was really at the center of rock music in those days. My boyfriend was a musician and I managed a little rock and roll band. My whole life was music. I had always been attracted to the opera and theater of course because of my experiences in Santa Fe, so I always went after ushering jobs so that I could see productions.

I started to make friends with some individuals with the American Conservatory Theater in San Francisco. This was while I was still working at the bank. There were a couple of people whom I grew very close to. Because of them, and later, because of my musician boyfriend who had a friend who was an acting coach, I was invited to join the group of acting students. This friend of his was going to be teaching an improvisational acting group. I think my boyfriend actually even said to me "Shit, or get off the pot." I said, "Okay, fine — point taken!" I joined the group and it was a year of wonder because I had never explored that side of myself. I was always the wallflower sitting on the sidelines and watching everybody else. By the way, I always tell people that the best therapy in the world is acting classes or just to take an acting class. At that time, I was shy in every way even though I was running stores which gave me a chance to open up and be the mistress of my domain. Acting was a whole different thing.

My life changed because of the acting. I wasn't so available to other people because I was now focusing on myself, so it was around that time that I met John. Shortly after we met, and had had all of these conversations about acting, he said, "Well, how would you like the opportunity to get in front of the camera?" It was at that moment when he said that, I said, "Why are you asking me this question and what do you have to do with it?"

It was at that point that I realized he was talking about an X-rated film and I said, "No way."

He said, "You know, this is a straight role. You don't even have to take your clothes off. Haven't you wanted this?" I thought, "Yeah, you have, kiddo." I accepted the offer and I went and met a gentleman by the name of Robert McCallum, but his real name was Gary Graver. He made some very fine little adult films. He was the cameraman and the director which is a hard job. He had worked very closely with Orson Welles. He was not what I would have expected. He was just a young, good looking, California guy with a wife and a small child. I went, "Whoa, this is interesting." I took the role and recently had a chance to watch it again, but I was so embarrassed because I was so bad in this role. What the heck, it was my first time. It was intriguing and I loved the art of filmmaking right away. It was called *V: the Hot One* (1978). The storyline was much the same as *Belle Du Jour* (1967), the Catherine Deneuve film. After that came *SexWorld* (1978), that was the next one.

In McCallum's story of obsession and sexual deviance (in which Parker made her screen debut in a non-sex role) *V: The Hot One* prominently featured Annette Haven, John Leslie, and Paul Thomas. Haven heads up the all-star cast in the title role as Valerie, the high society wife of an esteemed attorney that secretly lusts after other men and women.

The late John Leslie, a gifted actor who often performed under McCallum's direction, is known for assuming some of the meaty and seedier roles in adult films before directing many of his own pictures and movies. In January 2011, Kay attended Leslie's memorial service in Los Angeles. She had known about his culinary skills, but was surprised to learn of his other talents. John Leslie was a brilliant painter, professional singer, and blues musician in Marin County. Leslie often played harmonica in a band when he wasn't directing.

Word kind of spread fast in those days — once you had appeared in one film people started talking about you, and I guess, because I was older than most of the girls at that time there was a call for older characters. I started to get calls right away. *Sexworld* (1977) came close after *V: The Hot One*. It was never about money. If it had been about money, it would have been an entirely different thing. It was about something else that I came to realize later on, what was guiding me to go down this path.

Again, John called and said, "There's a director in town and he's one of the best directors in the [adult] business. There's a great role for you in this movie called *SexWorld*." It was another take-off, this time on the movie *Westworld* (1973). It was a story about places people go to fulfill their fantasies and this was the X-rated version. It was a very big budget film and I think it took almost two weeks to shoot it. That was a long time for that genre. I don't know what drove me to even say, "Okay, I'll go meet with the director," who was a guy by the name of Anthony Spinelli; that's the name he went by. It was Sam Weston [Sam Weinstein].

A lot of people don't know this about Sam or Antony Spinelli, but he had actually been a mainstream director who had made a film called *One Potato, Two Potato* (1964). I guess it was in the early 1960s, but it was the story of an interracial relationship and it wasn't time yet. It had no trouble getting distribution in Europe. It actually won an award at the Cannes Film Festival, but he couldn't get distribution in the United States. Anyway, it kind of devastated him and I'm not even sure what happened after that, but one thing lead to another and he started directing adult films.

Many years later, I was having lunch with Sam and his wife Roz, who was just the sweetest angel, and we were talking about those days and she said, "You know, he had a huge crush on you." I said, "Nooo…" and she said, "It's true, he always had a big crush on you!" It was very sweet. The whole family was there and that was the last time I saw Sam. Actually, he died of Alzheimer's disease. Sam was great.

Anyway, Sam was very talented and very gifted as a director. We sat and we talked. He was very straight with me and said, "Honey, we'd really like you for this movie. Will you dye your hair red for me?"

I said, "I'll do it but I won't perform sex."

He said, "Well, this is a sex role, it just is."

It was and it is, and the rest is history. I've been a redhead ever since.

SexWorld

Semantics

You say my sons are drifting
Here lies the difference; ergo
Fearful you see them drift
Joyful I watch them flow

— MAUDE MEEHAN

It was a defining moment in my life. Once you've done film, you've done film. There's no going back, and I went ahead and I did it. I don't know if "terrified" is the right word, but I felt like a fish out of water. Because I was older, I could only take my lead from the young women that I was watching so I tried to get tips from them. "How am I supposed to do this?" That was the director's job, essentially. In the art of filmmaking, things are shot incrementally so you can shoot one part of the scene and still you haven't done anything sexual. Then you shoot another part, and now you've done something sexual but you haven't gone all the way. The next part is penetration and once you've done that, there is no turning back. That's kind of when the panic struck me! Then, once it was over, it was over. It was just loaded — it was such a profound moment.

The make-up man on that movie was a guy who had made up some of the most famous women in the world. I don't remember his name, but he was an older guy at that time. He'd done up Elizabeth Taylor and he'd done everybody for one reason or another. I was sitting there and he was telling me stories, and then, here I am. It was just amazing.

Kay and Sam Weston. COURTESY OF KAY PARKER

In *SexWorld*, I play a frustrated housewife and my fantasy is this blonde guy played by Joey Silvera. He was playing a robot, essentially. The character's husband is a wimpy guy so she wants a real man. I used to do college presentations where I would show clips from the movies in order so I would show the progression. I wanted to make it interesting and entertaining, and I'd talk about myself and explain what I was doing, and my reaction to what was going on.

They loved it. It was very successful. I had many friends who were teachers in several colleges. One of the scenes I would show is where Joey Silvera slaps me back and forth in *SexWorld*. In that particular scene, we had obviously rehearsed it and had it synchronized, but when it came down to shooting it, something happened and we were out of sync with each other. He actually slapped me and he chipped my front tooth. My father's front tooth was chipped in exactly the same place. When he chipped my tooth, the adrenalin was pumping. We were in the middle of the scene and we continued until Sam yelled, "cut" and I wasn't sure if I was bleeding or not. I mean, the slap was pretty hard. It didn't really hurt but it stung me a little bit. I ran to the make-up room just to see and I was fine, but my tooth was chipped. I looked in the mirror and I saw my father looking back

Kay Parker and Joey Silvera in *SexWorld*. vcx

at me. It was interesting because I hadn't even thought about my parents at the time that this whole thing was happening. It was one of those moments where I thought, "Okay, now we have to reckon with this. What about mom and dad? Am I going to tell them?" I never did tell them and both of them are gone. They were so removed, certainly from my life. I found out years later that my niece's husband actually found out about me, but they love it! They love it and are just so intrigued by it. I'm their exotic Auntie Kay. They would call me something; I'm not quite sure what! *SexWorld* is the first time that I performed in a sex scene and it was pretty dramatic.

SexWorld plays like a Magical Mystery Tour sexual adventure whereby the players on the bus are mystified as to what kind of erotic encounter to expect. They know only that a customized experience will unfold once the bus arrives on the grounds of Sex World. As each guest is interviewed privately by the Sex World consultants, they are encouraged to share their deepest and most intimate sexual desires without realizing they will soon find themselves in the middle of a fantasy-sexscape. Kay Parker portrays one of the weekenders whose fantasy is to have sex with an aggressive man possessing supersized equipment. She finds herself in a stark white room next to a three-tiered bed. After her male suitor (Joey Silvera), arrives, Parker informs him she is waiting for someone else and asks him to leave. He smacks her hard across the mouth and throws her on the bed — fulfilling her fantasy to be dominated as he roughly overtakes her amidst cries of ecstasy while her unassertive spouse watches through the window. The scene is powerful and lascivious. John Leslie and Desiree West are also most effective. They set the sheets on fire after some terrific verbal foreplay as West's character (talking funky rap) teaches the "white boy" a thing or two about "black sugar." Sharon Thorpe and Johnny Keyes put the finishing touches on this above average picture in a sensuous scene with Keyes reprising his role as the black stud in *Behind the Green Door*. Keyes is even dressed in the same white leotard he'd worn years before with the hole cut out in the front displaying his genitals.

I got rave reviews from those around me. My co-actors all raved, so that was great. In those days, the reason we took so long to shoot is because they would usually cut an R-rated version of the film also for European distribution. They covered themselves so that they could distribute it in different markets.

There were some films where the person I was working with was a good person, a nice person, and we were friends and the sex was sweet and we had a good connection. There were other times when it was very difficult because I couldn't get a connection with my partner. Keeping in mind that I had just come out of a year of this acting class and what actors need to have is a connection. Otherwise, you end up being technical.

For a fish out of water, Kay evidently was usually able to establish a connection with her co-actors and created some remarkably magical sexual moments on-screen following passionate overtures of foreplay with her leading men only too happy to oblige. To this day, she and former co-star Richard Pacheco (Howie Gordon) have remained friends. It is not surprising that Pacheco, along with intellectual and artistic peers John Leslie and Herschel Savage, was one of her favorite on-screen partners.

There were some actors around who were good little actors. Richard Pacheco was kind of like me in a sense, because he was so above everybody else. I think he came from a theater background. He's still a good person and we e-mail each other occasionally. Somebody, a friend of mine, who has always been a little bit of a groupie, sent me a picture from a movie that I did with Howie called *The Seven Faces of Dr. Lau* [aka *The Seven Seductions*, 1981]. It was a take-off on the Tony Randall film [*7 Faces of Dr. Lao*, 1964]. We had to shoot a love scene on a ski plane up the coast North of San Francisco on this little island in the middle of a lake. It was nice except for the mosquitoes! Recently, my friend sent me a picture from this love scene in the lake and there I'm sitting. We both look so pretty. My boobs, which I always thought looked way too big, were actually beautiful! I sent it to Howie and he said, "Oh my god. We were so young and so beautiful, and I still love those boobs of yours!"

I said, "Yeah, well, they're hanging a little lower these days!"

Kay also enjoyed a palpable onscreen chemistry with Paul Thomas, the classic-trained actor that transitioned to adult performing in the mid-1970s, and later became one of Vivid Entertainment's premier directors. *7Into Snowy* (1978) is an adult film parody of *Snow White and the Seven Dwarfs* (1937) produced by Dave Friedman and his partner William Allen Castleman. As the wicked step-mother Fedora, Kay and her assets are front and center while she envelops the role of the devious widow (her husband died while the two were on their honeymoon) commanding her lovers: the chauffeur/woodsman (played by Paul Thomas), and the secretary (Bonnie Holiday) to seduce her step-daughter portrayed by the lovely Abigail Clayton. Thomas and Parker partake in a rough and ready sexual interlude as a prelude to Thomas's scenes with Clayton whom he ends up protecting from Fedora's evil potions and maneuvers.

Where's the *Porno* Star?

Like many of the women of her class, Kay Parker completely defies the stereotypical "Porn Star" stigma which is made even more obvious when you meet her in person. As a spiritual educator and counselor, Kay's training as a guest speaker while touring the college circuit during her days as an adult film star, fostered a confidence and wisdom that beautifully tempers her edgier persona as a rebel. As the saying goes, you don't know a person until you've walked in her shoes. On-the-job training is sometimes the optimum life coach.

I was specific about what I'd do and what I wouldn't do in films. The one girl-girl scene that I did is set apart from all the others. It's in a movie called *Health Spa* (1978) which Cass [Paley] produced.

Kay Parker and Paul Thomas, *7 Into Snowy.* VCX. COURTESY OF KAY PARKER

It might have been 1979 or the late 1970s. It's a quality little film with a young actress by the name of Abigail Clayton. Abigail was nursing her baby at the time so she had some boobs. Anyway, it was set at the health spa and I ended up having a girl-girl scene with Abigail, and it was so sweet. It was directed by Emily Smith who was also an actress. It was a beautiful love scene. There was nothing that hard about it at all. Of course, the music was very dramatic and we did have a premiere for that movie. I always remember being in the theatre that was full of paparazzi, and that scene got a standing ovation. I was very proud of it because it was my first girl-girl scene. I didn't know what the hell I was doing and I'm not naturally inclined towards women, but Abigail was so sweet. I looked at her and said, "Abigail, I don't know what I'm doing," and she said "don't worry about it, leave it up to me," and it just turned out beautifully. Even today, it's still very effective because it was a lot of eyeshots. That was another of the pieces that I would show in my presentation because it was directed by a woman.

It's interesting, when I was lecturing, I'd walk in the room and people would say, "Where's the porno star?" Particularly, the women who came out of that era, we had an opportunity to do things differently. It is true that I think we were a whole different ilk than the people who are in the business today. My absolute truth is this: Individuals that would use any of the negative terms about us are usually speaking from their own personal experience and the women that they are seeing or observing, are mirrors of themselves or of their own issues. That's how humans are. Most definitely, some of us are from dysfunctional families, and at some point, have been exploited or objectified. I'm not going to say that's not true, but I have found that those individuals that have the most heat on it — and I've met them — the placard holders — I look at them and I say, "Oh my gosh, I'm so sorry for your pain."

This is a wonderful little story that comes to mind and it is in my book. The very first TV talk show that I was on was a show in San Francisco called *Front Line Video*. The producers were all very young and very hyper and made it sound very appealing for me to be on the show. My intention was always to just share because I've always come from a place of wanting to share my experiences for the purposes of healing. This was my first time on a show like this so I was naïve, but I listened to the producers and didn't ask too many questions. Once I was there, it was just me center stage with the audience and the interviewer or the moderator. I didn't know there was a group of individuals in the audience who were so full of rage and so hurt. All of a sudden, that was all focused on me. I looked at them, and I thought, "Oh my goodness. What's going on here that you would direct all of your rage at me as if I'm responsible for everything that happened to you in your life?" The producers wanted a show and they wanted it to be lively and interactive. The good news was that after I was bombarded with all of this rage which made me feel like shit — it was very hurtful — suddenly, there was another person in the audience who stood up and acknowledged me and my work and said, "We're aware of Kay's body of work". Even by that time, my work had become known. It was so great. The person who had stood up was a strikingly beautiful woman with long blonde hair by the name of Kat Sunlove. Kat was a well-known dominatrix, who has since gone on to be a very outspoken lobbyist for the Free Speech Movement. I've said in my book that everybody should be grateful to Kat because she has done an amazing amount of work for the Free Speech Movement, and I think, continues to unto this day.

COURTESY OF WORTH MENTIONING PUBLIC RELATIONS

Since the early 1980s, Kat Sunlove has been involved in the adult industry as a performer, journalist, educator, publisher of *Spectator*, and a lobbyist for the Free Speech Coalition since 1997. With a Masters in Political Science, a year of law school, and many years of political activism, Kat is well suited for the challenges of advocating for the interests of the adult industry. Better known as "Mistress Kat," Sunlove wrote a weekly advice column on erotic dominance and submission in the early eighties for *Spectator* and later for the national magazine *Chic*, earning her the label of "the Dear Abby of S/M". Along with her life partner, Layne Winklebleck, Kat designed and taught a popular workshop series: S/M for Loving Couples, the first-ever serious educational workshops pertaining to this sensational and misunderstood topic. Today, Sunlove spends most of the year in Costa Rica, but was recently in New York City in June 2012 to join friends for the wedding of Veronica Vera and Club 90 reunion.

Anyway, these individuals in the audience were seeing me, as a reason somehow for their life's pain and issues which I thought was very interesting. After the show, I went back to my hotel room and I cried, but I cried for their pain not my own because I realized how many of those individuals are out in the world and I wanted to help them. Their issues were fundamentally sexual having come from abuse and their own shame which is taken on from parents by the way. They had no idea that they were, in fact, objectifying me.

One girl stood up and said, "I'm from New York, and I am so horrified." I think this was before the Rudy Giuliani reign when he had a lot of the peep shows and theaters around New York closed. She said that when she walked down the street to her work or wherever she had to go, that she would have to walk past the theatres and that it made her feel dirty and so on. When she said that, I thought, "Okay, so you've got the shame. It's not the theatres that are making you feel dirty, you already have that." This was just rubbing salt in that wound. I looked at her and I said, "I know this is probably going to offend you, but why don't you walk another direction so that you don't subject yourself to that?" To me that was a logical response because I don't enjoy that part of the adult entertainment world either quite honestly. That response just tended to make the small group that she was with even angrier. I thought if you don't already have that pain scar or whatever you want to call it—I call it "the shame bug"—if you don't already have that, it doesn't push your buttons.

I had a phrase or response with some of my friends that I used up until a few years ago. I don't do it so much anymore, but if they would lament or start to talk about somebody who had rubbed them the wrong way or that they had an issue with, I would look at them and say, "Who in you?" I have one friend that I dearly love and he looked at me once when I said that to him and he said to me, "I hate it when you do that, but I love it when you do that." I had to do that because I couldn't condone blaming someone else for something that exists within us. Blame the shame.

This is all of the different stages of the work that I do to help people to free themselves. When you truly reach the point of spiritual maturity, then the emotions which are God-given and are red flags become flat and they can't hurt you anymore because the buttons are no longer there to be pushed. In my mentoring, I help people to get to that point.

Taboo

In 1981 Parker's movie career and personal journey reached an apex when she was invited to star in the first of a series of films titled *Taboo* directed by one of the early pioneers in the business on the west coast, Kirdy Stevens, and written by his wife and long time partner Helene Terrie. Stevens and Terrie started producing Nudist films (primitive, innocent shorts) in the mid-1960s prior to the couple's conversion to the mail order business with the advent of hardcore loops in 1967. Stevens was frequently arrested on obscenity charges and defended by the late Stanley Fleishman, a constitutional lawyer specializing in First Amendment Rights.

True to its namesake, *Taboo* (1980), the launching pad that became part of an innovative series of pictures dramatizing volatile sexual scenarios, examined the subject of incest between a mother and her grown son. This was not the first time Parker had appeared in a role depicting incest. One year earlier, Kay and John Leslie engaged in a sexual encounter as sibling physicians overseeing an institution for the criminally insane in *Lust at First Bite* (aka *Dracula Sucks*, the softcore version), the 1979 adult film variation of Bram Stoker's novel *Dracula*.

In *Taboo* Kay Parker's starring turn as a newly single woman embarking upon the controversial act of sexual relations with her own offspring (played by All-American Mike Ranger), resulted in *Taboo* becoming one of the highest grossing adult movies to date. The picture is included in Volumes 1-6 — recently released as a set. There are twenty-three films in all within the *Taboo* series extending from 1980-2007. Kay also appeared in the second and third sequels released in 1985 and 1986 with Juliet Anderson and Dorothy LeMay. Parker explained the significance of selecting the role that transformed her life.

> *Taboo* is the one film I am best known for which makes it ironic that it was an incestuous role. Again, obviously, I pondered deeply and looked at the prospect of playing that character from many different facets, and I had to deeply reckon within myself when I took the role because I had known women who had experienced incest. I knew how prevalent it was and that it is a very sensitive issue. We should make the statement— the feedback that I have received from many individuals is that people don't take the storylines of these films seriously. However, for me it was a serious issue, and I looked inside and I talked to my guides and I said, "Why would

I even consider this?" Then I realized that somebody was going to do it so why not me? I could at least bring some consciousness and sensitivity to it. Now a lot of individuals who have an issue and who have the scars would say, "That's a fine excuse." All I would say is that I was guided to do it, and because of that I have an even bigger platform today to do my spiritual work and healing, so that was just a path that my destiny took me down. I'm totally responsible for it, and yet, that movie was a very defining point in time for a lot of reasons. I wrote about it in a chapter of my own book.

Beautiful and endearing, Kay delicately handled *Taboo's* frowned upon (and in some countries outlawed) subject of incest in her taut portrayal of Barbara Scott, the mother of a teenage son, cast aside by her husband of several years for a younger woman. Lost and disillusioned, Barbara seeks comfort from her best girlfriend Gina (played by Juliet Anderson), and hooks herself up as a receptionist in the office of a male friend that happens to be secretly in lust with her. Concurrently, Barbara goes on a blind date with a friend of Gina's and winds up at a swing party, much to her dismay. Angrily, Barbara shuns the advances of her date and others, but her libido is awakened. Upon returning home and seeing her handsome, strapping son Paul (Mike Ranger) naked and asleep in his bed, she enters his room and begins to perform fellatio. Startled from his slumber, Paul isn't certain at first if he is dreaming or awake, but he welcomes his mother's advances as he had fantasized earlier about making love with her (and peeked in on her while she undressed) on previous occasions. The Parker/Ranger session is passionate and hot, making one temporarily forget the two are supposed to be related by blood. Juliet Anderson (she keeps two playmates on standby throughout, Don Fernando and Miko Yana) supplies comic relief as Barbara's friend who, rather than offering any kind of real advice to her distraught girlfriend, gets turned on and masturbates when Barbara privately confides her indiscretion with a heavy heart. Adeptly, Parker expresses the emotions of a woman torn between doing what she believes is right, but ultimately responds helplessly to her physical urges. It is understandable why this performance has become the focal piece of Kay's body of work.

Helen [Terrie] wrote the storyline. The husband and wife team, she wrote it. It was around the time when films were starting to present the female perspective. That was her justification for it. They're a very nice Jewish couple in the Valley and what is always so fascinating, you know, is the fact they were married and had two children. In fact, a few years ago they had won back the rights to *Taboo* when they went through numerous lawsuits to retain rights of the movie. They had sold them and finally won the films back later from VCX. I had gotten a call from Steven their son one day who said that they'd digitally re-mastered the film and were going

COURTESY OF KAY PARKER

to release it on to DVD. They wanted to know if I'd be interested in doing a commentary. We did and we worked out the finances. I've never seen it by the way, except on YouTube. They didn't send me a copy. I just let it go. It was no big deal. Anyway, I said to Steven, "Now that you're a grown man and you're doing this is this the path that you chose for yourself?" He had sort of this attitude that *Taboo* had impacted his life in a huge way and I said, "Yeah, we had actually shot the pivotal seduction sex scene in your bedroom." I think he was a fifteen-year old boy at the time. I had this conversation with him and I got the impression that this was not necessarily his choice. Well, of course, it was his choice, but there was reticence there. It was interesting that he was going along with this, but I guess he was helping his father out.

Often times, the producers weren't on the set and they didn't oversee the script. They just said, "Give us the hottest and the wildest because that's what we're going to sell." As video became more and more of a reality that became the criteria. It was sad because we kept saying to them, "You're going to lose your female audience." The female audience could grow.

I used to have women come up to me at conventions and say, "Thank you."

I'd say, "Thank you? What did I do?"

They'd say, "Because of you, my husband and my sex life is better." To me that was the best testimony. It was the best thanks and gratitude that I could ever receive. I think the women — I can't speak of the women of today and it would be unfair of me to do so, but as a group, we were able to create. It was a transition time from stag movies to video and during that time, we were able to get in there and make some classic movies with story lines and weren't focused upon shaved genitalia. Pornos weren't really focused on the sex even though they were sex films. Yes, there certainly was a formula and we strove to get the formula broken. You can probably talk to a lot of women of the golden era who will say this. There was a formula, and it was something like seven sex scenes per movie with one girl-girl scene, and one orgy scene. If the storyline didn't have that formula, it wasn't saleable. We strove to convince the producers that that was not true and that you could run the storyline throughout the film without compromising anything and have it be very sensual. There didn't have to be an orgy scene, and there didn't necessarily have to have a woman-woman scene. If was if there was a storyline, or if there was a build-up of eroticism, people have a tendency not to fast-forward. We tried to convince the producers of that. Ultimately, money wins over so they got to the point certainly as the video era came upon us and the video awards began, then they sold out again. "Let's just pump as much sex into it as we can. Whoever has the hottest sex is going to sell the video."

PHOTOGRAPHY BY KENJI

At the time, there were also several women directors. My own personal logo was, "Put the heart back into sex." Up until that point, it had been the raincoat brigade. It had been stag films primarily, but the advent of video really broke the market open because now women could watch the films in the privacy of their own homes. That was the impetus, I think, for a lot of us to strive to do stories with women characters that were strong and empowered and I think that we were relatively successful until the internet.

For me, the way it was at the time, it was an opportunity to do some acting, but most definitely to make a difference. I think that people have to recognize that sex wasn't a huge part of the movies. Even though they were X-rated, most of the movies that I was in, and I was only in about fifty which is nothing compared to most of those individuals, had story lines. In some cases, we had hundred page scripts, which was unheard of. They were movies. They were like Hollywood "B" movies with sex in many cases. Not all, but some. We were pioneers, and many of us tried to do what we could do to bring the female perspective into the films. That was it and then the golden era was done.

Many of us felt that it was a good time. I think that's why it's called the "Golden Age" because we were pioneering and of course, those women who were more intelligent — we really applied ourselves to make a difference and to bring quality and some sensitivity, and certainly, to empower women through what we were doing. I can remember many times being on talk shows with a group of my peers and that's what we were talking about. We were saying, "This is why we were there." We were even on *Oprah*. Seka and Veronica Hart and I were Oprah Winfrey's guests on *A.M. Chicago* just before the launching of *The Oprah Winfrey Show*. We met her and that was cool. She was doing her job. I think where she was at the time was to do her job the best way she could with her particular brand. That was fun and it was a good experience.

It's all very paradoxical. As I say, there was this window of time that lasted about ten years where we had the opportunity to insist in some cases that eroticism was not about penetration and bump and grind. A lot of men feel the same way as women. Still to this day, I get e-mails saying, "Thank you for your body of work. We get never get tired of watching it because of the quality and sensitivity."

The God Factor

By the mid-1980s, Parker began to ease out of classic adult films as a performer excluding appearances in special projects of interest. Kay guest starred with her good friend Seka in Seka's debut as a director: *Careful, He May be Watching*, released in 1987. In 1985, Kay adopted a different role as a PR executive for Caballero, one of the largest and most lucrative adult entertainment studios founded in 1974. Its empire was built upon a colossal collection of classic sex loops with major golden age stars as headliners. Parker's one and only directorial effort came in 1994 when she helmed the instructional video *The Tantric Guide to Sexual Potency* with well-known feature performers Sharon Kane and Jon Dough demonstrating to viewers how to prolong the sexual experience while achieving greater satisfaction.

Parker fully recognizes that her choice to have worked in sex films is a confounding, complex issue, and not a decision she made lightly. As a woman, Kay has worn many hats, yet she bucks any notion that she fits the traditional feminist model.

I know many men in my life, actually, who are feminists more than I am. My dearest friend and my mentor and a gentleman who is fully self-actualized will often say, "I love women and I'm here to help empower women". Certainly, at this point, women constitute sixty percent of the spiritual energy on this planet. A lot of the men are still lagging behind. They are stuck in the ego and stuck in their limited left- brain. Women have always been more willing to go into the right brain and into the creativity and explore the sixth sense.

In terms of being a feminist, I would never call myself that because even during the day when women were burning their bras, I was on my soapbox, appealing to men and women to come together and harmonize. I so appreciate feminists and women like them who have spoken out, but if you're speaking out angrily, it's still the same as men speaking out angrily. It's like the pendulum swinging too far to the other side. We know a whole generation of women who want to be more like men because of how we've been treated and because of the dominance of the male. We still live in a male-dominated society, there's no doubt about it. To me, it's more about balance. It's not about running off, putting on pants and entering the corporate world because I find a lot of women who have done that have moved way over into the left-brain and that's not what we're after. What we're really after is harmony and peace that comes from the balance of the two. That's why I would never really call myself a feminist.

Kay cautions young women and men contemplating entering adult entertainment as a career choice and explains that ideally, it's about building a bridge to a higher ground.

My guidance for anyone considering entering the adult entertainment business has always been "Think very carefully." It's like with children; they're going to do what they're going to do. The more you tell them not to do something it's more than likely their impetus to do it. It's not an easy industry. Filmmaking is filmmaking. It's grueling, and can be long, and it's tedious. If you're going to do it, you're going to do it, but women need to think doubly or triply about it because it takes its toll on the emotional body. This is where a lot of people have that idea about women being objectified and abused. If you take a young lady, a little babe, who has been scarred in some way, and put her in front of a camera and you pump her full of ideas of success and stardom, it can be extremely damaging in addition to the damage that's already there. We have seen that and I think we still see it, but I think it is part of any industry. It happens in Hollywood. If you introduce drugs or a lot of alcohol into this whole equation, then the confusion begins.

I don't drink and I don't do drugs, and by the time I was in movies, I had a rule that if drugs were on the set, I'd walk. Then, if you add to that the one other component called sex, it's even more of a fragile scenario. I've seen it in the music industry and Hollywood today. My advice to young individuals with aspirations of entering the business: Think very hard about it and do some research. Read some of the books about performers because it's not easy, and it's not glamorous. I was emotionally strong, even at that time. I'm intelligent and I'm well educated so I was aware of what was going on all the time.

Actually, to really address this properly is from a spiritual perspective which is where I'm coming from. I met a young gentleman from the Chicago area who had been a priest, and he had defrocked himself because of the corruption in the church. He became a counselor and a learned psychologist. He was a funny guy because his calling card had a very buxom blonde on one side so he may have been a sex or a marriage counselor of some kind. He was profound in his own way. He had written and self published some very controversial books where he talked about the corruption in the church. He had a blurb on one of the front pages of his book essentially that said in all sexual relationships we're ultimately looking for a deeper connection to God. I'm paraphrasing, but that's why I say we're really on that journey of finding out about what we are. The

COURTESY OF KAY PARKER

more pronounced that desire is to have a deeper connection to God, the more we want to take our clothes off and get naked. I think if given half a chance any actor would do a sex film because it's really ultimately about their search for themselves. That's what life's about. For me to have gone through the process that I went through, of subjecting myself to that and going through it, was, in a sense, about stripping myself down to my core so I could discover who I was.

To whom much is given, much is expected.

In terms of being on the cutting edge not only as a woman, but also as a woman who has left her mark in a proscribed business often held up to scrutiny by the outside world, Parker moved in a defined direction when her past employment experiences segued to her present work as a spiritual teacher. Upon compromising to the external forces she believes have guided her as she continues to flourish in the Light, every day is a new opportunity and challenge.

While strolling with Kay in the summer of 2011 in the beautiful rose gardens at the Santa Monica bluffs where she had resided for over thirty years, I was awed by her inner beauty and her devotion to her belief system. Even during that pivotal time in her life, Kay is not one who waivers from the truth or manifestations realized through the power of her spiritual commitment. Nor does she lose sight of her sense of humor or forget how she arrived at this place in her life. As we waited at a crosswalk across from the bluffs, Kay shared a funny story that had occurred several years ago in a similar location to where we were standing. A police officer noted that Parker jaywalked across busy Ocean Avenue and started to write up a ticket for the minor infraction. Upon request, Kay handed him her identification. The officer suddenly looked her up and down, and with a glimmer of recognition in his eyes, he exclaimed, "You're not *the* Kay Parker, are you?"

Kay smiled and answered, "I'm Kay Parker." The officer smiled back at her and began to rip up the ticket. Stunned, she said to him, "You're not supposed to do that, are you?"

Grinning, he replied, "I can do anything I want."

Utilizing her credibility as a beloved legendary adult film actor, in the summer of 2011, Kay was in the preparatory stages of spreading her message of peace and love internationally specifically targeting the male population. For the first time in more than two decades, Kay Parker decidedly resurfaced as the identifiable erotic icon. Her new campaign "Putting the Heart back into Sex," had already started into motion as she was featured with three other famous adult stars (Amber Lynn, Nina Hartley, and Asia Carrera) in a September 2011 article for *Playboy* Magazine written by acclaimed journalist Mike Sager. Kay also booked guest appearances on talk radio and television programs, and spoke to students at the San Francisco Institute for the Advanced Study of Human Sexuality (IASHS). Since our visit in the summer of 2011, and after a trip to Asia in the winter of 2012 to further continue her spiritual work on a broader scale, Kay has relocated to Northern California which is home for now. She will be traveling to Scotland in the fall of 2012 for a speaking engagement. (For those interested in arranging a one-on-one spiritual guided session with Kay, she can be contacted through her website at: *www.kaytaylorparker.com*)

When you're on a spiritual path, you have to be willing to let everything go for the sake of that experience of going deeper. I'm always going through that in my life. I'm going through a process of that right now where my finances are totally shot. It's been such a tough year, but in the end, there's a reason for it. I have a sign above my office door: "To whom much is given, much is expected."

Kay in Santa Monica.

That's really another byline to my autobiography. Because of the job that I took on in this lifetime, I have to be so clear and so clean, and especially right now because there's another sort of threshold that we're moving past in terms of spiritual growth and the collective willingness to move forward. It's almost as if I'm going through another clearing. It's not comfortable at all, but I know what it is and I have got to go through it.

Since I draw from everything, and since I believe that there are no mistakes and that there's a reason and purpose for everything, that path that I went down — every aspect of it in its own way was perfect. Would I to do it again if I had the opportunity to do it again? I can't even begin to answer that question because it was as it was. When people ask me what I would have done differently, I say, "I don't know." Maybe it would be to become a better business-woman! Seka used to wag her finger at me — we have a wonderful bond — she used to say, "You're not taking care of yourself."

That was not my way, but I really believe that what happened was supposed to happen, and as I've said, later, I came to understand why I went down that path. It continues even today. It's kind of like a gleaming paradox in my life. There's a reason for that also, but in one sense, it keeps me humble. I'm very careful and I have to be extremely cautious in terms of my own application with people. I have to be careful how I interact with individuals. Certainly, with those who contact me on the internet. It was always my intention to respond to every e-mail, but I have to admit there are some e-mails that come through occasionally that I just have to erase. It's not appropriate that I have to deal with them. I shoot them a shot of love and that's it.

The career was a piece of my past that brought me to this point with wisdom and understanding. In terms of sharing parts of my past with neighbors that don't know about that — it's not necessary. Sometimes it comes up, but it's like with my family in a sense. At that time, they would not have understood, and it wasn't necessary to expose them to that. It was my path to go down and for me to deal with, not for them to deal with. I didn't want to impose that upon them and would not impose it upon certain people. Then there are other people — a lot of individuals that I've counseled and I'm speaking in terms of the male populous, have known about the past. For some reason it has been a plus and I'm very clear with people that my work is strictly spiritual counseling. If they have an issue, and they want to heal and they're willing to do the inner work, then certainly, I'll do the work with them. If they're coming to me thinking that we're going to do some kind of hands on work, sorry. That's not what I do. There are times when just because of my past and because they know I've gone down that road it somehow gives me an opening that other therapists wouldn't be able to attain. We can speak about sex, but I make it clear that we talk about it only in terms of it being about you and your soul.

Once in a blue moon, a person hasn't known about me and something comes up in the reading or in the sessions and it's rare, but I would say, "Look, I don't know if you know about my past but..." I introduce it into the session and somehow it's like a key that opens a door to a part of their consciousness that had been locked before. They've allowed me to go through it just in terms of counseling, and somehow, it was a healing for them. It's been very gratifying from that perspective.

There is a book called *The Artists Way: A Spiritual Path to Higher Creativity* (1992) written by Julia Cameron. What I understand the significance of it to be is about having a lot of creativity in your life and giving it equal time. How that translates to me is spending equal parts of time living in the right brain. I've realized over the past several months because I've been going through a lot of financial stress, that I have been doing that. It's ironic because I tell everybody else that you need to exercise and have your creative time and meditate. The last couple of days I've been realizing that I need to do more of that. I love to write — to me writing is the ultimate creativity. It centers me and when you're inspired to do it, it comes from your soul. I need to dedicate myself to more writing, and particularly, I'm working with a woman to restructure my book so I think it's going to be more about pulling the spiritual principles out of it and highlighting them which I'm looking forward to.

What I'm doing today is assisting in the uplifting of consciousness on the planet. That's it, in a nutshell — anything that I can do and anyway that I can do it, God's already using me to do this. I'm here to join the ranks of the other amazing souls on the planet who are working towards this end. I interact with some very profound individuals who are involved in global consciousness. I don't believe that this planet third dimensionally will ever attain peace because the collective ego is still too involved. We're moving toward a time of planetary ascension, meaning a dimensional shift, and at that point, those who are spiritually ready and equipped will move forward and they will experience peace. It's a good time to be alive — it's not an easy time but it's what we came to do.

I believe that there are truths and realities in every religion on the planet. Then there are, of course, the lies that deal with corruption that has essentially come from men who have been so-called

COURTESY OF KAY PARKER

leaders in a specific religion and structured it for their own purposes. Another aspect of my work is to illuminate and show people their egos. I created the website to give people ideas and tools. God works in mysterious ways. If you want to have a session with me your life will change, so be ready for that. It's powerful and I've been prepared for this for many eons. There has never been a time like this in all of our recorded history. That's what 2012 — the end of the Mayan calendar, is all about. There are already monumental changes happening — the age of corruption will eventually end. All of the corruption is being highlighted; we're discovering it and it's going to continue to happen. It throws many people into a state of chaos, and fear, and dread. To a large degree, my work assists people in trying to understand it from a spiritual perspective so that they can understand their part in it. It might not eliminate the challenges, but it gives them more clarity so that they can handle what they're going through in a more cohesive and intelligent way. Every person that I speak to or impact these days, it's as if it goes through you and into so many other people. It is about being a channel for the light which is consciousness and intelligence — which is love.

My friend says to me, "You are the ultimate love bunny." Who I am, is not Kay Parker. That's not who I am. My career is not who I am. Who I am at this point in my life is a spiritual conduit. That's who I am.

15

Juliet Anderson
"Aunt Peg"

Juliet Anderson is one of the most ferociously seductive temptresses to have entranced golden age audiences. Anderson moved swiftly up the echelon of adult performers in her fortieth year after accepting the role of a housekeeper in Alex de Renzy's *Pretty Peaches* (1978). With the subsequent unveiling of her alter ego, the insatiable, shoot-from-the-hip, "Aunt Peg" Norton, Juliet became an instant sensation and recurring screen character following a scene whereby Anderson instructed her virginal "niece" (Sharon Kane) on the finer points of sexual gratification during a ménage à trois. Initially introduced in the *Swedish Erotica 1* loop, the scene was later implemented in *Aunt Peg's Fulfillment* (1981) granting Juliet the distinction as an influential figure and consummate actor of vintage adult movies.

The eldest of two daughters, Juliet Anderson was born Judy Carr. Raised in Burbank, California by a Big Band trumpeter and his wife, money was scarce for the small family, but love and affection was bountiful. Juliet spoke with humor and awe when recounting her parents' uninhibited sexual compatibility vividly recalling how they would often sneak away and make love. She credited her mother and father for instilling in her a carefree and healthy attitude about her own sexuality.

Contrary to her later years as an indomitable blonde Cougar, Juliet's childhood was often lonely and isolated after she was diagnosed with Crohn's disease. The illness produced debilitating symptoms that sent her to hospitals and prevented her from participating in regular girlhood activities. Vowing to not allow the condition to consume her, Juliet eventually studied art and English in college, and taught conversational English abroad to foreign students for several years before settling in San Francisco. There, she proceeded to hook up with a friend for some casual

"I've always had the philosophy that it isn't how long you live, but how well you live, and I don't mean by money, but by how much you experience life and get out of it."

JULIET ANDERSON (1938-2010)

sex and the encounter became the impetus for her job search. Shortly after answering an advertisement in a newspaper seeking to hire nude performers, Anderson made the acquaintance of director Alex de Renzy and her fate was sealed.

Juliet is also renowned for mentoring Nina Hartley as is evidenced in the Anderson directed venture *Educating Nina* (1984). Anderson schooled Nina in similar style and sexual techniques influencing Hartley's hardcore performances throughout her profession as an actor and a stage performer. When Anderson's career which included a traveling one-woman show in addition to a long list of magisterial film credits came to a close, she applied her unique gift of touch for counseling purposes and enjoyed a satisfied and satiated, clientele base.

On January 11, 2010, just four months after she was interviewed for this book, Juliet Anderson passed away quietly in her sleep, but "Aunt Peg" lives on forever.

In like a Lamb

I was born in Los Angeles in 1938, and my sister was born four and a half years later. I absolutely adored my mother and father, and vice-versa. My father was a jazz trumpet player in big bands until he got tired of needing to be on the road so much. This was the late thirties and early forties. He played for Warner Brothers in some of the musicals, and occasionally, at parties, but he couldn't really make a living that way. He was a very shy person and not willing to do all of the things that were required to have success in those days so he didn't keep a high profile. That's why his name doesn't mean anything unless you look up Fred Carr, and then maybe it might be mentioned, but he's not known today to the public. He certainly could have been but he chose not to. Anyway, that stopped my father from being in the music business and it just pretty much broke his heart. He loved my mother and didn't like to be away from her so she travelled with him and then, when I came along, they took me along.

I have fond memories of my mother and I, and the other men's wives and girlfriends. I was the only child of the forty-piece Pinky Tomlin Band — and we traveled by train across country to places like Chicago so that the women could be with their men. Finally, when my sister came along four and a half years later my father just said, "Uh, uh...It's too much. I want to stay home and be close to my family," and that's when he quit. He wasn't prepared to do anything else. All he had was a high school education so what are you going to do when you're in your late twenties without any experience in anything else?

Pinky Tomlin (nicknamed Pinky mostly for his flushed complexion) from Eros, Arkansas got his start in music playing with the Louis Armstrong Band on a riverboat when he was sixteen. Tomlin became a Big Band leader during the thirties and forties whose signature hit song "The Object of My Affection" was recorded by Ella Fitzgerald. Juliet recalled when she was a young girl; she would occasionally be invited on stage alongside Pinky and his orchestra, and danced excitedly to the Big Band swing ensemble. Anderson's ongoing battle with Crohn's disease however, made her world small and she learned to find different ways to occupy herself during extended periods of absence from school.

I had no friends. I was very shy and very nerdy — no friends. I had a couple of friends, but nobody I remember. There were very, very few because I was sick and they formed little cliques and so forth behind my back and they had excluded me. For many of my years in elementary school and high school, I was home sick and I had home schooling. I was very smart. I've always been very smart and curious and so forth — I simply couldn't go to school most of the time so that part wasn't good. I was skinny because I wasn't absorbing all the nutrients from my food and the Crohn's manifested itself in severe diarrhea. I wore glasses, but I had pretty, long blonde hair and everything, only I was not comfortable with my appearance and I didn't have any communication skills.

I tried piano lessons as a girl. When I was young, my parents broke down and let me have some piano lessons. There were definite abilities, but I knew I wasn't supposed to do that with my life. So much of what I did was also controlled by how I felt because I had these spasms and attacks. I very much loved to read. I didn't like television and I still don't. I don't have a television. I'd love it when we'd go on vacations to the beach and experience nature, but my parents really didn't go up into the mountains and take walks or anything like that. I had a dog, but I didn't have any cats. Now I do, I've made up for it with four cats. I really didn't have any hobbies that I can think of.

I did very well in school. I loved to study and I loved doing my homework. I could just sit out on the balcony and look at the trees blooming or butterflies, or watch dragonflies. I really paid attention to what was happening right then. We lived on a very limited income or a tight budget. I just lived in the moment and felt happy to be alive. I really didn't know from day to day how I was going to feel, and whether I was going to be able to stay out of the hospital. It was necessary to appreciate what was just around me. I seized the moment of living in the moment. I still live fully.

Juliet's parents made little attempt to conceal their own affection and sexual desire for one another leaving a lasting impression upon their eldest daughter as they snuck off to enjoy a little canoodling whenever they felt the impulse to be alone.

My family was so loving and supportive, but more than anything, they showed it. They didn't say one thing and do something else. First of all my mother and father met when they were sixteen and still in high school and immediately loved each other and said, "That's it. We're for each other and nobody else." They absolutely adored each other. My mother and father got married when they were twenty years old or something; they showed their love by hugging and kissing all the time. It was, "I love you honey," or "Oh, I love you too, darling." They both had jobs, but even when my dad was in the music business, I remember that they would set times aside, and apparently often where they would make love and they would lock the door. If they were out on the road, then they would take me to stay with one of the other couples in another room and my mother would say, "Your father and I are going to make love and we'll come back and get you in just a little while." When we were at home living in our house, they'd said, "Okay, you girls fix your own breakfast because we're going to make love this morning," and they'd lock the door and you'd hear them through the walls exclaiming, "Oh, that feels so good! Oh, I love you!" They'd be laughing, and moaning and groaning, and they were loud. I grew up with that as a normal thing.

They told me, "Your mother and father are very lucky, and we're special and you're special. Don't expect other people to be as affectionate as we are, but hopefully, you'll be that way too one day." I grew up with this attitude, and as a result, look how I've turned out! I've always given credit to my parents, even now when doing the work I do because I'm still educating people about sexuality.

Whenever I get a client who comes back a second and third time I will call mother, and sometimes, I'll put him on the phone. He'll say, "Dottie, I think Judy is wonderful. She has helped me so much and I know she learned it from you." Isn't that something? Sometimes, I'll call her and tell her that I've found someone who I was able to pass along some wisdom to about the importance of sensuality and sexuality and cuddling and hugging and kissing, and all of that. Even about sex because people want to know about it. They don't know about it. They are afraid of all of that.

When I got to be twelve — now remember, this was still in the 1940s — there was one book out at that time about sex to read to young people. It had no pictures, but just a few diagrams drawn in black and white of female genitalia and a male — that was it. My father and my mother, mostly my father, would sit down with me while my mother was cooking dinner and he would read to me all about sex — what was available. He would embellish it a bit, more specifically. I remember, saying, "You mean you put that…" or I'd ask, "What is the name of that thing again?"

He would say, "It's called a penis". I'd knock on the coffee table and say, "You put your penis inside Mommy's pee-pee?" I thought that was so cute!

He'd say, "Well, it's not her pee-pee, but it is real close. It's where the babies come out. Where you came out when you were a baby." He'd explain that it felt wonderful and that's what men and women do when they love each other. Can you imagine how wonderful that was for a child of ten or twelve-years-old to have that good of an education?

Neither one of my parents grew up in a religious household. Actually, my parents had neglectful parents. I never had grandparents, so to speak. They never asked us to spend time with them or to do anything with them. The one grandparent I had was my paternal grandmother. She was a real sweetheart and really, very lovely. She would have us over occasionally to stay overnight, but she died of breast cancer at age forty. We had no aunts or uncles, so it was just my parents and somehow, they escaped any kind of indoctrination from society or whatever. In fact, as far as religion, they were very open with us and said, "We don't believe in a God in the sky or a man up in the sky looking down and making judgments. It's called being an Atheist. You are very free though to choose any path you want to lead." I couldn't imagine doing anything other than that because I respected them so much in their honesty and that sort of thing.

As a young, curious teenager eager to fit in, Anderson decided to test the waters of conventional religion when she joined the Presbyterian Church.

At one point, because I was so lonely and such a nerd in my late teens especially after I'd had a serious surgery for the Crohn's, I wanted to see if I could be a part of a community, and if I would make some friends. One of the neighbors belonged to the local Presbyterian Church and so I went with them to try it out and went to Sunday school. Almost immediately for me, I felt that this was bunch of BS. There was no way that I could honestly embrace this. I'd have to lie which I don't do, but I was going to pretend for a while because I really wanted to make some friends. I even got baptized. After a while I thought, "I'm not a person to lie. It's not me." I'm still that way. I like to say and it's true that the only time I will lie is to save my life. I stopped going, and again, my parents had supported me.

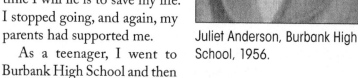

Juliet Anderson, Burbank High School, 1956.

As a teenager, I went to Burbank High School and then Long Beach State College. I didn't know for certain what I was going to do because here I was an artist and what are you going to do if you're going to be true to yourself? I was very gifted in the artistic field. I eventually had jobs there and put myself through college. Oh, my god, I worked thirty hours a week, plus carrying twelve units in school as an Art Major, and then I had hundreds of hours that I needed to put in toward projects so I only got two-three hours sleep a night. Sometimes, I'd go to the room where we did paintings or ceramic, and use my jacket as a pillow and just lie on the table to get some sleep. I did all of this, which is amazing when I look back with this very serious ailment that I had, and still have, which is Crohn's disease that acted up terribly.

Crohn's disease is an autoimmune disorder causing inflammatory bowel disruption usually affecting the intestines, but it can also occur in the anus. People with a family history of the illness, Jewish heritage or smokers may be susceptible to the risk of developing Crohn's disease. Symptoms can include fever, severe abdominal pain, and water diarrhea. Crohn's can be treated with various pain medications along with a proper dietary regimen essential to maintaining a healthy lifestyle as it aids in reducing symptomatic flare-ups.

I've treated it with diet which kept it at bay; that was the most important thing to do. After a couple of years of college, I still got these terrible attacks and I thought, "Well, maybe I'm not going to live to be much more than twenty so I want to live my life fully for as long as I am here." I've always had the philosophy that it isn't how long you live, but how well you live and I don't mean by money, but by how much you experience life and get out of it. Look for the good and just have a good time.

Timing and Inspiration

About halfway through my college career, I switched from Art to English, and still kept Art as a minor because I thought I couldn't make a living as an artist. That would have been too hard because I knew I was going to stay single. I graduated with a degree in English and Art, and then I said, "Now what am I going to do with English because I'm not going to teach in the school as a school teacher?" I couldn't do anything where I'd have to be totally depended upon because of the Crohn's and the diarrhea, and the pain. Finally, at age twenty I moved to Japan to be with the first great love of my life. Actually, I had one more before that that was short-lived, but it was a real heart connection with both of these guys.

The one I joined in Japan was in the U.S. Navy. I moved there because he said, "You would love it here, Juliet." By the way, my name in those days was "Judy," and not "Anderson" — I created "Anderson" and "Juliet". Because I was drawn to Asian art, automatically, he'd told me "Everywhere you look, it's everywhere and we're stationed very near a fishing village. There is so much beauty around that you would love it, so get on the plane and join me!" That started my many, many years of traveling, not as a tourist, but going and living.

I travelled to Japan and married Bob, and stayed there for two years with him. We agreed that when we came back to the United States we'd get a divorce because we didn't want a traditional marriage. I'd made a vow not to get married or to have kids because of the Crohn's disease. We agreed to get a divorce when we came back to the States because we wanted to remain friends and not end up as a bickering couple. I've always been very independent anyway and he loved that in me. Here we are still friends after all of these years.

Bob is in prison for life for a crime he did not commit, in New York. He has been incarcerated for thirty years. They will not let him out. He doesn't have a family to return to; I communicate with him through letters. He has no place to go. He has one daughter, but she does not want or can afford to support him or have him come there, and there's nobody else to take him in or anything. They're not going to just put him out on the street. It costs thirty thousand dollars per year, per inmate. Life is not fair.

Given the fact, her ex-husband was awarded the maximum sentence for his crime; I asked Juliet if Bob was convicted of first-degree murder. While recounting some of the circumstances of the trial in her mind, Juliet did not wish to elaborate further.

I do believe him when he said what happened, I really do. I went to the trial and when I heard how rigged it was — what had happened, I was thoroughly disgusted. That's enough. After that, I was in California, and then I went to Europe just for a trip. I checked out some countries to see if there was somewhere I wanted to live, I had come back, and things had not changed here — the same thing about pouring all kinds of money into senseless wars and my tax dollars were going to the military to support immoral wars against people all over the world. I just couldn't justify that. I left again in the late 1960s.

I lived in Spain, Portugal, Italy and Greece and I stayed two and a half years in each place. Each time I would come back to America to see if things had changed. I was teaching conversational

American English, because in Europe, they learn formal British English, but it doesn't prepare them for visiting the United States and actually being out amongst the people on the street. I taught privately and I made money, frugally, and I enjoyed the country. I learned the language of each country and had a good time — and a lover. I've always been serially monogamous except in the films. I've always had a lover. I like to say they stand in line, but anyway...I lived in Greece, and then the last country I went to was Finland where I worked for the Finnish Broadcasting company. It was a fluke how I got the job.

One of the main tenets of my philosophy is all of life is timing and inspiration. The timing has to be right and then you have to be inspired. I happened to arrive right at the time when somebody decided to leave the Finnish Broadcasting Company. It was the Foreign Service Department in that people spoke English. They were mainly from England. They all spoke English and they needed somebody to make radio programs in English about Finland. They would go all over the world to educate any small English speaking population anywhere about Finland. They would get people to visit Finland and get them to understand Finland. As it happened, I was so naturally good at it that I moved to the top just like that. Here I was, only a few hours off the plane, and I got invited to this meeting and somebody said, "Oh, I'll take this opportunity to say I'm quitting and going back to Canada."

The person who brought me said, "Well, I think I've found somebody who can take your place." They asked me if I'd be willing to give it a try, and I said, "Yeah". I'd always been good at English.

Juliet thoroughly embraced her assignment with the Finnish Broadcasting Company which eventually enabled her to personally fraternize with locals in various communities at a grass roots level. Anderson's work options abroad totaled approximately eighteen years.

When I got to these countries, I realized that I had a niche there. What I always did was go to the Embassy right off the plane and I'd say, "Here I am. What do you think I could do?" "Where could I fill in with these requirements — these skills?" I found out that nobody else was doing that. In Finland, I got paid for being nosy. I loved to talk to people and find out what inspired them in life, how they'd gotten to where they are, what their talents were — like what you're doing. It was a form of journalism, but it didn't include photos. I had a few words that I needed in Finnish that I could take out and around the country when I was interviewing a farmer or a sailor, or that kind of thing. More often than not, I took someone with me who spoke Finnish. They would tell me, "Don't try to learn Finnish, it's too difficult. Even we don't speak it."

There's no other language like it. I learned enough Swedish [the second official language in Finland] and spoke English. I'd travel all over the country and interview these fascinating people and even foreigners who were visiting, and in the cultural arts, theater groups and symphony orchestras, and find out what their experiences were. I had so much fun. I also contributed to a magazine about the same thing and on the side, I taught a little bit of conversational American English. I stayed there for a long time.

I came back here to California and settled in the San Francisco Bay area. I had never lived there, but I chose it because of its culture and its multi-ethnic, multi-generational diversity. I moved there with that in mind and I knew I could grow old there and still be accepted. I moved to the Bay area not knowing what in the world I was going to do, but I had faith my past experiences would help me. I was a total film virgin. This was the end of 1978.

I was quickly running out of money. I found a place in downtown San Francisco — a studio apartment which was great. I paid first and last month's rent and then I had only two hundred dollars and I thought, "My Gosh! I've got to get some work here. What am I going to do?" I had a neighbor, a man, and he had a Swedish accent or something so we laughed about the fact that I had been in Finland and it was close to Sweden and his parents were from Sweden and so on. I was very horny and I was used to having regular sex so I quickly propositioned him at the beginning and said, "Hey, how would you like to have some sex? I'm really feeling horny and I'm attracted to you." Of course, he wasn't about to say no. As you saw me in my films, I was very pretty. I'm just naturally very sensual. We had some great sex. I don't mean just lie back and spread my legs missionary position. I've always been very creative with lots of different positions and it was good. It was fun. We did that a couple of times, and later, I said, "Eric, could you give me some advice — I need some help. Could you point me into a direction of what kind of work I could do? I need some money and I have no idea what I could do."

He said, "Well, you're so good at sex. I'd certainly see if I could get some work in the area of sex." I said, "What? Get a job by using sex?" I said, "I don't want to go out on the streets and be a prostitute."

He said, "No, no, no". He said, "I just saw something in the newspaper." He went back to his apartment, and got his paper

PHOTOGRAPHY BY PAUL JOHNSON

and came out and just showed me the classified ads. It was a little two-line ad, no picture or anything, just a tiny advertisement. Talk about fate for him to be looking through there and see this and it said, "Attractive women over eighteen wanted for softcore sex show, short hours and lots of fun. Good pay."

He told me, "I don't know what it is, but the theatre is right down the street three blocks from here in downtown San Francisco." He said, "You have nothing to lose by going to check it out." He was right.

Juliet's *Pretty Peaches*

I called the number, made an appointment, went down there scared to death and there was this young woman down in the basement of this theater. It was a regular movie theater. She was eighteen years old and I'll never forget her name, Milvia. You have to understand, I knew nothing about professional sex other than the prostitutes of course. I understood prostitutes and brothels. I understood sex for pay brothels because of having lived in Europe. I went in to apply for the job, and Milvia looked at me and I introduced myself. She said, "Lift your shirt."

I said, "Really?"

She said, "Yeah." I've never worn a bra. I have these lovely large natural breasts. It was just a little cramped cubicle in the cellar of the theater, so I lifted my shirt up and she said, "You're hired." She told me what it was going to be. She said, "We have movies. We also have a short little stage show and you'll work with other gals, but you don't have to do anything you don't want to." It wasn't a lot of money, but it was something. I certainly wasn't prudish. When she said I was hired and I said, "That's all?"

She said, "Yeah."

I said, "No, I want to show you something else." I turned around, and lifted up my skirt and showed her my behind. She started laughing and said, "You're doubly hired." She added, "Oh, my god, Alex [de Renzy] will love this."

I said, "Who is Alex?" and she said, "He's the owner of the theater. He'll also want to meet you, but he's in the middle of shooting a movie right now and so it'll be a little while, but you'll get a call." I went home and that evening I got the call. He said, "I've never heard Milvia so excited. Can you meet me tomorrow?"

I said, "Yes, sure." I wasn't doing anything. I went down there and he agreed. He said, "You're definitely hired for the show, and by the way, I'm shooting a film and there's a part that hasn't been cast yet," which was true, he wasn't making it up. He told me, "I was wondering if you might like to be in it. It's not difficult or anything. It'll only take a short time and it's just for one day, but I'll give you two hundred dollars." Now, see that was a lot of money. Nowadays, ladies get eight hundred dollars for a fourteen-hour day. I'm talking about the girls who are no one — just starting out. Then the stars, they get thousands, you know. Apart from that, I know nothing about it. I don't keep track of anyone and I know zero.

Within the hierarchy of the adult movie industry, it is generally understood first-rate actresses are the faces consumers see on a cover. Up until a few years ago, these females were the highest paid performers comprised mostly of contract girls who made approximately four to five feature films per year. At one time, their earning potential was around the one to two thousand-dollar mark, excluding any outside income earned while on the road. Prestige female stars were afforded the luxury of selecting onscreen partners and could approve or nix a specific sex scene, while "B" and "C" list girls were often hired for more specialty work such as fetish roles or sex acts involving anal/double penetration. One of the top four male performers of all time (and rated the #1 porn star by AVN), "Porn's Ambassador" Ron Jeremy commented a few years ago on the pay scale for all categories of X-rated performers. He confirmed that typically, women could earn up to two hundred and fifty thousand dollars per year. In contrast, men might earn an average of three to four hundred dollars per scene, and one hundred dollars per scene if the male is a novice. If those numbers are indeed accurate, not much has changed since the infancy of hardcore in the late 1960s and into the early 1970s when aspiring male actors earned on average approximately fifty to seventy-five dollars per scene or per film. Up until recent years, women ruled in the sex industry and it is because of the women that pieces of product were/are sold. However, in the current market with increasing competition stemming from live webcam sites and amateur productions sold over the internet, most major companies have dropped all contract actors.

Anyway, [de Renzy] said, "Well, I've got to make a couple of calls, but here's the script. Your part would be that of the maid. It's near the beginning." I opened it up, I was reading through the maid and

I came to the part where the maid has sex. The sex part was that the maid jumped on the bed and dove into a woman's pussy and started licking her. Up to that point, I'd never been with a woman. I read that part, I screamed and Alex covered his mouthpiece of the phone and said, "I'll be right with you."

My heart was pounding and I said to him, "Oh, my god! What is this? I've never done — do you mean to tell me there are movies like this?" I'd never heard of the X-rated film business in my whole life. I'd been living abroad. He was very patient and he explained. He said, "This is the X-rated movie business," but he said, "Look, you don't have to do it if you don't want to. You'll still have the job here."

I said, "Well, I believe I was given this opportunity for a reason and it would be really foolish of me to pass it up because I like to learn new things."

He said, "Atta gal. Good for you." He sent his assistant over to pick me up the next day and we went out and bought a wonderful French maid outfit for me: black stockings and a sexy black slip with a little white apron and a cap. They picked me up and took me there, and I did that one scene and I absolutely loved it. I did it with the gal. They had to pry me away from her when it was my time to have my scene with John Leslie. It was *Pretty Peaches* (1978), of course.

Anderson claimed her knowledge of sex films was next to nil, but to the naked eye, it's hard to believe *Pretty Peaches* [aka *Alex deRenzy's Pretty Peaches*] is Juliet's hardcore debut. Anderson conducts herself as a pro in the film considered by Alex deRenzy his best all round picture which presents buxom beauty, Desiree Cousteau, in the lead role as a ditzy amnesia victim following a car accident. A calamity of sexual scenarios result as Cousteau tries to restore order to her memory. In an uncredited role, Juliet appears as the Swedish maid Katia and becomes entangled in a threesome with (bearded) John Leslie before devouring an actress by the name of Flower. Anderson goes at it with gusto, eagerly lapping Flower's limber body all over while Leslie penetrates her through the back door.

John Leslie was my first man I worked with and throughout my entire career; he was my favorite. We had the most incredible chemistry. We absolutely had a ball. I went on to make dozens of films and I was in the industry for six and a half years, but John Leslie was my very favorite. He was intelligent and funny, a good actor, and we just had so much fun; it was extremely obvious on screen. I was having real orgasms. I tried different positions and I made up the dialogue on my own. They just let me make up the dialogue. They'd give me the basic premise of the story and then tell me to just follow through with what I'd say to people. I had that reputation.

COURTESY OF WORTH MENTIONING PUBLIC RELATIONS

Shortly after her star power was recognized in *Pretty Peaches*, Juliet was thrilled to have an opportunity to perform with John Leslie again in Anthony Spinelli's *Talk Dirty to Me* (1979). Considered one of the finest 1970s porno productions, high praise credited to *Talk Dirty to Me* is largely due to Leslie's sexy swagger, and cool, confident style as a lothario looking to outdo his less fortunate buddy Lenny (Richard Pacheco) in the art of wooing women. When Jack (Leslie) sets his eyes on lovely Marlene (Jesie St. James), he bets Lenny he can seduce her in three days, but first, he must pinpoint exactly what it is that ignites her loins. Jack quickly discovers through his liaisons with other willing females (Cris Cassidy, Sharon Kane, and the dazzling Juliet Anderson) that the key to Marlene's heart is dirty talk and lots of it — something she secretly fantasizes that he does to her.

Once again, Anderson's sexual appetite is voracious. She doesn't hold back in her scene with Leslie — matching him every nasty step of the way as if she owns his member. Their chemistry is palpable with the two actors bursting out in laughter immediately after Juliet rubs Leslie's juices all over her lips. The mega success of *Talk Dirty to Me* spawned several sequels with John Leslie starring in the recurring title role.

I recently looked at an old film and I can see it from those early days and I thought, "Oh boy, were we ever a great couple." We didn't see each other outside of the films. John Leslie and Mike Horner — those two were my favorite male co-stars.

"Aunt Peg"

I never had to do anything I really didn't want to. Once when I performed with John Holmes was one time I didn't enjoy my experience and another one was Johnny Keyes. The chemistry was not there with Johnny, and then John Holmes would be forceful with women and hurt them with his large cock so I chose to tell him right at the very beginning, "Let's do this scene and make it good and do it the first time through. Let's enjoy ourselves so that we can get it done and go home. Let me tell you, if you try to force your big cock in and hurt me, I'll cut it off and I mean it. So be gentle. You're more than a big cock and I know that so don't act like an asshole. Don't tempt me." He was gentle.

Juliet's reservation about performing with Holmes is undetectable as the two immediately get down to business in a three-way Swedish Erotica segment with Sharon Kane playing Juliet's wide-eyed niece. The scene was groundbreaking as it simultaneously launched Anderson's brand new persona "Aunt Peg," as the aggressive forty-something sex fiend who consumes men and women with equal exuberance. The landmark ménage-a-trois loop with Holmes and Kane was later incorporated into *Aunt Peg's Fulfillment* in 1981.

I really liked Sharon Kane who played my niece in the *Aunt Peg* series. Because Sharon was blonde and I was blonde, I suggested that she be my niece coming to visit her aunt on school holiday. That was the story line. She came to see Peggy Norton which I took out of a hat: Peggy Norton. I was "Aunt Peggy". While she was visiting me one of my boyfriends/lovers came over and it was John Holmes. I can't remember exactly how we got into it, but I think maybe he and I were making love in the next room and she came in and got down on her knees. I was down on my knees, probably licking his balls and stroking him and sucking. Suddenly, she just looked at his big cock and said, "Oh, my god!

Juliet Anderson and Johnny Keyes, in *Aunt Peg.* vcx

Aunt Peg, it's so big!" You know, more to enjoy. Then we both started to suck it. Well, you couldn't really suck his cock, it was too big, but we started licking and tonguing his cock. So here I was, corrupting my niece. The name "Aunt Peg" stuck. That was probably 1979-80. It just took off. I mean, that name "Aunt Peg" was America's favorite aunt. I was an original. It was not only the name, but it was also the trademark of the black stockings and garter belt — the garter belt could be a different color. I would go and buy garter belts that were purple or pink or whatever, but if I couldn't find the color I would buy a white garter belt and dye it to match my outfit. I had a scarf around the neck, a garter belt and black hose — always sheer black hose and high heels. That was Aunt Peg.

Traditionally, the garter belt, silk stockings, high heels and dainty scarf fastened delicately around the necks of female performers were customary touches first introduced in Swedish Erotica loops. The marketing brainchild was conceived in the mid-1970s when Swedish Erotica (owned by Caballero, one of the largest producers of pornographic material in the mid-late 1970s) decided to glamorize the steady stream of females showcased in their numerous vignettes. Evidently, the aesthetically appealing costuming trend later became a popular grooming trait for various adult feature productions.

Anderson played Hollywood producer Peggy Norton in the primary offering of the "Aunt Peg" series titled *Aunt Peg* (directed by Anthony Spinelli as Wes Brown) illustrating her involvement in numerous liaisons with the most popular performers of the decade. With various Swedish Erotica loops melded together to create this montage feature, Juliet is partnered up with Seka, Serena, Jamie Gillis, Mike Ranger, Mike Horner, Billy Dee, and others in impressive and vivacious displays of copulation. *Aunt Peg's Fulfillment* is a continuation of the established trademark "Aunt Peg" series as Peggy Norton (Juliet Anderson) personally auditions prospective actors for an upcoming film project starting with Johnny Keyes as Tyrone Tips. Peg handles Keyes' manhood aggressively, and shows no mercy while giving the startled job applicant head as her niece Sheila (Sharon Kane) sleeps in the next room. Later that day, Peg arrives at her office and proceeds to chew up the furniture and a few unsuspecting co-workers and friends (Richard Pacheco, Erica Boyer, and Suzanne French are all featured) before retiring for the evening. At home, Peg is up to her tricks again as she entertains two male companions played by Mike Ranger and John Leslie, each one unaware that the other is in her apartment. Humorously, Peg dashes between two rooms to effectively service her pals. In each and every segment, Anderson commands the screen with confidence and diabolical flair. The previously filmed three-way interlude between Anderson, Holmes, and Kane appears in the middle of the film.

I have a compilation: *The Best of Aunt Peg* that I've been selling for a long time because I get it from the owners of the *Aunt Peg* films. The owner [Ted McIlvenna] has the largest collection of pornography in the world. It's the Institute for the Advanced Study of Sexuality [IASHS] in San Francisco. I've known them for a long time. I give talks there periodically and they've been making this compilation for me and duplicating it for many years. There is *Aunt Peg* (1980), *Aunt Peg's Fulfillment* (1981), and *Aunt Peg Goes to Hollywood* (1981).

"Aunt Peg" does Hollywood

Lisa DeLeeuw and Rhonda Jo Petty, along with their (on-camera) boyfriends, Jeff Conrad and Kevin James all vie for spots in Aunt Peg's Hollywood porn project titled *Aunt Peg Goes to Hollywood* (aka *Aunt Peg Goes Hollywood*, 1981). With a couple of embedded Swedish Erotica clips utilized to bump up the sex scenes (including a hefty dose of anal scenes), everyone wants to get in on the action, from directors (Ron Jeremy) to cinematographers to projectionists — in this final submission of the "Aunt Peg" franchise. Anderson is her usual feisty self, but only appears in one scene, along with Jeff Conrad and Little Oral Annie who is introduced. Conrad travels with Peg to her Mexico hideaway, and after he is greeted by Annie (smiling like the Cheshire cat), the two horny women entice him into the bedroom and put on a stimulating show leaving him no choice but to join in.

Again, I created the stories. I collaborated with the director [Paul Vatelli] and said, "What do you think?" We had this background because we'd shoot them in people's houses for the most part and at different locations. I'd ask, "Who are my co-stars?" We'd sit down the three or four of us, and put our heads together and we'd talk about what kind of fun we could have today and, "How about this?" or "How about that?" The ice-cream truck would be out front and we'd say, "Oh, well, we could have ice-cream and spread it all over our bodies…" We'd have fun.

I remember I also liked Jodie Maxwell and I liked working with Kay Parker. I can't remember the others. I didn't like Marilyn Chambers because she had a very nasty attitude from day one. She walked into the set — she strode in and pushed everybody aside and said, "Get out of my way, I'm Marilyn Chambers."

When I went up to her and said, "Oh, I'm so glad I get a chance to meet you."

She said, "Get out of my way, I'm Marilyn Chambers." Here, we were meant to be in a film together. She had bodyguards, security guards who came with her. She was very spoiled with a very nasty attitude, but you'd never notice it in the film that we were in together because I made a point of being good at stopping it at that. I never would have chosen to do another film with her. I wasn't alone, other people said to me, "Don't take it personally, that's just the way she is."

In the sequel to *Insatiable* (1980), *Insatiable 2* (1984) Juliet played Morgan Templeton, a writer spending quality time with Sandra Chase (Marilyn Chambers) in order to gain better insight into Chase's sexuality and the many taboos to heighten her sexual experiences. During her research, Templeton is enlightened about her own sexual fantasies and learns inventive ways to achieve gratifying orgasms through her personal interaction with Sandra.

Although Juliet was in her fortieth year when she made a career choice that was life changing, I wondered if or how her decision affected her small, closely knit family.

My parents always supported me in anything I did because they knew that I would make all the right decisions. Even if they weren't the best ones, they knew I would learn something. I'd gone to other countries and I'd lived in other countries, and they knew I had quite a few lovers. They just said, "Be responsible, don't get pregnant, and don't hurt people." When I decided to get into films, I realized that they were going to find out at some point and I didn't want them to find out from somebody. I made an appointment to go down to San Diego.

Anderson took a proactive approach when she decided to be upfront with her mother and father about her porn career. If Juliet's conference with her parents unfolded exactly as she described it, truth is indeed far more surprising than fiction.

I flew down from San Francisco and I asked them if they would sit down when it was convenient, I'd like to have a little meeting with them because I had something to tell them. The three of us gathered in the living room of their small apartment. They sat down and I said, "I have something I want to tell you because I don't want you to hear it from somebody else and it's bound to get out. I know you made me promise not to get into films." They made me promise not to get involved in regular films, or be a musician or singer or something like that because they knew that even though I probably had some talent, women always had to provide sexual services to the men who would hire them. They didn't want me to have to go through that, so I promised them I wouldn't. I said, "I know I promised you I wouldn't, and I haven't all of these years, but then something came up just recently. I had no idea what I was getting into, and nobody forced me by insisting upon any kind of sexual favors. I didn't have to put out for anybody. I am in adult films and I don't know if you know what that means. It means explicit X-rated films — sometimes it's called "porno." I have very quickly become a superstar. Believe me, I had no idea it was going to happen."

PHOTOGRAPHY BY PAUL JOHNSON

One can only speculate whether Juliet truly had no previous knowledge of the adult film industry in 1978 as she indicated during our interview. Wikipedia and Juliet's own autobiography (on her former website) documented that in 1963 Anderson was employed as a receptionist for a filmmaker of Nudie films in Florida. She had also appeared in a sexploitation movie in 1963. The Internet Movie database *(IMDb. com)* lists Anderson in the credits for two sexploitation films directed by Barry Mahon in 1965: *The Beast that Killed Women* (uncredited), and *International Smorgas-Broad*. Mahon's first production, *Cuban Rebel Girls*, released in 1959 was the last picture for Hollywood star Errol Flynn which also co-starred one of Flynn's girlfriends Beverly Aadland.

> I told my parents how it happened and that it completely surprised me. I didn't even know that the adult industry existed because I'd been out of the country for so long. They looked at each other and looked back at me — I can see it right now — with big smiles on their faces. They said, "We know it already." Somebody they knew came to them and told them. They had actually gone to a theater. In those days, you had to go to a movie theater. It was before video. My parents told me that some friends of some people they knew went and saw me. I said, "Oh no! I'm sorry." They just started laughing. They said, "Don't worry about it. You're a grown-up gal and if you can't take care of yourself at this point then it's too late."

One Woman Dynamo

For the longest time after her movie debut, Anderson didn't see herself onscreen until one day she eventually bit the bullet and went to a theatre incognito.

> I remember I got a wig to disguise myself and go with somebody to see the film. It took a while for them to edit and all that. But what I quickly figured out is that I couldn't live on what I was making in the films — still, that was very little money so the way that I supported myself through those six and a half years was creating one woman stage theatre — not strip shows, but theater.

Spurred on by her reputation as a fêted celebrity, Juliet decided to kick things up a notch and spread her wings as an actor by exposing extensions of some of the personalities she had developed within the framework of her films to a broader audience.

> I was my own manager and I booked myself all over the country. I would create characters like "Carol the Cook," "Elaine the Engineer," "Helen the Housewife," "Nurse Naughty," and my

PHOTOGRAPHY BY PAUL JOHNSON

favorite, "Elaine the Executive". These were parodies to dispel the myth that there was any separation between being sexy, and intelligent, and funny, and older. That's what I did in the films — dispel those myths and that's what I did with this show. I had fun creating these characters. I created these great shows. I was my own agent and booked myself in, and I had them find me a hotel room.

While Anderson continued making films and traveling with her stage show, she cleverly managed to take advantage of other profitable sideline opportunities such as personal appearances and phone sex, in addition to operating a mail-order business selling her own product.

They'd feature my films at these events — they'd show my film and even women came. Then, they'd have the live show. I had to do five shows a day. They were an hour and then I'd stand out in the lobby for Polaroid photos — the line would be around the block. I was the biggest star the Mitchell brothers ever had at their theater in San Francisco. The line was clear down to Market Street of people waiting to get into the theater. They would wait in a long line to get their picture taken of me wearing a garter belt and hose and heels sitting on their lap. Then I'd autograph it and I'd charge ten dollars. With the shows and the films, I was able to make three thousand dollars a month. That's what we did, about one film a month or something like that.

I was very much an anomaly in that industry. I wasn't aware of it at the time. It was later that I found out how very different that I was. Not only being older, but being unafraid to show that I was intelligent and funny, and really enjoyed what I was doing and having real orgasms. The other women didn't like it at all. They were there to make some money. They didn't really enjoy sex. They had to have other jobs, or they had boyfriends or husbands who would support them because you didn't make any money. No, they didn't like it at all and they were in it for a very short window of time.

For those fortunate enough to have witnessed Juliet Anderson in action either as the feisty man-eater "Aunt Peg," or as another one of her ball busting cast of characters, it would be futile to suggest she didn't seem to enjoy her work, and definitely more than the average actress. Consequently, it is not difficult to accept that Anderson did experience authentic orgasms on camera. "Exploitation" is not a word found in Anderson's vocabulary when referencing her own experiences in adult entertainment.

> If women let themselves be exploited, I imagine they were. I can't really speak for the other women; I just know that I never was. I never allowed myself to be. The directors who wanted to do that didn't hire me because I had a reputation for being independent and not putting up with nonsense. I did a very good job when I was in front of the camera and I made it easy for everybody because my scenes could often be done in just one take. They just gave me the basic outline of the story, and I created my own dialogue and I immersed myself in the feeling of just being there. I wanted to enjoy myself and I wanted my co-stars to enjoy it and have some fun, too. I had a positive attitude, but I also saw it as corporate America. The big boys were making lots of money and we working folk were not. That went for the directors and the crew as well as the cast. The rumor is that I made three producers millionaires. That's just a rumor, but I certainly lined the coffers of the corporate people who financed these productions. It's big business.

The term "big business" with respect to the pornographic film industry since the advent of hardcore movie productions is putting it mildly. In the mid-1970s, it is estimated in the United States that approximately five-ten million dollars of revenue was realized from the production of X-rated films. By 1979 (one of Anderson's primary years in the business), gross annual revenues of upwards to 100 million dollars were yielded in the state of California alone. Today's global figures encompassing everything from adult oriented films to internet sales and magazines are close to a staggering ten-fifteen billion dollars.

> I like men and I like women. It doesn't mean I like all of them. I think women should not be objectified. Women are as intelligent as men are. There are intelligent men and there are intelligent women. There are also men and women that are not so intelligent, but it is a man's world unfortunately. Women are often objectified and they're not really supposed to like sex. I have never really understood feminism other than to say, "Hey, just because I am a woman doesn't mean I shouldn't have equal rights." A person's sex is irrelevant to me whether they're gay, lesbian, male or female — it's

what's inside of a person. In other words, people are not their labels. Let's not label people, but accept them for what they really are and what's inside.

No matter who she was paired with, Anderson maintained a high level of professionalism at all times thinly veiled through her assertive and domineering MILF personas leaving audiences wanting more. Prominent appearances by Juliet in films that followed the aforementioned productions are *Taboo* (1980), *Fantasex Island* (1984), *Reel People* (1984), and innumerable others. In the ambit of directing, Anderson's name will always be synonymous as the brains behind the succinct success of Nina Hartley and her eminent virtuoso performance as an acting student studying the effects of fantasy upon one's sex life in *Educating Nina* (1984).

Ageless Desire

After I got out of the business, I tried to figure out what I was going to do. I was exhausted, and it was quite by accident that I was at a place called Wilbur Hot Springs: a natural hot springs, along with a woman friend, just relaxing. I saw an announcement that a lecturer at a school of massage was going to be giving an intensive three-day workshop on massage at Wilbur coming up soon. It was going to be ten to twelve hour days. We both looked at each other and thought, "Hmmm, why the hell not?"

I thought, "Until I figure out what I'm going to do next this would be really worthwhile, just to be able to give to family and friends." That was all I intended to do. I somehow had sensed that during whatever last film I made, it was time to quit and I always paid attention to instincts. We signed up, and returned and took the training. Instead of my keeping things non-professional, both of my teachers took me aside and told me I had the gift of touch and for me to use it wisely. I thought, "Oh, my god, maybe this is what I should do next," but I quickly found out that you can't support yourself just doing massages. It's very, very hard work. I wasn't going to have anybody sharing my expenses and that's when I added the Tender Loving Touch. I've been doing the two for twenty-two years.

While teaching, counseling, and providing massage therapy to customers utilizing her customized techniques, Anderson additionally offered sexual healing for those from her select group of clientele requesting extra attention and willing to pay for her special services. As another means to strive for financial independence, Juliet cleverly launched a line of educational videos preaching the virtues of sex after sixty. One of the more well known from the list is *Juliet's Masturbation Memoirs Volumes 1 & 2* costarring Annie Sprinkle and Scarlet Harlot (1995), where she explains how orgasms provided relief from the pain she endured as a Crohn's and rheumatoid arthritis sufferer.

Juliet poses in mauve for friend and photographer, Paul Johnson. This was one of her personal favorite pictures. PHOTOGRAPHY BY PAUL JOHNSON.

After undergoing a complete hysterectomy at age fifty, Anderson discovered due to of a lack of essential hormones she could no longer climax during vaginal intercourse. There is medical evidence to support the fact that the cervix plays a major role in orgasm as it dilates during intercourse to prepare for conception and is highly sensitive to touch. If a women's cervix is removed during a hysterectomy, the sensitivity to the cervix area is lost during penetration by the penis because the nerve endings that respond to stimulation no longer function. Anderson turned to perfecting masturbation techniques in order to relieve her sexual tension and manage her pain.

> I do body work. I am a massage therapist. With Tender Loving Touch technique, I use my entire body very slowly and very gently all over the recipient's entire body. I have a real gift of touch. My clients can completely relax and go into an altered state. I do this and get them very relaxed, and then I give them a real nice massage. I also do some relationship counseling to help couples to learn to talk with each other, before they are yelling at each other.

As founder and expert practitioner of the Tender Loving Touch application and in accordance with her own body, Juliet effectively expanded upon the fundamentals of her program to serve as a basis for a distinctive film venture in 1998.

Amazingly, at sixty years of age after appearing in a few 1990s movies, Juliet's film and directing career(s) were officially semi-revived when she, her partner, and three real-life couples over the age of fifty performed in *Ageless Desire* (1998). Drawing from a cornucopia of sexual techniques spanning more than four decades, Anderson explicitly demonstrates the finer points of lovemaking for seniors in this notable project where she is still every bit a Goddess.

> *Ageless Desire* was actually my production. They let me on the set and said, "Why don't you take over, Juliet? You have a better idea of what's going on. We'll take a smoke break, you go ahead." In most of my films, I was actually directing while acting anyway. I was just creating what was going on. I'd whisper to people, "Let's move over here," and that kind of thing. Yes, I'm a born director in and among other things in my mind. Other people would just say, "Yeah, you're just bossy." I see things in a larger context and how they're going to fit together, that is sort of instinctive. I didn't

mean to be irritable, it's just that I have a vision and can see things and other people don't. It's a talent and it has been recognized by many. There were often jokes on the set. Director Anthony Spinelli said to me, "Oh, I'm so glad to see you Juliet, now I can pretty much just take the day off." I would be on-camera very aware of what was going on to the extent that he didn't have to pay attention or follow my every single move. I multi-tasked and I also satisfied something in me. I really enjoyed doing it. No one was forcing me.

Like many former porn personalities, members of Juliet's family don't necessarily share the same enthusiasm or reverence for Anderson's legacy and superstardom, as did Juliet, and especially, her fan base. Anderson's achievements in the adult entertainment field are plentiful and range from her induction into the Legends Hall of Fame in 1996, to her XRCO Hall of Fame award in 1999, to her Lifetime Achievement Award in 2001 followed by an honorary doctorate from the Institute for Advanced Study of Human Sexuality in 2007.

My family does have regrets, of course. Even my conservative sister and her daughter and husband; they know and they are not happy about it because they are conservative and we don't talk about it. I don't hide it. When I've gotten awards, I have certainly written to them and told them, "I'd just like you to know that I've gotten a Lifetime Achievement Award by the Adult Entertainment Industry for the years of work that I did and it's a real honor". You know, that kind of thing. I got every award that was out there. The only thing I haven't gotten yet is director. That would be for *Ageless Desire* made over ten years ago.

Out like a Lioness

It is reported Juliet Anderson passed away peacefully in her sleep on January 11, 2010. Juliet's quiet passing is a fitting end to the life of a classy woman who still manages to turn-on fans of her exceptional work in vintage adult films years after she gracefully closed the door on her central role as one of the first Cougars in the adult industry. When she died, Anderson left behind a close group of chosen friends, four cherished cats (all of whom have found homes thanks to Annie Sprinkle), and a timeless legacy epitomizing the true meaning of "ageless desire."

The women of my era definitely have left a legacy, and if for no other reason people will always enjoy things about sex whether they want to admit it or not. We gave people an outlet for their suppressed sexual desires. The legacy is that the women who really made their mark which I introduced, is that a woman can be intelligent, funny and sexy, and sometimes older like Kay Parker and me.

PHOTOGRAPHY BY PAUL JOHNSON

Women don't have to be real young for these sex scenes. Having a bit of experience is definitely appealing.

After I stopped doing films, everybody went their own way. I ran into Nina Hartley quite by accident when she was giving a talk right down the block from me. I was completely surprised to find out that she was there. I introduced her to the industry. It was nice to see her, but I'm not going to see her again. She has her own life and I have my own life. Everybody, when they quit, they went their own ways so that was it. That's fine. I always wish them well and hope that they're happy and enjoying whatever they are doing.

I tell very few people what I used to do. I still get recognized though. If somebody really followed that genre and look at me they will often say, "Oh, my god, it is you." For me it's a little touchy when we're on the public transportation and somebody says loudly, "Oh, my god, it's you! I loved you in films, you were so sexy!" Then everybody turns and looks at me. People are so thrilled when they run into one of their idols.

I go to a lot of concerts, especially classical music, but I like many different genres. I love theatre and some of the performances that I get to see are because I usher in several venues. I like foreign films and I'll often go to movie theaters to see the films because I chose not to have a television. I like to read and I am a very good, creative cook. I love to have people over and entertain. I take walks. Actually, I have very few friends. I'm somewhat reclusive, but I have a few and I cherish their friendship. I also get a massage on a regular basis. It's very therapeutic. I'm very good about how I spend my time. I like it quiet, and I'm not interested in going to places that are very noisy and crowded. I'm the cat lady. I've got four, or four have got me.

I feel very fortunate and blessed, and I have had and continue to have a really full and enjoyable life. I would prefer not to be as sick as I am with the Crohn's disease, but that could happen to anybody. I have chosen not to have any children whether legitimate or illegitimate. I have no children, grandchildren or great grand-children. I am happy in spite of this very unpleasant ailment that I have which can cause me severe pain, but I make the most of the good days. As for the other days, I lay low. One of the reasons I'm happy is because I was not expected to live beyond twenty, so every year is a gift. I feel good and all of my body is natural. I've chosen not to have any face-lifts or augmentation. I feel very fortunate. I feel very lucky that I am alive and I live in a nice place. I live simply, but there's lots going on, so I count my blessings.

I especially love nature. I live in the foothills by the Bay. I walk all over — it's not necessarily to get from point A to point B. I like to walk up in the hills. It's so beautiful overlooking the San Francisco Bay. I'm near John Muir Woods and everything is right here. I just need to go with somebody because I don't have a car anymore. I crashed mine and didn't replace it because I can get around almost anywhere with the public transportation. I don't have a car or a television. Boy, do I save a lot of money so I am a throwback to some past generation. Yet, here I was having all this wild sex! I had an amazing life!

16.
Seka
"The Platinum Princess of Porn"

Dorothiea Patton hails from the state of Virginia where she is the daughter of industrious blue-collar parents and one of a multitude of relatives. As a child, "Dottie" was a rough and tumble tomboy who reveled in wide-open spaces examining bugs or pulling mischievous pranks with siblings and various cousins. A plain-looking girl in her adolescent years, by the time she was sixteen, Dottie had transformed into a beautiful young woman and won her first Beauty Pageant while still in high school.

Marriage at eighteen provided a means to independence and freedom, but Dottie quickly discovered she was not destined for a life of bare feet and a succession of pregnancies. After she and her first husband parted company, Dottie began dating a man who owned several adult bookstores showing eight-millimeter loops. Appalled by how unkempt some of the early female performers appeared, she decided she could present a more aesthetically appealing package for consumers and set about to prove it.

Shortly after arriving in Las Vegas where she did her first nude photo layout, dyed her hair platinum and adopted the stage name "Seka," (borrowed from a Vegas blackjack dealer meaning "kind girl" or "little darling" in Serbo Croatian) the tomboy from Southwest Virginia had arrived. Poised and glamorous, with white blonde hair Seka resembled Marilyn Monroe and possessed obvious star power that has since left a lasting impression amongst devotees of the Hollywood counterculture.

Seka's introduction to hardcore film audiences was in *Dracula Sucks* (1978) sporting an all-star cast of veteran performers. Suddenly, she found herself the object of her male co-stars' sexual desires. Once the sultry blonde bombshell came into view for the first time before legends Jamie

"Take control of your life. Don't let somebody else control your life. If you're thinking about getting into the business, get an education first. Go to school. Go to college and think about what you're going to do after this is all over." SEKA

COURTESY OF *SEKA.COM*

Gillis, John Holmes, John Leslie and Paul Thomas, she swiftly established the pecking order by refusing to participate in a scenario where she felt her boundaries would be compromised. Taking control of her career has been Seka's mantra as is evidenced in her becoming the first female star to become a contract girl for Swedish Erotica. In 1981, Seka's fame was at its peak when she personified her namesake in *Inside Seka*. Five years later, Seka was the first adult film star to appear on *Saturday Night Live* with boyfriend and comedic genius, the late Sam Kinison.

For enthusiasts of the vintage adult genre, Seka is an institution. She is one of a few golden age legends who continues to make public appearances and has astutely honed her innate business sense to ensure she remains a marketable commodity. Since her arrival as an adult entertainer, the unified feeling shared by fans and contemporaries alike is one of respect and reverence. Seka is credited for redefining the female face and vision of erotic cinema.

Mountain Mama

I was born in 1954, and I grew up in the southwest part of Virginia — down in the tip of Virginia next to North Carolina and West Virginia in the mountains. I'm a hillbilly. I have a tremendous amount of family. We didn't have babies. Please, we had litters. I have one brother and one sister, but my mother's family is quite large and we had lots of children. Today, I have about four to five hundred living relatives that are close relatives on my mother's side, and about the same on my dad's side.

Life in the mountains was good. Even though I didn't have a lot of brothers and sisters, I had lots of first cousins and second cousins and everybody just grew up together. You're never alone. It's not like being an only child or whatever. If one parent couldn't take care of the kids that day then everybody just got together and they went to somebody else's house or all played together, so it was like having lots of brothers and sisters. Both my parents were employed doing factory work. When you come from a big family, if your parents are at work then you go to your grandma's house, or your aunt's house, or your uncle's house, or your cousin's or whatever, so there was always someone around.

I didn't have a lot of friends when I was in school — in grade school. I was just like a little ugly duckling child. They used to call me a "little Biafra War Orphan" because I was skinny, and I didn't have any front teeth. I was a tomboy and I didn't like wearing dresses. I didn't want to be a girl. Girls didn't have any fun. They couldn't go and play with worms and dig in the dirt — I wanted to be a boy. I don't know that things have ever changed. I still like to dig in the dirt and play with worms! You can take the girl out of the country, but you can't take the country out of the girl.

As a youngster, Seka emulated iconic cinema idols such as Brigitte Bardot, Marilyn Monroe, and Sophia Loren. When she started to grow into a striking young woman, the spunky teen mustered up the nerve to enter a couple of prestigious beauty pageants in her vicinity and did quite well before broadening her horizons.

I won the high school beauty pageant [Miss Hopewell High School] and Miss Southside Virginia. The high school one was a moderately big pageant and Miss Southside Virginia wasn't as big. That one scared me to death because I had to do a bathing suit competition. I did not want to do that.

I graduated from high school, but during the time I grew up it was more about getting married and having a couple of babies and that sort of thing. It was what everybody did. I was never interested in having children. I never wanted to have children. I liked them well enough, but I never wanted to have any. It's not that I'm not maternal. I love other people's children, but I figured it was hard enough to take care of myself. How could I take care of something else, you know, or anyone else for that matter so I was never interested in having children.

I met my first husband while I had a job selling shoes. He played pool across the street all the time and he was eleven or twelve years older than I was. He was 6'6" or 6'7", and I was like, "Wow, that's a really tall guy and he goes in and drinks beer and plays pool! He's a bad boy! I think I'm interested in that!" The person I was dating at the time was from the same church that I went to and he was shorter than I am. Everyone always wants the taboo. Anything that you can't have, you want, because if you can have it, then there's no challenge to it.

After I got married, my husband wanted kids and I said, "No, I'm not having kids, at least not now." It was about, "Well, we need to start having children," and I'm like, "No, no, no." That was probably what broke the marriage apart. He was sort of demanding that I have children and his parents wanted children and I said, "I'm not going to do that." That's the worst thing you can say to me is, "You have to do that," because I'm going to do everything in my power not to do it. I'm very defiant! I was still a baby. I was only eighteen. Really, the reason I got married was to get out of the house because I knew there was more out there than just the various minute parts that I had already experienced. That's another reason why I probably got divorced too. I had started to listen to rock and roll music — you know, the devil's workshop — bad girl — and I'd had sex for the first time. It wasn't until the day after I got married that I had sex the first time. I didn't even have sex on my wedding night because I was scared to death and I locked myself in the bathroom. Suddenly, it was sex, drugs, and rock and roll. I was like, "Wow! This could be fun! I think I need to be single!"

Sex wasn't what I expected, but I don't know what I was expecting. Still, I thought, "this is pretty nice". It has stayed that way all these years. I know a lot of women who don't enjoy it after a certain period. It's like after they get married and have children they don't want to have sex anymore. I think, "*What* is wrong with you? It's fun and it feels good!" I suppose some women feel tugged on. I know a lot of women who don't have children that don't want to have sex. It's like there's something missing there that got left out when the recipe was being put together. I was in first grade in 1960, so obviously, I didn't ever think about sex until around 1970. I've always been known for my timing though so it was perfect timing, I suppose.

I think most people know that I owned six or seven adult bookstores at one time after separating from my first husband. That was eight-millimeter films. You had the peep shows at the back that were the quarter machines. The way that I had my store set up, I could see all the way down the back so I could see all the projectors running. I'd never really watched adult films before. I wasn't offended by it — just didn't know that much about it.

Blonde Fire & Dracula Sucks

Seka's decision to embark upon a career as a sex performer was predicated upon the simple belief she could present a more appealing image in front of the camera rather than some of the plain girls she observed from her vantage point as the proprietor of adult themed stores. As an eager, self-assured woman, one could argue her motivations were purely business oriented. In the early stages of her career, Seka had a partner.

Ken Yontz, a fellow that I was dating — I was never married to that man, thank the Lord — had the adult stores, and then we eventually got more and more stores in Virginia. When the film would break, you'd have to take the movie projector out and splice the film back together and re-open the booth so that people could watch it. I started seeing a lot of the movies, and I saw what women looked like in the movies and I thought, "This is just a travesty". It wasn't that they weren't pretty women. They could have been pretty women, but the bottoms of their feet were dirty and they had pimples on their butts; no make-up, stringy dirty hair, and I thought, "This is horrible!" No wonder women were perceived at that time as if they were a piece of meat. It was no wonder they weren't admired, and they weren't put up on a pedestal and they weren't treated like the Goddesses that we are. I said, "You know, I think I can do this and do it better" and I think I did. That was part of my intention. That's how I started.

According to some sources, Seka's boyfriend and business partner, Ken Yontz, was controlling and possessive over Seka throughout their tumultuous relationship. Acting as her manager during her rookie years in the business Yontz occasionally performed with Seka and others in some of her early works from 1978-1982. Emphatically, Seka reiterated during our interview that she and Yontz were never husband and wife and claimed any information to the contrary is false. Nevertheless, the young, determined, aspiring star was well aware of her worth. After her first nude photo layout in Las Vegas garnered Seka a good deal of attention, she set her mark on breaking into the adult film business. Intuitively, she understood her potential to become a great asset to the industry. Inevitably, Seka loaned an intangible quality of class and raw animal magnetism to an atmosphere where she could utilize her beauty and home spun smarts to the max. Others followed her lead.

I can remember when I started in films and I'd be working with other women and I would look at them and say softly, "Why don't you go get cleaned up a little bit?" If we got undressed to get dressed for a scene and they started to walk around barefoot, I'd say, "Why don't you put on a pair of shoes so your feet won't get dirty?" or, "Why don't you put some body lotion on so your skin's not so ashy and chalky looking?" Just to help.

They would say, "Oh, I never thought about that." That's something I would have done if I'd been getting ready to have sex at home with somebody I knew. You want to be nice and clean and smell good, and feel pretty about yourself. If you don't feel attractive about yourself, how can you feel attractive to somebody else?

The platinum hair was a mistake. In the beginning, I just wanted a few streaks of blonde in my hair and when the lady finished it was pretty much all white. I was devastated. Afterwards, I thought, "Hmmm…I like this. Maybe God messed up." After all, there's the avocado and the platypus. I think that maybe he forgot to add the blonde hair for me. This was somewhere around 1975, 1976.

The country girl got her feet wet by appearing in a few loops in Baltimore, Maryland prior to debuting under the guise of her new persona "Seka" in her first big screen release which happened to be a porn adaptation of the 1931 classic Hollywood horror picture *Dracula*.

Technically, *Dracula Sucks* (1979) wasn't the first movie that I'd done, but it was the first full length feature movie that I did because I'd done some little eight millimeter loops and things like that and then moved to California and met Bill Margold. He was the one that was instrumental in helping me to get a lot of magazine work first — print stuff, and then I did the features. *Dracula Sucks* was the first one, and I believe *Blonde Fire* (1978) was the next one.

The Freeway Films Production *Blonde Fire* was shot before *Dracula Sucks* (aka *Lust at First Bite*, the hardcore counterpart), but released afterwards as was often the case with many of the earlier erotic features. Set in South Africa, Seka appeared in the beginning and at the conclusion of *Blonde Fire* effortlessly winning adult film fans over as private detective Johnny Wadd's (John Holmes) hot blonde San Francisco squeeze. The apex of the picture, a beautifully crafted, choreographed sex scene is filmed from the top of a ladder producing a highly desirable effect as the actors make love on blue crushed velvet. According to director Bob Chinn, Seka requested a rather robust non-negotiable sum for a partial day's work, but he knew she would be worth it as he indicated in his following reminiscence about Seka.

I was in San Francisco getting ready to shoot the Johnny Wadd movie, *Blonde Fire*, when I first met Seka. My first impressions on meeting her was that she was beautiful, blonde, bold and businesslike, and I knew immediately that she was going to be a big star. She knew that she was going to be a big star. She had come to California from Virginia with her boyfriend Ken Yontz to be a big star, and I could read the determination on her face. Here was a woman who would do what she said she was going to do, and be what she said she was going to be. Here was a woman who already owned adult bookstores back in Virginia who one day just decided to embark on another phase of her career.

I had already finished casting *Blonde Fire*, but I wanted her in my movie so I hastily added a part for her. It was a small part but it opened and closed the film and fit in well with the "blonde fire" theme of the film.

Seka was certainly a diamond in the rough. She was also an extremely sharp businesswoman. There was no negotiating her salary, which was high — much to the chagrin of my production manager. For her part in the film, we managed to negotiate hiring her for a half-day, which put a dent in our contingency cushion but still kept us within budget. *Blonde Fire* was Seka's first feature film appearance even though the second film she made was released before it.

In the veteran stacked picture, *Dracula Sucks* included Jamie Gillis, John Leslie, John Holmes, John Seeman, Annette Haven, Paul Thomas, Kay Parker, Mike Ranger, Serena and Bill Margold. Seka portrayed a nurse overtaken by Dr. Stoker (Holmes) in a mental institution operated by sibling administrators John Leslie and Kay Parker. Utilizing highly potent seductive powers and a hypnotic voice, Jamie Gillis makes a very convincing Count Dracula as he seeks out and overpowers unsuspecting nymphets (Haven and Serena) and others in his wake. Seka's titillating sexual rendezvous with Paul Thomas situated inside of a parked car, chronologically appeared before the Seka/Holmes rape scene. It had actually been filmed after her scene with Holmes.

It wasn't really a rape scene with John Holmes in *Dracula Sucks*. Supposedly, it was, but between John and I that could never have happened because we just liked each other too much. It was very interesting that during the *Dracula Sucks* shoot, I walked into the castle and Annette Haven was coming down the stairs in her peignoir looking like an angel, and all the guys were sitting at a table off to the left having breakfast. There was Jamie Gillis, John Holmes, John Leslie, John Seeman, Paul Thomas — I don't know if Bill [Margold] was actually sitting at the table. I know he was in the room. I walked in and those guys turned around and looked at me, and I was just frightened to death because it was as if I was just a big side of beef hanging there. It was like, "Oh baby, there's new meat!" It just really scared me, and the majority of the men got up and said, "Hello," and introduced themselves and I was very star struck because after all it was John Holmes and Jamie Gillis, for god's sake. I mean, what else could a girl want?

COURTESY OF *SEKA.COM*

As coordinator of the *Dracula Sucks* film project, Bill Margold stated he had arranged for Holmes to take Seka's virginity, metaphorically speaking, which produced some disgruntled campers who also wanted first dibs. The calamity that ensued on the set created a domino effect still etched in Seka's mind.

The first time that I said, "No, I'm not doing that" happened in *Dracula Sucks*. There was a particular actor, who decided that he wanted to work with me before John [Holmes] got to work with me and he wrote a scene in. It was the first feature film for me and I was scared to death. The scene he'd written wasn't in the script and I said, "I'm not working with you." It was a very demeaning thing that he wanted to do and he got a little nutty and said, "Oh, you'll never work again."

I said, "I don't care. It doesn't bother me." He finally pissed me off enough that I took off my shoe and I winged it at his head, and told him to go fuck himself and walked out. The shoe was a Saddle Oxford and they weighed about five pounds apiece. They were huge, they were heavy, and I was glad because I really wanted to hit this person in the head with the shoe and I walked off the set. I would not work with this person until he apologized to me on set. I didn't do the scene and they finally took it out of the script. He pouted for two or three days about it. He refused to work with me because he thought it was going to hurt me, but as most of us know, the women are the ones that draw people to watch these movies more so than the men do. Finally, he had to apologize before I would ever work with him.

It would seem that Seka eventually accepted John Leslie's apology. In 1985, she and Leslie teamed up for *Blonde Heat* regarding the pursuit of a Maltese dildo with Leslie in the lead role as the gumshoe.

That was the only controversy I ever really had on a film. It had to be my first one too! I figured, I might as well get it out of the way, you know. I think I was the first woman at that time that ever said, "I'm not comfortable with that. I really don't want to do that." I think women were afraid to say they would or wouldn't do something because they were afraid they wouldn't work. Whereas, I didn't give a rat's ass — I didn't care. At the time, it was, "I'm not compromising myself for anyone." I don't care what field I was working in. If I'm walking down the street and a man is a gentleman, he's going to step aside. If you do compromise yourself, you'll feel bad about yourself and life's hard enough as is so why should you make yourself feel bad?

A few hours before John [Holmes] and I were to do our scene that we had to do in the barn, he said, "Come here. I'd like to talk to you." We sat down on a stump out front of the castle and he said, "Let me tell you something. Always respect yourself and don't ever do anything that you don't want to do. If you want to say 'No,' you say 'No,' and don't feel bad about saying 'No.' Just be true to yourself." I've always remembered that and I've always stuck by it. I don't know if that's something that helped me to take my shoe off and wing it at this other person's head or not, because I was so pissed off at that moment. I really wasn't thinking except that I knew I wasn't going to do what this other person wanted to do. From that point on, John was always my favorite guy.

Learning the Ropes

Seka began to augment her feature film work by appearing in Swedish Erotica, Blue Vanities, and Erotica Collection loops. She illuminated how the process of shooting and performing in an adult movie was not unlike acting in a typical Hollywood film. Apart from participating in actual sexual intercourse, it was all about lighting and angles.

I was horrified because I didn't think I looked good. Not the sexual performance because I knew that was good, but the acting part I thought was horrible because I know I'm not an actress. Quite a few people in the adult business are quite good actors and actresses, but I'm not one of them. I don't care because I've never considered myself an actress. Jamie Gillis was very good. He did some off-Broadway stuff and studied in theatre. I've just considered myself a performer. I've never professed that I am an actor. I don't think I can act. I know I enjoyed what I did so that wasn't acting. I enjoyed what I was doing. It was real. I'm a performer period, but not an actor. I couldn't act my way out of a paper bag.

I was completely okay with performing. You do get more used to seeing yourself. The first time that you see yourself nude and having sex — it wasn't that I felt intimidated by that by any stretch of the imagination, but because I had seen other people in adult movies, I was like, "Oh man, I was so horrible." I would cover up a shot using my arm and you couldn't see me giving head. It's just the little things that after a while you learn how to suck cock on screen. It's not as if you're at home in your bedroom. It was, "Okay, it doesn't matter how uncomfortable you are, it looks good to the camera." After a while, it becomes natural. If you're giving oral sex to the man, it's natural to put whatever arm is facing the camera down to the side or over your head so that the camera can see it. It's the same thing that any actress or performer would do in any other kind of movie. You learn where the camera is and where your lights are to make the scene work. Just because you happen to be performing sex, doesn't really make it any different than if you were doing any other movie, it's just that you learn your craft. After you learn your craft, then you learn to enjoy it within those parameters.

In adult films, everybody always has sex on top of the kitchen counter that is hard and cold. If you look at these movies, they take place in a bathroom stall, on a cement floor, on a chair or on a kitchen counter. *Puleeaze!* People don't do that! Once in a great while if you have a wild hair up your ass, so to speak, you might want to get crazy and have sex in an alley way or something. Generally speaking, most human beings, if they're watching an adult movie they're laying in bed where it's comfortable. It's like, "Oh baby, we can go to the alley-way or the elevator," but that's not what normal human beings do.

The niche group of actors who worked together during the golden era is identifiable to adult fans because of their individuality which made it relatively easy for purveyors of sexually explicit material to feel a sense of kinship with the actors.

The first time you have sex with someone in a film it's not always the best because you're not familiar with each other's bodies. When we were working in the late 1970s, we worked together a lot because there weren't that many of us. The fans could get to know you.

In 1980, Seka portrayed Ilsa, the Nazi Secret Service Officer in *Prisoner of Paradise*. The role, a spin-off character from the 1975 film *Ilsa: She Wolf of the S. S.* enabled Seka to have fun by unleashing her "Hyde" alter ego as her character taunts and tortures three American captives: sailor Joe Murray (John Holmes) and two nurses (Nikki Anderson and Brenda Vargo). Stranded on a remote Pacific Island outpost during World War

II, the American prisoners are subjected to various forms of physical and sexual cruelty doled out by Ilsa and the other German officers, as Murray struggles with his own demons to become courageous. Despite some of the antics deployed for effect in *Prisoner of Paradise*, after learning her lesson on the set of *Dracula Sucks*, Seka was determined she would not allow herself to be pushed around again.

Seka and John Holmes.

In *Prisoner of Paradise* for example, in the scene where I looked as if I was beating the girl with the riding crop — I would not do that. I did not do that. I said, "I will not beat this woman with the riding crop."

They said, "Well, you have to."

I said, "No, I can tell you what you can do is you can move her. You can get the motion of me moving my arm. You can put a pillow there for me to hit and you can put a sound effect in later. If you want, you can spank her butt and make it red, and make it look like she was hit with a riding crop. Or you can have somebody else do it to her and have me doing the motion, but I will not do that because it's not something I'm comfortable with." That's because it's not going to be true. It's not going to come off as looking true, or convincing, or anything else. They finally said, "Okay." They really wanted me to beat this woman and I wouldn't do it because it was not a spanking. Those things really hurt your butt or any part of your skin that you smack with riding crops. I wasn't about to do it. We eventually figured out another way to do it without me physically having to do it...I'm a convincing German, Nazi bitch though, huh? It was funny.

Gail Palmer (Parmentier) is often attributed as the lead director on the set of *Prisoner of Paradise* and other adult pictures because of her personal relationship with porn distributor Harry Mahoney at the time. Bob Chinn, who actually directed the lion's share of the scenes, once again shared his memories of having had the opportunity to work with the platinum megastar.

> *Prisoner of Paradise* had a much larger budget enabling me to cast Seka in a starring role. She was perfect as the cruel, over-the-top, Nazi SS officer stranded on a remote Pacific island outpost during World War II. Most people don't realize that this film is simply a strange surrealistic fantasy about a stranded sailor who must become a hero while coping with his own personal demons by rescuing two nurses held captive by psychotic Nazis who perform sexual experiments on them. Seka did, and we had a lot of fun shooting this picture. I found Seka to be very easy to work with. I found her to be smart, efficient, down to earth, and a rarity in this business — a true professional. She is indeed a "Golden Goddess."

Inside Seka

In 1980, Seka embodied two signature roles in feature films which proved to have a long shelf life in the adult genre. All decked out as a futuristic alien in *Ultra Flesh*, Seka is sent to the earth to cure the male populous from impotency in the star-studded vehicle directed by Svetlana. Also launched that year was *Inside Seka*, a collaborative directorial effort with Joe Sarno and Ken Yontz, co-starring Ron Jeremy, R. Bolla, and George Payne. By the time the quasi-documentary was released, Seka's platinum locks were almost as famous as Seka herself. The star became immortalized when the film's publicity team rolled out her new title: "The Platinum Princess."

That was Video-X-Pix. When I did *Inside Seka* they put "Platinum Princess" on the box and it's stuck all these years which is why I still have to have my hair this color! I do like it. I've gotten used to it after thirty-some years.

Inside Seka is the vehicle that truly showcased Seka as the glamorous porn diva she is. Stylishly dressed throughout in crisp, white blouses and tailored skirts with an opal pendant and gold diamond rings adorning her necklace and fingers, Seka's elegance certainly doesn't detract from her ability to get down and dirty when the scene calls for it. She does so while wearing gorgeous lingerie and hose with matching stilettos as she and various partners set out to pleasure one another. Touted as samplings of Seka's real life sexual engagements she makes love with Ken Yontz throughout the story while tales of her many erotic liaisons, are depicted.

One of the standout scenes is Seka's tryst with the lovely Merle Michaels who almost rivals Seka with her fashionably coiffed hair and nails. The two ladies kiss sweetly before getting undressed and move fluidly into the sixty-nine position. Passionately, they bring one another to explosive climaxes before a third party (Ron Hudd) joins them. Ron Jeremy's now infamous auto fellatio scene is included in this film which spectators might wish to fast-forward through if this isn't your particular preference. To Jeremy's credit, the procedure is executed with his typical humor and good-natured manner while in the role as a company Foreman. None too pleased his three employees are being blown by Seka, he complains to deaf ears until Seka tells him to "go blow himself." He decides to do just that.

In the closing scenes, Seka, Yontz and another couple (Sofia Solana and Anthony Mann) slip into Plato's Retreat in New York. After sipping a few drinks poolside for a while, the foursome joins in the fun as they enter the "Mattress Room." Here, orgy magic is happening in a Fellini-like fantasy, an amalgamation of tongues and exposed body parts within a cloudy den. Interestingly, Yontz is described in Seka's own written words during the closing credits as her "husband" of six years which could infer a common-law marriage.

My film work was something I did and I enjoyed doing. I made very good money at it, but I never really thought a whole lot of people would see it. It wasn't something that really concerned me whether they did or they didn't because I wasn't embarrassed about it or ashamed of it. I had no idea that it would last this long. No clue whatsoever. It wasn't my intention to go to Hollywood to be on the silver screen to be a star. I went there because it was something that I chose to do and that I wanted to do, and I was living in California so what was the downside? At the time I was thinking, "Wow, I can get paid. I can have sex with a hot guy that's going to be really good sex. I have a great afternoon. I get laid and I have an orgasm and I walk out the door with money in my hand." Damn! Bonus!

On the other hand, there are so many different emotions — not so much emotions, but trains of thought. At first, I really didn't think of it as a business. I had no idea it was actually going to be my career. I didn't think of it that way. In the beginning, I thought it was fair. I was getting paid good money. After the first time that I did an autograph signing at a convention in Chicago, the light bulb went on because they had printed five hundred pictures for three days. I thought, "My god. What are they thinking? I'll never go through five hundred pictures." Well, the first half of the first day we were out of pictures. That's when the light bulb went off and I said to myself, "Holy crap. I'm not getting paid enough money. We're going to have to even out the playing ground here." So I asked for more money and I got it.

In addition to demonstrating a good head for negotiating on behalf of her own best interests, Seka reinforced the importance of having been part of a tight recognizable group of entertainers. Up until 1981, adult performers were still a small community of people which allowed for selectivity of on screen partners. Seka counted the men and women whom she truly enjoyed working with almost on one hand.

I liked John Holmes, Jamie Gillis, Mike Ranger and Randy West. What I liked about John is that he was respectful of me. He always treated me very kindly and he treated me like a lady. So did Jamie Gillis. There was something intriguing, and dark and kind of sinister, sexy about Jamie. Mike Ranger was just like the All-American California boy. Cute, very cute, and very nicely built. He knew how to use everything he had. I liked Randy West just because he's Randy and he's gorgeous. He looks better now than he did before. I also liked working with Serena, Kay Parker and Jesie St. James. I enjoyed working with Jesie St. James because she was easy. She was easy going; she wasn't a prima donna. She wasn't prissy or "I'm the star here, I've been here longer than you have". She treated everyone equally and so did Kay Parker. Serena was interesting. She was very quirky — hippie-ish. She liked everybody and she was very kind, and still is very kind. She's just a very sweet human being. I absolutely love Veronica Hart. She's my all-time favorite person in the business — Veronica and Kay. I think that's a good line-up of people.

The old saying goes, "There's a new one at the bus stop every day that has run away." There were a lot of runaways back then too, but the people I worked with weren't like that. We were just a small group of people. Little did we know that they needed us more than we needed them; we were already established and helped build their inventory and their empires.

Seka took a break from films in the early 1980s when she resumed photo layout work and travelled on the road to feature in nightclubs. Stirrings about a reputed problem with substance abuse in the eighties caused the truth to become distorted.

There is one thing that a lot of people do not know. I did not do drugs or drink when I was working. When I was actually doing movies, I knew about pot and I knew about cocaine. I didn't do them. I didn't even drink much then. I didn't start drinking until I hit my mid-late thirties. When I was actually performing and making movies, I didn't do drugs. I just wasn't interested in it. Did I do it afterwards? Absolutely, and I had a good time. I would do it again if I could, but I can't. I'm too old. I would kill myself. I'm surprised that I'm still alive. I know it was said that I was in rehab for a year. That makes me laugh because I don't know anybody that goes into rehab and stays for a whole year. Did I do drugs? Absolutely! Did I abuse them? You're fucking right I did and liked it! When I decided it was enough and that I couldn't do it anymore or I was going to kill myself, I put it aside and never did it again. It didn't bother me, I didn't experience symptoms of withdrawal — nothing, because I'm not an addictive personality. Do I think about it sometimes? Absolutely, I do. I think, "Oh, my god, it'd be nice to do a big fat line right now". Would I do it if it was in front of me? No, I wouldn't do it.

Drugs were part of the entire entertainment industry. It wasn't just the adult entertainment industry. Because people so objected to adult entertainment, it was just another tool that they could use to try to stab and bring down the industry which is bullshit. I'm not going to lie about having done drugs. That'd be silly because too many knew I did it so if I lied about it, many people can crawl out of the corner. When I said, "I'm done," I was done. I stopped and that's it. When I realized that I was not only in the process of killing myself, but that I was going to die if I kept doing this then I stopped doing it, period. I liked me too much to kill me. It was like, "Damn! I'm fucking up!"

COURTESY OF *SEKA.COM*

The drug use wasn't a grey area for me, but I think that it was for a lot of people. The statement that this one person made saying that I was in rehab for a year did piss me off. It didn't hurt my feelings, but it pissed me off because number one, it wasn't true, and number two, they said it because I didn't want to work with them.

What a lot of people don't realize about drugs in general, is that you can be a drug addict and you can use drugs, but you can use drugs and not be an addictive personality. You can put it down and not pick it up again. People that have problems with drugs, just like people that have problems with alcohol are addictive people. It's the same thing as people who can't eat one chip only. If I have any addiction at all, it's food. I love food. I'd be eight or nine hundred pounds if I let myself because I love food and I love to cook and eat.

I did one movie after the period when I'd stopped making films and that was *American Garter* (1993) [directed by Gloria Leonard and Henri Pachard]. It was my last film, except for the one that I produced, *Careful, He May Be Watching*. It could have actually been before that, and then I did *American Garter* — that was the last film that I did. I was doing drugs at that time, not on set, but it was in my life. After I was done, it was like, "Okay, I can't do this anymore. Goodbye. Let's find the next new thing to play with."

"The Platinum Princess" Meets "Brother" Sam Kinison

In 1986, Seka became the only celebrity in adult films to make an appearance on the widely watched television show *Saturday Night Live* after a chance encounter with comedian Sam Kinison led to a romantic liaison. Kinison, a converted preacher known for his outrageous comedic executions generally delivered in a loud and raucous rant, died on April 10, 1992 in Southern California. The vehicle he was driving was struck by a seventeen-year old drunk driver.

Sam was fun. We had a good time. It wasn't anything that was serious, serious. It was mid-late 1980s. I went to see him at one of his shows, and I was laughing my ass off and he wanted to meet me because he liked my laugh. I ended up travelling with him for several months. We had a very good time together, but it was difficult being around Sam because of his drug use and my drug use at the time, too. Eventually, we just parted. He lived in California and

I was in Chicago, and I wasn't going to move to California. We were connected off and on — more on, for a period of about two years.

Sam was an amazing comedian and he was very, very smart. He was a preacher. He'd studied theology and it was hard to argue with someone who has studied theology. It really is because they're very smart people. Most comedians I find are very intelligent. The stuff he could come up with off the top of his head was amazing. Because of the drugs, it just got very bad at times and I couldn't do that anymore. I don't think he could either. He finally straightened up and was on the straight and narrow as far as his drugs and alcohol were concerned when he had the car wreck and got killed. He'd been straight for about a year I think — maybe a little less. That was devastating. He was such a great talent and it was such a loss. He'd just gotten married. *Back to School* (1986) with Rodney Dangerfield was hysterical.

Sam Kinison.

Saturday Night Live had wanted Sam to do the show. He'd already done the show, and there was controversy over something he'd said or done and then they wanted him back. That was when I'd just started seeing Sam. He said, "I'll only do it if you have Seka on". He figured he wouldn't have to do the show again, and then they agreed so he had to do it.

I started the show with "The Church Lady". Dana Carvey used to live in the building that I lived in, in Chicago. "The Church Lady" and I did the whole "It's Saturday Night in New York," or whatever that whole thing is. I was very well known at that time. I don't know if it is on YouTube, but I have it somewhere on VHS tape and I can't find it anywhere.

The following dialogue is excerpted from the "Church Lady" skit that appeared in the fourth episode of the twelfth season of *Saturday Night Live* in November 1986. "Church Lady" played by the brilliant comedian, Dana Carvey set the table for Sam Kinison and Seka's entrance.

CHURCH LADY: "It just gripes my bottom that, right now, they're getting ready for their dirty little sex show! I just don't think we should have to *stand* for it! In fact — well, gosh, darn it, I'm not gonna stand for it! I'm gonna put a stop to this! Gosh, darn it! Where is Mr. Kinison? Where is this *sinner*? Where is this insurgent? Where is he, I know he's here! Where is that diabolical disciple of depravity?! Has anyone seen that paunchy prince of perdition?!"

(Church Lady finds her way into a back hall, where Kinison stands with his girlfriend, Seka)

"Oh, that — oh! Look! There they are! The sinner! There they are! Oh! Look at you!

(Stops, notices Seka)

"Seka? Oh, I've only seen you in — well, what are you doing here with this *awful* Sam Kinison? He's a *terrible* influence!"

SEKA: "Stop trying to run my life, Church Lady. "

(Tosses her hair)

CHURCH LADY: "Well! Apparently, some of us don't care too much about our little reputation, *do* we? Isn't that super?!"

(Seka makes a flagrant display of feeding Kinison from her fingertips)

CHURCH LADY: "So — well."

SAM KINISON: "You know what you need?"

CHURCH LADY: "What's that?"

SAM KINISON: "Well, you need what I was *just* about to give to her."

CHURCH LADY: *(Glances back and forth between Kinison and Seka)* "Well, I have no idea what you're *talking* about!"

SAM KINISON: "I call it a *real* touch from God!

(Pulls Church Lady down and gives her a big, wet kiss on the lips. The Church Lady is flustered as he finally releases her and then turns to face the camera with a fury)

CHURCH LADY: "Live from New York; it's Saturday Niiiiiighttt!!"

Careful, He May Be Watching

I can only speak for myself but I never felt exploited, taken advantage of, demeaned or any of those things. I chose to do what I did. It was my choice, no one else's. I was not guided by anyone to do it. I liked what I did. I got paid well for what I did. I didn't do anything I didn't want to. If you're going to do something, be proud of what you do. Own it and make it your own, and if you feel like doing something else after that, it doesn't mean you tossed it away, it just means that you've added something else to your collection. Yeah, I did that and I did it well. Now I'm going to do this and I'm going to do it well, as well!

Careful, He May Be Watching (1987) is a film that I wrote, directed, produced, raised money to produce, and I played two parts. I own *Careful, He May Be Watching*. Residuals on the film were offered to me. They said, "We'll pay you X amount of dollars and you can have so much on the back end." I didn't trust it. I knew I'd never see the money so I took as much as what I could get up front and be done with it. You would never deal with a lot of the same people twice, and you never knew who was where, or doing what and it was nutty. I just said, "I want this amount of money — take the rest and do what you want." People of my era helped to build a place where people do get residuals or could own their own companies. We didn't at the time because we didn't know any better.

In every respect, Seka's rendering of two contrasting personas is superlative in *Careful, He May Be Watching*. As the married thirty-something Jane Smith, and porn star Molly Flame, the story is a representation of a hefty portion of the female population with a private desire to be more unreserved in the bedroom. Wearing shorn platinum hair enhanced by carefully applied eye make-up and lined lips all serving to highlight her high cheek bones, Seka is a Goddess of grace and beauty.

By day, Jane Smith is the unassuming wife of a handsome airline pilot Bill (played by the actor sometimes dubbed "Clark Gable of Porn," Mike

Horner). After hubby leaves for work, Jane morphs into a hot new adult screen idol Molly Flame. Disguised in a red wig, designer sunglasses and a full-length fur coat, in her anonymity as Molly, Jane is free to explore everything onscreen she is too frightened or timid to attempt in the arms of her husband. In a hilarious recreation of a real porn set, Jon Martin plays a stud for hire and is severely reprimanded by the director Harry (Misha

Careful, He May be Watching. VIDEO-X-PIX. COURTESY OF *SEKA.COM*

Garr) for climaxing inside of his superstar partner rather than pulling out for the money shot. When Harry bellows that his "talent" won't be receiving a check for his shoddy work, the stud shouts back, "I don't give a fuck! Besides, I don't accept checks. I'm only paid in cash!" Meanwhile, Jane's husband is about to get a little on the side himself. Bill begins to fantasize about one of the flight attendants, Miss Cummings (Shanna McCullough). In his daydream, he engages in a sexual rendezvous with her, only the fantasy soon becomes reality. Afterwards, Bill suggests to his wife that Miss Cummings join them for a threesome. Up until this stage, Jane has turned down Bill's offer to share their bedroom with another woman, but after "Molly" experiences a little girl-girl fun with another big star Annie (Kay Parker, who does a great job in the dominant role), Jane is finally open to Bill's idea. In the end, everybody winds up happy and satisfied, and Jane's alternate identity continues to be concealed from her spouse.

Toward the end of the 1980s, major changes in the direction of Seka's personal and professional life took hold. She and Ken Yontz finally parted ways after spending more than a decade together. In 1988, Seka testified before the Meese Commission in an opportunity to join her co-workers in opposition of the report's conclusion (with unfounded evidence) that viewing pornography produced harmful effects upon society.

I did testify in front of Edwin Meese and the Senate Subcommittee on First Amendment Rights and things like that. That was a fight worth fighting because it was for freedom of speech for everyone. It wasn't just for women. As human beings, we have to stand up for ourselves and be self-thinkers as leaders and not followers. Do what's true to your heart. We're all human beings, and it doesn't matter what your gender is.

After more than ten highly successful years in the business, excluding her return for the aforementioned movie *American Garter* in 1993, Seka made her departure from films and began to consider new prospects.

I walked away from doing films because I didn't want to disgust people by taking my clothes off in front of a camera and having sex at fifty-five! I'm not going to do that to my fans. I mean, my god, they've been supportive of me all these years, why should I devastate them? I don't feel bad about the way I look, but it's just not something that I want to do anymore. When I was twenty-five and thirty years old, when I had sex, there were things that didn't move. I'm not ashamed of the way I look now, but a lot of things move and when things start moving, it doesn't look all that great! So no, Mommy won't be doing that!

Yesterday and Today

I think that my career has influenced my life in a positive way. I don't have any problem with my friends knowing or my neighbors knowing. Either they accept me for who I am, or we're not friends because I don't have time for that kind of narrow-mindedness. What I did does not change the kind of person I am or the kind of human being I am. Either you like me because of the kind of person that I am, or you don't. You don't like or dislike me because of what my career choice was.

My family had all known my plans before I did the first film. I told them what I was going to do, and I wanted to be the one to tell them so they didn't have to find out from a neighbor or a friend and be in shock. I wanted to let them know ahead of time what I was going to do and their reaction was, "If you think it's going to make you happy, go ahead." They were very supportive and still are to this day. I'm lucky that way.

I think of myself as a very independent thinking, very self-assured woman who is comfortable in her own skin. I know what I want and I know what I like, and I know what I don't like. If I've helped pave the way for any women, I hope it's because they've seen that it's okay to be a woman and not because they have to fight to be a woman. I don't think we should have to fight to be a woman or a human being. I think it's our right.

Like many other women with her past employment record, Seka discovered it wasn't easy to modulate from adult entertainment to regular work, but she accepted her lumps and was patient. Seka wisely advised the younger generation of sex performers about how to be smart when considering work in the adult business.

Own your own name. Do your own register. Do your trademark. Do your copyrights. Own your own product. Own your name so that people can't rip you off. If you have photographs done, own them. Take control of your life. Don't let somebody else control your life. If you're thinking about getting into the business, get an education first. Go to school. Go to college and think about what you're going to do after this is all over. What are you going to do when you're fifty-five years old and you're not in front of the camera anymore? How are you going to support yourself because what you did in your past is never going to go away — trust me, it's hard to find a job. Society is not as forgiving as we are to one another. It is like, "Oh yeah, you'd make a great receptionist at a hotel or whatever," but once they find out that you've done adult movies you're gone. Society today might be accepting of sex, but I don't think they are accepting of sex performers.

I've bartended off and on for thirty years. Trying to find a bartending job at times was very difficult but it was great. They liked me because I was pretty and I had big boobs so I would draw lots of customers in, but a lot of places once they had found out that I had done adult films, I was gone. "We don't want that element around us." It was okay if I was a customer, but I couldn't work for them. That stigma remains today. Still, I wouldn't change anything because to me if you want to change anything about your life or your career, then you have regrets and I don't have any regrets. If you change anything about your past, you're not going to be the person you are now. I like who I am so I wouldn't change anything — except the color of my hair. It would be naturally blonde.

To her credit, the entertainment industry warmly remembered Seka years after she'd stopped performing in movies. In 1997, she was hired to host a Chicago radio program called *Let's Talk about Sex* on 97.9 FM that enjoyed a three-year run every Saturday evening from ten pm until two am. During her time in Chicago, Seka kept tabs on her two favorite sports teams: the Chicago White Sox and Chicago Cubs.

The reason I got the radio show in Chicago was because of my name, but even when I worked as a bartender and was let go I looked at that as someone else's stupidity. It was all about them. It wasn't about me because I was still the same person. I was a great bartender. It didn't change my ability to do something. It was their perception.

I think the filmmakers and performers are lazy in today's movies. There's no story. Not that ours were so great. They were trite but there was a reason to have sex. There was a beginning, and middle, and an end. Instead of the scene opening and everybody's naked and everybody starts screwing. It's like "Oh wow. That's exciting." What's sex without foreplay? You might as well not do it as far as I'm concerned! It's like taking a pitcher out of the bullpen and throwing him right into the game before he warms up. It's no good.

I don't think there is any individuality in the way they look. They all look the same and they just seem so robotic. Everybody has big blonde hair, and big, pumped up lips, and big, pumped up boobs. When I was doing films, there were red heads and brunettes and blondes. The guys all looked different when I worked. Now they all look like they're pumped up on steroids with all these muscles which I don't particularly like myself. I like a guy to be fit, but all these ripping muscles? I can't grab a hold of anything. It's like trying to grab a cement wall. I want to grab a hold of some meat and hang onto it! I'm sure they're all very nice people, but as far as films go, it's just not exciting. It's so violent. To me, violence and sex don't go together. If you like a little S&M, if you like a little B&D, okay, no big deal. Climaxing in some girl's eye to give her pink eye or choking her with your cock until she pukes or passes out? That's sexy? I don't think so. What is sexy about that? It's violence. If anybody should feel violated, it's the people of today. I think we've just become so desensitized to everything that there's no passion anymore. I don't watch porn because it's so disgusting to watch.

Again, the difference between when I was working in movies and the girls and guys who are working now is there were only a handful of us. We didn't have a different sexual partner in every movie we did. You got to become familiar with the other person so there was some sort of camaraderie and communication, and you could see that you were comfortable touching that person, or being in that person's presence. It made it more realistic, whereas now, I don't know if anybody works together more than once or twice. For ten years or so, there were about eight or ten-twelve guys and eight or ten-twelve girls and you worked together so it was like you were going to visit an old friend.

Golden Moments

In 2002, Seka's international fame inspired two Swedish filmmakers, Christian Hallman and Magnus Paulsson, to create a unique documentary that set about to track down the star in a flattering exposé which also contained several career highlights. *Desperately Seeking Seka* culminated in a final interview with Seka unpredictably revealing her excellent culinary skills and affable, fun-loving nature. After playing at various movie festivals the DVD was released in 2004, and includes many bonus tracks. To date, Seka is one of a few female icons in adult entertainment to have been made the sole subject of a documentary. In 2012, she was interviewed for another documentary, *After Porn Ends*, which examines the careers and post adult lives of some of the biggest names in the industry.

I think the women of the golden age of porn have definitely left a legacy. We helped open the doors for the ones that came behind us in the same way the ones who were in front of us did. We made it easier for them to work and to get more money, to get paid better and to own their own names, to own their own businesses within the industry. We paved the way for that. I feel that we were able to let young women know that it was okay to be an adult entertainer and to feel overwhelmingly proud, classy, and good about themselves rather than saying, "Someone forced me". I've seen a lot of girls who do that, when, in actuality, they weren't forced to do anything, but it was easier for them because that was their way out. It was, "Oh, I was forced to do this, and now I can get out."

You have to remember that nobody's going to take care of you, but you. My motto with people is, "Sweetheart, it's you first — after me. It's always, me, me, me, and then maybe you." Once I've taken care of myself I can help you, but I can't help you unless I have taken care of myself. It's a lot like loving yourself — if you don't love yourself than how can you love anyone else? Damn, I love me a lot! I think that's why I'm fortunate enough to have a lot of friends. I have a tremendous amount of friends and I don't mean friends that you can toss out a name, but very good friends that I've had for twenty-five, thirty, thirty-five years. I think it's because if you can't like yourself, you can't like anybody else. You can't take any shit from anybody. There's no time in life. Life's too short. Smile and have a good time. You don't have to be rich to be happy.

I met with Seka in Montreal in September 2009 when she traveled there on a business trip with her husband. We went out for champagne and crêpe breakfast at one of her favorite little nooks in the picturesque French Canadian city before heading back to her luxury hotel room to chat. At fifty-five years old, sprawled out on the plush, king-sized bed in her spacious room, Seka is as glamorous (and at times wily and bombastic) as one might expect as she punctuated her entertaining tales with boisterous laughter. Since relocating to Kansas City, Missouri, Seka continues to root for her favorite sports franchises and when time allows, she books time to make special appearances at Adult Shows and the occasional Horror Conventions. Seka is also busy polishing her autobiography. Towards the end of our morning together, her twinkling eyes danced when I asked about her life today.

Life is good. My love is my husband and my cat, Jake. She's a female named Jake. She's sexually challenged but that's okay. She's an old girl, so it doesn't matter!

Unfortunately, Seka's beloved Jake passed away in 2011 but she has since adopted a new kitty, Miss Tippy, to fill the void.

I like to dig in the dirt and play with bugs and grow my garden and cook, and do a little travelling. I have girlfriends in the neighborhood and we have our little girl's night once a week. We go out and have drinks or a light dinner. I live in Kansas City right now. I don't plan on living there forever. I'd like to eventually be in Costa Rica or Panama City. I want to be somewhere where it's warm all the time. I'm tired of the cold.

One of the most memorable days in my life is when I got married to my current husband. It was on August 23, 2006. I got married in the Grand Caymans on a little island on the beach, without any shoes. It was beautiful. It was a nice breezy day and we were right on the ocean. Friends and family came down. I'm going back there in November because my nephew, who was my husband's best man, is getting married on the same beach in the Grand Caymans where we got married. My husband has no kids which worked out well because neither one of us wanted children — little ankle-nippers! I'm in the process of writing a book which I'm pretty much done with — I just haven't closed it up. It's going to be called *Inside Seka* and it will have the cover of the movie, *Inside Seka*, because it's the most recognizable movie that I did. I hope it will be out in a year, but I've been saying that for two years. I'm finished, but I just have to finish putting it completely in order. Everything's written and the pictures need to be put together, but I know exactly where everything is going to go. I've just been lazy. As you know, or anybody who writes or does a book, there are certain times when something hits you and you just stop. It's not that it is writer's block it's just that it's not right yet. It's just not the right time. I'm also very involved with my website: *seka.com* — so people can come and visit me there.

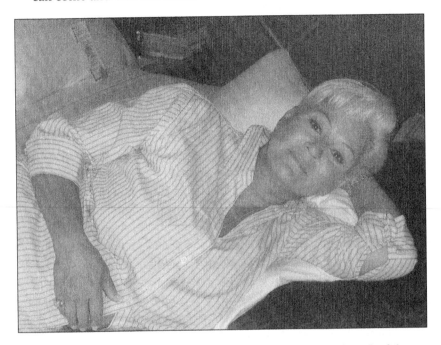

As someone who is pleased to be a part of this book and of the legacy of golden age women that I feel were special, I'd like to say thanks to everybody who was there and was supportive. I couldn't have done it without everybody who was supportive of me. I truly and gratefully mean it. Thank you.

17.
Kelly Nichols
Kiss and Make-Up

The most spellbinding feature when observing Kelly Nichols (born Marianne Walter) face-to-face are her amazingly luminous eyes. With Susan Sarandon-esque charm and a voice that echoes comedienne Ellen DeGeneres, the auburn-haired Nichols is an intricate mosaic of personas. Raised in the San Gabriel Valley, the only girl in a family with five brothers steeped in the Catholic faith by parents with good intentions, Kelly made a secret pact to herself that she would remain a virgin until she was eighteen. She kept that pledge. As a young woman conflicted by her religious beliefs, Nichols converted to fundamentalism in her sophomore year where she discovered a sense of belonging in a leadership role and achieved a kind of hierarchy within the group. One year later, Kelly received a partial scholarship to study commercial art, but dropped out and moved in with a boyfriend. While contemplating her next move, Nichols strode into the offices of Sunset International Agency and signed an agreement to do nude layouts for *Hustler, Penthouse* and *Swank* magazines before ultimately moonlighting as a make-up artist. The modeling work not only brought Kelly steady income and stability, but it instilled within her a newfound confidence within the presence of men. Encouraged to obtain her SAG card by an agent who recognized her unique acting talent, Nichols soon received offers for small roles in legitimate films. She was cast as Jessica Lange's stunt double in the $80 million grossing film *King Kong* (1976), and made waves in low-budget softcore horror flicks namely *The Toolbox Murders* (1978) where she is billed as herself, Marianne Walter.

A string of appearances as a stage performer at Sex World in New York City enabled Kelly to transition to hardcore films in 1979 where she turned out compelling performances in *Roommates* (1981) along with

"I've let them know that their mother was in naked pictures early on and that I was in naked movies, but you don't give your kids valium, you don't give them alcohol, and you don't give them porno. You take it as it comes." KELLY NICHOLS

co-stars Veronica Hart and Samantha Fox, and *In Love* (1983) in which she won Best Actress Award from the Adult Film Association of America (AFAA). Nichols also received a Lifetime Achievement Award from the Free Speech Coalition and she was inducted into "Legends of Erotica" in 1996. Although her career as an X-rated actor officially closed in 1984, Kelly reunited with former co-star Tom Byron in 2009 to prove to herself she still "had it," and passed with flying colors.

As she works to maintain control over her sobriety, Nichols' immediate plans include reaching out to faithful fans and admirers via the internet as her continuity in make-up artistry for adult productions keeps her active and connected to old friends in the business. When she's not preoccupied with future projects or working her matchless magic for actors on movie sets, Kelly retains a deep and liberal connection with her two grown daughters.

I spoke with Kelly Nichols via Skype late fall, 2010.

One Love

I grew up in a large Catholic family in the suburbs of L.A. in the other Valley called San Gabriel Valley. I was the oldest and the only girl with five brothers. My mother was very Catholic, my father was Lutheran and then he converted. They moved to San Gabriel Valley after they met at the University of Chicago. They're both intelligent people. My father worked two jobs while my mother raised the first three of us, and then finally, he was able to make enough money working for an insurance company in his one job to quit his second job.

I went to a parochial school. My mom did everything she could to make sure that I could go to parochial school and become a real good little Catholic girl. I attended Catholic school up until my freshman year and then they couldn't afford it anymore and they put me into public school. It was the best thing my mother could have done because going to Catholic school was like living in a bubble. You're not really getting any real information. Living in suburbia was a bubble, so I was put into a bubble within a bubble within a Catholic bubble.

My parents were happy. My dad was overworked and my mom was pretty much Catholic and had all of these kids and took care of them. She was raised with the "spare the rod, spoil the child," philosophy so the three of us who were the oldest, were pretty much disciplined by corporal punishment, literally. When my father quit his other job, he kind of came down on her and made her stop doing it so much. She was from the Midwest and had kind of a staunch attitude towards things. It was "spare the rod, spoil the child," but at the same time when it came to sexuality, my mom never really discussed it with me. I think she wanted me to be married before I did anything is what I kind of got a sense of, but she never said anything. She never actually put sex down to me so I never had any words in my head that indicated sex was wrong or bad. Even when I was in the Catholic Church, the nuns didn't talk about sex. Nobody talked about sex. I assumed it was something that was a bad thing to do until you got married, but no one ever said that. I didn't have to feel guilty to enjoy myself!

I liked art and used to draw all of the time and I played guitar. I was either drawing, playing guitar or reading. I played with my brothers, or babysat my brothers, more likely. That was kind of it. I didn't know that I was a loner. I wouldn't call myself a loner at the time, but looking back, I can see that I was pretty much a loner. I was considered a freak in elementary school. I was the one the kids teased. I was the tallest one in class and I had size ten feet in grade eight. I was the proverbial ugly duckling. I had a wicked sense of humor, but nobody shared it, so I bonded with guys more than I did with girls because my mom kind of raised me as one of the boys. I played asphalt football with them and had very few girlfriends.

The only type of acceptance I received came from a Jesus movement in my sophomore year and I became Born Again. We used to meet in garages and have sing-alongs and meet in church parks and stuff. I got very good at quoting the bible and became kind of a leader for a while. I got five liturgies introduced that they literally still teach today at my old high school. I was involved in setting up a Christian newspaper. It made me feel like I was doing something. It started out not to be a fundamentalist group. It started to be where we'd meet in coffee shops and sing and give about testimony and stuff, and then later, while I was still in high school, I sort of glommed onto this First Baptist kids group. They were Born Again but they were like in a Junior League and they belonged in the choir. They didn't drink or dance, but they still had a lot of elements that were in the other group and for some reason, I got more into this. Probably because I saw them all of the time and I was gaining some kind of seniority in that group, so for a while it was good. Then I properly decided myself "this is bullshit" by my senior year. I didn't see that they were any better than the Catholics were. I sort of thought there was more behind it because they were explaining the bible, and then I realized that so much of Christian belief is how to do context thinking and it really kind of made me check out other religions. I clearly went through that religious self-questing which did lead to something else. After a while, you just kind of accept a world religion and a world God.

I remember the first time it blew my mind. I dyed my hair and they all looked at me and thought it was a sin. I was ostracized, and I thought "Well, if that's religion…" It was very much a wake-up call. I didn't join the group to date guys or anything. It was a social group and it was cool for a while.

Catholic Girls Start Much Too Late

Kelly's years of diverse religious influences, beginning with her early Catholicism indoctrination instilled a certain ethical code she aspired to honor. Those conditions included a self-made vow to refrain from sexual experimentation until she was late into her teen years. Once Nichols permitted herself to let her guard down, she realized her capacity to attract and seduce males. Unsure of her future, Kelly compiled a short mental list of what she didn't want out of life.

I made a promise to my mom that she doesn't even know I made, but I promised her in my head that I was going to wait until I was eighteen to have sex and I did. I picked up a boy who liked *Star Trek* and played paddle tennis. He was twenty-two. The summer after high school I did that and got it over with; I felt I just needed to get it over with so I'd know what everybody was talking about.

It was terrible. He was terrible. I got emotional and started crying. He looked at me as if I had five eyes and it was like, you know, someone's first time and painful and just dumb. It didn't stop me from doing it because I realized afterwards that it was a real power trip. If you can get a guy to stand at attention — guys really pay attention when they're sexually interested, and all of a sudden, I realized that I could get them to pay attention to me that way. It made me embrace the power of it and made me realize what a powerful thing it was.

I ended up with a partial scholarship to art school and I needed to pay for it, so I started to go away for about six months. I was working at a Bob's Big Boy and I wasn't making any money, and I was getting really tired of being used as a baby sitter at home. I knew there was more out there. Where I lived was so land-locked. Their idea of career counseling was, "What do you want to be? Do you want to be a teacher?" or "Do you want to coach?" There were no real options out there. In fact, one of the options I almost took advantage of was the Navy. They came in and gave me a test and I scored real high on it. I tried to talk my mom into letting me join the Navy! I had a few more ideas than anyone was telling me in school, but she wouldn't let me.

I went to art school and it was formalized. It wasn't fine art; it was commercial art. I moved out of my house and my boyfriend at the time moved to another apartment, and he let me sublet his apartment. I just moved out overnight when I was about almost nineteen. I started looking in the Want Ads. I knew I wasn't good at waitressing and I wasn't good at typing. I just needed to do something so I could figure out what I wanted to be when I grew up kind of thing. I wasn't motivated to go back to college because it kept seeming that I'd have to move back home to be able to afford it. In my little trials and perusing, I found an ad for modeling at Reb's Sunset International. I called them up and they had me come in. Reb's a biker kind of guy.

Reb Sawitz, the oldest former agent in the adult business was a part-time biker and the landlord of an apartment building in 1968. Sawitz opened up his own agency, Sunset International, after he was solicited by Anton Stone and Associates and brought them out of the red. Starting in the late 1960s and throughout his time as a proprietor, Sawitz and Sunset International ran ads in local newspapers seeking nude models and talent for softcore and hardcore loops. They also hired performers for adult feature productions.

This was around 1975. I started doing nude modeling. At first, it was just about being chased around tables by photographers but it didn't bother me. It was kind of interesting because I had never liked my body that much. That was at first, and then I started meeting some real notable photographers who were shooting for magazines. They not only liked using me as a model, but they liked my make-up. All of a sudden, I was being paraded around as a make-up artist and doing nude shoots for *Hustler* and *Penthouse* and *Swank* and *Genesis* magazines. Then I'd do the rounds all over again. I'd collect different wigs and cut my hair differently and they just kept using me, it was great. I had a whole livelihood working as a nude model for many years and doing make-up. The modeling

PHOTOGRAPHY BY KENJI

paid better, but the make-up was more consistent. They pay much better now than they did back then.

It was fun. It was very fun. Every day was a different place and I enjoyed the photographers I was working with. It was challenging. I was very good at what I was doing, and I was learning the whole time. The more faces you have in front of you, you keep trying and

you just keep learning things. I would apply what I had learned in Art School or what I had learned as an artist. It also made me feel that I wasn't dependent upon the nude modeling so much. I'd also joined Hal Guthu's Agency. He was the one who always pushed the idea that I should get my SAG card and he thought I had all kinds of potential being an actor. He was the one who got me into *King Kong* (1975) and he was the one who got me into *Toolbox Murders* (1978). I was a straight actress also. A straight actress and a porn star!

Talent scout, Hal Guthu, who had an eye for spotting raw acting ability in Nichols and others, saw his instincts actualized when Kelly started to pick up work in mainstream films and "slasher" pictures. In *King Kong* (1975), she was hired to play Jessica Lange's stunt double, a grueling eight month shoot that also starred Jeff Bridges and Charles Grodin.

I also got a lot of non-SAG parts in screamers [films]. I have about seven credits in SAG films but the rest were low budget, softcore, horror films where we'd just get chopped up and run around. That's where I became known as the "Scream Queen". It's fun because I can go to conventions and people still know me as "Marianne Walter, the Scream Queen," and they want my autograph as "Marianne Walter". Then some of them will come and say, "Are you also Kelly Nichols?" I'll say, "Yes."

I saw myself actually die on screen before I saw myself in a porn movie which is kind of strange. In *The Toolbox Murders*, Cameron Mitchell breaks in. I'm taking a bath, and I'm masturbating a little bit and I have bubbles all over me. He comes in and I jump past him, and he chases me around the room and then he shoots me. We have dialogue for about ten seconds and then I run out and he shoots me and I die. I die in this chair with my eyes wide open and he puts this veil over my eyes. It's horrible! That's the first time that I saw something graphic of myself, really blown up.

In the visually gruesome story, the perpetrator played by Cameron Mitchell in *The Toolbox Murders* wears a ski mask and wields a collection of carpentry tools leaving a trail of dead females in his wake after a torturous rampage. In her portrayal as Dee Ann one of the stalker's victims, Kelly's presence in the exploitative horror picture considered by many critics to be mediocre in its genre left an enduring impression on slasher and porn fans alike. Nichols (as Marianne Walter) and Mitchell (in a non-sex role) later appeared in director Anthony Spinelli's *Dixie Ray, Hollywood Star* (1983) starring Lisa DeLeeuw and John Leslie as a private investigator.

I would have probably stayed with acting if love hadn't come along! I met my first husband and that kind of got me all messed up and questioning everything. He was sort of a neurotic alcoholic with many personalities. None of which I knew about when I first met him. He would shame me about the nude modeling, but he wouldn't mind taking the money. He talked to me about marrying him, and then he kept breaking up with me and getting back together. He could be violent. Then he moved to New York City, and called me from there and said, "You've really got to come out here and we can start all over again." I was so missing him and I was so hurt at that time. It was stupid. He said, "I'm doing camera work at a theater." I literally sold everything that I had, my car and everything. I did a couple of back-to-back magazine shoots and jumped on a plane, got there and found out he was working at Show World in New York. He was not operating a camera; he was actually operating on stage with another girl. I'd sold everything so I was stuck there.

Show World, the former adult emporium in New York City formerly located at 42nd and 8th Street operated in its prime years between 1975 and 1995 during an era where live sex shows (and peep shows) were the order of the day. In 1995, a zoning ordinance passed by City Council restricted adult theatre owners from operating in the heart of the world class city forcing Show World to eventually close down in 2001. The mezzanine has since been replaced by the Laugh Factory, and the one time upstairs theatre was leased to an off-off Broadway company in 1998. Young Marianne Walter, who ventured solo to New York City to hook up with her boyfriend in the late 1970s, accommodated his wishes by becoming his new stage partner at Show World

It wasn't a big deal. I'd been nude in front of the camera so many times and with another nude male model, so it just seemed like an extended version of that. I never felt I had to justify my feelings about it, I didn't really feel one way or another. I was used to being disappointed by my boyfriend. I was disappointed in him because he was the one who was always coming down on me for being in sexual situations because of what I did for a living, and there he is on stage. He said, "If you don't want me to be with other girls then be with me." He took me in and introduced me to all of his friends at Show World, and all of a sudden, it just seemed like a job. He got me to come on stage and do things for Show World with him various times. It was kind of a little naked lesbian community! You got to make up your own story and script it and go on stage. Find someone to fuck, get off, and then do it five more times that day. It was interesting. It was during that time that he introduced me to [director] Chuck Vincent, who was my Svengali: the one who first got me into the films. "Kelly Nichols" was created and then it took off! That's how I got into porn. If I hadn't been in New York, I would not have gotten into porn because it was just too illegal in L.A. at that time.

Opening Up

You're probably more aware of your feelings as a sex performer, but I still think that just by being a nude model and the way you are a nude model you are opened up. You're not just nude modeling, you are "opening up". In a gynecological way, you're opening up. If you can do that and pretend you're looking up at the sky or the sun, and just go off in that place in your head, you can pretty much do anything past that. You can have anybody shove anything into you or do anything, because it really is you in your own imagination.

When I was with a guy, I'd be in a caretaking mode and I'd want to make sure that he was comfortable and that he was getting hot and off. That's part of my power thing with sex. I've always liked the fact that guys get hard-ons for me so that was probably just like some complete sexual perversion I'd create for myself. You look at the camera and the lighting person and you just tune them all out.

Early on, I actually did more critiquing of myself to determine whether it seemed natural rather than giving the appearance of reading off of a script. Then the next thing was, "How does my body look?" I'm very critical of my body. So I'm not even thinking about the sexuality or the act. Apparently, I'm good because I make terrified faces and terrified faces depict orgasm. You just go, "Ah!" Ah!" Ah!" like you're going to explode! Oh, my god! People give you awards for it! It was later on I'd get letters from jail that these guys would write in crayon, and they'd say how much they enjoyed my work. You didn't realize whom you might be influencing. It's never a bad thing; it's just that you're in an insular kind of situation. When you were doing film, you didn't realize how few performers there were. That was pornography; it was distributed all over the world. There were only a handful of us so everybody saw the few of us.

Kelly validated the presumption that a vast number of adult entertainers felt encumbered by social protocol and values embedded in traditional religious denominations and that working in pornographic films helped them to break free. In fact, it's not as transparent as that.

I've often thought about that and I think that I am a closet exhibitionist. I'm a closet exhibitionist so it was a way of showing off as a ham. Whenever I was a thespian, I was always a ham. It was a way of showing off. It was also a way of getting a dollar value out of a body that I personally didn't think was all that great. If someone was willing to pay a great deal of money to look at me, to me, that was concrete evidence that my body was good enough. They were paying for it so that threw me for a loop that my body was okay because I never really liked my body that much. That was a part of it. Some of it could have also been a "fuck you" to my mom and

Harvey Magazine.

all of the Catholicism I was raised with. It's funny, because when I was working most of the girls were Catholic and most of the boys were Jewish.

It's just something as simple as not having any sisters and not being a boy, and wanting to be one of the boys but not having the body to be a boy. This kind of validated that I was a girl on some level too. Instead of being a boy, my career was such that I was able to put on lacey things and strappy heels and be sexy, and people thought I was sexy and pretty and that was a good part of it too. As far as my facial features go, I have been told I have marble eyes. I get the cross that I look like Susan Sarandon and when I smile, I look like Goldie Hawn. I wasn't against opening myself up wide, so I did put on lingerie, and put on make-up, and put on pretty faces and had people tell me how pretty I was. Many people have a job description where two thirds of the job they like and one third they don't. So, two thirds of my job I really liked and the one third? Well, okay, I'll just factor it out.

It was seamless in the beginning of my adult career because Chuck [Vincent] is gay. I'm talking about a man who is like an older uncle who is gay. I was introduced to him by my ex-husband who would normally flip out about something like that but he introduced me. Chuck promised him a part too, but he was looking for a brand new girl to create a new identity with and take her to Europe and pay her "X" amount of money.

Michigan born Chuck Vincent began his career in entertainment as a stage manager and director in regional theatre prior to helming his own production company, Platinum Pictures, in New York in the early 1970s.

One of the reasons I became an X-rated star too I have to tell you, is because the travel was fabulous. I got to go all over Europe to so many countries and I was wined and dined, it was just wonderful. I had never been outside of the country before. We were broke in New York and it was like, "okay". It was fabulous! Chuck liked the fact that I had been in *Penthouse* a couple of times and that I presented myself well, and that I could memorize dialogue because his films contained a lot of dialogue. We just kind of all agreed on it.

Nichols' first experience in a sex film was positive which made it easy for her to continue to accept offers and keep working.

I was offered my first venture starring in Europe where they did all of the exterior stuff, and then we went back to America where we spent two weeks shooting the hardcore which I did with Jack Wrangler who is gay. My first sex scene on camera was with a gay man and I had no idea until right before our scene. I was supposed to give him a blowjob in the car, and I was walking over to the car and someone said, "You do know he's gay."

I'm like, "Oh, man!"

Vincent's *Bon Appetit* (1980) introduced Nichols in the title role as Faith, an uneducated caterer stuck in a rut with an out of work boyfriend (Roger Caine). On a whim, she is retained for $250 thousand dollars by a "high society" Cougar (Gloria Leonard) to bed the world's best lovers in fifty days and provide a full report. Faith's assigned photographer (Randy West, with whom Nichols had apparently enjoyed a brief affair) must accompany Faith and document the proof — which he does with reluctance at first. Nichols is outstanding as "Faith" particularly when pretending to be a model posing for an artist (Ron Hudd) who becomes completely unglued by her seductive banter until he has no choice but to cave to the pressure in his jeans. Equally enchanting are Kelly and West; they network with one another smoothly when out of bed and with sexual enthusiasm when under the covers. Kelly's scene with Jack Wrangler (playing a Hollywood celebrity) is brief and appears towards the end of the film. Considering this was Nichols' debut hardcore feature, she is remarkably loose and relaxed with all of her conquests.

Wrangler (John Stillman), who was openly gay, married popular 1940s singer Margaret Whiting twenty years Wrangler's senior. *Wrangler: Anatomy of an Icon* (2008) is a recommended documentary about Wrangler's life and career. He died in 2009.

For starters, it worked because [Wrangler] had already done two successful films for straight people and the whole AIDS thing hadn't blown up in our faces yet. We were still coming off of the seventies a little bit and everything was still cool. I just said, "Okay, Jack. What do you need me to do?"

He said, "Oh, honey, put your head down there and I'll do all the work." He did. I just bobbed my head a few times, and he made "Oooweeee…" sounds and it was just the sweetest thing. We remained friends for quite a while. He was a good friend. I find it very humorous that the very first person I had sex with on my first film was gay.

In another Chuck Vincent treasure, *Games Women Play* (1980), Nichols, Veronica Hart, Samantha Fox, Lesllie Bovee, and Merle Michaels shared center stage as five models making men and breaking into the New York fashion scene. Ron Jeremy, Jack Wrangler, and Roger Caine fill the bill in the stud department.

I was actually working in a very interesting time in adult where all we were doing was creative positioning. There was no anal when I started. We started doing anal around 1984, but I wasn't in any of the anal movies. I accidentally had anal happen to me one time on a movie where somebody actually backed into the wrong place. It was funny and we all kind of just laughed at it. We didn't do complicated positions, or double penetrations, or ass to mouth or any of that stuff. It was just finding cool positions and utilizing them. If you go back and look at the old films, you'll see that the scenes don't last for longer than a few minutes, but we would shoot for an hour and a half. I wonder where all of that footage went for the movies! They just edited it down to here and the rest was dialogue. As long as I had dialogue to do, that was great.

In the premature years of the illegal pornographic film business very few sex acts seemed to fall under the restricted category as anal and double penetration scenes were often performed in loops, feature films, and Swedish Erotica montages. Risky maneuvers in sex pictures however, were designed to guaranty a bust creating mega publicity for films and stars resulting in raids of several adult theatres.

Probably primarily anal scenes were done in the sixties and seventies, but not as much then as later on. I noticed that when we were pulling away from doing it, there were a lot of amateur companies happening in the eighties before all of the Europeans started buying up all of our stuff. We were literally being overrun by amateurs with video cameras and the Europeans expected a little bit more for their money. When anal started being introduced as kind of a regular diet, I think the Americans started to buy it a little more and it became more accepted. When I was doing films, it didn't seem to add to anything, and I certainly wasn't called upon to do it. It never occurred to me to offer my butt up either! There's a big difference between what the Pussycat Theatre allowed on its screen, and what the smaller theatres showed in their back rooms.

Nichols' statements regarding the menu pertaining to her film work are worth noting: Kelly performed an anal sex scene with Harry Reems in *Society Affairs/Jet-Set Orgien* (1982*)*, and agreed to do a double penetration scene with Billy Dee and Rocky Balboa which can be seen in Alex de Renzy's *Dirty Girls* (1984). With the interpretation of the term "double penetration" (or "DP") evolving over the years to indicate the act

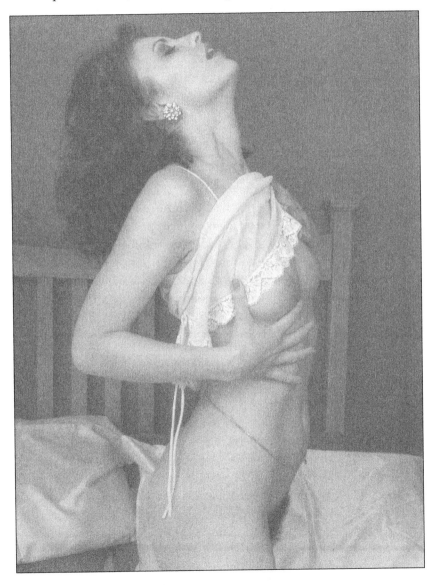

of inserting two penises into one orifice, it is possible Kelly is accurate in stating she didn't participate, but had instead been involved in a "sandwich" scene. "Sandwich" is the correct slang terminology for the insertion of one penis into the vagina and another penis into the anus simultaneously.

I'll tell you one thing, we didn't have a "no" list. The girls nowadays have a "no" list. I was called to work with any of the guys and I worked with them because I knew them all, there were like ten of us. There weren't that many of us and it was just not a big thing. I pretty much knew they all had my back and I had their back. We all were very at ease with each other.

In Love with Kelly Nichols

One of the reasons we worked in porn is because there was kind of a rebellion about it — there's still a little bit of that bohemian — fist to the man, kind thing that was in all of us. We just didn't play well with others. We did play well with ourselves, but not with others and it kind of kept us from circulating. I think when the adult stars starting getting more video, the Hollywood stars realized they had more opportunities to meet the porn stars who were interesting. Especially when you could start bringing video home, the stars really got interested in the porn stars because they didn't have to sneak into a theatre to see it, they could rent them. You certainly saw the girls partying more with the stars — the Charlie Sheens, and so on. Not so much when I was in it, we were really our own kind of dark little thespian group.

For many years, porn stars and Hollywood celebrities have gravitated toward one another, but no other "A" list actor has attracted media attention for his admiration of sex performers in quite the way that Charlie Sheen has. Tabloid TV reporters sensationalized Sheen's unique living arrangement in the winter of 2011 when cameras were invited inside of his "Sober Valley Lodge" to film Sheen and his two "Goddesses" (one of the girls was former porn star, Bree Olson, aka Rachel Marie Oberlin) at play. As the saying goes, nothing compares to the good old "golden" days.

I loved Samantha Fox. Veronica Hart and I are still very good friends. Sharon Mitchell, even though we never worked together, we're really good friends. We know one another well. Ginger Lynn is a sweetheart. I like Ginger. She knew the game really well. Those are really the Golden Girls.

By the early eighties, Kelly Nichols was no longer one of the new girls when extenuating circumstances caused her personal life to unravel. During the disintegration of her first marriage (Nichols was married to

PHOTOGRAPHY BY KENJI

writer Tim Connelly, aka former performer Dick Howard with whom she made appearances in several of the same early eighties movies, but apparently not together), Kelly used drugs heavily and began to show signs of bulimia, she started to binge and purge. Nichols also was the victim of an attack on her home. At the time, Kelly's parents were not around and the events of her life culminated in a feeling of loneliness and loss of self-control. Nichols decided to join the Marines; she was accepted after passing the physical and underwent stringent training. Meanwhile, Kelly was offered one of the leads in *Roommates* (1981) with a cast that included Jamie Gillis, Jerry Butler, Jack Wrangler, Veronica Hart, and Samantha Fox. Kelly put the brakes on her plans to become a Marine. Nichols is outstanding in the Video-X-Pix feature *Roommates* in which she shares the limelight with Veronica Hart and Samantha Fox as one of three friends rooming together in New York City trying to build a new future while hoping to put old habits behind them. In a show-stopping performance as Sherry, Kelly plays a coke-addled aspiring commercial actor whose penchant for a fix lands her in some dangerous and desperate scenarios. Manipulated by men (mainly Jamie Gillis in a particularly creepy and menacing turn) who use and abuse her, every single scene in which Nichols appears is marked by deep and intensely raw emotion. Additionally, Fox and Hart are both sterling in this irregular piece.

I worked with Jamie Gillis for one film (*Roommates*) and I think he was nominated for Best Actor, but I'd seen him around before that. We'd sit there and nod to each other. We had a place that was called Bernard's that was open until four am and any time of the day you could see three or four porn stars hang out with our peers. In Europe, we had a kind of community and there was a little community like that in San Francisco.

In a tongue-in-cheek nod to Kelly's brief brush with the Marines, Chuck Vincent directed Nichols in the campy *Puss 'N Boots* (1982) where she played Private Priscilla "Puss" Mason. "Puss" joins the army and instigates a series of mishaps between the female privates, soldiers, and civilians.

The early to mid-1980s were good years for Nichols in front of the camera as one feature film followed another. Adult fans were treated to Kelly in Roberta Findlay's *Glitter* (1983) with Shauna Grant, Rhonda Jo Petty, and Marlene Willoughby. Several other releases in which Nichols enjoyed prominent billing are *Pleasure Island* (1984) and *Dixie Ray, Hollywood Star*, an exceptional 1983 release directed by Anthony Spinelli. The incomparable Lisa DeLeeuw played Hollywood legend Dixie Ray on the downside of her career. Blackmailed by her ex for some compromising photos of herself, Ray hires a PI (John Leslie) to track him down. Nichols and Leslie's characters eventually find themselves together in a hotel room where they get nasty after some wickedly sexy foreplay. Kelly doesn't bother to remove her panties while riding the veteran actor cowgirl-style leaving Leslie drenched in sweat at the conclusion of the money shot.

John Leslie was funny because he reminded me of a soap actor. He was very witty but very on point. I'd say that the one thing that the boys in the business shared is narcissism. I think you'd have to be kind of narcissistic to be a porn star.

In 1983, Nichols commanded the lead in *The Mistress* as Karen, a young, single woman employed by an architectural firm. A consummate professional in most aspects of her life Karen's Achilles heel is her tendency to date married men. When her boyfriend/boss Carl (Eric Edwards) offers her a plum promotion and she accepts, Karen realizes there are certain strings attached. She is expected to sleep with potential clients (married and single) the firm is courting, or she must look for other work. When Carl stands Karen up at Easter to spend the day with his family rather than with her as he'd promised, a epiphany arises for Karen as she flashes back to an identical scenario with a previous lover (Randy West). Realizing she needs to change her pattern, Karen walks.

Nichols does a fine job communicating her character's hope and disappointment in this taut nugget of a film. She is easily the object of desire with her large, dramatic eyes and mouth, coupled with her quiet, gentle demeanor. Directed by Jack Remy, *The Mistress* co-stars Juliet Anderson and Richard Pacheco, both fulfilling non-sex supporting roles.

> I loved Ritchie [Pacheco]. We had the hots for each other but we didn't know it when we first met. He thought I was being cool and he thought I was into girls. I thought he was too cool for school, so I just sort of ignored him but I thought he was very cute. We came together later on, many years later when we did a shoot together. We ended up spending all night together because we had so much fun and we were like, "Wow, we should have known this about each other." He was just a good buddy and a good actor to work with. Richard Bolla (Robert Kerman) was also a good actor to work with.
>
> The film that I won Best Actress for at the AFAA [Adult Film Association of America], which would be equivalent to the Erotic Awards, is what I would consider my best work and is a film I did after *Roommates*. Jane Hamilton won Best Actress for *Roommates*. I won Best Actress for *In Love* which I did the following year. *In Love* is what I consider my most significant role because I did carry the whole film. Chuck cast me as the lead and I was pretty much doing lead stuff. I was almost never cast as a best friend or anything I was always a lead. I didn't realize what a gift it was until later on. That afforded you the most man attention, the most amount of money, and the most amount of dialogue.

In Love (1983) is the fifth film Nichols appeared in for director Chuck Vincent. It became the most significant picture of Kelly's body of work because of her pure and unfiltered embodiment of a woman in love. Jerry Butler is exceptional as Kelly's leading man, and once again, Jack Wrangler is part of the cast while Henri Pachard (Ron Sullivan) is credited as writer. The four-hanky picture is a classic.

Kelly Nichols with Jerry Butler in *In Love.*

One of the directors I loved was Henri Pachard. He had so much energy. He'd come on the set and he had a little glass of water and everybody knew it was mostly vodka. He'd be all fired up and he'd say, "Let's get this show on the road!" He'd be, "Let's get this party going!" He had more energy than the youngest of us on the set. He made it fun and it was just so great. Chuck Vincent was not as good a director, but he could cast people really well together. He would cast people who could work off of each other. Typically, he wouldn't have to direct, the people would direct themselves. He was very good at that. After video, it got sad because all of sudden they cut all of the dialogue out. That was one of the reasons I quit too because there was nothing in it for me after that because the dialogue was at least holding my interest.

I think that pornography is the microcosm of Hollywood in a lot of ways. It was interesting because the time that I was doing it, they were getting more dialogue — this was before Beta and VHS, and before you could rent the films and take them home. We were still competing with Hollywood films. *In Love* and *Roommates* were playing at straight theatres during the same time they were playing in porn theatres. In fact, they both got write-ups with [American film critic/columnist] Judith Crist. That was kind of interesting so Hollywood was getting nastier and we were getting closer to mainstream. We were getting closer and closer to the punch and then Home Video happened.

Big Bang Theories

Women such as Serena and Juliet Anderson were adamant their orgasms on set were legitimate while others such as Rhonda Jo Petty claimed responses to pseudo lovemaking are usually feigned. Nichols dished that it's a gift when a woman experiences a real orgasm in a sex film even though most of the moves and intimate overtures are carefully orchestrated.

I wanted to come across a certain way. I wanted to build the scene just as I would build my acting, so in my mind I wanted to be in control of it. When you really are having an orgasm, you are in anything but control. Lips are flailing; your eyes are rolling back in your head, so I tried to pretty much control and give the viewer what he really wanted. There were different times on screen where

I actually came because it was just hitting all of the right spots. I had about an eighty-five percent rate of controlling it and fifteen percent not controlling it. Now, the girls are funny. They're pissed off if they don't get an orgasm. The younger ones especially, but it's a job! You're laying on your back and getting paid for it, but it's quite physical. When you're getting into different positions and

Swank Magazine.

someone is pounding you and the size of the package delivering is bigger than the average guy because that's what you need to see on camera — that continual pummeling can be like a work-out. It doesn't necessarily mean that you're wetting up for it. You're taking one for the team and you just go on and close your eyes, and grab the pillow and murmur and act as if it's good. You've got to make sure that the guy feels it. In this day and age, they just take some kind of pill to stay hard, but back then, they didn't have any pills or anything like that.

While some of the actresses either faked or didn't fake their orgasms, the male performers had a lot more at stake in achieving an erection on cue, and afterwards, climaxing while a community of their peers and crew patiently (and sometimes impatiently) looked on waiting for fireworks.

The men who worked during the golden era period really had to earn their money. It was amazing to find one who could do it twice in one day — that was crazy. It's not just that they had to get hard for the girls — they had to get a hard-on in front of a multitude of guys. There are guys on the set, so you've got other guys looking at your junk. It's not always nice. The stagehands could be so sabotaging. They could say and murmur the nastiest shit and the guy would hear it. Some of them would do it just because they weren't porn stars and they weren't making the money and they would do it to deliberately sabotage the scene. Usually the environment was good, but you would have disgruntled people and guys who had been up too late or taking too much crank or whatever. It could be kind of nasty. If anything, I would be able to identify with the disgruntled make-up artist because I'm with him, I'm the first one to get there and the last to leave and I don't get paid that much.

The outside world has somewhat of an interesting view of porn sets and that the girls are being mishandled, but they're actually not. Unlike what Linda Lovelace was saying, we do control a lot as far as the actual work environment. We don't have a gun to our heads. If there was ever a set I was on as a make-up artist and there was mishandling of the girls, I would totally speak up and call someone immediately. Some of the little girls who have gotten into it, they went through grade school and high school knowing that once they got out of high school they wanted to do porn because that way they could meet musicians and some of the stars. You know, it's a real rock and roll career to a lot of people. It's the money and the rock and roll appeal. Guys will like them and they'll get to be in music videos and stuff. I would say that the worst thing is that they take them at eighteen years old before the girls really have a chance to know what they're capable of or what a good decision is. I really didn't get into it until my mid-twenties. I kind of wish they would do that with the girls now, but it will never happen because the age of consent is eighteen and the guys want to have their fantasies.

There are some girls where their mothers actually got them into the business and there are some girls where it's fine with their families, and some of them come to their awards shows. Sunny Lane would be a great girl to talk with. She's got a real open family and they've got a crazy relationship. She's had longevity; she's still in it. She's [porn director/adult actor] Tommy Byron's girlfriend. It's cute because when she goes to the awards shows she always takes her mother and her dad with her.

Since the legalization of sex films in the state of California, there has been debate as to the appropriate age for a female or male to enter the erotic movie profession. Hypocritically, society appears to have greater concerns about the welfare and potential for the exploitation of young women in X-rated movies than they do young men. A given individual's level of maturity definitely plays a factor. As a feminist who is also a porn star, Nichols made a point of clearing up misconceptions with a novel analysis of sexual performers.

I would say that having the right to use my body anyway I want to, is the ultimate in being feminine in a lot of ways. I chose to take on the profession whether I was a prostitute or a porn star. I like the porn star aspect because the guys get paid and you don't pay the guys. There's something when you're a pro, the guys are paying you and I think that diminishes the male. When the males are getting paid too, you're both on a level playing field. You both feel like you're a part of something.

I've gotten together with feminists through phone calls and sitting around in discussion. Ultimately, at the end of the day, they could not disagree with me that it was about standing up and deciding what we wanted to do with our bodies instead of the government telling us what we wanted to do with our bodies, or a boyfriend telling us what to do with our bodies. We are using that judgment. Like any job description, there are going to be ones who are going to cause trouble. Often times the trouble makers like squeaky wheels, made the most amount of noise. There will be the occasional kind of situation where some pimp brought his girl in and wants her to get tested and work or there will be an abusive director, but that doesn't last long because it's not tolerated. We've

Kelly Nichols (pictured top left) is featured with Veronica Hart, Candida Royalle, Annie Sprinkle, Veronica Vera, and Gloria Leonard. PHOTOGRAPHY BY DONNA ANN MCADAMS

never tolerated child abuse or anything, that's a whole myth. It's up there with the myth of fluffers. Mostly in the nineties, they were doing the scenario where how many guys can this girl fuck. They were marathon films and they literally needed tons of girls to keep the guys hard and then move on.

The term "fluffer" describes an individual on the sidelines hired to "blow" a penis in order to produce or maintain an erection in preparation for the male's imminent ejaculation scene. Although it is no longer commonly done, fluffers have served their purpose on porn sets over the past forty years. Former adult female performer Houston reportedly had sex with over six hundred men in *The World's Biggest Gangbang 3: The Houston 500* (1999), a colossal exaggeration. According to the movie's description, several "fluffers" were hired to keep the men hard so they could get the job done. In truth, male participants in gangbang productions are generally inflated artificially without the aid of fluffers. "Snuff" films continue to be part of the urban legend and contradiction congruous with the adult film environment. The term "snuff" cited earlier in this book is used to describe the alleged "snuffing" out of a participating actor during shooting — literally, committing homicide.

I worked for Roberta Findlay who did the film *Snuff* (1976). I asked her about snuff films and she said, "If that stuff existed it existed only in the hands of someone who paid to have it done and it would not be in public domain." It's something someone would do and then hand it off to the person who wanted to do it again and again. I think porn's purest form would be stuff that was shot in real time using real movies of the person. I guess you have something to that effect today when people film themselves in their own home. We worked in kind of a choreographed way that made it beautiful. It was false, but it was beautiful. It had its own kind of uniqueness and it was very art deco.

Nothing Lasts Forever

In the early eighties, young Nichols had the foresight to predict the course of the future for adult entertainment once shooting on videotape took hold.

At first, video films were quite expensive. The Video and Beta was about one hundred dollars or you could go to the theatre. I was friends with all of the guys at the Pussycat Theatres, and I used to be the one girl who would sit around and drink with them and I'd tell them outright, "Guys, you've got to change your business because people can take the films home and no one will go to your theatre," and no one did anything. They lost fortunes. I was just a little porn star in 1982 going, "It's going to change guys," and by 1984, it already had.

I think that technology pushes it where it's supposed to go and at this point it's kind of gotten weird and sleazy and chopped up because we're not making movies at all anymore. Movies don't sell at all. Why do that when you can go to a free website. There are a lot of free websites out there showing blowjobs and other things. On a free site, you can get a half hour of that and you don't have to put any money in. That pretty much puts caterers, make-up artists, lighting people, everybody out of the business except maybe the camera guy. That isn't as much the older guys because the older guys are used to corralling full groups of people to shoot. These younger

Chic Magazine.

guys come with a camera and shoot the girl who is sucking him off or somebody else, but it costs very little. There are so many girls right now. There are so many agents and so many agents have so many girls that it's the antithesis of when I worked. There were so few of us and now there are too many of us. There was some place to put it, and now there's no place to put it.

As a sage in her field, Kelly extolled particles of wisdom for young people coming into the fold.

I would tell kids today that there's not that much money in it. You'd be better off doing Escort service. I'm so fucking serious. If you really want to make money on your back, get with a good Escort service. The money is not that great in porn anymore and it's not as if anyone is going to see the evidence that you were in these films so your parents and your relatives will never see it. You'd have some longevity as an escort and you'd make more money than you would as a porn star. You work very hard as a porn star. They have the girls doing so much stuff these days. They come in and they have to do

the softcore, the hardcore, the softcore stills, the hardcore shoot —
cum in the face. Then they have to put all of their clothes back on
and do all of the dialogue from the beginning. The girls are there for
hours and hours when they actually shoot a movie. Even the parodies they've been shooting lately are running its course. They were
kind of the thing for a while and now everyone is doing a parody.

There are many web shows on the internet to create where you
could get invested in characters and they're like shows that you
would see on TV, but they are on your computer. I see people doing
sex web shows where you can actually track characters. There are
people out there who actually care about characterization. I have
a lot of fans that love my characters. There are a lot of men who
want to get their rocks off and get that much more, but they just
don't want to pay that much more because the price has dropped
so much. Why pay fourteen or twenty bucks for something that
you can get on the computer?

Putting aside the infinite differences between the old days and the new, I
wondered how Nichols might constitute the legacy of a "Golden Goddess."

A "Golden Goddess" legacy would probably be your "Golden
Goddess" on the silver screen. It's our best memories of a group that
brought something very interesting to the vernacular. Porn could
be in the gutter and awful, and so could low rent movies, but you
had people work hard to elevate and bring it up to a certain level
where the women were photographed stunningly. They were given
wonderful things to say and interact with their co-stars so that there
was a reason why they would fuck and make sense. It was just the
best way you could portray it. It was old fashioned and best way to
portray pornography. We've become like Old Hollywood. It's like
the old star system where the studio would groom the actor, and
he would come out of that studio and then they would push him
at the movie theatres. Then television came along and that became
a group of different kind of actors.

There were a lot of people acting before you had the golden star
who put their footprint down. Yeah, we had very few stars. We also
had a vehicle, a theatre. People would come to see a "Kelly Nichols"
production. They treated us like old school. No one is really standing out today. The girls who were huge in the 1990s are just scraping
by. No one even knows them now.

Family Matters

I actually quit the business in late 1984-85, and I met someone in New York, literally, the night I had walked off the set. Someone had ripped off my purse. My second husband at that time was cheating on me with another girl and I just walked off with this guy. We spent three days in a hotel and I just didn't want to come out. When I did, my second husband had kind of moved this girl into our apartment so I stayed at my girlfriends' and just sort of decided to quit the business. I quit him, I quit the business, and then the guy I had walked off with and I had a happy little mayhem — that's a little sponge I was using at the time as a birth control method. I got pregnant and decided to keep her. In 1986, I had my first daughter, and in 1987, I had my second daughter.

After meeting her third husband, budding screenwriter John Skipp and had two daughters (they later divorced), Kelly kept her hand in the business primarily as a make-up artist. She also appeared in sporadic non-sex or BDSM roles. According to her filmography, in 1996 Nichols also participated in a boy/girl scene with the late adult actor Jon Dough in *Night of Seduction*. Drawing from her reputation as a female star and skilled make-up artist, Nichols is one of the very few who kept a healthy balance between performing and other pursuits that didn't include capitalizing on her physical assets for financial benefit.

I moved back to California in the nineties and I started back doing make-up again. I had done make-up earlier on and then I had two kids so I actually stayed quite a bit with the adult industry because they knew me. I knew I could be there in a day and I wouldn't have to go on location. I would come home that night and it was my own people. They didn't pay as much as working as a performer in the industry, but you'd be taking home four to five hundred dollars a day being a make-up artist which was still more than working as a bank teller. It was fine for me and for my kids.

My kids know about me. I've let them know that their mother was in naked pictures early on and that I was in naked movies, but you don't give your kids valium, you don't give them alcohol, and you don't give them porno. You take it as it comes. There was one point when Melanie was thirteen and she had gone on Cass' [Paley] computer or something and found out my name. She said to me "I know who you are…You're Kelly Nichols…"

I turned around and stared at her dead in the eye and said, "Yeah, do you have a problem?" and she said, "No," and then I turned to Mikie [my other daughter] and I said, "Mikie, you got a problem?" and she said, "No, Mommy!" That was it. Melanie has asked me a

Over Forty, Adult magazine.

couple of questions since then and I showed her some [softcore] magazines of mine. Mikie is my little abstinent girl. She's just very nice and she doesn't like to hear about sex with anybody but her boyfriend, and she doesn't even admit to that. She's twenty-four years old and she's just very shy. Melanie is very open. We trade porn anime and whenever I work for some of the toy companies, I'll get her extra toys and stuff that I can bring home in a package and give to her. We have a great relationship, but it's polar opposite. It's funny though, no matter what your kids don't want to be like you!

I do have a dividing line between "Kelly Nichols," and "Marianne Walter". When I was working in New York, my family was on the opposite side of the coast. I didn't have kids then and I was in a relationship with someone who was a musician who later on got into the business. When I was in Manhattan working in the business, everyone called me "Kelly Nichols," nobody called me "Marianne," so I literally only had one name until I got out of the business. When I got out of the business, I added water to oil and had two kids so as soon as that happened I put a whole kibosh on the "Kelly" thing. I didn't let anybody know I was a porn star at all. I was just a make-up artist.

I could tell my mom I was a make-up artist because in the early eighties when I was being "Kelly," I was also doing a lot of make-up for MTV. I was doing some early contemporary things that were really kind of neat. I could tell her I was a make-up artist and not be lying to her face. It's just that I didn't tell her the whole truth. My brothers, they found out sideways in their own ways. My brother Steve is helping me work on my website right now so he has a healthy attitude about it. One of my brothers didn't have a healthy attitude about it and my other brothers haven't really talked to me about it. Yeah, you can't really be in bed and be in the family.

Second Chances

Early in 2009, Nichols made a brief comeback as a performer after a purported twenty-five year hiatus opposite the sexy male star Tom Byron in *Seasoned Players 8*. After initiating his adult career in 1982, Byron had a reputation in the late 1980s as a rocker before returning to the business as a performer, and eventually, a director. Kelly's calculated reunion was seamless as she rekindled her onscreen relationship with her long time friend. The result is ebullient as the hyped film touted that Nichols' return to movies would contain a surprise "first" for fans of the popular erotic performer.

Tommy Byron asked if I would do it and I was wondering if I could do it so it was kind of a personal thing. The money was good. It wasn't that, it was just that I wanted to be in the right frame of mind. I wanted to do it sober and I wanted to look as good as I could. I did it, and I had a lot of fun doing it. It was just Tommy and this cameraman. It was great. I felt I was in good shape. The guy who was handling the camera was a sweetheart. I'd known Tommy for a long time and I shot with him once when he first got into the business. He's sober now and he's in his own house, it's a beautiful house.

He totally took care of me — he took control of the whole experience. It was as if I'd never stopped performing. I was so comfortable and he got me into a new position I really liked. I thought, "This is good! I like this!" It was called the "lazy cowgirl". It looks like I did all the work, but he did all the work and it was really, really fun. It was one of his best sellers so I got strokes in the department

Kelly Nichols and Tom Byron.

of fans. They loved it. That's all I need to do. I feel for a woman my age to do guys is like taking two steps backwards. It's kind of pathetic. I don't mind playing around with pretty girls and stuff as long as they're over twenty-five. I don't mind talking to the fans either, but there's no need to prove myself by doing guys anymore. I have a boyfriend and that's fine.

Kelly and Tom Byron open their scene together in *Seasoned Players 8* by recollecting their previous on-camera encounter. Nichols recalled they had first met in New York, and that during vaginal intercourse she had appreciated Byron's assurance he would be gentle. Casual teasing and laughter preceding the film's sexual interaction creates a fun and light atmosphere. Kelly doesn't completely disrobe, but peels down to her lingerie with her plaid skirt pushed up to her thighs revealing a small, thin ring pierced through her clitoris. Soon enough, after giving rigorous attention to Byron's erect penis, Tom moves Nichols into a cowgirl position. When he finally ejaculates, it's reminiscent of the fountain show in front of the Bellagio Hotel in Las Vegas proving that during her twenty-five year absence as an adult star, Kelly hasn't lost her touch.

What I've been doing for the last ten years is content work with other girls. They'll come over and my boyfriend will attend to the two of us and we'll just play with each other and then she'll keep the content and I'll keep the content. I have a bunch of it saved up that I've literally done. I might do some live talks, but I don't want to work that hard, honestly. I'll just do the occasional content thing and see if that'll make a difference because there are a lot of classic fans out there. I'm actually working on two websites that I'm going to be on, but the only thing I'm going to do on it is just girls or me. I just got hired today to work with someone who is doing a show for Showtime. He wants certain porn stars to be on the show with him and then they'll sort of play and he'll comment on it while they're playing. Then he'll talk about it afterwards.

I asked Kelly about her experiences with alcohol addiction, something she has officially addressed in interviews and has no qualms about discussing. Nichols works at staying healthy and whole with the aid of her personal sponsor.

Actually, drinking was a problem when I was quitting doing adult work because I wasn't having fun and it had all gone to video. I felt I was just doing it by rote, and I was unhappy in my relationship so as I mentioned when I quit my relationship, I quit the adult. I'd have to say that some of the last shoots I don't remember doing because I was just drinking waiting to go on. It was not a good place for me to be at that point in Manhattan doing porn.

I go in and out of sobriety. I'm mostly sober and then I'll have a bad whatever and have to call up somebody to get me back on track again. That has been interesting. But I'm not drinking because the work is going bad and I'm not freaking out because I'm doing more work on my website, so I'm waiting for the next shoe to fall to make me feel like I need a drink again!

I like to work out. I like to read. I'm going to be learning how to use a computer better because I'm going to be loading up these two websites of mine. I've been studying to be an Herbalist seriously for a long time and Homeopathic Sciences. At some point, I'd like to do something with it. I'd like to get to a place where I'm not worrying about money so that I can actually go to school and figure out what I want. I'd like to take nutrition courses and find some kind of Homeopathic place I could go into. I still have quite a few years left and it's something that fascinates me, it really does.

I like to hang out with my daughters. My twenty-four year old daughter lives with me. My other daughter is twenty-five and she lives around the corner. The one who lives with me is going to be moving out in January and the other one is talking about moving in with her father. He and I are still friends. He lives in Eagle Rock, [California] so they'll be in the same state. I'm probably not going to stay here in Thousand Oaks. I have a boyfriend of nine years and he lives in Redondo Beach so I might get a place at least by him. It's too white man out here where I live now. It's not integrated enough.

You know, essentially, I was still raising my kids in my early forties. When you hit your fifties, you become your own person again. I've had to accept the whole empty nest syndrome. You really have to accept the fact that we only have a certain amount of time left so better fill it up.

18.
Veronica Hart
Thespian

For the self-described, "brainy, teenage nerd," Veronica Hart probably surprised herself more than her former classmates when she grew up to become a highly regarded adult film actress. Hart, whose poise, warmth, and shapely figure are her trademarks in addition to her inherent ability as an actor, was born Jane Esther Hamilton in 1956. She is one of the few female stars known equally by both her birth and stage names. Raised in Las Vegas, Hamilton gradually morphed from a geek to cheerleader to actor, and was an active member of the University of Las Vegas Modern dance troupe for eleven years. At age sixteen, Jane entered UNLV (University of Nevada, Las Vegas) on a scholarship and graduated with a Theatre Arts degree. For a while, Hamilton student taught at the local high school and at age twenty-two traveled abroad to England where she danced topless at the Stork Club, modeled, and in her words "mismanaged" a progressive rock group.

While serving beverages at the newly built National Exhibition Centre in London, Jane suffered an unfortunate accident involving a coffee urn which resulted in third degree burns extending from her right shoulder all the way down to her hip. She was hospitalized for two months. The consequences from the incident became a pivotal turning point: Jane returned home to Las Vegas and threw herself into repertoire theatre. A string of successful starring roles and favorable notices bolstered her confidence and Hamilton set off for New York City to make her mark. After a prospective mainstream work arrangement fell through, Jane discovered performing in live sex shows along with her musician boyfriend could not sustain the couple, but her innate acting abilities and natural sexual proclivity proved to be fruitful in the erotic film market.

By 1980, Jane Hamilton under her pseudonym, "Veronica Hart," rivaled co-actors and riveted fans with her standout performance in

"One of my goals when I got in the business was that I would be able to come out of this business and still enjoy my sexuality and making love." VERONICA HART

COURTESY OF JANE HAMILTON

Amanda by Night (1981) directed by Robert McCallum. She won Best Actress award from the Adult Film Association of America for Chuck Vincent's *Roommates* (1981) costarring Samantha Fox and Kelly Nichols. With razor sharp acting chops and evocative appeal, Hamilton established herself among an elite class of pornographic motion picture veterans. Excluding non-sex work projects, during the mid-1990s, Hamilton made the switch to director and has worked freelance for various adult companies garnering her Best Director accolades. Contemporary, mainstream movie audiences were treated to Jane's highly attuned skills in the landmark motion picture *Boogie Nights* (1997) where she portrayed a judge in a taut scene supporting Hollywood heavy weight, Julianne Moore.

In 2010, Jane moved back to Las Vegas to take care of her ailing mother (who passed away in the fall of 2011 in her ninety-sixth year) and currently works at the Erotic Heritage Museum. She also assumed directorial duties for the forthcoming biopic on the legendary Marilyn Chambers: *Marilyn Chambers, Sex and Life after Porn* for Gobos Film and Entertainment.

With her vitality and care-giving, compassionate nature, Hamilton remains close to her family, lifelong friends and to her animals. She enjoys a tight bond with her two grown sons who share in her sense of humor and lust for life.

I interviewed Jane Hamilton in the spring of 2010.

A Scent of Jane

Jane Hamilton is my real name. It's not a big secret, but I am "Veronica Hart," and I am "Jane Hamilton". Mark Twain had a pen name. The name changes depending upon the job I do. I usually produce as "Jane Hamilton" and if I'm directing or acting, I'm "Veronica Hart". I'm "Veronica Hart" in straight films too.

I was born in 1956. I grew up in Las Vegas and I had very nice parents. My childhood was great. My mom was mostly a housewife. I think she went back and watched children of the people who would go out in Las Vegas. She worked for a babysitting service to try to get her social security credit and when she was very young, she worked at a Woolworth's as a cashier. She was quite smart but her mother died when she was fourteen and her father died when she was fifteen, so college wasn't meant for her. She started leading an interesting life right away.

My dad was awesome. He passed away in March [2009]. He started out as a delivery boy and went to electronics school and then he went to radio and television school. My dad was essentially a radio-TV repair guy. I think he had worked at my mom's TV repair shop. He literally ran away with the boss's wife.

I had three sisters and an older brother. I'm the youngest by

In 1956. COURTESY OF JANE HAMILTON

seven years. My mother remarried my father and then had me. The sister who is next to me, the one who was seven years older, absolutely despised me growing up. You're the baby, and all of a sudden, this "thing" comes along, but I'm very close with all of my sisters. I've got great sisters — I've got a great family. It's a regular family, but I'm probably the black sheep–although I do have a nephew in jail. I've always been a successful black sheep until recently.

I was really loved. I think the nicest thing my parents told me was that I could do anything I wanted to do. My dad would tease me and say, "Oh, that's not bad for a girl." Just like that, just to get me riled up and feisty. We worked on cars together and I made doll's beds, and that's how I know how to do things in houses and build walls and put in floors and things like that.

When I was really a young girl I got a picture of a ballerina and on the back of it, under the frame where you couldn't see, I put, "My dream". I've danced since I was seven until I was about eighteen so that encompassed eleven years in all. I was a part of the UNLV Modern Dance Troupe. My dance teachers were my role models. Dorothy Frankovich, I believe, had a cousin or nephew Mike Frankovich who did some stuff in Hollywood. She was in the chorus line in some films and she had photos from some of the pictures in which she was involved. To me, that was very glamorous. I thought I'd love to do something like that. I was either going to be a veterinarian or I was going to act. I thought that if I didn't try acting, I'd always be a "what-if?" person. I'm still doing the acting in a half-assed sort of way. That's what I should be pushing, but I'm doing all of these other projects — producing and trying to raise money — raising money is not something I particularly enjoy.

Actually, two teachers that had a big influence on me were Mr. Schuman and Mr. Diet. Mr. Diet was ultra smart, but he was a bit of a prick to me, he really was. I was the only girl that was in the Science Club. We were hatching chicks before they should be hatched and carefully watching the embryos. I said, "Oooohhhh" and he looked at me and said, "If you want to say Oooohhhh' you don't belong in here. You can remove yourself from the Science Club."

I said, "No, I don't think so," and we just had that kind of a relationship. What really got me was that all the boys were making noises too, but he didn't comment about them. Then came Mr. Schuman who was so tough and such a jerk, but he

COURTESY OF JANE HAMILTON

opened me up to the whole world and to the idea that I wanted to travel. He taught sixth grade and his forte was social studies because he'd been all over the world. He showed us pictures of castles and hotels and architecture from his travels. I thought, "I've got to do that. I want to see some of that stuff." He was responsible for influencing me not being afraid to tackle the world. I used to like to go places by myself. I think I find it more difficult to do at my age, but I'd like to take off on my own and go have an adventure.

I was kind of a nerd as a kid because I was a little bit smart but it wasn't very fashionable to be smart. I was the kind of girl that you love to hate — that one that sat up at the front waving her arms because she knew the answers. Later, I decided not to do that, and I started being sexual and I became a lot more popular! I was a nerd-geek, but I was a cheerleader in junior high. I still have my megaphone. I went through that cheerleading phase. Then when I got into high school is when I got into the thespian part of it all, so I was in my element. As a kid, and while growing up, I was totally into rock music and completely an anglophile. I was into David Bowie and the blurring of the genders and the theatrical nature of it and androgynous aspect of it all.

My first big crush boyfriend was Jay Osmond from the Osmond Brothers. My friend [Dorothy Frankovich's daughter] had a crush on Donny Osmond so I couldn't have a crush on Donny — we both had a crush on Jay — he was a cutie. We made him pictures and we took them down to him. The Osmond Brothers were the opening act for Jerry Lewis and when we went down to talk to Jay, there was a misunderstanding and they thought that we wanted to talk to Jerry. They brought Jerry to see us and we kind of begged off, we weren't there to see Jerry. It was stupid because I still should have seen Jerry. Jay was in the coffee shop and we were directed towards the coffee shop, and he was in there with his family. We left the pictures there for him, the things that we'd made. I liked David Cassidy too.

In high school, I started to become more confident of myself. The football guys would talk to me from around the corner, but then, if somebody more popular would come along they'd kind of just leave. I really was a nerdy thespian. There was also a quality about me where people knew I was going to do something. I was definitely geared toward being famous or known for something. I had a feeling that I was different, I really did. I thought that the only way I could be able to exercise my uniqueness was to hang with different people. That insight first attracted me to celebrity.

Like Mother, Like Daughter

One of Hamilton's earliest sexual experiences as a mid-teen was memorable only because her partner lacked sensitivity and was more aggressive than she expected or is probably acceptable by today's standards. In hindsight, symbolically, the encounter became an empowering portal for what lay in store for Jane in the years ahead.

I was fifteen and my first was Patrick Quinlan, I think. He was very sweet and I figured it was time for me. We'd gone to see a concert and smoked a little pot, and gone to somebody's apartment. I had it all set up, and we were in bed and I was a little high. It hurt a little, but it was life changing. It was like, "Oh, my god, I'm a woman now and all that kind of stuff." I told him that was my first time and everything, and I asked him, "Was it yours too?"

He said, "Oh, no, I've done it about six other times with different women." I remember I was crushed. Later, I learned a big lesson. I was in my talent show at school and I was running around in my hot pants and boots at that time. I thought I was hot shit, you know — I was in the school talent show and I thought I was pretty cool. This guy came up and started talking to me and I was like, "Hi, how are you?" but it wasn't as if I was dying to be too talkative. Then I found out that he was the lead singer in the rock group that was playing in the talent show. I said, "Oh, hey! How are you? I'm Jane and I want to talk to you. Where do you play?" He was nice back and he asked if I'd like to help him pack up his equipment and take it back to his home. We smoked some pot and got high and he kind of took me by the hair and dragged me into the other room. I had panty hose underneath my hot pants. They made it down to my knees. He got me good and it hurt like mad. It was just like, "Whoa. I'm no good at this, man. This is something I'm just not good at." I was probably the worst lay he'd ever had. I thought, "Wait, I'm a Scorpio, we're made to be sexual."

He raped me in the sense that he didn't ask me, but I could have said "no" at any time, and I didn't because he was the lead singer of the rock group and I wanted to be cool. I wanted to go to bed with him. I got him, but it didn't live up to any hype about it, it was just painful and it was horrible. We didn't go to the same high school, but I would see him often at concerts and so on and I'd always be running up to him, and waving and saying, "Wayne? Hi, it's Jane, remember me?"

He'd be like, "Oh, yeah, yeah." Later, after I became "Veronica Hart," I saw Wayne. By then I had a little bit of experience. It wasn't the second time I'd ever gone to bed, and I'd been in the adult business and I was better. All of a sudden, he was so attentive. We had exactly changed positions. He was now the one going, "You're so gorgeous; blah, blah, blah." I ran into him in California. He was working at a studio. I think he was maintaining a studio. He was a good singer, that's what he had wanted to do. I was determined to fuck him and show him that I was a good lay. I wanted to let him know that I wasn't some lame lay. I discovered why it hurt had so much — he was hung like a horse!

We had a history of developing sexuality in our family, as I'm sure it does in any family. I did drugs and I couldn't talk to my mom about drugs, but I could always talk to her about sex. I would go out with the college president or the hotel manager at one of the big hotels and my mom would get a kick out of it. She'd ask, "Oh, honey, did you have fun?" It was her language for "Was he any good?"

Jane is pictured below with a high school boyfriend, Stan, as they prepare to go to the high school prom — not the same boy that had played in the band.

Jane Hamilton and her boyfriend Stan.

I was like, "Oh, yeah. He was great and we had a good time. He took me here and we had dinner." I'd just say that it was lovely and mom and I had an understanding that he was good and I probably would see him again. I think that the acorn doesn't fall far from the tree. Whatever you are, there's a good chance that's what your kids will have in them, too.

Jane's high standard of excellence in academics seemed as if it might pave the way for her to assume a more traditional and secure vocation as an instructor or a medical practitioner. In the end, she listened to her heart.

I went to UNLV right here in town. I got a scholarship for ten or twenty thousand dollars. At that point, I was either going to go to med school or acting, and I decided I'd probably just follow the acting. In that case, I didn't really need to go to one of the California schools. I got accepted at a couple of the California schools, but I chose to go to UNLV. Again, I was on that accelerated path. I graduated my high school at age sixteen and I graduated college in three years instead of four years. I did some summer classes and I did correspondence courses, and I was able to get out in three years. I graduated with a Theatrical Arts Major. I performed in the Eisenhower Theatre at the Kennedy Centre. I played Adela in *The House of Bernarda Alda* and we won at the American College Theatre Festival. I'd like it documented that I'm not a dummy and I had acting talent. I still like acting and I still do acting. Probably what I enjoy most for work in life is acting. I also student taught at the local high school. It was interesting because I was a nineteen-year old teacher teaching kids that were three or four years younger than I was.

In the drama program there are kids who try really hard and are so committed and are so lousy at it, and then there are other kids that barely show up but they just have innate talent and they're good at it. It was difficult for me to try and grade—you'd have to grade them on everything. You had to take all of that into consideration. I did enjoy teaching. We used to have a revue and put on lunchtime shows. There would be a kid who felt the performance wasn't going real well so he thought if he started cussing and throwing all sorts of swear words that it would elevate the performance; it was actually the blueest Neil Simon play I ever heard.

When I was in college, one of the cool things I did was travel one summer all over Europe. I was working as a PBX operator at

[The MGM Grand Hotel]. I had saved a lot of money and I went on one of the college trips that were chaperoned. There were probably about fifty college-aged kids going around and seeing Europe. We were lead by Dutch tour guides. That was wonderful. This was during the middle of college. I also went to Australia. I had met a guy and went to visit him in Australia. I kind of got the wanderlust,

COURTESY OF JANE HAMILTON

the wonder bug. I really enjoyed travelling around Europe and I spent a week or two after that tour with a friend of my sister's, a woman by the name of Kay Bailey who was just wonderful. She became my English mom. I really felt strongly that I needed to be in England so after I finished college — I have to credit my mom for this — I was saving money to be able to go back to England. My mom looked at me and she said, "You're miserable here, aren't you?" I agreed. She said, "Do you really want to go back to England?"

I said, "Yeah," and she said, "Well, go."

I told her, "Mom, I don't have much money."

She said, "If you want to stay there, you'll stay there and you'll figure it out one way or another."

I thought, "Oh, okay." I left the next week.

Changing on a Dime

When Jane arrived in England without an employment visa, she didn't allow the incidental issue to prevent her from pursuing fame and fortune. Hamilton took her place in line at a club audition for a dancer and waited on pins and needles until it was her turn to show what she was made of.

I went over there with a student work permit that I was able to get so when anybody asked me if I had a work permit I would say, "Yes," but it wasn't legal any of the time that I worked over there. I was never asked to produce it. I was dancing over there and modeling, and it was wonderful to model because I'd grown up here where I wasn't tall enough to model. If I'd have been taller, I would have stayed in Vegas and been a dancer and that would have been that.

I went to The Wendy Ward Charm School — there's a mentor for you. Maureen — she was a gal who was a model and was into fashion and I always wanted to be an actress or a dancer. Again, I knew I always would be something. Maureen was responsible for pushing me into that whole modeling dream. I learned how to do runway modeling. I could do the turns and do the moves and all of those kinds of things. I was only 5'6" so there was no chance of modeling in the States. In England, you can be short and be a model. I danced at the Cockney Club and at The Stork Club. It is mostly for tourists and they've got all of the English songs and so on. I had gone to a regular dance audition. It was pretty clique-y and everybody knew each other. I was the Yank that was just sitting there and they said, "Where are we going to get a topless dancer?" My little ears perked up and I thought, "Well, I'm from Las Vegas. We're known for some racy stuff. I guess I could do that." While I was in England, I went out with a guy whose father was sort of an equivalent to Dean Martin except that he appealed to the old dears. His name was Max Bygraves and he was quite famous at the time. I went out with his son, Anthony [Tony].

Max Bygraves, the likeable all round British entertainer appeared on several of his own television programs starting in the late 1940s showcasing his diverse range of talents.

I think it was very difficult for Tony to follow in his father's footsteps. He had worked with a very talented musician. I know they did some jingles and some television. He performed for a while, but I don't know exactly what happened. I kept in touch with him for a few years and then I think he got married and they had three or four kids. Their family was wealthy. That was fun.

I also mismanaged a rock group over there. I got them a lot of gigs, but we never got any kind of a recording contract. We travelled all over performing, but it was very strange because they were kind of into more progressive rock and traditional rock and that was right when punk was really breaking. I tried to steer them in that direction, but they had their own ideas about music and the course they wanted to take so it was kind of tough. I lived in London for about a year and a half, and then I moved up to Birmingham because that's where this rock group was from.

Hamilton fell in love with Britain's culture and practices. As one who is versatile and able to customize her skills depending upon what the situation demanded, Jane began a temporary assignment working as a server for attendees of a newly constructed centre. After a short duration of employment, an unexpected meeting with fate caused Hamilton to put her life temporarily on hold.

They had just built the National Exhibition Centre over there. It was in the West Midlands right in the middle of the country and a lot of conventions were held there. I worked as one of the dolly birds on the convention floor, inviting people to come to the stands. I remember I toasted crumpets for a month at Wimbledon.

I think that was for gas fireplaces or something like that. I did all sorts of crazy stuff. I worked for a car lease company at one of the auto shows when leasing cars was a new idea. I worked at many different jobs and I was always in the newspaper for one thing or another, a fashion show or for something else. That leads us to the accident.

I was working at the National Exhibition Centre and I was on one of the stands. I was serving drinks: alcoholic, and coffee and tea. They had an old style coffee maker and the water would percolate up into a funnel that was on top that held the grounds. When all of the water had percolated up into this top-heavy piece of equipment, the machine was supposed to shut off and then it would just drain back down through. The mechanism on the machine was broken and it didn't shut off so I would have to take the pot with the grounds and set it down [off the burner]. I was bending down to pick up a cup and a saucer and on my way up, I hit the side of the counter and the coffee poured out. It got me from my shoulder all the way down my side. I didn't know anything about how to treat hot burns at the time, but what they did was the worst thing that could have happened. If you have clothes on, you get them off because clothes keep the heat in close to the skin. You need to strip the person off and you need to throw ice over them. You need to stop the burn from heating your skin. Years later, because I had actually told this to a gentleman that I was working with, he was able to save his girlfriend who had a pot of coffee pour out on her at craft services. He immediately tipped one of the ice coolers onto her. It saved her and I felt good that I had helped to prevent a severe burn.

Anyway, nobody knew what to do. They kept me in my clothes and I stayed in those clothes burning and soaking until I got to the hospital. By that time, they were third degree burns. My right hip was taken out and my right shoulder. For the longest time, you could see the imprint of my bra on my back, etched right in. I had skin grafts and everything like that. I spent about a month and a half to two months in the hospital. They use a dry method with their burns over there. We use a wet method that is more susceptible to infection. The dry is less susceptible to infection but it's horrible because you have a tendency to grow into your bandages. When they remove them, it tears everything off and then you have to start again.

It is possible Jane initially experienced what can be classified as a "deep partial thickness" burn that extends deep into the skin and can progress to a third degree burn category especially if it is not treated properly at the occurrence of the accident. As Hamilton mentioned, early cooling of a minor or serious burn is imperative, as it will help to counteract pain and extent of skin damage. A "spill scald" is one of the most common types of burns. If it progresses to a third degree burn, the patient will generally require skin grafting and hospital stay in order to monitor the healing process and ensure that infection does not result. Fortunately, Jane did not have a history of physical or psychological problems which can greatly hinder a burn patient's prognosis for recovery.

> Here I am, a model, a dancer, an actress — after my boyfriend [at the time of the accident] and I got home and I got into bed with him the first thing he did was turn out the lights. I just cried. I really thought that was it, that I'd never be able to be sexy to anyone again. I kind of felt finished, you know. It wasn't true. I dissolved my relationship with him and got with somebody else who was very kind and very loving, and got back on my feet. Then I moved home.

Introducing "Veronica Hart"

Jane returned to the comforts of home and the theatre which helped to resurrect her self-confidence and esteem. While on stage in Las Vegas, Hamilton enthralled audiences by appearing in several theatrical productions adapted from and/or inspired by books and films and won raves for her incarnation of inspiring characters. Jane's exceptional stage performances and eventual movie auditions caught the eye of a casting director which inevitably provided the framework for what lay ahead as an actor in adult oriented features.

> I had a real good run back home. I played Susie in *Wait until Dark* at the Judy Bailey Theatre [in Las Vegas], and I played Lulu in Pinter's *[The] Birthday Party*. In a community theatre, I played Frances Black in *Light up the Sky*. I did all that and then they were making a movie called *Going in Style* (1979). It was with Art Carney, Lee Strasberg [and George Burns]. That was the one where three old guys knock off a bank in New York City and have a vacation in Las Vegas. I went out on an ad for casting and met the casting director here in Las Vegas and he said, "You know, you really should move to

New York." I also had a guy contact me because of an article/review that had appeared in the newspaper and he said he was starting into the music business. Because I'd been in England and been involved in the music business there, he called me up and said he would be interested in starting up a studio with me in New York. The casting director suggested that I move to New York, and the other guy who wanted me to partner with him in the music business wanted me to move to New York. I was twenty-two years old at that time.

I moved to New York and the gentleman that I moved with was an agent. It was quite eye opening. He was a relatively callous, New York Jewish gentleman. I'd never really been around that kind of personality before. We were up at his friend's resort and I think his friend had just had a heart attack or something. He'd just gotten this big resort up and running and I said I didn't think anything was worth having a heart attack over. I had just been in the hospital for a couple of months and it was all fresh in my mind. He didn't appreciate that comment so that was pretty much the beginning of the end. I knew I had to move out. I looked in *The Village Voice* and I found a couple of places to go. One of the places I went was to a gentleman called Roy Stewart. It was a loft and I moved in with him. He had seen my acting pictures and my modeling resume and he knew that I enjoyed sex because we had some casual sex.

He said, "You should be in the [adult] business." I couldn't imagine that. When I'd gone to Australia, I'd seen some loops at Kings Cross, in Sydney. I think that was the first time that I'd ever seen anything like that. I had been a topless dancer of course and I'd seen *Les Folies Bergere* and all of the shows on the strip — they all had the topless acts and I was a bit of a nudist myself. Anyway, this girl came out and she did a strip, and then they showed the porn. I thought it was fun but there was no acting in it. It wasn't something where I said, "Oh boy, I can't wait to do that." I considered myself an actress. Roy said, "You'd be a really good actress," and I said, "Well, I am a really good actress, but I'm not going to do that. I'm not a prostitute."

Hamilton's impressions while watching a sex film for the first time weren't necessarily compelling, but with a good script and smart dialogue, she recognized the work was something she could possibly warm up to while putting her training and experiences as an actor toward something potentially redeeming.

He took me to the [Show] World Theatre. I think it was at 54th street in New York at that time, and I couldn't believe it because it was a real movie. There was sex in it, but there was acting, and dialogue, and costumes. I haven't a clue what film it was, but it was enough to go, "Oh my god. This is a real movie. Okay, I could do this. This is something that I would like to do." I always liked

"Veronica Hart." COURTESY OF JANE HAMILTON

sex and I liked to act, and by that time, all of my friends at college were doing anything except making money at acting, so there was a chance for me to do that.

I went around and met everybody, but nobody was shooting anything. I met Chuck Vincent and Shaun Costello. I did *Pandora's Mirror* (1981) with him and a couple of other movies. I met a couple of filmmakers but nobody was doing anything. I found another boyfriend at that time, Billy McKeever, and he was a struggling musician. I was still staying at Roy's place paying him rent and I was working at *Psychology Today* — that was slave labor. I was making no money and working hard and they would try to get you to work overtime or stay late. People ask me if I've ever been taken advantage of and I say, "Well, yeah, I worked for *Psychology Today!*" It was just a job to pay the rent.

I was trying to get money together to go with Billy back to Vegas so that I could see my folks for the holidays at Christmas, and Roy said, "Why don't we do some live sex shows?"

I said, "Oh-Kay…" Roy's thing was he wanted to put you in front of the camera, but he'd always fail miserably. He was a great lover, but when he went to do it in front of other people, he would always fail. That was very difficult in a week of live sex shows because he couldn't perform. I literally blew my brains out during that week. What it did reveal to me was that those shows weren't so bad. I did get paid. I got enough money to get Billy and me back to Las Vegas and decided that I had a new career when I got back. I would be doing the shows with Billy, and not Roy. Roy was my landlord and Billy was my boyfriend. I would be making love with him anyway and it was very exciting for the first day.

We got there and it was so exciting. I think we made love in the dressing room and then we went out and did our first show. That was great, and then I think we went back and fooled around some more. When it came time for the second show — nothing happened. Billy's dick was just dead so we learned to pace ourselves — he could only ejaculate maybe one or two shows out of the day and then we'd pretend the rest of it. Billy was a musician — I'm the one who got him into it.

As Jane and Billy began to cultivate their act at the infamous Show World in New York City, Hamilton learned that everybody has a breaking point — especially when performing live sex.

Billy and I were doing the shows and then the movies started picking up. I started doing the movies and it had gotten to the point where basically, [Billy and I] would do anything but make love as a couple. If your job is making love six days a week, six shows a day — it got to a point where I had conjunctivitis so I had to wear sunglasses, and I was on my period, and I had a cold or something.

It just dawned on me that I couldn't do it anymore. I always liked to make love, I always loved sex, and I realized that I had to stop this. It was very tough because it had been a way for my boyfriend and me to make a living. Essentially, I was telling my boyfriend that I was taking away his living. I could go and I could strip, and not have to make love and make the same amount of money. He had to get another girl to perform with him. It was easier for girls to get guys to perform with them than it was for guys to get girls to perform with them. It just wasn't good for me anymore. I've always had good enough sense. I will try anything, but once I realize it's not good for me, I do stop. It may take a while to bring it about, but I do.

Somewhat relieved, Jane immersed herself in the transference from live sex shows to regular film work. In little time, her efforts paid dividends not only in the way of income, but more importantly, with critical praise. Her competence as a performer resulted in a touchstone of new heights.

I got into the films and the films were great, and I would always work around my scars. I still don't wear sleeveless outfits much. My garter belt helped cover up because I often wore garter belt and stockings. I worked in San Francisco or New York. They'd fly me out to San Francisco and I worked on the west coast, and we worked in New York. This is the late seventies, early eighties. When you went outside of New York, you shot with a script that had no reference to the sex. You'd tell everybody that you were making a low budget feature. I didn't do loops because that wasn't acting, and I didn't do tons of layouts or anything like that — I really considered myself an actress. I was twenty-two years old so 1978 to the tail end of `78 and the beginning of `79 is when I started in films. Then it would take them until 1980 before the film was released.

A Scent of Heather

Jane's first official film credit is in a movie titled *Woman in Love: A Story of Madame Bovary* (1978) in which she played a model and performed with Ron Jeremy along with supporting stars Laurien Dominique, Samantha Fox, and Vanessa del Rio. *Confessions of Seka* and *Urban Cowgirls*, both released in 1980, contained scenes where Jane is paired with one of the most likable male veterans in the business, Eric Edwards. Hamilton appeared with Edwards at least five times during her career as an actor.

Eric Edwards was my first one going in and my last one going out. He's a nice man and a great guy. There was [also] another guy who had never done it before and as far as a turn-on goes, that was more of a turn-on than the guys who had worked with everybody and their brother. To take somebody who had never made an adult film before and to get them to relax and start thinking about everybody not watching them and trying to get them to pay attention to you — it was great to pop somebody's cinematic cherry.

After exhibiting some fancy footwork in her first few appearances, by 1980, adult directors commenced to hire Jane for principal roles where she proved she could adeptly carry a story. Hamilton learned to be careful about angles — and keeping her feet clean.

A Scent of Heather (1980) is the first film that I'd starred in, but I made a lot of other ones before that. I can't remember which [sex scene] was first, but in *A Scent of Heather* I thought, "Oh my god, they can't shoot my nose that angle because I look like a pig." I've since had it fixed. I had the strangest nose, and if it was caught the wrong I did look like Miss Piggy. I think in one film there was a beautiful scene and I put my feet up and my feet were dirty, so I thought, "My god, I'll always have to watch that." When I'd see a blemish, I'd think, "Why didn't anybody say anything?" That, more than anything, had a lot to with my directing. I will stop a scene and I will get make-up touched up on a beautiful woman who is having a little problem which pisses a lot of people off. I will make sure that feet are clean. Those little things are important to me.

A Scent of Heather is an enchanting period piece examining the topic of incest. Newlyweds Heather (as Veronica Heart) and Frederick (Paul Thomas) discover they are half-brother and sister just prior to consummating their wedding vows. Virginal Heather is willing to keep their dirty little secret private in order to enjoy sex with her new groom in their boudoir, but Frederick wants to do the right thing. His method of coping with the surprising information is to emotionally detach from his new bride. Frederick proceeds to screw the female help (Vanessa del Rio and Tracey Adams) at the manor while in the midst of fantasizing he is bedding his half-sister/wife, while poor Heather remains chaste. Feelings of guilt soon consume Frederick as only he is partaking of the sins of the flesh. He arranges for Tom the chauffeur (R. Bolla as Robert Kerman) to seduce his unsuspecting spouse in an abandoned barn. The sexual episode that envelops the pair becomes a critical turning point—Heather can't seem to get enough erogenous stimulation. Soon, she skips the pretense with available mates in her radar and encourages them to assuage the heat between her loins. The epilogue takes on a bit of a twist once Heather and Frederick uncover the truth — they come to understand their family heritage is even more confounding than they had initially thought, but get the green light to finally seal the deal.

In her debut as a primary player, Hart's polish as a trained thespian endows her with the capacity to bear the weight of her character rendering her a likeable heroine and one who is unashamed to cross the threshold into womanhood without second-guessing the authority of her libido. Hart's fantasy scenes with Paul Thomas are sexy, but it's hard not to root for Heather and her unlikely suitor Tom. Hart and Richard Bolla make a beguiling and unpretentious couple.

As it is with stripping, when you're involved in a performance what you're doing is not on your mind, but when you eventually see what you're actually doing, it's a completely different thing. It's much easier doing it than watching it I think because you're actively involved. There are these other feelings and there are other things going on around you. It's similar to when you look at a picture of yourself and you say, "That picture is good, or that picture is bad. This was shot from a good angle, but this wasn't." You get to know about yourself. When you hear about the Hollywood divas who want a certain side to be shown, they've learned and actually paid attention and they care about it. They know what kind of light is flattering and that's all because they pay attention to the detail. I was more interested in my acting than my lovemaking. That still interests me more than adult films.

Bobby Kerman [R. Bolla] who was in *Scent of a Heather* was one of my favorites — we did tons of stuff together. I first met him on that set. We were getting ready to do a sex scene and we were shooting the shit, and he asked me what my dad did. I'm very close to my mom and dad — my daddy passed away a year ago. He was very special and he was a "man" as far as I was concerned. I grew up a lot like a boy because my dad never said I couldn't do anything. He always led me to believe that I could do whatever I wanted to in life and I was certainly capable of doing it all. My dad had worked out on the Nevada test site and I told Bobby about this. All of a sudden, my dad was the cause of all of the ills of the world. I said, "Wait, this is my dad you're talking about. You don't know my dad. My dad is amazing." Here he was telling me that my daddy was the cause of all of the evils in the world. Then we had to do a sex scene and I thought, "I've got to fuck you — okay." I gave him a great grudge fuck and then we became the best of friends after that. Bobby did *No Way Out* (1987). He was the F.B.I. guy in that film and he did some legitimate acting afterwards for a while.

More recently, Robert Kerman played the tugboat captain in the highly popular 2002 film *Spider-Man* adapted from the Marvel Comic book series starring Tobey McQuire.

To get to where we originally started with the burns — you don't have to be a psychologist to know that in my life I didn't think I would be able to turn one person on. I think that was a lot of it. What better thing is there than to get into something where I was going to turn the world on? I think that was a part of what motivated me. I don't think it was a conscious motivation. If you look at a lot of girls at that time, many of them were making up for some kind of something. I'm not saying we're victims or anything like that, but you look for kudos in something else when you feel deficient in a certain area. Whether or not they were missing out on love from their parents or seeking attention — it could have been anything like that.

Amanda by Night & Sex 101

"There once was a hooker who thought she was a human being. Can you believe that?"
AMANDA HEATHER IN *AMANDA BY NIGHT*

There are certain kinds of girls who come into our business that get absolutely chewed up and spat out. For her, it's the worst business. I've seen the other type of woman that comes in and a lot of times, it's with some suitcase pimp or some husband who's got some kind of fantasy that he wants to fulfill with his wife. All of a sudden, she gets a sense of her own power. She gets a sense of her own sexual power and she gets a feeling that maybe she does count for something, maybe she is cool. You see these women actually blossom. The business is not always good — it's not always bad, it depends upon the people that you get involved with and your own personality.

When touching upon what vintage adult film fans believe is her most significant starring work in films, Hamilton affirmed that one of her powerful pieces is *Amanda by Night* (1981) directed by Robert McCallum. In her spirited portrayal of Amanda Heather: a gold-hearted, high class prostitute on the verge of becoming extinguished when friends and enemies become one, Veronica Hart (Jane Hamilton) is given ample latitude to explore the moral parallels influencing one's choice to work in the sex trade.

As the film opens, Heather has set her sights on upward mobility after making a decision to leave the business, but agrees to one last favor for her pimp and sometimes boyfriend Friday (played by Jamie Gillis). Friday, who plans to open a new club, has requested Heather send over a couple of girlfriends: junkie Gwen (Samantha Fox) and Bev (Lisa DeLeeuw) to entertain a shady city Councilman Blakely (played by the terrific John Alderman)

Amanda by Night. CABALLERO HOME VIDEO

with some S&M exercises in exchange for leniency on zoning restrictions. Immediately, Gwen and Bev get into character. The women dole out supercharged verbal and sexual abuses during role play just as Councilor Blakely anticipated, but when Gwen makes her departure (likely to go do some smack), Bev remains behind continuing to lay insults upon Blakely even after the sex games conclude. Blakely tells her to "knock it off," but she continues to get riled up until he becomes forceful and kills her in his swimming pool. Shortly afterwards, Gwen's dead body is also discovered — apparently from a drug overdose. The film quickly shifts into a murder mystery and one Lt. Ambrose Hart (R. Bolla/aka Robert Kerman) is on the case. Lt. Hart starts to nose around and begins with Heather who was the last person to see her two friends alive. Understandably, she tells him to get lost, but like all good private dicks, Hart is persistent and doesn't take "no" for an answer. As he delves more deeply into the particulars surrounding the dead girls, Lt. Hart discovers the dirty truth behind the inner workings of the police department and its intrinsic relationship with local politicians. Hart and Heather grow to become friends and eventually lovers, after he saves her from obliteration. The picture wraps with a promising future on the horizon for the pair.

Through Veronica Hart's potent incarnation of Heather, one could easily interpret *Amanda by Night* as a parable for individuals (primarily women) working in the adult film industry often misunderstood by outsiders as immoral and depraved. The story touchingly magnifies the point that they are indeed worthy, compassionate, and capable of giving and receiving genuine friendship and love.

Hart was honored with a Best Actress award from the AFAA while director Robert McCallum was voted Best Director by Critic's Adult Film Awards. Jamie Gillis, Samantha Fox, Lisa DeLeeuw, Ron Jeremy, Jon Martin, Eric Edwards, Arcadia Lake and Pat Manning all make viable contributions in one way or another in this film. For a sexually explicit movie that is also a heavy weight both in the acting department and in its narrative, viewers need to look no further than *Amanda by Night*.

Probably a film that received more critical reviews than *Amanda by Night* is *Roommates* (1981). That played a midnight showing in the Village for years. Judith Crist of *The New York Times* reviewed that. I think it's a very interesting film because it's not a very sexy film. *Roommates*, is one of those true to life films they don't make anymore. It's about three girls and it wasn't such a nice story. It was more about how real life can suck and it's very dramatic. I have some lesbian friends that asked me what I felt was my best film, and I said, "*Roommates*". Kelly Nichols is in it and Samantha Fox and they both gave amazing performances. Afterwards, my friends said it was an amazing movie, but such a downer, they were so depressed. The last thing they wanted to do was make love. It certainly had plenty of jerk-off material but it had so much more of a story line.

In *Roommates*, I had a scene with Jerry Butler. He was playing a gay man who was my best friend, but he decided that he wanted to try it with me. My husband got very upset about this. We weren't married at the time. I'd said that it had felt like love. It wasn't love. I wasn't in love with Jerry Butler, but the way we were doing our job with all of the candles and the quiet, it was luxurious and it felt like love.

The Veronica Hart/Jerry Butler love scene in *Roommates* (reviewed in chapter 17) is as elegant as Jane's description. One could believe Jane and Jerry are genuinely making love in their sequence together consummating the relationship and desire felt between characters within the context of the story. Hart/Hamilton is marvelous in *Roommates*, which allowed her to display her range and dexterity as an actor whether she is featured in a sex scene or non-sexual interaction with her co-stars.

The strength of Jane's early 1980s film work is also evidenced in her leading role as the cagey (blonde) Wanda Brandt drafted by a stock brokerage firm to seize control of a Wall Street corporation in *Wanda Whips Wall Street* (1982). Hamilton sizzles and pops when the plot calls for erotic measures, and when she's playing it straight, she's as steadfast as ever.

Fucking can be many different things. There is a fun fuck and there's the old porno fucking, cowgirl style where the two bodies are apart. You can have some rough, not-so-nice sex if the guy's an asshole, but that might be the kind of sex two people like if they're both into it. Sex is all of that. It's like eating a meal. Sometimes McDonald's does it. Sometimes you're dying for French fries, and sometimes you want to sit down to a Thanksgiving feast. They both can be very satisfying. Something nasty in an alley way or a quick hand job before you go into a restaurant can be really fun, as well as a six hour tantric lovemaking session. All of that can be fun and all of that should be fun.

Most people only watch adult material so that they can jerk-off. I've had guys tell me, "Why do you bother acting with people who can't act and sets that are bad and there's not enough time to do it in? Why bother to even have any kind of a story?" Then I have other people who actually tell me that they miss the days of the story and they like to get involved, and they like to know the people. I guess it depends upon your point of view. I think it depends if you are watching the film with a person. I've never watched a film for the sole reason of getting off. Well, I guess maybe I have. One terrible experience stands out when I was seeing someone. The guy turned on the video and was fucking me, but he was definitely watching the video and not watching me at all. I felt just like a live marital aid and that was very strange. Most of the time, I don't watch adult films unless I'm making them or seeing someone else's work or seeing what's out there. It is funny because probably the people who make adult films are the least likely to actually watch them. I would say there are many people who make sex films who know little about sex. That's okay, because I think it's wonderful that people make movies that turn them on. I came into it from the exact opposite end — I was more interested in the acting rather than the sex part of it.

Passionate about Love, Fantasies & Directing

In 1988, Hamilton caught the directing bug when she co-directed Jeanna Fine and Alexis Firestone in *Tales of Ambrosia* along with her friend and colleague Candida Royalle for Candida's own production company Femme. Jane's years of experience as an actor parlayed into a smooth evolution into her directorial career, she was able to effectually transfer her knowledge and vision behind the camera lens. By the early-mid-1990s Jane's days as an actor were limited to special projects such as the cult film *Bloodsucking Pharaohs in Pittsburgh* (1991), considered by many to be Hamilton's best non-porn role. Jane decided to move into directing full time in 1995 and was able to inject new life into her career through her first solo effort, *Right Connection* (1996) for VCA. In 1998, she rolled out one of her personal favorite ventures, *Love's Passion*, the first of three movies Jane believes are her best.

> *Still Insatiable* (1999), I had a little cameo in, and *Torn* (1999) with Ginger Lynn, I also had a little cameo. As far as directing, there is one film that I did is called *Love's Passion* (1998) which is more about romantic love. It's about being so in love with someone that you just want to be fucked everywhere and everyplace just because you love them. I've been accused by my guru of being in love with love and I think I am. I'm very much in love with the idea of romantic love. I love the notion of love. I'm a horrible romantic. Romance, as far as I'm concerned is being able to do the dirtiest things you can possibly do with that person, and being able to fall asleep with them and then look at that person in the morning and carry on about your business and get up and fix breakfast or look after the kids. When you can be that abandoned and that free with the person you love it's easy to do stuff with strangers. It's easy to be this little piggy-slut that you want to be. If you own that and face that person and continue to share with them — to me that's the ultimate, when you can live out your fantasies and everything.

There are a lot of women who don't want to own the responsibility of being sexual creatures. That's not me, but we know from polling women that there are tons of women with rape fantasies and everything. Does that mean they really want to be raped? No, but they want to have abandonment and they want to be relieved of the responsibility of wanting crazy sex. That way, they're still a good girl;

COURTESY OF JANE HAMILTON

they haven't done anything wrong; they couldn't help it, it was forced upon them. Somebody made them do it as far as a choice. How do you portray that common women's fantasy without saying that it's okay to go out and rape a woman? *Edge Play* (2001) was my attempt at that. The premise for the film is there is a society that you could join to have women's fantasies fulfilled. A situation would present itself and you could either say the code word or you'd pass on it so it would be ultimately up to you if you were going to indulge yourself in that fantasy or if you weren't. I directed this film and it was with Marilyn Chambers. *Edge Play* was fun and that was shot in four days.

Love's Passion and *Edge Play* are two of my favorite films, and *Taken* (2005). My husband wrote *Taken*. That was meant to be an R-rated film, but I shot six days on that which is unheard of these days. *Taken* is another one that a lot of people thought that I shouldn't have made because it's a story of a woman who is abducted and who falls in love with her captor. If you only look at it three quarters of the way through, you think, "Why is she making a movie about this?" If you follow it to the end, you will understand this is a woman neglected by her husband who falls asleep and has this whole dream of being abducted because she wasn't taken care of. The message is not that women need to be abducted. The message is that it doesn't matter if you've been married for a number of years or have children you're still a vital, sexy woman who probably has desires. That was my message, not that women need to be taken out and raped but if you don't take care of stuff at home, you might have to do something about it, or if anything else, a woman spends a lot of time daydreaming about it. When *Playboy* [channel] played it, they cut out the whole abduction part where the woman falls asleep and wakes up at this guy's house. They would not show what they felt to be coerced sex. My boss stuck up for me because he saw what I was trying to do. I give him credit for that.

Obviously I made films that I cared about and that's why it's difficult for me to go out and sell myself as a director right now because I don't have any burning passions. I also produced a horror film called *Parasomnia* (2008) of which I'm very proud. I think it's the best movie in which I've probably ever been involved. *Parasomnia* was an actual movie that we shot and I spent two and a half months on that. It helped bankrupt me, but I'm really quite proud of that. There's a chance that I might see a little bit of money out of that. Who knows?

Parasomnia is an intriguing independent horror movie about a young hospitalized woman (Cherilyn Wilson) afflicted by parasomnia. The condition causes people to sleep for extended periods only to awaken for brief intervals. After a visitor (Dylan Purcell) falls in love with the patient during a period of "awakening," he moves her to his apartment to protect her from a fellow patient and murderer (Patrick Kilpatrick), a man who convinced his wife (Sean Young) to jump from a building while under hypnosis. Jane Hamilton appears as a TV reporter.

I think, in adult, I absolutely have done everything I've wanted to achieve. I could make more films, but I'd like to try other things and do other things. It'll happen or it won't. I don't know; I don't care. It's like love. Love might happen to me again, or it might not. I'm lucky that I've had the love that I've had, and I'm lucky that I've made the movies that I have made. I'm hopeful, but I'm still going to be okay if it doesn't happen.

One of Hamilton's great loves, her late husband, Michael, was her collaborator in life and in what she considered her finest movie projects and other initiatives including *Electric Blue*, a softcore TV program for the Playboy channel that first aired in the early 1980s. The couple learned how to pool together their individual strengths in order to form an alliance and complete work they were both proud of — which included two sons.

Michael was an artist, a great guy. He had a master's degree from Columbia University. He'd shot *A Night of a Hundred Stars* and the Toni awards and a lot of commercials and that kind of stuff. He actually ended up in the adult business because of me. He wanted to come out to the west coast and do straight stuff, and obviously, the entrée I had was in adult. If you read Georgina Spelvin's book [*The Devil Made me do It*], he's "Iron Mike". Iron Mike is one of the guys she writes about, and that is actually my husband. She talked about her "Michael," and I talked about my "Michael" and I got married to him. At the AVN awards, I went to introduce her to him and she just about fell over because my Michael was her Michael. It's a small world but I still wouldn't want to paint it. He was a cameraman and he was a lighting director. He was my lighting director for almost everything I ever did except at the end when he got to be too sick.

It was tough at first because I didn't know the production side of the business very well. I first started producing before my oldest son Christopher was born — he's now twenty-seven. We started working on *Electric Blue* stuff for the Playboy Channel. I started into producing that long ago. I'd just gotten out of the business and he was going to be my cameraman. I didn't know a lot and he was very short with

Jane Hamilton, Michael, and their young family, 1980s.

me. He was very impatient with me. I was learning and I just said, "Hey now. I'd like to keep the money in the family, but I know there are a lot of clients who are much worse than I am and you're very nice to them. You treat me like one of your clients or I'm not going to work with you again." He did and I did, and we had a life-long working relationship together. At first, he was expecting me to know stuff that I didn't know. I sure learned, but at first, I didn't know since I haven't been on that side of the business before. I hung out with the crew mostly more than the cast. I gravitated there, and anyway, he was great after we had that initial talk. It all worked out quite well.

We were together for twenty-seven and a half years because we were together for a year and a half before we got married. He's the father of my two boys. During the last ten years, we were on and off in our relationship. Towards the end, I had relationships with other people. He passed away a year and a half ago. I got him a kidney and liver transplant and he ended up passing away from cancer stage four, metastasized cancer. Michael was sixty-nine when he passed. He was eighteen years older than I was.

Boogie Nights

Many people unfamiliar with sexually explicit films first hand have at least seen or have knowledge of the first Hollywood picture to attempt to emulate the golden era of adult filmmaking titled *Boogie Nights* (1997). Directed by the self taught, San Fernando born maverick, American film-maker Paul Thomas Anderson whose more recent film *There Will be Blood* (2007) was nominated for eight Academy awards, *Boogie Nights* (inspired by the life of John Holmes) follows the rise and fall of a fictional 1970s porn legend, Dirk Diggler (played by Mark Walhberg). The mass appeal of the picture (nominated for Oscars in three categories) is responsible for putting Anderson on the map as one of the most masterful and exciting mainstream directors of the last two decades. Hamilton, who was hired by Anderson to play a family court judge, believed the role of Diggler's lover and fellow porn star Amber Waves (portrayed in a scintillating performance by Julianne Moore), is the incarnation of a few select porn Goddesses, including Hamilton. In 1999, Jane was rehired by Anderson to appear as part of his ensemble cast in *Magnolia*. Hamilton was also in the popular TV series *Six Feet Under* in 2001 in addition to other mainstream roles, but it is her commanding turn in *Boogie Nights* film buffs won't easily forget.

> *Boogie Nights* was great. I was really excited about it and found out that Paul [Thomas Anderson] is a big fan of mine. That was exciting to learn that someone in the straight world knew of me. Ron Jeremy is responsible for putting us together. Paul wanted to get to me and Ronnie knew how to find me. He got the two of us together and I went down for a reading and everything, and I got the part of the judge. Paul said he would never put me in one of his movies as a porn star, a prostitute, a hooker, or anything like that. [Former adult performer] Skye Blue is also in the film and [adult

performer] Summer Cummings. Those girls were the chicks that were in the hot tub scene. Skye is a producer and director and does a lot of *Playgirl* and adult stuff.

On the day we were shooting the scene, I was sitting there and Julianne Moore was in the make-up chair next to me. I didn't want to be rude and I didn't want to say anything to her. I thought that maybe

Jane Hamilton in *Boogie Nights.* NEW LINE HOME VIDEO

she had to concentrate. She really didn't say "hi" to me and I didn't say "hi" to her. I tried to give her, her own space. We weren't leery of each other but maybe just a nice "hello" or something and that would be it. I was thinking, "Oh my Gosh. Okay, here we go." She certainly wasn't mean or anything, but she wasn't friendly. Looking back, I probably didn't appear very friendly either. She'd never been around somebody from our business. She had no idea what we were like.

We were on the set and I said something to her or she said something to me about Annette Haven. Now, I like Annette but she's a nut case. She's a hypochondriac and she's a nut case. I kind of said to Julianne like, "Oh yeah, she's great." or something to that effect.

Then she said, "Oh, my god, did you find that…" and all of a sudden it broke the ice and we were chatting like there's no tomorrow. Julianne is just one of the nicest gals you'll ever want to meet.

I went to a couple of openings with her because I was in *Magnolia* (1999) for a second too. You'd probably miss me. My name is on the credits longer than my face is on screen. I played the dental assistant in *Magnolia* that harasses Bill Macy. He's also a lovely man, by the way. Whenever I run into Julianne, it's always, "Hello. How are you?" It's been years now since I've seen her, but for a while, I was running into her a lot at openings and premieres. She was always just the kindest, nicest, down-to-earth person. I have such respect for her; she's such an amazing actress. It really made me feel good that she took the time to address me as a fellow actor and to acknowledge me. I had a quick, but small relationship with her. It was very thrilling for me. She's just a lovely, lovely person.

Mark [Walhberg] and some of the guys came to one of my sets because they wanted to see what an adult film was like. I think I was doing something for [adult company] Adam and Eve at the time. It was one of my house party videos or something like that; they came over and hung out, they were just nice guys. I didn't pay too much attention to them because I was directing. They just observed and talked a little bit; they hung out near craft services. They talked to some of the actors to get kind of an idea what it was all about and what we were about, how we worked. What it was like on the other end.

Jane's role in *Boogie Nights* as the family court judge is crucial to the story as porn star Amber Waves (Julianne Moore) battles her estranged husband in a courthouse for shared custody of their young son. In an ironic and powerful scene, Amber's husband (played by late adult performer John Dough) manages to convince the judge his wife is unfit to jointly raise their son, not only because of her involvement in pornographic films as an actor, but also because of her struggles with alcohol and drugs. The final shot of the segment shows Waves crying alone outside by the courthouse wall, devastated by the judge's ruling.

I filmed that courtroom scene in one day. I think there were about four or five takes and that was it. I was probably in make-up longer and then there was the lighting. After they see everything, they ask you to go away and then they light it and shoot it. I did feel great to be a part of it. A lot of people in our business really didn't like that movie. It makes it look like our business is a violent business; that we're about being violent. You know, when you make a film you have to realize it's not reality. If you notice many of us are well spoken and can put a sentence together so that makes us uninteresting. We're kind of like regular people. If you want to uncover somebody, you have to go for something dramatic. P.T. Anderson is a filmmaker. It wasn't a historical piece. He took dramatic license. We wouldn't have shot where he had a shooting; that would have never happened. We wouldn't shoot in San Fernando Valley at that time. This was pre-1980s.I just saw *Boogie Nights* again a couple of weeks ago and it was very interesting to see it on the big screen. I didn't remember it being so violent and so off the wall. There were always those characters around and especially at that time, everybody was doing blow. It wasn't just us — doctors, lawyers, everybody — it was the time when that was going on; it wasn't just our business that was out of hand. Look at the music business. We're lucky that any of us are still alive, I am sure.

A Renaissance Woman

Jane Hamilton is anything but naïve when it comes down to how outsiders might critique and dissect her profession. She is not willing to yield to those who don't know her, nor can she be untrue to who she is at her core. Sometimes leaving well enough alone is all that is required.

I don't usually volunteer the information about my work unless it's appropriate or unless I'm bored and I want a reaction. I don't usually share who I am with neighbors. First, because it's not necessary, it's not that I wouldn't share but I don't think it's got anything to do with our relationship. I'm not concerned about what they do too much. I'm concerned about them being a good neighbor. Do I hide what I do? No. I'll tell you what, because I do movies and many of them are low budget, I wear many hats. We were doing a show where we needed a police car and after finishing up at about two am, I drove the police car home at night. I drove it to my house and when I woke up on Saturday morning the whole neighborhood was a buzz. They got all excited and I was dead tired, I'd gotten home at three or four o'clock in the morning and I'm going, "You guys. It's a prop car. I used it for a shooting in a movie; it's a prop car. Everything's fine." They were okay, but it was funny. I do happen to have the best neighbors in the world and we watch out for one another's houses. How much do they know about me? I don't know.

I don't think it really matters. There are family friends of our sons. They've grown up together and our kids have known each other their whole lives. We are best friends and they know everything about me, and they've been in my movies. They've done extra roles in my movies and stuff like that. They've been great friends and there is definitely not a problem.

COURTESY OF JANE HAMILTON

For Hamilton, choosing the scenic route has brought about an acute self-awareness. It's taught her that having the right to succeed or fail is one of the most beneficial and practical tools a woman can possess in her arsenal. Any regrets Jane might have are few and far between.

Nobody forced me to choose the path that I chose. I chose it myself and I'm very glad. What other genre would I be able to be so successful as a star and as a director, as a producer, an occasional writer, and as an editor? Where else could I do all of those things and be successful, be given a shot and given a chance? A feminist means being able to make your own choices in life even though they might be unpopular with people and other women. I am a feminist and this is one of the only jobs where the women are paid more than the men are so I consider myself a major feminist. I'm able to make my own decisions about my life and choose the kind of work that I want to do. I have control over my body and I might use my body or my brains as little or as much as I want. Anybody who decides to go into sex work that has a choice of doing other things, I think they are feminists. You have to be.

A lot of people have a feeling about women, especially, that they get into this area of work because they can't do anything else. They are perceived as victims and they have to do this as if it's their last holdout or they are forced or something. That's not always the case. That's what helped us to get out from under the whole prostitution thing — it was a choice and both partners are being paid. It is different if you're a woman who can't do anything else, but this has helped me to be a better person. It's helped me to be okay. When you meet actors or actresses who don't have any recognition yet, they're just neurotic people. "Look at me. Here I am." Because I've been able to be a star and have fans, I don't need that anymore. I'm comfortable in my own skin and I feel fulfilled. I have some kind of validation that I am special. Therefore, I don't have to go around and ask if I am special. Like I said, it's not for everybody, but for the people that it's good for, I think it can be a real saving thing.

There is something in my personal past I would change and it has nothing to do with adult. It's tough for me to even think about so I'm certainly not going to discuss it. There are decisions that I made that might have influenced people's lives and maybe not for the better. It has to do with family and animals. Those are the only things I regret. I have regrets that the last time my dad was sick I waited so long to come here to Las Vegas. I had been back and forth and I needed money very badly, and I had a job so I stayed for the job. I cancelled the one over the weekend which is when he died so I have that regret. I also have regret that I didn't take my husband to the beach one last time to see the ocean. I told him that we were going to hang out and then I was working and didn't get a chance before he passed. I don't regret any of my decisions in porn. I don't regret the choices I've made. I regret that the choices I've made that have had such an impact on my family and my kids.

Somebody once told me that being a porn star was one of most selfish things you can do. I didn't understand that and I was completely pissed off at that comment, but upon reflection, I think he's right.

He said that because you decide to do what you want to do you kind of just say, "Deal with it" to parents and your family, and to your loved ones. Somebody came up one time and asked my dad about a picture of me, and said, "Isn't that your daughter, Sid?"

My dad looked at it and said, "No, that's not my daughter." I think when my family could be proud of me, they were. I'd always said I would never get married and I would never have kids. I met my husband and the first I wanted to do was to get married, and have his kids. It was a biological thing. I met him and I fell in love with him. I wanted to marry him and have his babies. This business affects your life in a lot of different ways. My children; especially my older one has been very affected by it. I didn't realize it until now and he's going to be twenty-seven. I wasn't aware of it until he was about eighteen and he kind of pointed it out to me. It's been a difficult life, but I think as a result, my boys are much nicer to women. They're not the kind to sleep around. I think they have a pretty damn good respect for women.

The kids have been very good for the most part. My children are cool, I love them — we get along great and we're best friends, but at the same time, they are much more conservative than I ever was. They grew up with a mom who pretty much anything goes so the good things are that we're completely close and they are completely loved, and the bad things are that they've got a very outspoken mother who tells them probably way too much information. Now, my kids are much closer to me when they were growing up. We sit and we'll party together, and smoke and joke and laugh. They're my favorite people in the world, actually. They're very interesting and I think they're funny. They're sarcastic and they're cynical and enjoyable people.

[Renowned erotic photographer] Suze Randall really was my mentor in showing me that you could be in our business and you could be normal. You could have a family and the kids were going to be okay. You could work in our business and still be a good mom. I remember when I first started hanging out with her we'd take Holly [Suze's daughter] to the beach and watch her in the water. Holly's a big photographer now. She's taken over the business and she's a lovely gal. She's a wonderful gal. We use her when I shoot for Adam and Eve.

It's been very interesting financially. It's been tough for me financially lately, and I mentioned to one of my sons who is a PA

(Production Assistant) with me — he works on sets — I said to him that I may go back and do some Cougar scenes or something like that. He said, "Mom, do whatever you've got to do, but I don't want to be on that set." That's my younger son. He's fine with it, but my older one said that if I did that he would never speak to me again which is pretty radical, seeing as how close we are. That's how much he really doesn't like it.

In addition to occasionally accepting credible roles in television and movies in recent years, Jane has also flirted with the notion of making a return to the classroom.

I could go back to teaching today, but I probably would need to pick up a few credits. I've thought about it, but with my history teaching kids and with the internet, it just opens it up to bad stuff unless I was teaching at the college level. High school — I could be accused of all sorts of things because of my sexual background. When my kids were little, I was a substitute teacher in New York, off and on for about a year or so. I was working here or there once or twice a month. They would call me when a teacher was absent. You really have to be careful because you get all sorts of labels. Being a mother, I was completely freaked out by the possibility that people might think I'd be inappropriate with my children. They figure that if we are liberated sexually we must be deviates.

I got my sexual drive from someplace. I'm a sexual being. My mom is still very sexual. Her dementia demonstrates itself in her sexuality. She constantly has me screwing the caretakers and the caretakers are constantly running off to get married. She told me her caretaker proposed marriage to her a couple of weeks ago. She's been very sexually charged her whole life. It was very difficult because my father was unable to make love to her. I would talk to them and tell them that you don't have to have a penis to make love, but that didn't seem to make sense in their minds especially for men. It's just still a very much a part of her — her whole sexuality. My mom and dad were very demonstrative. I know now that when my mom used to pass my dad and they'd both laugh she was reaching behind and cupping him. I'm also very affectionate.

I tell you, I've been in a position where I couldn't get laid to save my soul. The last time I was in one of those moods and I went to go out, I wanted to go dancing. I couldn't get into the place that

I wanted to get into and I wasn't going to stand in line and wait. I went to a bar and this young kid kind of next to me — I wasn't trying to pick up a kid, but I was out trying to dance and have fun. He looked at me and said, "Yeah, I can kind of see how you might have been good-looking once." It's called "aging". I'm lucky because I've got a lot of people who say nice things to me. To be

COURTESY OF WORTH MENTIONING PUBLIC RELATIONS

honest with you, I think way too much emphasis has been put on sexuality. I think that if we had a healthy society we wouldn't focus so much on it, but I just wish that everybody got five hugs a day from somebody. I believe it would calm down the world and I think we'd have fewer wars and we'd have less everything. People get so uptight over sex.

Relax, It's Just Sex

"You can't leave a footprint that lasts if you're always walking on tiptoe." MARION BLAKEY

When asked to speak about the legacy she has behind for classic film fans, Jane is frank about her distinguishable contributions to the adult industry.

My legacy is that I was the girl-next-door that you would be able to have a shot. I definitely wasn't a pity case. I don't think I was the most gorgeous and I don't think I was the sexiest, but people liked me because I was a regular person. I like myself more now. Some people want to get back to another time or they want to have a do-over and be back in school. Oh my god, I'd never want to do that again. I've had more than enough of everything. I think I was able to show that smart, intelligent women choose this type of profession and again, being the type of woman or person that most people wouldn't think would be involved in adult, I believe that's what our legacy is. I think society tends to dismiss us as a bunch of bimbos who can't put a sentence together so I feel that's the deal. My legacy is also that I tried to make films that depict sex in a realistic way. That's what I tried to do.

When I met Jane during a girls' lunch at Penny Antine's home in North Hollywood in the summer of 2011, it was evident from her friendly, easy-going nature that can become impassioned depending upon the discussion at the table — she is the quintessential girl next door. Pleased to reveal that day she recently found love again with her high school sweetheart Stan, Hamilton continues to keep the wheels in motion while setting aside time for life's fundamentals, not to mention primal urges.

Apart from my work, I like to care of my animals. It used to be working on my house, but I'm so sick to death of that. I don't want to do it anymore. I love to read, I love to make movies. I love to talk to my kids and my family. I have a big social circle as far as gals I e-mail [including Club 90 friends]. I hang out with very few people. I'm very much a homebody. I will go out, don't get me wrong, I'm

not a recluse, but I'm not a real partier. I'm happy to be home with a few friends. That's who I like to be around and my family. What I'm very proud of most are my two sons. All this other stuff is work. I'm proud of my family, I'm proud of my sister. I'm proud of my family, and my little kitty; that's what really counts.

What I like to do more than anything is to connect with people. That can be on a friend basis and it can certainly be sexual. What I like to do in my spare time is I like to still make love and get close to people and share intimacy. That is so important to me. That was one of my goals when I got in the business: that I would be able to come out of this business and still enjoy my sexuality and making love. Thank god, I've been able to do that.

19

Julia St. Vincent
From *Exhausted*
to *Boogie Nights*

When filmmaker Julia St. Vincent decided to direct the first erotic documentary about legendary porn star John Holmes in 1980, she never imagined her movie would become the inspiration for *Boogie Nights*, the critically acclaimed motion picture that enlightened mainstream audiences about the hardcore film industry during its glorified golden era.

In the early 1970s during summer breaks from secondary school while living just outside of San Diego, the teenaged St. Vincent left her family home to work part time as a filing clerk, and eventually, became the bookkeeper for Freeway Films, an independent Los Angeles adult company owned by her uncle Armand Atamian. Atamian, known primarily for the success of the Johnny Wadd dynasty was an enterprising and ingratiating figure in the 1970s adult entertainment scene. Along with partners Lee Frost and Bob Cresse, he produced sexploitation films in the 1960s, prior to realizing his niche in hardcore pursuits. Atamian passed away suddenly in 1980 leaving his niece to assume full control of business operations. Faced with the task of ensuring Freeway's survival, St. Vincent shrewdly took stock of the company's greatest resource and prepared to produce and direct an original documentary featuring Holmes. The result, *Exhausted: John C. Holmes, The Real Story* (1981) combined interviews with the star and people on the street, interspersed with Johnny Wadd film footage and an original title song written and performed by St. Vincent. The film's New York release in the fall of 1981 synchronized with the sudden disappearance of Holmes on the run from the law due to his connection to four unsolved murders in Laurel Canyon the previous summer.

"When I made *Exhausted* people said it was just a fluke and in a way, it was just a fluke. It really was a case of being in the right place at the right time to make a film. It was kind of incredible that it went as far as it did. That film grossed over a million dollars in 1982." JULIA ST. VINCENT

COURTESY OF JULIA ST. VINCENT

Inspired and influenced by St. Vincent's conception and subject, in 1997 director Paul Thomas Anderson introduced the world to *Boogie Nights* featuring pornographic film characters Dirk Diggler (Mark Walhberg) and Amber Wave (Julianne Moore), both composites of Holmes and St. Vincent along with other notable players fashioned after actual industry personalities. Impressed by Anderson's fastidious attention to detail, Julia acknowledged Anderson's homage to her own successful cinematic effort, yet she is reticent about the intimation that *Exhausted* is her legacy.

St. Vincent has lived many lives since planning her exit strategy from Freeway Films and the shadows of the adult entertainment industry just a couple of years prior to marrying and giving birth to two children in the mid-eighties. Still guided by her entrepreneurial rock 'n roll spirit, Julia reaps the benefits from a profitable business and keeps her finger on the pulse of the latest trends to penetrate modern culture. Characterized by her raucous sense of humor tempered by subtle sensuality, St. Vincent continues to reside in balmy Southern California and wouldn't have it any other way.

I interviewed Julia St. Vincent in the fall of 2010.

Sweet Captive

I was born in a small naval hospital outside of Boston, Massachusetts in the 1950s. My dad was in the Navy and I'm the youngest of three girls. We moved when I was four years old to California and I grew up in a little suburban town outside of San Diego. After we moved to Southern California, we bought our house for sixteen dollars. Back then, you could buy a house on the Navy fund for nothing. They put sixteen bucks down and bought this house and I think my dad was deployed or whatever and it wasn't long before my dad was gone. I don't really remember him being there. My stepfather was in the picture before my mom divorced my father. She met him at the store. I believe he was a manager and she worked at night, but at one time, she also had a job during the day. We didn't have a lot of money. This was a single parent household pretty much. It was a military household where the father is never there. Anyway, she would come home after working at the bank at night and since everybody was in school except me, I had to sit by her bed while she slept all day. I guess I played with dolls. I played with whatever I could, books and toys. I just played by the bed. To this day, she tells me what a good kid I was because I would sit for hours. I said, "Okay, I sat for hours and now look at me, I'm a total loner." My sister is two years older than I am and would have been in kindergarten or first grade, so I guess I sat there until noon or three in the afternoon. I remember that my sisters and I were close up until I was about ten. They were both older than I was so they were off doing important things older kids do. I think my mom remarried when I was about five or six.

My stepfather was ridiculous. He was a cowboy and his parents were Germans from Michigan. I didn't know at the time he was a cowboy. I didn't realize this until I was into my late thirties when it hit me one day, "Oh my god, these are songs my dad was listening to". Then, I suddenly remembered that he wore a cowboy hat and I realized that he was a cowboy. Even for those days, he had a vintage truck that he would fix up and it had the wood rails. Eventually, he owned a gas station and there was a farm across the road from it. I remember at one time, he had a bunch of goats and all of them died but one. One of the goats was all screwed up so they gave it to us to nurse which was kind of silly because we weren't allowed to have animals in the house. All of our animals lived outside in the freezing cold. California isn't that cold but they could have died from the chill. I used to walk that goat on the leash, but he didn't last very long. It was only about six to eight months. We had a Cocker Spaniel, too.

It was a regular family, but my stepfather was very strict and my sisters were always getting in trouble. I was always taking the blame. He was abusive with his punishment, but in those days it wasn't necessarily considered that bad. My mom used to chase us around with ping-pong paddles to try and spank us so we used to break the handles off of them. She used a hairbrush and he used a belt, but that's just the way it was. Up until the time we were teenagers it was a pretty normal but strict house. I remember him staring at me from the other side of the table and I was nervous because you could get into trouble for stupid little things. You had to wipe your mouth and say, "excuse me" and do all of the things that perfect people with a lot of class had to do, but we lived in the suburbs we didn't live in Beverly Hills. There was a lot of dysfunction in the families around us too. I think a lot of people there were military families. We were middle class people. We were on the lower spectrum of middle class.

I loved school. I was a good student. There were five or six of us kids who hung out together in the early years. I was good until about puberty and then stuff went the other way. Up until then I was very happy, and had a lot of friends and had a lot of fun. There was dysfunction but it wasn't the whole highlight of my day.

I sang when I was a little girl and I played the violin. I played violin in the school band in elementary school. I wouldn't try to do it nowadays! I got into trouble in kindergarten for singing opera. I was put in the corner for about an hour for singing opera. Nowadays, they would put a person on YouTube and you'd be famous for a week. At that time, you weren't supposed to sing opera because you were supposed to sing like a little kid. My mom sang opera at the house so I would sing along with her. We would sing harmonies in my house. My sisters and I learned the harmonies and we sang all of the Christmas carols. It was okay, but I was a tomboy and I liked to run around with the neighborhood boys.

All in the Family

My family heritage is Armenian so they were immigrants. My grandmother and her husband worked for years in the shoe factory. They didn't have any money, but they ended up raising kids who had college degrees and they were enterprising kids. For having come from that background, to do as well as they did — they all died with money. They weren't hurting for anything.

My uncles came to all of our Christmas dinners that were at our house. Often my grandmother or my grandfather would come and stay with us for a period. I'm not sure why that was, but everyone seemed to end up at our house. My mom would cook dinner and my uncles didn't like each other; they would fight and argue and they were also a little perverted, but at the time what did I know about that? I didn't know. There were signals when they chased us around and grabbed us. Just little signals like that, but it was a totally accepted thing. My mom didn't realize or think it was a problem. These were her brothers and I guess she just thought they were uncles who were being silly. They used to argue and my Uncle Armand used to tell hilarious jokes, but they were inappropriate jokes. My mother would ask if he was pregnant because he was fat and he would say something like, "Yeah, I'm going to have a baby elephant, do you want to see his trunk?" You know inappropriate comments in front of a little kid. My mom would shut them up and then they would act normal. They would always be at our house for the holidays.

Julia recalled that in the 1960s, her uncles became affiliated with the adult entertainment business in New York and Los Angeles. Her Uncle Armand's first joint production came a few years later.

I remember my Uncle Armand was an engineer at Litton Industries [specializing in electronics and early computers] which was a big company back then, and my other Uncle Gil — I'm not sure how but he got involved in pornography and ran sixteen millimeter films, eight and sixteen millimeters through New York. He had theaters there where he would run these films and he'd go through the alleys or whatever and deliver them. He earned a ton of money from doing this illicit activity and he was a millionaire. Gil owned a huge home that had eleven rooms with a pool and a sauna room, and it was out in the country outside of Boston. My other uncle was an engineer too, but Armand ended up getting involved here in L.A. making the films. He had a friend out here that he probably met through his brother Gil. So it was kind of family helping other family members to get involved in this business. I will say this; they were all a little perverted. They were very inappropriate around us girls, yet no one realized it, no one knew that. When I visited Gil back east, he would do sinister little things that were totally improper.

Slaves in Cages

Armand was involved in film production with his associates before he had his own company. He was involved with sexploitation producer Bob Cresse. That's where Armand got started, with Bob and director Lee Frost. They were all buddies. Gil had been involved first and he knew people — it's likely that he came out and they went to the racetrack or whatever. Armand met these guys, quit his job and started doing those kinds of films.

My sister, who was a natural born artist, designed the posters for the movies. It would have been the late 1960s. My uncle had her put together some posters and logos at first. We knew what they were doing, but we didn't see the movies or anything. They were just bad words on paper and they weren't that bad. The cast had some women who looked kind of like hookers. We knew that, but we didn't see any nude people.

The first company was UTA [United Theatrical Amusement] and the second company was Phoenix. The office was two rooms in an apartment. That's where they did all the mysterious stuff because UTA was a legitimate company. Phoenix would have been around 1970, and it was actually more of a company on the books. They had UTA and then they had Phoenix that produced the sleazy movies that Bob Cresse made. UTA was built to distribute Cresse's movies and Dave Friedman's movies, and then they got a few other people on board and distributed their movies too. Armand was the guy who was responsible for all of the posters and the trailers and all the one sheets and theatre cards that go in the poster holders in the front of the theaters. He shipped all that stuff out for those guys. It was his original job. Armand used to distribute all of the things that Dave and Bob Cresse were making, and a couple of other porn people of that genre of porn. Their friend Lee Frost also got work in the legitimate end of things. He would be making regular films and then come over and help Armand and Dave make the sleazy films because that was his little voyeur thing. Armand had actually acted in a film called *The Animal* (1968), but again, what he did for the most part was theatrical distribution. He would ship the films out and then get them back, and ship them out to the next guy. He ran them like that.

Bob Cresse seemed to have had somewhat of a specious reputation: Once while out walking his dog, he (and his dog) was shot in the stomach by police while assisting a woman in an alley he believed had been mugged.

The first film Armand made was *Slaves in Cages* (1971). For those who know anything about that genre it was relatively abusive toward women, and weird, dark stuff. Nowadays, people tend to make it seem like the exploitation era was fun, but in reality, it was kind of dark. It was kind of a sick little thing — guys beating off, peeping Toms, and there was murder and rape and all kinds of stuff going on in those movies. Because they had such low budgets, they didn't show too much and didn't mix too much violence with it. I guess that would get have gotten people busted a little bit quicker.

The original grindhouse stylized film *Slaves in Cages* produced by Armand Atamian was directed by sexploitation sultan Lee Frost under the pseudonym Carl Borch. As a marketing scheme, the Phoenix International Films release was billed as a Denmark production, but was actually shot quickly in Los Angeles. *Ride Hard, Ride Wild* (1970) and *The Captives* are additional early Phoenix productions advertised as European/Denmark films. Under a similar title, Freeway Films eventually produced the hardcore feature *Sweet Captives* (1979) with Rhonda Jo Petty in the starring role (co-starring Paul Thomas), though the two films are quite different. Another effort titled *Sleazy Rider* (1972) was produced by Cresse and Atamian, and directed by (sometimes) actor Roger Gentry. In 1973, *Sleazy Rider* and *Ride Hard, Ride Wild* were paired together at the box office.

Julia, along with her two sisters, was often sent to reside with relatives on a temporary basis while enrolled in high school in San Diego. The three girls also traveled to Los Angeles on different occasions to help at their Uncle Armand's burgeoning film company in part-time employment.

We'd go up there for a week or so in the summers to work in the office. My sisters would go and then I'd go. It seemed that we all took turns. There was one time when we were there together, but that was only for a couple of weeks. I'm not sure why my mom kept letting us go or shipping us to other people's places. I suspect it's because she couldn't deal with us. Anyway, we'd go up there and do filing and box stuff up and all kinds of miscellaneous things. Armand had the office on Cordova Street and next door to him was Dave Friedman. Originally, I worked as a file clerk at the back and then I'd leave because I had boyfriends or I'd go back home. I don't really remember the entire sequence of events. Armand would teach us how to work because teenagers don't know how to work. I would end up working there for a summer doing theater records where they'd order something and they'd put it on a card and you'd put it into a machine. It was the first of its type, a computerized system using cards because back then they didn't have computers. We happened to have one of the first derivatives of a computer for the business.

Eventually, I did the bookkeeping. A few years after the movies were put out I was still making those reports. At first, Armand distributed for other people, and eventually, he distributed for Universal — big companies. Back then, they used to mix porn with big companies. Eventually, they opened up a partnership with my Uncle Gil. I didn't know at the time that Gil was a partner. Armand would tell me to do the books and to cut off twenty-five percent, and then add ten percent back on. I didn't know why he was doing it that way. My Uncle Gil was angry one day and started yelling at me. He called me a "lying cheater". Armand looked at him and said, "Don't say those things to her. She doesn't know." I didn't know who the partners were. I was told to add and subtract things so I did.

Freeway Films

They started Freeway Films in the early 1970s. That's when Armand started to make films on his own because up until that point everything that Armand did was for his buddies. My uncle must have had a lot of energy because he was doing the exploitation films, and then he was doing the films with Dimension Pictures such as *The Thing with Two Heads* (1972) which was a legitimate production Lee Frost directed starring Rosie Greer and Ray Milland. They were very campy movies back then. While he was also doing work for Universal Pictures, he opened Freeway Films right around the same time. He was good actually, with business. Freeway opened in the office next to us on Cordova Street, and then later, it was moved up to Hollywood. The office was moved to appease Damon Christian really.

Damon Christian was hired as a producer for Freeway Films when Freeway decided to branch out to produce sophisticated films that eventually became hardcore in nature, including plans to resume continuation of the popular Johnny Wadd series. As her Uncle Armand integrated into the adult filmmaking business as a venture capitalist, Julia's mother found it challenging to raise her youngest and most independent-minded teenage daughter while having marital difficulties. With much uncertainty in her home life, St. Vincent found it difficult to concentrate on her studies.

I think my mom was overwhelmed having to take care of kids. When I was fourteen, she had shipped me to Boston for the summer and when I got back, she told me that she and my stepfather were getting a divorce. She said, "Oh, by the way, your dad doesn't live here anymore and we're divorcing."

I was like, "What?" That's when I started getting into trouble and having problems. The next year she shipped me again, but by then I was the age where people ran away so that didn't work. When I was seventeen, I hitchhiked to New York and graduated there. I was in school in New York until January when it was freezing cold. I remember I went to someone at the school and said, "I want to graduate early. If you guys don't graduate me I'll probably never graduate," so they did it. I didn't even have enough credits. I'd missed so much school by that time from having problems. I was seventeen and a half.

St. Vincent's strained relationship with her mother during her teen years inspired her to do a fair bit of traveling on her own and make new friends. She hooked up with a band and had several opportunities to demonstrate her impressive singing talent as a part-time vocalist. When she and one of her boyfriends eventually broke up and the funds ran out, Julia contacted her Uncle Armand for assistance prior to returning to work for him at Freeway Films. During her absence, Freeway Films produced *Beach Blanket Bango* (1975) starring Rene Bond and Ric Lutz, a send-up of the Frankie Avalon/Annette Funicello MGM feature *Beach Blanket Bingo* (1965). Freeway also released *Confessions of a Teenage Peanut Butter Freak* (1975) with Rex Roman, John Holmes, Helen Madigan and Constance Money.

> I told Armand that I needed money and I needed a ticket home and he sent me the money. It was just like the Beatles' song "Ticket to Ride" because he sent me the ticket to get back home. Armand was the guy who saved everybody and he had money. My mother was divorced and she never remarried again, but she never gave me anything.

Between the years 1975 and 1978, Atamian and Freeway Films, one of the top production companies of its day generated the final five and best Johnny Wadd pictures of the series and became the largest distributor in the world of the Johnny Wadd domain. Freeway is duly credited for proficiently turning Johnny Wadd into a brand unrivaled in the industry. With superior production values, Freeway's library of Johnny Wadd features stand apart from low budget productions of the era. Over the next couple of years, Julia fulfilled different roles in the company when needed while her uncle hoped to finally secure her in a permanent, full time position.

> Armand was like my refuge. He was the one I went to when I didn't want to go home to my mother; I'd go to Armand. I

worked for him at Freeway Films when he was making *Liquid Lips* (1976) and *Tell Them Johnny Wadd is Here* (1976) — that was a summer job for me. It just so happened that they were making those films when I was there. The previous films had been made at Bob Cresse's apartment or they'd do shots on the street or something, but it wasn't hardcore porn. They'd switched over to hardcore because actress Felicia Sanda who was hired to do the one scene with John in *Tell Them Johnny Wadd is Here* was not originally supposed to do a hardcore scene. I was working at Freeway that summer when those two Johnny Wadd films were shot, and then I came back and they were making *China Cat* and *The Jade Pussycat* in 1977. I think Armand would be in production and he'd call me and say, "Come up here." I'm not sure how I happened to end up there every time they were doing a film, but I believe it's because he called me.

St. Vincent recounted how she and her female co-worker were present on the set of *Tell Them Johnny Wadd is Here* the day actress Felicia Sanda broke away from the script and engaged in hardcore sex with Holmes rather than the softcore scene that had originally been written. For a young naïve woman, St. Vincent described the experience as shocking, yet intriguing, to witness the spontaneous fusion unfold.

I was on the set of *Liquid Lips* when I was still a kid so I was sneaking around and peeking in windows and stuff, but it was exciting to be there because there were lots of people around and cameras and everything. The other girl who worked in the office and I would run back inside and Armand would tell us to get back to work. We'd sneak out again and go see the next scene and he'd not really impose penalties on us. We'd sort of sneak around until we almost got in the way and then he'd tell us to leave. Honestly, I think he knew he was kind of my father so I believe he was trying to curtail my activities.

I had gone up to San Francisco when they were shooting *The Jade Pussycat*. Armand had sent me up to San Francisco to watch Damon Christian during the production of *The Jade Pussycat* to make sure he wasn't screwing around. I walked into one of the hotel rooms and Georgina Spelvin took all of her clothes off and was running around naked. I was like, "Oh my god! What am I supposed to do?" I ended up sitting in John's room because he was the only normal person in the room. Everyone else was doing weird things and laughing. They were all much older than I was and they were naked. Imagine a twenty-two year old girl with blue jeans and pink high heels. I was sort of a disco girl but had no experience with that kind of a situation. I thought to myself, "What? You guys are going to strip and start screwing each other?" I don't know, but it

COURTESY OF JULIA ST. VINCENT

was strange which is why I ended up hanging out with John because he was sort of like a big brother or something that was not naked. I hung out a little with Damon, but he was right in there laughing and cajoling with all of the naked people. There were other sets where people would try to get me into a threesome going, "Come on, we'll do it right now. Just close that door. Let's go in that closet."

I said, "No, I've got to work." They didn't understand that I had a job, although frankly, I'm sure if I quit doing the job I'm not sure that anything would have happened. It's not as if my boss would come in and say, "You didn't do your job!"

I had originally been the file clerk. Then the bookkeeper would leave and Armand would get another bookkeeper and he wouldn't like her. He kept enticing me to come back with money, or a new car or whatever it took to get me to come back to L.A. to work. I didn't want to go there. I believe he gave me a new Pinto, one of the first compact cars made.

So I was there when they filmed *The Jade Pussycat* and I stayed with Freeway probably a year. Then I left again because Damon Christian and I got into a fight and I got sick of him. He drank and he would bitch at me and treat me terribly. When I left after *The Jade Pussycat* nobody wanted me to leave, but I couldn't work with Damon. He'd slave me to death and when people would come over he'd yell at me and say, "Go get me coffee." It was humiliating. At one point, I got up and walked out so that was why I quit because of him. I had also worked for a while at Crown International Pictures that did the film *Coach* (1978) with Cathy Lee Crosby and some other movies that were sort of B-rated movies and were legit, low budget. I got tired of it though because they made me a clerk and a receptionist. I had gone back to San Diego and got in a band and then I screwed around for a couple of years, but I ended up returning to Freeway. When I came back later, they were going into production with their last two films before Armand died.

Moving On Up & Mr. Wonderful

When Julia returned to work for Freeway for what became her longest and final period, the company was about to go into production with *Sweet Captive* (1979) and *Sweet Dreams Suzan* (1980). Both pictures highlighted star Rhonda Jo Petty and were directed by Lee Frost. Unbeknownst to everyone at the time, the productions would be the last two movies made by Freeway under Atamian's reign.

I had been in Lake Tahoe with my boyfriend and I'd had just had surgery. I was in the hospital. Armand bailed me out of that, too. I went back to Freeway and that's when he invited all of his buddies over like John Holmes, and Lee Frost, and everyone was there telling me what a great opportunity it was to go back to work for Freeway. Armand would buy me any car I wanted. He bought me a Toyota Supra, a little sports model. It was a brand new car and I was to get so much money per week and holidays paid, and all these things to convince me to come back to work. He told me that day that he'd fired his girl Joyce. I'd been back working there for a couple of weeks and I said, "You fired her. Who's going to do her job?" I started to work as a print booker and bookkeeper for Freeway up at Hollywood and Vine. Damon Christian wasn't in there at that point; he had been gone. Armand got rid of Damon because Damon was cheating on Armand with Joe Steinman [head of Essex Pictures] and a bunch of other people. Damon made an under-the-table deal with Joe and Joe gave him the money to run a big company that was somewhat successful. Armand hated Joe because of that.

In the 1960s, Columbian born Joe Steinman started Essex Video, an adult production company and distributor located in Northridge California. Alongside Caballero Home Video and Video Company of America, Essex grew to become one of the largest pornographic production firms in the United States during the 1980s. In 1988 Essex Video declared bankruptcy owing its creditors including filmmaker and cinematographer John Derek (husband of actress Bo Derek until his death in 1998) nearly one million dollars. Derek had made *Love You* (1984), an explicit sex film he sold to Essex consisting of cast members Annette Haven, Wade Nichols, Lesllie Bovee, and Paul Thomas in a tale depicting a couples' romantic getaway weekend.

They convinced me to stay. For a while, I lived with Armand and then I got an apartment. One thing led to another and I started hanging out with "Mr. Wonderful" [John Holmes]. I spent time with Mr. Wonderful at night when no one was around. I had actually gotten a little house and my boyfriend at the time lived there for a couple of weeks before my uncle kicked him out. Armand said to me, "Do you want me to have some people break his legs?"

I said, "No, just put him out." He did and let him go. It was weird and my boyfriend left. He didn't want to leave because he was pissed off and he knew how it was coming down. I had the opportunity to be with people more successful than he was. Besides, he was abusive toward me. I wasn't very good at picking people at this point in my life. Not that I ever was, but I kind of just picked the next person that walked around that was attractive. He was a good-looking guy, you know. He had a good body and he was a musician, and I thought he was cool. He left and then it went on from there. I started hanging out with Mr. Wonderful. He was actually the main reason why my boyfriend had to leave.

Adult Film Association of America

Julia grew to know John Holmes quite well and embarked in a romantic relationship with him lasting a few years. Together they socialized with people in the industry and often spent down time at St. Vincent's Hollywood home. At the time, Julia kept her friendship with Holmes private from her uncle and their colleagues. During the initial stages of their relationship, Holmes's excessive use of cocaine and freebase hadn't yet become problematic. In the interim, St. Vincent stepped up to become the youngest board member of the Adult Film Association of America.

After I came back to Freeway, I got my own house and I started hanging out with all the porn people. I had never done that before because I was younger than they were and I just never did it. At the same time, Armand started sending me to all of the meetings for the porn business. They were producer meetings. He really didn't want to go himself so he'd send me there and he would go out gambling. I usually went by myself. I don't remember Armand there but he might have gone once or twice. I would go to the all of the conventions. I would have been between twenty-two and twenty-four years old at this time. The people at the producer meetings were [directors] Ann Perry and Carlos Tobalina and his wife Maria, and Joe Rhine, who was the First Amendment attorney — that was Ann's husband. Joe Steinman was the head of Essex, which was one of the largest companies in the world making pornography at that time, and Dave Friedman who was the President of AFAA. Every Friday, or every other Friday, we'd have these meetings and then we'd all go to dinner. We'd have meetings with several industry people, but the top guys would go to dinner. I went along because I was the Kewpie Doll in the group.

St. Vincent laughed while recalling how Holmes would often suggest she dress in appropriate professional business attire for AFAA board meetings rather than in jeans and high heels which she customarily wore. Julia wasn't about to conform her personal style or her fashion preferences for anyone.

I was the youngest board member of that group. I would go to dinner with all of the big shots and one day they asked me, "Do you want to be on the board?"

I said, "Sure, what do I have to do?" They said, "Nothing, you just raise your hand whenever we do it." They had a big meeting and there were about a hundred people, and somebody nominated me. I was voted in as one of the board members. There was a President and a Treasurer and there were approximately five board members. I remember that I was the youngest board member and I attended the conventions. It was probably about a year.

Rationale

As a woman who grew up working behind the scenes for Freeway Films, and eventually, looked through the lens as director of an erotic movie, Julia confessed she can't conceive why an individual would choose to expose oneself in sex films.

There were times they'd be shooting a scene and we'd be in the background watching them and I'd turn to Bob [Chinn] and say, "How the hell do they do this?"

He'd say, "I have no idea.' I hate to say it like this, but how could these women allow themselves to be put in a position where the whole world was going to find out? How much is that worth, two hundred dollars? How do you have sex in front of people for two hundred dollars? I can't imagine it. People will tell me that they were poor. Do you mean to tell me that they didn't have a single relative to stay with; I find it hard to believe. I guess if you were an addict and working in adult films and you don't have any one to support you because they'll kick you out. Back then, people didn't know about how to deal with addiction.

One of the girls, [porn actor] Danielle, thought she was so cute that she believed she'd be famous. She was a little girl that I took in for a while after Armand died and she eventually ended up living with Gloria [Leonard] and Bobby Hollander. I talked to her extensively about what she was thinking and I've talked extensively to Rhonda [Jo Petty] as well. I know that girls came in believing that they were something special because guys would tell them how special they were and they were too naïve or confused to recognize the truth about that. When you take advantage of a person who is confused, then you are exploiting them. That's like me telling a mentally challenged person, "Let's go rob a bank." How would they know? "You're going to be famous on TV with a gun in your hand, let's do it." I mean, how did Patty Hearst end up with a gun? She was a hostage who ended up in an environment where weapons were being used and all of that was going on. It's kind of the same thing.

When I was working for Freeway, I'd get on an airplane to go somewhere and someone would ask me what I did. I'm a very talkative person, and I would end up telling them and I can't tell you how many times I'd be embarrassed. Some people would really want to hear this stuff, but there were other people that just looked at me like "What the hell are you doing?" It was embarrassing to me because I was kind of raised with the message that you don't get into movies. You don't do anything like that. I had really no discretion about the people I spoke to and no censorship of my own which is typical with me, so I'd tell them my life story. There were people there who would go, "What? Why would you do such a thing?"

I'm wondering, do these women never travel and run into people who know? How do they deal with that? Do they pretend it doesn't exist when half the world disagrees with what they do? I couldn't handle that. There's a difference between how I think and how a lot of other people feel about it. Even back then, you knew this was something that was not a vehicle to real stardom. I mean, come on, everyone knew that. I guess some people just thought, "Oh well, I can just do this instead of real stardom." Personally, I never wanted to give up the idea that I'd be rich and famous or whatever, in legitimate terms.

Exhausted: John C. Holmes, The Real Story

Armand Atamian was diagnosed with cancer in the fall of 1979 and died six months later. Julia had grown very close to her uncle, and suddenly, while still grieving over his death she found herself in the position of conceptualizing a way to sustain the company's success. St. Vincent found she was able to kill two birds by devising an idea for an inventive film project.

Originally, the reason I made *Exhausted* is because my uncle had died and I was really floundering around trying to figure out what to do. I was going to the producer meetings and hanging out with some very ambitious people. One day it hit me, "You can't call yourself a producer if you don't ever produce anything." I hired a management consultant to help us to figure out what to do with the company, and we all kind of brainstormed the idea and tried to determine what we had for assets in the company. It turned out that what we had the most of was Johnny Wadd [footage]. That

John Holmes in *Exhausted* raw footage. COURTESY OF JULIA ST. VINCENT

turned into, "Well, we should make a film." That really incubated for a long time. We didn't immediately make a film. I started shooting these interviews with John mainly because I realized he was going to die one day soon. As far as the process goes, originally, it was shot on sixteen-millimeter film with this camera guy Kenny Gibb. I paid him to shoot interviews with me and with John in the back of this studio. That's why the original footage looks so bad besides the fact that John looked terrible. It was the original footage shot.

The original interview footage for *Exhausted* filmed in December 1980 shows Holmes looking rough and fidgety. As the star chain-smoked while positioned between two potted plants, St. Vincent posed several questions. Because of his relatively accelerated decent into the usage of freebase, Holmes was unable to remain focused and instead, laughed and danced around her queries. At one point, he turned to camera operator Kenny Gibb requesting a time-out. The twenty-minute raw footage did not appear in the 1981 release of the film, but it was introduced as one of the extra bonus features when the documentary was re-released on DVD in 2001, twenty years after its making. Julia expounded upon the reasons why she believed it was advantageous to produce the picture.

> The film was really a way to give John a thousand dollars and to give me something to do. In the back of my mind, I realized that a bunch of situations would be involved: John would realize he's not a bad guy and he would get out of the dumps. In the case he died I would have that footage of him and I'd become rich, but there were lot of little things going on and that was how it was shot. Then it was put in the can until the next year, at least four or five months. We started editing in some of these other movies [Johnny Wadd clips] to it but we really didn't have enough to do anything with it. I had hired a few people to help me and one of these guys said, "Let's go and shoot some more footage". We ended up going to Chicago and we did "man on the street" interviews there because we had already done them in Hollywood. We got more out in the open with regular people footage. We also interviewed Seka in Chicago. Then we came back and edited all of that together.

Cowgirl on the Forefront

In addition to the Holmes interview segments, Seka is the only other adult film star interviewed for *Exhausted*. At the time of production, Seka and Holmes had worked together in many feature films and Swedish Erotica loops, establishing a believable rapport as porn royalty. One of their most celebrated outings is the final Johnny Wadd film *Blonde Fire* (1978) produced by Freeway Films and adapted into *Exhausted*. When she was interviewed for this book, Seka spoke about St. Vincent's adept capabilities as a filmmaker.

> I was put up at the Hyatt Regency Hotel in Chicago when I was invited to do the interview for *Exhausted*. Julia was very thorough and professional. She knew what she was talking about and she had obviously done her homework. I found that to be an interesting little tidbit at the time because often many people would interview you and they had no clue what they were doing.

Especially in the eighties — she was doing something that men didn't even have the balls to do. She was definitely one of the cowgirls on the forefront.

As the first director and female to produce a feature motion picture about an erotic film legend, Julia made a distinction between her docu-

Julia St. Vincent Directing *Exhausted.* COURTESY OF JULIA ST. VINCENT

mentary and contemporary biographical films. She addressed how an effort such as *Exhausted* was atypical of movies being made during that time frame.

It is different making a real film than it is to do what I did because essentially *Exhausted* is a compilation of films. I already had the material. I could do it at home now the way people do with YouTube. You get films and stick them together and then you need supplemental footage of people talking or something else happening in order to make it work. In 1981, there were no documentaries in the adult genre. I don't think any documentaries were made in this fashion at all. You could say it's more similar to Reality TV today or whatever. There was nothing else done like these "man on the street" interviews. It was partly due to the fact that I didn't have any money that I had to do it that way. I did it on a sixteen-millimeter print and then it was sent it into the lab and they created the whole thing. It was kind of fun, actually.

While in the midst of writing narrative, conducting interviews, directing, producing and editing the picture, St. Vincent added a personal touch when she wrote and recorded the film's title song "Running out of Love." The following is a sampling of the song's lyrics illuminating Julia's professional and private analysis of her film's subject:

> *"The words of many seem to whisper with the wind.*
> *The eyes of many gleam when he walks in,*
> *He is the man of love; he is the sigh,*
> *He is the mystery; he is the lie.*
> *Ten thousand held him close, but he was free.*
> *He is the mystery; he is the sigh.*
> *He is the man of love. He is the lie."*

When you're making a movie, you get to do anything you want. You get to be the singer and the song- writer. There's no one around to say you can't do it. At one point, I tried to sell that song to radio stations but nobody bought it. I don't think I really tried very hard though, I just sent a couple out to see what would happen. I should add that when we looked at the footage we decided that we needed another interview with John.

We dressed him up and we put him in there, and we did the last shoot at Laurel Canyon. That's when he was a freaking mess. I took him down to Ludwig's [a high-end Men's boutique in Los Angeles], and got him a nice suit and fixed him all up. Originally, I had really wanted him to look the way he does in the outside interview footage, but I couldn't figure out how to get what I saw in my head on film. At first, there was sort of a disconnection between the idea of how to get someone to look good on film and actually executing it. I suddenly realized, "Oh, you've got to put him in nice clothes and surround him with a lavish set." I was relatively young so I didn't really recognize at the time that was the issue.

The film was shot incrementally, but at that point, when the outside footage was shot, John was almost a total mess. It was a miracle that I got anything out of that; it really was kind of a fluke that it came out as well as it did because you're dealing with a drug

Julia St. Vincent interviews John Holmes in *Exhausted*. COURTESY OF JULIA ST. VINCENT

addict who is rambling. At the same time, I suppose for a film it's a good thing when somebody's rambling because now you've got footage. Shortly after we finished shooting, John was wanted [by the L.A.P.D. in connection to the July 1, 1981 multiple murders in Laurel Canyon] and then the film still sat around for quite a while until somebody said to me, "You better hurry up because I heard that someone else is doing it." I thought to myself, "seriously?" That put a fire under my ass. I could have gone on indefinitely never putting that movie out. The reason that *Exhausted* sat in the can for a while is because I had to keep rekindling an interest in it. It turned out that no one was actually doing a documentary on John, but another producer had told me it was happening. When they said it I flipped out and went, "Oh, my god," so I started working my ass off to try to get it out and that coincided with John being arrested. I broke that film in October. I can't remember the exact date but John was arrested in December of 1981.

St. Vincent ended her relationship with Holmes prior to his Wonderland escapades in the summer of 1981. While Holmes was on the run from the law *Exhausted* opened in New York City. The release of the film coinciding with Holmes's disappearance triggered a wave of publicity that couldn't have been strategically planned. By the time *Exhausted* reached The Pussycat Theatre in Los Angeles, it was both a critical and profitable success.

October is when it was first released in New York City. We went to do a screening there and I'm confident that my partner called the cops. He started handing me money and said, "Call the papers right now."

I said, "What do I say to them?"

He said, "Tell them you're at a screening and they're busting your film." I started dialing the *New York Post* and everybody had this story the next fucking day. We were making phone calls and the cops were on their way while we were dialing. Then the cops would arrive and we'd get in an elevator — jump out, then jump in — because they were undercover. They followed us all the way back to our hotel room and then we got on the phone with *The New York Times*. I said, "Do you guys want an exclusive on this?"

They said, "Yeah". They asked, "Who has it?"

I said, "Just, *The Post*," so he said, "Yeah, we'll take it." I knew the people at *The [New York] Times* because they'd already interviewed me before when John had disappeared. From there, the guy in New York booked it at the [New York] theater. Thank god, because this was my last dollar. At this point, I had borrowed fifteen-thousand dollars from my mom. Back then, that was a huge amount of money. I had already put ten thousand dollars into the film and I had borrowed about forty thousand dollars on credit for the prints. I was nerve-wracked wondering if anybody would buy the film, and then New York said, "we'll take it'. They ended up running it for six weeks and holding it over. The next quest was whether the Pussycat Theatres would take it. They ended up pulling down *Deep Throat* (1972) to take it. That's when I realized, "Okay, you're going to be alright." *Deep Throat* had been running almost ten years and they were trying to figure out how to take it down because it was losing money. They couldn't come up with a film to replace *Deep Throat* and then they put *Exhausted* there and put up the bright lights waving in the night. We had a big old party up there with the *L.A. Times* and the TV networks came and it was kind of fun. When *The L.A. Times* and others came they weren't there to cover it, they came because I knew them. By now, we were friends. It was a private party. That night I was the Debutante of Porn, yeah.

Exhausted: John C. Holmes: The Real Story contains a series of hardcore footages extracted primarily from the Johnny Wadd movies directed by Bob Chinn and produced by Freeway Films during the years 1975-1978. With a tagline that boasts: "14,000 Women knew him intimately!" what

makes *Exhausted* a truly innovative venture is the rare interview segments with Holmes filmed between 1980 and 1981. Captured in an array of moods from provocative to pensive to playful, the dialogue portion is reinforced with candid and funny comments provided by random people on the street who supply opinions about the controversial and well-endowed porn legend. St. Vincent also shot Bob Chinn directing staged scenes from an unfinished Johnny Wadd script, *Waikiki Wadd*, depicting Holmes as the charming private dick chatting up Laurie Smith and Laura Toledo. Later, he makes simulated love to the two girls in a hammock. Ominously, the date on the

Original cover art for *Exhausted.*

clapboard for the exterior interview footage reads June 25, 1981, only four days prior to the robbery of L.A. nightclub owner Ed Nash resulting in four deaths at 8763 Wonderland Avenue. Thirty years later, very few documentaries have been produced about X-rated film legends. *Exhausted* is the first of its generation.

The 2001 DVD re-release of *Exhausted* is accompanied by special features: Julia's Diary, Cast Bios, and St. Vincent's own engaging commentary presented in an upbeat and humorous tone. Julia is joined by her old friend and contemporary Bob Chinn, along with Gloria Leonard for a retrospective on Holmes and the golden age of adult filmmaking.

The Legacy of *Exhausted*

It was an unlikely scenario. When I made *Exhausted*, people said it was just a fluke and in a way, it was just a fluke. It really was a case of being in the right place at the right time to make a film. I had nothing else going on and there was nothing stopping me. I

Holmes and Bob Chinn are interviewed (by Julia St. Vincent) in *Exhausted.*
COURTESY OF JULIA ST. VINCENT

had to figure out how to survive the world I lived in. It was kind of incredible that it went as far as it did, and I was able to accomplish that with literally nothing. That film grossed over a million dollars in 1982.

At the time, it had the biggest video contract ever done. It played outside of the pornographic film world. It went into Georgetown University and other regular theatres. It was a *hardcore* movie! When *Boogie Nights* came out [in 1997], that was the second fluke of the whole thing. Why would you think after sixteen years something as obscure as that film would come back into anyone's consciousness? Most people would put it away as I did and think, "Okay, that was fun and maybe someday you'll do something else with it." That was just something in my closet. How do I view it in the bigger perspective? I don't really think this was up to me at all. It was just a weird set of circumstances.

Weird set of circumstances or not, *Exhausted* proved to have staying power. While still enrolled in high school, award-winning director Paul Thomas Anderson created a thirty-minute documentary shot on video, *The Dirk Diggler Story* (1988) about a promising 1970s porn star modeled after John Holmes. Almost ten years later in 1997, St. Vincent's documentary became the impetus for Anderson's feature film *Boogie Nights*. *Boogie Nights'* two lead characters, Dirk Diggler (Mark Wahlberg) and Amber Waves (Julianne Moore) are eerily reminiscent of Holmes and St. Vincent as their professional and personal relationships intersect when Waves creates a documentary about Diggler. In the film, Waves interviews Diggler and his director Jack Horner (played by Burt Reynolds) in a scene precisely duplicated in dialogue and set design from the Holmes/Chinn interior interview segment in *Exhausted*. Anderson also copied famous scenes excerpted from two select films of the Johnny Wadd series: *The Jade Pussycat* and *China Cat*, and even paid tribute to St. Vincent by naming the Melora Walters' character Jessie "St. Vincent" an amalgamation of her surname and golden era porn actor Jesie St. James. Anderson endeavored for the authenticity angle when he hired adult film actors Veronica Hart and Nina Hartley to embody key players in the Hollywood account of the pornographic film industry during the 1970s at the peak of the golden age. The cover image for the *Boogie Nights'* special DVD edition strongly resembles the original artwork for *Exhausted*.

When I found out about *Boogie Nights*, I was sitting in the country on a ranch and I had no idea what was going on outside my door. Cass [Paley, director of the acclaimed documentary *Wadd: The Life & Times of John C. Holmes*, 1998] called me and I didn't even really know who he was. I forget how he even found me. I guess my friend Lee knew him and he got me.

If I played any role in any of this — and this is just the theme of my personal belief— but if you really set out to do a good deed and I earnestly was trying to do that even though it may have been a little misguided, but because of the good deed, years later *Exhausted* is remembered. Even though I'm certain there are fundamentalists who will say that's a lie. You take lemons and you make lemonade. I earnestly believed that all I had were lemons and I had to fix it somehow. At the time I was trying to make another human being believe that he was better than he was, and plus, I had to survive. Honestly, and I'm not trying to say this is true — but I think I formed who John is to this day. He is perceived a nice guy because people have seen that film. He really wasn't that nice. I created a monster. I was trying not to fail and I was trying to help someone see himself differently. I mean, that really was what motivated me

Dirk Diggler (Mark Wahlberg) and Jack Horner (Burt Reynolds) are interviewed in *Boogie Nights*. NEW LINE HOME VIDEO

behind everything else. I'm not particularly motivated by the idea of making a million dollars. I do say that — that I'd like to make millions, but that's not what I was trying to do. That's kind of where I think I probably differ from people who are in the porn business and that's really why I'm not in the business anymore because it's all about the money. To me, it was more about cause than it was about the money. It's difficult to get through something if you are just doing it for money. If my uncle had been in some other business than I would have done the same thing somewhere else in a different genre, but unfortunately, I didn't have any uncles that were regular producers!

I really do think the reason that *Boogie Nights* came out is because I did make John appear somewhat nice. Therefore, he was a fascinating guy. If I'd portrayed him as a guy who was just having sex with a bunch of people I don't know that it would have lasted this long. There is nothing profound in the fact that someone had sex with people. The domino effect is that because I made *Exhausted, Boogie Nights* was made, and because that film was made, *Wonderland* was made.

Beyond *Boogie Nights*

Spurred on by the popularity of *Boogie Nights*, Hollywood took another crack at cashing in on the public's fortuitous interest in porn legend John Holmes. In the fall of 2003 *Wonderland*, directed by two relative newcomers to filmmaking, James Cox and Captain Mauzner, was released by Lions Gate Films. The film chronicled real life events leading to the robbery set up by Holmes (Val Kilmer) at the home of L.A. nightclub owner Ed Nash (Eric Bogosian) followed by a multiple homicide in Laurel Canyon. *Wonderland* strikes a chord during certain segments, but due to its unsympathetic characters, harsh content, and misrepresentation of certain incidents, the production was unable to capture the success or the same demographic that made *Boogie Nights* a triumphant undertaking.

I always wondered if Paul [Thomas Anderson] didn't know somebody in the business because he got really close to me with the Julianne Moore character in some respects. There were many little things in there that I thought were parallels, but they could have just been completely coincidental although I did wonder if he might have known someone. Anyway, the homage was very nice of him even though we ended up with legal issues.

Initially, when plans were made for the DVD release of *Boogie Nights*, *Exhausted* was slated to accompany it to make the product a dual set until a legal infringement compromised the marketing strategy.

I should qualify that by saying it wasn't something that I was doing vindictively. I was just a little pissed that there was no credit. Everyone ripped me off. The video company that got involved totally ripped me off. They pretended to own *Exhausted* which they denied. They swindled Newline and Criterion into believing that they had the rights to give them. It was a business proposition. There wasn't insult on the work that Paul Thomas Anderson did, but I wasn't getting paid a single nickel for DVDs that my film was put on. Then when lawyers get involved, it kind of snowballed. If someone came and had legitimately asked me if they could pair *Boogie Nights* with *Exhausted*, and given me a percentage, or something, I would have been fine with that prospect. That was never offered to me as a counter offer. If they'd made that offer it would have been different, but nobody made that offer. I may have miss-stepped somewhere, but I didn't know any other way to do it, and I reached out to those guys to try to talk about that, but who am I? According to them, I'm a miniscule part of life. In other words, you don't go and take *The Little Engine that Could* and recreate it without talking to the guy who wrote that book and said, "Hey, we're going to redo this, are you interested and we'll cut you in".

I have a feeling that whole thing got confused because of certain people who had no right to get involved. I think they shot some scenes [for *Boogie Nights*] down there at their company and so they were the big shots of the day, I really don't know. Having said that, I thought *Boogie Nights* was really a good film and made well. Except for the fact that I was depicted as a porn star, it was real to life, yeah.

Bigger Picture

St. Vincent is genuinely humbled when asked about the impact her film has made historically on contemporary cinema. What is most important to her is that people and fans of the adult genre understand the motivation and cautionary measure communicated in her project.

My legacy is minute in the scope of all of humanity, but if it was only pertaining to one little section, I'm not sure. I think P. T. Anderson passed along the message that I was trying to show and that is quit messing with people because they are making poor choices and help them instead. I think that's what he was trying to say as well — that people were confused. People were just doing what they had to do just as I was trying to do with John. An opportunity was there and I took advantage of it. You could say the same thing with all of the women who do pornography. That's what they do, they take what they do have and use it. If you're one of these judgmental people, you should get off of your moral code because people did whatever they thought was right and what they could do at the time; they might have not thought of the bigger picture, but so what?

I honesty do believe that they're coming from a dysfunctional screwed up situation though — most of them. I don't think in the whole time that I worked in that business that I really met anybody — women who acted in films that were coming from a real holistic viewpoint. That's what I meant earlier about them being preyed upon on by people. It's really a hard business. Young girls get

COURTESY OF JULIA ST. VINCENT

involved in it thinking that they'll become something, but they're not. You're going to get paid some money and then it's all over. The damage has been done to you.

I think there's a difference in the overall attitude in today's porn. The women are in a different environment because the attitude is more open about the adult industry now. People are not as judgmental today as they were years ago. There were many judgers back then so it's not as bad for people now. You can actually survive without being beat up about it at this point. As far as the women go, I'm not sure about caliber, but I still believe that people who enter pornography are in some manner dysfunctional and haven't resolved their issues. Otherwise, you would make a different choice. If you're twenty years old and if you have it presented to you to have a choice of being in pornography or being in a commercial or a bit part in a movie, I would take the bit part as far as I could take it. The other point is that people around you are telling you that you should be doing it, and you don't realize on the other end what it's going to do to your life. It's not a healthy thing.

St. Vincent, who has been gone from the pornographic movie industry for more than twenty-five years, remains cautious about sharing her past with people who might not understand. Coinciding with the 30th anniversary of the 1981 release of *Exhausted*, in the summer of 2011, Julia made a rare public appearance at a downtown L.A. venue where she introduced her documentary to members of the media and a group of vintage film fans. While gauging the age range of the audience, a mixture of youth, middle-aged, and older, not surprisingly, eyes were riveted to the images on the screen as many absorbed the film for the first time since its release. Gram Ponante, an adult journalist in attendance that evening, commended St. Vincent for her unique presentation of an adult film icon. He wrote, "Aside from the interviews, which are priceless, the collected sex scenes in *Exhausted* are beautiful. Holmes took his time with his partners and it's refreshing to see so many natural, fleshy beauties again including Seka, and the perfect Annette Haven. There can be no argument that Holmes was famous for a reason, and this loving documentary is worth watching."

For me personally, it's not even as severe as other people, but you can always use that as a way to beat yourself up — that you're not as good as everybody else is because you did pornography. You cannot run for public office without that coming out somewhere along the line. It's been a long time for me, but you can always use it against yourself in some manner. Other people can bring it up and mess with you. Again, if you say to someone, "I was pretty successful at one point, I made a movie," and they ask you what it was and you tell them they say, "Oh, a porn movie? That was really something." There's always a way to get beat up, but I guess in the bigger picture they could beat you up over any damn thing.

I got married to get out of the adult business. I tried to change my life and the thing that I thought was, "I don't want to raise children and have Mommy going off to work with a bunch of people that are stripping and screwing each other." I couldn't see how that and a newborn baby could fit in the same picture.

St. Vincent's children are now grown. When she's not working in her home office, Julia, a larger than life personality in every respect is funny and often spontaneous. She loves to walk her dog along the ocean boardwalk or take off for an adventurous road trip on the spur. I had an opportunity to accompany Julia and her dog alongside the ocean in Carlsbad late one afternoon in July 2011. While we observed kite boarders near the shoreline on a picture perfect day, St. Vincent reflected upon her past in the pornographic film industry. Years ago, she recorded her experiences and is saving them for a rainy day.

It's not that I have anything personal against pornography, but I don't like the way it can affect someone's life. People get hurt by it. Sure, it is fun when you're a kid and everything, but when you grow up and you look around and you see what choices you have, some of them are limited because of that. Everybody can come out and try to question my opinion, but I've been there and I already know what they have to tell me. Even the women who came out sort of unscathed don't make a lot of money today at age fifty because of pornography. They're broke. You can only use your body for so long. It's not even the same thing as being an actor because an actor like Betty White can get old and still accept parts. What kind of part in porn do you want to see an old grandmother doing?

20

Laurie Holmes
New Dawn for Misty

At forty-nine years old, Laurie Holmes (born Laurie Rose) is an apt example of what it is to be a survivor although she'd be the first one to proclaim she's nobody's victim. As the youngest of three children from a nuclear family in New Mexico, Laurie was not unlike any other little girl growing up in the southwestern United States during the late 1960s and 1970s. The daughter of a military man and kindergarten teacher, Laurie grew rebellious in nature during her teen years. She was sent to live in foster homes before becoming pregnant by her boyfriend at age sixteen. When she was unable to reclaim the carefree years she'd lost before becoming a young mother, Laurie entered adult movies in 1982 to support her young son and chose the stage name "Misty Dawn."

In her first feature film, *The Best Little Cathouse in Las Vegas* (aka *For Love or Money*, 1982) Laurie co-starred opposite her favorite veteran actress at the time, Rhonda Jo Petty. Although her tenure as a performer was sporadic, her petite stature in conjunction with a high-spirited girlish essence and well-formed figure, made Laurie popular with male audiences.

Shortly after her introduction into the triple X industry, the young performer fell in love with legendary porn star John Holmes (fresh out of L.A. County jail for contempt) after becoming smitten by him on the San Francisco set of *Marathon* (1983). A few months later, John invited Laurie and her son to move in with him and became a mentor to his ready-made family.

After joining the ranks of the new breed of female adult performers in the early 1980s, Laurie starred in her own feature vehicle for VCX as psychiatrist Dr. Misty Banks in *Dreams of Misty* (1984). In 1985, Laurie put her acting career on hold and became an office clerk for Penguin

"I am a fighter. I fight for what I believe to be true no matter what the cost. It has often cost me dearly." LAURIE HOLMES

PHOTOGRAPHY BY CHARLES BIGGS. COURTESY OF LAURIE HOLMES

Productions, an adult video company Holmes formed along with his partner Bill Amerson. Granted the responsibility to balance the books and preside over accounts that had fallen into arrears, Laurie eventually became Vice-President of Penguin and watched it turn a healthy profit during its short term in operation.

Before he passed away from AIDS-related causes in 1988, Holmes bought Laurie a car for her twenty-fourth birthday and encouraged her to make a fresh start away from the industry. With her son in tow, Laurie relocated outside of Los Angeles where she found work at various jobs that included dancing and bartending. After giving birth to another child, the young mother drifted back to pornographic movies in 1999 where she met her second husband Colombian born Tony Montana. Later, Holmes found employment under Dr. Sharon Mitchell at AIM.

In 2003 at age forty, Laurie finally hung up the G-string for good and hasn't looked back. Nor does she encourage young aspiring starlets to follow in her footsteps. Employed full time in the medical community, Laurie resides in the Colorado Mountains and has a new lease on life. She concentrates on the elements she believes are essential to her well-being: love, family, friends, nature, and a dog named Miss Beto. Laurie manages to retain a few vestiges belonging to her untamed youth however demonstrated by her continued passion for politics, rock and roll music, driving in the high country, and a propensity to speak her mind.

I interviewed Laurie Holmes in the winter of 2011.

Budding Rose

I was born in Albuquerque, New Mexico. I had a very good and happy childhood. It was probably better than most kids' childhoods. My father was a military man. He came from nothing and worked very hard to become somebody. We had more material things than many other families did in our community because of my father's success. While I was growing up, my mother was a kindergarten teacher. She was also a hard worker and was admired by many, yet both my mother and my father always had time for us kids and for all of our many activities. I have one brother and one sister; I was the baby.

I had many dolls and I was into gymnastics and took various lessons during my childhood years. I was a cheerleader in YAFL [Young American Football League] in New Mexico. I was a Blue Bird and a Camp Fire Girl — the whole works. My family went on many summer vacations together. It was the seventies and it was all grand.

During my early years, I had problems in school though and I wasn't very popular in grade school. Then one summer I blossomed into something that I wasn't ready to be. Upon returning to school that fall, all the boys wanted me. The attention I received was a little overwhelming, but I enjoyed every single bit of it. In the eighth grade, I was expelled from one school and in the middle of the year, I started attending another. The girls were terribly jealous towards me and I remember running to the bus away from them so that I wouldn't get beaten up. That incident clearly isn't as pleasurable as the memory I have of walking down the hall and noticing that the boys were literally bending over and grabbing themselves while gazing at me. That image is still etched in my mind. For better or for worse, all of the positive attention was coming from the opposite sex — for sure.

COURTESY OF LAURIE HOLMES

By the time I reached high school I was totally out of control; I hated any kind of authority. I was going to do whatever the hell I wanted to and nobody was going to tell me any different. I was sixteen going on thirty-something, or at least I believed that at the time.

My first love was at the age of fifteen. My parents did not approve as he was about eight years older than I was at the time. That didn't stop me. By the time I was sixteen, I was living in foster homes because my parents didn't know what to do with me. I saw one psychologist after another against my will, of course. Finally, one of the psychologists said to my mom, "She thinks she's grown up and you're not going to stop her. She's going to have to go out in the world and find out what reality is like for her own self". Shortly afterwards, I moved to a different state with my boyfriend and it wasn't long after we'd started living together that I became pregnant at the age of sixteen. I was far too young for motherhood;

I know that now. By the time I was eighteen, I was back at home living with my parents with a baby. I was working at a stupid little clerk job, riding around town with a baby on the back of my bicycle while living under the rules of my parents. I didn't like it one bit. It was during this time when a girl friend of mine and I reconnected. She told me that she had been shooting porn movies and making good money. After hanging up the phone with her, I called her back a few minutes later and begged her to turn me on to these people. For a young mother living at home with her parents, it sounded like an exciting lifestyle as well as an opportunity for me to make enough money to get away from the homestead.

Cathouse

In 1981 during the beginning stages of her adult film career, Laurie was enthralled by the attention and glamour the new and alternative Hollywood lifestyle afforded her. The money was better than what she managed to earn as a sales clerk and she welcomed the sense of family unity.

At that time, they were still shooting thirty-five millimeter movies. I was definitely star struck. In my mind, it was just like Hollywood: "Take 1," "Scene 5," "Rolling" — boom — "silent on the set," and "Action!" What eighteen year wouldn't be Hollywood bound at that point? The fact that we were making decent money to do this too — wow! And the catering, oh my god, did they do some good catering back in the day! This was not McDonald's fast food. Having your hair and makeup and wardrobe done was very cool. I remember that I stayed in a huge mansion with a pool and tennis courts and game rooms. Believe me, it was really quite an experience for a young girl.

My first movie was called *The Best Little Cathouse in Las Vegas* (1982) with Rhonda Jo Petty who was starring in the lead role. Rhonda became one of my favorite actresses for the longest time.

Directed by Hal Freeman, Laurie made her film debut as "Misty Dawn" (not to be confused with the contemporary porn starlet Misty Dawn) in *The Best Little Cathouse in Las Vegas* wherein she played one of the young prostitutes at the brothel owned and operated by Rhonda Jo Petty. When the IRS lands on the premises of the bordello to ensure the company's finances are not overextended, the girls use their assets to effectively keep Big Brother at bay. During the time of the production, Laurie was eighteen years old and she appeared even younger. Much to the delight of adult film fans, with some exceptions, Misty Dawn would become known in the industry for convincingly depicting females more youthful than her years.

PHOTOGRAPHY BY SAM MENNING. COURTESY OF LAURIE HOLMES

Valley Girl

Shortly after I finished the movie, someone told me that if I really wanted to be in the industry, I needed to go to the San Fernando Valley. One of the girls gave me a few phone numbers and hooked me up with a place to stay and someone to pick me up at the airport.

Laurie soon found a home with a group of performers living together above the former Seven Seas nightclub owned by restaurant manager/ nightclub owner Eddie Nash (Adel Gharib Nasrallah). The friends became known as the "Hole in the Wall Gang" because of their tendency to knock down walls to expand their residence for new tenants.

> In the early years, I was star struck and found it all to be extremely exciting. After a while, I found that it wasn't what I had initially thought. I didn't get as much work as when I first started working just like everyone else, and there was always someone new or prettier coming along. I found it was hard to cope with feelings of rejection at such a young age. It was very difficult. You are so young and you try to hide those feelings. I know I did, but still, they are there inside of you to deal with.
>
> Back in those days, the industry was the forbidden fruit so to speak, and if you chose to work in porn, you certainly didn't do anything to bring heat to anyone in the industry. There were unspoken rules that you just abided by. It was dangerous which made it that much more exciting, and it was also illegal which made it that much more profitable too. We believed that if we brought heat to anyone in the business we would be killed or something bad would happen to us. Back in the day, the Mafia ran the adult business — it's as simple as that.

The Feds believe that as early as Gerard Damiano's *Deep Throat* (1972) and probably earlier, Mafia involvement particularly in the areas of financing and distribution of sex films has been an open secret. It is alleged members of the Peraino family who belonged to the Colombo crime syndicate were instrumental in loaning funds and overseeing the production of *Deep Throat* and other illegal X-rated films. This trend continued over the years throughout the porno chic era and beyond. Whether or not it can be verified, other porn producers living in the L.A. region such as Bill Amerson have openly claimed to have had mob affiliations.

Late 1982, Laurie and a friend drove up the coast to San Francisco where she was hired to co-star on the set of *Marathon* (1983) featuring luminaries Jamie Gillis, John Holmes, Ron Jeremy, Bill Margold, Don Fernando, Sharon Mitchell, and Drea in a story centering on various sexual activities during a Masquerade party and at a hospital. While on set, the young actress was introduced to Holmes who had recently been released from a four-month stint at L.A. County jail. Within a few months, the couple began to cohabitate at the home of John's friend Bill

Amerson in Sherman Oaks, California. Toward the end of the year, Laurie and John moved out of Amerson's home and into their own apartment, along with Laurie's young son.

In 1983, Misty Dawn appeared on the box cover for *The Newcomers* directed by Roy Karch and produced by Bill Amerson. She joined Peter North, R. Bolla, Shaun Michelle, Cara Lott and Summer Rose in a story-

COURTESY OF LAURIE HOLMES

line that perfectly captured the early 1980s climate of adult filmmaking by showcasing a bold new generation of female starlets paired with seasoned performers. Concurrently, the industry was transitioning from film to video. Laurie is one of the first newcomers to have worked on the cusp of both mediums including loops. Under her stage name "Misty Dawn," Laurie made a few more movies during the next couple of years including the third installment of the *Taboo* series supporting Kay Parker, Pat Manning, and Mike Ranger. She also had a primary role in the wildly entertaining video *California Valley Girls* (1984).

In *California Valley Girls*, Laurie is featured as one of four "Valley" girls hired to work for an escort service owned by Becky Savage and Shaun Michelle. The quality story is actually a star-studded commentary on the 1980s San Fernando Valley girl scene which hosts veterans Ron Jeremy, Paul Thomas, Herschel Savage, Eric Edwards, and John Holmes. Along with Cindy Shephard, Desiree Lane, and Dominique, Laurie does a great

Misty Dawn, *Newcomers.* vcx

job feigning an authentic "Val" accent. The multi-faceted still photographer Kenji wrote the hilarious theme song for the film.

Subsequently, the young starlet had her first starring role as Dr. Misty Banks in *Dreams of Misty* in 1984. Misty Dawn portrayed a psychiatrist treating sexual repression in her patients by imparting samplings of her own erotic fantasies shown in sequence revealing the various desires and fetishes originating in her childhood. (Pat Manning and Nick Random are both exceptional as Misty's parents.) Laurie has said she felt she was not mature enough to portray the lead in the film at that time, but she is quite believable as the sexy Dr. Banks, and had an opportunity to extend her range as a young actor while enjoying a variety of partners including Marc Wallice and Scott Irish. Laurie eventually gave up performing for the first time in 1984.

Family Business

While Holmes continued to support the family making movies, Laurie concentrated her efforts on raising her young son. In 1985, she demonstrated her capability as a business administrator when she was hired to organize the office affairs of John and Bill Amerson's joint venture Penguin Productions. Penguin was a start-up company between the two long time friends that produced movies on video for adult audiences. Remaining behind the scenes only, Laurie did not make an appearance in a Penguin feature.

When John and Bill first formed a business partnership and started up Penguin Productions, I was supposed to help get the office organized. It wasn't John's intention for me to work there. It was Bill Amerson's idea to hire me on as secretary and after he got a taste of my office skills, he moved me to office manager. Later, I became Vice President of the company. At the very end of my employment there, Bill incorporated the partnership right out from under John. It was challenging working with Bill because he played many head games especially towards the end when John was very sick [with AIDS]. Bill Amerson knew that I wasn't sick with HIV and there were many times when he flirted with me. On a few occasions, I remember that he chased me around a desk.

I believe that I did a great job running Penguin. The books were right on the money, maybe sometimes too much on the money.

Bill had hired his children to work at Penguin and they didn't always feel they had to adhere to my business standards. Bill had also hired his sixteen-year old daughter [Denise] to work in our porn office, and I was concerned about that in addition to the fact that at that time, the industry was still illegal. Many of the porn companies were getting raided all around us, but not us, which is interesting when I look back on it. I had to try to explain to my warehouse people why Bill was talking to the Feds behind closed office doors which was tough — I wanted to know the answer to that myself. I went into my office and shut the door, and discovered that holding a glass up to the wall really works. When I went home that night and told John about what and whom Bill talked to the Feds about he blew a gasket. That was the end of my employment at Penguin and the end of the relationship between John and Bill Amerson.

For the record, Laurie did not wish to divulge exactly what it was that Bill Amerson shared with the Feds when she overheard his one-sided conversation.

John was very proud of me at the end of his life about this. He felt I handled myself better than he had expected, but the games were getting to be too much for me to handle. To this day, I really dislike head games.

Mental Toughness

Laurie and John married in Las Vegas in January 1987 just fourteen months before Holmes's death from AIDS-related causes. Saddened and embittered following her husband's passing, Laurie left Los Angeles and attempted to make a new start as a dancer, doing bartending work, and through other means of employment. She found it difficult to re-invent herself and felt torn and stigmatized because of her work in the adult entertainment industry. After giving birth to another son, Laurie eventually returned to the San Fernando Valley where she re-established herself as a performer, and later, met her second husband Tony Montana on a film set. She and Tony were married in 2001.

Through the years of bouncing between dancing and performing in sex films, Laurie developed an addiction to methamphetamines and alcohol. She illuminated the cyclical grind of life in Porn Valley.

I danced from age twenty-nine to thirty-five, and even at that age it was rough. I needed the speed to get me there and keep me dancing throughout the night. I needed the alcohol to cut the chase of the speed. The sugar in the alcohol also gave me a false sense of energy and security. In my experience, ninety-nine percent of the girls were in the same boat I was. There was usually one girl in the

PHOTOGRAPHY BY KENJI

entire bunch that didn't need the drugs or alcohol, and usually, she was the youngest one.

In many ways, stripping is much harder on your body and your psyche than doing porn. When you are in a movie, you have wardrobe, a make-up artist, and a cameraman looking to get the best angle on you. When you are stripping, you don't. Women are stripping because they can no longer get work in the movies. It takes a lot of energy to dance all night, so like I said you have got to have something to get you there and keep you there. You know in your mind that you're not the same hot sex object that you used to be and the competition is fierce, yet when you come out on stage everyone is expecting to see the way you were, not the way you are now. It takes even more drugs and alcohol — and some tips — to make you feel like "you've still got it," until the next day when you wake up, look in the mirror and your reality and mortality is staring back at you. Then you turn around and do it all over again. It is rough enough for a regular aging stripper, but to have the expectation of being what you used to be on top of it — yet, if you were to use a different name other than your porn name, nobody would come see you at all.

I think it's extremely sad that many of the girls don't know how to become normal working people after porn, and they have such little self-esteem they think they can't do anything else but rely on their aging and abused bodies. It's a vicious, psychological cycle enhanced by your over-the-hill aging body. Again, I stripped for roughly five years and I would never do it again. I feel sorry for those girls. Porn was much easier and prettier.

A few years before bowing out of movies indefinitely, Laurie was asked by director Bob Chinn to make a non-sex cameo appearance as a moll in a movie project Chinn modified from an original Johnny Wadd script he'd written years before titled *Magnum Love* (1999) with Billy Glyde, Veronica Hart, Chloe, and Mike Horner. Laurie's final film came four years later.

The very last movie that I performed in was titled *Voyeur Vision* (2003). I was forty years old and used the name "Misty Dawn" for the very last time. I had left the industry several times and returned. This would be my last movie. I looked great and wanted to be remembered that way.

A more mature version of her former self, Holmes retained her sex appeal in *Voyeur Vision* playing one of the temptresses to entice a Federal Agent employed by a United States Senator in a special program designed to prove prostitution should be decriminalized.

When Laurie finally retired from performing, she was hired to work in various capacities for adult film production companies situated in Las Vegas such as Hollywood Video and VCX "The Home of the Classics."

Not one to mince her words while addressing the subject of the contemporary pornographic movie industry, Holmes believes there is a distinct difference between the current genre and her era even though she acknowledged the business was flawed during the time she was employed.

I feel that the industry today is disgusting. Don't get me wrong, it's always been a meat market, but there was a time when, even though the industry was a sex industry, it had class and it had art form. The golden peak years of porn are gone forever — we could never bring them back. Today, it is how many cocks can be shoved up an ass at the same time. It's about gangbangs and degradation. Psychologically, I believe it was damaging years ago when we were being filmed having relatively normal sex, but the outcome of what the people in the industry today are going to have to deal with afterwards is far worse. What will the long-term repercussions be for those people? To be exploited for doing things that society doesn't accept is bad enough, but being exploited for doing things that are totally sexually abnormal in society's eyes is even worse. I believe we will see many more suicides in years to come, not to mention, the physical damage these individuals are doing to themselves. I recently watched a woman shove a dildo larger then a baby up inside of her rectum. She will probably be wearing Depends diapers by the time she is thirty-five.

I consider myself a very strong person. Even so, there were times that I thought about suicide. All I had to do was pull that trigger and I wouldn't have to deal with the fallout from porn anymore. There are three reasons why I didn't ever follow it through. My two sons were the two main reasons, and not wanting to give the industry that much satisfaction was the third. We are worth more dead to the industry than we are alive. Our content is worth more money to the production companies after we are gone. You are a dime a dozen alive to them otherwise.

If I could go back in time and change anything in my life, I would have never worked in pornographic movies. I have to wonder how different my life would have been. The problem is that even if it's something you think you know you're getting into at the age of eighteen, what the hell does anyone really know until forty? A vulnerable person can be convinced of just about anything at a young

age, but until you have experienced life, the world, relationships, and all the ups and downs sociologically — I think the statistics speak loud and clear.

Many times, I have been scrutinized or judged unfairly because of my involvement in the adult industry. Sure, nobody ever held a gun to my head or twisted my arm to do it. Still, I feel I was a victim. I was a young kid, and woman, and exploited many times with nothing more to show for it than the fact that I survived it all. I believe that porn tears down the moral fiber of a person's sexuality. It destroys lives, relationships, futures, and families. If you think that it doesn't, ask a porn producer if he would want his own daughter fucking in front of the camera and engaging in sex acts so physically challenging that can actually physically and psychologically destroy her later. He will tell you "No," I guarantee it. We didn't subject our families to pornography. We did our thing on the set and then came home to our families — all of us. There was a reason for that.

Despite her strong feelings about having participated in performing sexual acts before a camera, more importantly perhaps, Laurie understands that no matter how much a person's life can change after leaving adult film work, portions of the past remain a constant.

You know, once you are involved in the industry it just becomes a part of you forever. It's not that you are close friends with everyone forever, but you see each other or hear of each other now and then as years go by. It's a part of your world away from your world if that makes any sense. Unless a person has ever been a part of the industry it is hard to understand us, but we share a connection that never ends.

Health Risks

I would discourage anyone, male or female from doing pornographic movies and so would John Holmes if he were alive today. The way he felt in the end was that it was despicable. John wanted health insurance benefits, and yes, some counseling as well as education and financial building for what he truly considered his people. He wasn't named "The King of Porn" until long after he was gone and not until they discovered how valuable his content was. In fact, he felt as if the industry had literally turned their backs on him while he lay dying of AIDS in his hospital bed. I witnessed this so I know. I think his dying at that point was a desirable option for John as this was his belief in the end.

Ironically, Laurie has borne witness to two husbands suffering from the same devastating disease. Since Tony Montana's 1999 positive HIV diagnosis, Holmes has taken it upon herself to make sure he receives all of the health benefits attainable in order for him to remain relatively well. At present, Montana's condition is stable and he is in good health. Holmes has kept herself abreast of contemporary procedures and medications used for HIV treatment that are exorbitant in cost, but necessary to ensure quality and longevity of life. Laurie and Tony are still legally married but no longer live together. Montana resides in Los Angeles, and the couple continues to remain good friends.

My second husband, Tony Montana, is still living with AIDS today. Once again, he isn't given the time of day by many in the industry. I feel sad for him because his entire adult life was spent in the industry and this is what he has to show for it. Even though AIDS testing is organized within the industry today, it is very important for people to understand that it is not a guarantee. Tony tested positive during the time when AIDS testing was already in place as others have done. Even if a person never contracts HIV, the potential for an individual to contract many other STDs is

Laurie and Tony Montana. COURTESY OF LAURIE HOLMES

highly likely. STDs, such as herpes for example remains with you for the rest of your life.

It is believed that performers today are restricted from working without an HIV and/or STDs test that is older than thirty days, but that isn't always true. Even though you are required to show proof of testing and the test can't be older than thirty days, it still isn't a guarantee because you don't know what the person might have done last night, last week, or anytime during the last month. Nothing should be assumed. They must have a notarized test that can't be older than thirty days.

If it is assumed that the person you are going to work with has all of their current tests up to date, it's still possible that the same person could have ingested meth [amphetamine] or something else during the past week, or had some kind of a kink-fest of their own with people outside of the industry. This happens all the time. Ever had Herpes in the eye? It happens and you can go blind from it and it's ugly. How about gonorrhea of the throat? If you still think doing porn is appealing, it's not. Don't think for a minute that porn won't affect or even destroy the rest of your life, because it will. It will come back and affect your life time after time when you least expect or want it to.

Between the years 2001 and 2003, Laurie was part of the work force at Adult Industry Medical (AIM) located in Los Angeles. Under the supervision of Dr. Sharon Mitchell, she counseled and administered drug tests to industry people and to those outside of the industry potentially at risk for HIV and other sexually transmitted diseases. As reported incidents of exposure to STDs and HIV continue to be tracked and defined due to new government legislation in the state of California, adult film studios will be required to pay for all regular STD testing. Individuals must be qualified by an occupational physician under Cal-OSHA (California Occupational Safety and Health Community) before returning to work while employers are responsible for notifying performers where to go for STD testing at designated locations presently being established. At the time of this writing, many sex performers are using Talent Testing Services based in Florida but with draw stations located across the United States.

New policies under Cal-OSHA (legislation was passed in January 2012) require that all potentially harmful medical waste including used condoms, razors, and laundry must be disposed of in a specified container to be picked up and removed from premises of use. Additionally, it is recommended that mandatory washing of body parts containing fluids between sex acts, and sex toys employed during scenes are sterilized after use. Although the recommended use of condoms has been in effect since 1993 for adult film production companies and performers, it had not been enforced or made mandatory by law until 2012. Many porn studios such as Wicked have long required their actors wear condoms. Heavy penalties are to be imposed upon studios for refusal of compliance of obligatory condom use of performers (yet to be implemented). Many insiders believe the new compulsory acts will drive the production of pornographic films out of L.A. County. According to the adult news reported by AVN and X-Biz, at present, Cal-OSHA regulations do not apply to content trade, webcams or personal websites.

My experience working at Adult Industry Medical and personal conflict while trying to counsel young people entering into the business was a delicate matter. Of course educating people on STDs and protocol was easy. However, there was a fine line we didn't dare cross. We couldn't really discourage someone from entering the biz as we would be running off business and agents would no longer send us their talent if we did that.

Keeping Watch

In 1998, Laurie published *Porn King, The Autobiography of John C. Holmes* compiled from audiotapes Holmes himself had recorded a few years prior to and leading up to his death in March 1988. In February 2012, *Porn King* was re-released by BearManor Media with additional writings by Holmes, updated information, and revisions to some of the original text including new material added by Laurie in her personal memoir in the book's final pages.

My relationship with John was very special then and maybe in some ways even more special today. At the time when John came into my life, I really needed someone older and wiser to guide me. John used to say that I reminded him a great deal of himself when he was younger. I think, as much as I needed guidance, John had the need to save someone — maybe metaphorically, his younger self. In much the same way today, I feel the need and desire to want to help others understand the devastation that porn can do to their lives. I think I know and understand John better than anyone else for when he passed away I took on all of his battles. I have fought those battles ever since his death along with my own battles. It hasn't been an easy task. He was my daddy.

I remember John telling me how I needed to make a diary. On one hand, I think that somehow, he knew what was in store for me and he wanted to prepare me; there were other days when all he

Laurie and John Holmes. COURTESY OF LAURIE HOLMES

wanted was for me was to leave it alone. I think he realized that if I could just break away clean it would have been better for me, but deep down inside, he knew I wouldn't be able to just leave it alone.

I hated how it all came down in the end. I loved him and I still do. I've wanted the record to be set straight about John and about the industry and I've made every effort to do so, sometimes blindly. I have faced forces far greater than I had ever imagined I would have to face. People don't always play fair. The media is a beast driven by the greed behind each and every medium.

I believe that John has never really left me. He keeps an eye on me from a different realm perhaps. There were times when he felt that maybe I wasn't going to make it this far and now he watches and is at peace because I have survived. There is some meaning and purpose, and importance behind it all. I know I will join him one day and I look forward to that day, but for now, I must live this life.

Kodak Moments

When asked if she believed the word feminist could be applied to her sense of individuality and her desire to openly share personal opinions and beliefs about the adult industry at the risk of ostracizing herself, Laurie weighed the reality of the term before responding. Likewise, she put her own spin on what a "Kodak moment" means to her and grew thoughtful while once again considering the full impact of her life experiences.

I really don't think of myself as a feminist. I really can't conceive of the meaning behind such a word. I am feminine and I am myself. I am strong, but as far as being independent, I really don't know if I always want to be self-sufficient. It's nice to have someone to lean on sometimes. I am a fighter. I fight for what I believe to be true no matter what the cost. It has often cost me dearly. Is it because I have paid such a heavy price at times that I could be described as a feminist? I really couldn't tell you.

I wonder is a "Kodak moment" actually a moment caught on film or is it a moment, a memory, or a feeling you only wish could have been caught on film. I always enjoyed modeling for a still camera more than I did filming actual sex scenes. You could pose or be posed. Your make-up wasn't all messed up the way it was in a sex scene and that's always a plus. There were moments when I just knew that I had given the cameraman a great picture. There were times when the camera really loved me. Unfortunately, other times the camera didn't love me at all, very much like life.

There have been many times in my life when I felt great sorrow. After all, that is all part of life. Of course, I felt great sorrow when John died. I feel great sorrow for all of those that didn't survive. I feel great sorrow for the ones that haven't faced those demons yet, and know that they will have to someday. I feel great sorrow for the shame that I brought to my family to this day, and even though I have been forgiven, I feel a great amount of guilt and shame and I have to live with that every day. I am very guarded in my community. I don't want people to know who I am and what I have done in my past. I know from experience that it doesn't bring about anything that is positive. At the same time, I believe I am a terrific person. If people would take the time to get to know me, they would be amazed. It's all very hard to deal with sometimes and there are days when it makes me feel sad.

I never really played the "victim" card because I was mostly a victim of self-infliction. Therefore, I had to blame myself first. I was a young girl. I was star struck — it was exciting. I let myself be a part of it and I was exploited for it, and I have to deal with that. You can become very jaded at times. I reached a point of not knowing what normal lovemaking was. I would be with someone outside of the industry and I would be waiting for the trapeze artist to fly down from the ceiling. It suddenly dawned on me that maybe this normal guy didn't know all of the freaky positions that I knew. One day, I just realized, I wasn't normal. I had to get back what I had lost and that was my own self. Like many others, I had turned to drugs to deal with my emotional pain. At first, the drugs helped to enhance euphoria, but in the end, they only numbed what I didn't want to feel. I knew that if I was going to survive anything, my first step was to get off drugs. I had to get back to where I belonged and although I took the long way home, I did eventually make it. Once here, I could begin to heal from the life that I had lived. I don't think I will ever be completely healed but at least I can live with myself now.

In the summer of 2007, Laurie and I arranged to meet at the Hamburger Hamlet in the San Fernando Valley for lunch. Laurie had suggested the restaurant would be an ideal place to get together since it is where many business dealings involving the production of sex films were made and squashed over the years. As I sat waiting for her to arrive, I glanced out the plate glass window from my spacious, hardwood booth to notice a small, girl-woman with long, dark brown hair pulled back into a barrette briskly approaching the door of the establishment. In person, Laurie is even more petite than she appeared in films. Unafraid to admit her foibles, Holmes is direct and has a big heart.

Now drug free for over five years, Laurie defined what love, honesty and honor mean to her. They are words she believes are traits of a mutually rewarding relationship not only with the new partner in her life, but also with her family. Fulfilled in her current employment within the medical profession in a position that gives her pride, Laurie hopes to upgrade her education in the near future.

Genuine love to me means truth, total respect, and trust no matter what. You have to trust one another over and beyond. You

Laurie Holmes and Miss Beto. COURTESY OF LAURIE HOLMES

have to admire and learn to grow with one another and not apart from each other. I really do believe in a monogamous relationship sexually. That is a significant part of love. When you let others into the bedroom, you break down the pillars of a relationship. Love goes right out the window. I have met someone new, a very nice man. We live high up in the mountains in Colorado. We have a wonderful, monogamous relationship. When we started to get serious, I told him everything. I don't believe you can start a relationship based on lies. I told him about the past and that it was just that — the past. He accepted and understood.

The relationship I have with my family today is probably better than it has ever been. My kids are grown up and on their own now, they are both doing great. I am the lucky one; my family has forgiven me. For many girls who have worked in the porn industry this isn't the case.

I have a regular job with a normal paycheck. I have my own little office at a select location. I do my job and nobody breathes down my neck. I work better that way. When I am not working, I really try to just enjoy life, whatever that may be. I love to go to music concerts. Rock 'n roll never forgets, you know. In the summers I spend a lot of time outdoors going fishing, hiking, and going jeepin' up in the high country. I really love my mountains in Colorado.

I would like to be remembered for my heart. Like John, I believe that I have a heart of gold. I would like for my friends and family to remember me as someone who was strong enough to have survived things that I should have never been a part. Although my life hasn't been as rosy as people would have liked it to have been things happen for a reason, even if that reason isn't always clear or understood. I want them to remember me as a whole person and not only my mistakes. There is a very sweet part of me worth remembering. I am porn free, drug free and couldn't be happier about it. I am at peace with my life.

21

Ginger Lynn
Turning the Page

Ginger Lynn Allen bubbles with childlike exuberance and a zest for life that is palpable and contagious. Her kinetic energy, in tandem with her soft curves and a sultry coquettish sex appeal, turned the erotic film industry on its ear when she splashed onto the adult entertainment scene in 1983. A Rockford, Illinois native, Allen is candid about her dysfunctional family history, yet she has not allowed adversity she suffered as a child to impede or impact her life in a negative way. Always one to make the best of circumstances and opportunities, Ginger welcomed the move to her grandparents' home at the age of thirteen after bearing a difficult relationship with her mother. Once settled within the comfort of family who loved and nurtured her, Allen blossomed as she continued to cultivate a healthy alliance with her father.

Despite an IQ of 142, Ginger managed average marks in elementary and high school, but participated on the gymnastics team and attended several rock concerts with her close group of girlfriends. Instilled with a strong work ethic, Ginger worked part-time throughout her educational years and entered the world of retail after graduation. In 1982, Allen moved to Southern California to accept a job offer at Musicland; she was joined by her boyfriend a short time afterwards. In order to supplement her income, Ginger answered an ad as a stripper for a bachelor party. When she followed up on an advertisement for the World Modeling Agency in Van Nuys, Allen immediately recognized the potential for financial security and stardom. Ginger demanded a healthy sum for her initial two feature film appearances in *Surrender in Paradise* (1984) and *A Little Bit of Hanky Panky* (1984) and got it in a single unprecedented maneuver that has continued to be her trademark throughout her career. Shortly thereafter in a groundbreaking business move that fostered a new

"I'm the first contract girl ever in the adult film industry, and I'm the only one left who has not sold out, or let them buy back the original deal that they made. I've had the longest shelf life in the history of adult film actresses."

GINGER LYNN ALLEN

COURTESY OF GINGER LYNN

trend and altered the stigma of sleaze often associated with adult material, Ginger's name, face, and image launched Vivid Entertainment on
the glamorous box cover *Ginger* (1984) that eventually opened the door
to her own video line. Many fans are not aware that Ginger's mainstream
film credits are almost as extensive as her erotic work, an achievement
most adult actresses are unable to obtain.

As of 2011, Ginger Lynn was still active in the adult business attrib-
uting her longevity, legendary status, and many successes to careful
navigation and planning. She is protective of the fragility of life and
prioritizes the things that are dearest to her heart, most importantly her
teenage son.

As one who has been consistent about documenting her (almost) fifty
years in diaries and journals, Ginger is presently working on an autobiography that will detail many elements of her life including surviving her
2000 cervical cancer diagnosis, and her long term 1990s relationship with
notorious Hollywood actor Charlie Sheen.

My interview with Ginger Lynn was conducted in three parts toward
the end of 2010 and early 2011.

A girl named Ginger

My parents met in Illinois, got pregnant and had me. They had
a good old-fashioned shotgun marriage. My father was seventeen
when I was conceived here in California at the air force base. My
mother was almost nineteen years old and I'm the first-born child. I
have one natural sister and two stepbrothers. I grew up in Rockford.

My real name is Ginger Lynn so without me making that choice
consciously, my name has turned into a blessing in disguise. Ginger
is not very common. My great grandmother's nickname was Ginger
because she was feisty and had red hair. I was also born with red
hair — it's an auburn ginger color, like a chestnut — that's my
natural hair. When I moved to California, I dyed my hair blonde.

I grew up in your normally dysfunctional family. I don't think
there is anything as normal and I don't think there is anything
such as a "normal" childhood. You can be rich, you can be poor,
you can be religious or hippies whatever the case may be. Every
childhood has its dysfunction which at this point, is normal. My
mother is what I consider a psycho bitch and has absolutely no
remorse whatsoever for her actions. She's a sociopath. Her mother,
my grandmother, died in an insane asylum. My grandmother was

a hooker in the south and was impregnated by a Native American Indian who had been adopted by a Southern Baptist minister and his wife. The Southern Baptist Minister and his wife adopted the Native American man who impregnated the hooker, and my mother was born.

After my parents married, they began to have difficulties. My father was much too young and my mother was way too nuts. When my mother was home, it was a nightmare. When my father was home, even though he was an alcoholic, there was always a lot of laughter and a lot of joy and a lot of fun. My father had a sharp tongue and a quick wit, and he's funny and entertaining. Even if he had a few drinks or he was shit-faced drunk, it was still joyful.

I believe I was probably about eight or nine when my parents separated for the first time and that continued off and on — back together — apart again until I was eleven when they finally divorced. My mother, being raised by a southern Baptist minister and his wife, was taught to believe in hell and damnation and God would punish you for everything you did. The Baptist minister had the philosophy that you spare the rod and spoil the child. I remember my mother telling me stories that she wore burlap sacks to school. They were very, very, poor. Being that she was punished in a physical way growing up, she continued the cycle. My mother was not only mentally ill but she had tendencies toward physical and verbal violence. When my parents separated and finally divorced, there came a point where I was done with it all. I knew I didn't have the same belief systems as my mother did. I had a breaking point one night and moved out of my mother's home.

The night that I left my mother's home, there was an altercation and a beating. I had gone to bed and I'd forgotten to brush my teeth. I got up and went into the bathroom, and began to brush my teeth. My mother came in and said, "Get back to bed." I went back to bed and then I snuck out to brush my teeth again. She came in and she started wailing on me with a belt, and at thirteen, I was just stunned. I remember grabbing the end of the belt, not the part with the buckle, but the end — I had it in my hand and I put it into a noose and put her around her neck. I said, "You ever fucking touch me again and I will kill you." I meant it. There's no doubt in my mind that I would have, could have, killed this woman. The phone rang and it was kind of one of those moments when you're suspended in time. Everything stopped and I let go of the belt and my mother went and answered the phone. It was my grandfather. I knew it was my grandfather. I started to scream and scream. At the time, my grandparents lived about six blocks down the road so my grandfather called the police — he was a Deputy Sheriff. He showed up and the police showed up. My mother had suddenly changed into this little baby blue nightgown. I was bleeding with welts on my back and she was running around with her nipples and tits hanging out. I put everything into a brown paper grocery bag, took everything with me and got into the car with my grandfather. My mother said to my grandfather, not in these exact words, but close, "Give me five hundred bucks and you can keep her." My grandparents brought me to their home without a question and I lived with my grandmother, my grandfather, and my father. That was my freshman year in high school. Because he was seventeen when I was born, my father never really had a childhood so when he moved in with my grandparents as a newly single man he was out and having fun. My grandparents had become the main caregivers from the time that I was thirteen and on.

My father's parents were wonderful. My grandmother is the woman who taught me how to have patience and to believe in myself. She also taught me to knit and to sew and design jewelry, and she really inspired the creative side of my personality. They were integral in my upbringing. My grandparents are gone now, but they were and they will always be my two favorite people in the world. I also have to include my dad today. My father is a recovering alcoholic. Now, somehow, when I hear myself saying these

COURTESY OF GINGER LYNN

words, it sounds like your stereotypical porn star upbringing or background, but I believe that any and every family has their colors and mine just happens to have a few more colors than most people's do. Things are good with my dad today, fabulous. I talk to my dad every day. He's a wonderful, wonderful man.

As Ginger grew older, she retained close ties with special friends. Along with her grandparents, her small circle became her salvation.

Even as a young child, school was my playground. It was my escape. There were four of us, and I was the fourth in the wheel. I was very, very close with a girl named Pattie. When I lived with my grandparents, it was a house in a cul-de-sac with a park across the street. Pattie was my best friend and is still my best friend to this day. We have known one another since we could walk in the park. Her house was on one side of the park and mine was on the other. I also had two other girlfriends, another Pattie, and Michelle. Those three women, Pattie, Pattie, Michelle and I made up the Four Musketeers. With the exception of Pattie, the other two women are gone already. Pattie died of pancreatic cancer about four years ago, and Michelle died of alcohol poisoning three years ago. There's a lot of comfort in a small town that you would never get in a big city, but there's also a lot of down time, a lot of poverty. People tend to find solace in drugs and alcohol, and unhealthy lifestyles. So unfortunately, although I made three fabulous friends growing up, two of those three are gone and one remains. Pattie moved out here to California in the late 1980s-early 1990s, and she now lives about two hours from here. People from Illinois have good hearts and most of them will be there for you no matter what.

Rebel, Rebel

Hobbies for Ginger were plentiful and diverse as she described her most impressionable teen years with high hopes of becoming a rock 'n roller.

I was definitely not the popular girl in school. I had my little quirks and cliques. I didn't have the money to dress the way that a lot of the other girls did. The friends that I had, for the most part, were a wonderful little group of misfits. None of us became cheerleaders or the popular girls. I wasn't a jock, although I was on the gymnastics team. I wasn't the "brain" although I have a 142 IQ. When we had our Student of Education courses, they'd have the statewide event with a thousand kids who came from all over the state and I took second place. The only reason that I didn't take first was because I'm mathematically challenged. If anything, I was

the "alley" girl. I was the girl who went to every concert there was. I
wore the Van high tops and the concert t-shirts and the blue jeans.
I had the long straight hair, but not really a hippie chick. I graduated in 1980 so disco was popular then, but I was much more of a
rock and roll girl. I was a huge Led Zeppelin fan. I still am. I also
liked AC/DC.

I did a lot of sewing and I did a lot of art projects. I can shoot
a gun; I can shoot a rifle. My grandfather used to take me to a
shooting range where we would line bottles and cans whatever
we could find along what was left of the walls of the camp, and
just shoot. I grew up riding on the back of my grandfather's police
Harley and then moved onto my father's Harley. I've got a photo of
me, it's probably the earliest one, and I'm no more than about nine
months old on the back of a Harley. I'm in my little bassinette with
my grandfather's police cap. We go to Sturgis, South Dakota every
year for the bike rally. My father called me up a couple of weeks ago
and he said, "I'm tired of hauling your ass on the back of my bike!"

I was thinking to myself, "I don't think I've gained that much
weight."

He said, "You're getting one of your inheritances early. I'm giving
you my first Harley. I'm giving you my Sportster. Take your course
and you'll have your own Harley." It's a Sportster, not my favorite
Harley, but a wonderful one to learn to ride on.

You know, I had my first job at eleven. I vacuumed Joseppi's
Restaurant which was right down the street from my home and
I think I made $1.65 per hour. I worked from the time that I was
allowed to work so that I could have money to get the things that
I wanted to have. I was the talking Christmas tree at our local
department store. I'd sit in a box underneath this big tree and pull a
little lever down, and talk to the kids. I directed cars in the parking
lot at Bingo while my grandmother would play Bingo. We would
go on Friday nights where my grandfather was the Sherriff on
duty. I'd say that my first real job was when I worked at a clothing
store during my freshman year in high school. I was involved in a
special program where I would go to school half a day and work in
the store during the other half while I became manager. I believe
it was Junior High School. I kind of thought that I would work in
retail, and eventually, own my own store and design my own clothing, but my dream when I was growing up was that I wanted to be
a rock and roll star. My girlfriend and I were going to be the next

Heart. I got my first guitar at thirteen and I took guitar lessons at a couple of places. One was Charlotte's Web and another one was Nielsen's. Cheap Trick is from my home town of Rockford and [the lead guitarist] Rick Nielson's father owned a music store where they sold instruments and sheet music and gave lessons. I learned to play guitar and I was reasonably good at it. When I first wanted my family to hear me play, everybody sat on the front stoop, and I was out on the lawn with my guitar and I sang "Mr. Tambourine Man". My father had remarried at this point. He had actually remarried in 1980, but his fiancé and her two children, my stepbrothers, moved in a couple of years before that. My brothers, and my sister, and my dad, and my grandparents, and my step-mom were all sitting on the stoop and I was playing my heart out. When I finished no one said anything. All of a sudden, my dad, who is hysterical, started laughing this gut wrenching belly laugh and said, "You sound like a dog scratching his butt on a nail board!" I can't carry a tune to save my life! I pretty much hung it up after that.

I always knew that I didn't belong in Illinois. I wanted to leave and I always wanted to go to California. I had bigger hopes; I had bigger dreams. I wanted everything that there was to have in life. I always said that I would never get married until I was at least thirty. I wanted to have a career and even though I didn't know what it was, I knew I wanted it.

In 1981, my grandparents moved to California. It was my grandmother's dream because she wanted to be where it was sunny. When I was growing up my grandfather used to buy and sell twin model trains. That was his hobby. Our basement was a giant train track. It was an entire city, state, country — made up of trains. He sold all of those and bought a fifth wheel and sold the home that he and my grandmother had built from the ground up to my father, who still owns that home today. They moved to California and built a house in Lucerne Valley. I was supposed to go with them, but I chose a boy instead. I'm not a good picker when it comes to men.

My grandparents had moved out here and I was working in retail part-time in Illinois. At night, I was a cocktail waitress in a bar so I had three jobs. A phone call came when I was at work and it was my father's brother. My Uncle Donny said, "I need you to get on a plane, your grandfather had a heart attack. He's in the hospital and they're scheduling a triple bypass. He has lost his will to live and if anyone can make him live it's you." There was pressure there because I was nineteen or twenty. My uncle bought me a plane ticket and I packed a suitcase and came to California. My grandmother couldn't stay in the house because she had to be close to the hospital. She lived in a trailer and I stayed with her while going to the hospital. When my grandfather recovered from the surgery, he couldn't speak. He couldn't feed himself, and he couldn't take care of himself. He'd just given up and it didn't matter whether I was his favorite person in the world and he had me on a pedestal or not, I don't think he wanted to go on living like that. My grandfather died the day after his 65th birthday. He died November 3, 1982. I didn't go back home after that.

California: Making Ends Meet

While I was here in California and my grandfather was passing, I had been working as an assistant manager at a Musicland store which was back when we still had record stores. I went into the store at the San Bernardino location and said, "I'd love to work out here." They doubled my salary — they gave me a thousand dollars to move and made me a trouble-shooter at one of their stores. It was my job to go in and get locations out of the red and into the black. I've always been good with people. I can sell you anything. I've sold everything from stereos to Santa Claus. When I came here, I had my suitcase that I'd left town with and got my apartment and different furnishings, and things that I thought I would need at the time. I thought California would be fun and free and easy — that's what I had imagined growing up. In reality, it wasn't that at all, but it was wonderful and beautiful. There was the ocean and the sun and people didn't judge you, and they didn't have attitudes. It was much easier for me to fit in than it was in Illinois. I didn't stand out here. Actually, my bodyguard, my Nanny, my Manny, is from my hometown. I met him out here in 1992. It's amazing — two of my best friends that I've met in California are from my hometown in Illinois. We've just gravitated towards one another.

I was working in the music store seventy hours a week and life was a little more difficult than I thought it was going to be financially. I was in charge of hiring and firing people — that doesn't make you the most popular girl around. I was so lonely that I bought two cats that lived in my trailer with me, Blondie and Rio. The band Blondie was very big at the time and Rio was the name

of a song by Duran Duran. I had Blondie and Rio, and a different boyfriend from Illinois decided that he loved me and he came
out to California with his Corvette and the payments that went
along with it. He was living with me and I was paying his Corvette
payment. On top of that, I'd gone from a two bedroom, split-level
apartment in Illinois at a hundred and sixty-five dollars a month,

COURTESY OF WORTH MENTIONING PUBLIC RELATIONS

to a three hundred odd dollar studio apartment with a pool that had no water in it. It was a home to rats. Now I had a boyfriend living with me, and I couldn't quite make it.

I've always been a survivor. I've always made things happen no matter what I had to do so I looked in the newspaper and answered an ad for stripping. It was for a bachelor party. It was for two hundred dollars and it was a lot of money. I thought, "I can do this." I got my little boom box and my cassettes and picked a few songs, and got my outfit put together. My boyfriend drove me to this bachelor party gig. Well, I hadn't thought it through. Sometimes I tend not to think things through completely. I got inside and I went, "Fuck! These are all men! I'm the only woman here." I just didn't think about the fact that I was going to be in a room full of men getting naked by myself.

Apart from winning a wet t-shirt contest at a local gym, Ginger had little experience with nudity before a group of testosterone driven males prior to being hired to strip at the bachelor party.

When I got the bachelor party, and walked in there and saw all of the men, I just realized "I can't do this. I can't get naked in front of all these men." I left. I went outside and talked to my boyfriend and he went inside. I took his car and left him there. It was shitty and mean thing to do. I was scared. I was young. They beat him up and the whole thing was ugly. I went back and got him and it was horrible. He was a very nice guy. He was the quarterback of the football team and he did have a fabulous job in Illinois. He designed microchips for computers, and back then that was groundbreaking so he did have potential but he and I were having difficulties.

I answered another ad in the newspaper which was for figure modeling. It was in the Orange County newspaper and it advertised five hundred — five thousand dollars per day. I was living in Orange County at the time and I drove up to Van Nuys, California and walked into World Modeling Agency. I did my test the next day. Jim South was working there at that time.

Highly regarded by mostly everyone in the business, Jim South is responsible for helping to instigate the careers of many of the popular pornographic film actresses of the 1970s and eighties. In 1987, South became embroiled in a legal battle when World Modeling Talent Agency was charged with hiring the underage Traci Lords (born Nora Louise Kuzma) to do nude modeling and sexual performances in films prior to the legal age of eighteen. When it was discovered Lords had intentionally falsified her date of birth in order to obtain a government passport (issued to her under the name Kristie Elizabeth Nussman) to gain employment in the adult business, South was cleared of all charges.

Among other claims made against South in her autobiography *Traci Lords: Underneath it All*, (2003) Lords stated that South supplied her with drugs and alcohol in order to lure her to comply with his offer for adult work. Since making a fresh start, Lords (who, ironically still uses her porn moniker) has enjoyed moderate success in "B" feature films, television, and as a video pop star. In addition to Ginger, many other performers such as Christy Canyon and Laurie Holmes who also began their careers in the adult industry under the direction of Jim South, have sung South's praises and are vehement that Lords' accusations are completely unfounded.

When I walked into Jim's office, there were eight by ten framed photographs of a dozen or so beautiful women on the wall. Every single one of them was stunningly beautiful. The only one I remember specifically was Shauna Grant, a blue-eyed blonde who is no longer with us. I think it was the first year that I was in the industry that she shot herself in the head. I wanted to be one of the girls on the wall. I just thought they were so pretty. My new goal was to be a wall girl and I think I was a wall girl within three days. I was up there as soon as the photographs had been taken of me and printed. I probably posed for every major male magazine over the next three months.

I don't know if you want to call it anal-retentive or OCD, but I take notes and write and write, and I can tell you everything about every single day from the time that I did it and who I did it with — not by memory, but by notes. I still have my journals, my diaries, and daily planners from day one. Those three months I worked on average twenty-six to twenty-eight out of thirty days.

Ginger was paid well for the *Penthouse* shoots and did her first girl-girl photo layout with the beautiful adult performer, Hyapatia Lee. Comparatively speaking, *Penthouse* paid far more than wages Lynn received at her regular day job. A few months after she started photography work, Jim South approached Ginger to consider additional opportunities. When South suggested she might want to consider doing films, Lynn was initially appalled by the notion of branching out.

> I was paid one hundred and fifty dollars to do the layout and I saw Hyapatia get paid two hundred and wondered, "Why is she getting paid two hundred dollars when I only got paid one hundred

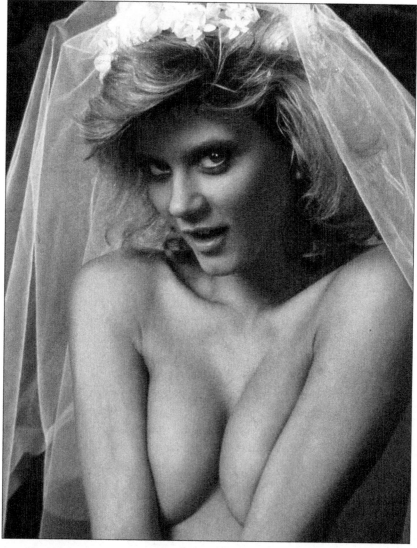

COURTESY OF GINGER LYNN

and fifty?" It was between a hundred and fifty and a thousand dollars per day, but a thousand dollars was huge and few and far between. I think I made twelve thousand dollars per year working seventy hours a week for Musicland, and I made five thousand dollars for one day for *Penthouse*.

Jim had actually started to ask me to do commercial work for a while and I soon found out what "commercial" meant. I had been thinking that "commercial" meant television commercials. In the adult world, "commercial" means sex. If you do a commercial scene, it's a sex scene. When Jim told me what it meant, I was — I wouldn't say I was disgusted, but I thought, "Wait a minute. How can you think of me in that way? I'm not that kind of a girl." At that point, even though there was Shauna Grant and the wall girls, I still thought that a certain type of woman or a certain type of girl did those films and that I wasn't that type of a girl.

In school, I'd had sex for the first time at thirteen. I lost my virginity to my puppy love. He was fifteen and I'd had a crush on him at the park since I was probably five. We were together throughout my entire high school years. He walked me to every single class, every single day. We were going to get married. You know, I'd been with other men after we broke up, so I was by no means a virgin. I don't know if it goes back to my great grandmother in that I thought that porn was similar to hookers. At that point, I did feel that way. I think that a lot of people did. Porn was not popular. It was very taboo and not part of the norm. It was underground and you didn't watch it. If you did, you didn't talk about it. When my agent asked me to do this, I guess "mortified," would be the best word to describe how I felt. Not because of the act, but because he thought that I was "that kind of a girl". I said, "No". I wouldn't even think of it.

One day there was a beautiful woman with red, shoulder length hair in his office wearing a long, white gown and a cigarette holder and a script. She was articulate and intelligent and I asked her, "You're not a porn star, are you?" I had my own stereotypes and my own preconceived notions of what "that kind of a girl" was, yet looking at this woman helped me to make my decision. I'd seen photographs of other women but I'd never had the opportunity to meet one of them. When I decided to make films after speaking to this woman, I walked back into Jim's office and I said, "Okay, I'll do it, but I want a thousand dollars per scene. I want script approval and I want cast approval." Jim was on the floor rolling around laughing and said, "You've got to be kidding me?" It wasn't that I was full of myself or had a big ego. It was just that this is how I had wanted to do it. When I believe in something, I stick to my guns and I stand my ground. I believed in myself and that's what I thought I was worth. I didn't know this girl from Adam, but at the same time, if I was going to do it, I was going to be a different caliber.

Surrender in Paradise

In the early-mid 1980s, adult pictures were not produced at the rapid fire pace they are today. According to Ginger, approximately ten films were made a month so there was ample opportunity for performers, directors, producers, and photographers to become acclimatized to one another's personalities and preferences. More often than not, Ginger recalled that the west coast arm of the industry would often congregate in South's office.

Ginger's first two films were shot back to back and directed by Svetlana who began co-directing adult movies during the latter part of the 1970s until 1986, often in conjunction with her partner David J. Frazer. As a test drive, Lynn first appeared in an eight-millimeter loop with Ron Jeremy.

Svetlana and her husband David were casting a film. They wanted someone who had never been in a film before who had the girl-next-door look and a spunky attitude. I guess I fit that bill. They agreed to all my terms. They were doing two films simultaneously. They did *Surrender in Paradise* (1984) and *Little Bit of Hanky Panky* (1984). I agreed to do the films. I had three sex scenes in each movie and we were shooting on the Island of Kauai, Hawaii. I hadn't been out of the United States up until this point. I signed the contracts and I agreed to my leading man. Everything was fabulous and wonderful, and I got home after signing the contract and I went, "Fuck! I don't know if I can do this and I just agreed to be the lead in two movies! I have all of these people depending on me and relying on me and what if I can't do it?" I went back to my agent's office the next day and I said, "Jim, I don't know if I can do this."

He said, "Well, we'll do a trial run." The trial run turned out to be two eight minute, eight millimeter films — no audio, to be shot the same day. When I walked in, there was a big, hairy guy, and when

I got closer, it turned out to be a man by the name of Ron Jeremy. We were doing the scene and the cameras were on me. I was on all fours in doggie style with the camera in front of me, and Ron Jeremy behind me. I was wearing bright red lipstick, and I turned toward the director and he said, "Would you lick your lips?" I licked them, but not sexily. I went from my nose to my chin and then

PHOTO COURTESY OF SUZE RANDALL, *WWW.SUZE.NET*

around in a circle. I didn't know what "lick your lips," meant. Ron was behind me and I thought, "Okay, he does feel good as long as I hold my breath and don't look at him. If I can get through this, I must just enjoy myself!"

During our interview Ginger was emphatic she is not a fan of Ron Jeremy and once alleged to the adult press she was raped by him more than twenty years ago. No charges were laid. In the excerpt below from a 1999 AVN piece discussing the incident, Ginger's friend and mediator between the two parties, Veronica Hart/Jane Hamilton, commented.

"Ginger has always felt that Jeremy raped her. That's been her story from the beginning, that's how she remembers it," Hart said. "She came home, he was at her place; he split a screen to come in. Ron does not remember it as a rape. They both believe their own story. Ron, in his mind does not believe he raped her and she in her heart knows that he did. And never will the two meet."

I got through that and the second scene was shot in the same day. It was either two hundred dollars total or two hundred for each scene. The second [loop] was with Tommy Byron. I love Tommy. He's just always been like my big brother. We had a fabulous scene and I found that there was not a problem with me on camera. That's how I made my first two films.

It's hard to imagine Ginger was new to adult films while observing her in *Surrender in Paradise* — a fantasy about several women shipwrecked on an island with an escaped con (Jerry Butler). Equipped with a fair amount of poise and passable acting ability, Ginger displays a shy demeanor and genuine sweetness as she reciprocates easily with Jerry Butler, in conjunction with a sexual abandon highlighted by her vocal emanations. Her fresh face and tiny frame might give one the sense she is naïve and fragile, but Ginger clearly appeared to be a cut above her fellow actors in this initial outing.

In the second film shot on the island of Kauai, Hawaii *A Little Bit of Hanky Panky* (aka *Hanky Panky*), Ginger easily handled her share of dialogue and sex scenes. Playing husband and wife, Lynn and Ron Jeremy converge on the beach during the first half of the movie to enjoy some back door sexual fun. Jerry Butler, Jamie Gillis, Bunny Bleu, and Stacey Donovan form the balance of the cast in this appealing movie about a couples' Hawaiian getaway which becomes a retreat for breaking down sexual barriers. Taking into consideration Ginger wasn't particularly enamored by her cast mate, her scene with Jeremy is seamless and sexy.

In 1984, Ginger and Ron Jeremy were paired together again in *Supergirls Do General Hospital* directed by Henri Pachard (Ron Sullivan). More than twenty-five years since their first on screen encounter, in 2010

Ginger Lynn and Ron Jeremy.

the two AVN (Adult Video News) Hall of Famers were cast together in a send-up of the *SAW* horror franchise in the movie *Drill a Porn Saw Parody*. Jeremy was quoted at Lukeisback.com in June 2010 stating the two stars got along famously and that their sex scene together was "exceptional." Evidently, it would seem that Lynn and Jeremy were able to put their personal differences aside in order to synthesize their individual brands for the financial benefit of the studio, consumers, and one another.

I started back in the day where movies were still shot on film and we actually had premieres. I did a film called *Kinky Business* (1984) and there was a scene in the shower, I vividly remember with Tom Byron. I was on my knees in the shower with my hair stuck to my face and matted down. I was sitting in the movie theatre at the premiere for the film and all I could think of was how silly I looked. My cheeks were sunken in and I looked like a fish. I got up and left the theatre and I cried. I thought, "I'm a cock sucking fish." You know, I've always been a passionate person and I've enjoyed sex from the first time I had it, so that was the first time I watched how I looked doing it and I didn't care for that look. Ironically, I won Best Sex Scene for that particular scene that year.

PHOTOGRAPHY BY KENJI

Leading Men

My favorite men from that day — the ones who always tripped my trigger and made me smile were Jerry Butler, Tom Byron, and Peter North. I worked a lot with Harry Reems and we had a good connection, and of course John Holmes. I was cast in *Girls on Fire*

Ginger Lynn and John Holmes at the premiere for *Girls on Fire.*

(1985). I believe that was my first film with John. I'd seen him in photographs but I wasn't familiar with his work. I knew only that he had a giant dick — that's all I knew. There were rumors flying around at that time that he'd been involved in murder, in one way or another. My first memory of John is when we were at the airport going to San Francisco to shoot the film *Girls on Fire*. I used to smoke pot a lot back then, and I had been on a plane a couple of times and I had my pipe in my pocket. John and I were going through security together, and I pulled my pipe out and I said to him, "Do I put this in the tray with my keys?" I was very naïve at the time, and I remember John grabbed my pipe, pushed me through the metal detector, and he put my pipe in with his things in a little bowl and walked straight behind me. He then ripped into me, you know, "What's wrong with you? What were you thinking? You could go to jail! We could all go to jail!" We were rebels at the time. We were making films undercover, behind-the-scenes. It was illegal to do it so during my first interaction with John he kind of rescued me and took care of me.

Girls on Fire, loosely based on *Some like it Hot* (starring Marilyn Monroe, Jack Lemmon and Tony Curtis, 1959) starred Jamie Gillis and Bobby Bullock as Danny and Greg: two insurance hustlers trying to keep out of sight of a mobster's side kick Rocco (John Holmes) at a lingerie show. Dressed in drag, Holmes sneaks into Ginger's hotel room to keep out of sight and is accosted by her at gunpoint. Lynn demands he lift his dress to make certain he doesn't have a gun concealed somewhere and they proceed to have sex. Lynn and Holmes exhibited great sexual heat and always made for an exciting porn couple. According to Laurie Holmes, John and Ginger Lynn also indulged in a brief affair.

Dressed in a white, satin evening gown and diamond earrings, Lynn accompanied Holmes to the lavish premiere for *Girls on Fire* in February 1985. The event was hosted by Ron Jeremy at the Pussycat theatre on Santa Monica Boulevard.

I liked John. He made me smile; he made me laugh. He was a gentleman, and he had a huge cock. We had an incredible amount of passion and great chemistry together. We made several films together and all of them are wonderful, and all of them were fun. You know, he was just fabulous, and according to Laurie [Holmes] and a couple of other people, I guess I'm one of the few women ever able to help John get a full erection. It was a big ole wiener. It was huge! No one will ever compare to John. John was bigger than life in all respects.

One of my all time favorite films is *The Grafenberg Spot* (1985). Another one of my other favorites is *The Pleasure Hunt* (1984). There was something magical about filming in San Francisco. The producers, the directors, the stars — there was a different attitude up there. As free-spirited and open-minded as Los Angeles is, San Francisco is even much more so. The films I did for the Mitchell Brothers, the films I did for Bill Amerson and Bob Wolfe, and everybody in San Francisco, it was just like going on vacation and fucking, and getting paid for it.

The Grafenberg Spot is a seductive, good-looking Mitchell Brothers film about a contemporary couple, Leslie and Michael (Ginger and Harry Reems) compatible in every way except that when aroused during cunnilingus Leslie orgasms a stream of clear liquid onto her lover's face. Michael is deeply disturbed by Leslie's eruptions, and the two have a falling out. Leslie seeks comfort from a sexual disorder specialist (beautiful Annette Haven) and begins to fantasize about other male lovers (John Holmes and Thor Southern in a stimulating three-way) during a visit to a welding shop. In turn, Michael hits the nightclub scene and through his encounters with many women (including Amber Lynn and Nina Hartley), he discovers that they too are hip to the mysteries of the "G" spot and comes away with a new perspective on Leslie's quirky habit. Eventually, the couple reunites with a newfound respect for one another, and immediately become engaged in exceptional make-up sex. Ginger and Reems are both terrific in their scenes together, and individually, within this prestigious "A" list cast. Traci Lords was part of the original cast, but her scenes were later deleted due to her being underage at the time of filming.

Not Vivid

Ginger was the first porn star to introduce her own exclusive line of videos through Vivid Entertainment directed mostly by the late, former Hollywood effects specialist Bruce Seven. However, Lynn does not acknowledge she was a Vivid girl, and instead prides herself on her individuality. While associated primarily with Vivid, Ginger was featured in some of her most popular films: *Ginger* (1984), *Ginger Effect* (1985), *Gentlemen Prefer Ginger* (1985), *Ginger and Spice* (1986), *Ginger Snaps* (1987), and *Ginger Rides Again* (1988) — a sampling of the entire Ginger Lynn/Vivid collection of movies.

I've never been a Vivid Girl. I've always been "Ginger Lynn". There would be no Vivid without Ginger Lynn. A Vivid Girl, in my opinion, is a generic flavor of the day, video of the month, video box cover with legs. No personality — the same tit job, the same nose job, and the same implants in their asses. They are cookie-cutter women with nothing. Very few Vivid Girls are anything more than a Vivid Girl, just like *Stepford Wives* (1975). They have no name and they have no face. They are generic so I find it completely and totally offensive to be put into that category.

I started Vivid. I helped Hirsch. I went from distributor to distributor signing autographs. I'm Ginger Lynn who helped to start Vivid. They used my face, my personality and my name. They made me an offer I couldn't refuse. I'm the first contract girl ever in the adult film industry, and I'm the only one left who hasn't sold out, or let them buy back the original deal that they made. I still have eighteen films that I own a piece of that I will not sell ever. I've had the longest shelf life in history of adult film actresses.

Traci Lords & Federal Prison

When underage Traci Lords stepped into the limelight to compete directly with Ginger for a share of the market, things began to heat up quickly. Unbeknownst to Lynn or to anybody else at the time including agents, directors, and producers, Lords made her debut as an adult performer allegedly at age sixteen (and possibly earlier, at least with photo layouts). The controversy that transpired regarding Lords' underage film work after she was found out hung like an albatross around the neck of the (then) illegal industry, but not before Lords and Lynn collaborated in several film projects apart from the aforementioned *The Grafenberg Spot* in 1985, and *Kinky Business* in 1984.

Traci Lords and I did several films together. The day I met her was in the parking lot. I don't know if it's still called Gelson's [Market] now, but it was Gelson's then on Van Nuys Boulevard across from Jim's office. Prior to Traci coming into the industry if there was a big film being made, I was in it. When Traci came along, there was definitely some competition. I won't deny that and maybe some animosity there. The day I met her she had her hair in curlers, she was wearing Lycra shorts with the slits up the sides in the parking lot of the grocery store and we're going to do porn. You know, you want to be as subtle as possible and she had her tits hanging out. I swear like a truck driver, but she made me look like a nun. She was just the most foul-mouthed little bitch I've ever met in my entire life which made for great chemistry on-camera. We hated each other from day one. There's no doubt about it.

Those Young Girls (1984), a script written by Lynn paired Traci Lords with Harry Reems, and Ginger Lynn with John Holmes. The film also featured Lynn and Lords in a girl-girl exchange and Lynn, Reems and Lords together. As the result of Lords having been underage at the time of production of the Paradise Visuals feature, allegedly, all prints and copies of the original picture were destroyed excluding the intact Lynn/

Holmes scenes implemented under a new Paradise Visuals title *Ginger Lynn: The Movie* (1988) in addition to the inclusion of several other stars and multiple pairings.

Talk Dirty to Me 3 (1984) cast the two young actresses alongside elite vets John Leslie and Jamie Gillis, and *New Wave Hookers* (1985) again showcased Lynn and Lords prior to the industry's knowledge of any foul play opposite Jamie Gillis, Jack Baker, and Rick Cassidy along with co-stars Tom Byron, Peter North, and Steve Powers. Gillis and Baker play a couple of greasy dudes turned pimps once they put their noggins together and hire all of women they can to guaranty a steady flow of cash and pussy. Miraculously for them, all that is required is a diet of new wave rock and the girls are agreeable to doing anything in pants. In her blonde, beehive hairdo and Madonna-esque studded leather, Ginger chants, "boys, boys, boys…," as she makes a memorable entrance. What follows is a titillating double penetration scene with "nerds" Tom Byron and Steve Powers yielding the greatest impact as Ginger doubles her pleasure. All Traci Lords's scenes contained in movies (including *New Wave Hookers*) produced prior to her eighteenth birthday have apparently been demolished with augmented footage reinstated.

It came out that Traci was underage and I was questioned in 1986. I was to testify on her behalf against all of these film producers and I refused. The U.S. attorney became involved and my attorney said, "You need to go before the Grand Jury." I did, but I have a very bad memory. I didn't recognize anyone. I looked at lots and lots of photos and I was unfortunately unable to help the prosecutors. Before I'd testified, they said, "If you don't, we'll make your life very difficult." My grandfather always told me that one of the worst people in the world is a snitch — bottom of the barrel — scum of the earth. You know, I loved my grandfather. He was a very well respected man as well as being a cop. He made choices and decisions and he had integrity and grace. I wasn't willing to do anything on behalf of this woman and compromise myself.

Five years later, almost to the day, I was indicted for federally subscribing to filing a false tax return. They'd spent *five years* investigating me. Someone was paid one hundred thousand dollars a year to read every interview I ever did, watch every movie I ever made, look at every magazine that had hired me to do layouts. They tried to charge me with tax evasion. I'd already paid my taxes. The whole thing was over two thousand, eighty-seven dollars and two cents.

I was facing six years in federal prison. I served four months and seventeen days in federal prison.

During her 1991 trial, father and son actors Charlie Sheen (whom Ginger had been dating at the time) and Martin Sheen wrote letters to the court vouching for Lynn's character, but to no avail. Hypocritically, Lords who demonized the adult entertainment industry in recent years, and made accusations of exploitation and worse, legally changed her birth name, Nora Louise Kuzma, to her pornographic persona Traci Elizabeth Lords obviously in an effort to bolster her earning potential.

Jail was one of the most challenging and difficult times of my life. The things that I saw and the things that I went through in such a short period are unbelievable and I wouldn't wish them on my worst enemy. It was a huge growth period for me. It was frightening; it was fantastic; it was unbelievable. I walked in wearing "come fuck me" shoes, and I walked out wearing one "come fuck me" shoe and the other "fuck you" shoe.

Dispelling the Myths

In 1985, Ginger enjoyed top billing as the daughter of renowned psychiatrist Jeremy Lodge portrayed by Jamie Gillis in Kirdy Stevens' *Taboo 1V: The Younger Generation*. The continuing drama again fleshes out the inner desires and consequences suffered when mothers seduce sons, sisters give way to attraction for brothers, and daughters entice fathers.

Sisters Robin (Ginger Lynn) and Naomi (Karen Summers) are expelled from private girls' school after Naomi is discovered in bed with her boyfriend. Both girls fear the wrath of their father who happens to be conducting weekly therapy sessions at his home for incest addicts. Behind Lodge's back, his beautiful wife Alice (played by the luscious and talented Cyndee Summers) has surrendered to her repressed feelings for Dr. Lodge's brother Billy (John Leslie), the biological father of her daughter Naomi. Alice and Billy are finally caught red-handed in the act of a sexual tryst by Lodge. Following some ugly name calling the doctor banishes Alice from their home just as the two girls arrive home from school. Naomi, whom Lodge accuses of being just like her mother, opts to leave with Alice while Robin chooses to remain at home to look after her father. Several conquests are experienced between cast members throughout (including Joey Silvera in the role of a drama coach) until eventually the psychiatrist, believing incest and infidelity are linked, finally succumbs to his lust for his loyal daughter Robin. Lynn and Gillis close out the excellent film in a passionate and naughty act of consensual coitus.

A couple of years after entering the adult business and with dozens of performances under her belt, Ginger suddenly found herself on the fast track to self-destruction. She discovered a trusted friend in renowned, erotic photographer, Suze Randall. Eventually, Lynn spent time in a drug rehabilitation and treatment facility and began to accept offers for low budget, mainstream film work. It is Ginger's belief that at the very least, the adult entertainment industry is merely a mirror image of mainstream Hollywood with similar baggage and toxicity. The microscope is magnified more intently upon the sex industry.

1984 and 1985 is right after my parents found out I had started doing adult films. I was disowned. My father took my grandmother down to watch my porn. It was brutal; it was very difficult. It took a couple of years for us to reestablish our relationship which became stronger. The whole trauma, the drama, the tragedy of my family discovering what I did was terrible. I love my family and they essentially disowned me.

I went on a downward spiral for about two or three weeks. Suze Randall is someone who had always been involved with her girls' lives. She cared about them. Suze Randall is unlike any other woman, ever. I believe she's the first photographer to shoot her own photos of pubic hair. She was integral in my career, and she is the person who introduced me to Seka. Jane Hamilton is another wonderful woman, director, friend, and porn star. Suze heard I wasn't doing well and that I'd been doing cocaine for about three weeks straight and she drove to my house. It was at the top of a mountain — one road in and one road out to get to it, and she just came over. She'd brought a joint and smoked it with me, and said, "Get your shit together now." She told me to incorporate.

She sat me down and said to me, "You're really someone special and you're going to throw it all away if you live through this." She saved my life and helped me to become the woman that I am today. Suze is the woman that I admire and I respect the most in this industry.

Recognized as the world's foremost prolific erotic photographer for over thirty years, Suze Randall began her career as a nurse and midwife at a London hospital where she worked until the late 1960s. When she attracted press attention by photographing fashion models including supermodel Jerry Hall, Randall's brilliant, stylish portraits afforded her employment as the only female staff photographer for *Playboy* magazine for two years. After leaving *Playboy*, Larry Flynt snapped Suze up to shoot for *Hustler* Magazine. Randall believes her personal technique was crafted by her years spent with *Hustler* as she learned to perfect her artistic flavor and style by utilizing creative posing and lighting. From there, Suze worked freelance for prestigious adult magazines such as *Penthouse* enabling her freedom to capture her female subjects in exquisite settings. Throughout her career, Randall has guest appeared on numerous radio and television shows; she has been profiled in *Vanity Fair* and in the esteemed *Photo District News*. In 2004 after a ten-year hiatus, Randall launched a DVD line featuring photographs highlighted by her trademark erotic intensity. Her highly successful video website *www.suzevideo.com* offers everything from erotic mini features to documentary footage. Additionally, an impressive and extensive library of Randall's finest work encapsulating over ten thousand of her striking images is available at her website *www. suze.net.* Currently working as a freelance photographer, Suze kindly contributed some of the exceptional pictures observed in this book. It is Randall's belief that her unique approach to photography helped her girls to look and feel beautiful. She said, "I love the erotic art medium. Beauty and sexuality are powerful. I enjoy empowering my models, helping them shed their self-doubt, watching them blossom."

After Suze left, I wrote a fourteen-page letter to my father. He cried and I cried, and not long after, I did my very first AVN [Adult Video News] show, my very first Consumers Electronics Show [CES]. One of my favorite photos is of me wearing my Sears dress in Rockford, Illinois where I was selling donuts. I signed autographs at the CES wearing the same dress with my dad standing next to me.

You know, even though I've had my bouts with drugs and alcohol, I never want to miss anything. A lot of people do drugs to zone out or be mental midgets and not be aware of what's going on. Alcohol will do that to me, but the drug that always called to me more than any other was cocaine. Part of that is due to growing up in Los Angeles being in the entertainment industry, going to the Playboy Mansion, being on porn sets and being involved in mainstream Hollywood as well as adult. I did many more drugs with mainstream actors than I ever did with porn actors, by far. It's not even close.

One of the things they told me during one of my stints in rehab is that people with my chemical make-up or imbalance that have the energy level that I do often times choose cocaine as their drug of choice. The way most people feel on cocaine is my natural state. It almost balanced me. Today, I will drink socially, but I don't do drugs, I don't smoke pot. I can't remember the last time that I did

Ginger Lynn with her dad at the Exxxstacy Show, Chicago, 2010.
PHOTOGRAPHY BY SCOTT CHURCH

a drug, but I will always be an addict. I will always be an alcoholic and I will always have that gene or desire that will never go away. It's my disease and it will always be there.

I find that balance is the key to my life today. Moderation is okay and at this point and in my living with the disease of alcoholism and drug addiction, I need to balance. Any drug addict or alcoholic out there reading this book will tell you if you're an alcoholic or an addict, you can never drink or do drugs again. I'm not an idiot. I know the rules but I've never played by them.

The abusive nature of many of our childhoods is not exclusive to the adult entertainment industry. I think that many, if not most actors or entertainers performers and musicians have come from abusive backgrounds whether it is verbal or whether it is physical.

Something dysfunctional in our childhoods prompted us and that applies to anyone in the entertainment industry — mainstream and otherwise. They are people who have the need to be loved, wanted, admired — they want to be somebody else. I wish that people would not point the finger only at this part of the industry. I know my story. I've told it before, but every time I tell it and I think back and hear myself saying it, somehow it sounds like I'm a victim when I see myself as a survivor. I just hate to perpetuate the image. I've exploited myself. Have I allowed other people to do so? Not without it being my decision. No one has forced me to do anything without me being a part of it.

It's much easier for me to be "Ginger Lynn" than to be "Ginger Allen". If I'm pretending to be somebody else, or if I'm taking one piece of my personality, one piece of that entire pie that is uninhibited and I'm showing you that part, that's easy. It's showing you the whole pie that's hard for me. I don't think that's exclusive by any means to the adult entertainment industry. You know, I was with Charlie Sheen for five years and if you were to go through his family history, there is the shit and the secrets that don't come out. Many people have the same and some more so in the entertainment industry.

Falling in Love

In the winter of 2011, Charlie Sheen was fired from his mega hit TV show *Two and a Half Men* after going on a verbal rampage to the media where he publicly criticized executive producer Chuck Lorre and Warner Brothers for preventing his work continuance following a short rehab stint in his home. The rehabilitation resulted from a three-day party binge in January 2011 in Sheen's mansion which sent him to hospital with severe abdominal pains. Lorre and company resumed the fall 2011 season after hiring (*That`70s Show*) actor Ashton Kutcher as a replacement for Sheen, while CBS reached a settlement with Sheen in September 2011 granting the actor an immediate $25 million dollar payout and $100 million over the next ten years in syndication. Sheen will star in a new tailored made HBO show slated to air in the fall of 2012 titled *Anger Management* after the film by the same name. In March 2011, *Los Angeles Times* reported Ginger Lynn was auctioning off several personal items given to her by Sheen during their five-year relationship in the early 1990s. The two met on a film set that starred Sheen's older brother, Emilio Estevez. Apparently, Charlie had been a long time fan of Ginger.

In addition to doing adult work, I've done many things outside of the porn industry and of course, dating Charlie Sheen and all of the mainstream things that I did. I've never been one to mince words. I speak my mind. I have no problem doing that, but I do get myself into trouble. I met Charlie Sheen on the set of *Young Guns II* (1990). Charlie wasn't in it, but he came there to meet me. When I came

Ginger Lynn and Charlie Sheen.

back from that set, I sold the house and bought another house, and started dating Charlie. As I'd mentioned, Charlie and I were together nearly five years. Everything was fabulous. Here was an actor who was secure and would let me do what I want. He's a bad boy and he doesn't answer to anybody. Then there was the evening where he'd just gotten so much flack from his parents, and from his agent, and from his manager that without going into too much detail, basically, Charlie had arranged for me to fake my death, change my face and my hair. He had a surgeon already set up. He was crying, asking me to marry him and telling me how much he loved me except no one could know. I would have to fake my own death. I almost did it if it weren't for the love for my family. He had a fake ID and the whole thing ready so that he could still be with me, but not have to deal with the outside pressure. Here's a man who had found that balance and who could deal with it in every way, and then you had the family.

Everybody loved him on *Two and a Half Men*. It's *so* Charlie. The Charlie that I knew, that I dated, that I was involved with from 1990 until 1995 is not the Charlie that I know today. The Charlie that I met and that I consider my one and only true love is the one that I knew when I was with him. Absolutely, there is no doubt.

I don't want to go into a lot of detail about it, but we started dating on February 13, 1990 and publicly stopped in 1992. We continued to see each other until June of '95. That will all come out in *How to Meet a Boy and fall in Love* which is the book that I'm working on right now. I knew Charlie to be a very good man, and I dated him throughout some of the most difficult times of his life, some of the most publicly disgraceful things. There were so many judgments made about many things, and again, the sensationalism. Nobody knew the person. Nobody knew what was really going on.

He will always be very, very special to me. The times that we had together, the things that we did together, the places we went, the feelings we shared — he's just always going to be with me. I'm embarrassed to say this but I still dream about him. He's still deep, deep in my heart and my soul. There was a bond and understanding, and a friendship and a passion that we had that I've never had with anyone prior to or since. I could finish his sentences. I knew what he was thinking. I still feel him even though haven't seen one another since my son was born. Between Charlie, my father, and my grandfather, they are the three men that I will always hold up as standards for any other man.

In a quote from the *L.A. Times,* article which appeared in the March 7, 2011 publication, Ginger was insistent that Sheen was not verbally or physically abusive toward her during their years together and she wished him well.

"I do want him to be healthy and happy," Lynn said during an interview last week.

"We all have demons. We all fight them," she added, alluding to Sheen's well-publicized drug history and tangles with his bosses. "We fall down, we get back up. I've done it. Everyone I know has done it. It seems to me, without knowing any details that right now, Charlie is going take a little different course. Hopefully, he'll rise again; he'll be like the phoenix."

Ginger Lynn *Turns the Page*

I cannot choose one thing in my career as my favorite because there are so many different things that make me excited. If I did, I'd have to choose something that makes me most proud.

Although she has accumulated many honorable nominations and awards over the years as a celebrated adult film starlet, Ginger believes her credible acting parts in television and movie projects unrelated to her erotic work are equally worthy. In 1993, Ginger turned in an admirable performance in the "B" Hollywood lesbian themed movie *Bound and Gagged: A Love Story* co-starring Karen Black. The movie is considered Lynn's best porn-free outing. When the hard rock metal group Metallica solicited her in 1998 for a starring role in their music video cover of the successful Bob Seger song "Turn the Page," Ginger wasn't interested at first. Eventually, she was won over by the extremely sensitive nature of the material. It is difficult to take your eyes off of her in the powerful piece.

I was on the road with my entourage. I had a mainstream agent and have been part of the SAG since 1986. I've done more mainstream work at this point in my career than I had adult. Most people don't know that since my mainstream films aren't publicized with me being in them. My theatrical agent called me and said, "Metallica's doing a video and they'd like you to be a part of it." I thought, "I'm more Aerosmith. I'm into Zeppelin. I'm AC/DC; I'm not Metallica." I'm not a heavy metal girl and never really have been. I had done a video for Styx a few years prior to that for Tommy Shaw. I just didn't want to be the bimbo. I didn't really know what they wanted except that they were a heavy metal band and they wanted "Ginger Lynn" to be in the video. I thought, "Enough," and I said, "No". My agent called several times and every time I would say, "No".

I was in Waco, Texas and my hair was in a ponytail. I was wearing overalls and had no make-up on. I had my son, my Manny, my bodyguard, and my assistant with me and the front desk manager called me over and said, "You have a phone call from your agent." If my agent's calling me in a hotel lobby, it's got to be important so I was thinking it was another big film. I'd done *NYPD Blue*, so I thought it might be something else like that. I went over, took the phone and he said, "Jonas Ackerman is the director for Metallica. He did Madonna's *Ray of Light* and he has done all of these award-winning videos. If he asks, will you please meet him? They are filming in two weeks and he just wants you to meet with him. Just go in and if you turn it down, just forget it." He said, "I know you'll be flying soon, but when you get off the plane he'll be at the Chateau Marmont Hotel [in Los Angeles]. Meet him there and he wants to discuss it with you."

I wasn't being a prima donna; I wasn't being bitchy. I just really, really wasn't interested. I said, "You know what? I'm in overalls. I've got an entourage with me. I'm not taking my hair out of the pony-tail. I'm not putting make-up on. He can see me as is. I'm going to meet with him and he's got twenty minutes. I'm going to have my family down in the lobby and I'm going to get them something to eat. So that's what he gets." I walked in and Jonas told me the story that they were doing a remake of the cover of the Bob Seger song, "Turn the Page". I loved Bob Seger. When I ran away years before and was supposed to be at my grandparents' for my high school graduation down in Florida and I was hitchhiking across the state, I listened a lot to Bob Seger. I thought that Metallica was going to bastardize the song. They were going to ruin it. Jonas told me that all these years he has wanted to be a mainstream video director, but that there was always somebody who said that he couldn't. He said, "I've been directing circuses, *Cirque de Soleil*, in Sweden all of these years." He said, "I'm good at it and I've made a lot of money, but it's not who I am. It's not what I want to do, but it's what I did to get where I am today." He told me, "We all make choices and we do what we have to do in order to do what we want to do. At some point, we turn the page, we make it different."

He was telling me this story about a woman who is a stripper and a hooker who has a little girl. Child Services had taken her daughter away. She's got her back and she's living out of a car and stripping from town to town. In the video, and in between of all the clips where the band is singing the song, there's a talking portion of me with my hair back just like I wore it in the eighties. I'm dressed in a jump suit and one of the statements I made was — and these are not my words, these are Jonas' words — "If I had the chance to do it all over again, I would make the exact same choices." As an actor, the words that Jonas wrote were so real to me and I felt them to my core. It's a very, very emotional video and at the end, this woman picks up a john and takes him back to her room. Her daughter is on a mattress on the floor. The guy beats the shit out of this woman and her daughter wakes up. You see this little six-year old girl holding a stray black cat while the john throws a lot of money at the mother before walking out the door. That's when it's time to "turn the page".

With all of the talking head pieces in-between, I had more feminists and more people and fans sending me money. They were thinking that I was living in a car after watching the video. It was so real to me

Scene from Metallica video "Turn the Page".

and it was what could have happened. The video was banned from MTV because of my performance. Jonas wrote the script — I did not. They did show violence in the video but there was good reason.

To bring it full circle, two years ago Jonas, who has directed Madonna and is so amazing — he was given his American Music Video Award — he called me and asked me to present him with his award because he was the most proud of *Turn the Page*. It was because we understood each other. *Turn the Page* video I did that was directed by Jonas Ackerman is the most intense piece of work I've done and the one in which I am the most proud. It's the first thing my dad ever saw me in, my dad had watched me in "B" movies, but when he watched me in the Metallica video, he called me and said, "You know, Ginger, I have to tell you, you are a really good actress and I'm very proud of you." My dad knows me very well and he was just so proud of me. Between not wanting to do it and then doing it and it becoming so personal and my dad being proud of me, it's just a piece of work that means the most to me.

Also worth mentioning is the 1999 adult film *Torn* (directed by Jane Hamilton) Ginger co-wrote about a woman torn between lovers. The film is touted as her triumphant comeback. Lynn had done selective work as a sex performer in the years leading up to this project, but seemed to be back with a vengeance as she took on three men in her first scene, and appeared in almost every subsequent one. What is also interesting about the film is the conspicuous use of condoms.

Ginger continued to be choosy about her appearances in sex movies, and kept her eye out for alternative movie and television endeavors.

I also did a series called *Skin* for Jerry Bruckheimer in 2004. We filmed thirteen episodes and eight of them aired. We were up against *Two and a Half Men* and *Vegas* when we premiered. Everything Bruckheimer touches is gold. Part of the reason that project was pulled is because we were on the set filming the last episode when a "cease and desist" order came through from my son's biological father.

Due to a gag order, Ginger could not confirm or deny rumors her son's alleged father is porn mogul, Steve Hirsch.

There were two main men in the story and one of them was based upon my son's father. One of the characters lived in Los Angeles and was a corrupt politician — the other is a pornographer with a heart of gold. Again, I didn't write the show. I just played my character. My son's father happened to be at a Bruce Springsteen concert sitting next to one of the producers who told him the story line, and within a few days, he ordered a "cease and desist". My son looks exactly like his father, only with a little more gentleness that came from me.

Ms. Mom

What has been the best ingredient for balance in my life has been my son. He's an amazing thirteen-year-old boy so I don't have the luxury of making choices today that may end my life. I'm responsible for a beautiful human being who has his whole life ahead of him. It's my job today to guide him and be the woman who can instill good things into my son and be there for him no matter what.

We have a very open communication. We're very close. He is familiar with porn, of course. He knows that I'm an actress and he knows that I have two different names that I use for work. He said,

COURTESY OF GINGER LYNN

"Why are you Ginger Lynn Allen in *American Pie* [*Presents Band Camp*, 2005]?" "Why in *The Devil's Rejects* (2005) are you Ginger Lynn Allen? You're Ginger Lynn on Facebook." He's picked up on that. I know that he's done searches on friends of mine — you really can't go on the internet and not see the name "Ginger Lynn" connected to porn at some point. I've opened the discussion up many times and asked, "Is there anything you want to know about me?

Are there any questions that you have?" I would bet my life that he knows, but he isn't ready to discuss it. He's very well adjusted so it's not a factor. There aren't any signs of it becoming difficult, but I have spoken to a therapist as well as my parents about, "When do we have this conversation?" I want him to hear it from my mouth. He loves the fact that Mom is famous. He likes it when we go places and people want my autograph.

He's definitely my son. He's all honors in all of his classes. He's been MVP of the football team for three years. He's on the snowboarding team. He's been at that school for eight years and I know everybody on a first name basis. They call Sterling the "Sterling Allen Show" because my son is the class clown. He is the jock. He's the brain. He just got an award from the thespian society for over one hundred hours on stage. He's an amazing, healthy, well-rounded, wonderful child. I have a little card that I keep that he made for me a couple of years ago that sits in front of my sink in the bathroom. It says, "Mom, I love you." There's a row with a little red card that says, "Our adventures never end" and "never" is in capital letters. We get each other. We laugh. We talk. We banter. He's very deep and very insightful. I'm a Sagittarius and he's an Aries, a fire sign. We butt heads, but we have a bond. We just have a fabulous relationship and I'm truly, truly blessed with my son. I'm pretty much a happy, lucky girl.

This is the house where everyone has been coming since my son started going to school when he was five. Halloween was his favorite holiday and it still is. Every year we would have a party. It would start at noon on Saturday and go until noon on Sunday. I'd have games planned and an overnight. We've done that forever, but I remember that first year and those first five parents. I thought they were all going to move in. They brought their kids, they were all there, but you know they were camping out. Within an hour, they found out the schedule and the list, and the games and the friends that I had employed to come and help with the party, and suddenly, they were all gone.

One of the parents who came to that first party are Southern Baptists and extremely religious. Yesterday, my son went snowboarding with one of them and I was asking him about their phone and its options. He is in a porn star's driveway telling me about their sermon and they know exactly who I am, and what I do, and they call up and ask if they can drop their son off.

On New Year's Eve, somebody knew I was going to be home because their child was coming over and word spread — all of a sudden, I had seven teenagers. Someone phoned and said, "Can we bring our son over so that we can have wild, crazy sex?" Pretty much everyone in the neighborhood knows who I am. The people who live on one side of me own the pre-school that my son attended. My neighbors on the other side, our children have grown up together and we go everywhere together. He's been in a private school his entire life and I'm very involved in his activities so I know every teacher, every staff member and every janitor. They're wonderful. I've had teachers ask me for autographs and movies for their friends and boyfriends. Living in Southern California is definitely a factor, and I think because my son goes to a private school they just get to know you better. It's much more intimate. Most children who are actors or whose parents are actors are in private school for various reasons. There are several reasons why I chose private school for my son. One of those reasons is that I consider education a top priority, but there's also life experience. Next month we're going to Maui. I travel extensively with my son. I can take him out of school and they understand life experience. They encourage it.

I don't think I could live any other way. Then again, if I were to go back to my hometown it would be okay because I'm a celebrity. It just depends. I'm sure there are places where it would be very difficult to live the life that I've led. If I wasn't so recognizable I could hide and get away with it, but I don't want to hide.

Both Sides of the Fence

The most difficult part about the choice that I've made in my career is relationships with men. I meet men who want a relationship with me but they're swingers. When I'm in a relationship, I want to be monogamous. I want it to be one-on-one. For the most part, the ones who are accepting of my career live a lifestyle that I don't. My career and my life are two completely different things. I'm not a swinger and I'm not the sexually free woman that you would think that I am. I don't live up to my reputation off camera — as far as my lifestyle. I've been engaged nine times but I just can't go through with it. My work has made relationships very difficult. I've had some long-term relationships. I've had some fabulous ones, but I don't know if I'll ever get married. Eventually, and inevitably, they get hang-ups.

My first longest relationship that I had was five, almost six years. It was with a man who was a photographer in the adult film industry. He had never seen one of my movies. Our relationship was fabulous — he didn't want to swing — we had great times. We were in sync in every possible way. The cause of our breakup came during the time I was hired to work on *Young Guns 11*. The night before I left, he had a few too many to drink and he was watching his girlfriend go from porn into mainstream. He was not able to go from porn into mainstream. He became angry and said, "You've got one foot on this side of the fence and one foot on the other side. You're never going to make it, who do you think you are?"

I said to him, "If you ever speak to me this way again, it's over." I went off to make the film and before I came back, I got a phone call from him. He had chosen for the first time ever to watch one of my movies. He went through my things in the garage and found some of my movies, and watched them. He called me up and said, "You're a fucking cocksucker. You whore." Here, we were almost six years together. I went from the woman that he had asked to marry that was wearing his ring to a "cocksucker" and a "whore". I had filmed in adult at that point almost five years. We'd already bought a house together and we were talking marriage. His career wasn't making it, but mine was in the mainstream so even that long into the relationship there was a backlash. It still came back to the "Ginger Lynn" factor.

There is someone out there for me. I'm not looking so that's probably why I'm not finding that right one. My number one priority is being a parent. Even now, I'm dating a wonderful man and we've been dating for eight months, but every once in a while he'll go "Oh, my god, I'm dating Ginger Lynn!" I always want to be able to take care of myself, but I love it when someone will take care of me. I love the opportunity to be strong and to be independent and make my own decisions, but I would never want to be in a position where I don't feel like a lady or a woman or a girl that needed or wanted a man to be a man for me. I don't want someone to control me. I don't want him to own me. I want him to stand beside me. When it comes down to the end of the day, I want to cook his dinner. There's a part of me with old-fashioned values. I want the man to be the man. I've been wearing the pants for so long it scares me. If I had to say if I had more masculine or feminine qualities, that'd be a tough call.

"MILF" is not a Four Letter Word

Ginger joined Christy Canyon as a co-host on *Night Calls* for Playboy Radio at Sirius Satellite Radio in 2006. Since leaving the position, Lynn continued her involvement with various film projects and maintained a healthy balance between mainstream options and her adult work. In March 2010, fans were surprised to see Ginger turn up on an episode of *Dog Whisperer* with host Cesar Millan along with her Rottweiler and teenage son. In 2011, Ginger returned as co-host with her long time friend and former co-star, Christy Canyon in the newly revamped Playboy Radio's Sirius Satellite Radio show *Spice Radio* which recently integrated the long time running *Legends of Porn*.

With sexual credentials like Lynn's, offers for employment in erotic movies today generally showcase her in roles where she is able to utilize her years of experience in pairings with younger men. Occasionally, Ginger teams up with old comrades such as veteran Tom Byron. Lynn and Byron's genuine attraction for one another is ultimately conveyed in *Seasoned Players 4* (2008) where they generate palpable heat. The segment opens with a slightly rounder Ginger warming up the audience as she happily regales Tom with her memory of the first time the pair made one another's acquaintance in 1984. From there, the two continue to laugh and banter back and forth — at one point Lynn claimed that because of great guys like Tom, she remained in the business. She also shared that her scene with Byron in *New Wave Hookers* was her personal favorite in her history in front of the camera. Byron contended Ginger was one of the few women he'd worked with who wasn't shy about participating in anal sex, and admitted he prefers working with old friends rather than with new talent. After things progress to the bedroom scene, Byron buries his face into Ginger's derriere and Ginger obliges by taking Tom's rather stiff organ into her mouth. Keeping the mood playful, Byron shifts Ginger into position so that his penis can easily glide into her rectum and they shuck back and forth until Tom climaxes onto the surface of Ginger's rear end with a close-up camera angle confirming he expelled a substantial shot.

I do a couple of films a month. I don't do the big movies where I have to be on set twelve to fifteen hours a day. I save my acting for the mainstream and my performances for the adult. I turn down more mainstream films than I do adult. It depends on the type of role that is offered. If you want me to be the naked girl in a mainstream movie and there's no meat to it, I'd rather fuck on film.

There's a major film in the works with one of the biggest directors in Hollywood. He bought the rights to a short film that I did a year or so ago. They're planning on making it into a series right now. I don't want to give away the title or who it is, only that it's a television series and a real life cartoon. The director and creator of this series is one of the head animators on *The Simpsons*.

PHOTO COURTESY OF SUZE RANDALL, *WWW.SUZE.NET*

At present, I'm doing a lot of Cougar work. It's fun. At this point, they need to be taught — it's so frightening that these guys think this is how you have sex. I say, "Okay, stop watching porn today. Everyone needs to watch porn from the seventies and eighties. Get over the pubic hair and watch the real stuff."

James Deen is one of my favorites. As far as new guys go, in all honesty, James is the only name that stands out. I couldn't tell you most of their names. I talk with them and get to know them a little when I get there, but they are not memorable. They don't know how to fuck. Back in our day, men were men. There was no Viagra. There wasn't anything like that. Today, you've got these twenty-year old guys who are on Viagra who walk in with a hard-on and it's not because they're twenty-one. It's pathetic. They're not porn stars. They are young guys taking Viagra who fuck like my dogs. It's not just the directors or the actors who are unenthusiastic and don't know what they're doing, the guys try to fuck the way they think a porn star fucks.

I continue to move back and forth between the two worlds. I've got a lot of eggs in my basket right now. I've got my own production company that is getting ready to launch. My book is coming along well. I need ten more of me, I really do. It's difficult a lot of days to balance porn, motherhood, business- woman, athlete, sister, friend, and girl that dates. Last weekend, I just hung three paintings that I did. I do acrylic on canvas. I design and sell my jewelry. I love to cook. My grandfather taught me how to cook. My days begin and they're over way too soon. I just don't have enough time, but it's all good. There really isn't anything negative in my life. My girlfriend says I juggle a lot of glass balls so I have to be careful because when I drop one it's going to break. I'm well organized and I work out of my home. I try my best to never do housework in the day when I'm home so I do prioritize.

Legacy of Passion and Innocence

Many porn purists believe the legalization and regulation of sex films in the state of California in 1988 resulting from the Freeman decision is a double-edged sword. The ruling vindicated the industry, but it also quieted the rebel rousing and free spirited energy that propelled the pioneers who reigned throughout the golden period of adult entertainment — leaving the current erotic movie industry suspended and in somewhat of a pillaged state. With the advent of internet and webcam voyeurism gaining in popularity in the post-video era, the production value by studios is almost negligible and the genre itself seems frigid and indifferent. Not surprisingly, there is revived interest in the classics and vintage actors. According to former and contemporary performers, the existing movement in adult films is all about acrobatics and "extreme" sex leaving a veneer of a storyline and honest sensuality in the dust. After all, there are only so many ways to skin a cat.

It's different today than it was back in the sixties where it was all about wild and free sex. They were free and easy and out there and everybody was doing it — those are the people of the seventies who were in porn, but the women of the eighties were the women that changed the face of porn when it was dirty, and naughty, and taboo, and unacceptable. I think that those of us who came after, and the people who grew up watching our films — I believe we will leave them with a sense of passion and innocence in sex. Today, there is no passion, there is no innocence, and it's not just in the adult film industry, it's the entire medium — listen to the radio, read the magazines.

There are those of us from those Golden years that will leave an impact on the future and on people to come in the entertainment industry as well as the film industry. Unfortunately or fortunately, depending on the person, I also believe that many of us will not leave anything. You know, there are people who don't even know who "Aunt Peg" is. Juliet Anderson just died a couple of weeks ago [January 2010]. She was the original, the first Cougar — the first MILF. We spoke about her when I was at the show in Vegas recently. I had a long line of people coming up and a couple of girls who were standing nearby were saying, "Who is that? Who is that?"

To have a long shelf life or a legacy in the world is rare. Personally, I was able to break out of the adult industry and into mainstream because my face, my image, and my persona have been in many different areas. You hear my name — you know it. Whereas, if you were just a porn star, not that there is "just a porn star," but if you didn't grow above or outside of that box people will not know who you are in two years, much less twenty. We're kind of a dying breed.

I don't know if this is a compliment or an insult, but a guy recently came up to me at a show who was twenty-something and he said to me, "My grandma told me that the very first porn I had to watch was you. I love your movies!" His grandmother raised him and when he became sexual, she said, "This is how you do it." So maybe there is somewhat of a legacy. Maybe people will know there is passion in sex!

In the summer of 2010, I met with Ginger at the Exxxstacy Show in Rosemount, a suburb of Chicago. Lynn was at a booth signing autographs and as good fortune would have it, she took a moment for a break. We walked outside of the Hall and stepped onto the long escalator down to locate a place to talk in quiet. We found a spot along the steps, just inside the shadowy bowels of the convention centre. After making ourselves comfortable, I was immediately at ease. Ginger has a remarkable way of giving one the sense they've known her for years and during our brief time together that afternoon, I felt as comfortable as I would chatting away with an old girlfriend. When we returned to the center, Lynn's father was waiting for her at her booth and we were introduced. Ginger bore a definite resemblance to her dad, and it was obvious the two had an intrinsic and tough bond. In a heartbreaking twist of fate, only a little over a year after our meeting, Ginger's father was seriously injured in a motorcycle accident and passed away in October 2011.

I'm the exception to the rule in the adult film industry. I'm not the norm and not by any means would I recommend any woman to get into this industry or any man for that matter. Unless you are strong, extremely strong and you can deal with the judgments and the accusations and all of the bullshit that goes along with it, it's not for you. Now, there are many more things that are wonderful if you know how to deal with it and if you have the right mind set. Most people don't.

I would definitely have to say that the choices that I've made and my history in the adult industry have had a positive impact on my life. I wouldn't be the woman that I am today. I wouldn't be as open-minded. I wouldn't be as dignified. I wouldn't have as much courage. I wouldn't have the balls to stand up for myself. When I got into the industry, I was barely turning twenty-one. I was from Illinois and I was shy about life. I didn't really know how to have relationships, how to talk to people or how to stand up for myself.

I did grow up quicker because of my work, but I became more of a woman because of it. I wouldn't change it for the world.

I wish I would have been a little wiser with my money or had someone that guided me. I've been extremely fortunate though and have done very well in the industry, better than ninety-nine percent of the women and I have things to show for it, but there's still that retirement fund I'm working on. On the plus side, I'm able to ask for what I want. Not just in the bedroom, but in life, in general. It has given me a sense of security and not because of the sexual aspect, but a sense of security as "I'm a woman," and I made these choices and I will stand up for myself. I do stand up for myself because I've had to fight to a certain extent, the public perception and negativity, at times. I've learned how to hold my head high so it has definitely been positive. My personal motto is this: If it feels good do it, but don't hurt anybody in the process, especially yourself.

22

Amber Lynn
The Blonde Panther

Orange County, California generally conjures images prevalent in the popular TV show by the same name depicting affluent white privilege, texting teens languishing on perfectly groomed beaches ambivalent to the sun's harmful rays while surfer boys gauge the wave action in anticipation of their next big adventure. Growing up in the OC for Laura Lynn Allen however, was anything but idyllic or opulent. After her parents' complicated break-up at age three, Lynn was placed in foster care for a period of four years at which time her mother convalesced in a hospital following a mental breakdown. Tragically, at age seven and shortly after Lynn finally left her foster home, her mother was killed in an automobile accident leaving Laura to be placed under adoptive guardianship.

As she grew into an attractive young woman, Lynn took advantage of the omnipresent sunshine and mild temperatures offered by the allure of the Orange County coastline. With her ultra tanned skin, precocious sex appeal, and bleach blonde hair, Amber set her sights on a modeling contract while destiny seemed to be in her corner in 1983 when she crossed paths with Althea Flynt, wife of the magazine mogul, Larry Flynt, at one of West Hollywood's prestigious nightclubs.

After modeling for *Hustler* and *Penthouse*, the natural next step was a meeting with the successful west coast director, Bobby Hollander. Hollander cast Lynn in her first film *Personal Touch III* (1983) with Bunny Bleu and Lisa DeLeeuw. Lynn's second film role introduced her to the enigmatic veteran of the blue screen, the dangerously hypnotic Jamie Gillis who became a long time lover and sage in her life as he took on the task of masterfully guiding her career. Lynn, along with another burgeoning nymphet sharing the same middle and surnames, Ginger Lynn Allen, ascended the rungs of stardom quickly in the San Fernando Valley

"I wanted this bright, shiny persona. That's what the industry gave me the ability to do. I was able to recreate something new and exciting that didn't have all of this heartbreak and tragedy. That's why I got into the industry and just took off." AMBER LYNN

while enjoying the friendly camaraderie and competition that bonded and branded the two young starlets. Headlining in clubs and excessive drug use soon overshadowed Lynn's adult career, and eventually Amber's reckless lifestyle caught up with her as she began to lose the people and things she loved and had worked hard to sustain. Lynn has been clean and sober for more than a decade.

Throughout the rough patches in her life, Amber's altruistic nature has prevailed as has been demonstrated through her nurturing support of The Youth AIDS Foundation of Los Angeles, and more recently, *We Are the World XXX*, a filmed fundraiser for the late director Henri Pachard (Ron Sullivan) who passed away from cancer in 2008. After remaining silent throughout the debacle of the Sullivan project, Amber hoped to set the record straight by agreeing to be featured in this book.

I spoke with Amber Lynn in December 2010 and January 2011, shortly after veteran John Leslie passed away.

Orange County Kid

I was a kid from Orange County and I came from a severely broken home, a traumatic childhood and upbringing. My birthday is in September and I'm actually born in 1964. I know that IMDb.com and Wikipedia state my birth year as 1963, but it's not true. I don't even know how they got that date. I've tried to go in and correct all of the misinformation about me on Wikipedia because there were many misleading statements and in the press, opposite of what the truth is.

I was taken away from my mother when I was three years old. I was placed in a foster home because my mother and father had a very traumatic break-up and divorce. My father had cheated on my mother and had other children with another woman. In a nutshell, my parents had a daughter before me along with a son that was my older brother who became [porn star] Buck Adams. The little girl was born with holes in her heart and she died when she was two years old. My mother was going through the process of hospitalization and surgeries trying to save my sister's life during my parents' marriage. She became obsessed with having another girl and it ended up destroying her relationship with my father who then became involved in another relationship. I guess he didn't break off his relationship with my mother and his children though. It exploded, and we all wound up going into foster care when I was three years old. My mother was then institutionalized with a nervous breakdown. Back then, they didn't have rehab. They just thought you were crazy and especially if you were a woman. They'd just lock you up in the nuthouse. Today, if you have a drug or alcohol problem there's help out there. I was in a foster home when I was a kid and there was a lot of abuse. It wasn't sexual, but it was physical. It was a frightening thing that I went through.

When I got out of the home and went back to my mother, within that year of returning home, my mother was killed in a car accident in front of me. My life was spared because I was thrown from the car. I was seconds and inches from dying and I witnessed my mother's death. I was almost decapitated in the car. This all happened by the time I was seven and a half years old. I suffer from PTSD and there was a kind of a huge splitting in my childhood. That's what children do when they suffer from traumatic events because they are too young to interpret. They split so that they don't go into shock. I didn't find this out until years later in therapy and I was able to leave myself to create a character and be someone completely different. Now in my mid-forties when I look back at it squarely, even with all of the recovery, it's still huge. In my memory, I had a short relationship with my mother, but a few things my mother had said to me always stuck. Her words formed me on the very little information that mattered. My mother was a Lithuanian Jew. She had wanted me to marry once and she wanted me to be a wife before I was a mother. On these little things, I rely.

When I came into the industry, I was a kid. I was escaping from all of that past. I was so ready by the time I got on the road to come to L.A. and be an actor to get the hell out of what had happened to me as anyone could imagine. I was going into modeling and got into the industry by accident. I had come to Los Angeles from Orange County where I had been modeling to get into the magazine side of modeling. I wound up getting involved with *Hustler* and *Club* and *Penthouse Magazines*. There was a photographer named Jay Stephen Hicks who shot me for *Penthouse* and that was my focus. These people separated the model from the porn actress. At that time, it was very important that you were separated. Girls who modeled for Men's magazines didn't necessarily do porn and now they are kind of required to do so much more than what we did.

Anyway, I'd met Althea Flynt before I did films with Clive McLean who shot me for *Hustler*. That was, I guess, how they had

noticed me. I'd gone to the Rainbow with some of my girlfriends.
We would go up to the Starwood and we used to see bands play. On
one of the nights we went to see this band called Y & T [originally
known as Yesterday and Today] which was a really big deal, and
we ended up over at the Rainbow. A guy pulled up in a red `64
Corvette; I'll never forget it because the license was the year of my
birthday. A black limousine pulled up right behind it and it had
a naked lady on it and out of it came Althea Flynt. At the time, I
didn't know who it was. I thought it was someone like Joan Jett —
she had this shocking, cropped, black hair and black leather pants
on. She came in and they invited me to their table, and we started
drinking. They said, "I want to shoot you". I was already interviewing with Stephen Hicks, and had done some shooting here and
there and they shot me right away for *Hustler*. Clive McLean and
I became very close and we actually dated and had a relationship.
We stayed best friends for my entire career. We were dear, dear
friends and I spoke at his wake when he passed away years ago.
It broke my heart. That was how I got into the industry through
Clive and Althea.

Althea Flynt was born Althea Leasure in Marietta, Ohio and experienced a shattered childhood mirroring Amber Lynn's. Orphaned at
eight years old after her mother and grandfather were fatally shot by her
father who then turned the gun on himself, Althea resided in the care
of nuns for the duration of her childhood and teen years. At seventeen,
she met her soon-to-be husband, Larry Flynt, while stripping at his
club in Columbus, Ohio and became *Hustler* magazine's first centerfold.
Eventually, she was promoted to co-publisher. With full-blown AIDS,
Althea drowned in a swimming pool in 1987 at the Bel Air home she
shared with Flynt, just a few years after taking Amber Lynn under her
wing. She was thirty-three years old.

I got into the limo with Althea that night and she took us
down to a restaurant down the street. She had a magazine she was
doing about rock stars and we were up there trying to meet rock
musicians. She was interviewing The Police and Sting and we went
over there. She was just this great woman. We had a kind of weird
connection. She thought I was some kid who was partying and
they wanted me for *Hustler*. That's how we rolled back then. One
thing led to another.

Rolling

John Leslie's death changed my idea about doing this interview because his passing triggered many memories and it triggered the first time I met John. I was going to do a film for the late Bobby Hollander who was actually the man who discovered me and got me into the industry. I went over to meet Bobby Hollander for a go see, to talk about a part in a film where it was planned for me to do a single, pretty girl scene. It was not sex and it was not supposed to be hardcore or so it was promoted to me. I was just a magazine model, but I guess he had seen me in a magazine so I went there and he pulled out a pipe and I got loaded with him. It was the first time I had ever experienced smoking cocaine. The next day I was on a [porn] set and I made my first movie.

There were drugs involved and they were definitely used as a ploy. The first time I smoked cocaine I had no idea what I was doing. I thought that I was smoking grass. I had done grass in bongs but I had never done freebase. I didn't even know it existed. Now, you can't rape the willing. Let's just be honest. You can't rape the willing and I was willing. You make the decision. The decision is laid out right in front of you no matter how the manipulation occurs. You have a free choice to walk across that line or not. You have to take responsibility and accountability. That's the deal. Were there manipulations? Of course there were. That's business, in all business. The bottom line though good or bad, is that's how I got in.

On that same evening, I met Shauna Grant in Bobby's living room. She wound up shooting herself in the head a month later. When I saw her, I thought, "Oh my god, she's so beautiful. If she could do this, why shouldn't I do this?" I saw her a few times during the course of this visit. She had been living out in Palm Springs and I presumed she was coming in to hang out with Bobby. They were close and he had managed her career. That was the big story that was handed to me, that he had made her who she was and he was going to do the same for me. I thought, 'Wow, this is not so bad," and then the next day I made the film. They set me up really well. The first film was done on the drugs. The second one was done with Jamie [Gillis] and John Leslie and they were huge stars. It was on the second movie I was named "Amber Lynn".

The late Bobby Hollander directed pornographic films from 1979-1995 and is one of the first pioneers in his field to transition to videotape. It is believed that Hollander, who discovered famed actress Shauna Grant, provided the inspiration for "The Colonel James" character in *Boogie Nights* (1997) superbly personified by actor Robert Ridgely (who memorably portrayed "The Librarian Cop" in an episode of *Seinfeld*). Married for a few years to Gloria Leonard, Hollander died of a brain tumor in 2002.

I used to hang out on Newport Beach all of the time. I always had a tan and I was a very dark-skinned, little surfer girl. I went by the name I had grown up with which was Lynn. All my childhood friends called me "Little Lynny" and they thought this name was definitely not sexy so we started to kick around names on the set. I went from meeting Shauna Grant, and Ginger Lynn, and Jamie Gillis, and John Leslie, and Danielle — a lot of people don't know who she is now, but she was a big star back then and one of my very first close friends. They had plans for me from the minute I walked through the door. Jamie saw me and said, "This is my girl-friend," and he and I became a couple. I had a support system and Jamie ran my early career. He made sure I got the same money that Ginger was getting at that time. He knew what Ginger was being paid, and he said, "Amber's getting the same because she's worth it," and that was it. Jamie was really behind all of that and he gave me the support that I needed to say "no" to things. Once I got my foot in, I loved it. It's not that I wasn't willing it's just that it wasn't my idea. Let's put it that way.

The second movie I made was called *Centerfold Celebrities 4* in 1984. I think the reason I had met Shauna Grant was because she had made one [or two] earlier. I went to stay in the hotel where they were going to shoot this film and I was to meet Jamie the next day, but John Leslie was at the hotel and he grabbed me coming through the lobby because I was the new actress. We had a little affair in the room that night. I loved John Leslie and I was always very close to him.

I talked with Bill Margold recently, and he said that people used to do things back then as if it was a handshake. I picked up the phone and called John's wife immediately after I heard about his death, and offered her my condolences and sent my love. He was an incredibly special human being and absolutely one of my favorite people of all time. You know how they have the "Sexiest Man Alive" on the cover of the cover of *People* Magazine. I always picture John Leslie's face on there. He was so sexy, and he was just so masculine, and smooth and classy. He was brilliant and dirty. He was just all of it. Jamie was all of those things in a different way. As friends and buddies, and as a team, they were an era. They were wonderful.

PHOTO COURTESY OF SUZE RANDALL, *WWW.SUZE.NET*

I'll never forget the day I set eyes on Jamie. He came into the make-up room where he would always hang out and I was sitting in the chair. Here he was this older, revered actor in the industry and they were making a big deal of him. He had this beautiful curly hair which I loved. To this day men with curly hair is one of my things. He was very elegant and this wonderful talented actor. I was just sold on it all. When I met Jamie Gillis, I just thought he was a nice Jewish boy and he was. He was crazy and sexually deviant, and all of those things that other people have talked about he could absolutely be, but he was also a brilliant man and he was really the love of my life in that respect. I was very young and Jamie knew everything about me. He knew where I'd come from, he knew what had happened. When I got into the industry I didn't want people to know who I was and where I'd come from because then people would always judge me as the kid from the broken home, or that I'd come out of foster homes. I didn't want that. I wanted this bright, shiny persona. That's what the industry gave me the ability to do. I was able to recreate something new and exciting that didn't have all of this heartbreak and tragedy. That's why I got into that industry and just took off.

Centerfold Celebrities 4 (1984), the fourth installment of the series directed by Bobby Hollander is a difficult to find item. The original series contained footage of Hollander casually interviewing young starlets new to the business that had previously done centerfold work. He would often pair them with veteran performers such as Jamie Gillis, Ron Jeremy, and John Leslie for their initial hardcore scenes. An early critic's review for this title claimed Amber Lynn (billed as Amber Lynn Lane) and John Leslie's love scene simmers and is very sensuous. Helga Sven, Tantala Ray, Jamie Gillis, Nick Random, R. Bolla, and Sasha Gabor also co-star. Amber also appeared in the fifth installment of the series *Centerfold Celebrities 5* (1985) opposite Jamie Gillis. Interested fans of the early-mid-1980s adult stars might want to consider searching Ebay for the titles belonging to this series.

I met a crazy woman in *Centerfold Celebrities 4* named Tantala Ray who was a dominatrix. I saw her do a scene where she tied up a guy and abused him. She strapped on a dildo and fucked him in the ass, and I loved it. I was like, "Ah, this is insane!" That was where Jamie and I made this connection. Jamie ended up highjacking me, and he took me immediately away on the second movie. It wasn't before the monster in me had already woken up. I had serious problems with drugs and alcohol when I was with Jamie and all through my life and career. It wasn't always when I was on set and there were periods when I would not do any at all, but it wasn't until much later in my life when I was able to label it for what it was. A lot of it was my unresolved stuff that I had never faced, plus the fact that I was in complete denial.

Jamie and I did a lot of sexual things. He took me to the Pussycat Theatre and I would wear these short skirts and high heels, and this was like our couples night out. Most couples go out to the movies on Saturday night; the movies we went were at the Pussycat Theatre and I was dressed like a trollop. After a while, the guys in the theatre would recognize me, know who I was, and know who Jamie was. They would get all turned on just by being in the room with us. He just thought it was the hottest thing. We would go home afterwards and we would have this great sex with each other as boyfriend and girlfriend, committed people to each other. We didn't have a lot of sex outside of our relationship until the relationship broke up because Jamie had an affair with [performer] Careena Collins behind my back. That was devastating for me. We really had this very all consuming, totally in love thing for years. We lived together. Actually, I woke up this morning and the first words out of my mouth were, "If I did have one thing to do over again, I would have married Jamie."

The Lynn Girls

After Amber got her first tastes of stardom there was no shortage of film appearances throughout the meat of the 1980s as her lengthy filmography reveals. Lynn boasted performances in well over a hundred videos between the years 1984 and 1989 and many were starring or prominent roles. As Amber ignited heat in the loins of her male fan following with her sassy, pouty lips and sinewy, lithe body, she soon came face-to-face with her rival in the adult scene, Ginger Lynn. The Lynn girls shared the limelight as friendly competitors resulting in a delectable smorgasbord for their admirers, particularly when the two were cast in the same film.

I met Ginger Lynn shortly after the night that I worked on that set with Jamie. He took me home and that was it, we lived together from that minute on. The following week he took me out to Harry Reems's house, and Ginger was there and I met her. She said, "Why don't you come outside?" and she started feeding me tequila on the patio and then she had sex with me. That was the first time I had ever been with a girl. Ginger was like that and I just thought, "Oh my god. She's so beautiful." Once again, I thought, "If she can do this and she's so beautiful, so can I". She

Ginger Lynn and Amber Lynn. PHOTO COURTESY OF SUZE RANDALL, WWW.SUZE.NET

was brand new and she had just gotten back from Hawaii. I think we left there and went up to the Playboy Mansion or something. It was just a crazy time.

I love Ginger. I fell in love with her the minute I saw her. We were very young and we had a good connection, and she's an amazing girl. People often talk about our personalities where Ginger is the sweet one and I'm the ball buster and I'm wild and loud, but she's the one that if you get her mad, you won't want to get in her way. Whereas I'm the one who will hesitate and won't say anything until I'm so angry I'll just explode.

As is often the case, behind every successful erotic performer is an enterprising figure. Cleveland, Ohio born Reuben Sturman became the biggest distributor of adult magazines by the late 1960s after his meager start as a comic book salesman. During his prime, Sturman allegedly became of the most powerful men in America as an unstoppable profiteer in the business of selling sex. The businessman and organized crime affiliate was convicted of tax evasion in 1989 and sentenced to ten years in prison. An influx of legal woes encroached upon Sturman's ability to operate and thrive. He was charged with extortion and died in 1997 in a Lexington, Kentucky Federal Penitentiary, but not before staging an escape from jail in Boron, California. He was later apprehended in Anaheim. It is believed Sturman arranged to have several porn stores bombed and people murdered. In the mid-1980s, Amber Lynn and Reuben Sturman developed a professional arrangement.

I remember Ginger and I used to do the trade shows together, and I worked with Reuben Sturman for Vidco. I was his contract player. He was the big dude, the godfather of the porn business back then. Stevie Hirsch was just starting Vivid, Ginger was contracted to Vivid, and they would put our booths together. Ginger and I were always signing autographs together: "Ginger Lynn and Amber Lynn," and we'd be side by side. We were at a Trade Show in Chicago one time and we went to go shopping. Ginger wanted to go over to the mall and check things out. I'll never forget, the elevator door opened and out walked this girl. She was a long legged woman and she said, "Oh, are you so and so?" We were like, "Yeah."

She said, "Oh, I'm Porsche Lynn." Ginger looked at me and she looked at Porsche, and she said, "How dare you call yourself Porsche Lynn?"

She looked at us and asked, "What is the big idea?" Ginger was just this little tiny thing. We were all promoted by three different people. The thing of it was that from the gate everyone knew that my name was Laura Lynn Allen and Ginger's was Ginger Lynn Allen. When they met me, it was like "Wow, you've got the same name as Ginger!" Ginger wasn't anybody at that time. She was

brand new in the industry. She was not some famous icon. She was just this new girl who had done a couple of films. They said, "Oh, you kind of resemble each other so why don't you call yourself Amber Lynn?" We never thought it would be a thing. When I got into the adult business, I never in a million years thought that somebody would recognize me on the street and say, "Can I have your autograph?" The thought never even crossed my mind. My idea of the industry was that we were doing these dirty little films and we were making money for the studios, and yes, there was a camera involved, but not that they would be shown somewhere, where people that I would see out in the real world would see them. I imagined the people who would look at those films as little shady guys in raincoats.

Once I got in, it became this real competitive thing where Ginger was doing movies and I was doing movies; we were doing movies together. She got this big name and then I wanted to be that big. Then I was big and she was big. Then Christy Canyon came in and there was a third arm to the whole star thing. Ginger and I were at a show in Chicago one time and we said, "I want to be picked up in a limo," and they said, "Okay". We said, "I want make-up artist Lexie [Alexis Vogel] on all of our movies," and they said, "Okay". Then it was "Our movies are going to be catered!" and they said, "Okay". We literally dictated the treatment on the set. We were able to create the star system and did so just like the rock and rollers. Ginger used to have M&Ms on the set and I wanted peanuts, and she wanted plain and we got things. We were kids and got certain stuff. She always wanted the make-up artist to do us differently. She liked to look very plain and played down and very girl-next-door. I wanted nothing to do with that. I wanted lots of make-up and hairspray and tiny costumes and my push-up bra, and that was it. I had a very rock and roll eighties style and she had a completely different look. That's why we were able to co-exist.

I remember Ginger and I worked very closely on *The Grafenberg Spot* (1985). We both wanted that film to be very good. It was her movie, her vehicle, and they brought me up to be on it. That was one of the ones where she wanted to make sure we were very different.

The Grafenberg Spot (highlighted in chapter 21) is a well-crafted, good-looking film, written, directed and produced by the Mitchell Brothers. In her first segment, Amber Lynn (with her pixie face and trademark, voluminous "eighties" hair) plays a patient that Annette Haven (in the role of a physician) encourages to orgasm through direct stimulation of the "G" spot while Leslie (Ginger Lynn) looks on. The Lynn girls, unquestionably beautiful here, are especially noticeable because they are featured together. Later, Amber teams up with Harry Reems to provide him with an extremely unrestrained blowjob. In the "outtakes" features, Amber and Reems are clearly having a good time together as they practice for their forthcoming scene. Lynn taunts him to "come all over my tits," which he does with colossal effort. Notable cast members include Nina Hartley, another brand new blonde acquisition to the fold, in addition to Rick Cassidy, Lili Marlene, and Thor Southern.

> The movie that my fans never fail to mention, as a favorite is a film by Suze Randall called *Love Bites* (1986) with Peter North, Harry Reems [and Traci Lords]. Back in the day, before they were popular, I was in this MILF scene where a conservatively dressed woman carrying a brief case and wearing a suit, gets on an elevator and is bitten by a love bug. She proceeds to attack two men [James Miles and Rick Savage] in the elevator sexually, and have her way with them. It was way back in the eighties, and it is probably the most popular scene I've ever done because through the years people never fail to mention it wherever I go. The role that I played in *Trashy Lady* (1985) was a very significant one as well. It was a period piece. Those are the films that I think probably stand out the most for me.

No longer in her freshman year, Amber held her own with veterans Jamie Gillis, John Leslie, Harry Reems, John Holmes, Eric Edwards, Peter North, and Rick Savage (a former ballet dancer before working as an actor and performer). Lynn proved to be a quick study and her ability to personify a character on camera in addition to performing blistering sex scenes, was evidenced by her feature role as the voluptuous, hard-boiled moll Rita in *Trashy Lady* (1985) co-starring Ginger Lynn, Harry Reems, and Savage. Set during 1920s prohibition, Rita, a gorgeous, tough-talking broad with a penchant for men, money, and mayhem is hired by a bootlegging gangster Dutch (Harry Reems in a great acting turn) to teach his fancy new girlfriend Kitty (Ginger Lynn) how to become a fast, foul-mouthed dame with the same exceptional ability to handle men in the sack as Rita. For their warm-up session, Dutch pays a young newsy Jimmy (Tom Byron) a handsome sum to be a guinea pig so that Rita can school Kitty in the finer points of fellatio and intercourse. Comically, after Rita shows Kitty the ropes, Kitty straddles Jimmy the kid while Rita seats herself next to the bed with one watchful eye on the make-out session. She applies polish to her (already) heavily lacquered fingernails, fixes her white blonde, curly coiffe, and admires herself in the mirror. Kitty turns out to be an A-plus student, and while she prepares for her first rendezvous with Dutch, Rita pays a conjugal visit to her man Louie (Herschel Savage) in the slammer for his part in illegal activities. Louie is none too happy to hear that Rita has been making frequent visits to Dutch's place, but she explains she was only helping Dutch groom his girl. Louie softens and tells Rita how much he's missed her — and her body. In a fantasy sequence, Rita proves how much she's missed Louie as she gives him some imaginative head. Louie reciprocates with impressive cunnilingus that leaves her breathless. They consummate the deal, and shortly afterwards, Louie is back on the beat with the boys with Rita continuing to call the shots. Cara Lott, Bunny Bleu, Mark Wallice (as Mark Wallace) and Rick Savage co-star.

Toxic Twins

Soon after establishing herself as a rising young star, Amber's older brother and former boxer/bouncer, Buck Adams, debuted as a performer in 1984 in *Body Shop* for VCX. Amber and Buck, along with Melissa and (the late) Lisa Melendez are in the minute category of porn siblings to have worked as actors during the tail end of the golden era.

There is a myth out there that my brother and I hid that we were siblings until we were booked to do a scene together and we had to confess. That is not true. The truth is that my brother came to the set and I introduced him to John Holmes as my brother. I don't think I did say anything in the very beginning, but it wasn't something that we really hid from people. Actually, I don't think I told John on the set of *Body Shop* (1984) he was my brother, but they didn't book me a scene to do with my brother. There was never any reference to that, but people say it all over the place. I definitely introduced him to John, and later, my brother had his own career. When my brother came into the industry there was a period when we were in involved together, but I went off and started dancing and he stayed and blazed his own trail. He had his own success. He was his own person, and he was incredibly talented in his own right. In fact, my brother taught me a lot about directing. He was always very reluctant for us to stand together because there was always a competitive shadow for both of us. We used to go everywhere together. Actually [Aerosmith front man] Stephen Tyler used to wear a shirt that said, "Toxic Twins," that referred to him and [guitarist] Joe Perry. I used to have those shirts and that was my brother and me. We were like that. We loved, and adored, and respected each other and we were fiercely competitive rivals at the same time.

When Amber introduced Buck Adams to John Holmes on the set of *Body Shop* in 1984, Holmes was employed as a line producer and actor for VCX. *Body Shop* (directed by Bill Amerson under the name Bill Williams) takes place in a mechanic's garage where the girls, headed up by Madame Jackie (Amber Lynn) along with her boyfriend Russ (R. Bolla), give a new definition to a "lube and oil" job. As the joint proprietor of the girls' outcall service centre, Jackie/Amber is decked out in white short-shorts, stiletto boots, and a tiny red shirt. She joins in on sexually ambitious outings with R. Bolla and Scott Irish while big brother Buck, in his first shot as a porno performer, engages in a three-way with Tracy Duzit and Pamela Jennings on the hood of an automobile. Adams actually burned his leg on the carburetor during his sex scene because he didn't think it would be prudent to stop the action midway in his first time out. The incident left a permanent scar.

Amber and Holmes worked together in more than a few films beginning in the 1985 release *Rubdown* where they had hot sex in a Jacuzzi, another leading role for Amber. Lynn portrayed one of three girlfriends (along with Bunny Bleu and Kimberly Carson) that decide to open their own escort service after one of the girls (Carson) is sexually harassed by their boss (Harry Reems). Overall, *Rubdown* (directed by Bill Amerson under the pseudonym Bill Williams) is not particularly memorable, but some of the sex scenes are undeniably torrid.

Lynn, Holmes, and young Tom Byron made for a dynamic trio in *The Adventures of Dickman & Throbbin*,' the 1986 parody of the 1960s *Batman* TV series. In the best scene of the spoof, Amber, playing the naïve, teenage starlet Brooke, is sexed-up by the pair of "sexorcists," Dickman and Throbbin' (magically appearing in a cloud of dust) in her bedroom. Dickman (Holmes) delivers a funny tongue-in-cheek monologue about Brooke's pussy while Throbbin' (Byron) punctuates his dissertation with humorous lines such as "Holy Hemorrhoids, Dickman!" or "Holy douche bag, Dickman! I think I'm going to throw up!" It's a bit of a stretch to imagine Amber Lynn in the role of a wide-eyed virgin, but the video scores points for ingenuity and flavor. Keli Richards, Pat Manning, Joanna Storm, Mark Wallice, Peter North, and Steve Powers co-star.

John always said to me, "You're too pretty and you're too big boobed." He liked much more natural looking girls. I was still brand new when I first worked with him and I remember he could not

Rubdown. VCX. PHOTOGRAPHY BY KENJI

get a full erection. Everybody was doing drugs back then. It was the eighties and it was part of the deal. It was the porn industry and that was part of the make-up of the industry.

Love, Stardom, and other Drugs

My mentor was probably Jamie. Jamie taught me everything. Jamie taught me how to fend for myself in the world for the first time. Here, I had lost my mother and my father died when I was eleven. I had my brother, but in the early part of my career, I was hiding my career from my family so Jamie is the one who helped me. He was sort of like the John Derrick to Bo — that's what Jamie and I were like.

Sexuality is very empowering. The funny part about it is that I'm completely the opposite in my personal life and the way I run my relationships. They don't match. I often will say, "What would Amber do in this situation?" I've come to that because there is no problem for me in that respect. She would always do what's right for her. She'd have no problem. With me, I tend to second guess myself a little more so there is a difference in the personalities. When you're an actor, you break down a character. They try to decide what they look like, what they dress like, and who they are. They bring life to the role. Jamie was a Shakespearean actor and was very brilliant and highly trained. Early in my career and in my experience through Jamie, I decided to create the persona under the same idea. For me "Amber Lynn" was everything that Laura always wanted to be. All of the things that I really wasn't capable of this persona could be. Often times, I acted in ways when I was doing a role that wouldn't be comfortable to me as Laura. Me as "Amber Lynn" is a very assertive personality and a ball buster. People will say, "She's nothing like that in real life. She's much more of a romantic and sultry." I am a different person. I'm sure Tom Cruise isn't blowing up buildings in his real life either.

Amber continued to turn heads and provided inspiration for countless male fantasies with her expressive vocal exuberance in the midst of many of her starring roles opposite some of the hottest men and women in the X-rated business.

At the time I began, we were just crossing into the video age. I'll never forget the first time somebody recognized me. I was coming out of the Pussycat theatre with Jamie, and I was wearing a pair of white hot pants and white pumps and they had zippers on the sides. They were completely short. We were walking across the street on Western Avenue and a cop sped up and slammed on his breaks, and stopped right in front of us. He turned into the driveway and two cops got out of the car and said to Jamie, "You get over here and put your hands on the hood of the car."

I looked at them and I said, "Why?"

They said, "Don't ask any questions. Just get your hands on the hood of the car."

Jamie said, "Officers, officers, please. What is going on?" They thought I was a prostitute.

Jamie said, "That's not a prostitute. Look!" He pointed across the street at the Pussycat theatre and right in front of the theatre was a giant poster of me that was from the movie I had just done called *If My Mother Only Knew* (1986). I had on the exact white hot pants that I was wearing that day, and I had gum in my mouth and I had this little hairdo. They looked at the poster and they looked at me and they looked at Jamie, and they let go of me. They'd had my hands behind my back because they were handcuffing me. They let go and they said, "Oh. That is you."

They were in complete shock and Jamie said, "Guys, guys, guys. Calm yourselves down. She's not a prostitute she's an adult film actress." That was so amazing because at that moment I was shaking it off and then I thought, "Yeah, I'm an actress." They recognized Jamie right away. When I was out with Jamie people knew who he was. Jamie was incredibly famous. He and I would go to restaurants in small areas and people would know Jamie immediately. He had this deep voice and he would clear his throat before he would ever say anything. If he wanted you to listen to him, he would clear his throat and he would look at you so that you would go, "Oh," and then he would say what he had to say, but he would always clear his throat first.

Jamie hated drugs. He loved to drink wine and he loved to smoke those certain cigarettes and have his coffee. One of the reasons Jamie said he hated drugs is because he watched drugs destroy me, and our relationship. He saw that I got into the industry because I got high on freebase and freebase was the kind of drug that would completely unleash your inhibitions. I was *on* the minute I got high and Bobby Hollander would give tons of it out on his sets. Jamie knew that drugs destroyed our relationship in the end. I went away on a movie set and went to work for Svetlana on a film called *Miami Spice* (1986), and once again, we're in Miami and somebody broke out a big bag of whatever. I would get up in the morning with all good intentions. I would have told him that I had sworn off drugs forever and that I was never going to do it again. There were months when I would do absolutely nothing and we would go back to a blissful life, as blissful as it could be because we had a very normal conventional relationship with a bond and an agreement, and an understanding around it.

You will find this with most people in the industry in spite of the lifestyle. The commitment to the union in the relationship is always very deep and very true with any of us. If you look at me and Jamie or John Stagliano and Karen or Nina Hartley and Ira — people have these very stable commitments where you can't get between it. It's a very strong bond.

COURTESY OF WORTH MENTIONING PUBLIC RELATIONS

When I was still living with Jamie they had called me to go to Europe to work in a bunch of films and the first place I went was Paris. I wound up jumping on a plane with Sharon Mitchell and I had the time of my life. Mitch and I went to Paris during the craziest time of my career, and we made boatloads of money and we came back penniless. We just partied and I hooked up with this Parisian biker gang and made one of them my boyfriend. I wound up having to call Jamie. I'd spent all of the money and ended up getting into a lot of trouble, and filled up two shopping carts with our belongings and left the hotel. I had to call Jamie and I had to say, "I need you to get me a ticket home," and he did. I had lost my passport and he got me a ticket home. I remember getting off the plane and he was waiting for me in the airport because he was my rock. I opened my hand and all I had was a handful of coins. I handed him the coins saying, "Here you go. This is my purse." The idea was that I was going to go to Europe and make all of this money and we were going to buy a house, and get settled. I was there for four months and spent the money aimlessly, and partied and it was just insane. This is what the industry does. It feeds off of that, and especially if you have an addictive personality. Jamie and I ended up breaking up, and as I mentioned, he had an affair with Careena Collins that I never forgave him for until years and years later. He said it was my partying, that destroyed the relationship. I said it was his affair. That was it.

The Amber Lynn Show

After I left the relationship with Jamie because he had been such a stabilizing force, I spun way out. I went out and I decided that I was going to get out of the industry and get clean, the year that I moved to Canada. A club owner came down and gave me a call, and said there was another club owner that wanted to meet Ginger and me. They wanted us to go to Canada and dance. I had never danced in my life. I didn't know how to dance. I was a porn star not a dancer. They said, "That's okay, all he wants you to do is appear at the club."

I said, "Maybe that would be fun." We went up and then Ginger called me literally, the night before we were to board the plane. She was going into a legitimate acting career at the time which was around the same time she had started to become involved with

Charlie Sheen. She said, "I know that I promised to do this thing with you, but my manager thinks it's a bad idea and I'm going to take this career for all it's worth. You're going to see me get an Oscar one day."

I said, "You've got to be kidding. They don't give girls like us Oscars, Ginger. What are you thinking?" The man who I had danced for in Canada had success with my show. Ginger didn't show up, and he flew up Tracey Adams and she came and did the show with me. It was a huge success and we made tons of money and later on down the road, Ginger wound up coming up and dancing but not for a long time. Tracey and Roberto Rovella [the club owner], who was my boyfriend started bringing in other acts. He brought in Marilyn Chambers and Seka, and he brought in Barbara Dare and down the road, I think, Christy Canyon. I know Porsche Lynn was also there and Danielle and lots of people would start dancing. They would make a lot of money and they would go home happy. I started going from club to club to club in Canada because Canada had already been featuring specific dancers long before I ever got to it. In Canada, they had feature dancers that would come in and they would put on these wild and elaborate shows, but they didn't really have names other than for the contest they'd win by putting on these shows. They'd do dance shows like Miss Nude Canada and they'd win these titles and travel the clubs and do elaborate shows with fire and costumes. When I came in [Roberto's] idea was that he was going to use porn stars where everybody would have an idea who the porn stars were. He brought me into the club and had the dancers show me how to dance because I didn't know how at first. He put me in a costume and put me up on a stage, and advertised it and it was gangbusters.

At the time when I met Roberto, I was living in Jamie's house. I went up to Canada and I danced, and then I started a relationship with Roberto and we lived together. He had helped me to start my dancing career. We did it together. He owned the club and I was the feature entertainer. We were actually engaged to be married and I had a ring on my finger. It was a beautiful diamond ring. We were going to do all kind of things together. Then we broke up and he went off with some other dancer, and I moved back to Los Angeles. It was an extremely devastating break up for me. Then I just went on the road. I had a friend I had met in the industry and she went out on the road with me as my tour manager. Together, we built

"The Amber Lynn Show" which was the biggest and highest grossing show up until that time ever known in the adult entertainment industry. It was huge and it was successful everywhere I went. That friend actually wound up being involved in a very devastating situation that happened to me later on where I was robbed. Some people that were in the industry did it. She was part of the situation. It

PHOTO COURTESY OF SUZE RANDALL, *WWW.SUZE.NET*

was another actor in the industry, and it was something that happened that was completely betraying. Drugs, greed, or money was probably the motivators. There are a lot of people out there who prey on the girls because the girls are making all of this money and often are partying and unclear — foggy or unstable — whatever is going on and they wind up in precarious situations. I had my wits about me, but we would be partying at least a couple of nights a week because that was our job to party when we were in the clubs. Patrons are buying you drinks — it doesn't have to be drugs — they are buying you drinks and your job is to entertain. After the shows, everybody is drinking and it is part of the festivity. It doesn't have to be outlandish. It's just the course of the day, and at the end of it, it's a grueling schedule.

I was dancing for between four to eight hundred people in a show on weekends. One time I danced in New York City and I broke all records. There were twelve hundred people to see my show. It was at Goldfinger and there was a line around the building to get in. News cameras came and they asked people if they were protesting the strip club and they said, "No, we're waiting in line to see Amber Lynn". It was on the news.

I danced in Toronto many times. I would go up there and I danced for the House of Lancaster, and Spiro, and people thought I was coming in from the States, but the truth was I came up from Niagara Falls. It was a great deal and it got me out of the business. I was no longer making films but I was living off of the name I had already created in films. I was keeping it alive by traveling, and touring and doing the dancing. It was a brilliant transition.

I was dancing in Canada when I found out about John Holmes being sick because he called me. He never told me that he was HIV when we worked in the Italian movies together: *Carne bollente* [aka *The Rise of the Roman Empress*, 1987] and *The Devil in Mr. Holmes* (1987) in the fall of 1986. He never told me that, but he called me up and asked us to send him money and we sent him money. He said, "I'm broke and I'm destitute and I don't have any money, and I'm sick and I need help." I remember going up into the office and talking to him and saying "I'm really sorry" and everything and he never said to me "I had HIV when I worked in a movie that you were in and I'm sorry." He might have even told me that he had AIDS, but he didn't tell me that he had exposed me to it. I had worked with him, but he didn't tell me he'd had it on the set. In fact, the person that told me that he had it during the time that we went to Europe was my brother. My brother had Bill Amerson call me. Bill Amerson was the guy that was behind him. I had left the industry and the industry was not testing, and then all of a sudden, there were all of these rumors going around. I was up in Canada and my brother had Bill Amerson call me and say, "You need to get tested because you worked with John and John was HIV positive." This was after John died. He literally waited until after John died to tell me. He waited to tell everybody. I got tested and I was like "Wow". I wasn't actually exposed to him in that respect. You'd have to have some exposure to their semen. I remember when I was working on the set with him, at one point, he actually pushed me away from him and I took it as a slight.

In a fortunate twist of fate, all of the women who worked with Holmes in the two Italian films tested negative for HIV, including Tracey Adams and the former Italian pornographic actor, model, singer, and elected member of the Italian Parliament, Ilona Staller (aka Cicciolina).

Later on, Jamie and I almost got back together. At the time, I was engrossed in traveling on the road and dancing, but Jamie came back to me and said, "I want us to get back together and I want us to do this again." I was making money hand over fist. I was literally carrying my money off of stages in trash bags. I was so into working and involved in the whole grind of being a star and out there touring that I was not focused or interested at that time in our relationship.

We talked about that recently when Henri Pachard was dying. Jamie said, "I wanted to come back to you and I wanted us to get together and I wanted us to get married. I would have given you anything you wanted." I wanted to get married and I wanted to have a baby. I wanted a normal life and I couldn't get that settled, I just couldn't.

"Angel"

From what I saw, Marilyn Chambers was bigger in public acclaim than I ever saw anyone else, even bigger than Jenna Jameson was. Jenna Jameson is great and I love her and think she's done tremendously well. She took a lot of ideas that were already created by other people and just made them big. All of the things she's done with her career, like traveling and dancing, were already created by me, and Ginger and other people — she took it to another level. Marilyn was doing all of these things for the first time. When my star got handed to me — they don't just hand it to you — you have to have some kind of credibility that says

PHOTO COURTESY OF SUZE RANDALL, *WWW.SUZE.NET*

you're the biggest or whatever. I was dancing and I went to the O'Farrell Theatre to do my booking for the first time as a dancer. I got there and I broke Marilyn Chambers' attendance record the first time I was there. She had made that place famous for her sex shows. I broke her attendance record which is why I was recognized as the number one star. Jamie was there that night. That's when I met Aerosmith and Stephen Tyler. They came to my show, and I was in my dressing room and there was a knock at my door. I said, "Who is it?"

A voice answered, "Stephen Tyler."

I said, "You've got to be kidding." My personal assistant grabbed the door and we were laughing because we thought it was a joke. The door opened up and there he was behind the door. I almost wet my pants. I went out on stage and they were there to see my show. Jamie was there backstage, flitting around wearing my fur coat. He was so proud of me. They wanted me to go on stage with them in San Francisco. I couldn't go to Aerosmith's show. They wanted me to open with them for this song "Angel" which they had done. The story goes that Stephen Tyler would write songs to porno that he had on his piano. He wrote that song to a porno called *Pink 'n Pretty* (1986) that starred me, and Porsche Lynn. He was a huge Amber Lynn fan. He had known what I was wearing in the movie and the color of garters that I'd was wearing. I wound up flying to Sacramento the following week and I started dating their keyboard/ sax player for many years. His name was Tommy Gimbel. I dated him and we flew all around, and that was the deal.

One leads to the other. In 1992 I was about to turn twenty-eight, and at that time, Victoria Paris was my best friend. She and I had a friend that was the head of the Youth AIDS Foundation of Los Angeles. Through the course of a dinner, he revealed to me one night that they wanted to do something for my birthday. They had been bugging me about having a big party for me. I had been working very hard traveling on the road and I was not comfortable with people just having a party for me. During this conversation, he revealed that his Foundation was in trouble and at risk of its doors being closed. The Foundation had been spearheaded by Aaron Spelling who had kind of developed it around the *90210* show as kind of a press thing. They used to go out on the streets and to train stations and collect kids that were getting off the buses. They were runaways from all over the country coming to Los Angeles to become actors. They would find them on drugs and involved in prostitution, and they'd be infected with HIV if they were needle users and so on. They had this whole operation going where they provided shelter for these teens and those who had HIV. They were trying to get them off the streets and using clean needles. Back then this kind of work wasn't usually done. In spite of the fact that it had been formed for press purposes, they had left it behind and now it was about to go under. I said, "We're going to do a benefit." We had absolutely no idea how we were going to make this thing happen, but we all had good intentions and we made an agreement right there that we were going to do this benefit. We set out to do it and we got everything single thing donated. We realize that society judges the adult business and considers us pariahs, but the truth of the matter is there is a community that exists within the industry, that is very strong. We do have a kind of camaraderie of sorts.

The Bel Age Hotel [in Los Angeles] was donated and we had the event at this beautiful location. It was the first time in the history of the adult entertainment industry that any money knowingly had been accepted by the outside from an adult entertainer. Money was raised and it was turned over to them. The most significant thing about it was we got on the phone with every contact we'd ever known in the adult business and asked for donations to help put the thing on by buying a seat, ticket or table so that one hundred percent of the money would go to this cause. We wound up in the *L.A. Times*. We wound up in the *New York Post* and others. We just got much attention and worked so hard to make this thing happen. We had famous actors. We had Larry Flynt and big names for this charity benefit that was put on by the Adult business. Everybody was in full gowns and black ties. It was an amazing thing that we all walked away from with warm hearts and extreme pride to have been a part of. I learned so much throughout the course of putting the AIDS benefit on that when I went away and got into my own twelve-step program, and got into recovery, I learned a lot about being of service. A part of what I do for my own recovery is to go out and try to be of service to others.

Over the years, I've had so many people misrepresent me, or my motives at times in the industry. I've heard people tell stories about me that I think if I was half the person that I hear people say I am or have those kind of motives, I would not be able to live with myself. When that happens, you don't have any control and there's no way to go back and change or restructure things. I do notice that the filters that the industry relies on can often sensationalize things on purpose to get a good story. I look at things and say, "Oh my god, that's not me. That was never me."

We are the World XXX

For the first time documented, Amber shared her side of the story regarding the controversy, misunderstanding and allegations that punctuated an attempted fundraiser effort devised by Lynn to assist a dying comrade and long time member of the family of X. It all started with an idea.

Bill Margold is the guy whose office I ended up in the first time when they sent me on the go see to do the Bobby Hollander film. I absolutely adore him. I've known him for many, many years and I know the good and the bad. I know that this industry, regardless of who wants to admit it or not, is better off having had Bill Margold as the captain in the story and what he has been to the industry,

Bill Margold. PHOTOGRAPHY BY KENJI

than not. He's a brilliant man. I made films with Drea [Margold's ex-wife] in the early part of my career. Bill is just Bill. He doesn't become another person when you turn your back on him. That's why people have such a hostile opinion of Bill because whatever he is thinking of you, he is telling you. He won't stab you in the back. If he wants to stab you, he'll stab you right in the front. That's just Bill. I will tell you one thing, if I was on a sinking ship and I wanted to know there was going to be one person on that lifeboat I would want it to be Bill. He would not think twice about putting his life on the line for anyone in this industry whether he liked you or not. He is not about the individual. He is about the common cause and movement that this industry entails.

No matter how far away any of us go, when you turn around one day and realize you've gotten really far from the ship, you go,

"Wow, John died. Jamie died. I'm in trouble. My brother passed away. We did *We are the World*" — who do I turn around and call to get the status? Bill. Everybody thinks that way. Like Bill or not, if you need to make a phone call one day, it is mostly Bill's number that everyone remembers. He's the reason why this industry continues to survive. I can't tell you how many times in my career when I've had resentment toward someone for something that's happened and I'll say, "That's it, I never want to hear that person's name again."

He'll go, "Oh, you'll get over it, don't worry."

I'll say, "No, I won't!"

He'll go, "Yes you will." The next thing you know a couple of years will pass and I'll say, "Do you remember when blah, blah happened?"

He'll say, "I told you you'd get over it. We're family, kid. And that's the way it is."

I thank God for him.

Bill Margold, a graduate from Northridge College with a Journalism degree, is also the founder of PAW (Protecting Adult Welfare).

One day I found out that Henri Pachard [Ron Sullivan] whom I had a lot of respect for and had worked with early in my career, had cancer. They were broke — penniless, about to lose their home and they were appealing for money basically, trying to get handouts because they were so desperate for money. They had appealed to several people I knew so I immediately said, "What can I do to help?" That's just who I am and it's who I've always been. I went to Bill Margold and said, "Bill, we've got to help Henri Pachard."

He said, "That would be wonderful kid, but the bottom line and the sad truth is there is really not a lot of money in the PAW Foundation to help anybody anymore." The benefits that had been put on to raise money were not making much money anymore. There was no money in PAW to help him. What I saw immediately were two things: There was a fire to be put out and that was the fact that Henri Pachard needed help. The bigger picture was that we needed to get some money either in the PAW Foundation or into a Foundation that would be there for these people that get sick that have no insurance. It happens to all of us, and it has happened time and time again to people in this industry who have wound up broke or with no money. They end up with HIV or whatever and there has been no one to turn to for help. I thought, "Let's do something about this." Bill Margold is always willing to help and I got this idea to do another benefit. I thought we'd figure it out as we go. We each grabbed our contacts and sat down in Bill's living room, and got on the phone with Henri Pachard, who was incredibly sick. The truth of the matter is they weren't interested in what we were doing really. The day Bill and I were to go to Henri Pachard's house to tell him what our plans were, he was sick and his wife said, "Just do whatever and if you get anything out of it that would be really great." I believe she was focused on her dying husband and she had little faith that I could pull it off. The industry doesn't really come up against these situations where they try to help one another. That was the thing supposedly, of days gone by. And I knew if I could get Bill — Bill might rub certain people the wrong way, but he loves you and I'm a ballsy woman who everyone knows is not afraid to speak up and speak out and people will listen. They might not like what I have to say but they have to stop to hear. That's what we did and we started to get things going.

What happened very quickly, and what I was told soon after was that if I handled the money I would be liable if the bottom came out from under this thing. I thought then that we could create it as a PAW benefit. Whatever money came in was to go to the Henri Pachard fund, which we created as a 501(c) (3).

The reason we did that is because as a tax benefit I could not accept money from people on behalf of Henri Pachard. If he accepted the money directly, there would be tax issues and laws that would have come into play. When you do a 501(c) (3) there are a couple of things that are law, and one of them is you have to have open books. Number two, is that any money collected has to go into the benefit, and then be paid out after it's accounted for. This is legal.

A 501(c) (3) refers to an American non-profit, non-tax benefit for a charitable cause.

Behind the scenes, this thing was inches from death at any moment because there was no money. Everybody would contribute time, but people would not contribute money so I sold them on the idea that this would be completely non-profit. Everybody who worked on the production: from the person supplying food to the lighting person to the actors to the crew, was not going to get paid. Their time was going to be turned in as non-profit, but in order for everything to be successful right to the end including the distribution, had to be donated. In order to be non-profit and a benefit, money collected would have to go into the Henri Pachard fund to be accounted for and then obviously back out to be distributed from this fund. Then, all of these other things would come into play like taxes.

People said "I'll do grip and I have a truck," or "I have a camera and I'll shoot," and "I'm an actor and I'll work with so and so and then I'll donate my scenes." A handful of people were willing to be a part of the production based on the fact we were doing this film for Henri Pachard. There were many holes in the boat and in the eleventh hour, the production was going to close down and fail. There was no money to buy film to shoot. We couldn't get anyone to donate film because film costs money so I got a poster distributor to print out a stack of posters that I took to L.A. Erotica with some pictures of myself that Wicked had given me to use. I sat there and signed pictures for donations. It was actually PAW who got these posters created of some of the actresses. In turn, they would go down and sit in the booth for a couple of hours, and sign posters and put it in the PAW fishbowl.

We counted up the money to see how much film we could buy and in the end, I literally borrowed money to go out and buy what we needed which was a dozen rolls of film. There was a cameraman named John Keeler who worked very closely with us on this. There weren't enough people to put this project together so I got on the phone and asked everybody I knew to come in as a favor. We turned it into a PAW benefit and there were a lot of people who were there because they wanted to do a good deed that were friends of Ron, but there weren't enough to create a production. We got people to come in who were friends of Bill's. We asked other friends to come out, and certain people showed up just because they were going to work with certain talent and that certain talent was going to work for nothing. We worked every angle we possibly could to get this thing and it turned into a benefit. We had the opportunity — just like what had happened with the Youth AIDS Foundation — we got to be a part of this bigger picture of doing good.

The film was shot and people were not showing up for their committed spots and they were not showing up with their equipment that they had promised, and they were not coming across.

Certain people were showing up too loaded to do what they had promised they would do. I had to run this thing and it was like trying to thread a very tight needle. We had time constraints and we had fire codes and we had things that weren't arriving, and here I was trying to make this thing happen. Everybody was getting mad at me, the captain, because feathers were getting ruffled. I would say, "No, we're going to keep going! All hands on deck and we're going to make this thing!"

They said, "Oh, well, you're not being nice to me!" or "I'm upset," and so on. Drama was going on, but when all was said and done, we got the project shot. We went to go into post-production. At some point, I got a call that said there had been some money that had exchanged hands directly around the production through Henri Pachard. I needed to confront that.

We had procured this whole thing that we had done, a huge production which had gotten a lot of press so it wasn't as if we could say it never happened as a non-profit. I'm the one who was spearheading the whole thing. If they turn it into a profit-making venture because somebody's going to give them cash underneath the table that they don't want to claim they received — they get to run off with the money and I'm the one left with the criminal charges. Meanwhile, Henri Pachard's life is hanging in the background. I said, "What do we do about this?" We had decided early in the game that it was going to be a 501(c) (3) and the law required that we do things a certain way so we had to continue on the path we'd originally planned. We couldn't go back now and redo it. Everybody was screaming at me and I said, "We can't go back and recreate the wheel." The production couldn't have existed or been completed if we hadn't turned it into a non-profit.

Vivid Entertainment sought to purchase select scenes to use for their own proposed revision of the film.

It was Vivid and Paul Thomas who was a part of the production. I got on the phone with PT who, up until that time wouldn't even take my calls because he was busy shooting the latest huge Vivid movie which is understandable. He's a big director. PT said to me, "Just give us the scenes!"

I said, "I can't do that because I promised these workers who gave me their work under an agreement." People had agreed to work for us on a specific day to give me their craft which was just like giving me money out of their pockets. When they come in to give me their work, it is like sweat equity. I told them that they wouldn't be paid and neither would anybody else profit. When they decided, that they would have to use their own box people and their own distributors and their own replicators and whatever it was because Vivid doesn't work any other way, I said, "You can't do that because that was not the original agreement. This one time, you've got to work with us."

He said, "We won't do it."

I said, "Well, I can't rip off everybody I've made all of these promises to so I have to take a stand."

Saving our Own Lives

When Vivid was arguing and saying they were going to do it a certain way, I had Wicked Pictures ready to take it. They were going to distribute it exactly according to the 501(c) (3) requirements. They were willing to set aside any idea of profit and just put it out and make sure that our original conception was going to be followed. It went back and forth, and eventually it was killed off. They were too many chiefs trying to run the last part of the show. Evil Angel was involved and wanted it at one point, and everybody just started squabbling in the middle and it got killed. I took a stand for everyone who was standing behind me who had worked a day or two or more for free and had helped me make this thing happen. It's not just about Henri Pachard it's about the whole industry making an agreement to do this benefit together. You know what they did. They went to the press and they threatened my reputation and said things like, "We'll burn you to the stake!"

I said, "Do your worst." I looked at Bill and I said, "Bill, I know what the agreement was and you know what it was and if the agreement is going to change I don't have a problem with that, but what I have to do is give these people the option to opt out." What that meant was there were many people that were involved in certain scenes that wanted to pull their releases. If they pulled their release then that scene fell apart. PT started screaming at me on the phone saying, "Fuck these fucking actors and these porno people! Nobody gives a shit about them! They don't even give a shit about each other!"

I said, "Guess what, PT? I give a shit about them. I wouldn't have this piece of footage if it wasn't for them and they matter to me and I'm not going to let this go." What happened was cute. The cameraman, John Keeler, called me up knowing I'd been sober for years and said to me, "I really need a meeting".

I said, "Let me help to get you to one. Let me meet you here." He met me outside of a 12-step meeting and said, "With all of this drama going on I don't want anything to go wrong, so why don't you give me the master and we'll make a master copy of it? I can give you back the master and we'll both have a master and everything will be fine." He stole the master tape from me. The footage had been shot on my film that I had borrowed the money to buy, and we're standing here in the middle of this giant dispute and these people are saying, "If you don't do this, blah, blah, blah…" And John Keeler ran off into the night with the master.

Amber explained she had willingly given up the master to John Keeler in good faith, expecting it to be returned to her within twenty-four hours. She suddenly found herself in front of a firing range.

My brother, God rest his soul, called me up in the middle of this and said, "No, sis, I'm not going to work on this production because when this is over these people are going to hand you your ass. You know it's going to happen, so prepare yourself for it." That was before everything started to unravel. I always ran to my big brother who has been a mentor in my life just because he was my big brother, not because of a professional relationship. I said to him, "What'll I do?"

He said, "Just do yourself one favor. You keep those releases and that paperwork separate from the film." I handed John Keeler the tape and even though I had the releases I said, "Listen, you can have the film of the people who want to go, but not the people who don't want to go. You can't have that." They said they were going to destroy my reputation and they went to the press, and there was this whole coalition of people who were going to go on and call me all these names. It was a bunch of bullshit because they had no idea of the agreement that was formed that day, nor did they know whether Ron Sullivan had agreed to it. The idea behind it was that Ron had no money and was desperate for money, and if the production didn't happen, he was no worse for that. If it did happen, then he would have benefitted in any way that he could have and he would have been grateful for it. Everybody called me and said, "You need to step forward and tell them the truth."

I said, "I am not going to piss on a dying man's grave no matter what he does to me. I'm not going to do that because I'm not that kind of a person." No matter what kind of a person is coming at me, I can't do that and I held onto those releases. I sat down in my living room with a few volunteers. We bought envelopes and we wrote a letter that said: "The original production that was going to be a non-profit production as I promised you when you came to work on it in whatever capacity has now been stolen from me and is going to be put out as a 'for profit' production. I'm now returning your release to you. You can decide whether you want to be a part of the new production based on this new information. Whatever you decide I support you and I appreciate your effort on my behalf. Thank you very much." We hand wrote each and every envelope and we made sure that every person was re-granted back their release and given the opportunity to return that release immediately over to Ron Sullivan.

We never went to the press and said anything. The other side did go to the press and burned me at the stake and said Bill Margold had robbed the coffers. It was bitter, incomprehensible lying. It was unbelievable. They thought they could get me to give them the releases because many of the scenes had people who had volunteered to be a part of them and no longer wanted to be a part of them because of the way they were going about things. It was done in a way that was strong-arming and a lot of people said, "I don't want to be a part of that. That's hate-mongering." It was horrifying behavior and that's not what they had come there to do. We all kind of just kissed it goodbye. The truth of the matter is that Ron's wife holds the original footage to the original movie that was made out of complete love with the PAW benefit that was called *We are the World XXX*. The whole idea was that the adult business got to come together just like the original *We are the World* for the bigger picture. At any time, the movie could be resurrected, and it could be put out as it was originally intended.

I folded my hands after I made a decision that I felt had the most integrity which was to give everybody individually their personal opportunity to say "Yes" or "No". A lot of people got together and they made a new production. It is my understanding that they went out with their hair on fire and tried to create. It didn't go off so well.

I'm not really sure, but whether they like this or not, the truth of the matter is if they would have left us alone the production would have been an absolute success as it had been intended. Any profit that would have legally come at the end of it through the 501(c) (3) that was accounted for and metered out would have gone exactly where it was intended which was to the Henri Pachard fund, and

Amber Lynn. ADULT VIDEO NEWS

then moved forward to Dolores Pachard. The sad thing is it never benefitted anybody, including Ron Sullivan. Horrible things were said that were untrue about Bill and me, that we were stealing money. There was no *money*! We had potluck on the set where people brought their own food and ate out of their own bowls.

A huge deal was made about me putting myself on the box cover.

It was suggested that it was some evil maniacal move on my part to keep other people from being on the box. That was the biggest joke of all. After being up all night long on the set shooting, I went in to reshoot a scene with Ron Jeremy and one of the girls because he had had some performance issues during the scene. He wanted to be his best and I respected that so I arranged to bring these girls together because we'd worked into the night in the freezing cold. By the time we got the scene shot Ronnie was beat and tired. He made this great move to say, "I'm going to fly the girls down, and I'm going to show up on the set, and I'm going to perform at my best." We opened the set and arranged for him to come in. I kept talking about what I wanted the box cover to look like, and the photographer was there and I said, "Humor me for a minute. Let's just get this shot so that we have a back up." It was never intended to be anything more than a backup. On the box cover day when we were supposed to do the shoot, nobody else showed up. I was standing there with dirty feet and a pair of flip-flops, and I grabbed this ball and they shot a picture of me. It wound up being used as the box cover because there was such an argument about who was going to get to shoot the box that nobody could ever see the forest for the trees. There were so many people fighting.

Once again, I looked at Bill and I had tears in my eyes. I said, "Bill, don't they understand what we're trying to do?" The bottom line was it wasn't just about Henri Pachard and it was about Henri Pachard, but it was about every other person including John Holmes when he called me up twenty odd years ago when I was in Canada and said, "I'm sick. I'm broke and I need help." He was calling everybody he had ever known and had worked with in the industry and asking for handouts because that's what his life and career had been relegated to, and he had nothing left in the end. My vision along with Bill's, was that together, we were trying to create something. We didn't know what it was going to look like down the road. We were concerned about getting funding for people who were sick such as Ron, who needed it at that moment.

"No Legacy is so rich as Honesty."
WILLIAM SHAKESPEARE

Maybe that is my legacy that I was able to come in and accomplish something on behalf of the industry and for the industry that couldn't have been done if I hadn't been there. Maybe if I hadn't done the AIDS Benefit years before, the children's organization would never have accepted money from the Adult industry. If they would have allowed me to finish *We are the World*, it wouldn't have been only that one time it could have been another time. Who knows how many people we could have gone on to help and maybe even create a Foundation? We could have set aside a week a year and have people donate whatever they do. There would have already been a model in place. I was trying to create a model to be able to do it again and again.

Eric Edwards was sick with cancer at the same time as Henri Pachard and I was trying to say to everybody, "Ron is sick and this is going on and so is Eric Edwards and so are other people." We can only do so much and Mitch [who had helped Eric Edwards find a place to live] can only do so much, and everybody can only individually no matter how great they are, do so much.

I felt like there were a lot of things I could have done differently. There are moments that I do regret as far as the production itself. The group who attacked the project and me failed to realize was while I was on that set helping Ron, my own brother was dying and about to pass away within months of Ron. Buck had been fighting his own alcoholism and addiction for years, and instead of me focusing on my own family, here I was trying to help Ron. What was in play in those moments was that I was going to continue to stand for what this industry has always stood for and that is the freedom to choose. I wasn't going to take anybody's choice away.

I had a talk with my brother and I realized at that moment after they went to the press, if I had known it going in I wouldn't have had anything to do with this situation. I had worked my ass to the bloody bone to help these people. Let me tell you this: I'm not rich. I'm not a rich woman and so it's not as if I'm some rich do-gooder working on some charity. I was taking time away from my life and my family and my own dying brother. You know, there are people always standing on the outside of the industry just waiting for us to do something unlawful. I go back once again to the Traci Lords issue as a case in point. If you know that the propensity exists for them to turn on you like that, you're standing on your own.

According to articles that appeared in the adult press in 2008, Lynn was indeed lambasted by the media and by others, including Ron Sullivan's spouse who contested Amber's motives were not genuine.

They got caught up in the whole force of destroying Bill and me and then they just ran off and created some kind of shoddy production. The original was a beautiful production. I created this satire similar to *Saturday Night Live* called *We are the World XXX*. Larry Flynt played God and he was very good. I went into Larry Flynt's office and shot him. He was going to be at the end of the movie and it was just brilliant. It was really a great piece from an artistic standpoint.

It would be very difficult to get Bill Margold to be a part of something like that again because he watched me cry. I even said to him the other day, "Bill, maybe someone could approach them and see if they do want to finish the film? If they do our door is open."

He said, "I can't believe you would even consider it after all you've been through." Bill says it clearly, "It's the playground of the damned." These people are not necessarily going to be your upright type of individual. They ended up taking one of PT's scenes and they put together something. I don't know if they made money or not, I hope they did, but that was the end of it. When that happened, I thought I just had to admit my failure. It was like failing falling forward. It's okay to fail when you skin your knees. You're bound to have failure, but if you go all out and you fail while you're doing your damndest and your best with your integrity and heart intact and stand up for yourself, then it's okay.

It was a brilliant, overwhelmingly positive experience because I got to see who my friends were and who my friends weren't and that's a gift. We often go through life thinking people are not our friends. When we get into a real place where the shit hits the fan and we're vulnerable, somebody will come and we'll realize he or she were in our corner all along. The opposite is true, people that I thought were my friends wound up not being. I realized in the end that I wasn't in charge or control ultimately and I cannot force my will no matter what I am trying to do and make them see what I want them to see.

At the time of this book's publication, *We Are the World XXX* remains unreleased.

Big Brothers

There are good and bad parts of my career. Things I would have done differently like most people with anything you do. Relationships I had ended in ways where I could have done better. There are always things I could have done better and I could have done worse. I have made a lot of friends along the way, and there are people I look back on today that I absolutely love and I pick up the phone and I talk with them. I always got along really well with Annette Haven. I loved her from the minute I met her. She was kind of like a mom. The other person I got along with was Seka. People said I was like the 1980s version of Seka, the blonde bombshell. I give it to Seka. I love Dottie to this day. She's somebody whom I revere and look up to and respect. We will always be friends. I always got along with Marilyn Chambers, too. I never had a problem with Marilyn. I was very sad to hear she died. I always got along with all of them. Every time someone in our industry passes away, Bill takes it very hard. It also causes him to face his own mortality. You can only get so old in this industry and then there's nothing left for you anymore. There's no way to make money anymore. For me, Bill's been there since the day I set foot in the industry and is like a big brother. He's still there for me, regardless. He has been steadfast.

Buck Adams.

It's funny, because I really feel like my brother Buck communicates with me and it just felt like he wanted me to participate in this book. My brother was very upset over the whole *We Are the World* fiasco and when all of that was coming apart, Jamie had gotten in touch with me. There is always something good to come out of anything. Jamie got back in touch with me, and during those conversations with one another, we made all of these amends to one another. We'd had this relationship that had kind of ended prematurely and traumatically and we had some hard feelings, and then through these conversations that came about because of the film we had changed all of that. We were able to really form a loving bond with each other.

Then my brother passed away and that was the most devastating thing that's ever happened in my life. My brother died literally, in my arms in the hospital. Again, my brother and I were estranged at that time because he had fallen off the wagon. He had gone back to using and I was desperately trying to control that and stop him. My motive behind that was I wanted him to be there to see his grandchildren grow up, and have his grandchildren have him be a part of their lives and upbringing. I wanted to force him to be something he wasn't so that he would continue to be there for them. I couldn't change him into somebody else and when I got to the hospital, certain people didn't want to let me in because they thought I was going to go in there and control everything.

The thing I had to do right there in that hospital room was get on my knees and make amends to my brother. Mostly, it was about accepting him for everything he was and everything he wasn't. He was my hero and the day I walked out of that hospital room, I knew what my job was from that day forward to focus on what was left and that was our family. That was it.

When my brother passed away, I wouldn't have buried him if it weren't for Bill Margold — again. He came to my rescue and got a location. My brother passed away with nothing. He was in the middle of building a studio and they ripped it out from under him and gave us nothing. We really didn't even have the money to buy a plot to bury him. We had to pull it all together and we were able to get my brother taken care of. His ashes are still with his grandchildren and his family because that's where we believe he wants to be for now. Bill hand designed and printed the programs for my brother's funeral. He didn't want to, but I said, "Bill if you don't help me do this, it won't get done."

He said, "Okay."

We printed this lovely program for Charles Steven Allen, aka Buck Adams: "A brother, a father, grandfather, friend, and legend." Everybody came and all my brother's best friends: T. T. Boy, and Brad Armstrong, and John Doyle, and Bill Margold, and all the people that loved my brother. They all showed up and we gave him something that we knew would make him proud.

"Aunt Lynny"

There was a very significant time in my life when I wanted to leave the industry behind and that's when my great-nephew was born, Noah. He got to an age where he could understand and he's still very young, but he could understand or compute that knowledge. He did know that his grandpa Buck was a director and he knew his Aunt Lynny was very famous. When he was a toddler, we were in a Denny's and he was very protective of me. He backed up against me and I felt him put his arms around me. I looked and I didn't realize what he was doing, but there were a couple of guys across the table at the diner were looking at me because they recognized me. He saw the look on their faces, that kind of leering, excited look. He held his arms around me as if to say, "That's my Aunt Lynny!" I realized that there was going to come a day when that would maybe come to pass. When he got to be older, I wasn't working in the industry anymore and I decided that I wanted to close that book.

When Buck's daughter Christa was young, I was at the height of my career and she was a baby so there was no way to hide it. You couldn't have told Christa anything that would change her opinion of her dad or her Aunt Lynny. She just was one of those kids. She has a very open personality anyway. Her husband is in punk rock band so they're kind of like, "Wow, cool!" She was kind of raised with it. It was explained to her and she kind of accepted it and it was okay, but I could see where a child may not accept it. The bottom line is it's about acceptance. His grandpa has now passed away, but one of the things I always wanted Buck's grandchild to have is a very healthy idea of women and of his aunt. I didn't want that to be fractured at a young age because he got information that he wasn't yet old enough to be able to hash out. I was worried about that. He's only eight now and he's too young to be subjected to this kind of information.

I think that if I'm being totally honest, I know that there have been crossroads in my life where because I had been in the adult industry it cost me things such as relationships. I don't regret my past and I don't wish to shut the door on it, but there are a lot of things in my life that have come from my time in the industry. It's not specifically, because I was in the industry that I wound up in recovery for drug and alcohol addiction, but certainly, the lifestyle I was living supported all of that while I was in it. I had to include it. They lived alongside each other — the persona that I created and the lifestyle supported it. I went out and got sober, took my time away and got into recovery. Then I went back into the industry because I wanted to know what it was, what it felt like, what was different about it.

I was in a relationship where the man I was in love with had nothing to do with the adult industry, he had actually been a music producer. We had been in recovery together and we both had lived other lives in the past. He wanted to move on from that and form a new life together. It definitely was in his face. Even though we set out with all good intents, he didn't realize how big it was. I've been in Costco or K-Mart with my significant other long after I was out of the industry and had people walk up and say, "I know who you are." There's just no way for me to deny and say, "You must be mistaken." I would never do that anyway, but there are times when you might want to just like any actor who doesn't want that private moment intruded upon would feel that way.

Amber Lynn, The Legend Continues...

I don't have a lot of photos from anything anymore because when I got out of the industry and I was living with my last boyfriend — we were going to get married. Part of the agreement between us was that I wasn't involved in the industry anymore and I got rid of everything. I have had people say that if I want to be in a successful relationship then I should just not tell them. I thought it would be shocking to have someone fall in love with me and then find out I'm "Amber Lynn," or whoever if they hadn't been told. It'd be horrible. I would feel completely betrayed if somebody hid something like that from me.

I live in Santa Monica now about a dozen blocks from the beach. It's a nice little area. I like to go out and I do my own marketing. It is part of my day so lately, I've been trying to get out and get more exercise by forcing myself to walk. I sort of wound up here a little while back by default. I had moved over here to be in a relationship with my boyfriend and when the relationship didn't work out, I ended up stuck in Santa Monica. This is a situation where he ended up being violent, and got arrested. It was very sad, but it does depict again how people sometimes cannot handle the personas that go along with the women in the industry. They meet Laura, yet there's always this "Amber Lynn" character.

Since Amber's career in erotic films began, she has left and returned to the industry several times. In 2008, during the months she attempted to get *We are the World XXX* off the ground and her brother Buck was still alive, Amber made a strategic comeback rekindling her on screen fusion with Tom Byron as a certifiable MILF in Byron's *Seasoned Players 4* (2008). As is customary in all of the montages in the *Seasoned Players* series, Byron and Lynn had a sit down before preparing for intercourse to chat about the old days. The long time colleagues discussed how much

PHOTO COURTESY OF SUZE RANDALL, *WWW.SUZE.NET*

they'd enjoyed working together when they were both new to the business, and tried to recall their first film together. In jest, Byron made mention of Lynn's partying ways back in the day, but was quick to add that he had liked cocaine as much as the next person had.

Of all of the women featured in this particular series, by far, Amber Lynn is one of the most well preserved with her finely tuned body, and long, stylish hair augmented by luxurious doses of blonde. Dressed in a tapered, black business suit (at Byron's request) with a camisole underneath, Lynn bashfully admitted it'd been a while since she'd had sex and confessed she couldn't remember how large Byron was when considering condom size. Amber clearly stipulated the terms of their arrangement prior to the session — no anal sex and Tom must wear a condom. Byron teased that her requirements clearly weren't "old school porn."

Once things start rolling, Byron is seated adjacent to the bed where Lynn is positioned. Partially dressed, she begins to deep throat him with enthusiastic precision. They continue to change positions and keep things lively and loud. Lynn rides Byron reverse cowgirl style, and ultimately, he orgasms from in behind her framed in extreme close-up.

In addition to Seka and others, more recently, Amber was involved in the highly successful documentary *After Porn Ends* (2010) directed by Bryce Wagoner which examines the lives of several industry luminaries before, during, and after their careers. The compelling and poignant film will be available on DVD August 1, 2012.

I've been working on my transition forever into the real world. Often the real world doesn't even want this transition as much as they judge us and believe what we're doing is wrong or immoral. At times, I've humbled myself and said, "Okay, maybe you're right. I'm going to leave this industry behind and I'm going to go into the real world and I'm going to become an everyday Joe." They don't want you there, they don't. I've been in business and other careers where they've been in shock if they'd have found out who I was. I find that they don't come out and say it out loud. I've been involved in real estate. It comes out as this weird experience that is often hostile and passive aggressive in a work environment that actually, ended up costing me my business at one time. I still work in real estate and have my license, but it's not my primary occupation. At this time, I work as a PRA which is a Personal Recovery Assistant. I work with people who are in detox so that's my primary occupation. I'm not working in films today and I don't do any dancing. I'm getting ready to work on my memoirs. I'm writing my book and doing that so I'm not entirely associated with the industry today. It's not that I wouldn't be — I was just writing down some numbers today and getting ready to make some calls about holidays to wish people Happy Holidays [2010], so that's what's going on for me.

In July of 2011 when we met for dinner, Amber had recently resumed her dancing career as a headliner in the San Fernando Valley. Lynn has seen hundreds if not thousands of girls come and go in the industry and she is celebrating almost thirty years as a Hall of Fame woman in the business. During our lively conversation at L.A.'s landmark Silver Spoon diner (which has since closed and recently reopened under new ownership) in West Hollywood, Amber made it known she is pleased to be in a position of power and feels she no longer compromises her personal goals or her career aspirations. Lynn has been the recipient of some cosmetic surgery in recent years, but it is flattering and she appeared to possess a rock hard body beneath her black, fitted, Lycra mini-dress. As compelling in person as she is in movies, Lynn continues to be a major draw on the Los Angeles club scene.

One of the things I did that I didn't expect to do is at one point in my career I fell flat on my face. I had to pick myself up and I had to admit that I had problems and issues that had nothing to do with the industry, but that were my own. I had to face those issues and find out that I was only human. We aren't immortal. These personas that we create are not really who we are. We are actors and entertainers and this life is hard on all of us, and any of us. Our hearts break and our knees skin and what we go through is to find out that we're just human beings having to get by. It is a very odd industry because it allows you to live in the illusion for such a long time. It has nothing to do with reality through these personas like "Ginger," and "Amber," and "Traci," and "Christy," and so on. We're just trying to live our lives.

For many years when I got into the industry, I could not wait to leave behind the kid from Orange County that I came into the world as. I loved it and wanted only to be known as "Amber". When I got out of the industry and I transitioned and moved on into my normal life, it became imperative for me to be able to make a distinction between when I was acting or working or performing, and when I was home and I was myself. I think with any actor or performer they need to have down time. For many years because of the type "A" personality that I am, I wasn't able to do that. Everything is done in hindsight. If I only knew then what I know now, I would have done things then the way I am doing them today.

23

Christy Canyon
Doubly Delightful

If there was an individual you'd want next to you in a foxhole during battle in enemy region, Christy Canyon (her real name is Melissa) would have your back. Tenacious, loyal, territorial, and not to mention voluptuous with natural 36 double D breasts, Canyon's determination and overtly feminine attributes have earned her a badge of honor in an industry that unconsciously discriminates the girls from the women. Proud of her mixed Armenian and Italian heritages, Christy has maintained her childhood was not abnormal. Rather, she is a child of the seventies — the generation of divorce and latchkey kid phenomena.

When her parents' marriage dissolved while she was still an infant, Canyon and her older sister were raised by her mother and a couple of stepfathers in what would become porn's mecca, the San Fernando Valley. In order to distance herself from her mother's husband, Christy moved out of the house at seventeen and worked two part-time jobs to pay the rent in what the squeamish might consider a tawdry L.A. neighborhood. As fate would have it in 1984, Christy met a young, blonde stud, Greg Rome, while waiting for a friend and she was introduced to the forbidden fruits of adult entertainment. From that point, Canyon met with one of the most respected agents and gentlemen in the business, Jim South, at World Modeling Agency. South immediately took Christy under his wing and arranged for her to do exotic photo layouts and her first loop for Swedish Erotica with Ron Jeremy. Canyon had reservations at first, but any opposition she might have felt about working as a sex performer evaporated when she was cast opposite new industry pros Ginger Lynn, Traci Lords, Tom Byron, and Jamie Gillis in back-to-back Paradise Visuals projects *The Night of Loving Dangerously* (1984) and *On Golden Blonde* (1984).

"I don't want anybody's judgment in my life. You've lost the right to be in my life if you have any little bit of judgment. I am who I am, and if it's great, that's okay. If not, that's okay too. I don't have time to be everyone's friend." CHRISTY CANYON

Since Canyon's entry into pornographic movies, lifetime highlights include her ten-year contractual agreement with Vivid Pictures. She is equally proud to have earned a Marketing degree at the Fashion Institute of Design and Merchandising while on the road dancing. During two decades where Christy dominated the industry as a leading female star (Adult Video News rated Canyon one of the top twenty porn actresses of all time), she is reputed to have dated countless men including celebrities such as Max Baer Jr., Robin Williams, and director Adam Rifkin. In recent years since her retirement as a performer, Christy has customized a rewarding designation as the daily host on the Sirius Satellite Playboy Radio program *Night Calls*. Since April 2011, Canyon now shares hosting duties with her old friend Ginger Lynn on the newly reformatted Playboy Radio program *Spice Sex Circus* airing daily in the afternoons. The program also incorporates the popular weekly show *Legends of Porn*.

In 2003, Christy wrote a successful tell-all memoir titled *Lights, Camera, Sex!* Today, Canyon's new role and responsibility as a doting mother to her three treasured young children supersedes everything else.

I interviewed Christy Canyon in November 2010.

Ordinary People

I was born and raised in Southern California and second generation to boot. I'm half-Armenian and half-Italian. My childhood experience was very seventies. I grew up in that whole kind of New Age "wowie" stuff. My mom was on a macrobiotic diet, and at one point, she had an actual pyramid in our house like a pup tent. She'd put fruit under it and she'd meditate under it.

My parents divorced when I was one. Dad was in and out. I was never abused and have no sob stories, just the product of a seventies childhood. My dad died in 1990. We did stay in touch with our father after my parents divorced. I have an older sister [Clair] and we stayed in touch with him, definitely. We lived here in the Valley and he lived about two miles from us. Both of my parents got divorced and remarried about three times so it seems like every time he got remarried, he had more step-kids and so on, so we saw him on average about one weekend a month. It was what it was. We don't harbor grudges. My parents were young when they had us, they were in their early twenties and they did the best they could do. I have no ill feelings; I have no chip on my shoulder. I just realized they were just young. I can't imagine having two kids at twenty-two.

My mother is still alive. She had a mental breakdown a couple of years ago and she's in a home now. I see her about twice a month but it's tough, because again, I have young kids and you have to prioritize. It's the kids, me, my job, and I hate to say this, but then it's my mom; it's kind of the way it is.

As a child, I did have a lot of friends. I was a good "C" average student. I didn't really care about learning — isn't that horrible? I loved going to school because I loved my friends and I loved recess. I loved making money. In elementary school, for example, I would sell my pencils to the boys. A girlfriend and I would draw stick figures, like nudie figures, and sell them to the boys. Even at a young age, I always knew that I could make money. I was never good at languages; I was never good at instruments. I was good at sports and I was very athletic. I was on the tennis team in high school, but I was more of a social butterfly. My sister is the opposite, she didn't have that many friends, but she was brilliant — a straight "A" student and fluent in three languages so we're really opposites.

COURTESY OF CHRISTY CANYON

I was very close to my mom. I really loved my mom. I was a momma's girl and she was my world. She was a single mom raising two kids and worked as an accountant. She was so full of love for us. We didn't have much money, but she was a wonderful mom when we were growing up. We always knew that she loved us and I always wanted to be like her, independent and strong, and able to take care of myself. She was a fine guiding light for me to realize that women could be in charge of their own lives. I really was a happy and contented child. It was tough though with my parents' divorces and it was hard when my mom had boyfriends over to our house. It certainly wasn't a rose-colored glasses world, but then again, what is really? For ninety percent of the time though, it absolutely was.

Until I hit about twelve everything was pretty damn good and then my mom married this guy that didn't like me and I didn't like him. At the time, he was the president of a huge music publishing company. It was the eighties and he made good money, but he was a real pompous ass and we just didn't get along. He was jealous of the time my mom spent with me, and of course, as a fourteen-fifteen year old, I was jealous of him. When I was about sixteen, I really started to rebel. I dabbled in drugs, nothing major, but I got really drunk one night at sixteen at a party and got a DUI (driving under the influence). Thank god back then you only paid something like a fifty-dollar fine. Sixteen is when the trouble really began because I didn't have my mom the way I did when I was younger. She would say "goodnight" to me and he would say to her, "Jackie, come in here and look at this!" It was almost as if he was competing with me. Now when I look back, that's when my mom's mental issues started to kick in. As a mom myself, no motherfucker is going to get in between my kids and me. I think she thought, "Oh, I'm forty, I should be married," so she was going through her own stuff, and sadly, it did affect me.

Christy was an early bloomer and it wasn't long before the boys at school started to take notice. She was able to channel the male attention using it to her advantage and smartly, Canyon managed to resist sexual exploration far longer than most of her girlfriends.

With boys, I was a huge flirt. In sixth grade, I had started getting my boobies and I felt like that was powerful. Even in sixth grade, I knew that people would love it. I was very flirtatious. This sounds young for L.A. in the eighties, but it wasn't young — I didn't lose my virginity until I was fifteen and a half to a guy from Thailand that I was dating for about six months. I was definitely a flirt, but not a loose girl. I dated him for probably a year and then maybe in my twelfth grade — when I was seventeen, I really started to sow my oats a little bit, but not that much. I slept with probably half a dozen guys. Then I got into the business and I figured out what sexuality was, but before I got into the business, I was not very promiscuous with actual intercourse. Some of my girlfriends were twelve and thirteen when they lost their virginity. My first sexual experience certainly wasn't a one-night stand. He was my true blue love. It was scary. I knew that I wanted to and I think he was kind of expecting it, but still, it was very scary. I don't remember much of it, it was kind of a blur, but I certainly don't remember it hurting. I remember I didn't bleed and I think he got a little offended and thought that maybe I wasn't a virgin. The next morning I cried to my sister, "I lost my virginity." I wasn't like, "Hey! Hey! It's gone!" It was more like the ending of my childhood. Then suddenly with this same boyfriend, it was lights out. We did it in cars, we would go to cheap motels; we would do it in bathrooms. It was like, "Oh man, this is awesome." We were just like bunny rabbits.

New Kid on the Block

I moved out at seventeen and never finished high school. In June, I turned eighteen and three months later is when I got into the adult business. My life just started to downward spiral from the time I was sixteen and started spinning out of control. At sixteen and seventeen, I didn't really know what my emotions were. At seventeen, I moved into an apartment in Hollywood by myself. It was a dump, but it was my dump. I didn't have to put up with anyone; it was my own place. I was working part time at a clothing store and part time at a health food restaurant on Sunset Boulevard called The Source. I just couldn't survive. Two part-time jobs at minimum wage — it was expensive.

I had some crappy little MG Midget that was breaking down all the time, so I was standing outside my apartment waiting for my friend to pick me up and I met this guy Greg Rome. He was a cute little blonde boy, a surfer type, and he pulled over in a white Trans-Am with the gold eagle decal on the hood. He said, "Hey baby, you're so cute. What are you doing?" He was around nineteen. I told him I was waiting for my friend and that my car had broken down.

He said, "Why don't you wait in my car where it's air conditioned?" I was so ballsy. Here I am at seventeen living in the centre of friggin' sleazy Hollywood. It certainly wasn't cleaned up like today, and yet, I never felt in danger. I'd walk to my apartment building at two in the morning after going to a club. I know that there were hookers and pimps. Everyone was fine, thank god. No one ever tried anything on me that I didn't want to have tried on me. Anyway, Greg told me I should be a figure model. I was truly naïve. I thought figure modeling was hand modeling or body parts like feet. I didn't know that much about the adult world but I had seen *California Valley Girls* (1983) and thought it was awesome.

He said he would show me what figure modeling was, and he pulled out a *Hustler* magazine that had photographs of him. This was the kind of magazine where the guy's dick was three inches away from someone's mouth and very soft core compared to the

stuff now. I just remember thinking I was kind of excited. I just sat there and looked at it. It was a pretty girl in the photo and he was good-looking. It was a Ron Vogel shoot — there was a pretty girl with a tree and a boom box in the back and I thought, "Wow." I remember thinking I wasn't afraid or grossed out. He gave me Jim South's card from World Modeling. He said, "If you ever want to do it, it pays two-hundred dollars a day."

I sort of said, "Okay" but I put that business card in my drawer. It wasn't like, "Great, thanks!" and then I shredded it.

About two months later I had pennies to my name, I was like a hamster on one of those rusty wheels. I just couldn't catch up to myself. I remember late one night I called the number on the card and there was Jim South's southern drawl and I just left a message saying I'd met Greg Rome and he told me to call him. The next morning Jim called me back and I went to see him the next day. That was the beginning of "Christy Canyon".

I love Jim South. I have nothing bad all these years later to say about him. I hear about all of these horror stories on my radio show that these girls have with their agents. I just thank my lucky stars that I was in the business at the time that I was. There was clearly a level of class to the industry during that time and mystique when it was kind of a hidden thing. Hush, hush and underground. I love the people from my era, I really do. They're a great group of people.

I started with magazines first: layouts for probably the first couple of months. It was the boy, girl, girl, girl thing, and a couple of hardcore shots, but it was with Greg Rome and I felt comfortable with him. When I called him and told him I'd gotten into the business, he asked me if I knew all of the positioning. I really didn't. I knew the missionary position at the age of eighteen. He took me to this goofy place that they used to have in the eighties before the health department kicked in. They were these buildings on Santa Monica Boulevard and you could rent a Jacuzzi room. There was a Jungle Room, and a Medieval Room, and you could rent Jacuzzis. Greg rented one and he showed me all of the different positioning: doggie style and spoon. I didn't even know these existed. We had a bottle of champagne. It was tough and I wouldn't want to go through it again, but damn, I look back on it and I really had a great experience. I really learned a lot about sex though making films. This was toward the end of 1984.

Loving Dangerously

Like many of her sister newcomers who had already started into the adult entertainment business as it melded into the video-age by the early-mid 1980s, one of the very first brand name performers Christy worked with was Ron Jeremy. Their friendship and onscreen compatibility was immediate and they were paired together many times over the course of both careers.

I believe my very first piece of filming was a loop for Caballero with Ron Jeremy. I think it was shot on Beta-Cam. It was the new high-def of that era. It was a little more expensive to rent. I was scared to death. Oh my god, I was scared. Jim told me it was a loop. I said, "Okay" not even thinking what a loop was. I thought it was some new kind of layout or something, and then I saw the camera. I called Jim and I was going on. He said, "Well, I told you it was a loop and you have to do it because they're already there and they have a budget." He didn't try to trick me because I could have walked out. I'll never be a victim, but I told myself, "I can do this." If you see that first loop, I think it was *Swedish Erotica #57* with Ron Jeremy and I in bed, and then another couple in bed next to us. A big, buxom, German girl named Stevie [Taylor] and I don't remember who the guy was [possibly Rick Cassidy]. We were having sex in the same bed. Up until that point, I'd never shared a bed with anybody. It'd be lights out, in the dark, doing missionary, so it was scary.

Ron was adorable. He made it fun because he's just a hoot, but I remember I came home crying. I wondered if I'd crossed the line because I'd done sex on film. It was even different from doing stills. There was something about going to live film. It was almost the ending of this footloose and fancy-free modeling thing. I knew I'd entered into a whole new dimension.

At that time, I wasn't talking to my family. My sister was in London going to college and she was always my ally and friend. I really felt alone. I called Jim South and said, "I don't want to do that again."

He said, "Well honey, I've lined you up for something else for Paradise Visuals, but after the next two films *On Golden Blonde* (1984) and *The Night of Loving Dangerously* (1984) in tandem, you don't have to continue".

I said, "I can't do it again." I didn't want to disappoint him because Jim was like a dad to me. It was kind of a tough time. I asked myself, "Do I do it?" I didn't want to do it, but this man had been so kind to me. I really was very conflicted at that point, not only about films, just about life! The other thing too was that the money was just so nice. Here I was working two jobs making one hundred dollars for each job for the week, and suddenly, I was able to make five hundred dollars a day. I just remember thinking, "I'm going to do it. I've made the choice to do it." I didn't want to alienate him. He was somebody stable in my life at that point. It's not as if I felt like it was gross; it's just that I knew I'd entered a different dimension and that my life would never be the same.

I asked Christy what she believed might have happened at that point had she been insistent with Jim South about not returning, or if South explained the ramifications of what Christy had chosen to do. Canyon was emphatic she was determined to make up her own mind and that no one coerced her or influenced her decision. In her autobiography, Christy admitted Jim South represented to her the father figure she longed for after her own father had put his girlfriends and various relationships ahead of Christy and her sister.

I don't remember if he had gone into detail about anything at all. If he hadn't, I still would have done it. That was my new chosen path in this world. There was the money and I knew I couldn't go home. I just knew that wasn't an option. Working two jobs obviously wasn't an option because I never had any money. Suddenly, they were like my family. The reasons the girls got into it back in the eighties is different in comparison to what I hear on my Playboy Radio show. They get in it now to cross over to mainstream. They get into it now for whatever reasons. We got in it because we were rebels. It was the best "fuck you" to your family. We were rebellious! You couldn't get more rebellious than that. "Hey, I'm making porn."

The next films I promised Jim I would do was for Paradise Visuals: *The Night of Loving Dangerously* and *On Golden Blonde*. I've got to tell you, I showed up on the set after having conflicting thoughts about it and then I met Ginger Lynn and Traci Lords and Peter North and Tom Byron, and suddenly, it was like a whole different vibe. It was fun and we had catered food, and it was really an *amazing* experience. Ginger Lynn, bless her heart, the first scene of the day was with her and then Jamie Gillis was coming in — he was a good man and I remember telling Ginger, "I've never been with a girl."

She was so fabulous and said, "Don't worry, Christy, I'll take care of you." She really put me at ease. She put this raspberry lip balm on her puss lips, and suddenly, it was an amazing feeling.

PHOTO COURTESY OF SUZE RANDALL. *WWW.SUZE.NET*

Between Swedish Erotica and Paradise Visuals' two movies, it was like day and night. I said, "Jim, book me. I love this." I mean, Peter North...come on, how fucking hot is he. You didn't need much time to either sink your chops into it or realize, "You know, this isn't for me."

The initiative for the 1984 Paradise Visuals feature *Night of Loving Dangerously* is derived from the 1982 Mel Gibson vehicle *The Year of Living Dangerously*. Since the original hardcore movie contained scenes with Traci Lords, it is a rare occurrence that anyone might still have an original VHS copy in his or her possession. The plot outline (compiled from a series of online reviews) is as follows: Peter North portrays George, a disabled, retired police officer earning a new living as a private detective. George is hired by his ex-wife Janice (Lords) to assist in tracking down someone blackmailing Lords's husband-to-be Greg Harrison (Jamie Gillis). After a meeting and some nookie with Harrison's daughter Louise (Canyon), George further investigates the situation at hand while participating in several erotic sketches with various partners. Christy's spotlight with Peter North is followed by a girl-girl scene with Ginger Lynn, and later, with Lynn and Jamie Gillis. She does not appear with Traci Lords. *Night of Loving Dangerously* was directed by Michael Phillips.

Canyon's second official feature *On Golden Blonde* (1984) is loosely inspired by the storyline in *Heaven Can Wait* (1978). Having borrowed its title from the poignant Hollywood hit *On Golden Pond* (1981) starring Henry Fonda, Katherine Hepburn, and Jane Fonda, Christy plays Alice, a gorgeous young woman furious that her young life was cut short as a result from a mix up in heaven. Through means of atonement, Alice is sent back to earth in order to test drive different bodies, each of which is blonde-headed much to Alice's displeasure. Alice proceeds to encounter various sexual experiences before deciding upon the chassis that she likes best. Apart from the obvious gratuitous sex and audacious Canyon breast exposure, this movie is fairly typical of efforts made to sexualize popular Hollywood films. Also featured in the Paradise Visuals production (directed by Michael Phillips) are Ginger Lynn, Jamie Gillis, Gina Carerra, Peter North, Marc Wallice, and Tom Byron.

I don't recall seeing myself on screen right away. I don't think I could afford a VCR at that time. I went to a local newsstand though and I remember seeing myself on a box cover and thought, "Oh my god. That is so cool. I'm on a box cover [for *Dirty Shary*, 1984]. I'm a star." I remember going to the newsstand with a girl name Lora Lee [aka Heather Wayne], and the director who went by the stage name [Harold] Lime took the two of us to Musso and Franks on Hollywood Boulevard in the heart of Hollywood. Afterwards, we'd go to the newsstands and look at our magazines — it was a rush. It was a thrill; it was fun. I felt like this was my family and I felt pretty once again.

The one year I wasn't getting along with my step-dad and my mom was picking him over me and my dad was out of the picture, I really felt like I wasn't pretty. I felt that no one wanted me and it was as if the adult community loved me. They weren't abusing me. It was just friggin' sex back then. It wasn't friggin' fisting and double dildos. I look at what I did and I am proud of everything I did. I wouldn't take one thing back.

Canyon quickly adjusted to life within the X-rated terrain. Due to increasing demand for her presence, she worked continuously almost immediately after her career began as she vied against Ginger Lynn and Traci Lords (still in the running) for chief female spot in the adult market. Releases such as *Dirty Letters* (1984), *Hollywood Starlets* (1985), *and Wild Things* (1985) represent a modicum of Christy's prodigious filmography directed by Michael Carpenter, Bruce Seven, and Alex deRenzy, respectively.

In the early days of Christy's calling, she and Traci Lords were often paired in films together which served to bolster Christy's career once controversy surrounding Lords's age began to swirl. Most of the features co-starring Canyon and Lords were able to be salvaged with Lords footage removed and replaced with new material excluding one known title *Battle of the Stars 1* (1985).

Christy continued working for Paradise Visuals, and received considerable screen time in *W-Pink TV*, a 1985 production featuring Canyon and Ron Jeremy as the two leads. As television news hosts, Christy and Jeremy are in cahoots when they take over their network and turn it into a late-night sex show. The network's secret agent, Scorpio (Harry Reems), arrives incognito on the scene determined to get to the bottom of the mutiny. All hell breaks loose in the studio when Canyon eventually seduces Scorpio, followed by an orgy with participation from the bulk of the cast including Marc Wallice. *W-Pink TV* is an orchestration of veterans and freshmen together in various sexual acts, including a notably steamy scene between Jeremy and Canyon. Christy also appeared in a masturbation exhibition. The 20th Anniversary Special Edition DVD of this title (re-released in 2005) presents an interview with Christy Canyon and Ron Jeremy facilitated by Bill Margold. The stars enter into a lively discussion with Margold about the 1985 shoot with a special appearance by Laurie Holmes.

Here's the deal, you had about three actors to choose from back then. I loved them all, but my favorites were Ron Jeremy, Peter North, Tom Byron, and Marc Wallice. I loved Marc Wallice with that banana dick. He was totally stoned out of his mind all of the time, but he was a great guy. The only real drugs I ever did and it was for a very short time, was coke. It was maybe only for a month or two out of that part of my life. I was friggin' doing it when I was sixteen at our prom for school. It was such a 1980s type of thing. I certainly wasn't an addict, but I'd do it on weekends and things. Toward the end of the eighties there was a period where Heather Wayne and I were totally into it — we were doing it hard and heavy. I'd still show up to work and I'd know my stuff. Actually, the only time my sister was ever worried about me [being in the business] was when she came over one time in 1984. I was doing drugs with Heather Wayne and she said, "Just don't go over the edge." It was a little warning but she never cut me off, and was never too worried that maybe I wouldn't survive what everyone perceived in the eighties — that it was a dirty business. Anyway, one morning I remember waking up and saying, "Okay, I'm done." That was a very short period of my life. I never drank on sets, never got into pot, just coke for a tiny period of my life. Not my porn career, but my life. I don't blame my drug use on the business and I didn't get it from people in the business except maybe one time from a director. I had my own source on the side and I would just do it on my own, and go to a club and dance all night. I was a weird loner. It certainly wasn't to get through work. I never did it on set, except one time when the director gave it to me. I haven't done drugs since I was probably nineteen. It was great; it was fun. I can't even imagine doing it now, but I got it out of my system long before I became a parent. I feel like if a person doesn't experiment with certain things, it might come back to bite them at a point. If it doesn't come back, then good for the people who don't experience that. I learned not to worry about what other people do.

Going Straight

Unlike many of her girlfriends and fellow 1980s adult actors who achieved the echelon of stardom rapidly after making literally dozens of films, Christy took a break from performing for a few years starting in 1985 and decided to re-enter the straight working world. Since Canyon's filmography shows several releases between 1986 and 1989, one can safely assume the videos were produced prior to her departure and released later. Canyon's decision came on the heels of a toxic relationship she experienced with boyfriend Michael Paulsen. According to Christy's memoir, *Lights, Camera, Sex!* Paulsen didn't appreciate the fact his girlfriend was a porn star.

You know, I quit the business in 1985 not because I didn't like it, but I was dating a guy who owned Paradise Visuals, a guy named Michael. You know what I was working twenty-nine out of thirty days. I really just needed a break. I never quit because I didn't like it, I quit because I was burned out and I was in love with this guy.

Simultaneously, at age nineteen Christy decided to enter one-on-one therapy with a trusted counselor to try to restore the broken relationship with her parents.

My mom and I didn't talk when I was seventeen. I had moved out and gotten into porn. I think when I was about eighteen I bumped into her and I got this surge of energy. It was like, "You fucking bitch, you kicked me out!" and I kind of got a thrill out of it. She got teary-eyed and said she knew I was working in something related to the adult industry. At the time, I remember I felt like saying, "What did you think I was going to do woman?" I had gotten into the business in `84, and we connected in `87. Then when I got back into the business in `89, she cut me off again. I worked for my dad from 1985 to 1989.

I went to work for my dad in accounting and in the Christmas tree business, but I still had unfinished business in the porn part of my life. After I returned to films my mom cut me off again and at that point, I thought, "I can't live my life for you guys." I realized that the porn business meant as much to me as my blood mom and dad did. When my mother cut me off, I thought, "How could you do that?"

I said to myself, "Well, my mom will have to be mad at me, I have to be me." Being a part of the business provided a huge sense of family for me. I think it was two years later, my mother wrote me a letter to say, "I love you no matter what." I wrote her back and said, "If you want to repair this then we have to go see a therapist together." We had stuff from ten years ago at this point that we needed to talk about. She was willing and we went. Obviously, it wasn't what we had together when I was a kid because I wasn't a kid anymore and there was a lot of water under the bridge, but I was finally validated. It didn't matter what I did. I was a good person. I just happened to fuck on film for a living. It wasn't a big deal to me.

Contract Stardom

After Christy's return to sex films, she re-emerged in 1989 with her own video line aptly christened Canyon Video and reaped the benefits of a sole proprietorship. Within a year, she became one of the very first and most celebrated contract girls for Vivid Entertainment signing an eight-year deal with breaks along the way during the 1990s. Canyon explained that her initial agreement with the large production company in 1990 became paramount to her status in the adult industry in terms of popularity, celebrity, fan-ship, and financial gain. She contended that Steve Hirsh and Vivid provided her with a viable opportunity for endurance and prestige in a business that has evolved into an extremely fickle field in the years since she has left. Eventually, Canyon grew to trust and admire former adult actor Paul Thomas hired by Vivid Entertainment in 1985 to direct, a few years following his stint in jail for cocaine smuggling. In one of Christy's better than average efforts made in tandem with Vivid and Paul Thomas in the director's chair, is the 1991 release *A Portrait of Christy* co-starring Rick Savage, Peter North, T. T. Boy, and Joey Silvera.

Christy is on her game in this entertaining portrait of Christine (Canyon), a criminology student embroiled in a set-up between an ex lover with a huge debt, and a slick nightclub owner by the name of Jimmy G. (Rick Savage). Christine devises a method to pay back her ex-boyfriend's loan by appealing to Jimmy to take her under his wing as a shadow. She informs him she'll do whatever it takes to return the inordinate amount of debt racked up by her former lover. Feigning sincerity, Jimmy teaches Christine how to deceive others by walking her through different underhanded scenarios (sex is part of the deal), until eventually, she realizes she's become a pawn in a game of extortion. Prior to getting revenge, Christine engages in a blazing hot three-way with Peter North and T. T. Boy that is as remarkable for Christy's seductive talk as it is for the scorching sex. Canyon really appears to be into it, and North and T. T. Boy most definitely are. After the boys extinguish their loads, Christine returns to find Jimmy, surprising him and her ex (presumed to be dead) when she pulls out a loaded pistol. In an explosive conclusion in more ways than one, Christine handily takes care of the double-crossing dudes, keeps the millions in the briefcase, and assumes possession of the nightclub. In the role of Christine, Canyon reminds adult fans that sex films are supposed to arouse while Rick Savage does a crack job as the crusty mobster. This is a very entertaining flick.

GOLDEN GODDESSES

I don't mean to be wishy-washy, but I think that the eighties are such an important part of my life. That's what solidified my name out there. It made me who I am. Jump to the nineties. I think being a Vivid Girl contract star was equally as important, but in a different way. It's like comparing apples and oranges. They were both hugely important and had big impacts on me as a person, me as a porn star, and me as someone down the road when I ended up quitting the films altogether. They both are such a huge part of my life.

It gave me complete acceptance that I was at the top of my game of my chosen road. Ginger will never say she was a contract girl. In my nineties era at Vivid, the crème of the crop during the eight years I was there were Hyapatia Lee, Jamie Summers, Raquel Darien, and Savannah — bless her heart up above. Jennifer Stewart was short-lived, but very popular for her little time in the business — and Janine. There were some great girls in the nineties because I was there for so long I was able to know them. Barbara Dare was also a Vivid contract star, but she quit right when I got on board.

Hyapatia Lee (aka Victoria Lynch) is one of the first known Native American women to have worked as an erotic actor in the hardcore adult video business next to Jeanette Littledove. Lee's biography states that her mental health issues namely "dissociative identity disorder," enabled her to perform sex on-camera under the guise of one of her "personalities." In 1993, Lee left the business, and in 1998, her fans were astonished to learn she had died from diabetes. It is believed Lee staged the hoax hoping to seek financial gain from anticipated increased sales of her movies.

Savannah (born Shannon Wilsey) is perhaps the female James Dean of her generation and genre. As an adult star, Savannah was one of the most dominant and popular adult actresses of the video-age during her short term between the years 1990-1994. She was also famous for her reckless activities on and off the porn set, and died from a self-inflicted gunshot wound to the head after surviving a car crash at age twenty-four. Two years prior to her death, Steve Hirsh and Vivid Entertainment handed Savannah her walking papers due to erratic and unpredictable behavior.

Steve Hirsch is such an amazing person. We signed a contract in 1990 for one year and it was all on honor and trust. The contract was three pages long. To this day, I love Steve Hirsch. I truly love him. Again, going from Jim South to Steve Hirsch to Playboy Radio, I have been spoon fed and coddled for the entire time. When I danced on the road for nine years, one bodyguard traveled with me on every single trip. He didn't miss one trip because I treated him as an equal. I continued dancing for about three years after I left Vivid, but I always knew he was my right hand and my left hand. Clubs provided bodyguards, but he was my sanity on the road. If I stayed at the Radisson so did he. If I stayed at the Sheraton so

PHOTOGRAPHY BY KENJII

did he. I would fly first class, if the businesses had money so did he. One time our flight got cancelled and we got on another flight and they only had one first class. I said, "Okay Joe, I'm taking first class, but at meal time we'll switch because I know you want the good food." I respected him and I knew that I needed him. I could have gotten any flunky to do it but I wanted that man at my side.

Despite working a full schedule in the early 1990s while under contract to Vivid and on the road as an exotic dancer, amazingly, Canyon found time to earn a post-secondary Marketing degree which became a necessary asset as a bankable star in her profession.

I kept my adult career separate from my other career. I went to college in 1990 to the Fashion Institute of Design and Merchandising. I got an AA in Marketing. It was a nice experience, not because it was college, but it was so great because I went on Mondays and Tuesdays and then I'd go on the road dancing. I'd take a red eye on Tuesday night, go strip for a couple of days, come back on Sunday and be back in school on Monday. It kept me balanced and kept my head sane. I always knew I needed two separate lives because if I got engulfed in just the porno life it wasn't going to be a good thing. No matter how much I loved it, it's too intense to live that life all the time and it's not my whole life. I have other talents too. Not that I ever did anything with my Marketing career except that I learned how to market myself.

Intolerance

When asked what it meant to be a Feminist, or about notorious tarnished female performers such as Linda Lovelace or Traci Lords, Christy articulated her thoughts at a rapid fire pace.

I never understood the true definition of the word "feminist" — the women who burned their bras and so on. I always looked at the feminist movement as something I never fully understood. Parts of it I like — equal pay for equal work, but I'm also feminine. I happen to like my bras and I paid damn good money for them so I'm not about to burn them! There are things about the feminist movement that I don't like. You always hear that they say porn takes advantage of girls. I believe Linda Lovelace jumped on that bandwagon after she got out of the business. I don't believe in that part about feminism, but what I know about the feminist movement is that there are parts I get with respect to equal rights, but I'd also like the right to make a porno.

Traci Lords is very anti-porn. She's kind of a trip — a real wacko. I personally don't care what she did; it didn't affect me. If anything, Lords being underage at the time of filming made my films more valuable because so much of my stuff was with her, but I just don't like her hypocrisy. She left the business and then kept the [stage] name Traci Lords. That's not your birth name woman! Hypocrisy is my number one pet peeve. People who complain about other people, be it their race or sexual preferences, whatever, it's because they're trying to hide something.

Back to the feminist question: I'd like a guy to open my door, but again, I'd like to have the right to decide whether I should fuck on film or not. As God is my witness, not that I believe in that religious bullshit, but as Mother Nature or whoever is watching out for us up there as my witness, I have never been taken advantage of as a woman. Granted, I may have made X amount of money to do a film for Vivid while the owner made XXX amount of money from that same film. I had a right not to be a Vivid Girl. I also had a right to get off my Armenian ass and produce, direct, star, and distribute films, but I didn't want to do it all. No one took advantage of me so that part of the feminist mumbo-jumbo I don't believe in.

Canyon's opinion about those who assume the role of another person's keeper triggered an arc of emotions pertaining to a variety of topics.

I don't like it when people try to tell other people how to live their lives. Who has the right to tell a woman she can't have an abortion — or these losers who sit outside of the jail when they're going to put to death a murderer? Put a bullet in his head already. Maybe that's the Armenian in me but I'm a firm believer in Capital Punishment in certain cases when there is no shadow of a doubt. Criminals are never going to be rehabilitated. Some people might be born with mental issues, but I think a lot of it is childhood related, and a lot of it is abuse in the household. I don't know how they fix that, I just know that a guy that has raped children many times — cut his fucking dick off. You want to live. Great, but you just won't have a dick anymore. As a mom, if I knew a child molester, I'd flip out. "Get yourself off my street." Put them all on an island. Some people have lost the right to be around civilization. I just have no patience for that. Granted, some of them are mentally ill, as I've realized with my mom's mental illnesses. She has a problem, I mean, this woman freaked. She was insane and was put into lock down a couple of years ago.

Garden Variety Porn

Canyon doesn't consider that the women of today who work in porn have attained anything remotely close to the same stratosphere she and her generation did, and the ones preceding her in terms of credibility, finesse, and duration. Moreover, Christy doesn't foresee a promising future for the young females and men of today who aspire to be "Porn Stars."

Revolutionary women in the adult business like Marilyn Chambers and Gloria Leonard who successfully opposed some of the anti-porn advocates such as Catharine MacKinnon are examples of women Christy admires and respects.

I had known Gloria's husband, Bobby Hollander. We're all kind of intermingled. I know pretty much all of the old-timers. These new girls come on the radio show and then they'll come back again six months later and I'm like, "Oh, have we interviewed her before?" They don't make an impression on me like the old-timers do. They really don't. They have no distinguishing qualities. They're cute with perfect bodies and fake boobies and that's all fine and great, but they don't stick out in my mind once they leave the show. I'm looking at them and I think, "Woman, if you can make a porno, anyone can." I don't know if you want to publish this, but a lot of the girls are sort of like street urchins. Well, in reality they are one cut above a streetwalker. The last couple of years a lot of them got into the business to make a name so that they can call themselves a "porn star," even though I don't consider them a "porn star". They're a "porn hole". You're not stars. Who the hell are you after doing three scenes to call yourself a star? They do it so they can build up a clientele list so they can hook on the side. It is true. I'm not talking about the New Sensation contract girls or the Wicked, or the Vivid Girls. I'm talking about the girl who does the double anal scene for five hundred dollars. There is the garden-variety girl who gets into it, has the face that can stop a clock, but she'll do anything. I think Jenna Jameson and Terra Patrick were truly the last of the superstars. A few are filtering in like Tori Black I suppose, but she won't be a superstar. In a few years, no one's going to know Tori Black in the way people know Tori Welles.

Possessing beautiful and dramatic characteristics, Tori Welles began working in pornographic movies in the late 1980s and had a ten-year run before marrying an adult director (Paul Norman) and giving birth to two children. Like Canyon, Welles was a Vivid Girl and one of the best known throughout the duration of her career.

With respect to pecking order, Sasha Grey, one of the most popular girls the adult movie industry has produced in the last five years, managed to cross over the proverbial line into mainstream work with recurring guest spots on HBO and other networks albeit, in type-cast roles. Most notably, Grey played the porn star girlfriend of Hollywood superstar, action hero Vincent Chase (Adrian Grenier) on the program *Entourage* in the 2010 season. Grey was also cast as a high-class call girl in the 2009 Steven Soderbergh film *The Girlfriend Experience*. Since leaving the pornographic business, Sasha was recently criticized by parents for her participation in a reading program for American schoolchildren.

Marilyn Chambers and Christy Canyon.

Sasha Grey has been on our radio show. She's a very pretty girl, I've give her that. I've never seen her work so I don't know her acting abilities, but she's not going to be a superstar, not in my opinion. She's as big as she's going to get in this day and age. The mystique is gone. It's so in your face now which is good I guess, but they don't know the star system the way they used to. There are way too many girls and the companies can't afford to promote the girls the way they used to do. The internet has definitely helped a lot of people, but the porn business like the music business has been hurt by it. Everything's watered down. It's certainly more acceptable and mainstream, but I think another huge thing is the money is not there anymore. Not that we made a lot, don't get me wrong, but the production money was there. You had a five day shoot with Vivid. You had cool locations.

I've noticed on my show that when I started five to six years ago, I'd ask the girls how many films they'd done and finally after a couple of times one of them said to me, "Christy, what are you talking about films? I don't do films I do scenes."

I said, "Oh my god, you girls don't do films anymore." With the exception of the top three companies, there are no films. It's about how many scenes you have done. You show up, you get stuck in a hole with three or four dicks, and you're out of there. To me that is the huge difference. The glamour of it is gone. It wasn't mainstream back then, but they had make-up, they had hair, they had scripts, and they had catering. Now I think the girls do their hair and make-up so the production has gone downhill compared to what I was used to. Maybe the girls like it, I don't know. I'm just glad I had a nice little production behind me. I liked getting there at eight am in the morning and doing hair and make-up. Doing your first scene, taking a lunch break, chat, do another scene and take a dinner break. It was just like a real set with some sex mixed in. I came from the superstar era of porn. Just like the 1990s had superstar models. There aren't superstar models anymore the way we had in the seventies, eighties, and nineties like Claudia Schiffer, and Linda Evangelista, and Cheryl Tiegs. That was the era of a true superstar. I made a huge impression, but in fifty years, no one's going to know me because all of the performers will be dead.

Comeback

Christy Canyon left the business again in 1993 before returning in 1995 and reconnected with Vivid. She continued the same trend juggling films with her dancing career and said she retired from the road for good in 2001. For a short time, Christy directed a few movies for Paradise Visuals, the company that had been the genesis of her start in films. Canyon has a list of approximately two hundred movies (including compilations) containing scenes in which she appeared throughout her feature movie career.

When Christy returned to the business for her final few years in 1995, she made a film with Vivid that mirrored her comeback suitably titled *Comeback*. Christy played a parody of herself: a porn superstar coming out of retirement after a few years absence to reclaim her position as the principal female personality in the X-rated genre. The movie is a day in the life on set as Christy's agent Max Hardcore (Tony Tedeschi), her director PT (Paul Thomas playing himself), and the rest of the cast and crew (featuring Asia Carerra as a shy girl in craft services) all mill about in anticipation of the sexual fireworks Canyon is known to elicit. Unfortunately, things don't exactly go according to everyone's expectations. Christy becomes reluctant to step onto the sound stage after her agent inadvertently speaks out of turn — Max excitedly exclaimed about the prospect of copious loads of semen brought about by Canyon and her oral capabilities. Turned off by Max's brash and insensitive remark the X-rated film diva refuses to put out leaving Tedeschi, PT (showing good humor), and the others in a quandary. Keeping herself pre-occupied during her no show, Canyon masturbates while observing others (Dallas and T.T. Boy) doing the nasty prior to helping Jenteal overcome her nervousness about a girl-girl scene. Canyon and Jenteal engage in a passionate exhibition, topped off by a fervent sex scene between Christy and Tedeschi (wearing a condom) but only after Canyon agrees to return to work once they arrive at a sizeable sum for her expertise. Christy is very vocal and descriptive when placing her carnal order with Tedeschi — she instructs what she wants him to do to her, characterized by licking and thrusting which serve to intensify the sizzle. Afterwards, Christy is satiated and raring to go as she enters a jungle scene with Steven St. Croix. PT sets the stage and the two actors go to work. St. Croix, excited to work with the busty legend for the first time, climaxes before PT and company are able to catch the money shot. Frustrated by the amateur-hour antics of his male star, PT remedies the premature expulsion by suggesting that a third performer be added to the twosome. Canyon suddenly remembers how special the girl working in craft Services is and invites Carerra to join her and St. Croix. The three make movie history while Carerra and Christy become BFFs as is later revealed inside Canyon's boudoir in a comical conclusion.

Christy's final movie role in 1998 for Vivid Video with Janine Lindemulder is titled: *Where the Boys Aren't 9*. It was released in 1999.

Gemini: The Twins

I'm very lucky that I live in Los Angeles in the Valley where everything's accepted for the most part. I avoid people who knock the porno business to me like the plague and have not had much confrontation.

In recognition of her birthday on June 17, Canyon has spoken in interviews over the years about how her personality fits the qualities known to be associated with the Gemini astrological sign. With two major aspects, duality and contradiction belonging to the central theme of the Gemini sign Christy has described herself as two distinct characters: Christy the uninhibited porn legend, and Melissa the complicated, tenacious woman who has fallen in love several times.

Consistent with the contrary twin Gemini personas, Canyon stated she practiced condom use in all of the films she made for Vivid, yet claimed to have engaged in unprotected sex with all of her male co-stars (in connection with Vivid) prior to production. In her private life, Canyon conceded she did not practice safe sex. Although she excelled at portraying the throw-caution-to-the-wind, seductress on screen, in her personal life, Christy is far more pragmatic, particularly about money matters. To her credit, Canyon is financially solvent because shrewdly, she handled her own career.

When I'm not on radio or I'm not acting, or I'm not dancing, I am Melissa. I am the other person. I don't mix my two selves. I've always kept the two personalities separate and I've never appeared on the raunchy type of radio show like *Howard Stern* or on *The Jerry Springer Show*. I've never allowed myself to knowingly go into harm's way. I don't need the publicity. When my book came out, I was offered to go on the *Howard Stern* show, but I didn't feel comfortable so I didn't do it. I didn't need the money and I didn't need the extra promotion so I've never really had someone attack me because of my choice of being a porn star.

I don't want anybody's judgment in my life. You've lost the right to be in my life if you have any little bit of judgment. I am who I am, and if it's great, that's okay. If not, that's okay too. I don't have time to be everyone's friend. I have no problem with it and I cannot have anyone in my life, family or not, that has a problem with it. If you're not in charge of your life, they'll eat you up and spit you out for breakfast.

I give nothing but props to this business. They allowed me to find out who I was in this world. They allowed me to find out sexually who I was. They allowed me the ability to earn a decent income and sock some away in the nineties and to really be proud of the person I am. I've learned to love my body because I'm not a twig. I've learned to love my Armenian hips. I'm never going to be

the Barbie Doll body and it's not a rock hard body, that's for sure, but they seem to love it.

I got into the industry at a time when we worked every day because they could not create enough videos to satisfy the customers' demand. We all got paid three-four-five hundred dollars. When I took my four-year break and then went back in the business, I went with Vivid for the most part and I had a nice little contract there. I was one of the few girls that got residuals and when they went to catalogue, the owner cashed me out on the titles. When we stopped doing the films, he said he couldn't continue my dollar-a-take royalty because he was only making one dollar and twenty-five cents. I took a pay out on everything and didn't make any more royalties. I'm comfortable.

The only misnomer Christy has made, according to her, is in the area of matrimony. Married and divorced three times, presently, Canyon prefers to be in the company of her children when she isn't working for Playboy Sirius Radio.

I don't have time to date right now. My life is seriously my kids and my job. I get asked out, but I would rather be in bed reading *Junie B. Jones* books to my daughter — but the thing is, I did all of that. I've had hundreds of lovers. They were all great for their time and once their time was up, they were done. It's funny. My book doesn't go into my three marriages. The book is the onset of my career and until I quit and when I was going to start dancing.

My first husband Bob was a contractor who worked at an old house I remodeled. It lasted from July of 1995 until August of 1995. I knew it was a mistake as I was saying, "I do." I was turning thirty and I thought, "I should be married by now." Thank god, we didn't have a big wedding. It was funny, but he was kind of cute in his tool belt. Suddenly, I married him and he just got to be this lazy bum. I would come home and he would be sleeping on the couch. He was so dispensable. He got comfortable real fast, and I thought, "Oh fuck." It was a good thing I had a pre-nuptial agreement and I just kicked him out. Then I married a guy in the business who was an actor in the seventies. His real name was Tim Connelly, but he went by Dick or something. I don't even know his stage name. He was a writer for a while and then he worked for AVN [Adult Video News]. We got married in July of `96 or `97 for two and a half, three and a half years. I was on the road stripping at the time. We fought all the time. It was the most toxic relationship. I'm a very kind of Zen person and I don't like arguing, and it was just a mistake so we divorced. We had no ill feelings at all — it just didn't work out.

Tim Connelly, Christy's second husband went by the name "Dick Howard" in his 1970-1980s adult film appearances. He had been married to former 1980s porn actor Kimberly Carson prior to his relationship with Canyon. Connelly and Carson had two children together before Connelly apparently left Carson for Kelly Nichols. Since leaving the industry as a performer, Connelly worked as an editor and a writer for Adam Film World and more recently, AVN under the pseudonym Jeremy Stone.

Canyon's third husband, Grant, is someone she had known since high school. The two friends re-established a connection many times throughout the course of her career in movies.

I married my last husband in July 2001 and we were together for about six years. It just didn't work out. You know he's a great guy; they're all great guys! I can't knock any of them. I think guys have a really hard time with the fact that I'm really independent and I think that's a really big turn-off to a lot of guys. At first, they're really into it. They think, "Wow, she has her own money. She's got her own place!" and so on. I think the thing they fall in love with is eventually what they hate about me. I don't need anybody. I want somebody, but I don't need anyone and I think that's a big blow to a lot of guy's egos. I think learning at a young age that I couldn't rely on my parents at all ties into the way that I am now. I could never rely on anybody.

"It is easier to build strong children than to repair broken men." FREDERICK DOUGLASS

At the time of our interview in the fall of 2010, Canyon shared, she was the proud mother of two adopted Asian children, a girl and a boy. Since our initial conversation, she has adopted a third child, a two-year old girl from China. After adopting her son, Christy had not withdrawn her name from the list of Americans desiring Chinese children. She was contacted by the agency in 2009 to gauge interest in adopting another child. Canyon hadn't expected to adopt a third child, but felt that if she'd refused, in her mind, it would be the same as choosing an abortion. Admirably, Christy recognized the link between her patchy childhood and her desire to be a good mother. She is determined to learn from mistakes.

The only way that my childhood has impacted me has been in a good way. Because of not feeling wanted — that is what has driven me to adopt children from orphanages. I want to give somebody a chance. If I have changed children's lives in this world, I am a better person.

My daughter from China just turned seven. She's in grade one now because of the age cut-off. She was too young to throw into kindergarten so she was in kindergarten at a private school and now she's at another school. My son is from Vietnam and he is now two years and eight months. They are the greatest. They're beautiful. My daughter was thirteen months when I got her and he was eight months. They are the loves of my life, they really are. I started late. I was thirty-eight when I went to China to get her six years ago.

My daughter was at her seventh birthday party and there were twenty of her friends there, and everyone was running around at this place called "My Gym". She was laughing and having fun. I thought, "You wouldn't have gotten this in the orphanage." I was still with my last husband when we adopted the little girl from China. The first one I got with him. I think that three kids are enough. I'm forty-four. The problem is now all of the countries are closing or you have to be married for five years, so they're really making it undesirable to adopt from foreign countries. For a while, you could get a kid out of there in about three months. Now I'm hearing it's taking about two years. This is because we were under the Bush administration, it's harder to adopt from foreign countries. Everything that motherfucker touched got fucked up. Democratic or Republican, I don't care. I voted for Schwarzenegger a couple of years ago. I just thought the man had such a goddamn big ego he'd never fail. Boy was I wrong. I am a Democrat by heart — the Republicans have attacked our business a lot, but I vote for who I truly believe is the best.

The funny thing about adopting Asian children: I've had Born Again Christians at three different times get mad at me for not adopting within the state. I've just said "My God. He doesn't care where I adopt from." In porn I've never really had anyone put a negative spin on me, but it was when I chose to adopt kids from outside of my country that I got hit with a backlash which I find fascinating. If they only knew I was a porn star, then all hell would have broken loose. That was the only time I ever felt anyone was judging me and it wasn't for my porno career. How's that?

I needed to get out of my system the films, the dancing on the road. I needed to cleanse that part of my life. I did it for ten years and then I said, "That's it, now I want kids." I only ever wanted Asians. I kept on hearing how the little girls are abandoned in the fields and I just always thought there should not be a kid unwanted. Granted, I can't adopt a million kids, but I think that any healthy young kid would get adopted. I certainly didn't want a drug-addicted child. I don't mean to be mean, but my energy level only goes so far. That is what it came down to, and then I applied for a second child in China a year later and they just started to slow down so I switched real fast to Vietnam and I got him.

I'm single now and that's how I wanted it. It's just my path, it really was. I didn't want to be pregnant or get a sperm donor or a boyfriend. I really wanted to adopt. My family medical history isn't that good — you know, Mom went cuckoo, Dad died young, and I thought, "You know what? I really could make a difference in this world." My mom was a great mom until we got to a certain age and then I think her brain started playing tricks on her. I just feel like maybe some of the faults that my mom had like dating a lot of men made me not want to do that. I don't want my kids to feel like there's somebody new all of the time. Again, my parents did the best job they knew how to do.

When my father passed away in 1997- `98, we had reconnected and we had made amends. I loved him. Sometimes when I go through a bad period, like when I got divorced or you know how you have a cruddy day sometimes? I'll sit down and I'll cry and say, "Goddammit, Dad, why aren't you here?" I miss having parents now because my mom's not together. She's doped up on some kind of anti-depressants all the time. Thank god, I have my sister who is two years older and who has always been my best friend through thick and thin, and good and bad. She is the only stability I've had throughout my entire life. She lives five houses away from me! It's wonderful. My sister is another one of the main reasons why I really wanted to adopt kids. There are no guarantees my kids will be best friends, but I want to give them the opportunity. My sister has one child my daughter's age and one who is a teenager. We're a small but mighty family.

Talk Radio

Suffice to say adding up the trials and tribulations of the erotic film actress, Christy Canyon's life is charmed. Canyon's legacy as a Vivid Girl, a highly sought after feature dancer, and most meaningful of all, her place as a conscientious parent, demonstrates she is a gleaming example of an individual who discovered life after porn. For more than six years, Christy has enjoyed a successful career as a talk show host for Playboy Radio at Sirius Satellite Radio.

In the summer of 2010 while at the Exxxstacy Show in Chicago, I had an opportunity to be a guest on Christy's radio program. Invited to speak with her about the development of this book, it was my second experience as a guest on her show. As a host, Canyon is well prepared, sharp and professional, yet she is spontaneous with a devil-may-care attitude that is endearing and fun. Christy explained how the radio gig happened.

It was good timing. When my book came out back in 2003, I went on Playboy Radio to promote it and then I went back again. At the time, I had a publicist for my book and then they called the publicist six months later and said, "Oh, we're doing 'Legends of Porn' week, can Christy come back?" I went in a couple of times and did Playboy TV to promote my book. Then they called me one time and asked if I wanted to co-host one night because Julie or Tiffany [the regular hosts] couldn't make it. I became a go-to-girl with one of the girls and I really wanted to do it. I got thinking what a fun job it would be. Then one time when I was guest hosting they told me that Julie was getting married and moving to Florida. I remember on the inside thinking, "I want her job!" but played it real cool. They said they were going to test some people and I happened to be one of the girls they tested. A month later, I got the job. How lucky am I? Ginger and I used to be co-hosts and then Vanessa Blue came on as my host. I do the show three hours a day five days a week.

Christy has worked with a few different co-hosts on the Playboy Radio show over the years since Ginger Lynn left. In the spring of 2011, Ginger rejoined Christy in the newly formed radio program "Spice" and Canyon is ecstatic to have her back. Due to her busy schedule with the two radio programs "Spice" and "Legends" along with her commitment as a mother, Christy temporarily abandoned her plans to write a sequel to her autobiography, *Lights, Camera; Sex!*

I started a follow-up but then I got my daughter and my job at Playboy and then my second and third child. I don't have time to even look at my e-mails, let alone continue my second book. It's definitely on hold. It's probably a quarter of the way done. My book doesn't include my children because it was published a year before I got my daughter.

Adult Video News (AVN) award.

I still do my website: *www.christycanyon.com.* I love it and Vivid runs it for me. I can post all the stuff and do the photos, but I don't know the damn html — I'm not that computer friendly. So again, ten years later, they're still coddling me. I love that company. They don't make any money off of it; they're just great people. I also have stuff that I sell on e-bay and it's a lot of fun because there is a lot of "Christy Canyon" memorabilia. It's a good little side business.

When Christy's time isn't consumed by her family and her job, she occasionally becomes sidetracked by politics. Disheartened by current global economic issues, Canyon touched upon how and where American tax dollars might best be served for the greater good of everyone before concluding our conversation so she could pick up her oldest daughter from school.

I am fully on board with spending our tax money not in the way in Iraq bullshit, but putting up mental health facilities. I have no problem with cleaning up our own backyard. If you really want to help people, go to Africa and help the AIDS babies, don't spend it on a fucking war just so that Cheney could get the oil out. That's my opinion. The whole Bush Administration has turned me off of government. I had no problem with it when Clinton was President. I voted for Obama, but the man got handed a pile of junk. People complain that the man hasn't done anything, but that man has eight years of a spending spree to undo. He's fighting an uphill battle. I think he steps up one and the Republicans push him back two. They need to work together which is what's wrong with the country now. They're all fighting. For the first time they need to think about the country. I'm at the point where I don't even watch the news. All I can do is take care of my family and that's it. I'd rather be watching *CSI: Miami.* It's escapism.

24

Raven Touchstone
Innocent Taboo

Penny Antine began her career as a scriptwriter in the adult industry in 1984 under the pen name Raven Touchstone when the genre was in the midst of a transformation to video.

As a youngster who endured a turbulent mid-west childhood, Penny found salvation through her love for reading, writing, and theatre; at six years old, she joined the Cleveland Play House in Ohio and became enthralled by the world of fantasy, costumes, and thespian training.

In the mid-1960s, Antine transplanted to Southern California to pursue an acting career, and performed with "A" list Hollywood stars such as Doris Day and Richard Harris. She won a small role in *Caprice* in 1965. Penny also accepted a non-credited part in the 1968 film *The Valley of the Dolls*, and appeared in guest stints on popular TV shows of the decade such as *The Beverly Hillbillies* while continuing to cultivate her writing as a sideline. She hoped to become a novelist one day.

After a hiatus as a wife, stepmother, and businessperson, Antine renewed her commitment to writing while assuming a position as a personal assistant for the haughty actress Eva Gabor. In an unexpected turn of events, the developing scriptwriter was hired to compose her first story for adult director Scotty Fox under the VCX umbrella. The result was *Intimate Couples* (1984) with Herschel Savage and Jacqueline Lorians. Thus began Antine's love affair with the adult entertainment profession which allowed her to exercise her creative outlets in inventive and exciting new ways.

Penny recounted what a rush it was to shoot pornographic movies in California during the mid-eighties while production and performing in sex films was still illegal. Excitedly, Antine described how she and members of cast and crew would be blindfolded and driven in vans to film locations always staying one-step ahead of the L.A.P.D. More

"Part of the attraction of working in the industry is the fact that it is an outlaw industry. It's a taboo industry. Sex in this country is so fascinating because it's still taboo except everybody wants it." RAVEN TOUCHSTONE

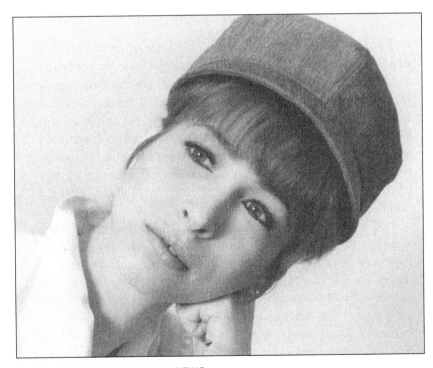

PHOTO COURTESY OF PENNY ANTINE

than twenty-five years later, Penny marvels at her own endurance in an unconventional career that has paved the way for her to hone her craft as a writer, costumer, and erotic photographer extraordinaire.

At present, when she's not writing scripts Antine and collaborator Rob Clampett (son of Robert Clampett, the animator for "Tweety Bird") are working on a series of film exposés about various facets of the sex industry, an endeavor shaping up to be a massive but rewarding project. In her spare time which is not as abundant as what she would like, Penny is writing her memoirs.

Antine once remarked her childhood resembled that of Francie Nolan, the lead character in her favorite book, the classic novel *A Tree Grows in Brooklyn* (1943). Francie Nolan had wanted to grow up to be "somebody." While garnering admiration and accolades in a profession unchartered by most, Penny Antine has indisputably proven she is somebody.

I interviewed Penny Antine in the summer of 2010.

The Curtain Puller

I was born in Cleveland, Ohio and I grew up in theater. My mother and my grandmother took me to a play in an amphitheater at Cain Park when I was four years old. I think the show was *St. Joan — Joan of Arc*. What a play for a four year old to experience. I was so entranced by it. I have no memory of it, but I've heard this story many times: my mother, my grandmother, and my family have told me that I was completely riveted to what was going on, on the stage. When the actors came out to take their bows and there was all this applause, I stood up; I looked around and started crying. I said to my mother, "I want to do that."

In Cleveland at that time, there was the Children's Theatre. I think it might still exist. It was at The Cleveland Play House [established in 1915] which was America's first repertoire theatre and it was extraordinary. The Children's Theater was called "The Curtain Pullers," but you were not allowed to start in the Children's Theater until you were six. I think I got dancing lessons until I was old enough to enroll in theatre. At six or so, I started at The Cleveland Play House and it became part of my soul. I adored it. Actually, it was my salvation.

I grew up in a very volatile home with a mother who was a rage-aholic and a father who was an alcoholic. I probably would have drowned in this life had I not found my calling which was the Arts. By the time I was eleven, I was assisting the teachers at The

Play House. I became the leading juvenile actress there in the adult productions as well as the children's productions. The whole of my summers were spent at Cain Park Children's Theater. My winters were at The Cleveland Play House Children's Theater. When I got into my teens I was working at Musicarnival part time, which was a Musical Theater in the round. I apprenticed in costuming. I loved sitting in the costume room and just wallowing in the smell of old costumes. I would sometimes take them and wear them at school. I did costumes for plays at high school, because I had apprenticed at the Play House and Cain Park and at Chagrin Falls Valley Theatre so I learned how to do that. Years and years later, in porn, I wound up doing a lot of costuming. I have a costume room in my home. I must have over ten thousand dollars worth of costumes. As a kid I learned costuming, I learned props. I learned all of it because I did it all.

I had, in one sense, a significant childhood because I had such a great passion. There was not one minute of my childhood when I was ever bored. There was always something to do. My little friends and I from the Play House made up our stories. We had reel-to-reel tape recorders in those days and we would tape our stories taking on the various characters. We were always busy. We'd be in the basement making paper mache animals or writing plays, or making costumes. We were always doing something creative. I won a scholarship singing in Cain Park Main Stage Theater when I was fifteen years old. I was a musical comedy type singer. During that summer and the summer after that, I actually worked in the main stage adult theater rather than in the kid's theater. By the time I was seventeen years old I was teaching drama in the summers at another little theater. In my last year of high school, I actually didn't stay for the prom or anything like that. I left and went to New York. I wanted to be a Broadway star.

I moved to New York to pursue my career as an actress. I turned eighteen when I was there and I hated New York. I didn't like the feeling of the city. It was too much cement for me. I was overwhelmed by the coldness, and the rush and the subways — I just didn't fall in love with it. After about four months in the city, I went back to Cleveland and contacted my father who was in California. I had not seen him since I was eight years old. Now, ten years later I was eighteen. I contacted him and asked him if he would send me money for a plane ticket to California. I figured I could pursue my acting career in California. He did and I came out and I moved in with my dad and my stepmother. She was wonderful. He was a jerk. I never did like him. He had abandoned me when I was eight years old and I had longed for my daddy for the next decade. What a disappointment to find him at last and not even like him! He was a bonafide jerk. I loved my stepmother and felt sorry for her because she was married to him. I stayed with them until I got an apartment and a job. I joined some acting classes and started working in movies and TV out here.

To backtrack a little bit to being a very little girl: I loved to read and I loved to write. I wrote poetry and I wrote stories. I still have stories I wrote when I was eight, nine and ten. That was kind of a second passion of mine. Acting was first, writing was second, and singing was in there somewhere. I had a career as an actress and I did that consistently for quite a few years. I was in *Caprice* (1967) with Doris Day and Richard Harris. It was just a small role, but it was actually my first major movie. I also did a pilot called *Judd for the Defense*. I played the girlfriend of the lead girl, and I did the original movie *Along Came a Spider.* There was one made years later with another cast, but the cast I was with was Lee Marvin and Lee Grant. I did a lot of things like that during those years. I was in *Planet of the Apes* (1968), and I was in *Valley of the Dolls* (1967). I played a small part in that one, but it was fun. I was in a lot of plays in little theatre around town. Some were musicals. I also took the usual acting classes. I was on *The Beverly Hillbillies* as one of Nancy Culp's Biddle Bird Watchers.

On the side, I worked as an artist and sold my pieces at outdoor art shows on Melrose Avenue. Actually, I remember being on an art lot selling my things the day the astronauts landed on the moon. We were all gathered around a television set someone had bought and somehow plugged in somewhere. It was an exciting time to be alive and be young.

I continued working as an actor and an artist, and along the way, I got married to man who had five kids. I fell in love with the family and became like a second mom to his children. He was a singer. He's long gone now. We got into Shaklee Corporation and made a ton of money at it. We did very well. Shaklee is a direct sales company. It was the first time I did something that wasn't connected with the arts. He was very good at the sales program and I was very good at doing the product pitch. We became coordinators quickly, made a good deal of money; bought our first home and so on.

Penny and her husband had actually met at a club where they were both singers. Her husband performed with Benny Goodman and Tommy Dorsey bands. Eventually, he retired from his career as a singer when interest in Big Band jazz fizzled after Elvis Presley and the rock 'n roll phenomena began.

Years before the trend for healthy living via the supplementation of vitamins and minerals was in vogue, Shaklee Corporation was founded

Penny Antine and Nancy Culp on the set of *The Beverly Hillbillies.*

in 1915 by nutritional vitamin guru and San Francisco chiropractor, Dr. Forrest C. Shaklee. In 1956, Dr. Shaklee employed a multi-tiered marketing strategy to sell his product "Shaklee's Vitalized Minerals," another revolutionary measure that conveyed an environmentally consciousness raising message to prospective consumers. Shaklee Corporation has grown over the past few decades to sell organic biodegradable cleaning solutions worldwide.

I had agreed to give two years to this endeavor before I went back to my own life, and by the time the two years had passed, we were quite successful and secure so I began the next real phase of my life: writing. I thought I'd be a novelist. I was a major reader of literature. I wanted to create something great so I began to write my first novel. It was horrible! I realized how much I didn't know about writing, so I went back to school to study creative writing.

After a while, the marriage didn't work out. We got divorced and I went off on my own. In 1984 I was working for [Hollywood actress] Eva Gabor as her personal assistant and I was still selling my artwork. I had rented a darling little house and advertised for a roommate. I

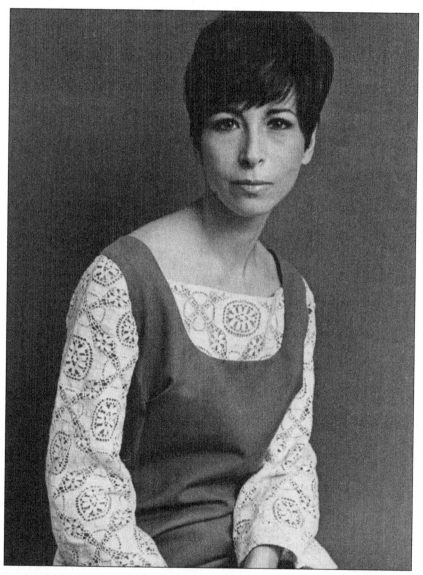

PHOTO COURTESY OF PENNY ANTINE

took on a nurse named Mary Westerfield. As fate would have it, she had lived next door to a porn director named Scotty Fox. She told me when she moved in that Scotty was looking for writers. Well, at that time, I was also trying my hand at writing screenplays, and I said, "Well, I could talk to him". By then I had written many things, and I'd ghost written some books and published stories. I met with Scotty and he gave me the basic five sex scenes: boy-girl, girl-girl, girl-girl-boy, and boy-boy-girl. It sounded like a dance — dah, dah, dah, dah, dah! He told me he wanted twenty page scripts and how many characters and so on. I wrote a few treatments for him and he took them and sold them so I started writing these porn scripts.

"Do those movies have a *plot?*"

I hated working for Eva Gabor. She was the Bitch of Buchenwald, a most hideous human being. When I started writing scripts for Scotty, I began working on the sets as well so I quit working for Eva. I figured I'd be in porn for about ten minutes. I would make enough money to find what I wanted to do next. Of course, what happened is that I fell in love with the business and started making so much money that I couldn't leave.

That first script was called *Intimate Couples* (1984) for VCX. Scotty Fox directed it and John Holmes was the line producer. He and Scotty came over to my house while my roommate was leaping around her bedroom screeching, "John Holmes, John Holmes! The biggest cock in the world is in my house sitting on my couch!" It was hilarious. John was very diligent about going over every line making sure he understood everything I wrote. He made sure he knew how they were going to shoot it. That was the very first script I had ever written in the business. The second was *Just another Pretty Face* (1985) starring Traci Lords.

Again, this was back in 1984, which is when I got into it. In 1985, I went onto the sets and started working the actors on their dialogue. Then Ginger Lynn was put under contract to Vivid, and Scotty started directing for Vivid. I wrote the first Ginger movie for Scotty which was called *Ginger* (1985). Then I wrote the second and the third one. After the third Ginger movie, they fired Scotty and kept me. They brought in a director named Bruce Seven. Bruce directed the next seven Ginger movies and I wrote them all and worked alongside Bruce assisting him and working with talent on their dialogue — costuming, anything that needed to be done. Then Bruce went on to other things and they brought in Henri Pachard. He just died a little over a year ago.

The late Bruce Seven was a special effects wizard in straight Hollywood prior to entering adult films in 1970 where he shot bondage loops as a sideline. Seven graduated to camera operator in 1980 when he was hired to shoot primarily bondage features for Bizarre Video. He teamed up with pornographic performer John Stagliano in 1983 to create a joint production company Lipstik Video. Lipstik Video, a lesbian centric collaborative venture, produced Seven's first full-length feature *Aerobisex Girls* (1983). In addition to working on Lipstik's fetish line, Seven freelanced as a director for the start-up company Vivid Entertainment. Bruce Seven passed away in 2000 at age fifty-three from complications arising from the combination of a stroke and emphysema.

Discussed throughout this book, the colorful and imaginative director Ron Sullivan (Henri Pachard) initiated his career in the adult genre in the late 1960s while directing several films for 42nd Street grindhouse moviegoers. His first film, *Lust Weekend*, about a couple abducted by a sex cult was released in 1967. In 1969, Sullivan was the associate producer of the politically incorrect satire *Putney Swope*, written and directed by filmmaker Robert Downey Sr. (who also had a minor, but key role in *Boogie Nights*). After assuming his nom de porn, Henri Pachard, in the 1980s Sullivan directed and produced an abundance of hardcore sex films until his death from cancer in September 2008 at age sixty-nine.

> Bruce and Ron both became like brothers to me. We were all close to the same age and wanted to make the very best movies possible. For the next six, seven, eight years, I wrote every show that either of them directed. I was on the set assisting them. I was working on the sets with them and I was just having an absolute ball. I loved it. I loved the people. I loved the whole thing.

One of the benefits Penny didn't bank on when she agreed to create sex stories for adult companies was the sheer caliber of talent she would be writing for.

> Going back a little, when I had first agreed to write a few scripts for Scotty Fox, he gave me several adult films to watch, as I had never seen one before. My impression of the porn industry was pieced

together from things I'd heard or read about: men and hookers in hotel rooms naked except the males kept their socks on. The porn craze of the seventies — *Deep Throat* (1972), *Behind the Green Door* (1972), *Devil in Miss Jones* (1973) — were all movies I read about but had never seen. Scotty gave me *Story of Joanna* (1975), *Devil in Miss Jones*, and one or two others. *Story of Joanna* and *Devil in Miss*

Jamie Gillis.

Jones blew my mind because of the quality and the stars. Jamie Gillis was a terrific actor, perversely sexual in a way I had never before seen portrayed on the screen. I loved his talent and his style. Georgina Spelvin of *DMJ* [*Devil in Miss Jones*] was such a fine actress, so deep and rich I could hardly believe I was watching porn. She was long gone from the business by this time. I hoped that one day I would meet her if only to tell her how much I admired her work.

After seeing Jamie in *Story of Joanna*, I hoped I would be writing porn films long enough to write something glorious for him to perform. As it turned out, he was cast in one of my movies for Bruce Seven in a role in which he wore a goofy Peter Pan outfit with wings. Fortunately, it was just the first of many roles I was fortunate enough to happily write for him over the years. He was in a class all by himself. There will never be another like him.

Blame it on Ginger (1986) and *Silver Tongue and Hot Rod* (1990) are two early feature films written by Antine and directed by Henri Pachard. Both productions showcased Jamie Gillis in fine form. *Blame it on Ginger*, a sex-laden adaptation of the hilarious Hollywood hit *Blame it on Rio* (1984) paired Ginger Lynn and Barbara Dare as two vacationing friends attracted to one another's fathers (Jamie Gillis and Joey Silvera) with Tom Byron and Peter North co-starring as the girls' love interests. The video combines zany situational comedy with passionate sex scenes and is a model of the taut, well-constructed stories Antine had started to write.

A virgin no longer in her incipient career as a scriptwriter for erotic films, in 1986 Penny was commissioned to assemble the storyline and dialogue for what became the final Johnny Wadd movie, *The Return of Johnny Wadd* (1986), in which John Holmes reprised his role as the lusty private dick. Fashioned eight years after *Blonde Fire*, *The Return of Johnny Wadd* was released by Penguin Productions and directed by Patty Rhodes-Lincoln. Antine had not penned a story about a hard-boiled detective before, but figured she had nothing to lose. Shot on video, *The Return of Johnny Wadd* is mildly reminiscent of the earlier Johnny Wadd movies that made Holmes a household name, but Penny's dialogue is slick and snappy, and Holmes, Kimberly

John Holmes and Kimberly Carson, *The Return of Johnny Wadd.* ADAM AND EVE. PHOTOGRAPHY BY KENJI

Carson, Sheri St. Clair, Mai Lin, Melissa Melendez, Bunny Bleu, Buck Adams, Billy Dee, Dick Howard and Nick Random all rose to the occasion.

By that time, I was cranking out maybe three scripts a month and it was just another script. Actually, the first movie I saw of John's was *Insatiable* (1980) with Marilyn Chambers and I was impressed with a couple things. One was the scene where he kind of very manly picks Marilyn up and moves her down. That scene really got me. I thought, "Wow"! He's so masculine. He's so male in that scene. That movie really impressed me. I thought that was very good. The other thing that impressed me was the size of his dick.

I watched a number of the Johnny Wadd movies in order to get a hit on his character. I watched that genre of film in regular movies because that's not my forte. I just sat there and I wrote it. I figured it out. They told me how many sex scenes it would contain — they always do. What combinations they wanted. Sometimes they'd tell me the actors they're going to use in different roles and I can write for those people because I know of them. It never seemed to me to be a big deal. It only became a big deal after John died when it was the last Johnny Wadd movie ever made. As far as I was concerned, at that time, there'd be ten more.

When I started, video had just moved into the home. People were buying VCRs and renting or buying videos and adult film companies were springing up like Vivid, and Wicked, and others. VCX and VCA were among the old warhorses. Some had been around since the 1970s when porn hit the big screen. There was a great influx of people from mainstream. Granted, Ron Sullivan had started years before, but he came from legitimate theatre. I think the last thing Bruce Seven had worked on as a Hollywood artist was Sam Peckinpah's *The Wild Bunch* (1969). He was the one who figured out how to get the bullets out of the gun, smash into the person's head, and blow his brains out. He was a special effects artist who had always loved porn. Because he had developed lung disease, he found he could not keep up the pace of working for the mainstream studios so he came over to the porn world. Paul Thomas came from the legitimate stage. A lot of people did, and so did I, so there was a great energy alive at that time. It was electric. It was palpable because we all wanted to make good porn, good movies with sex.

Featured in previous chapters, Paul Thomas or "PT" as he is more commonly known today became a leading man in adult movies after jump-starting his career in sex films in 1974. A trained actor, Paul Thomas is remembered for portraying the Apostle Peter in the 1973 film *Jesus Christ Superstar*. Thomas was also a member of the original cast for the production of *Hair*. For the past few years, PT has been actively involved in the industry as a freelance director after having worked with Vivid as a mainstay for two decades. Thomas mentored under Ron Sullivan, and according to Antine, is now one of the wealthiest people in the adult entertainment business.

Penny recalled how impressed she was by PT's "astounding range of talent" when she first met him in the mid-eighties on the set of *I Dream of Ginger* (1985) where he played the male lead. When she asked him why he wasn't working in Hollywood, Thomas replied, "I've already done that. Out there I'm just another handsome, talented, brilliant performer…" Then, with a grin, "In here, I'm a star."

In the very beginning, we had some good actors but there were also a lot of kids in the business who couldn't act. It was just like a little repertoire company. It was very small. There were not novices with a camera who thought they could direct. We had real directors who had actually studied the art. When you look at the quality of some of the people who we had in those days — there was Jamie Gillis who was a fabulous actor. Rick Savage was a wonderful actor. You had Sharon Kane, and you had Sharon Mitchell. I was able to write wonderful stuff for Sharon Mitchell, for Sharon Kane, for Rick Savage, and for Jerry Butler. It was a great bunch of people. They were actors. They all came out of theater.

John Holmes was smart. He was an intelligent man. He was not stupid. Harry Reems was an intelligent person. He may have gone crazy and gotten religion, but he had intelligence — and Ron Sullivan, and Freddy Lincoln, and Alex deRenzy. You had a wealth of fine talent so it was exciting and it was fun. I always liked Buck Adams a lot. My interactions with Buck were always on the set. Buck had a lot more talent than he thought he had. I did a great photograph of Buck.

Coupled with creating something new was the fact that we were outlaws which made it an absolutely wonderful and exciting time. Companies were willing to pay so we got paid pretty well. Because it was a small group of people, we worked all the time and the money just started to flow. It was just remarkable and we started making wonderful films, terrific movies. I'm proud of all of that. People say, "Well, it's just porn!" It's MY porn. People today still say to me, "Do those movies have a plot?" It was fun being an outlaw. We had to leave the area to shoot our movies because the cops were after us. There were these two cops, Como and Navaro, and they were the ones who were busting everybody. We would go up to Big Bear to shoot and up to Riverside. We'd go to San Francisco. There were many days when I would arrive at the airport and meet the rest of the cast and crew there. We'd also drive up near the San Francisco area where we were shooting. We'd shoot two or three movies at a time and then come back. It was interesting because a lot of the time we shot in the home of one of one of the City Councilmen. His name was Jack, I think. He had this incredible home that had a big area like a studio. I think there was

Buck Adams. PHOTOGRAPHY BY PENNY ANTINE

an indoor underground pool in this house. It was an incredible property. We shot there a lot because the laws up there were much looser regarding shooting porn.

Excluding minor exceptions, for several years the community of San Francisco was welcoming and virtually immune to the regulatory laws that made the production of pornographic movies illegal in the state of California during the 1960s, `70s and `80s until the Freeman ruling in 1988 finally lifted the ban.

In the beginning, I remember going on shoots with Scotty Fox where they would put us all in a big van and literally blindfold everybody so that no one would be able to tell anybody where they'd been. It was such fun. Who gets to do something like that?

So Much Beauty

I was in porn for many years and saw so much beauty. I could not put it into words. It was actually in 1992 that I decided I needed to get some of what I saw on film. That was when I went to school to study photography. It was precipitated a few years before by a scene we were shooting a scene for *Ginger and Spice* (1986) in a big fancy bathroom in a large home. Ginger Lynn was in the bathroom, naked. She has got this pale, beautiful skin with blue, blue eyes and blonde hair. Her hair was tied up on the top of her head in a little ribbon. She asked for a glass of wine so somebody brought her a glass of wine. I was in there because I was running dialogue with her. She was in a bubble bath with her script in hand, and in comes Barbara Dare who was in the same scene with her. She has this beautiful olive skin and dark hair, in absolute contrast to Ginger. Her hair was also tied up in a little colored ribbon on top of her head. Here, you had these two beautiful girls both naked with gorgeous bodies, and Barbara said, "Ginger, can I get in with you and run lines with you?"

Ginger said, "Sure". Somebody brought Barbara a glass of wine and she sat at the other end of the tub. These two young, fabulous women are in a bubble bath with a script in one hand, a glass of wine in the other, their hair tied up on top of their heads. I looked at that and I said to myself, "I would never be able to find the words to really convey how beautiful this is. I need to go study photography." That's what sent me to school.

I loved Ginger. Ginger was like a kid sister to me. I wrote all of her Vivid movies and I was on all of the sets. I helped her with her dialogue and when she got a column for *Club* Magazine called "Pillow Talk," I wrote that column for her. I was "Ginger Lynn" on paper. She'd bring me her fan mail and we'd go through the letters and pick out the ones that were the best for her to answer. I was also writing her monthly fan letter. I think I was the only one in the industry who was invited to her baby shower.

Due to Penny's unique situation as a woman who functioned behind the scenes in the sex industry for more than two decades, I was curious to learn if she observed evidence of exploitation of the women or men hired by the studios to facilitate the material written by scriptwriters such as Antine.

The girls are not exploited. I can't say one hundred percent because there are some people who will exploit everybody, male and female, even the crew. I've seen a clip of a so-called producer/ director with his camera in hand, literally shooting a little deaf girl who was crying. He kept forcing her do to more and more. It was a masturbation scene and it was completely hideous. It was

"Leena as 1940s's babe." PHOTOGRAPHY BY PENNY ANTINE

shown to me by Savannah Jane who is also a deaf porn actress and she was out to get this guy. I saw that clip maybe a year or so ago when I was interviewing Savannah Jane for my documentary. Those things definitely exist. There are creeps in this business, but I haven't worked with them. My experience has been different. I have worked with the Paul Thomases, and the Michael Zens, the

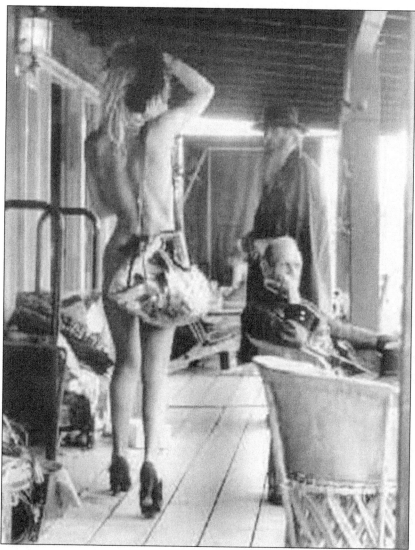

"Shame" PHOTOGRAPHY BY PENNY ANTINE

Bruce Sevens, the Ron Sullivans — directors who have respect for the people they work with.

In twenty-five years in this business, I personally have never seen a girl or boy forced to do anything. They all sign on of their own volition. They are paid well. Some of these kids are not very well educated and would be working at McDonalds. Some of them shouldn't be in the business. I've seen girls who feel so guilt-ridden about it. I always would say to them, "You don't belong here. Go do something else. It's too hard for you." This business is good for some people. It's not good for others. Those kids don't usually last very long because they spend their whole time crying and they wind up not being there — guys too. I think, for the most part, the only people who are exploited are the people who put themselves into a position to be exploited. Certain types of women and men have a specific mindset about sex. They understand it's a job. These people function well.

People were interesting when I started. They were [also] really screwed up. They were drugged-out or they were this or they were that, or they came in because they had such horrible issues with their parents. Today everybody is pretty much level. They come in with their datebooks and their agents and their lists of the people they will and they won't work with. They come, they do their job and they leave. A lot of girls come in just to work to make a name in porn so they can go dancing on the road and be a feature, and make a whole lot of money. That whole thing has changed.

People like Porsche Lynn [who started as a performer in 1986] find their way somehow into the industry, and it becomes the place where they work out their life "stuff". It is so with many people. Sometimes they stay a long time and sometimes they don't. Sometimes they stay forever and just move into another area of the industry, but unlike any other work place in the world they find their way here into the porn industry because for some reason it's the best place for them to work out their life issues.

Porsche not only had that incident as a child [where she witnessed her father shoot and kill her mother before turning the gun on himself], but she was abused by all sorts of people after that. How does a child survive this kind of treatment? Porsche has this incredible spirituality which she found in her search while working and living in the porn world. I believe she's a prime example of someone who came in here to work out her life "stuff". I think

Sharon Mitchell is another. She had a bad drug problem for a number of years. Look where Mitch went with her life. It's remarkable. That's often a part of it. We tend to fall down before we come up.

In 1986 Penny wrote the script for the overlooked video production *Innocent Taboo* (directed by Scotty Fox) starring Eric Edwards and Porsche Lynn as part of an ensemble of actors showcased in several scenes. The storyline exposed a different twist on the term "familial ties" as two sibling brothers marry sisters and the newlyweds rediscover the meaning of family unity after sampling a new love potion. The film's amusingly ironic tagline, "Being bad has never felt so good!" could also serve as a mantra for members of the Adult culture.

Porsche Lynn gained far more than bargained for on the plus side when she decided to become an erotic film performer. Unfortunately, external factors can cause one to lose footing. Lynn's former colleague and handsome cast mate, Eric Edwards, a graduate of New York's Academy of Dramatic Arts with over five hundred films under his belt, has spent much of his post-porn years as a single parent battling alcoholism and more recently, cancer. Penny had an opportunity to see Edwards recently while attending John Leslie's memorial and said he looked happier and healthier than he had in ages.

People aren't as much fun anymore because they're too sane today. They're not emotional messes, most of them. Part of the attraction of working in the industry is the fact that it *is* an outlaw industry. It's a taboo industry. Sex in this country is so fascinating because it's still taboo except everybody wants it. Today, all the kids are dressing like the BDSM community or porn stars.

Penny's observation about today's breed of porn performer appears to be precise, that they adopt a clinical approach to their work and are seemingly able to emotionally detach in order to be effective on camera. Penny drew from her own observations as a woman in a man's land when asked about the pitfalls of the business with respect to females who are not necessarily grounded or strong.

I believe most of the women who are running companies and directing porn are feminists. I'm not sure about all of the girls who work in front of the camera. I don't believe all of them have come in with a feminist attitude. They come in sometimes more out of desperation.

There was a little girl years ago when I was working with Scotty — I say "little" girl because I was at least twenty years older than she was but she was certainly of age. She was married and had a baby and her husband did not know that she did this work.

"Sweet Reunion" PHOTOGRAPHY BY PENNY ANTINE

She was doing it because her husband was having trouble keeping a job and she needed to feed her child. Her husband thought she was modeling. This girl was on a shoot that was busted. The cops dragged her in and she cried and begged them not to tell her husband. They said that if she would name names, they wouldn't tell her husband. She named the names and the cops went right to her husband and told him. He took the baby and disappeared and she was left absolutely bereft and alone because of these friggin' cops. Here was a girl who was doing porn to feed her kid and tried to make a better life for her family. That was just a devastating story for me. I think her porn name was "Pam" but I'm not sure. This would have been around 1985.

There was a group years ago that some of us women were in called "The Pink Ladies". One of the functions — and Nina Hartley would do this — she would make the girls understand that they didn't have to do anything they didn't want to do. She would teach them that they had power. She would also teach them that hygiene was necessary. Unfortunately, that group didn't last. Everybody just kind of grew up and went on, but it was certainly worthwhile.

It is presumed that (perhaps in another universe for the purposes of discretion) most males would jump at the opportunity to indulge in lascivious experiences with some of the sexiest women in adult movies if given half a chance. Jokes have abounded for years about male porn stars "having it easy" and how they are the envy of the have-nots. In reality, performing on cue is not as easy as one might think. The niche group of men that had long lasting careers during the "old school" porn era is considered by their peers to be athletes in their field. They definitely had their "mojo" working without the benefit of enhancements.

In the past, before Viagra, the guys would be so terrified. They would come in and they wouldn't be able to get a hard-on. They couldn't perform and they'd be so humiliated, you'd never see them again. It's not for everybody. It becomes a mechanical thing with the men. It's mental. Again, there were those who could do it. [Canadian born] Peter North [aka Alden Brown] could do it every time, and he'd shoot fifteen feet high into the air. You'd have thirty people standing around applauding him.

I remember being up on a shoot in Big Bear. I think it was with Peter North and Tommy Byron. They were on the couch discussing how they were able to get it up every time. It is a process. There were those who were brilliant at it, they were like athletes. They were able to focus their energy, and they knew how to do this and they were magnificent. There were others, who were hit or miss. Then, of course, Viagra fixed it for just about everybody.

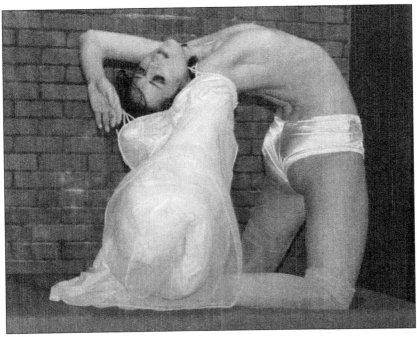

"Olivia" PHOTOGRAPHY BY PENNY ANTINE

The Artist doesn't see things as they are, but as *she* is.

While thriving within a world many outsiders deem demoralizing, subversive, and even perverse, Penny's capacity for capturing shimmers of raw beauty, elegance, and human spirit, so eloquently evidenced in her photography transcends in every thread of her work and life. She doesn't waste moments.

I loved doing photography and I know that I had a gift for seeing. Ten people can shoot the same thing and the photographs are all going to be different.

There's a saying I have tacked up in my office: "The artist doesn't see things as they are, but as he is". Everybody is different. We shoot according to who we are and what we are, that's how we see things. I don't think I've done my most significant work yet. In fact, I'm doing it right now. I can't say I've loved every single thing I've written, but I've loved writing, I loved photography and I adored acting. Acting was my first great love. I was so young and so vulnerable. I thought I could never love anything that much again because I would never be that young and vulnerable again. As I'd mentioned, I've also loved singing, but I can't do that anymore because of my Meniere's disease.

Antine has suffered from Meniere's disease (named after the French Physician Prosper Meniere) for several years of her adult life. Meniere's (aka Labyrinthitis) is an inner ear disturbance characterized by hearing loss and/or imbalance, vertigo and tinnitus (ringing of the ears). Penny wears binaural hearing devices that augment her residual auditory ability improving speech discrimination and understanding in most listening environments.

I started buying certain costumes because I knew if I left them at the studios, they would more or less end up as a rag on the floor. I bought some things that were so outrageously beautiful, some things from the thirties and the forties. I would buy them myself and then rent them to the companies. I had respect for these garments. I still have some of them, but a lot of them I've sold off. I've pretty much sold most of my vintage clothing.

I've loved every single phase of my creative life. I've been fortunate to have great friends who share my love of the arts, writers and actors, and directors and singers. In that sense, it's been an outstanding ride. I've had an incredible life. My enrichment has mostly been interior stuff. I did make very good money for many, many years in porn. It's not happening anymore because the industry is going down "la toilette" because of the internet. As wonderful as the internet is, in many ways it's destroyed the entire adult industry.

I think I was the first woman to come in and write actual scripts for the porn industry. I believe I was the first woman to do that. I was there right at the beginning of Home Video. All the major features that were made in the 1970s were written by men. I was writing for video and that was a new concept and technology. I've written probably five hundred or six hundred of them in the past twenty-five years. Everything from *Debbie Does Dallas: The Revenge* (2003), to *Heart of Darkness* (2003), *Jekyll & Hyde* (2000), *The New Devil and Miss Jones* (2005), to my favorite *CineSex* (1995) or *Bobby Sox* (1996) which won my first Best Screenplay award. *Throat: A Cautionary Tale* (2009) won Best Screenplay. If I never won a thing, I'd still have to say I loved it! I think I was responsible for boosting the quality of movies being done in the video era.

One of Penny's wishes during her early days, to meet Georgina Spelvin came true when she was asked to write the script for *The New Devil and Miss Jones* in 2005. The movie was produced by Vivid, and Spelvin, the star of the original film was asked to appear in a cameo. The *New Devil in Miss Jones* (directed by Paul Thomas) is definitely worth seeing and would especially be of interest to fans of the original production directed by Gerard Damiano. Antine's excellent script is the integral ingredient that breeds life into the inner turmoil and pathos experienced by the lead character, Justine Jones, the fictional heroine embossed by Georgina Spelvin.

In *The New Devil in Miss Jones*, the mousy Miss Jones (Savannah Sampson) awakens one morning to an upside-down day. It is her birthday. Justine begins to experience brief memory lapses and can't seem to get grounded as she prepares to go to work as an editor for a successful publisher of Romance novels. Along the way, Justine is confronted by sexual imagery: anonymous people are copulating in public, in a warehouse, on tables and in chairs. Feeling like an intruder in a frightening dream, tentatively, Justine participates as a voyeur to what she consciously considers acts of indecency. The conduct excites her though, as she eventually melds in with the faces in the crowd and becomes entangled in a ménage a trois. Afterwards, Justine has remorse about what she allowed herself to become involved in, but she can't seem to stop the fantasies (or is it reality?) from consuming her thoughts.

We soon learn Justine is not like her co-workers. She is quiet and reserved and doesn't mix easily. Her colleagues mock her and she retreats into her shell. Justine's boss, Miss Devlin (Jenna Jameson), invites Justine into her office and attempts to seduce her by intimating that Justine wants to share her desires. Confused, Justine becomes upset and suddenly finds herself in the Ladies' bathroom. She stumbles upon an attendant (Georgina Spelvin) who informs her it's "getting late" paraphrasing the white rabbit in *Alice in Wonderland*. Justine thinks to herself, "Late…for what?" Before departing from the bathroom, Justine encounters a young custodian Ted (Dick Smothers Jr.). She answers inappropriately when he tells her he cleans toilets after she asks why he is there. Ted wishes to chat with her, but she quickly brushes him off and he is left alone.

In the next scene, Justine is outside in bright sunshine seated naked by a swimming pool. Jordan (Nick Manning), a friendly, well-built co-worker appears on the deck. Justine allows herself to fall for his charms and Jordan leads her into an extravaganza of sex, leaving her temporarily satiated. In the next scene, Justine reconnects with her boss Miss Devlin. The two women approach one another with ferocious passion as they display impressive acrobatic maneuvers.

In her final sexual encounter, Justine indulges herself sandwiched between two males (Anthony Hardwood and Mario Rossi), and when it's over, the clock in her head is ticking faster. She is once again face-to-face with Miss Devlin who reveals to Justine her real identity. Miss Devlin leads Justine back to the last minutes of her life, the day she took an overdose of pills and died on her living room couch. Stunned and terri-fied by the reality of her demise, Justine senses her fate and while trying to reconcile why she is being punished for committing an act of suicide, she learns an even more startling truth, that her "act of selfishness" also caused the death of another. On cue, Justine's thoughts are interrupted again by the bathroom attendant who reminds her that time has indeed run out for Justine. Spelvin leads the fraught Justine down a stark, white hallway into a small room where she must live out eternity, unreciprocated in her attempt to be pleasured by Ted, the custodian she'd abruptly dismissed earlier when he had only wanted to talk.

Savannah Samson gives a quality lead performance in this film which would have undoubtedly been a challenge considering how good Spelvin (who is tops in her cameo) was in the original. Additionally, the art direc-tion and musical score are well matched to the material, and the sex scenes dovetail neatly within the framework of the story. *The New Devil in Miss Jones* picked up nine AVN awards in 2006 including Best Screenplay by Raven Touchstone and Dean Nash. Antine is proud of the success of the film, but more importantly, she is pleased to have made a new friend.

More than twenty years after the original film was released and well into our friendship [she always says we were twins sepa-rated at birth], Georgina and I sat in my bedroom watching her interview for the 25th Anniversary version of the original *DMJ* which included bits of the original movie. I asked her how she felt watching it after all these years. She said, "A bit embarrassed. You know my family and all." She was now in her early seventies with graying hair, an impish grin and a generous heart.

"You never expected to become an icon?" I asked.

"Hell," she said, "I never thought anyone would ever see the movie!"

Penny Antine with Jane Hamilton and Georgina Spelvin.

Although there are far too many to give attention to here, in looking at some of Penny's other favorite storylines it is apparent Antine is a prolific writer who is gifted at creating atmosphere. She is also meticulous with dialogue and plot. Not only that, but Penny's actors are appreciative of her efforts as she is able to vacillate between grit and the sublime which the following film synopses exemplify: *Cinesex* (directed by Michael Zen and released in 1995) features popular nineties starlets Asia Carrera and Leena. The pros harness their talents, incandescent sex appeal and beauty in this story contrasting two disillusioned women pining for different realities.

Weary of her life and her fiancé, a stripper (Asia Carrera) longs for a meaningful, romantic relationship and imagines herself as the star in one of her favorite classic Hollywood movies. Next, a tough-talking icon of the silver screen (Leena) desires to experience unbridled sex, and steps out of the celluloid to exchange places with a diehard fan. Their adulterated fantasies reach fruition when the women inhabit one another's lives. (Alex Sanders and Steven St. Croix assume the supporting male roles.) *Cinesex* won Best Film, Best Art Direction and Best Screenplay at the AVN awards and was followed up by *Cinesex 2* (1995) starring Asia Carerra, Lisa Ann and Kaitlyn Ashley. In 2008, the movies were released as a two-box set.

Throat: A Cautionary Tale (directed by Paul Thomas) stars the mysterious beauty Sasha Grey as Julie Garrett in this reprisal of the original Gerard Damiano film *Deep Throat* (1972). When the film opens, Julie's dead body is being examined by a mystified coroner. He discovers rolled up bills contained within a condom inserted inside of her vagina. Detectives Joe Gillette (Tom Byron) and Byrd Smith (Penny Flame) attempt to piece together the final weeks leading up to Julie's death. Through flashbacks, we discover Julie was born with an unusual congenital defect — her clitoris is in her throat. The story backtracks through Julie's life, and we learn she had capitalized upon her oddity in order to support herself and her aspiring suitcase pimp boyfriend. Julie's initial paid sexual engagements begin in a sleazy peep show theatre catering to a handful of lonely male souls (Herschel Savage is great in a cameo as Jacob King, a Hasidic Jew). She is taught by a fellow performer Lane (Aliana Love) how to use her rare gift by deep-throating dildos the size of a baby's arm for practice. Soon, Julie becomes addicted to the deep throat technique and for the first time in her life, she is able to achieve a climax in her tonsils rather than between her legs. Strong-armed by her boyfriend, Julie graduates to blowing strange men, one-by-one, in a trailer until she is rescued by a seemingly concerned promoter Danny Quinn (Evan Stone) as he informs her point blank, "You don't have to do this, you know." Julie takes up with Quinn at his Southern California residence and he treats her like a queen until he realizes the cash cow he has in his midst. Quinn signs Julie up to star in her first porn film with the "biggest" male star in the business Dante DeMarco (played by muscle bound/steroid fueled Lee Stone). Julie is not agreeable to the proposition, and angrily, she lets Quinn know but the deal is already inked. Reluctantly, Julie makes her way onto the set and begins to perform fellatio on DeMarco. The sequences of events that transpire from this climactic point are disturbing and tragic, begging one to question if Antine's refined script is a partial commentary on the pitfalls of the adult industry, or simply an example of what can happen when one becomes addicted to the pleasure centers in the brain. What stands out in this story is the capacity of disconnect exhibited between the actors during sex. It's hard to discern if the disassociation is intentional to further enhance the moral of the plot, or if this is typical behavior in today's brand of porn. In and amidst the expletives exclaimed during every orgasm, most of the actors appear robotic and even bored. On the plus side, Grey is a beautiful young woman and a fine actor uncovering a kind of curious Mona Lisa smile at times during her performance.

Early in 2011, Sasha Grey announced on her Facebook page she was leaving the adult business for other pursuits. Penny Flame (Flame now goes by her real name, Jennifer Ketcham) who played the troubled alcoholic detective in the story's subplot, has also left the business. Apparently, Flame is a very good writer as can be observed on a blog she has written for a while: http://becomingjennie.wordpress.com. *Throat: A Cautionary Tale* cleaned up at the 2010 AVN awards with Best Screenplay award going to Antine.

Early on, I didn't know that anybody even knew who I was other than the people I was working with. I was in the business for three years, sitting at home, doing my thing, and working quietly on the sets with my people. I was never a publicity seeker. I was at an XRCO Award Show and I think it was the second or third year I was in the business, I was walking down the hallway and a guy came up to me and said, "You're Raven Touchstone, aren't you?"

I said, "Yes, I am."

He said, "I was in a movie you wrote and I have to thank you for the role you wrote for me. I loved playing that role." I was absolutely floored.

"Well, thank you so much," I said. Then I went into the Ladies room and a girl came up to me and said, "You're Raven Touchstone, aren't you?"

I said, "Yes, I am!" I couldn't believe it! Then it happened a third time that night. It was at that point that I realized I had a career. One night during one of those events the kids out in the audience all just stood up, and screamed and cheered for me and I was just so touched by that. Everybody in my personal world knows what I do. I've never been secretive about it.

The Best of the Best

Inside Penny's North Hollywood home is a wonderful assortment of esoteric pieces, pictures and posters duly representative of her contrasting tastes, her spirited nature and varied passions. In the front hallway hangs a framed photograph Antine shot of Hollywood couple Roy Rogers and

Dale Evans holding hands back in the 1960s when she was a part of their circle of friends. In the summer of 2011, I was invited to a girls' lunch in Penny's home along with Georgina Spelvin and Veronica Hart. It was a treat to be privy to the valued friendship and mutual respect shared by these very unique, unorthodox women while engaged in conversation around the kitchen table. Afterwards, Penny brought us to a converted guest house behind her patio to reveal the treasure trove of garments and costumes she has collected, not only from her years of experience as a costumer, but as a fan of beautiful fabrics and designs. It is Penny's belief that inside or outside of porn, life is what you make it as she shared some proud and poignant Kodak memories.

Every five years I throw a birthday party for myself which I plan as a reunion for many of my old friends. Most of them know each other and we all have history together. Usually, the friends from Los Angeles show up, but the ones who moved away do not. This year I threw my "every-five-year party/reunion" and everybody came. My girlfriend Pat who has been close to me since we were nine years old and who was a roommate, both in New York and L.A., came down from Northern California. My darling friend Pamela, my roommate when she was nineteen and I was twenty-one years old and who is now a major archaeologist in this country, came in From Pennsylvania. My Southern Belle girlfriend Lucy came in from New Orleans. My closest male friend in the world, Ted Kristian, along with his lover Allan and our friend Carol, all came up from Palm Springs. Gail and Erwin Flacks and Su Ann Bamer, another past roommate, came from Las Vegas. The rest live nearby. All thirty-three of them, friends from my childhood, from the sixties, seventies, and eighties, some of them the great loves of my life were all here to honor and renew our friendships. After a long evening of eating and schmoozing, I sat them all down in the living room, and starting with the one I had known the longest, told them all how I had met each one and how they were connected to each other. I told funny stories about them and some of them told some about me! It was one of the most extraordinary evenings I've ever experienced: with love and joy, and gratitude. I'm the luckiest woman in the world to have such friends.

Over twenty years ago, several of my friends and I organized an intervention for an alcoholic girlfriend of ours. Eleven of us had gone through our paces the day before with the interventionist, and now we were facing the actual event. It was a frightening prospect for us to take over the responsibilities of her life, including her nine-year old son if indeed she agreed to go to the Betty Ford for thirty days which had already been arranged for her. We formed a circle, held hands, and then a great "whoop" came out of us all as our clasped hands came up in the air in the center of the circle. It was a whoop of anxiety and of hope. Later that night after we had done the intervention and had all gone out to dinner together, we'd taken her to say goodbye to her young son. After we'd all hugged her with tears soaking our faces, we stood in a group, waving goodbye as her sister and another friend drove her down to Palm Springs to the Betty Ford Center. That experience was a Kodak moment I will never forget. She has been sober now for over twenty years and she was one of the thirty-three at my party this year. Moments like these, I consider the "Kodak moments of my life". Have I had any of these moments in my life in porn? Of course, I have. Holding Ron Sullivan just weeks before his death and knowing I was losing a close friend who was losing his life — that was a Kodak moment for me.

Back in the late 1980s, I went to Paris to do a shoot. Ron Sullivan was directing and on one of our days off, I took some of the girls, Barbara Dare and Bionca to The Louvre just for the experience of it all. At one point, Bionca drifted away from us. I found her standing before a huge painting, her eyes wide; tears running down her face because a little child in that painting spoke to her soul and touched her heart. That was a Kodak moment for me. Climbing up to Quasimodo's gargoyles with Rick Savage, and standing out there looking at the sun setting on all of Paris — my god, what a moment that one was. Sleeping in a broom closet in the hunting manor where we all stayed in Tours outside of Paris because Ron's snoring was causing the plaster to fall on my head. Yep, that was a Kodak moment. Getting my first AVN nomination and my first Best Screenplay awards — there are so many moments.

Currently, I am working with Rob Clampett who is the son of Robert Clampett, the famous animator who created "Tweety Bird". "Tweety Bird" just turned sixty-five recently. We are making a series of documentaries. Right now, we are doing men and women in the sex industry. It's not just porn, it's everything. We've got over a hundred hours now of taped interviews with porn stars, strippers, street hookers, escorts, sex surrogates, sex therapists, name almost any area of the sex world and we've got them. One documentary is on the women and one documentary is on the men. We've got dominatrix's, and we've got dominants, and slaves, transgendered men and women — all kinds of people. It has been an absolutely, extraordinary journey.

For example, the people in the BDSM community have opened their world to us and it has been remarkable. We have interviewed and gotten close to some outstanding people who really are worth an entire hour themselves. Once we've got the documentary finished we're going to do spin-offs of certain people. Their stories are outrageous and some of these people are outstanding. There's also going to be a book attached to the documentaries with a small chapter on each person. It will contain material that's not in the film documentary, and it will contain photographs of each individual which I am taking. We're even thinking of including a DVD with the book. It's going to be wonderful.

Being in the porn industry opened me up. I was a relatively small town girl. I was always a maverick, but I was also sexually repressed — that was the world I had come from. Being involved in the sex world enlightened me in every way. It allowed me to have relationships I would never have had otherwise and a life I would never have had. Listen, nothing is perfect, but my experience in this industry has been terrific.

25

Nina Hartley
Heart-On Girl

Throughout her twenty-eight years in the X-rated film industry, Nina Hartley, with her blonde, shoulder length hair, and vibrant, blue eyes comprehensively epitomizes the term "Golden Goddess." Leading by example as a health professional turned sex worker, turned authoritative sex educator and theorist, the tireless fifty-three year old self-titled "MILF," openly advocates for women and men to own, understand and embrace their sexuality fearlessly and without shame. Free of religious indoctrinations she feels create a culture of fear and guilt about an individual's inherent need to seek, explore, provide and receive sexual nourishment, Nina confessed she got into the pornographic film trade in part, so she could live out her own sexual fantasies without emotional commitment. Hartley admitted she is an attention seeker and believes the same is true of anyone who derives income as an entertainer.

Nina Hartley was born Marie Hartman in Berkeley, California just two years after her father was terminated from his employment. During the first ten years of her childhood, Nina saw her parents struggle for survival as her father coped over the loss of his role as breadwinner while her mother worked fulltime to sustain the family of six. In an effort to keep their marriage intact and family together, Hartley's parents dabbled in diverse spiritual outlets, finally settling upon Zen Buddhism which teaches: "life is subject to change, and disenchantment and suffering are a result of an attachment to things which are not permanent." Guided by her communicative and expressive character, as the exceedingly bright Hartley grew older, she joined a fantasy playgroup and realized roleplaying provided her with a means to exercise her demonstrative and extroverted persona that would eventually become her signature in adult movies. Hartley was transformed at seventeen years old when she watched

"A lot of my ability to be a healed person is because of sex and sexuality. It's not just my livelihood. I'm a true believer in my desire for every person to be at home in their body."

NINA HARTLEY

PHOTO COURTESY OF NINA HARTLEY

the Mitchell Brothers' pornographic adaptation of the erotic novel *The Autobiography of a Flea* (1976) on the big screen.

During her studies to become a registered nurse at San Francisco State University, Hartley auditioned as a novice dancer at a Sutter St. club that led to work as a peep show girl, and a stripper at the Mitchell Brothers' O'Farrell Theatre. She graduated magna cum laude in 1985, a year after she made her show-stopping debut as "Aunt Peg's" over eager protégé in *Educating Nina* (1984) produced and directed by Juliet Anderson. In addition to her extensive resumé of work in adult entertainment, Hartley played William H. Macy's promiscuous spouse in Paul Thomas Anderson's *Boogie Nights* (1997).

Over the past two decades, Nina has learned how to shrewdly combine her love for sex with business through the development of her own line of instructional videos (more than thirty-eight titles) that instruct about all regions of the sexual spectrum in a manner that is professional, fun, and educational. She published *Nina's Guide to Total Sex* in 2006.

Along with her mate of more than ten years, Ernest Greene, Hartley enjoys the domestic life, and when time allows, extracurricular sex partners, an arrangement the couple has successfully adapted to their lifestyle without compromising their union or legal partnership.

Nina wholeheartedly lives up to her reputation as the beloved and sexy, intellectual, iconic celebrity who gave birth to her career during the twilight hours of the adult golden age.

With my seatbelt firmly fastened, I spoke with Nina Hartley in June 2010.

Marie Hartman

I was born in 1959 in Berkeley, California to parents who were politically very left of centre. Berkeley is a very family-friendly place; at least it was at that time.

My father had been blacklisted in 1957 for being a member of the Communist party and had lost his very good, high profile, radio-hosting job in San Francisco. I have three older siblings so I was born after the fall so to speak, after my father's fall from grace. My mother had three kids in five years, and then five years later, I was born. The others are five, seven, and nine years older than I am. There was nothing in common so I was mostly alone and alienated from a very early age.

The first ten years of my life were spent with my parents struggling to get their footing. They had to figure out what was going on in their lives while grieving over the loss of success. My father suffered depression over losing his role as primary breadwinner. My mother was frustrated and had resentment over having to become the major breadwinner during a time when it wasn't common for women. All the while, they were trying to keep the family together. I know they must have bickered a lot. I don't remember fights in front of the kids, but I was lonely as a young child because my parents were very, very other focused. I grew up with a housekeeper. We had a housekeeper/nanny come in five days a week so I had non-parental care when I was very little. My mother had been born in Alabama; she'd had a housekeeper/nanny as well because that's just what was done then. It was considered normal. I don't know what job my father had when I was very little. They both worked, but by the time I was in first grade my father became basically, a househusband and we no longer had the housekeeper. We lived near a school and I got to walk to grade school and things like that.

If my parents had not been so focused on survival I would have been the apple of my parents' eyes. My mother's biggest regret was that she couldn't stay home and raise me. She wanted to do it right this time, she wanted to breast feed for longer and she wanted to do all of those things, so this was a real source of sadness for her.

I'm the most like my father, but I am a part of whatever aspects of their character and nature they have. I'm very scientific like my mother and very dreamy like my father. He was a very esoteric person and a writer while my mother had science interests. They've both been Buddhists for forty years which is something they discovered in trying to figure out what they were going to do. They tried everything, they tried marriage counseling, group counseling, bioenergetics, biofeedback, naked Tai Chi, guided mescaline counseling — this was the sixties in Berkeley, man. They never tried Hare Krishna thank god, but they were definitely seekers and early adopters of these early movements. My mother was also an early adopter of feminist critique theory and she was educated. They finally figured out that if they didn't find something they could do together, the marriage was over. They didn't really believe in divorce. They'd had a very romantic marriage that had been knocked for a loop. They found Zen and they really took to it, they liked the devotional lifestyle. My mother was typically Jewish, there's no monastic experience in traditional Judaism. My father was very Protestant, there's no monastic practice in Protestant religion, but they're both very monastic people. They like the community, they like the vows, they like the devotional aspect of the life of a monk and they've stuck with it for forty years. In sixth months, they'll have been married for sixty-three years.

"Monastic" defines a devotee of a specific faith whereby its followers such as monks or nuns spend time in seclusion for the purposes of meditation or prayer. A Monastic strives to remain free of the distractions of the secular world and follows strict rules designed to assist with the daily guidance of believers. Zen Buddhists also practice formal disciplinary measures in order to seek wisdom and enlightenment.

I myself am an Atheist, but I do understand the appeal and the value in the devotional lifestyle. Even in Atheism, you have principles that you live by. Atheism has a value system that you try to embody which is one of the things that's kept me going all these years. It's not just my own need and love for attention, but because I have a mission to get to talk about sex and sexuality, and sexual expression out there in the world from my own experience. It's not just theory such as "Let's study pornography and develop a theory about it that supports my icky feeling about it." Most people who write about pornography have a tendency to impugn all kinds of motives that introduce hostility to pornography. Their paranoid conspiracy theories drive me insane. People don't like to have to take personal responsibility. "We're all victims". There are identity politics and victim politics, but there needs to be some relaxation. My childhood does affect how I act today. However, that being said, and I am liberal, there is that personal responsibility.

Emotionally disconnected from her older siblings and often her own parents during her childhood, Nina immersed herself inside of a world of books, music and films. As a young girl, Hartley's mind and imagination were keen, and early on, she was able to differentiate between herself and other children creating a feeling of estrangement from her peers.

As a child, I had a tremendous fantasy world — I wanted to go study chimpanzees. Helen Keller was an early hero. I've had a good Liberal Rights upbringing. I must have read *Gone with the Wind* twenty-two times, unfortunately. I love Revisionist History to the max — I'm into the Civil War. I love costumes and dramas. I loved *The Sound of Music* (1965), and I love musicals. I used to work at the Renaissance Country Fair. There was a fantasy playgroup in America called The Society for Creative Anachronism (SCA). Back before we knew the term "computer geeks" this was a group of people who got together to recreate Medieval England. It's a fabulous nationwide fantasy playgroup. I grew up doing that kind

XRCO awards, late 1980s.

of stuff on weekends. It's a lot of fun and we'd enter tournaments. I really loved costumes and playacting from a very early age, although, I was too shy in high school to be on stage. I became a part of the costume department. I don't love clothes that much. I'm more of a nudist, but I do love costume and theater and theatrical things. They make the kind of kinky sex I have nowadays really a lot of fun because of the costumes and role-playing, and things like that.

I'm very intellectual and I like music, but, I was not music talent in high school. I still don't play my iPod. I can't work and have music on in the background. Music means something more to me than noise. I can't think with words so if I have to listen to it, and if I try to think with words, it's just distracting. I never have music playing here in the house when we are just hanging out or anything like that. I'm a jazz fan and I love dance: modern, jazz, tap, ballroom. I never did ballet. I have the wrong body style for it. I was not competitive. Sports or team sports did not compel me at all. I've never been competitive in a way that my blood races and my heart rate will go up at the idea of beating somebody. It doesn't interest me at all. I've not come to like sports as a spectator, although I've grown to like American football and basketball. I like watching golf, but I don't have that individual competitive drive.

By the time I was ten, my father said I came home from school one day and said, "I'm an oddball." I knew by eight that I was not like other kids. I felt very alienated from them. I don't know why I felt alienated. I realize now that I was a queer child, but I wasn't gay. I don't know how many gay folks you talk to who know by first grade that this is who they are. They spend the next fifteen years getting okay with it before they come out of the closet and tell their parents. I wasn't gay, but I knew I wasn't like other kids. It had nothing to do with sex, because I wasn't having sex, I was ten. I was interested in sexuality already at age ten. At that point, it was about plumbing. How does it work? What's it called and where's it located, that kind of thing. It wasn't about how sex pertained to me personally, but it was about sex as a concept.

I made out in high school at the theater wrap parties, but I didn't have intercourse until I was eighteen. If I'd had better social skills, I would certainly have been doing fellatio and hand jobs sooner. I was interested in boys. I would have liked to have done it with girls too because by the time I was twelve I was interested in girls, and by the time I was fourteen, I realized I was a bi-sexual person. That was the good thing about living in the seventies and Berkeley because early on, I had labels for these desires that I had. Because I wasn't raised religiously, I had no shame or guilt. It's like being Jewish. Terms like, "hell," "sin," "damnation" were not part of my language. I never had a moment where I wondered what was wrong with me. I thought, "Okay, here's a label and there are other people out there who are like me! I need to go and find them." It took me a long time to find them, but I realized there are a lot of people out there who are like me and we are now finding each other. I definitely was not an early adopter when it came to sex. I didn't know how to be alone with anybody.

"Why sex, why not the violin?"

I wondered if Nina attributed her home environment as part of the reason why she sought affirmation through her unusual career choice, despite alternative and easier paths she could have chosen given her superior intellect and knowledge.

Certainly, nature versus nurture is relevant and what part of our environment triggers certain responses located within our genes to express themselves. I was a very thinking child. Our family had a relatively high IQ. Values, inquiry, examination and those kinds of things were a part of my growing up. I've often said that if I hadn't been so exhibitionistic, and if I wasn't considered attractive enough to be an exhibitionist, I would have been a mid-wife and very active on the weekends. It turned out that having a camera present coincided with the fact that people considered me pretty enough to pay me to do this. I don't know why sexuality became my thing. My father asked me, "Why sex, why not the violin?" I clearly was designed to study one thing my whole life. It could have been studying bacterium in a laboratory, it could have been studying gorillas in the Congo, it could have been pottery in Japan, or it could have been anything for all of these years. It turned out for me to be sexuality, both as an interest for my own needs, and as a health professional. I tend to say I'm a scientist and that is a constant. Pornography is my laboratory and I've had a steady stream of subjects.

There are a lot of people who get into porn who don't have these ideas. They are needy and aren't all positively affected by their experiences in porn, but there are also people coming into porn who are victims of American culture. They are usually Gentile and Christian denomination, so they're not only coming into porn with their own issues, but they have that entire cultural guilt, sin, shame, damnation, hell element that has them conflicted about their sexuality. I grew up in the seventies and I don't have a conflict about my sexuality because the seventies manifesto told women that we

have the right to live our lives the way we wanted it — to do it in a responsible manner and take responsibility for your orgasms. There is no "knight in shining armor". Learn how to give yourself orgasms. Learn how to give pelvic exams oneself — you know — consciousness-raising groups.

I was fourteen when Roe vs. Wade was decided. I knew to my core how important that was that if women do not control fertility there is absolutely no way we can be equal which is why I wanted to be a mid-wife. It's why I wanted to deal with women's issues and women's bodies. I'm still terribly interested. If I'd become a mid-wife I'd now be the nation's foremost authority on water births. That's what I would have wanted to do.

"Jane Roe" is the alias used by Norma McCorvey who filed a suit in the early 1970s citing that abortion laws in Texas encroached upon her constitutional right to choose to terminate her pregnancy. Dallas County District Attorney Henry Menasco Wade (who famously prosecuted Jack Ruby for the murder of Lee Harvey Oswald) was the named defendant in the case. On January 22, 1973, the Supreme Court overturned the Texas definition of abortion law effectively making abortion legal in the United States. The Roe vs. Wade decision ruled that a woman could abort her child during the first trimester of pregnancy under her doctor's guidance and without restrictions imposed on her or her right to privacy compromised. In an unusual twist thirty years later in 2003, Norma McCorvey (now a Christian) filed a motion in Texas to re-open her case and have the ruling overturned.

I wasn't so bold as to want to become a lay mid-wife, but I wanted the letters after my name to be a nurse-mid-wife. Then I realized that in our culture, sexuality is sick and sick people needed nurse's care. I also went into pornography to heal my own sexual issues so I just needed to go and study it a lot. Being a professional performer helped me because I could compartmentalize it. I didn't have to pretend to be in a relationship. I didn't have to care what you think about me tomorrow.

Nina's liberal childhood combined with a healthy, enriched education and self-awareness through the advent of books, resource materials, and role models, set the pendulum into motion. As a young teen, Hartley first discovered adult magazines and erotic writing. She realized the sexualized world was her oyster.

I got to be around nudist situations when I was twelve or thirteen years old and I loved it. I knew I wasn't supposed to stare, but I was completely fascinated by all of the different bodies and by what happened to boy's parts when they crossed their legs. When I was fourteen years old in 1973, it was the height of the sexual revolution and I knew this very swinging couple. They had a new

COURTESY OF WORTH MENTIONING PUBLIC RELATIONS

baby, and they had a waterbed and a padded frame and a full-length mirror, and a great collection of pornography magazines underneath the bed. At fourteen, both at their home and at a used bookstore in Berkeley, I discovered written pornography and loved it! I found that certain stories appealed to me and certain activities I thought were a lot of fun, sex activities and so on. Of course, I collected my share of *Playboys* and I loved looking at the women. I was never traumatized by looking at pornography. I never looked at my body and said, "I don't look like these women" because I'd also loved looking at classical art, and I recognized that even to this day I prefer a rounder more classically-shaped female. I never had the body image issues that American girls seem to have all of the time now.

I went to a couple of orgies in the seventies before I got into porn and as much as I always wanted to be at one, I was terribly uncomfortable because the people who were at them were Americans who had been messed up by the culture and I was intellectually, extremely evolved. I was already comfortable with my sexuality and could be with other people like me. My sexuality bothered everybody. I had a lot of boyfriends who were upset that I wasn't a monogamous person.

Now, we have the term "polyamorous" and the gay pride movement. Today, there are workshops on polyamory and how to negotiate polyamorous relationships. It's come a long way. Back then, in the seventies, "key" parties and wife swapping was shady. There was no word for what it was. People would call me shallow and fickle, and afraid of commitment. I just never fantasized having only one partner. This is going back to when I was eight or nine and I'd look at these after school movies with the schoolmarm having to choose between the rancher and the city boy. I never understood why she had to choose. I didn't even know about intercourse then, but I realized that it seemed to me that she shouldn't have to choose. I just never, ever understood that.

I believe that some people are monogamous, and for them jealousy offers a different function. For the most part, with jealousy there is a twinge of, "Hey, I don't like my partner doing that." I do believe that sexual jealousy is a culturally learned emotion.

I cured my own jealousy when I realized that jealousy is a function of insecurity and not about the person. Our feelings are never about the other person. Our feelings are always about us, about our story and our narrative. Another person acts as a trigger, a mirror, a conduit or whatever, but it's not their fault. Their behavior doesn't regulate my emotions. When I was twenty, I thought differently, but again, if I had been a monogamous person I would have said, "Jealousy is normal. I don't want him doing anybody else. I have a right to my feelings." I wasn't monogamous and I had fantasies of multiple partners. If I hadn't had the cultural support of me as a woman being able to have my own life on my own terms, I would have just said, "I can't have what I want. It's wrong. I'm too greedy. I just want too much." I got to have the life I've wanted with multiple partners. I didn't want multiple partners to be a problem with anybody. I didn't want to hurt anybody's feelings. I was just this way.

For me, the seventies were a good thing. They let me know that I could have the life I wanted. Jealousy was in the way of that. Jealousy was about our insecurity. That being said, if your partner is acting like a jerk, then that's a conversation you have to have. If you can tell that they're doing this to piss you off, then you have to have a discussion that might lead to the end of the relationship. The idea of, "You make me feel bad! You stop that." That is three-year old behavior. For many people when their sex issues are triggered, they revert to being six year olds because that's when our sexuality is stunted as a negative influence of their parents. "Don't touch that. That's your pee-pee. That's your gadget. That's your widget." There is no information. It's all very "bad". We put the adult behavior on top of that, but when it comes to sex which is a very primal thing along with our longing for acceptance and affection, all of a sudden, presto — we're back to how old we were when the initial trauma happened. It didn't have to be a molestation or rape trauma; it could just be whatever bullshit your family of origin laid on you about sex and the body. Our culture places such an unrealistic expectation on romantic love. "If you love me, you're supposed to accept me as I am." A person can be a very reasonable, mature individual, but when she gets her snit on, suddenly, she's five fucking years old. I don't fuck five year olds even if they're in the body of a twenty-five year old. It's about personal responsibility. It's not my job to make you feel okay. It's my job to check in with you and find out about your fears and to make sure I don't trigger them accidentally, but it's not my job to do your psychotherapy.

Feeding the Cookie Monster

One of the books I'd read when I was a teenager was classic Victorian pornography titled *The Autobiography of a Flea* (1887). I loved that story. It was so much fun! I was seventeen and a senior in high school when the adult movie theatre they still had in Berkeley that is no longer there was showing *The Autobiography of a Flea* (1976). I thought, "Oh, my god! I'll have to go to the movie." I was a virgin, and I'd necked in high school and I liked all that stuff, but it was like, "Alone with a boy? Are you crazy?" You had to talk to them. I decided I was going to see the movie. One day after school, I went into the theatre thinking, "Please don't card me." It was 1976 and they weren't going to card anybody. I sat down in the theater and I thought to myself, "Please no one sit next to me." A single female in a porno theatre was like a drop of soap in greasy water. The men just moved away from me. There was a ten-foot radius clear. I wasn't thinking it at the time, but I guess in a way I was trespassing.

The movie had Annette Haven, John Leslie, John Holmes and Paul Thomas. I ended up doing two of the three guys later which was funny. I was sitting in the middle of the theatre, I don't remember what scene it was but it was also a costume drama, which I loved.

The Mitchell Brothers' feature *The Autobiography of a Flea* is a porn revision of the erotic novel (written by a London lawyer, Stanislas de Rhodes) directed by (part-time cabaret singer) Sharon McNight. Set in France, the tale is told by a flea housed within the pubic hair of the heroine Belle (Jean Jennings) who details Belle's seduction. Belle enjoys multiple sexual encounters with the church clergy played humorously by John Leslie, John Holmes and Paul Thomas. The film delves into all of the taboo subjects of the original book with incestuous situations and satirical looks at the inequities in life.

Watching this movie in the middle of this theater, my inner Cookie Monster looked at the screen and said, "Me want to do that!" I wasn't expecting anything to happen, I just wanted to go and look at people parts. I wanted to see the movie because I'd read the book. Remember, I'd been into dance and musicals and theatre and the body, this had everything that I wanted. It had group nudity, it was about sex, and it was a performance. The film came out eight years before I made my first movie, but I knew then that was what I wanted to do. I wanted to start making porn the next year when I was eighteen, but I also knew that I was not emotionally prepared to be on a movie set. I waited until I was able to do it sober.

In the years before she became an adult entertainment star, Hartley was a college student and found employment part-time in a club as a stripper to help lessen the financial burden of working toward a career in nursing. With very limited experience as a feature dancer, the young apprentice picked up a few invaluable pointers from the experts.

I ran into a friend on the bus to school and she said she was dancing at this one place, and I said, "Really? That's cool. I didn't even know that existed." Then I went to the Sutter St. Cinema and did Amateur Night. It was also Amateur Photography Night. Guys could pay their ten bucks to get in and take pictures of the dancers. I was terribly excited that finally seven years after my first fantasy of doing this, I was going to be on stage! I got a cheesy costume — I didn't know anything about music. I didn't know anything about make-up and I wasn't even shaving my legs yet because I wasn't a leg shaver. I knew very little about feminine display and feminine dress, but I went into the dressing room with these women and I was terrified because they clearly were professionals. They were slapping on their bracelets and yakking with each other. They were confident and completely unfazed. They were all ringers: because they were there for the fifty bucks they got to show up and compete. They weren't going to win. I ended up winning because I was the only amateur. I saw some pictures from that day. I won and I got a job as a peep show girl where they were doing girl-girl shows. It was everything I wanted. I got some girl-girl action which is another reason why I got into porn because that's where the naked women were. People were watching, but they were behind a window so I couldn't actually see them. I got very comfortable with everything in a great environment. This is before I worked for the Mitchell Brothers and danced proper as a stripper. It was another year and a half before I graduated. I did a dildo show, and live, hardcore, girl-girl which was fun and it was great. It was actually fabulous. I did my first movie in my junior year. When I graduated in `85, I went into movies full time.

A few years prior to Nina's unveiling in adult films, at the age of nineteen, Hartley met and married her first husband David. The couple soon added a third party to the union, an anti-censorship feminist and activist (and member of Feminists for Free Expression) by the name of Bobby Lilly. Lilly and David had actually been involved prior to Hartley and David's meeting. In an interview Hartley gave to Sheldon Ranz

COURTESY OF WORTH MENTIONING PUBLIC RELATIONS

several years ago, she stated when the small group was still in full swing; Nina believed the threesome worked because of the stability, support, and perspective of objectivity that three can lend to a relationship. Hartley used the examples of a tricycle and a tripod as a simile to illustrate the security of three points in a ménage a trios. The triad apparently continued for twenty years before the group had a parting of the ways. Hartley no longer discusses the threesome or the situation since the termination of the relationship.

Buoyed by freedom from religious guilt, Nina claimed she was able to competently launch a career in adult movies with a crystal clear conscience about what she was doing. In her first feature film *Educating Nina* (1984) the nubile Nina Hartley made her debut along with her most remarkable asset, her rear end. Nina was escorted into the genre of erotic movies as a protégé under the guardianship of the classic golden age MILF, Aunt Peg, much to the delight of discerning spectators.

My husband at the time ran into Juliet [Anderson] at a grocery store and got her card. We sent her pictures and she put me in my first movie. She was a very interesting person and it was just very, very sad to learn of her recent death. Without "Aunt Peg," I don't know what would have happened. We'd already met a couple of agents, but eeewweeeoooo. I thought, "I guess I'm not going to get to do it." I didn't want to work for creepy guys. It was like Central Casting Agents, blah. Aunt Peg was a nice middle class woman, and well educated, so it was great.

Educating Nina

Educating Nina was my first movie in 1984. *Looking for Lust in all the Right Places* (1984) was also one of the first ten features [I did] shot on film, certainly. Shauna Grant had killed herself two weeks prior to my first movie in March of 1984.

Hartley's induction to the X-rated industry in *Educating Nina* (1984), a movie that was influenced by another Hollywood hit film *Educating Rita* (1983) starring Michael Caine and Julie Walters, turned out to be a big-league effort on the part of Nina for her first time to the plate. Hartley adopted the role of a young, ebullient drama student with an imaginative idea for her term paper on the relationship between individual's sex lives and their fantasies. She suggests to her classmates they act out various sexual fantasies submitted by audience members in attendance at a live sex demonstration. Appearing in two unforgettable expositions, Nina effortlessly gears up for some girl-on-girl combat with Karen Summers, and then cruises into pleasure seeking merriment with male stripper Billy Dee as the young attractive couple grind it out. Lili Marlene, Mike Horner and others help keep the feature lively until the closing scene where the

COURTESY OF WORTH MENTIONING PUBLIC RELATIONS

sensuous roundup is punctuated by director Juliet Anderson, Lili Marlene and Dan T. Mann. Hartley flaunts playful spontaneity, personal style and star quality in this preliminary submission emphasizing the point that young Nina is well educated indeed.

When my first picture was made in 1984, film was dying a brutal death. I was probably only in ten that were shot on film, so I was the overlap. Now, I did work with all of the performers. Back in the day, I worked with John Leslie and Joey Silvera and Billy Dee and Jamie Gillis, and all of the holdover men from the golden age. I worked once or twice with Colleen Brennan [in two 1986 productions, *Lady by Night* and *Getting Personal*], and I worked one time with Vanessa Del Rio [*Play Me Again, Vanessa*] in 1984-85. I did one movie [*Beyond Desire*, 1986] with Seka [and Francois Papillion] when I was "Who the hell is she?" They put me in a black wig because I guess there could only be one blonde woman in the scene.

Seka is a real pistol. She's only a few years older than I am, but when I met her, she seemed infinitely older because I was this naïve, college town kid and she'd had a real life for lack of a better word. There was no fluff about her. She was all business. Even today, you won't get a picture of her free. I say, "You go girl". Good for her. She knows what it is she's selling. She's had a harder life than some of us have and she's learned her lesson. Now she has a new husband and a nice life so I say, "Good for her." She still makes money being "Seka," which I think is amazing.

All of my experiences in adult films have been positive. Even situations where other people have said, "Oh, my god, they were horrible assholes. I really did not want to be there," things that other people would be upset over, I didn't even notice. Different people have different things that bug them. Again, my not having religion to give me grief about sin and damnation, I'm sure that is the primary reason why I've done so well here. I see what the business does to people and it just cripples them. I look at them and think, "Poor guy. There's nobody in the sky. It's okay."

It's interesting, in San Francisco, even before I got into the industry, it was never a problem to make sex films. L.A. absolutely, until 1988 before the Freeman decision, actively chased people around. You'd plan to make a movie, you'd meet in the parking lot and all get in the van and go somewhere else. It was really cat and mouse and they still managed to bust enough sets that there definitely was a climate of fear and of nervousness. They didn't want to arrest anybody; they wanted to terrorize them which they did. They wanted to terrorize the performers especially women into giving up the names of the people who had hired them. They threatened to charge them with prostitution and tell their family. You're talking about eighteen, nineteen, twenty-year old women. One woman did actually turn in states evidence to get Hal Freeman which is what started that whole chain reaction. He just said, "No, I'm not going to take this." On one hand, it was legal to make porn so we'd buy permits, and if a police officer came to the front door and said "I'm sorry," if they started to complain, as long as we had the windows covered and the permit to show him, he had to go away. He couldn't come onto the set to bother anybody. That's definitely a positive.

It's not entirely true that San Francisco's vice squad didn't make arrests or charge filmmakers and actors with obscenity and other offenses pertaining to the production of pornographic films prior to the Freeman decision. During the 1970s, the Mitchell Brothers were arrested in several instances, as were headliners such as Marilyn Chambers who appeared frequently at the O'Farrell Theatre. Often, police and/or proprietors of hotels or rental properties where films were made would look the other way. Former director Bob Chinn recently mentioned many of the sex scenes for his seventies films were shot at the Holiday Inn located at San Francisco's Fisherman's Wharf and the non-sex scenes were shot in Los Angeles. The crew would generally film late at night which resulted in exceedingly high electricity bills for the hotel. Eventually, after the manager of the Holiday Inn caught on as to the exact nature of Chinn's business, Bob was asked to leave along with his cast and crew. They were not welcomed back.

Contrary to what some of her contemporaries believe, Nina is adamant that eighties video porn is a step-up from celluloid.

People call the 1970s "The Golden age of Porn," but I call it a dark and dreary place. The grooming and the lighting got much better in the eighties with video. The cameras were smaller and required less light. The girls started shaving their lips so that you could at least see "it". The early porn isn't always so sexy when the grooming left a lot to be desired. People were very, very furry — him and her. Back in the seventies, most people didn't think they were doing anything revolutionary. It was like, "Oh, my god, let's get high and get paid a hundred bucks!" Why not? Nobody ever thought about a stigma being attached. Back then, if you stopped doing porn it was highly unlikely that you would run into anyone who would recognize you. If you wanted to, you could leave. Once video porn started, and once porn entered mainstream it was a lot more difficult. Now a lot of my early work that I did in the eighties is coming back out.

Nina is correct in asserting the first generation of performers didn't likely consider stigmatization when they set out to appear in early loops, eight or sixteen millimeter films. Forty years after the fact with video and DVD, in conjunction with the available preservation technologies combined with the internet, tube sites, and zealous interest in vintage works on the part of adult film fans, historians and production companies, industry pioneers have entered into perpetuity.

Naughty Girl

Some of Hartley's early movies produced in 1984 and 1985 are available as VOD and on DVD: *Butter Me Up* (1984), *Ball Busters* (1985), *Thought You'd Never Ask* (1985), *Shaved Bunnies* (1985), *Naughty Girls like it Big* (1986) and the award-winning *Debbie Duz Dishes* (1986).

Naughty Girls Like it Big (directed by Bob Vosse, known for the success of Swedish Erotica) is a recipe for success with attractive women, well-equipped men and hot sex scenes. Four gorgeous girlfriends (Hartley, Angel Kelly, Porsche Lynn, and Lili Marlene) hook up for a reunion and bring one another up to speed on the details of their past and current love lives. Their discussion quickly turns to the subject of length, and it becomes clear the four girls are size queens. Taking turns through flashback mode, the women vividly describe their libidinous experiences with well-endowed males (as the title suggests), as the chatter continues, the steamier the room becomes. Porsche goes first and gushes while detailing how she'd seduced a young virgin (Tom Byron) in a kitchen chair prior to Angel's confession about a tawdry first encounter with her former, sweet talking teacher (John Holmes) in the classroom after hours. Reluctant at first to kiss and tell, Lili shyly discloses an incident which occurred during a routine visit with her physician (Ron Jeremy) that included a third party (Alexis Greco) on top of the doctor's desk. Last, but certainly not least, Nina tops all three accounts when she divulges how she arrived one morning at a construction site, scantily clad, and after teasing the guys she proceeded to get it on with the two lucky stiffs (Mike Horner and Buddy Love, although neither one is particularly known as the "biggest" in the biz). All the sexy talk inspires Angel to call upon her accommodating boyfriend (Jerry Butler) who arrives just in time to entertain the girlfriends in bed. Nina appears to thoroughly enjoy herself in both

COURTESY OF WORTH MENTIONING PUBLIC RELATIONS

montages, and had no difficulty managing Horner and Love or the larger group. After all, Hartley was already a pro in 1986 after having appeared in dozens of movies.

> People probably thought in the beginning that I was on cocaine because it was the eighties, but I was just so happy to be there. I liked being there. I didn't need to be high. I have a mission — you can't be on a mission when you're not sober.

Hartley's performance in *Debbie Duz Dishes* (also directed by Bob Vosse) is nothing short of delightful. As a newlywed and former socialite, Debbie (Hartley) is overwhelmed by a mounting sink full of dishes in her new home just three days after her wedding to handsome hubby David (Mike Horner). Once David leaves for work, Debbie receives a call from her concerned Jewish mother who bluntly informs her: "Nice Jewish girls don't do dishes." Mom urges her daughter to have the marriage annulled. When Debbie explains the notion is preposterous because she and David already consummated their marriage, her mother is disgusted and abruptly dismissed while still in mid-sentence. In a style reminiscent of 1970s sitcoms, Debbie, as cheerful as ever (and almost naked) opens the door to a succession of visitors to the home. Kirby (Jerry Butler), a door-to-door salesman brandishing some rather unique genitalia attachments has Debbie enthralled when he offers to demonstrate an electric dildo device causing her to quickly climax after only a few thrusts. Next, he tries on a little gadget that helps to elongate his organ. Suddenly, Kirby has a brainstorm — he would rather Debbie assist him in getting hard in place of the gadget which she does lustfully. Shortly thereafter, Debbie's girlfriend Maureen (Keli Richards) arrives on the scene, hoping to talk some sense into her best friend about the dos and don'ts of married life. When the girls are interrupted by another houseguest Hank (Billy Dee), Debbie realizes Kirby is nowhere to be seen. The three head upstairs to the bedroom to find the salesman seemingly lifeless on the ground next to the bed. A green, gooey liquid is observed near his body and the girls determine the old house is haunted with deadly forces at play wielding some kind of potent sexual power over its inhabitants. Leaving little time for concern, the doorbell rings again, and Debbie is off to answer it while Maureen and Hank get to know one another better. Before the day is over, in addition to Hank, Maureen does the two deliverymen (Jon Martin and Roger Scorpio), and Debbie discovers she likes women as well as men.

In the final sex scene, Debbie takes on Jake (Herschel Savage), a weary tow truck driver with an imposing appendage. The movie's strangest moment occurs a few minutes prior to wrapping up when an Exorcist (played by cameraman, former producer and occasional 1970s non-sex performer Damon Christian) arrives to expel all evil forces by placing a ripe apple on a tee and whacking it as hard as he can with a driver towards the house. Amusingly, green goo flies madly away from the old home in every conceivable direction inferring the demons have been fumigated.

The premise for *Debbie Due Dishes* centering on a bored naive housewife with an overactive libido might seem outlandish and dated even by 1980s standards (and it is), but it's important to bear in mind, with few exceptions, adult themed material is not generally intended to be taken seriously.

Obviously, my involvement in adult films was partly for attention. Any performer is in it for the attention. Any entertainer is an
exhibitionist except that they usually leave their clothes on. When
a person gets onstage by herself and everyone is looking at her, she
has to be an exhibitionist. I happen to be a sexual exhibitionist, but
I'm also about doing it in an appropriate way. I'm not going to go
flash my boobs in a bar and chance getting raped. I've worked in a
strip club where there are rules and everyone knows what the deal
is. I just made sure that I was safe. When I gave them permission
to go ahead and film me, I knew there would be people imprinting
on me. I knew that I'd be under the radar. I just knew the power of a
good sex performance. I had a great time. I also had the five-minute
mother hen lecture that is delivered to new performers. What I tell
new performers is "What you don't do at home for free, don't do on
camera for money because it will eventually eat away at your soul."
I also want them to know why they are on a porn set and to own it.
If they're there to say, "Fuck you, Mom," know why you are there.
Today, more young women come into porn that don't have a need
to be high or stoned. They're freaky young people. Today, a polyamorous person or a sexual exhibitionist has a place to go. Instead
of worrying what they're going to be they can make a choice, "Oh,
I can go and make porn. That's cool." Again, if I had not been so
queer, I don't know how my sexuality would have evolved. I might
be in my second or third marriage, I don't know, but because I
recognized that I was bisexual and I'm not monogamous, I wasn't
even able to front as normal. Because I wasn't a heterosexual person
or a monogamous person, I was, by definition, "not normal". Porn
is the only place in culture where you can talk about sex somewhat
openly. People still snicker and say, "Why did you do it, why didn't
you do Hollywood?" I wasn't pretty enough to do Hollywood. I
wasn't talented enough. I wasn't driven enough. Hollywood turns
you away at the last minute every time.

Passion Within

Hartley began to rack up praise from critics early on in her career
(consisting of well over seven hundred titles) for her acting ability and
sexual capability. Nina often appeared alongside colleague Billy Dee in
feature showcases. She made an impact functioning as Dee's client in
Jack Hammer (1987), a detective story written by the late-1980s porn

personality, Viper, in which Hartley's character seeks to be penetrated by a custom dildo.

One year earlier, the affecting 1986 release, *The Passion Within*, with co-stars John Leslie and Annette Haven, is still regarded a personal best and is a very watchable love story/drama. Nina assumes the part of a lonely divorcee and writer, Abby, looking to meet Mr. Right. Her best girlfriend (persuasively played by the lovely Annette Haven in a non-sex role) has good intentions by introducing Abby to several candidates (Joey Silvera and Jon Martin do a fine job as indifferent, bumbling duds) each of whom fails to live up to Abby's expectations in and outside of the bedroom. While out shopping one afternoon, Abby mistakenly drops her purse in a parking lot. It is retrieved by Ted (John Leslie), an artist who has not only lost his creative muse, but he owes a debt to some under-handed characters. (Ted supplements his deficient income by sleeping with beautiful women married to powerful men, as is depicted earlier in a tempestuous sexual exchange between Leslie and Shanna McCullough.) Ted returns the purse to Abby, but harbors her diary and begins to learn about her life and yearnings. A few days later, Abby and Ted literally "bump" into one another again while out jogging, and are immediately mutually attracted. A tender romance begins to blossom. Abby and Ted manifest their passion in two beautiful love scenes analogous to watching a romance novel come to life — this is not a wham-bam job. As profes-sionals in their craft, Hartley and Leslie efficiently signify a true and veritable infatuation with deep warmth and affection.

Unfortunately, Ted's private life begins to wreak havoc once McCullough's ruthless husband (Richard Pacheco in a terrific non-sex appearance) discovers how his wife is spending his money. Hubby pays a visit to Ted's studio, informing Ted he's interested in showing the art-ist's unique sculptures at several art shows, on the condition Ted pay a price for his favor by imbibing in some male-on-male sex. Angrily, Ted declines the offer; as a result, Ted is roughed up by Pacheco's goons with more serious ramifications to follow if he doesn't comply with Pacheco's offer of compensation for pleasuring his wife. Unsure of where to turn next, Ted hurries over to Abby's apartment. Unintentionally, he confesses about having kept her diary while urging her to join him in leaving town. Stunned, feeling manipulated and hurt for believing in Ted, Abby shows him the door and cries herself to sleep. Back at the studio, Ted realizes in order to have any chance for real happiness and a future with Abby he must turn around his life. He accepts a standing job offer as an auto-mobile salesman, and after inking a heartfelt and loving inscription, Ted returns Abby's diary to her through the mail. Genuinely moved by his words, Abby forgives Ted.

The Passion Within (directed by Will Kelly) is finely scripted, deftly acted (including a nifty non-sex cameo by Billy Dee) and well suited for couples and individuals unfamiliar or even dubious about watching adult material. Hartley won AVN Best Actress award in 1987.

Pleasure Centre

Hartley's enormous wealth of experience as a 1980s performer and actor irrevocably lead to her role as an educator and sexual healer where the body, mind and soul are unified. There is ample resource material available to support the concept that the body, mind, emotion, and spirit are reciprocally connected. If a modification transpires with one of the components of the overall system, an interactive effect is encountered at all levels. Hartley is a proponent of the ideology there is a fundamental and concise correspondence between the four constituents. It is her belief the human body governs over all memory including sexual memories and memories the mind strives to block. Nina is convicted about educating others how to embrace the benefits of an intimate body-mind experience in order to embrace sexual freedom.

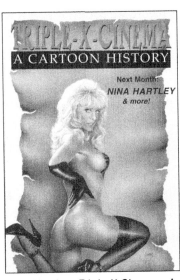

Nina Hartley, *Triple X Cinema: A Cartoon History.*

For me, sex is the thing. Sex is personal. As a seventies therapy person, there is all this stuff about kinesthetic memory and all of our ills can be addressed and healed when we learn to be at peace with our bodies now. Meditation is good for that, but some people have difficulty sitting still for five minutes. They're not comfortable in their bodies at all. Sex and sexuality is a primary way into the body to heal it because sex is so primal that when we're triggered, those urges can't be ignored, they can't be glossed over. Pleasure is a wonderful carrot to help us through the scary parts, and pleasure is our birthright as humans. Humans have an amazing sexual response cycle that has been stunted in every culture pretty much, and bruised, and hurt, and hijacked, and ill used, and misused. I write about this a lot. Even if I wasn't a pornographer and if I had not become a mid-wife, I'd have become some kind of dance therapist or something to do with the body, or birthing, or something that uses the body and not just talk therapy. Everything is stored in the body. All of our feelings are stored there and all of our memories and our experiences — even the ones that took place before we had words with which to describe them. When we can help a person to stay within the body, and stay within the pleasure, all sorts of things are revealed. It's certainly worked for me. A lot of my ability to be a healed person is because of sex and sexuality. It's not just my livelihood, but I'm a true believer in my desire for every person to be at home in his or her body. Once we no longer fight our sexual nature, fear it, condemn it, suppress it, or repress it — all this energy is released that can be used for other things. We don't realize how long we've been hitting ourselves in the head with the hammer until we can put the hammer down.

We all need touch. It's a universal human experience. We all need pleasure. We're all wired to have orgasms even though we may be individually different people. Sexual pleasure is an altered state of consciousness; it's like being on psychedelic drugs. You can fast for days, you can do dervish spinning; you can sing, you can do drugs, or you can pray. You can do sleep deprivation, you can humiliate the body and mortify the body. You can claim "God's here!" or you can really work on that pleasure angle. I work on the pleasure angel because I'm Atheist so that doesn't factor into my life.

I've had the "Born Again" experience. I've had the experience with a person that is of such incredible emotional depth and relief and letting go and acceptance and all those things. Even at the time I was having the experience I was saying, "Oh, my God!" If I was a God believer, I'd have to say, "I felt Jesus' love. God saved me." I was saved that day, but I don't have that language. I don't believe in God, so I've realized that the validity of this experience is a psychological state that can be tickled in the mid-brain and accessed on a reliable and regular basis through drugs or pleasure or prayer or whatever. I don't have a God story so I couldn't label it "Jesus". I think He was a human and I believe He lived, but that's about as far as I go with it. I believe man created God and not the other way around. For whatever reason, God gave us sexuality, or Mother Nature gave it.

It's amazing when you think about the human sexual response cycle, especially the female sexual response cycle. Clearly, pleasure is incredibly important for evolution and for human society, or it would not have evolved. We'd all have babies in April or May, but females respond to sexual stimuli three hundred and sixty-five days out of the year — we have no mating season. It's a whole different ball game. Not many creatures have sex for fun excluding a very few. It's unusual, but all things being equal, we can become aroused at any time. We can have pleasure without it having to be September!

Nina Educates the World

By 1994, Hartley began to broaden her objectives in the field as a sexual professional and activist (the star was once arrested in 1993 at a Free Speech Coalition benefit). She devised a premise that would warm her fans while instructing everyday people how to make love like porn stars. As a sexual healer, Nina utilized her background as a nurse coupled with her evolutionary first-hand experience in the adult business as a performer to forge a profitable agreement with Adam and Eve Productions. Hartley proceeded to create a signature line of videos that arouse, entertain and educate the public about sexuality. The videos contain self-explanatory titles such as *Nina Hartley's Guide to Cunnilingus: Under the Hood* (1994), *Nina Hartley's Guide to Anal Sex* (1995), *Nina Hartley's Guide to Oral Sex* (1998), *Nina Hartley's Guide to Spanking* (2005), *Nina Hartley's Guide to Bondage Sex* (2008) and *Nina Hartley's Guide to Great Sex during Pregnancy* (2009). As the consequent years of releases suggests with over thirty-eight titles, Hartley's movies have been well received.

I think the most important thing I've done on camera, obviously, are my educational tapes. I do think that most of my conventional performances are also important in that over twenty-six years they consistently show a woman having a good time and not just a cipher. A lot of my fans are fans because of a particular body part, but half of them at least, have written in with heartfelt thanks saying, "Wow, you really seem to like what you're doing." That really helped me to understand the lie and the smack put on men by people who say, "Oh, men just don't care," or, "They have no feelings," or "They don't care about women." It's so not true. Men are looking for a connection with women as much as women are looking for a connection with men. In our culture with sexuality, the artificial scarcity of sex created by the double standard definitely leave men not only wanting sex, but also intimacy and friendship with women in an affectionate, physical kind of way. For people to find most important about me that "I liked it," gave them hope that I wasn't the only woman in the world who liked sex for its own sake.

I can think of ten scenes that were one hundred percent acting. One percent of what I've done is one hundred percent faked and the rest of it, on a good day — fifty percent real and fifty percent enhanced. On a great day, it's ninety percent real and ten percent tweaked. I'm very happy about my entire body of work. I have to say the educational movies that I've done, and the educational engagements that I've done, speaking to Universities, speaking to future therapists of America, speaking to health care professionals, I'm most pleased about having done. Nurses are trained to be advocates, to educate and role model, to advocate for sexual literacy and sexual health and sexual freedom. I educate people about how to do sex in a more helpful way or a less horrible way, and I role model about how it looks. That's what makes me most proud.

The fact that I do have a college degree behind me, and one in the health profession does give me an "in" where a person who quote/unquote had "only" done porn for the past twenty-six years would not get an in. There are the ones starting out who are twenty-one years old that learn on their own. You can't tell them anything. A couple of women have listened and those who have listened have done the best. All I can do is put out the information and hope that when the *merde* hits the fan, they'll think, "Oh, I remember hearing about this." People have to learn their own lessons and will only listen when they're ready. I let go of attachment to them doing it; that is not my department. They have to live their own lives and make their own mistakes.

Our culture is extremely conflicted about sexuality and conflicted about the role of women. Someone said to me, "But, Nina, why is pornography important?"

My husband said, "Pornography is important because it is our dreams about sex." It has to be kept in the hands of people who care about the subject and care about the topic. Professional football should be left to professional football. Pornography should be left to the freaks and the queers. Sex is their life.

A very famous adult director named Bruce Seven once said, "Behind every successful movie is one man's hard-on." The people who do good work are the people who love the subject matter. The biggest problem in porn relating to my career has been because of the mainstreaming of it, because of the normalization of it. People came into porn that used to be widget salesmen. They weren't sexual

rebels, they weren't outlaws, they weren't sexually unusual people, they weren't queer or swingers or kinky or anything. They were just selling widgets. In order for porn to work, it has to grab you by the guts and the crotch or it fails as pornography. Pornography is designed to arouse you. If it doesn't arouse the people making it, how does it arouse you? It's partly desensitization, but more importantly, if the product being made had passion behind it, you wouldn't become desensitized. Feelings are contagious and the emotion expressed on camera should be real. If you're not numbed out by whatever your drug of choice is, it will get you.

Nina's inference to director Bruce Seven's statement "Behind every successful movie is one man's hard-on," alludes to the general assumption porn is made essentially for men to enjoy, which is undeniably true to a large extent. However, it is also true there is potential for all genders to be stimulated by a given product if it is created with the consumer's best interests in mind as Hartley suggested. Desensitization toward any kind of stimulus is almost inevitable when an individual experiences overexposure even if the object of a person's interest is made with good intentions. In order for certain individuals to remain motivated by sexual material, it is likely they might require alternative classifications of stimuli.

Years ago, I saw a movie in Germany when I was still brand new in the business. It was a day off and I went into town to an Adult Book store arcade to put in deutschmarks. You'd put in one deutschmark for ten minutes or whatever. I remember being stuck on this channel — the people were ugly, yet I was fascinated and I couldn't help but respond authentically in my body toward the scene. I did not like the people but it was so clearly hot for them! They were so deeply into it. I watched in some sort of fascinated horror. I've seen lots of porn, and I can still be moved by material that is made with passion and desire. Desensitization occurs when you are constantly bombarded with bland material. That has been the biggest negative effect of porn in the last couple of decades. The barrier to entry is very low, and the barrier to exit is very high. You know, I don't like horror movies, I don't like scary movies; I don't like SAW movies or any kind of hostile films or blood and gore. I've seen very few Freddie movies, and yet, humans are feeling animals and feelings are contagious — that's the way the brain works. Any good art form: poetry, music, painting, it moves us. If you show genitalia in action, it's pornography.

In the last ten years, the pendulum has reached the limit of how many things you can put into how many holes. What's supposed to be "hot" is excess so the only place porn has left to go is feelings. That makes a lot of people embarrassed, and don't forget, a large amount of people behind the camera themselves are conflicted about sex and relationships. I'd say twenty-five percent of the producers and directors have healthy relationships or are able to have relationships, and the rest are in some form of pain and discomfort over the state of their lives. They'd rather be making action movies; they'd rather be making cable with exploding cars and men with machine guns. Porn ends up being plan "B". You can't put porn on your resume. My husband is a fabulous editor; he could edit any number of mainstream magazines, but what do you put on that resume for the last twenty-six years? The skill sets are the same — spreadsheets and budgets. Again, because the subject matter is what it is and pornography enjoys the status that it enjoys, they watch you on Saturday, but they won't hire you on Monday. That has not changed.

Sasha Grey notwithstanding: Sasha is twenty-two years old. She has a great agent and a great manager, so she might be the first hybrid to enjoy real success in mainstream, unlike Jenna Jameson who only ever did straight adult films. Jenna never did any gangbang or any anal on camera and she has had a certain kind of success in mainstream, but Sasha Grey is crossing over a bit more so we'll see how it goes. The material available on her is much more extreme than Jenna or Traci Lords. Traci Lords has had minor success in some "B" movies, but Traci Lords only has one legal adult movie anyway.

Boogie Nights Revisited

Familiar with Hartley's work, director P.T. Anderson hired Nina to play the promiscuous porn star wife of the assistant director, Little Bill (played by William H. Macy), in the 1997 film *Boogie Nights*. Hartley's character humiliates her husband by randomly engaging in coitus in public forums. Like Jane Hamilton, Hartley's recollections of her experiences on the mainstream film set were mixed.

I had the best time in *Boogie Nights*. I was in the movie because the director was a fan although I did audition for it. Paul [Thomas Anderson] wanted me in that part. I found him to be a good director. He knew what he wanted and he was very calm on set. No histrionics, no waving of the arms, he was very good with me. He treated me like an actor, but nobody except for William H. Macy spoke to me on the set, no other performer. I think Julianne Moore found me terrifying. She never looked me in the eye. Heather Graham did stand next to me on the red carpet and let people take pictures of us together, but I knew that no picture would ever make it into the press. I also knew that I would never be used in any of the press junkets even though I could actually talk. I knew it would never go anywhere else.

It was like a regular movie shoot, but infinitely larger. Instead of one or two days, he had fifty days. I was on set for six days. There are five catering tables instead of one. There is a production manager, and three sub-production managers. Instead of one PA, there are six production assistants, that kind of a thing. A lot of it is "hurry up and wait," and make-up touch ups. That scene where I got shot was about eight or nine takes for that sequence which took most of the day. After each time, I'd have to take off make-up, put on a robe and so on. Having to remember to put my robe back on was the hardest part.

Boogie Nights, NEW LINE HOME VIDEO

I knew that I was hired not only because [P.T. Anderson] is a fan, but also because he wouldn't have to babysit me in the nudity portion. Mainstream performers are very nervous about being nude. They want the set closed with as very few people as possible. For them doing a love scene is very fraught with fear and insecurity so he didn't have to worry about whether or not I had a nipple showing. Anderson behaved appropriately toward me. He never suggested anything like "nudge, nudge, wink; wink". *Boogie Nights* is actually a Hollywood version of the industry. He got some of the details right, but it's the Hollywood version of an industry of which he is not a member, so many grains of salt.

Hartley's integral scene which takes place during a party sequence is pivotal to the subplot. Her explicit sexual exhibition at the social gathering is one of the final straws, serving as an instigator for her husband's (Macy) over the edge behavior on New Year's Eve. Unfortunately, it was not Anderson's intention to provide depth to Hartley's excellent porn star characterization which prevented the audience from having an opportunity to connect with Nina as Little Bill's wife, on any level other than her obvious profession.

Anderson left out two important scenes that would have made my character and Macy's character full people and not just cartoons. He had to cut off thirty minutes of a finished movie to make it fit into theatres. If he'd left out one minute of bad singing with Mark Walhberg, and one minute of that face stomping, my entire part could have been put in. That part he left out, even in the director's cut, are Macy and I arriving at that party where I end up doing that guy in the driveway and leaving that same party later that night. I was so pleased — when we were leaving the party, it was called a tracking shot. They set up some dolly shots so that the camera could move smoothly and Macy and I are just talking from the door to the car. He did that take about twelve times and did it a little bit different each time. I had to work on the nuance and the delivery and it wasn't even in the director's cut. I asked if he could make a reel for me to look at that, and he said, "Yes, of course." Of course, it never happened. To this day, I'm still annoyed because it was a decent little bit of acting and it made my character a full person which he clearly didn't want my character to become. What you see me do there is not a lot of acting. What really pissed me off is the fact that in the tracking two shot going from the party, I'm acting with William Freaking H. Macy, people! Here's proof.

Macy is a wonderful guy. He's a stand-up guy and a wonderful human being. He could not have treated me nicer. He treated me like a fellow actor and not a freak show. During the movie is when he proposed to [*Desperate Housewives* star] Felicity Huffman, that I thought was very sweet. The world needs more William H. Macy. Once the movie was over, I never saw Anderson again except at the party. I flew especially in from New York to attend the wrap party. I knew it was the only party like that I'd ever get to go to! It was a loud, dark, crowded Hollywood party so I saw Macy for a second, I saw Paul Thomas Anderson for a second. Don't forget, I was brought in as a curiosity more than anything else; after the movie came out I had offers to be in other things, but they wanted me sort of next week and I couldn't because I had a career and I was booked in the weeks following the opening of the film. After six months, the calls stopped coming. I knew they would. I realized that if I got any other work it would be the dancing bear kind of work and that didn't appeal to me. I'm very thrilled to have been a part of that film. John Holmes notwithstanding, porn is still about women. Anderson's film is a fictitious account.

The Bloom is off the Rose

If industry insiders such as Hartley believe sex films have become too commonplace even for pornophiles, what can ardent fans of the genre expect to see in the years ahead apart from what is already available? With a growing demand for Hentai (the Japanese term describing the depiction of pornography in comics or anime), computer games, urban porn, and other offshoots of human copulation archived on camera phones and (often freely) accessible through several mediums, anything is possible.

It is still in my experience a mixed bag at how mainstream porn has become because before 1992 you still had to mail order it, or go to a store yourself, get a movie and bring it home. That part was very positive. It did bring more women and couples into the viewing audience and help to normalize the experience, and help to make it less shameful and less horrible. The internet is really a mixed bag. Frankly, my husband wishes the internet had never been invented. On the one hand, yes, the internet helps connect isolated communities of sexual minorities. On the other hand, it did open up the potential for piracy. For the first five years of the internet, the people who got in there and who sold sex tapes and sexual things made money hand over fist. Now, of course, it's evened out and it's everywhere. Now, it's not as if we have to go see, we have to look.

I'm glad that mere nudity doesn't shock the way it used to. I'm a nudist and I wish people weren't so freaked out. People will never calm down about sex on a certain level because it's part of the cultural DNA with the Puritan heritage and the effect of Christian morality on all of the laws governing sex and sexual expression, and all of the laws governing birth control. In twenty-six years of porn, I am thinking overall that it has gone in a neutral, slightly negative direction: oversaturation of inferior product, over competition from piracy and free sites. The bloom is off. It used to be that showing naked breasts could get you money. Again, the biggest problem

with porn in our culture is that most of the people who create
the product have no particular interest in sexuality. They have no
theory. It's not coming from a place of art, personal drive, personal
fire or personal arousal so the porn industry deserves to collapse.
It's like the car industry — if you keep turning out garbage, people
are going to go to Japan. Porn has become the same thing — so

much bad product. All it has going for it is naked breasts. There is no feeling, no art, and no philosophical concept behind it.

People who are involved in this industry and doing porn, we are having fun. We love to get to go to work and make love with good-looking people. We get paid and we go home. One of the downsides of mainstream porn is that it attracts too many conventional people into it — people who are not rebellious and people who are not comfortable with sex. It puts them in a job that is not their trip, and then they become very conflicted about what they are doing and with or without the need to self-medicate, in order to go to work. Back in the day, it may have been a party atmosphere, but it wasn't "I have to take drugs because I'm so horrified by what I'm doing". For them, and for a lot of people, sex and drugs go together. I was so thrilled. I could not believe my good fortune. I got off on the sex. I got off on having my hands on other people; I get off on watching other people have sex because I'm a voyeur. I get off on the women because I'm bisexual. For me, except for my poor money management skills, porn is a job that I'm thrilled to be a part. I got to have sex and have a lot of different experiences without having that weird intimacy thing. I don't need to hear about your life or your last girlfriend or your mother.

One Legacy Fits All

One of the fascinating aspects in documenting the female contingent of the adult golden era is the fact that each woman featured is a unique and distinct entity with personal attitudes, experiences, and insights to contribute. Their combined years in adult entertainment, either in front of the camera, behind the camera, or on the sidelines in supporting roles have culminated in a collection of memories, emotions, wisdoms, and personal truths. It is clear there are several reasons why women might work in some sector of the sex profession. All participants in this book, no matter their demographic or background: socio-economic, scholastic, ethnic — whether they came from a volatile childhood or grew up in a healthy nurturing home emphatically admit they made their own choices, even those who might not necessarily have chosen porn if they had the opportunity to do it again. All twenty-five subjects are strong females whose collective input toward the classic erotic film/movie industry is immeasurable. Nina Hartley neatly underscored the personal legacies that she and her comrades have left behind.

I would say that the legacy is proof positive that the smack against women as being victims is a lie. I recognize all of the eighties Pioneers like Annie Sprinkle on sexual media and philosophy in terms of empowering women. You have women like Kay Parker, and Juliet Anderson, and me, and Sharon Mitchell, and Candida Royalle who are individual women who have individual

personalities and have their own way of doing things. I say that's good for them. They laid down their rules and people listened. They are not cookie-cutter women. They are not two-dimensional people. They are clearly unique. Annette Haven has a certain style of performing. Juliet Anderson had a way of being on camera. Kay Parker had a way of being on camera that was distinctly Kay Parker. You can't mistake Kay Parker for Candida Royalle because they are completely different. Their personalities would come through and they are clearly real people. Georgina Spelvin is another, and Seka, and Jane Hamilton. We can go look at them and see their individuality. That definitely is one legacy. There is proof out there that women can enjoy sex.

As it turns out, I get to be a public spokesperson, and as a feminist, I'm grateful that I get to talk about sex work from experience as opposed to theory. Most of the theory has been created by women who have a real problem with sexuality, and with gender roles, and with male sexuality, and so on, so they look at this material and project onto it all sorts of intent on the part of the creators who have no such intent. They are a bunch of people making money — it's a sexual enterprise.

All of pornography is hugely subversive in that it shows men and women going against every societal convention and living. I don't know about Canadian filmmaking, but in Hollywood, particularly today if a woman goes against convention sexually, something bad has to happen to her before the end of the movie. She will become lost or abandoned. She will end up in jail or alone. She'll lose her kids or lose her man, or go to prison, or become hooked on drugs, or lose her job, or lose her family if she — fill in the blank — has sex with a black man, has sex in groups, has sex without love, has sex for money, has sex with other women, has sex with toys. Pornography is sexual fantasy. Pornography is live cartoon. Pornography is a paid professional performance of a fantasy scenario. It is not a documentary. Now, it's slightly a documentary in that it's like a sports performance meaning how much dialogue happens before the sex starts.

Anti-porners have been saying for years and is one of the reasons they hate pornography is that it shows women as "whores by nature". I think, well, if pornography's *raison d'être* is to arouse; everybody in the movie is going to be in a sexual mode, the men *and* the women. Not all women are "whores by nature," but some are. I don't have a problem with that. I am a "whore" by nature meaning that I'm comfortable with a wide variety of sexual expression.

The legacy that these women leave us with is this: brave women who are willing to go outside of the cultural norm. Some of them have suffered consequences for it because there is no going back. Candida Royalle has done very well because she's developed a successful toy line and she's moved into producing. She's made a very elegant and graceful transition to businesswoman. Her last performance was twenty-eight years ago in 1984 so she got out before the video explosion. People know her, but she's not plastered everywhere. She's harder to find in the middle of action because she didn't do any video, only film. Annette Haven was the first real female to do it. She had very strong feminist principles and she was a big star. If she said she wasn't going to do a thing, she didn't do a thing and that was the end of that.

Porn and Family Values

As rosy as things may seem in Hartley's world in accordance to her ability to accept and resign herself to her own sexuality as well as impart her knowledge for the benefit of others, certain members of Nina's family haven't exactly always welcomed what some may classify as her hedonistic lifestyle with open arms. Recently, Hartley's father passed away.

No one in my family, frankly, makes much use of pornography. My mother did see *Behind the Green Door* (1972) when it came out. That was the porno chic era. Honestly, it's a kidnap/rape movie. There's no way around it. It's what it was. When my mother found out what I did, all she could remember was that movie and how horrified she was. Finding out what I did was very, very hard for my mother. Now, twenty-four years later, we are quite close and she has relaxed a lot, but when she first found out in 1986 it was very difficult for her as you can well imagine. Your youngest daughter is not behaving in a way that you would really accept or approve of. No mother wants her daughter to become a sex worker. Even though I'm fine, in our culture, it's not what a parent wants for their child. My family knows what I do, but we don't talk about it. My family knows little or no details, but again, we do not talk about it. I'll say, "I worked," or "I gave a lecture," or "I've been working a lot recently," and that's the extent of the conversation about it. It's not appropriate anyway to provide them with details. I do have adult nephews and nieces. My adult niece has said that she's seen some of my work and it did not weird her out, but she's a very cool person and she was probably watching educational stuff. My adult male nephews, I don't doubt that they've looked at some pictures because they have an aunt who does what I do, but again, we don't talk about it at all. I have one minor niece who I believe knows nothing and we all want to keep it that way until she's at least sixteen. I prefer eighteen, but she'll find out sooner or later. She's only a young teenager right now so if we could wait five more years I'd just be thrilled. The [relatives] who do know think it's cool that they're related to "Nina Hartley," but they did not grow up with me. I might as well be "Jane Doe" to them. These are second and third cousins. They're twenty-six years old, they already have tattoos — these are the children of my second cousins.

Once you get further out, there's no problem. In the immediate family, at one point, my uncle and his girlfriend came to see a performance of mine in San Francisco, and my cousin and her brother came to see a performance once at the back row. I did not know they were there until the end. That, I think, is it. That is the extent of my family's exposure to it and that was over twenty-two years ago.

For my sister, it would have been an unmitigated horror to do what I do. I think that when people are thinking about pornography, all they can do is project their own issues onto it. My sister imagines herself in front of the camera and could never do anything like this unless someone was threatening her children. For her, this is the strangest and most unusual job. She is monogamous. She's very shy and enjoys it very much at home, thank you very much.

Nina and Marie

Nina may be a construct, but she's built out of actual pieces of my personality. My real self, "Marie," is bisexual. "Marie" is exhibition-istic. "Marie" is not monogamous. "Marie" is expansive, and "Marie" is a nurse. I also have a bit of a people pleaser personality. Most of time when I meet new people, I'm "Nina" first. I introduce myself as "Nina". Once a person gets to be a certain kind of a friend, they get to know my real name. "Marie" is a name that doctors, lawyers and police officers know. I am very open with who I am with friends.

Hartley spoke about decisions she made years ago as "Marie," that eventually collided with her "Nina" persona. She has since purged any lingering negative feelings, and instead, used her experiences as a learning curve.

There's Nina, who is all this and a bag of chips and then there is Marie who struggled with her own issues. Finally, Marie's issues impacted Nina. My husband now says, "Nina took her host body and got the fuck out." As long as Nina got to go to work and do what Nina wanted to do, Nina didn't care if Marie was suffering. Nina didn't care enough that Marie was suffering to do anything about it until it became a question of living or dying. When I finally realized that if I didn't leave my marriage I was going to die, I went, "Oh my god! I don't want to die!" I fled, but it was a very bad situation.

Part of the reason I'm not in a better place financially is because I was just fucking stupid about money in the way that many people are and many women are. I was the breadwinner in my first marriage, but I was in an emotionally abusive marriage. I did not understand my power, and how to take it, and exercise it, and tell him to leave. I didn't get that. If I would have left my first marriage sooner and I would have managed my money differently, I should be rich. I allowed my messed up first marriage to drain all my money. Yes, I was young; they were older than I was. People can say I was taken advantage of, but I also did not choose to take control of my life until late in the game. Those are the only things I would have changed.

I wish I'd managed my affairs better and I would have more security now. I've made a lot of money for myself. I've made a lot of money for other people and because I was so artistic — being a hippie-dippy person, and quite frankly, being raised by failed Communists, you distrust the profit motive and the ambition motive and I did not pay proper adult attention to the business aspect of what I did. I was raised in the sixties in Berkeley by parents who were in full retreat from all of that, and that's something they did not impart to any of the kids. They had no money smarts to impart anyway so we did not get any. All my siblings have the same problem.

If I could do anything differently, I'd have paid more attention to the business side of things, and I would have gotten a business manager sooner. I would have gotten a bookkeeper sooner, and I would have honored my own happiness sooner and left my marriage earlier. I should have left my marriage in 1989 when I met the one man with whom I am now married. We have a wonderful relationship and he happens to be in the business. My ex had a great conflict about porn; they were from the Midwest. They did not like show business; they did not like being in show business. My current husband is a showman himself, he used to be in radio. He is a lovely, flamboyant character. I have a happy marriage to a former performer. He's also a writer, director, and producer. My husband is a wonderful man and we have a lovely, vibrant, actual marriage-marriage — not what I had before which was a sham marriage.

Hartley celebrates a long term, open relationship with husband Ernest Greene.

He's a tremendously fascinating person. I've known him twenty years and had an affair with him nineteen years ago. I've been with him now ten and we've been married for almost seven. He's been a non-sex performer. He's a BDSM guy so the films he's involved with are kink-oriented and with the flogging and the spanking, whatever — he's done that a long time, but behind the camera. He was the assistant director to a friend of mine. I was the lead and I liked him right away because, like me, he came to porn for a reason. He had something to say about sex.

In June of 2011, Hartley underwent surgery to remove non-cancerous fibroid tumors from her uterus that had plagued her for more than twenty years. Prior to her operation, several fundraisers were organized in order to assist with the cost of her recovery. Currently, she's back in business.

I'm working on a new project also to do with sex education and community called *Sexwise in the Community*. I'm trying hard to break more over into coaching, speaking, being a public intellectual about sex. I'm filming movies but they are not the bulk of my income anymore.

In addition to projects like Sexwise in the Community, an online social network she started in 2010, the majority of Hartley's movie appearances in recent years are restricted to MILF and girl-girl roles where she shows unseasoned players how it's done. In 2010 and 2011, Nina's filmography listed approximately twenty-five titles. Hartley enjoyed portraying former First Lady Hilary Rodham Clinton in Hustler's 2008 political porno satire *Who's Nailin' Paylin* with adult star Lisa Ann doing a send-up of former Vice-Presidential candidate Sarah Palin. In 2010, Tom Byron featured Nina on the cover of the twelfth release of his popular Seasoned Players line where she had sex with African American porn star, Sean Michaels, followed by an auxiliary scene with Byron from *Seasoned Players 2*. On camera, Byron thanked Nina for contributing to the success of his niche line after her inclusion in the 2007 release *Seasoned Players 2* proved a financial achievement creating a demand for more product of the same type. During the interview just prior to their scene, Hartley expressed how much she looked forward to reconnecting with Michaels again after eight years, and reiterated that her first sex scene had been interracial with Billy Dee. Michaels, in turn, lauded Hartley for supporting him when he first entered the business in 1989 after he'd experienced some negative backlash on the part of studios because of his skin color. In a positive way, a great deal has changed in the past twenty years with ultra male stars of color such as Michaels, Lexington Steele and others harvesting a huge fan following.

The Final Word

Because I'm a MILF, I'm a Cougar, I'm classic — I'm an icon — I'm trying hard to find a lucrative way for Nina to continue to make money for me. I've built this brand. I've spent a lot of time and effort building this brand "Nina Hartley". I've not diluted it, and I'm trying late in the game to get smarter about business and figure out a way to maximize the profit that I do have from this "Nina" person I have created. "Nina" enjoys a great deal of affection from the public. My name does stand for something, and I just have to find a way to monetize that. That's where I'm at now.

All life is good, but I tell young people that the choices you make when you're twenty do affect you when you're fifty. I'd say that eighty-five percent of sex workers have trouble with money in and money out. I don't beat myself up too much for being stupid, but I am sorry that I did not have a philosophy about money and I did not understand about money, and power, and all that that does.

I used to think that if I had kids in my mid-twenties it'd be okay, but the kid bug never really bit me badly and I married the wrong person initially so I'm not sorry today that I don't have children. I never really wanted them so for me being childless is not a loss or sadness. It's very hard to be a sex worker and be a mother.

During down time, Nina and Ernest Greene seem to have found the perfect way to amalgamate their love with their loves.

Nina and partner Ernest Greene. AVN

My husband and I like to have people over. We have friends with whom we are not sexual — we talk and chat, and then we have friends with whom we are sexual. My husband and I do enjoy at least once or twice a month, extracurricular activity with another woman. We like threesomes. I have a wide circle of friends who are potential sex partners and I go to my share of group sex situations because there are lots of us out there. I also have a special male friend that I see alone whenever we can make it work, and he has a special female friend that he sees if he can make it work so we are this way. My husband is more this way than I am. He has less jealousy than I do. It's hard to believe. I had to heal mine and he never had it.

My husband likes being married and he likes domestic life. He likes to go shopping and that kind of thing. At home, I like to cook and I like to read. I like picnicking, I like hiking in the woods and I like museums. We like hanging out together, doing errands, going to movies. We do like to spend a lot of time together. We enjoy each other's company a lot. It's very important. I never thought I would find someone I would still want to make love to for as many years as we have. I wasn't looking for it! I wasn't thinking that there was a man I'd want to make love to all of the time, but I've found one and it's so weird! It's fantastic!

26

Honorable
Mentions

I have dedicated the following pages to a group of women deserving of an Honorable Mention for beauty, talent, acumen, fame, longevity or all of the above. With such an extraordinary and magnetic range of women to draw from, it was difficult to narrow down to a small selection. I have personally chosen fifteen women for this section and provided a short summary on each one.

Without wishing to disregard any of the other female contenders who gave their all during the vintage phase of adult filmmaking, or classic adult film historians, critics and fans, I have deduced that a favorite actor or performance is similar to a preferable taste in music, or style of clothing. Since screening more than three hundred erotic films and loops over the past six years for two books, as one might expect, certain actors, films, performances and/or scenes have remained with me.

This year, 2012, marks the forty-year anniversary of influential pictures *Deep Throat* and *Behind the Green Door*. Along with the twenty-five portraits, I believe the following group to be an exceptional bonus assemblage of women further representing the period this book covers, bringing the total number to forty.

Here, then, are the finalists: Fifteen Retro Film Divas.

Linda McDowell

Linda McDowell (aka Claudia Grayson) began her short career in adult entertainment in approximately 1970-'71, combining modeling for several Men's magazines (including in the U.K.) with a handful of loops and short films. The late adult film historian, Jim Holliday, classified

McDowell as one of the most beautiful women in the history of the business. Blessed with an hourglass figure, large blue eyes, thick brunette hair, and a sexy mischievous smile, the irrepressible McDowell's most popular and famed appearances are when partnered with John Holmes in three designated Playmate Series loops titled *Playmate of the Year*, *Supercock*, and the aptly named *Wild Beauty*. McDowell displayed a remarkable sense of adventure and joy indulging in oral, vaginal, and (yes, even) anal sex with young Holmes who appeared unusually handsome sporting tamed wavy hair with a trim moustache. As the captain of the ship, Holmes precariously guided McDowell through the couple's anal voyage as she giggled and hugged an accent pillow.

Linda was also showcased in a threesome with Holmes and sidekick, porno-jock Rick Cassidy, while another loop featured a pregnant McDowell sandwiched between Holmes and Cassidy. Despite the fact, the two guys obviously got their rocks off, from a woman's perspective it is worth mentioning that Linda seemed completely at ease and playful in her maternal state. The loop is tasteful and fun and denotes the unsophisticated, innocent period in which it was shot.

McDowell and her blossoming tummy made another appearance in *Helen Bedd* (1973), one of her very few feature film roles. Linda demonstrated the proper use of a dildo to a friend (Sandi Carey) in a kitchen chair, in addition to engaging with various sexual partners as a supporting performer. *Helen Bedd* starred Sandi Carey, director Walt Davis, and the diminutive, seldom seen nymphet Barbara Barton (aka Gilda Grant).

Lovely Linda's chapter as an adult performer was limited to very few appearances. It is believed she may have passed away from cancer in June 2008 in Delhi, Iowa where she resided for many years along with her husband.

Linda McDowell will forever be commemorated on eight millimeter films, and undoubtedly, in the memory banks of many of the male populous where she continues to be regarded as one of the most desirable and superb creatures ever to have ever graced celluloid.

Rene Bond

Rene Bond (born Rene Ruth Bond in October 1950) is a standout pioneer performer beginning with minimal appearances in the late 1960s, particularly in sexploitation films produced by Harry Novak (dubbed the "Sexploitation King"). One of Bond's first films in which she appeared nude (and swinging on a rope) is the low budget "B" film *Country Cuzzins* (1971) involving the silly shenanigans surrounding the Peabody's, a hillbilly family in the deep south. Later, after receiving breast implants, Bond advanced to hardcore and S&M films in the 1970s, quickly customizing herself as a veritable rebel in her field. Rene also made waves in a couple of director Ed Wood's pictures: *Necromania* (1971) and *Fugitive Girls* (1974).

Encased within a tantalizing, tidy, curvy package, Rene and her boyfriend, sex performer Ric Lutz, were often paired together or as part of an ensemble cast in dozens of loops and hardcore features. Bond pronounced Lutz was her favorite on screen partner. Indubitably, Rene took delight in wearing the crown as a lusted after cult idol, particularly noted in Alpha Blue Archives' *Rene Bond, Sex Kitten*, a medley of seventies scenes underscoring her work with Lutz, John Holmes, Nina Fause and Virginia Winter (another beauty from her day). In footage excerpted from *Teenage Fantasies* (1971), cheekily, Bond introduces each passage by deep-throating unidentified males, demonstrating unabashed devotion to her technique and putting her personal stamp on every entry.

Rene's last known public appearance was in 1985 on the television program *Break the Bank* where she was a contestant along with her third husband. Tragically, Bond died in 1996 at age forty-five from cirrhosis of the liver, but her image as a blue screen icon is immortalized in the annals of

COURTESY OF WORTH MENTIONING PUBLIC RELATIONS

her untamed performances that lasted well into the late 1970s. An anticipated biography on Rene Bond is currently in the works titled *Rene Bond: America's Tragic Teenage Fantasy* by John Harrison slated for a 2013 release.

Cyndee Summers

Cyndee Summers (aka Anne Faulkner), a stunning redhead with a perfectly crafted body to match, was a frequent performer during the golden era of adult films in a career that overlapped three decades.

During her early years, Summers often joined steady boyfriend Rick Cassidy in loops and rudimentary pictures such as *Sex Picnic* (1971), *Penthouse Passions* (1971), *Panty Girls* (1972) and *The Winning Stroke* (1973). Dubbed "Lady Vanity" by adult historian William Margold (Summers had a habit of keeping a mirror on hand at all times) Cyndee blazed across countless cinemascapes as an ultimate male fantasy where she flaunted MILF authority even as a young woman in short films.

Continuing in the tradition of exploring the unconventional theme of incest, director Kirdy Stevens hired Summers to co-star in the 1985 film *Taboo 4: The Younger Generation*, the third sequel to the highly successful *Taboo* (1980). Summers was ideally cast as the sex-starved wife of sexual

COURTESY OF WORTH MENTIONING PUBLIC RELATIONS

psychiatrist Dr. Jeremy Lodge (Jamie Gillis) and becomes immersed in an affair with Lodge's brother (John Leslie), creating upheaval and dissention in the family structure. Luxurious and elegant to a fault, Summers handled the role with aplomb as she effectively elicited empathy on the part of the viewer for her plight.

In 1987, Cyndee appeared again with Rick Cassidy in *Divorce Court Expose 2* directed by porn auteur, Chuck Vincent whereby Cyndee is the recipient of a facial. Cyndee made her final appearance in *Swedish Erotica Featurettes 5* (1990, directed by Patti Rhodes-Lincoln) where she performed with co-stars Mindy Rae, Stevie Taylor and Mike Horner.

According to Wikipedia, Cyndee Summers is purported to have passed away in November 2009 at age sixty although that information has not been verified. Summers' trademark as a stealth feline with a wild, yet cultivated appetite for sexual variety renders her one of the true renegade women of the golden age.

Sandy Dempsey

Sandy Dempsey (aka Darleen Saunders/Tiffany Stewart) is a first generation adult performer easily recognized by an endearing overbite set off by her auburn hair; a lithe figure (sporting all natural, shapely breasts), and a butterfly tattoo on her right thigh — one of the original performers to have one.

Dempsey sparked off her career in adult entertainment in the mid-1960s when she appeared in Kirdy Stevens and Helene Terrie's experimental nudist films, along with boyfriend John Holmes and a group of unknowns. In 1967, Dempsey and Holmes (Sandy and Holmes appeared together in more than a combined twenty loops and features) were hired by Stevens and Terrie to perform in one of Stevens' first hardcore loops for mail order which can be viewed as a clip insert in the director's 1979 film *Me and Marla Strangelove*. Dempsey's initial full feature is listed as *Tough Guns* (1968) in which she assumed a non-sex role.

COURTESY OF WORTH MENTIONING PUBLIC RELATIONS

In addition to her extreme sex appeal and partiality, Dempsey had a knack for natural delivery of dialogue and floated easily between loops, sexploitation and hardcore films for directors Stevens, Walt Davis, Chris Warfield, Bob Chinn and others. Sandy also showed off her talent for the facetious in some of the sophomoric comedies of the era such as the softcore feature *Sex and the Single Vampire* (1972).

Wearing a big, floppy hat and bug-eyed sunglasses, Dempsey portrayed Sandra Hamilton in the 1970 release *Johnny Wadd* (the landmark film of the nine-part series) whereby her character successfully enticed the detective (Holmes) *not* to search for her missing sister by paying him handsomely in funds and sexual favors. *Little Miss Innocence*, released in 1978, is Sandy's final hardcore performance.

In the mid-seventies Dempsey left the adult business and is rumored to have died in a boating accident with possible foul play in 1975. However, as her filmography suggests, it has also been reported she is alive and well, and living in the South Western United States. Sandy Dempsey is one of the most dynamic and titillating adventurers of early erotic films.

Sandi Carey

Sandi Carey (aka Daisy Lay/Sylvia Duval) broke into adult films after starting out as a figure model in sexy magazines in the late 1960s. The petite, fine-boned, blonde Carey with large doe eyes was soon hired to perform in softcore, and also hardcore features coinciding with the late 1960s and the coming of a new era in filmmaking. Some of Carey's primitive appearances were uncredited roles, but by 1971, she had made over fifteen films mostly in the hardcore genre — some of which are difficult to track down.

Carey often co-starred with early contemporaries and friends Sandy Dempsey and Rene Bond as is evidenced in *Sex as You Like It* (1972), *City Woman* (released in 1974), and the softcore detective story *The Danish Connection* (1974) directed by Walt Davis.

Carey's delightfully coy on screen presence is maximized in the softcore feature *The Liberated Woman* (1972) about a frigid woman's entry into a world of swing parties and forbidden sexual delights. (The film's poster featured the graphic illustrations of gifted artist and former producer Linda Adrain). In 1976, Carey once again joined forces with the trio of starlets: Rene Bond, Sandy Dempsey and Cyndee Summers and put on a sexually supple performance in the opening scene of *A Touch of Sex*, a sultry story about a hot clique of California women hell bent on showing a city slicker the private pleasures of Los Angeles.

Sandi Carey was actively involved in the adult business on and off until the late-1980s, and held minor roles in a few horror pictures throughout the course of her film career as Sandra Carey. Sandi's final appearance in the adult genre was in a non-sex capacity in the 1987 sequel *Debbie Duz Dishes 111* starring Nina Hartley. It is alleged that Sandi Carey is presently living and working in Las Vegas.

COURTESY OF WORTH MENTIONING PUBLIC RELATIONS

Sharon Thorpe

Sharon Thorpe, the unconventional, captivating artiste began her career as a pornographic film performer in the early 1970s. She has been honored as one of the first five female stars to be inducted into the XRCO Hall of Fame on February14, 1985. Often featured wearing eye-

COURTESY OF WORTH MENTIONING PUBLIC RELATIONS

glasses in the early years, Thorpe (aka Joanna Savage and Julie Holmes) and her skill set were underrated. She was often cast in marginal parts; either presented as the BFF of the lead female character or as a mousey bookworm. Essentially, Sharon was an alluring and uniquely attractive character actress who soon won over film critics and fans with her solid acting capabilities and her passionate, sensual enthusiasm with partners.

Thorpe toiled through her service within the X-rated empire with all of the greats of the industry, and was often coupled with John Leslie and Clair Dia. Sharon played Leslie's first hook up in director Alan Colberg's (unavailable) feature *Tapestry of Passion* (1976) for Essex Films, entailing the resolution of a murder investigation.

Robert McCallum's *3:00AM* (1975) is considered one of Sharon's finest acting pieces. Thorpe summoned her inner "Mrs. Robinson," as a sexy thirty-something who consoles and satisfies the carnal yearnings of her neighbor's son (Charles Hooper) after the accidental homicidal death of his father. The act commences as a shy romantic union of two unlikely souls and evolves into a torrid interchange that becomes an instigator for the boy and his sister (Clair Dia) to embark upon their own incestuous sexual exploration.

Thorpe's touching and erotic scene with Johnny Keyes in Anthony Spinelli's *SexWorld* (1977) could be considered the seminal performance of her career. Juxtaposed against a preceding line-up of lonely hearts housed at SexWorld, a destination getaway resort on a tropical island that matches applicants with candidates promising to fulfill sexual requirements, Sharon and Keyes (reprising his role as the fantasy lover in *Behind the Green Door*, 1972) intuitively and lovingly anticipate one another's emotional and physical cravings. With bodies entwined, they effortlessly put a perfect exclamation mark on the weekend's curious rendezvous.

In the mid-seventies, Thorpe began to work in the areas of production and musical direction before leaving the adult business in the 1980s to pursue other opportunities. Reportedly, Sharon Thorpe presently resides in San Francisco and works as a real estate agent.

Annette Haven

Without question, Annette Haven is one of the most magnificently beautiful and adored golden era women with facial features and a form reminiscent of classic Hollywood. Having grown up in a strict religious environment, Haven married while still a teenager and divorced two years later. Shortly thereafter in the early 1970s, Annette left her home in Las Vegas and travelled to San Francisco where she began working on the dance circuit as a stripper and met pornographic actress Bonnie Holiday. Haven's first appearance in a sex film was Alex de Renzy's *Lady Freaks* (1973) which also starred Holiday. The two appeared in several productions together and lived under the same roof for a number of years, along with Holiday's boyfriend.

By 1975, Annette was a sensation and much sought after actor who patented her talent and exquisite beauty in some of the most preeminent and successful pictures of the 1970s and eighties decades. She had a reputation for setting the tone on a set and would not compromise her integrity and moral code for anyone. Many industry insiders and fans contend that Haven is responsible for transforming the sex film genre from grinder exhibitions into productions of prestige because of her poise and caliber of performance. It is said that Annette was considered for director Brian De Palma's *Body Double* (1984) in a leading role that was ultimately assigned to Melanie Griffith.

Haven is enduring as a virginal maiden in the Mitchell brother's hit film *The Autobiography of a Flea* (1976) and followed up as Johnny Wadd's

COURTESY OF WORTH MENTIONING PUBLIC RELATIONS

eye-popping main squeeze in the opening sequence of the Freeway Film production *Tell Them Johnny Wadd is Here* (1976). Throughout the pinnacle of the golden age, Haven continued banking on her marquee status by appearing in a steady stream of first-rate productions with some of the industry's brightest stars and directors. In her starring role in the outstanding picture *"V": The Hot One* (1978), Annette memorably performed with a fine selection of studs from the era: John Leslie, Paul Thomas, Joey Silvera, and John Seeman. *SexWorld* (1978), *Take-Off* (1978) and *The Grafenberg Spot* (1985) are other examples of exceptional films brandishing Haven's expertise as an actor and performer. Annette's star power shone within a career lasting almost two decades and she is an honored inductee of the XRCO and AVN Halls of Fame.

Today, Annette Haven lives in Sausalito, California, and will be turning fifty-eight years old this year. She has retained her classic beauty, and graceful, well-toned figure. Haven avidly communicates with friends and fans through Facebook.

Vanessa del Rio

Vanessa del Rio was born in Harlem, New York to Cuban and Puerto Rican parents in March 1952. Raised in the Catholic faith by a controlling father, a pious mother and overly zealous nuns, during her teen years, the voluptuous young maverick admired Argentine sex symbol/actress/model, Isabel Sarli and rebelled against the conventional rules and regulations established by her parents. Vanessa began to experiment with her own sexuality and tested the waters by charming suitors while asserting supremacy and control over liaisons. After leaving home at age sixteen, del Rio worked as a key punch operator and computer programmer before Go-Go dancing in clubs in the East Village. Eventually, she found employment as a call girl.

In 1974, the hot new starlet appeared in her first adult feature, *China Doll*, directed by Shaun Costello. Shortly thereafter, she became regarded as "America's first Latina Porn Star," breaking through all ethnic barriers. del Rio worked steadily in adult films from the early seventies through to the mid-eighties, thoroughly enjoying her time in the limelight on and off the set. While developing a reputation as a party girl, Vanessa utilized her star power to the utmost. She was arrested for what was deemed "obscene behavior" while headlining a strip tease act in Richmond, Virginia, and was charged with possession of cocaine and Quaaludes. During her time in jail, the adult cinema star reflected upon her childhood years spent in the Catholic Church, assessing the contrasts between her roots and her career in the adult entertainment industry. For a time, Vanessa disconnected herself from her porn persona. After making the decision to return to films, del Rio left the business again in 1986 when AIDS became a legitimate threat to the industry.

Acknowledging porn and rap make ideal bedfellows, Vanessa resurfaced again a decade later with a revamped profile manifested by her appearance in rap artist Junior M.A.F.I.A.'s video *Get Money*. The frequently recognized and well-respected del Rio, accepted cameos in additional videos and did occasional television spots while sustaining her work in adult films which officially ended in 1999.

Since disembarking from the industry, del Rio has been actively involved in maintaining her website: VanessadelRio.com. She is also on

Facebook where she communicates with many admirers and aficionados of her work. In 2007, German art book publisher, Benedikt Tashen, released a coffee table biography on the larger-than-life icon titled *Vanessa del Rio: Fifty Years of Slightly Slutty Behavior*. In a 2011 interview for *Media Take Out.com*, Vanessa avowed that if she had the opportunity to do it all over again she would have probably taken a shot at Hollywood.

In the same interview she proudly proclaimed, "Porn is the only industry where women are really in control." At age sixty, Vanessa del Rio continues to speak her mind, and as a gracious and durable celebrity, she frequently attracts new fans to her body of work.

Lesllie Bovee

Lesllie Bovee, another trailblazer with impeccable beauty and sexual allure, became known to adult fans after her feature role in Artie and Jim Mitchell's *C.B. Mamas* (1975) which co-starred luminaries Jon Martin, (the lovely and not forgotten African American actress) Desiree West, Joey Silvera and Paul Thomas.

Born in Bend, Oregon, Bovee (aka Lesllie Bovée) charmed spectators of X-Rated films with her unreserved and vociferous expressions of passion with many of her male partners. As samplings of her filmography will confirm, Bovee matched her sexual prowess with practically every male in her wake, and did so with such gusto it would be a tall order to attempt to challenge the legitimacy of her performances. Bovee's absorb-

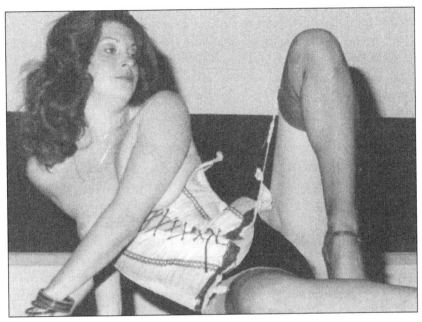

COURTESY OF WORTH MENTIONING PUBLIC RELATIONS

ing roles are plentiful, so to name a few is not to negate her contribution or dynamism in her field.

Eruption (1978) directed by Stanley Kurlan, is a porn parody of the 1944 film noir classic *Double Indemnity* in which Bovee portrayed Sandy Bevin (opposite John Holmes), a woman plotting to knock off her wealthy husband to gain full access of his fortune. Shot on location in Hawaii, Lesllie proved herself as a premiere leading lady in all facets of the film which contained murder, sex, intrigue, and plot twists. One year later, Bovee and Holmes starred together again in *The Senator's Daughter*, a highly entertaining spoof of the TV series *The Six Million Dollar Man*. Lesllie portrayed the kidnapped daughter of a senator taken to Tangiers where she is brainwashed and cloned. Upon her rescue by her bionic secret agent (Holmes), the two have (lots of) sex and fall in love. The film wraps neatly with a storybook wedding.

Bovee is equally credible in other notorious films of the 1970s decade such as *Ecstasy Girls* (1979) with Serena, Laurien Dominique and Georgina Spelvin. Mixing things up, she and Jamie Gillis were cast together in *Lustful Feelings* (1977) and *Blue Ecstasy* (1980), again proving Bovee was able to lend a darker edge to the embodiment of her screen characters.

Lesllie's farewell performance as an erotic actress was in mainstream director John Derek's 1984 picture, *Love You,* with Annette Haven, Eric Edwards and Wade Nichols. Long gone from the porno showground, the consensus is that Lesllie Bovee (now in her sixty-third year with a grown son) happily resides in New York City along with her husband of several years.

Mai Lin

Mai Lin (aka Miko Moto) is one of the first renowned Asian-American pornographic screen actresses of the classic film era. Born in Oakland, California in 1953, Lin enjoyed a long and flourishing career in front of the camera which can be attributed to her electrifying smile, nimble physique, and astounding stamina. Lin's legacy as an insatiable sexpot was kindled in the years following her 1976 unveiling in *Cracked Ice* co-starring Sharon Mitchell, C.J. Laing and John Seeman. The film launched Mai in a succession of more prominent roles in pictures that enjoyed a good deal of success.

Just one year into her career, Lin played herself in *Oriental Madam* (1977) as a genteel administrator, well versed at supplying girls for her clientele with deep pockets. Jade Wong, R. Bolla, Paul Thomas, Don Fernando, Eileen Wells and Herschel Savage all helped to round out the company. With effortless delivery, Mai seemed well suited to her craft, and during sex scenes, she was fully charged.

In 1980, Lin portrayed Sue Lee, fiancée of a sailor (John Holmes) during WWII, in *Prisoner of Paradise* (1980), the co-directed Gail Palmer/Bob Chinn vehicle containing footage from the Hawaiian island of Kauai and Northern California. Although Lin's character is killed off early during an attack on Pearl Harbor immediately following her intense love scene with Holmes, their sexual coupling is hot because of the sensuality exhibited between the two actors during foreplay. Caught up within the sexual interchange with his arresting and exotic co-star, in the final moments of intercourse, Holmes climaxes inside of Lin rather than providing the obligatory external "money shot." Director Chinn recalled after the scene was completed, the two actors remained absorbed while everyone else went to lunch. Lin discussed the film in the winter of 2011 confiding her only disappointment was that her own voice was not used in the finished edition of the picture.

During her membership as one of a designated troupe of golden age performers, Mai Lin was known to embrace all brands of sexual fetishes.

COURTESY OF WORTH MENTIONING PUBLIC RELATIONS

As an authentic star, whose career as an adult celebrity extended well into the early part of the 1990s. Lin, who works part-time as a phone sex operator today, expressed how her infamy as a sex Goddess has been a sore spot for certain members of her family which has led to occasional disagreements. Her notoriety also provoked discord in some of her inter-personal relations with non-family members outside of the industry. Even so, Mai remains sincere to her career in erotic films while accepting the reality that many people she encounters don't necessarily approve of her art. Mai Lin will always be affectionately remembered by porn enthusiasts for her spontaneity, and free spirited fortitude.

Desiree Cousteau

Desiree Cousteau (aka Deborah Clearbranch/Desiree Clearbranch), the radiant, curvaceous beauty with chocolate brown hair, is notorious for her signature, dumb-brunette routine observed in the majority of the Triple-X productions in which she appeared. Cousteau was an aspiring

actress from Savannah, Georgia who acquired a minor role (although it is uncertain if she actually emerged) in director Jonathon Demme's "B" flick *Caged Heat* (1974) about high jinks in a Women's prison starring Cheryl Rainbow Smith. The film's musical score was written by the founding member of The Velvet Underground, John Cale.

With her exquisite physical attributes, Cousteau accepted small roles in sex films once her mainstream options came to a dead end. She assumed the title role in the Alex de Renzy film *Pretty Peaches* (1978) playing the lovable amnesia victim "Peaches" who falls prey to a couple of lusty men (one of them being John Leslie with facial hair) that decide to rape her while she is unaware. Upon making the discovery Peaches is the victim of a car accident, the two fellows grow hearts and attempt to help rather than take advantage of their new friend. For her efforts, Cousteau won

Best Actress Award from the AFAA as the ditzy, bosomy Southern Belle unaware of the sheer potency her natural charms have on the male gender.

In conjunction with feature films, Desiree became a regular in Swedish Erotica loops, and worked with all of the celebrated male and female personalities of the era. Cousteau did not appear to have an aversion to receiving "facials," and was a trooper on set, although it has also been said she could be distant and not always comfortable socializing with her co-stars.

A few of Desiree's lasting film appearances contain content considered buoyant and frivolous, but entertaining nonetheless. Bob Chinn's *Hot 'n Saucy Pizza Girls* (1979) is a fun-loving venture showcasing Cousteau at her best. Desiree played "Ann Chovy," one of four pizza delivery girls (with Candida Royalle, Laurien Dominique and Christine de Shaffer) that take to skateboarding upon San Francisco's steep inclines delivering "special" toppings to Shakey Pizza Parlor's loyal patrons. Chovy falls into a sweet love affair with Inspector Blackie (John Seeman), and spends more time in the sack with her new beau than she does distributing pizzas — much to the chagrin of her co-workers and bosses. Also in 1979, Cousteau had a prominent role in *Hot Rackets* taking on Jon Martin and Mike Ranger in a hot tub at a tennis club, followed by *Inside Desiree Cousteau* (directed by Leonard Kirtman), one of Desiree's most well liked pictures. Cousteau excitedly describes how she transitioned from girl-next-door to adult film star as the story is told through explicit recollections of her employment featuring an assortment of popular sex stars engaging in coitus with Cousteau.

Many rumors have surfaced since Desiree Cousteau's departure from the adult industry in the mid-eighties. Some websites have claimed that Cousteau spent years institutionalized after leaving porn films, while others maintain she is a practicing psychologist in her home state of Georgia. One hopes the latter is true and that Ms. Cousteau is happy, healthy and at peace.

Gail Palmer

A Michigan born native, while enrolled in post-secondary school, Gail Palmer met a man who owned several adult theatres and bookstores and the two became romantically involved. Hyped in the illegal movie business as a director, producer and writer, Palmer worked mostly as a colleague in various adult film productions to which she has been attributed. Still, her name and face are tantamount to the 1970s and eighties

decades as a promoter of erotic pictures. Palmer was first granted directorial credits for *Hot Summer in the City* (1976) shot in Michigan for
Caribbean films. Classified as a roughie, the feature is a delineation of
brutality toward women.

According to Bob Chinn, Gail was eventually hired as a front woman
by Caribbean films strategically marketing the company's goods to males,

COURTESY OF WORTH MENTIONING PUBLIC RELATIONS

women and couples. With a bright and attractive young female representing Caribbean films it was believed consumers would inevitably open
pocket books to purchase more merchandise. Palmer made several television appearances and did publicity junkets in order to help reconfigure
the company image for their targeted clientele.

Gail received the director credit for two highly popular adult titles: *The
Erotic Adventures of Candy* (1978) and its sequel *Candy Goes to Hollywood*
(1979). Both films starred Carol Connors: the busty, statuesque, bleached-
blonde adult cinema star in the principal role as an inexperienced
twenty-year old, ripe for the sexual episodes that ensued as the result
of her gullibility. In the first, Candy (Connors) becomes familiarized
with miscellaneous sex acts through the advances of several horny males
anxious to get into her panties. The usual suspects are Don Fernando (in
the role of Manuel, the Spanish gardener who takes Candy's virginity),

John Leslie, Paul Thomas and John Holmes. Georgina Spelvin and Eileen Welles are featured in supporting roles, in the invigorating and droll flick. In the sequel, Candy indeed goes to Hollywood with dreams of hitting the big time, only to be misused by a shady manager (John Leslie).

In his forthcoming autobiography, Bob Chinn conceded that Caribbean's endorsement of Gail as primary director and producer of select films made sense to him so he went along with it. In an excerpt from his book, Chinn wrote about his working relationship with Palmer:

"Gail was a pleasant girl with a bubbly, effervescent personality who didn't hesitate to speak her mind and who took her job seriously. She also had a great sense of humor, which is always a big plus in my book. She was very compassionate, and happily, I got along very well with her. I really didn't care who received the credit of director as long as I received my salary."

In retrospect, Caribbean Films was prudent in appointing Gail Palmer as the face of their company. She not only fulfilled her position dutifully as assigned, but aided in softening the perception of the DNA behind the production of adult material.

Samantha Fox

Born in New York City, Samantha Fox's contribution to the adult film community and fans as a gifted actor and performer during the latter 1970s and into the first part of the 1980s is enormous. Not to be confused with the British pop singer Samantha Fox, the passionate and pretty X-rated star (aka Stasia Burgoff and Moran Moore), danced professionally prior to her transition into pornographic films. Fox was discovered by director Chuck Vincent who cast her as the lead in *Bad Penny* (1978).

While working almost exclusively on the east coast, Samantha became a predominant female figure in adult productions requiring an actor possessing diversified range. She always left audiences wanting more. Sweet and fresh one minute, and alternately domineering and rough the next, Fox shaped her characters depending upon what the scene called for. Often working with her boyfriend of a number of years, Bobby Astyr (according to Astyr, they met in *Double Your Pleasure* released in 1978), the couple generated more than a few unforgettable flashes of magic and chaos.

One of Fox's renowned roles is in the Roger Watkins (nom du porn, Richard Mahler) picture *Her Name Was Lisa* (1980). Samantha is outstanding as a hooker converted into a fashion model by a photographer, subsequently falling into a depraved pit of drug abuse, victimization and manipulation when a publisher puts her up in a swank penthouse so she can cater to his fantasies. In a particularly disturbing scene, Fox's character is brutally raped by Astyr and Randy West. In real life, Fox and Astyr lived in adjacent apartments for more than twenty-four years in New York City. When Astyr was dying of lung cancer in April 2002, Fox nursed him until his death at age sixty-four.

Along with co-stars Veronica Hart and Kelly Nichols, in 1981, Samantha won raves for an ensemble performance in Chuck Vincent's *Roommates* in her portrayal as one of three girlfriends sharing living space while hoping to make it in the Big Apple. Fox also left a lasting impression as the character Evelyn in *Outlaw Ladies* (1981) coaxing a socialite (Jody Maxwell) to extend beyond her sexual comfort zone to share in overpowering a sexual conquest (Joey Silvera) in a seedy motel room. Samantha has won coveted awards for her thespian work in more than one feature film.

In a 1984 video interview, Fox articulated that she had grown tired of her genitalia being exposed on camera, although she also stated she had enjoyed her work as an adult performer but wanted to explore other options. In recent years, reports that Samantha became a Christian have surfaced and that she no longer wishes to discuss her history in sex films. However, Fox apparently stays in touch with a few friends from the industry. Wherever she is today and whatever her beliefs may be, Samantha Fox will always be held in high esteem in the eyes of her comrades and fans.

Lisa DeLeeuw

Lisa DeLeeuw was born in Moline, Illinois in 1958. According to a 1980s interview, the top-heavy, well-rounded country girl (aka Lisa Woods and L'il Redhead) lost her virginity to two male friends just prior to her sixteenth birthday in the back seat of a Firebird.

Strawberry blonde Lisa was first introduced to erotic films in the 1970s through a boyfriend who had worked in an adult theater. At the outset, DeLeeuw found the movies unappealing. After working as a house dancer at the Mitchell Brother's O'Farrell Theatre in San Francisco prior to moving to Los Angeles to pursue acting, Lisa embarked upon a short modeling career in Men's magazines and made her adult debut in *800 Fantasy Lane* (1979). The picture, directed by Svetlana (deemed a tyrant according to DeLeeuw) starred Jamie Gillis and Bud Wise as two gas station attendants pretending to be wealthy oil tycoons to meet and bed beautiful women. DeLeeuw portrayed one of the bodacious females willing to fulfill the demands of the pair of con artists at 800 Fantasy Lane. Serena, Desiree Cousteau, and Nancy Suitor (another fan favorite with a remarkably short career in adult films) all co-starred.

Often cast as a strong, ballsy woman, Lisa won a Best Supporting Actress award for her role as Bev, one of two prostitutes (the other is played by Samantha Fox) paid to indulge in S&M games with a crooked City Councilor (John Alderman) in *Amanda by Night* (1981) starring Veronica Hart. DeLeeuw delivered a straight up, consummate depiction of a young woman hardened against the world who turns the tables on a powerful, but pathetic client only to meet her untimely fate.

Throughout her film career, DeLeeuw struggled with her weight. She was often told she would need to slim down in order to be hired. In 1983, Lisa was cast as the fleshy, alcoholic Althea Anderson in a tale about two competitive Country and Western singers in the entertaining *Up 'N Coming* (1983, written by Jim Holliday and directed by Stu

Segal), opposite Marilyn Chambers. DeLeeuw's performance is extraordinary and along with Chambers, Lisa performed all of her own singing
numbers. In another outstanding turn, DeLeeuw struck a convincing
chord as the independent-minded Hollywood starlet Dixie Ray, in *Dixie
Ray Hollywood Star* (1983). Set during post WWII, Ray hires a private
investigator (John Leslie) to look into the whereabouts of her absentee

husband and the two become sexually entangled.

In a 1980s interview excerpt at *lisadeleeuw.org*, DeLeeuw spoke fittingly about the perceptions and criticism of adult performers by those
on the outside turf of the sex industry: "If a club owner hires a singer,
he's giving her an 'opportunity,' but if he hires a topless dancer, it's called
'exploitation'. In both cases the performer is combining her natural beauty
with the craft and artistry she has developed."

Since she left hardcore films in the early 1990s, it is reputed Lisa died
of AIDS in 1993. Many believe the story was circulated by DeLeeuw
herself in order to make a fresh start. According to her friend and former
adult actor Jon Martin, Lisa DeLeeuw did pass away some time ago, but
not from AIDS. If true: R.I.P. Lisa DeLeeuw.

Porsche Lynn

Porsche Lynn (aka "Mistress Porsche Lynn") was born in St. Johns, Michigan on Valentine's Day in 1962. At age six Lynn experienced a traumatizing event when she witnessed her father murder her mother before shooting himself. After the incident, Lynn was raised for part of

COURTESY OF WORTH MENTIONING PUBLIC RELATIONS

her young life by her grandmother, and later, she resided in two different orphanages before the courts eventually granted custody of Lynn to her aunt (Lynn's father's sister).

Porsche said that she was physically and sexually abused during the period she lived with her aunt and uncle, but explained she escaped in scholastics and through her involvement in extracurricular activities: volleyball and basketball in particular. Porsche was a shy girl; she was not "the cheerleader" and had few close friends. As a young woman, Lynn admired and respected the life and work of Helen Keller.

Porsche attended Michigan State University for two years on a scholarship before working as a topless dancer in clubs to help finance her education once her scholarship ended. Lynn entered adult films in 1985 at age twenty-two, and enjoyed a fruitful career spanning seventeen years. One of her earliest appearances was in Kirdy Stevens' *Taboo V* (1986) with Amber Lynn, Colleen Brennan, Karen Summer, Jamie Gillis, Joey Silvera and Buck Adams. Admitting her experiences in films were an essential component toward personal growth, Porsche said she wouldn't change anything about her past or her profession. She is proud of her work in the adult industry but became bored with vanilla and formulaic sex films. Lynn emphasized that while dysfunction certainly exists within the adult industry as it does everywhere, it is not the only factor motivating people to become sexual performers.

Presently, Porsche resides in Phoenix, Arizona. She is an expert shooter and an active member of the NRA (National Rifle Association). At the time of our conversation in the spring of 2010, Lynn was involved in a long-term relationship with a man who is one of the country's best shooters. As a fierce believer in a human being's right to protect and defend oneself, Lynn contends there is a distinct connection between her penchant for shooting and her father's fatal actions. Needing to come to terms with what happened, Porsche developed a respect for weapons which became a portal for her to overcome her fear of guns.

Today Porsche works as a dominatrix teaching her clients how to balance the distribution of power using BDSM technique. Through fantasy role-play, her instruction is erotic in nature and utilizes consensual domination, submission and restraint as therapeutic tools pertaining to the restoration of power and equalization of authority. Porsche is a spiritually motivated person and espouses some of the same devout principles as Kay Parker. Lynn's website can be found at the following link: *http://doiaz.com/*.

Porsche Lynn avows that the legacy left behind by she and her peers opened the door for all females in the world to become Goddesses. She is fervent in her belief that sexuality is one of the most significant, and powerful rudiments of humankind.

The Flame

When you hold the light, you'll let go of the flame
I'll tell you, with a touch of my hand
But to you, it's all the same
When you know the smoke, you'll be sure to feel the heat
And the words seem alike from everyone you meet
For whatever comes near, keeps the fear
*   and the flame held in your hand*
Yet, even though it will always be here
The flame will never tell the man
Watch out for the fire and never say your name
For when you finally see the light
You'll let go of the flame

—JULIA ST. VINCENT

About the Author

Born in 1957, Jill Corinne Nelson grew up in Southern Ontario, Canada. During her childhood and teen years, Jill was inspired by her father, mother, and two older brothers in the fields of art, music, literature and travel.

Currently, Nelson resides in Southern Ontario and works part-time as a Hearing Care Professional. She enjoys spending time with her husband of thirty-four years, her two grown children, the family cat Greyson, and friends. Jill plans to chronicle personal experiences and expand into other realms in future writing projects.

Golden Goddesses: 25 Legendary Women of Classic Erotic Cinema, 1968-1985 is Jill Nelson's second book.

Index

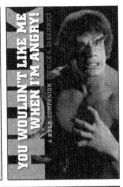

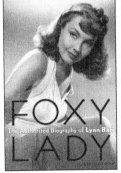
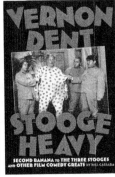

CPSIA information can be obtained at www.ICGtesting.com
Printed in the USA
BVOW11s0605180116

433315BV00010B/142/P